Women's Nonfiction

A Guide to Reading Interests

Jessica Zellers

Real Stories
Robert Burgin, Series Editor

Libraries Unlimited
An Imprint of ABC-CLIO, LLC

A B C **CLIO**

Santa Barbara, California • Denver, Colorado • Oxford, England

Copyright 2009 by Libraries Unlimited

Library of Congress Cataloging-in-Publication Data
Zellers, Jessica.
    Women's nonfiction : a guide to reading interests / Jessica Zellers.
        p. cm. — (Real stories)
    Includes bibliographical references and indexes.
    ISBN 978-1-59158-658-6 (alk. paper)
    1. Women—Books and reading—United States—Bibliography. 2. Reading interests—United States. 3. Readers' advisory services—United States.
    I. Title.
    Z1039.W65Z45 2009
    028'.9—dc22   2009026354

13 12 11 10 9   1 2 3 4 5

This book is also available on the World Wide Web as an eBook.
Visit www.abc-clio.com for details.

ABC-CLIO, LLC
130 Cremona Drive, P.O. Box 1911
Santa Barbara, California 93116-1911

This book is printed on acid-free paper ∞
Manufactured in the United States of America

This is for my colleagues at the Williamsburg Regional Library. Years ago I fantasized about working at WRL, a place that seemed like a haven of dedicated readers' advisors. Turns out the reality was even better than the dream: I'm honored to work alongside people committed to helping others find books to read for pleasure. Your love of books and your service to the public inspires me.

Contents

Series Foreword xi
Acknowledgments...xiii
Introduction xv

Chapter 1—Life Stories: Biography, Autobiography, and Memoirs 1
   Definition 1
   Appeal 2
   Organization 2
   Biography 3
      Women in the Professions 11
      Royalty and Rulers 15
   Autobiography and Memoirs 24
      Global Voices 30
      Women Warriors 37
   Women in the Margins 39
      Queer Identity...40
      Racial and Cultural Identity 43
      Religious Identity 55
   Consider Starting With 62
   Fiction Read-Alikes..62

Chapter 2—Personal Growth 65
   Definition 65
   Appeal 66
   Organization 66
   Psychology 67
   Celebrating Women..71
   Relationships 76
      Straight Romantic Relationships 82
      Queer Romantic Relationships 90
      The Single Woman 93
   Motherhood 97
      Fertility and Adoption 104
      Pregnancy, Childbirth, and Nursing 107
   Spiritual Growth and Meditation..112
      Christian Perspectives 120
      Jewish Perspectives 125
      Muslim Perspectives...127
      Buddhist Perspectives 129
      Hindu Perspectives 131

Chapter 2—Personal Growth (*Cont.*)
      Pagan Perspectives and Goddess Worship 133
  Consider Starting With 135
  Fiction Read-Alikes 135

Chapter 3—Health, Wellness, and Beauty 139
  Definition 139
  Appeal 140
  Organization 140
  Physical Health and Diet 141
      Sports and Fitness 144
  Body Image 147
  Cancer and Disease 153
      Eating Disorders 157
      Addiction 161
  Sexual Health and Satisfaction 163
      Menstruation and Menopause 169
  Emotional Wellness 172
      Midlife and Aging 174
      Recovery from Trauma 177
  Beauty, Fashion, and Appearance 184
      Cosmetics 192
  Consider Starting With 195
  Fiction Read-Alikes 195

Chapter 4—Women's History 197
  Definition 197
  Appeal 198
  Organization 199
  Women throughout the Ages 199
      Women's Bodies and Sexuality throughout History 206
  Women throughout American History 209
  Ancient and Classical Eras 212
      Religious Life in Antiquity 216
  Dark and Middle Ages 218
  Renaissance and Enlightenment 221
  Colonial and Revolutionary America 224
  Nineteenth Century 227
      The American Old West 230
      The American Civil War 233
  Twentieth Century and Beyond 236
  Women and War in the Twentieth Century 242
  Consider Starting With 246
  Fiction Read-Alikes 246

Chapter 5—Adventure and Travel 249
   Organization 249
   Adventure 249
      Definition of Adventure 249
      Appeal of Adventure 250
      Adventures in History 256
      Espionage and War...261
   Travel 265
      Definition of Travel...265
      Appeal of Travel...266
      Travel History 272
      Where to Go and How to Get There.............................275
   Consider Starting With ... .278
   Fiction Read-Alikes...278

Chapter 6—Feminism and Activism...281
   Definition 281
   Appeal 282
   Organization 282
   Feminism..283
      History of Feminism..283
      Feminist Theory, Concepts, and Beliefs 287
   Activism...296
   Consider Starting With ... .305
   Fiction Read-Alikes...305

Chapter 7—Women at Work 307
   Definition 307
   Appeal 308
   Organization...308
   Careers...308
      Women in Science and Technology 312
      Women Doctors, Lawyers, and Clergy 316
      Women Athletes..321
      Women in the Military 323
      Women in the Business World.......................................326
      Women Entrepreneurs..329
   Professional Guides...333
   Sexual Harassment 338
   Women and Leadership..340
   Women and Finance..344
   Consider Starting With ... .346
   Fiction Read-Alikes...347

Chapter 8—Women and Society..349
   Definition 349
   Appeal 350
   Organization..350
   General Social Issues 350
       Abortion and Choice 356
       Sexual Exploitation 358
       Sexual Liberation 361
       War, Violence, and Peace...363
       Women and Politics 366
       Working Mothers 370
   Consider Starting With … 373
   Fiction Read-Alikes..373

   Appendix: Further Resources...375
   Title/Author Index..377
   Subject Index..429

Series Foreword

In my foreword to Sarah Statz Cords's *The Real Story: A Guide to Nonfiction Reading Interests*, I noted that her book provided a much-needed map to "the rich and varied world of nonfiction."

The titles in the <u>Real Stories</u> series flesh out the map that Sarah drew and take us even deeper into the exciting worlds of nonfiction genres—Investigative Writing, Biography, Autobiography and Memoir, Women's Nonfiction, True Adventure, Travel Literature, Environmental Writing, True Crime, Sports Stories, and many others.

The titles in this series are designed to assist librarians and other professionals who work with readers in identifying nonfiction books that their patrons or customers will enjoy reading. The titles in the series will also help libraries evaluate and build their collections in the various nonfiction genres.

Similar to the titles in Libraries Unlimited's <u>Genreflecting</u> series, each of the volumes in the <u>Real Stories</u> series focuses on a popular genre in the nonfiction arena. Individual guides organize and describe hundreds of books each and include definitions of each genre and its subgenres, as well as a discussion of their appeal. Because readers' advisory is ultimately about making connections, recommendations of other nonfiction books and fiction read-alikes are also provided for each book highlighted.

With *The Real Story*, nonfiction lovers gained the equivalent of general guidebooks to fiction genres, such as <u>Genreflecting</u> or Saricks' *Readers' Advisory Guide to Genre Fiction*. With the titles in the <u>Real Stories</u> series, we now have even more specific guidebooks, similar to the fiction guides, *Make Mine a Mystery* and *Hooked on Horror*.

God, as 20th-century architect Mies van der Rohe reminded us, is in the details. The titles in the <u>Real Stories</u> series help us to better understand the details of nonfiction and thereby to better serve our users who read nonfiction for pleasure.

Robert Burgin

Acknowledgments

I am indebted to Kaite Mediatore Stover, the head of Readers'and Circulation Services at the Central Library of Kansas City Public Library and librarian extraordinaire. She saw me at a library conference a few years back, liked my shoes, and struck up a conversation that eventually led to my indoctrination into the world of readers' advisory. It was her gentle prodding that led me to write this book in the first place.

Of course, it would never have occurred to me to write a readers' advisory text, nor a book about women's issues, without a solid education. Dr. Mary Ellis Gibson and the other folks with the Women's and Gender Studies Program of the University of North Carolina at Greensboro nurtured my burgeoning feminism, and the faculty of the School of Information and Library Science at the University of North Carolina at Chapel Hill helped me discover that public librarianship is the best job in the world. Dr. David Carr in particular showed me the value of helping people find books to read for pleasure.

Library pals near and far have helped me grow as a librarian. My two editors at NoveList Plus, Katherine Bradley Johnson and Joyce Saricks, took a chance on a librarian fresh out of school and helped her refine her skills. Sarah Statz Cords wrote a superb readers' advisory text, which became a direct model for my own book; moreover, Sarah became a personal friend who commiserated during the trials of the writing process. Barry Trott commiserated, too, and persuaded me that faking my own death was inadvisable, looming deadlines notwithstanding. He and my other colleagues at the Williamsburg Regional Library endured my authorial grumpiness with grace and offered useful ideas galore; I am privileged to work among librarians who place reading on par with breathing. And Barbara Ittner and Robert Burgin were perfectly willing to risk editing a book about a genre that, in most people's minds, does not even exist. With their dedication to readers' advisory and tremendous knowledge of popular literature, they offered suggestions that improved this book immeasurably.

Finally, I am indebted more than I can say to my mother and father. When I despaired of ever finishing this book, they drove fifteen hours roundtrip to come clean my apartment and feed me. If that's not love, I don't know what is. Thanks, Mom and Dad.

Introduction

The Genre That Wasn't

Let us begin with a full disclosure: I am, at heart, a fiction-lovin' girl. This love affair began with *Hop on Pop*, by Dr. Seuss. I recall informing my mother that I could read the book perfectly well just by looking at the pictures, that I had memorized the words and therefore had no more use for them, but Mom said I should probably go ahead and read the text anyway. I took her advice to heart, and here I am, a quarter-century later, still reading fiction.

These days, my favorite fiction usually has fewer pictures than the typical Dr. Seuss book. (This is a darn shame, but I get my fix with graphic novels.) I tend toward speculative fiction, and I have this embarrassing weakness for paperback vampire novels, the trashier the better. To me, the most pleasurable fiction usually—not always, but *usually*—features a dead body, a ticking bomb, an alien life form, a werewolf, or some magnificent combination of them all.

Perhaps you begin to see why I don't read much Women's Fiction.

And yet . . .

And yet I like to read about women's lives. Of course I do: I am a feminist. When I was an undergrad majoring in Women's Studies, I devoured the literature. I studied the lives of ancient women in Sarah B. Pomeroy's *Goddesses, Whores, Wives, and Slaves: Women in Classical Antiquity*. I wept for Harriet A. Jacobs in her memoir *Incidents in the Life of a Slave Girl*. I encountered the lives of countless Russian women, thanks to the enlightened syllabi of Dr. Jeff Jones—who, unlike any other teacher of a general course on history I've ever met, emphasized women's history and social history every bit as much as political and military history. I swear I learned more about women's history from his survey courses than I did in classes *devoted* to women's history.

And it's not just women's *history* I like to read. I love to study contemporary women's issues. I love to read women's spiritual memoirs—doesn't matter what faith, I'm not picky, I just like reading about spiritual growth. I'm a sucker for books about sexual health, I regularly devour books about feminist activism, and darn if the best nonfiction book I read last year wasn't Susan Seligson's *Stacked: A 32DDD Reports from the Front*.

To summarize my personal reading experience, then: I do love to read fiction, and I love to read books about women and women's issues, and yet the only genre that seems to blend these two interests is Women's Fiction—one of the few fiction genres I regularly avoid. They tend to be too reflective, too leisurely, too contemplative for my high-octane needs. (And I have never found a werewolf in a Women's Fiction book. Never.)

I'm sure you're anticipating me here: it turns out that these books I enjoy reading are actually Women's *Non*fiction. That was easy, right? End of story. This genre I love is Women's Nonfiction.

There's only one problem: Women's Nonfiction isn't a genre. It's not even a reading interest, not the way African American nonfiction is. Women's Nonfiction isn't *anything*, because no one recognizes it.

With this book, I hope to change that.

Just What Is Women's Nonfiction?

Women's Nonfiction is that group of books written about women that isn't recognized by booksellers, libraries, or readers, but ought to be.

Ahem.

> Women's Nonfiction is a reading interest comprising titles that speak to women's experiences.

As I define it, Women's Nonfiction is a reading interest comprising titles that speak to women's experiences. It is not a genre, because the books do not collectively follow any particular conventions. A happily-ever-after ending for a romantic couple characterizes books in the Romance genre; a nonfiction narrative about a violent or criminal act characterizes books in the True Crime genre. Women's Nonfiction books, however, do not share a unifying genre convention. What they *do* share is a readership. Like other reading interests, such as African-American Literature, or GLBTQ Literature, Women's Nonfiction is written for a particular audience. Women (and men interested in women's issues) are the intended audience. More specifically, readers of either sex who care about subjects that traditionally engage women—such as health care, relationships, spirituality, and women's history—are the audience for Women's Nonfiction. The books tend to be read by women and written by women, but men do read and write Women's Nonfiction, especially in areas that have wide appeal, such as Adventure and Travel.

Women's Nonfiction titles may be found in every Dewey range in a public library, and in biographies, memoirs, and autobiographies; they may be found in every nonfiction section of a bookstore. They are present in every recognized genre and theme of nonfiction (True Crime, Sports Writing, Science Writing, etc.), but they often coalesce to form their own unique types and subsets; in this book, for instance, you'll find women-intensive groupings such as "Motherhood" and "Feminism," as well as subsections such as "Women's Bodies and Sexuality Throughout History," "Women Warriors," and "Menstruation and Menopause."

Do books authored by women automatically count as Women's Nonfiction? Heavens, no. Antonia Fraser's *Royal Charles: Charles II and the Restoration* is about a man, obviously. (Most of Fraser's other works are Women's Nonfiction, though; see the "Royalty and Rulers" section in Chapter 1 for suggestions.)

Books about women, then—those are all Women's Nonfiction titles, right? Well, no, not necessarily, not by my definition—though you are encouraged to disagree if you feel otherwise. If the subject of a book is a woman, but her womanhood plays an insignificant role in her story, then I do not consider it to be Women's Nonfiction. Thus

Wesley the Owl: The Remarkable Love Story of an Owl and His Girl, biologist Stacey O'Brien's memoir of her nineteen-year relationship with a bird, does not make the cut; a man could just as easily have had a long-term devotion to a pet (see John Grogan's *Marley & Me* for proof). Again, I define Women's Nonfiction as that which speaks to women's experiences. If a woman's story does not in some way address sex or gender —if a man could have been substituted in her place to similar effect—then it is not Women's Nonfiction. (I suppose you could call it Person's Nonfiction.)

Why Do We Need a Readers' Guide to Women's Nonfiction?

There is a prevailing myth that nonfiction readers are men and that fiction readers are women. The operative word here is "myth." My most successful library book display ever was "Real Men Read Fiction." I tell you, I couldn't find enough Cormac Mc-Carthy, Robert Ludlum, or Raymond Chandler to keep that display stocked. Maybe they're not big on Romances or Chick Lit (although surely there must be some male fans out there, somewhere), but men do indeed read fiction.

Women, in their turn, read nonfiction. Of course there are certain nonfiction titles that are gender-neutral; Mark Kurlansky's *Cod: A Biography of the Fish That Changed the World* comes to mind. But there are plenty of books written specifically for female audiences. From biographies of pirate queens to memoirs of surviving breast cancer, from social histories of women's daily lives in colonial America to studies of women's representation in the media, there are innumerable nonfiction books that are read primarily by women (or by forward-thinking men who want to know more about women). The problem is finding these books.

I just typed in "women" in worldcat.org. Results: 713,929.

I typed in "women" in my local public library catalog and got a far more manageable 12,484 results. Hrm.

I went to the mega-popular online bookseller Amazon. Results: 674,304.

Let's put on our library hats for a minute. Say a patron walks in and asks you for a good True Crime book. Let's further say that you personally despise True Crime; you've only read one title in your life (Truman Capote's *In Cold Blood*, of course), and you're never reading another again; the library bookmobile has borrowed all of the readers' advisory texts for the day, so God knows where they are right now; and the Internet is down.

(If this sounds unrealistic, you've never worked in a public library.)

Don't worry: *you can fake it*. March yourself over to the 364s and pull the books with the raggedy covers. When all else fails, you know that "raggedy cover" means "popular."

Now let's say the patron asks for a good True Crime book about women. Well shucks, you can handle that. Just grab a book with a raggedy cover and a pretty girl on the front; heck, those books are usually one and the same, anyway.

But now your patron asks you for a nonfiction book about women's relationships. What do you do? Well—you ask for further clarification. Does your patron want a book about improving her marriage? Does she want a book about sisters? About strengthening her relationship with God? (If so, which God?) Or would she prefer something historical, a book about courtesans, or about women who followed their men to war, or about queens who slept around?

"Oooh, all of the above!" your patron squeals. And to think, you loaned this book to the bookmobile for the day. Good luck to you. You're gonna need it.

Because Women's Nonfiction is not (yet) recognized as a reading interest or a genre, there is no convenient way to find the various titles. There's no road map to this terrain. Unless you're in a women's bookstore, you're not likely to see Women's Nonfiction books clustered in one browsable area. And in a public library, where nonfiction titles are almost always shelved according to Dewey, you're going to have to hunt through the stacks—and even then, you'll have to spend time perusing the book to get an idea of its content, tone, pacing, and style.

The book in your hands aims to make life easier for librarians, booksellers, and readers who want to easily locate Women's Nonfiction. Titles are arranged by genre and subgenre, and each title offers a brief annotation that discusses, as appropriate, the four big appeal characteristics of any given book: story/frame, writing style, character, and setting. Glance at the subjects below each title for a quick-'n-dirty summary of the book's content, or turn to the indexes to hunt for a specific subject, author, or title.

What Is Included

I dimly recall from my tenth-grade English class that Hercules had to perform twelve impossible labors. If memory serves, one of those twelve labors was to cull through all of the titles that are, or might be, Women's Nonfiction.

Very foolishly, I had allotted myself four weeks to collect, consider, appraise, and organize the titles I would annotate. In reality, the process wound up consuming nearly half a year's worth of evenings and weekends, and even then the titles were not set in stone. Only two weeks before my draft was due I realized I had forgotten to include anything on Mother Teresa; and the very day before my deadline I swapped out two books in exchange for different titles and plopped them down in a chapter I thought I had already finished.

I say this to illustrate the enormous difficulty involved in selecting and evaluating Women's Nonfiction. It is an incredibly rich, diverse, vibrant collection of books; sometimes it was easy to toss out an obvious stinker, but more often I had to struggle over which books to include and which ones to set aside.

Until that glorious day when Women's Nonfiction gains acceptance as a recognizable reading interest or genre, it will be the brave, or quite possibly foolish, bibliographer who attempts to qualify it. There is no ALA Notable Women's Nonfiction list.

There is no National Women's Nonfiction Book Award. Women's Nonfiction titles have certainly won awards, but they are scattered in all sorts of different areas.

Instead, I relied on other resources to find titles. Various women's bookstores, publishing houses, and extant bibliographies helped me out (read more about them in the Appendix), as did persistent, dogged searching in WorldCat and Amazon. I also relied heavily on lessons learned as a student of Women's Studies: as an undergrad I was fortunate enough to study women's experiences through a thorough, well-rounded curriculum, so I tried to apply this same thoroughness to women's experiences in my selection of titles.

For the most part, the books annotated here were published between 1993 and 2008, although plenty of classics and mainstays found their way in. Who was I to tell Margery Kempe to butt out? She wrote what may well have been the first autobiography in the English language, for crying out loud.

Also, most—but not all—of the books here have been written for a popular audience, though one person's popular book is the next person's doggerel. I endeavored to only include books owned by more than one hundred libraries in WorldCat, reasoning that readers would be assured of borrowing them via interlibrary loan, even if their local libraries did not own the title. I depended on reviews from journals such as *Publishers Weekly* and *Booklist*. I depended even more heavily on reviews from readers in Amazon: what ultimately matters is not what an individual reviewer thinks of a book but what ordinary readers think of it.

In some cases, especially with books on women's history, I included titles written for academic audiences. These are mostly books that general audiences will enjoy, especially if they can adapt to scholarly jargon. When I felt a particular topic needed to be addressed, I included scholarly titles simply because no popular titles have been written. In those few instances in which a book may be truly difficult to read, I have clearly warned readers up front.

My selection of titles was influenced by one other notable factor, perhaps the most important of all: I tried to present a fair balance of perspectives. If I simply included the obvious picks—the popular, recent, accessible titles—I would have been writing disproportionately about heterosexual WASP women. By way of example, it was very easy to find books about Christian women for the "Religious Identity" section; finding books about Hindu women was far more difficult. I have strived to include a variety of perspectives in each genre and subgenre, though I will be the first to acknowledge that I have not always succeeded.

What Is *Not* Included

As explained earlier, a great many titles got axed because they were too old, too scholarly, too rare, or even too common—that is, if a topic had already been covered thoroughly, I chose to leave the section with a manageable number of titles. There are, for instance, sixteen books in the "Beauty, Fashion, and Appearance" section, plus six more in the "Cosmetics" section; twenty-two other perfectly good books could have been used in their place.

The genres, subgenres, and sub-subgenres make an earnest attempt to cover the breadth of women's experiences, but there are some areas that are noticeably absent. Where, for instance, are the books on women educators? They *are* here, actually, but not grouped together in one spot. As I discovered, most books about women as teachers are far too scholarly and technical to be of interest to general readers. Popular writing about women teachers instead tends to be found in specific chapters in books about women; see, for instance, Kay Bailey Hutchison's *American Heroines: The Spirited Women Who Shaped Our Country*.

A few other areas are missing. There are no books about car repair for women here: zip, zilch, zero, none. Never mind that I personally find most of them to be condescending and sexist; the real reason for their exclusion is that books about car repair are not meant to be read for pleasure.

That point bears repeating: *the titles in this book are meant to be read for pleasure*; titles that are not meant to be read for pleasure are not included. By and large, that means that the books discussed here offer narratives, either in book-length form—with a recognizable plot, development, climax, resolution—or in the form of mini-narratives; collective biographies, for instance, usually feature discrete, unrelated stories.

Some nonnarrative works do find their way in, though. There are no books on car repair for women, but there *are* books on finances for women—five of them are included, actually. Although they do not offer the character or plot development in the same way a novel does, they are nonetheless enjoyable to read: they contain anecdotes and stories, trivia and food for thought, engaging writing and good pacing. It just so happens that they also contain practical advice. Self-help books and how-to manuals constitute a significant slice of Women's Nonfiction, and although they are not the focus of this book, those that blend entertainment with information and instruction are occasionally included.

Other types of nonnarrative books are included, as well. Although Harold Koda's *Extreme Beauty: The Body Transformed* does feature interesting text, the real reason to read the book is for the breathtaking fashion photos. It is a book to be looked at more than read. (Of course, one could easily argue that the "narrative" of this book is relayed in pictures rather than words.) And, I confess, a few reference books slipped in: for instance, *The Woman's Encyclopedia of Myths and Secrets*, by Barbara G. Walker, is too influential, too readable, and too downright entertaining to exclude.

Succinctly put, this book does not include titles that are no fun to read—though of course, you may hold a different opinion about certain entries. Generally speaking, you'll find narratives, or collective narratives, in these pages; nonnarrative titles, such as how-to books, are less common but not entirely absent; and there are even a few reference books, but only those that are extraordinarily enjoyable to read.

A Word about Antifeminist Books

In the course of preparing this manuscript, anytime I came across a text by antifeminists Phyllis Schlafly or F. Carolyn Graglia, I would cackle maniacally and toss the book from the roof, where it would conveniently land in the "to be burned" pile.

Well, OK. This is not actually true, but I did fantasize about it.

Readers will nonetheless notice a feminist slant to the books I selected. (Having an entire chapter devoted to feminism is a big giveaway.) Part of this is a function of unintentional bias—my educational background is in feminism, not antifeminism—and part of it was probably even *intentional* bias. I made a decent attempt to include a wide variety of perspectives, but I could have gone to greater effort to include antifeminist books—meaning books that undermine the principles of women's equality.

Why did I did not make this greater effort? They are written for women and about women's experiences; all feminist books are Women's Nonfiction, but not all Women's Nonfiction books are feminist. The answer lies in the book market itself. There are far more feminist than antifeminist books discussed here, but this is a reflection of the books that are currently available in bookstores and libraries. By extension, this is a reflection of the current reading tastes of the Women's Nonfiction audience.

But this guide does not merely parrot the book market. For every subject discussed here, I tried to faithfully represent the choices available to readers, but I balanced this with including niche interests. For example, it was easy to find books about the lesbian experience, but difficult to find books about the transsexual experience. Neglecting the "T" in GLBTQ would have been easier for me, but I didn't want to ignore this small but important population.

Likewise, I did include some books that contradict traditional feminist thought. They are fewer in number than the feminist titles, in keeping with the book market, but they do show up here. See, for instance, Katie Roiphe's treatise against the feminist approach to date rape in *The Morning After: Sex, Fear, and Feminism*, or Brian Mitchell's argument against women in combat in *Women in the Military: Flirting with Disaster*.

How to Use This Book

Organization of the Chapters

There are eight chapters in this book, each representing a specific genre, format, or reading interest in Women's Nonfiction. Three of these chapters are borrowed straight from recognized nonfiction genres: Life Stories: Biography, Autobiography, and Memoirs; (Women's) History; and Adventure and Travel. The other five chapters are less familiar and more subject-oriented: Personal Growth; Health, Wellness, and Beauty; Feminism and Activism; Women at Work; and Women and Society. Within each chapter there are sections and subsections, introduced with brief definitions and explanations of appeal. In addition, the eight chapters each kick off with three narrative sections that discuss the history and definition of the genre, the appeal characteristics of the genre, and the organization of the chapter.

The Annotations and the "Now Try" Recommendations

Within these pages you'll find 632 titles, each of which is accompanied by an annotation of approximately 100 words (or more, when the bibliographer couldn't help herself). The annotations offer brief summaries of the plot or purpose of the book—but, in recognizing that there is more to nonfiction pleasure reading than subject, the annotations also include information, as appropriate, on tone, style, pace, setting, and characters. Each annotation is followed by a listing of subjects, though this is something of a misnomer. Subject information (marriage, politics, the Civil War) is included, but if relevant, so, too, is information on place (Afghanistan, Europe, the Roman Empire) and time (Prehistory, Dark Ages, Nineteenth Century) and format and age (Graphic Novel, Memoir, Young Adult). For each book, bibliographic information —including original and most recent publication dates—is included, along with ISBN-13 numbers and page counts.

Following each annotation, you'll find a "Now Try" section, featuring one or more companion reads. These recommendations are based on similar appeal factors, whether in subject, tone, setting, or some other appeal. These read-alikes are based on my own judgment. Some were culled from judicious searches of Amazon's "Customers who bought this title also purchased" suggestions; some were suggestions from colleagues and friends; and some were just serendipitous good luck. Typically the follow-up reads are themselves Women's Nonfiction titles, though books with appeal to men and a few fiction suggestions do appear now and again.

The "Consider Starting With . . ." and the "Fiction Read-Alikes" Sections

If for some reason you do not have time to read every word of every single annotation of every single genre, skip to the cheat-sheet at the end of the chapter. The "Consider Starting With . . ." section lists a handful of books that are likely to appeal to readers of each particular genre. I hesitate to call them sure bets—I do not believe in the *existence* of sure bets—but each one of these titles has been chosen for its accessibility and broad appeal. Many of these titles spent time on best-seller lists, and all of them, in some way, offer a fine representation of, and introduction to, their specific genre.

Finally, you'll come to the "Fiction Read-Alikes" section. These titles, 109 in all, have been chosen because they share appeal factors with their nonfiction cousins. Don't be alarmed: there are genre titles here (and not just the obvious Women's Fiction genre; you'll see science fiction, fantasy, and thrillers, too), but they have been selected for their compatibility with nonfiction reading interests.

A Note on Language

Before the nice townsfolk of the book world show up at my door with torches and pitchforks, I'd like to explain my use of language. As any good feminist can tell you, language is a powerful tool, far more powerful than most folks realize. It can have innocuous, subconscious effects (do you ever say "firemen" when you mean "fire fighters"?), or—when it comes to matters of race and sex—it can have very noticeable, very significant meanings. It is this second situation that I want to draw attention to, so pray forgive a few brief semantics lessons.

Race. We generally recognize race as referring to the color of a person's skin. Ethnicity refers to a cultural and social heritage; it is usually, but not necessarily, associated with a particular race. In this book, I use "white" to refer to white people; I use "black" as well as "African American" to refer to black Americans; I also use "black" to refer to people with black skin color who aren't from America. The other common racial designations in use are Native American, Asian American, Latina, and Chicana. I use "Latina" to refer to women from Mexico, the Caribbean, and South America; "Latina" also refers to women (primarily Americans) who no longer live in those locales, or women whose foremothers lived in those locales. Finally, I use "Chicana" to refer to women of Mexican descent who presently live in America.

Sex and Gender. In this book, "sex" usually refers to a person's biology. Most people have either a female or a male sex; a few folks undergo operations to change their sex; and a very few are intersexual, with biological characteristics of both males and females. (I also happily use sex to refer to sexual relations between people.)

I use "gender" to refer to the social construct that is so often confused with sex. Though this is by no means universally accepted, I consider gender to be created by family, friends, the media, the environment: in other words, I consider it to be caused by nurture, unlike sex, which is caused by nature. Thus when I speak of gender, I refer to the trappings of womanhood (wearing makeup and skirts, being diplomatic, being intuitive); when I wish to refer to a person's physiological construction, I say "sex."

Note well: When I speak of someone's sexual preferences (i.e., when I speak of a person's identity as straight, gay, lesbian, queer, etc.), I use the phrase "sexual orientation," *not* "sexuality." I use the word "sexuality" not to describe an individual's preferences but to indicate the person's sexual awareness, interest, and identity.

Queer. Although "queer" was once a slanderous term, and is still often used as such, it has been embraced and reappropriated by the sexual minority community as a term of pride. It is now possible at certain universities to earn a degree in Queer Studies. I use "queer" throughout the book as a convenient shorthand to describe anyone who is not strictly heterosexual. It is far less cumbersome than "sexual minority" or "LGBT." Plus it's nice to steal back a word that was intended as an insult.

Labor. One last language lesson: "Labor," as used throughout the book, refers to work and employment, not the birthing process. (For that, I say "childbirth.") Note that I fully consider motherhood to be a variety of labor.

A Note on Style and Form

Sometime after I started working on this manuscript, Neil Hollands—my colleague, good buddy, and father to my cat (long story)—published his book *Read on—Fantasy Fiction: Reading Lists for Every Taste*. It is, and I say this with neither bias nor irony, the most entertaining annotated bibliography you will ever read. I read the whole stinking book, front to back. The table of contents alone sent me into a fit of giggles.

Although I doubt that any of you will stay up late with this book (but let me know if you do!), I have tried to capture at least a little bit of Neil's good humor and flair for words. There's no rule saying that annotated bibliographies have to be dull . . . is there? Don't be surprised to see the occasional uncalled-for personal opinion or the informal use of the second person.

Finally, I would be remiss if I did not acknowledge my debt to Sarah Statz Cords. Well before I got the first inkling that I might write my own readers' advisory text, I had admired her magnificent book *The Real Story: A Guide to Nonfiction Reading Interests*.

Then, as now, I referred to it frequently in the course of my duties as a readers' advisor at a bustling public library. But it was not till I started writing my own readers' advisory text that I began to appreciate how truly superb it is. With absolutely no shame at all, I have plundered her ideas and modeled my book after hers wherever possible. If this book strikes you as suspiciously similar to *The Real Story*, then I will take that as the highest compliment.

Chapter 1

Life Stories: Biography, Autobiography, and Memoirs

Definition

Quick! Think of a Women's Nonfiction book that doesn't talk about people's lives!

Having a hard time coming up with something? Me, too. Certain informational texts intended to be consulted on an as-needed reference basis—cookbooks, for instance —focus on information needs, not on people's lives. They generally aren't meant to be read as narratives (though if you've read or skimmed a cookbook from cover to cover, you're not alone). But it is the rare Women's Nonfiction narrative that does not refer, at least in part, to people's life experiences. Every single title discussed in the book you now hold in your hands could have arguably been categorized under "Life Stories."

> This chapter covers books that tell the stories of women's lives—primarily biographies, autobiographies, and memoirs.

To narrow the field, this chapter primarily covers biographies, autobiographies, and memoirs, though a few other types of works have snuck in; *The Diary of a Young Girl*, for instance, is the diary of Anne Frank, not her memoir proper. This is not to say that biographies, autobiographies, and memoirs do not show up in other chapters; they do, repeatedly, under their appropriate sections, though many of them could have been listed here.

There are countless life stories written by and about women, but only those that emphasize the unusual role of women's sex or gender are included here. Régine Pernoud's biography of *Joan of Arc* makes the cut because St. Joan defied gender norms to lead her people to victory in war. Tina Brown's biography *The Diana Chronicles*, on the other hand, is not here; although Princess Di was an extremely influential woman—not to mention beautiful and photogenic—she nonetheless acted within gender norms.

The Life Stories genre of Women's Nonfiction is dizzying in size. One could easily write a book—a *series* of books—about the cornucopia of titles written about women's lives. Such an enterprise would certainly include Princess Diana and other women (think Marilyn Monroe, or Madonna, or Jenna Jameson) who, for reasons of space, are not listed here. What follows are books about women who have acted outside the social norm to make a difference.

Appeal

The uber-popular celebrity magazine *People* is aptly named; we like to peer into the lives of other folks, see how the other side lives. Different readers prefer different details (What kind of clothes do they wear? How do they raise their children? What are their political views?), and different eras (ancient history, twentieth-century history, contemporary lives), and different professions (rulers, businesspeople, clergy)—but ultimately, it's very simple: people like to read about people.

Sometimes we read about people similar to ourselves. Struggling entrepreneurs can find inspiration in Virginia G. Drachman's *Enterprising Women: 250 Years of American Business*—but you don't have to own your own business to take heart from the tales of triumph over poverty in this collective biography. Likewise, Native American women can find a role model in Mary Brave Bird's *Lakota Woman*, but women (or men) of any background can take pleasure in her riveting story of race and class. Any given book in the Life Stories genre will affirm one person's experience while opening an entirely new world to another person. We read them both to affirm and expand.

The other reason to read Life Stories is to give a face to a concept. It is one thing to read about transsexuality; it is another to hear the voice of a woman married to a transsexual man in Helen Boyd's *My Husband Betty*. Books in the Life Stories genre permit us to become intimately familiar with a topic through the eyes of a person who lived it. This becomes especially apparent when the topic is history. Many people who avoid traditional history books will gladly read about times past if the focus is on character. A book marketed as a history of politics in sixteenth-century Ireland may have limited appeal, but Anne Chambers's *Granuaile: Ireland's Pirate Queen C. 1530–1603* speaks of daring and courage and adventure, just from the title alone.

Organization

The first section, "Biography," features stories of women who have made their mark as leaders, rulers, or feminists (or all three). These are women who have boldly defied gender norms, whether in the third century (see Michael A. B. Deakin's *Hypatia of Alexandria: Mathematician and Martyr*) or the twenty-first (see Carl Bernstein's *A Woman in Charge: The Life of Hillary Rodham Clinton*). The subsection "Women in the Professions" features women who have made their mark in fields traditionally dominated by men, and "Royalty and Rulers" features women who have made their mark in one specific field traditionally dominated by men, by ruling as spouses of government leaders or as government leaders themselves.

Like the Biography genre, the Autobiography and Memoirs genre includes books about women who have taken a nontraditional approach to the prescribed sex and gender roles of their various milieus. The "Global Voices" subsection features stories about women around the world, while "Women Warriors" includes stories of women in recent times and times long past who have joined the military to defend their countries.

One could argue that simply being a woman deviates from the patriarchal norm, but the women in the third subgenre, Women in the Margins, "deviate" in more than one way. In the "Queer Identity" subsection, you'll meet lesbians, bisexuals, and transsexuals who exist outside the mainstream heterosexual culture. "Racial and Cultural Identity" features books about women from minority races, ethnicities, and cultures, while "Religious Identity" features women whose identities are shaped by their faiths. Of course, "Women in the Margins" is a thematic selection, unlike the first two sections, so it includes biographies, autobiographies, and memoirs—but all with a specific focus.

Biography

> Biographies are life stories as told by a third party. In this book, the person whose life story is being told happens to be a woman.

Narrowing down the titles for this section was an excruciating process. I was tempted to direct readers to the biography section of their library or bookstore and to just grab a book with a picture of a woman on the cover. That would have been *much* easier for me.

Instead, I have chosen to focus here on biographies about women who distinguished themselves despite the obstacle of unsympathetic gender norms. Some of these women, such as Catherine de Medici, married into positions of power; some, such as Queen Elizabeth I, were born into it; others, such as Eleanor Roosevelt, had the wherewithal to transform their circumstances into positions of power. Yet others skipped "power" in the traditional sense, instead forging nontraditional paths to make their marks, as Judy Chicago did with her art.

The Biography genre comprises two subsections: "Women in the Professions" features books about women, past and present, who dared to choose careers that were traditionally dominated by men, while "Royalty and Rulers" features books about queens, chiefs, consorts, czarinas, and empresses.

Barry, Kathleen

Susan B. Anthony: A Biography of a Singular Feminist. New York: New York University Press, 1988 (2000). 426pp. ISBN 9780814711057.

In the year 1820, a rather normal Massachusetts family welcomed a rather normal girl to the world. Like other girls of the time, Anthony learned how to keep house, a necessary skill for the marriage that everyone assumed she would enter, and she bucked no gender roles when she took her first job as a teacher. In other words, shows sociologist Barry, Anthony's younger years were perfectly ordinary—but then something unexpected happened: she left her job in education to advocate for women's rights, embarking on a career to campaign for women's suffrage and equal treatment under the law. With her thorough research and engaging storytelling style, Barry traces Anthony's evolution from her traditional upbringing to her extraordinary role in the women's movement as a national star in the first wave of feminism. Read this biography not only to learn about Anthony's activist career but also to gain insight into her personal life, including her friendship with Elizabeth Cady Stanton and her unusual (for the time) decision not to marry.

> **Subjects:** Anthony, Susan B. • Feminism • First-wave Feminism • Activism • Politics • Suffrage • Labor • History • Women's History • Social History • American History • Nineteenth Century • America • Biography

> **Now Try:** Learn more about the personal lives of Anthony and four of her fellow activists—Elizabeth Cady Stanton, Lucy Stone, Frances Willard and Alice Paul—in *Sisters: The Lives of America's Suffragists*, in which historian Jean H. Baker deftly explores the societal milieu of the nineteenth and twentieth centuries to give context to the feminist accomplishments of the suffragists. Then meet more American women activists in *Nine Women: Portraits from the American Radical Tradition*. In this collective biography, Judith Nies paints portraits of women activists who made a difference, not only with women's suffrage but also with such issues as the abolition of slavery, the environment, and the Civil Rights movement.

Bernstein, Carl

A Woman in Charge: The Life of Hillary Rodham Clinton. New York: Alfred A. Knopf, 2007. 628pp. ISBN 9780375407666.

While myriad books revile Hillary Rodham Clinton, and while many others praise her to no end, Carl Bernstein's comes as close to neutrality as possible, considering that the subject is a woman who inspires the full gamut of emotions in her fellow Americans. Published in 2007, before Clinton announced her decision to change history by running for president, this biography considers the woman from her days as a child through her growing political awareness in college, from her position as Bill Clinton's most trusted political advisor through her meteoric rise in the United States Senate. Drawing on historical records and on interviews with family members, friends, and enemies, the book sheds light on Clinton's enigmatic personality, tracing the development of her politics and values and unflinchingly examining her triumphs and failures alike.

> **Subjects:** Clinton, Hillary Rodham • Senators • Rulers • Lawyers • First Ladies • Politics • Labor • Relationships • Twentieth Century • Twenty-first Century • America • Biography

> **Now Try:** The book *Living History* presents a more biased view of Clinton, but that is understandable, as Clinton herself wrote it. In this memoir, she reflects on her childhood, her politics, and her remarkable experiences as first lady. Then learn more about Clinton the woman and Clinton the political phenomenon in *Thirty Ways of Looking at Hillary: Reflections by Women Writers*, edited by Susan Morrison, in which thirty savvy writers such as Deborah Tannen and Katha Pollitt present their views—some critical, some hopeful, some conflicted—on gender, politics, and the influence of Clinton in America. Then read about another powerful woman in American politics with *Condoleezza Rice: An American Life*. Elisabeth Bumiller's biography of the former Secretary of State (the post assumed by Clinton under the Obama administration) describes

Rice's rise to power by drawing on interviews with her admirers, her detractors, and Rice herself.

Chesler, Ellen

Woman of Valor: Margaret Sanger and the Birth Control Movement in America. New York: Simon & Schuster, 1992. 639pp. ISBN 9780671600884.

Margaret Sanger is the feminist founding mother whom feminists hate to love and love to hate. As the founder of Planned Parenthood, Sanger's early advocacy for birth control makes her a pioneer in the fight for a woman's right to control her own reproduction; as an advocate for eugenics through birth control, she is a symbol of the racist history of feminism—and reader be warned, author Chesler treads very lightly around this controversial, disturbing side of Sanger's politics. With that caveat in mind, however, this is a fascinating biography of the woman who found herself in the American feminist limelight after she was imprisoned for opening the country's first birth control clinic in 1916. Filled with details about Sanger's two marriages and numerous affairs, this is an engrossing study of Sanger's personal life, her belief in sexual freedom, and her fight to give women access to reproductive choice.

Subjects: Sanger, Margaret • Birth Control • Abortion • Activism • Feminism • First-wave Feminism • Sexual Health • Health • Politics • Labor • History • Women's History • Social History • Nineteenth Century • Twentieth Century • American History • America • Biography

Now Try: Chesler offers a sympathetic apology for Sanger's racist attitudes as a function of the times she lived in; decide for yourself whether you agree with Chesler's interpretation by reading Sanger's own words in *The Pivot of Civilization*. Originally published in 1922, the book speaks eloquently to the power that women can wield in their own lives by having the right to birth control, while endorsing the use of birth control by the underprivileged and women of color as a means of large-scale social eugenics. Sanger's views clash with present-day sensibilities, and yet this is a thought-provoking read for those who want to understand the history of the controversial beginnings of modern birth control.

Cook, Blanche Wiesen

Eleanor Roosevelt. 2 vols. New York: Viking, 1992. 1,312pp. ISBN 9780747549758 (v.1) and 9780140178944 (v.2).

With more than one thousand pages already written, two volumes published thus far, and a third to be published in the future, this comprehensive biography of Eleanor Roosevelt takes time and persistence to read. But do not be intimidated: the books are long, but historian Cook crafts a compelling narrative with her engrossing writing style, shedding new light on one of the most beloved and influential women in American history. The first volume covers the years from Roosevelt's birth in 1884 through her husband's entrance into the White House in 1933, with a focus on her personality, her political perspectives, and her courtship and marriage; the second volume covers the first years of her tenure as first lady, from 1933 to 1938, with a focus on her activism, her complicated relationship with her husband, and her growing friendship with journalist

Lorena Hickok. Exhaustively researched, the biography relies on documents and solid history, rather than conjecture, to flesh out the story of Roosevelt's personal life and public politics.

Subjects: Roosevelt, Eleanor • First Ladies • Feminism • First-wave Feminism • Activism • Politics • Labor • History • Women's History • American History • Nineteenth Century • Twentieth Century • America • Biography

Now Try: Hear now from Roosevelt herself in *The Autobiography of Eleanor Roosevelt*. Published in 1961, just a year before her death, the book details her remarkable life story, taking readers through her childhood, her years in the White House, and her activism in the United States and around the world. With a focus on her experiences rather than on her personal relationships and private thoughts, the autobiography makes for a fascinating look at the remarkable achievements of a woman whose commitment to activism and feminism was well ahead of its time. For a much lighter read, turn to any of the *Eleanor Roosevelt Mysteries*, written by Roosevelt's own son, Elliott Roosevelt. *Murder and the First Lady* is the first in this delightful series, in which Eleanor Roosevelt takes up sleuthing in addition to her job as first lady.

Deakin, Michael A. B.

Hypatia of Alexandria: Mathematician and Martyr. Amherst, NY: Prometheus Books, 2007. 231pp. ISBN 9781591025207.

Very little concrete evidence exists about the world's first well-known female mathematician, but mathematical scholar Deakin takes what scant evidence there is and turns it into a fascinating biography of Hypatia, who lived in the third and fourth centuries C.E. As an intellectual, a philosopher, a religious thinker, and a committed celibate, this extraordinary woman developed algorithms for long division, studied conic sections, and understood the astrolabe. She devoted herself to the pagan philosophy of neoplatonism, and she shared her religious and academic knowledge with a large group of students—indeed, it was her influence with her students and with the civil authorities in Alexandria that led to her murder at the hands of a Christian mob. With exemplary research and accessible prose, Deakin studies the life and the death of a woman who made brilliant intellectual advances at a time when most people couldn't even read; the narrative itself is a succinct, quick read, though readers wishing to study her math in detail can turn to the appendixes for further insight.

Subjects: Hypatia • Mathematics • Astronomy • Science • Labor • History • History of Science • Classical History • Ancient History • Third Century • Fourth Century • Women's History • Paganism • Christianity • Religion • Greece • Europe • Biography • Quick Read

Now Try: For another carefully researched biography of Hypatia, turn to Maria Dzielska's *Hypatia of Alexandria*. In places she does speculate into the personality and character of Hypatia, but Dzielska's conjectures are informed by scholarship that is based solidly on historical documents such as the letters of the Hypatian student Synesius. Though the book focuses less on Hypatia's math than Deakin does in his study, Deakin's fans will appreciate Dzielska's commitment to pealing back layers of myth to reveal the real Hypatia. Then jump forward to the present day to meet Sarah Flannery in her memoir *In Code: A Mathematical Journey*. Like Hypatia, Flannery is a brilliant mathematician; she made headlines for her work with algorithms, an impressive feat in its own right—but now consider that Flannery was only sixteen years old at the time.

Fraser, Nicholas, and Marysa Navarro

Evita: The Real Life of Eva Perón. New York: W.W. Norton, 1980 (1996). 198pp. ISBN 9780393315752.

Perhaps you know Evita through the Andrew Lloyd Weber musical of the same name, famously played on the big screen by Madonna. Now meet this remarkable woman in this extensively researched biography, which, of all the many biographies written about Eva Perón, is one of the most balanced. This is no mean feat, as Evita continues to inspire equal measures of fanatical worship and disparaging criticism more than half a century after her death from uterine cancer at age thirty-three. Learn how an illegitimate child born in rural Argentina in 1919 grew up to become an actress and a mistress to Colonel Juan Perón—and eventually, to become the first lady of Argentina. Well researched and engaging, this biography illuminates the politics and personality of the woman behind the larger-than-life legends.

> **Subjects:** Evita • Perón, Eva • Politics • Labor • History • Women's History • Twentieth Century • Argentina • South America • Biography • Quick Read

> **Now Try:** A natural follow-up read is *Evita: In My Own Words*, ostensibly by Eva Perón herself, though reader beware: her family members dispute the authenticity of the text. If this really is the deathbed memoir of Argentina's first lady, however, it is well worth the read for the insight into Evita's vision of herself and her political philosophies. Another excellent companion read is *Evita: An Intimate Portrait of Eva Perón*, by Tómas de Elia and Juan Pablo Queiroz, which supplements a concise biographical narrative with a plethora of illuminating photographs and illustrations. Readers may also enjoy *Santa Evita*, written in Spanish by Tomás Eloy Martínez and translated by Helen R. Lane; this peculiar but beautifully written novel relates the journey of Evita's embalmed body following her death.

Holland, Barbara

They Went Whistling: Women Wayfarers, Warriors, Runaways, and Renegades. New York: Pantheon Books, 2001. 281pp. ISBN 9780375420559.

How shall we describe the women profiled in Holland's electric collective biography? Some of them were criminals (there's Bonnie Parker, of Bonnie and Clyde fame) and some of them were saints (literally, as with Joan of Arc); some of them exuded sexuality (think Cleopatra, or the lesser-known Lola Montez), while others decided that female sexuality could take a hike (there's the cross-dressing George Sand, and soldier James Barry, who was only discovered to be a woman upon his—or rather her—death). They came from different countries, different backgrounds, and different centuries, but one thing unites them: each one of these women decided to buck the social norms in pursuit of her own agenda. Briskly paced and catchy in style, this is a compelling social history, a tribute to independent women across the ages.

> **Subjects:** Adventure • History • Women's History • Social History • Global Perspectives • Biography • Collection

> **Now Try:** Looking for more ladies throughout history who decided to ignore social convention? Turn to *The Mammoth Book of Heroic & Outrageous Women*, edited by Gemma Alexander. With profiles such as "Lucrezia Borgia: The World's Wickedest Woman?" and "Mae West: The Bad Girl of Broadway,"

this captivating collection of mini-biographies takes us into the lives of women, some famous, some lesser-known, who refused to let gender norms stand in their way. Then consider a subset of adventurous women with *The Illustrated Virago Book of Women Travellers*. Edited by Mary Morris and Larry O'Connor, the book features gorgeous illustrations alongside writing by women such as Freya Stark and Mary Wollstonecraft.

Hutchison, Kay Bailey

American Heroines: The Spirited Women Who Shaped Our Country. New York: William Morrow, 2004. 384pp. ISBN 9780060566357.

Author Hutchison—who as a leading Texas senator has herself helped shape the country—presents an entertaining, enlightening look at the lives of influential American women past and present. Skillfully blending memoir, historical biography, and contemporary interviews, Hutchison considers movers-and-shakers in ten themed sections, including as "Education for Everyone," "Saving Lives," and "A Woman's Art." Stories of heroines from the past, such as Mary Baker Eddy and Sarah Winnemucca, share the light with contemporary women, among them Elizabeth Dole, Madeleine Albright, and Jackie Joyner-Kersee. Fun, informative, and highly readable, this collective biography shines light on women both famous and obscure who have made a difference in American history.

> **Subjects:** Activism • Labor • Politics • History • Women's History • Social History • American History • Eighteenth Century • Nineteenth Century • Twentieth Century • America • Biography • Memoir • Collection • Young Adult

> **Now Try:** For more stories of women throughout American history who have made a difference, turn to *Portraits of American Women: From Settlement to the Present*, edited by G. J. Barker-Benfield and Catherine Clinton. Arranged chronologically, the book presents biographies on twenty-four influential women, starting with Pocahontas and Anne Hutchinson and ending with Betty Friedan. Then turn to the biographies in *Lighting the Way: Nine Women Who Changed Modern America*, in which Karenna Gore Schiff examines the lives of nine twentieth-century women who had a profound impact on America's social and political landscape. Even the most famous among these nine women is, at best, moderately well known, so this will be a treat for history buffs who want to learn about forgotten figures from the past.

Levin, Gail

Becoming Judy Chicago: A Biography of the Artist. New York: Harmony Books, 2007. 485pp. ISBN 9781400054121.

A girl named Judith Cohen was born in 1939, but in 1970 she shed her old patriarchal surname to become Judy Chicago, the woman who would become a tour de force of feminist art in the late twentieth century. Best known for her controversial multimedia project "The Dinner Party," Chicago is a modern-day feminist icon, a woman who rejected the dominance of masculine norms in her art in favor of feminine imagery and values. In this compelling biography, author Levin draws on her own insight as an art curator to flesh out the details of Chicago's childhood, training, and revolutionary career. Based on Chicago's letters and unpublished writings and on Levin's interviews with Chicago's colleagues and friends, the biography reveals the complicated character and personal life of the artist while illuminating the significance of her remarkable career.

> **Subjects:** Chicago, Judy • Art • Artists • Feminism • Labor • History • Art History • Women's History • American History • Twentieth Century • America • Biography

Now Try: Hear now from Chicago herself in her two memoirs. Published in 1975, *Through the Flower: My Struggle as a Woman Artist* speaks with the raw urgency of a woman who is forging bold new inroads into the world of male-dominated art. The 1996 follow-up, *Beyond the Flower: The Autobiography of a Feminist Artist*, is more contemplative in tone as Chicago reflects on her career and muses about the directions that feminism in art should take. Readers wanting to know more about Chicago's most famous piece of art will enjoy her book *The Dinner Party: From Creation to Preservation*; published in 2007, the same year that her masterpiece found a permanent home in the Elizabeth A. Sackler Center for Feminist Art at the Brooklyn Museum, the book describes how the project came to be, while detailing the significance and meaning of the final product. To learn more about feminist art, try *The Power of Feminist Art: The American Movement of the 1970s, History and Impact*. Edited by Norma Broude and Mary D. Garrard, the book features art history, art criticism, and biographical information along with art reproductions.

Markey, Kevin

100 Most Important Women of the 20th Century. Des Moines, IA: Ladies' Home Journal Books, 1998. 192pp. ISBN 9780696208232.

Readers realize, of course, that any "Most Important" book will be inherently controversial, and this one is no different. (To my chagrin, Phyllis Schlafly is included, whereas my mother's name is mysteriously missing. Really, how is this fair?) With that caveat in mind, this is an entertaining and informative collective biography, packaged in a visually appealing layout and brimming with illustrations. But what is most appealing about the book is its intent: as the title says, the women have been chosen because of their *importance*—not because they necessarily did good things, or even bad things, but because their actions had a huge impact. Thus we see social reformer Eleanor Roosevelt alongside pop star Madonna, miniskirt inventor Mary Quant alongside Communist China's first lady, Madame Mao. Agree or disagree with the women included, this is a thought-provoking collection of concise, engaging biographies.

> **Subjects:** History • Women's History • Twentieth Century • Global Perspectives • Biography • Collection • Quick Read

> **Now Try:** Because it lays no claim to presenting the "most important" women of the twentieth century, Claudia Roth Pierpont's *Passionate Minds: Women Rewriting the World* is less likely to rankle readers' sensibilities—and yet the women profiled in this collective biography are by no means a vanilla bunch. The inclusion of Eudora Welty may not be a surprise, but readers may raise a brow over Doris Lessing—and as for Ayn Rand, well, the mere mention of her name has the power to provoke controversy. Those who liked the eclectic group of women in *100 Most Important Women of the 20th Century* will enjoy this engaging examination of eleven twentieth-century women writers.

Mattioni, Gloria

Reckless: The Outrageous Lives of Nine Kick-Ass Women. Emeryville, CA: Seal Press, 2005. 199pp. ISBN 9781580051484.

Ever heard of sled dog racer Libby Riddles? She was the first woman to win the Iditarod. How about Julia Butterfly Hill? This environmental activist lived atop a California redwood for two years to save it from loggers. Discover these and seven other courageous women who have dared to follow their dreams, despite prevailing social and gender norms. With photos, quotes, and captivating writing, this is an inspiring collective biography of outrageous women and their outrageous lives; filled with fascinating details about their struggles and triumphs, *Reckless* pays tribute to the bravery and independence of women.

> **Subjects:** Adventure • America • Biography • Collection • Quick Read • Young Adult
>
> **Now Try:** For more stories of remarkable women, turn to Katherine Martin's *Women of Spirit: Stories of Courage from the Women Who Lived Them*. Martin introduces each essay with a brief biographical sketch, and then the women themselves tell how they have found the strength to overcome obstacles and objections to make a difference in the world.

Miller, John, ed.

Legends: Women Who Have Changed the World through the Eyes of Great Women Writers. Novato, CA: New World Library, 1998. 128pp. ISBN 9781577310426.

It's hard to say what is the best part of this book: the fifty women who are the subjects of this collective biography, the portraits of those fifty women, or the authors who have penned the biographies. The concept is marvelous: an accomplished set of writers present their take on a variety of legendary women; thus Alice Walker writes about Zora Neale Hurtson, Joan Didion writes about Georgia O'Keefe, and Susan Cheever writes about Twiggy. Each profile is paired with a full-page photograph of the woman being discussed, making this a lovely, thought-provoking survey of some of the most interesting women of the twentieth century, written *by* some of the most interesting women of the twentieth century.

> **Subjects:** History • Women's History • Twentieth Century • Global Perspectives • Biography • Collection • Quick Read
>
> **Now Try:** Editor John Miller knows a good thing when he sees it: follow with his sequel, *Legends 2*. Using the same concept as in *Legends*, we meet such women as Donna Karan, Hillary Clinton, and Queen Latifah through the eyes of Coretta Scott King, Maria Shriver, Gail Sheehy, and others. Then, for a quirky companion read, try *Wild Words from Wild Women: An Unbridled Collection of Candid Observations & Extremely Opinionated Bon Mots*, by Autumn Stephens. This is a fun, lighthearted collection of quotes from a variety of women, from Emily Dickinson, Madonna, and Gertrude Stein ("Besides Shakespeare and me, who do you think there is?").

Pernoud, Régine, Marie-Véronique Clin, Jeremy duQuesnay Adams, and Bonnie Wheeler

Joan of Arc: Her Story. New York: St. Martin's Press, 1999. 304pp. ISBN 978031-2214425.

Literally tens of thousands of biographies have been written about Joan of Arc, the fifteenth-century French military leader who was first martyred and then sainted. Choosing which ones to read can be daunting, but a wise place to start is with the author Régine Pernoud, the French historian who until her death was one of the world's leading scholars of Joan of Arc. Pernoud's *Joan of Arc: Her Story*, coauthored with scholar Clin, translated from the French by Adams and edited by Wheeler, serves as an excellent introduction to the real person behind centuries of myths and legends. Based solidly in contemporary historical documents such as letters and trial transcripts, the book examines what is known, rather than what has been speculated. The resulting text may seem intimidating at first, but

Pernoud and Clin have arranged the historical sources within the context of a gripping narrative that illuminates Joan's character, her spiritual communications with God, her triumphs, and her rigged trial and death at the stake.

Subjects: Joan of Arc • Warriors • Spirituality • Religion • Christianity • Medieval History • Fifteenth Century • France • Europe • Women's History • Military History • History of Religion • Biography

Now Try: Those who enjoy Régine Pernoud's insightful analysis and keen scholarship will wish to turn to her many other books about Joan of Arc; perhaps continue with the biography *Joan of Arc: By Herself and Her Witnesses*, in which Pernoud achieves the remarkable feat of presenting historical sources in the form of vivid dialogue. And for another excellent presentation of the transcripts of Joan's trials, turn to theologian author Donald Spoto; his biography *Joan: The Mysterious Life of the Heretic Who Became a Saint* examines Joan's faith and convictions within the context of her heresy charges. Then explore Joan of Arc's life with a work of historical fiction, *An Army of Angels: A Novel of Joan of Arc*. With precise historical details and a captivating sense of setting, author Pamela Marcantel brings to life a passionate, willful Joan.

Women in the Professions

The "Women in the Professions" section celebrates those women, in times past and present, who have excelled in careers traditionally held by men. These are character-driven books that allow readers to explore fields such as aviation, science, and business, along with the barriers to women's employment associated with those fields.

Biskupic, Joan

Sandra Day O'Connor: How the First Woman on the Supreme Court Became Its Most Influential Justice. New York: ECCO, 2005. 419pp. ISBN 9780060590185.

In 1981, the United States welcomed its first female Supreme Court justice, Sandra Day O'Connor, who served for a quarter of a century until her retirement in 2001. (Only one other woman has been appointed since O'Connor, justice Ruth Bader Ginsburg.) Written by *USA Today* journalist Biskupic, a long-time Supreme Court observer, this fascinating biography focuses primarily on O'Connor's remarkable career, though it does not stint on more personal aspects of the justice's life, such as her childhood and her battle with breast cancer in the late 1980s. With a deft understanding of political science and constitutional law, Biskupic examines the trends of O'Connor's decisions and convincingly argues that she was the court's most influential justice, because hers was so often the swing vote in the court's 5–4 rulings. Based on O'Connor's personal papers, the biography offers an eye-opening look not only at the first female Supreme Court justice but at the inner workings of the judicial branch of the American government.

Subjects: O'Connor, Sandra Day • Judges • Lawyers • Supreme Court • Labor • Politics • Breast Cancer • America • Twentieth Century • Biography

Now Try: For a further glimpse into the life and mind of Sandra Day O'Connor, turn to two books that she herself has written. *Lazy B: Growing Up on a Cattle Ranch in the American Southwest*, cowritten with her brother H. Alan Day, takes us back into the 1930s and '40s, long before Sandra Day donned her black robes; this offers a glimpse into O'Connor's childhood, when she and her brother worked with cowboys and livestock on the family's ranch. Then turn to O'Connor's memoir of her later years, *The Majesty of the Law: Reflections of a Supreme Court Justice*, in which she shares her thoughts on American law and the Supreme Court; told in an eminently readable style, and with plenty of anecdotes about her fellow justices, this is one of the most engaging civics books you'll ever read. And readers keen to know more about the Supreme Court will want to try *The Brethren: Inside the Supreme Court*. Though written in 1979, Bob Woodward's examination remains one of the most informative and captivating books about the Supreme Court ever written.

Curie, Eve, and Vincent Sheean

Madame Curie: A Biography. Garden City, NY: Doubleday, Doran & Co., 1937. 393pp.

Of all the many, many biographies written about Marie Curie, perhaps the very best is the one written by her daughter, Eve; though published in 1937, its fifty-six editions attest to its perennial popularity. This is the story of one of the greatest scientists of the twentieth century, Marie Curie, winner of not one but two Nobel Prizes—one in physics, the other in chemistry. Told in Eve Curie's engaging, intimate style, the biography takes us through Madame Curie's childhood in Poland, her Parisian courtship, her stunning scientific achievements, and her tragic death from radiation poisoning at age sixty-six in 1934. With plentiful illustrations, including photos, letters, and pages from Marie Curie's notebooks, the book offers a fascinating overview of the only scientist—male or female—to ever win two Nobel Prizes in two different sciences.

Subjects: Curie, Marie • Nobel Prize in Physics • Nobel Prize in Chemistry • Science • Chemistry • Physics • Labor • History • History of Science • Women's History • Nineteenth Century • Twentieth Century • Poland • France • Europe • Biography

Now Try: Many excellent biographies of Marie Curie have been written—so many, in fact, that selecting one can be overwhelming. A good place to continue is with *Marie Curie: A Life*, by Susan Quinn; whereas Eve Curie primarily focused on her mother's science in the latter part of her life, Quinn fleshes out Curie's personal life with information about the love affair she entered in the wake of Pierre Curie's death, while offering insight into her role as a mother. For a biography that explores the scientific ramifications of Curie's discoveries, turn to Barbara Goldsmith's *Obsessive Genius: The Inner World of Marie Curie*. And for a mesmerizing fictional treatment of Curie, turn to Per Olov Enquist's *The Book about Blanche and Marie*. There are two female leads in this historical novel, Curie herself and her real-life lab assistant, Blanche Wittman—who, in real life and in the novel, lost both legs and one arm to radiation poisoning.

Drachman, Virginia G.

Enterprising Women: 250 Years of American Business. Chapel Hill: University of North Carolina Press, 2002. 184pp. ISBN 9780807827628.

American women entrepreneurs are not just a recent phenomenon. Sure, we know about Mary Kay Ash and Donna Karan—but what about Martha Coston, who in 1871 received a patent for her maritime signal flares? How about Marie Webster, who started a mail-order business for her quilt patterns in 1911? Discover women entrepreneurs from colonial times through the present in this inspiring collective biography. Plentiful illustrations and reproductions of historical documents bring their stories to life, while Drachman's expert analysis explains the contemporary barriers faced by businesswomen who dared to enter a man's world.

> **Subjects:** Entrepreneurs • Business • Labor • Gender • Sexual Discrimination • History • Women's History • History of Business • American History • Social History • Eighteenth Century • Nineteenth Century • Twentieth Century • America • Biography • Collection • Quick Read

> **Now Try:** Though more scholarly in tone than *Enterprising Women*, Angel Kwolek-Folland's *Incorporating Women: A History of Women and Business in the United States* is a good companion read for anyone interested in the historical impact of businesswomen in America. Rather than focusing extensively on biological profiles, the book seeks to survey the influence of businesswomen as a demographic since 1550. As much a history of women as a history of business, *Incorporating Women* explores the tensions between women's issues and business norms, shedding new light on an area of study that is typically neglected.

Maddox, Brenda

Rosalind Franklin: The Dark Lady of DNA. New York: HarperCollins, 2002. 380pp. ISBN 9780060184070.

Students in schools throughout the world learn that Watson and Crick discovered the model for DNA. What students rarely learn was that the real work was done by Rosalind Franklin, the assistant to Watson and Crick whose scientific research and photographs revealed the famous double helix. Whereas Watson and Crick won the Nobel Prize for their "discovery," Franklin was relegated to the back pages of history. In this thought-provoking biography, Maddox restores Franklin to her rightful place, showing how a combination of sexual discrimination and anti-Semitism conspired against Franklin, and how her untimely death from ovarian cancer shunted her out of the spotlight she deserved. Based on Franklin's letters and records, this biography paints a portrait of a fascinating woman, and Maddox's clear language makes the science accessible to the lay reader.

> **Subjects:** Franklin, Rosalind • DNA • Chemistry • Biology • Science • Labor • Sexual Discrimination • Judaism • Ovarian Cancer • Cancer • Health • History • History of Science • Women's History • American History • America • Twentieth Century • Biography

> **Now Try:** Continue learning about the importance of Franklin's work in *Rosalind Franklin and DNA*. Written by Franklin's friend Anne Sayre, this biography is a response to Watson's widely read book *The Double Helix*, which trivialized "Rosy" as an insignificant player. Based on Sayre's own recollections of Franklin and on her interviews with prominent scientists—including Watson and Crick—the book restores Franklin to the prominence she deserves for helping unravel the mystery of DNA. Then discover the story of yet another scientist whose crucial role in the drama of DNA has been forgotten. In *The Third Man of the Double Helix: The Autobiography of Maurice Wilkins*, you'll meet the scientist who first showed Rosalind Franklin's photographs to Watson and Crick.

Rich, Doris L.

Jackie Cochran: Pilot in the Fastest Lane. Gainesville: University Press of Florida, 2007. 279pp. ISBN 9780813030432.

You've heard of Amelia Earhart, but what about Jackie Cochran? She was, in fact, the better pilot: she broke any number of aviation records, she was the first woman to break the sound barrier, and she helped establish a corps of women pilots in World War II, the WASPS—which, as a colonel in the Air Force Reserve, she was more than qualified to lead. She was also a brash, forthright, frequently unpleasant woman, fiercely competitive to the point where she would lie and manipulate to outdo her colleagues; other women, such as Earhart herself, suffered from the lash of Cochran's tongue. Discover this bold aviator in Rich's eye-opening biography, which draws on numerous primary documents, including Cochran's letters, to paint a vivid picture of a complicated woman who made history in the skies.

> **Subjects:** Cochran, Jackie • Aviation • Labor • History • War • Women's History • Military History • American History • World War II • America • Twentieth Century • Biography

> **Now Try:** As we saw in Rich's book, Cochran was known to distort the truth when it suited her needs; thus readers should approach *Jackie Cochran: An Autobiography* with a grain of salt. Nonetheless, with the caveat that Cochran was not always the most truthful person, this is an intriguing read about Cochran's younger years and career as a pilot, comprising her own words and the voices of her friends and family, assembled here by editor Maryann Bucknum Brinley. And if you can't get enough of superstar women pilots, delve into the fictionalized world of Amelia Earhart in Jane Mendelsohn's *I Was Amelia Earhart*. Jackie Cochran herself would have approved; this beautifully written book presents Earhart as a deeply flawed, albeit compelling, protagonist.

Tuchman, Arleen

Science Has No Sex: The Life of Marie Zakrzewska, M.D. Studies in Social Medicine. Chapel Hill: University of North Carolina Press, 2006. 336pp. ISBN 9780807-830208.

Born to Polish parents in Germany in 1829, Marie Zakrzewska was determined to become a doctor and managed to become a hospital director and a professor of medicine by 1852. But when the scandal of her sex forced her to resign, she did not kowtow to sexual discrimination; instead, she immigrated to America, where—encouraged by Dr. Elizabeth Blackwell—she graduated from the Cleveland Medical College. With an academic but accessible style, Tuchman tells the remarkable story of Zakrzewska's success as one of America's first female physicians. Read this engaging biography to learn about the woman who defied the social norms of her time to lead the way as an educator and practitioner of medicine.

> **Subjects:** Zakrzewska, Marie • Doctors • Labor • Sexual Discrimination • History • American History • Germany • America • Nineteenth Century • Biography

> **Now Try:** Readers curious about female doctors in nineteenth-century America may wish to try *Pioneer Doctor: The Story of a Woman's Work*, by Mari Graña. Though considerably lighter in style than Tuchman's book, readers who enjoy the integration of fictionalized dialogue into their biographies will be delighted to learn about Mollie Babcock, a doctor who has unconscionably slipped into obscurity. In the 1890s, this pioneering woman decided, like Zakrzewska, to leave the familiar and to start a new life for herself; this is the story of how she went out West to practice medicine—and to campaign for women's rights, too, in her spare time.

Zimmerman, Jean

The Women of the House: How a Colonial She-Merchant Built a Mansion, a Fortune, and a Dynasty. Orlando, FL: Harcourt, 2006. 399pp. ISBN 9780151010653.

In 1659, the twenty-two-year-old Margaret Hardenbroeck set out from Holland to seek her fortune in America; by the time of her death, some three decades later, she had become the richest woman in New Amsterdam, having amassed a stunning empire based on business and real estate. In *The Women of the House,* you'll discover how a shrewd colonial businesswoman ambitiously traded goods in a man's world (though many readers will be disappointed to find that she participated in the slave trade). With excellent research and an engaging style, Zimmerman's book brings Hardenbroeck to life, along with the female heirs who followed in her footsteps.

> **Subjects:** Hardenbroeck, Margaret • Entrepreneurs • Business • Labor • History • Women's History • American History • Seventeenth Century • America • Biography

> **Now Try:** Readers who enjoy the thrill of discovering unknown women who defied the gender roles of their times will be delighted with two other excellent biographies. In *America's Joan of Arc: The Life of Anna Elizabeth Dickinson*, J. Matthew Gallman introduces us to a nineteenth-century advocate for women's rights and the abolition of slavery. As a friend of Susan B. Anthony and a fiery orator, Dickinson is a fascinating character, one whose story deserves to be known. Then skip over to England to meet Elizabeth Marsh in Linda Colley's biography *The Ordeal of Elizabeth Marsh: A Woman in World History.* At a time when few women traveled, Marsh was voyaging across the globe (though this did have its drawbacks—being captured by pirates and nearly being forced to join a harem chief among them). Filled with adventure and derring-do, this is a spirited story of a woman who didn't let societal norms prevent her from exploring the world.

Royalty and Rulers

Royalty and Rulers biographies tell the stories of women, past and present, in positions of power.

We are endlessly fascinated with women in positions of power, from both the past and the present. In the "Royalty and Rulers" section, you'll meet queens, empresses, and others who were at the very top of the social ladder. Some of them married into it, as we see in Antonia Fraser's book *Marie Antoinette: The Journey,* while others ruled all on their own, as we see in Wilma Mankiller's autobiography *Mankiller: A Chief and Her People.* These are character-driven books that emphasize the political realities and social conditions of each ruler's era.

Chambers, Anne

Granuaile: Ireland's Pirate Queen C. 1530-1603. Dublin: Wolfhound Press, 2003. 213pp. ISBN 9780863279133.

You may already know Granuaile as the stuff of myth; she has been immortalized in legends and songs as the impetuous Irish woman who ruled the seas in the sixteenth century. But Granuaile, also known as Grace O'Malley, was indeed a very real woman, as historian Chambers shows in this captivating biography. Chambers, who is both a scholar and a novelist, here turns her flair for prose to the chieftain who led her people to battle, both at sea and on land. This is a page-turning account of Granuaile's career as businesswoman, noblewoman, military chief, and mother, replete with vivid details of the ocean and land of Ireland in the 1500s.

> **Subjects:** Granuaile • O'Malley, Grace • Rulers • Leadership • Royalty • Pirates • Warriors • War • Politics • Labor • History • Women's History • Social History • Sixteenth Century • Ireland • Europe • Biography

> **Now Try:** Granuaile may be the most famous of the pirate queens, but she is in good company, as we learn in the fascinating book *Bold in Her Breeches: Women Pirates across the Ages*, edited by Jo Stanley. Though the book is more of a cultural history than a collective biography, readers who love learning about female pirates will discover swashbuckling women pirates from throughout the ages and across the globe in these academic but accessible essays. Try also the innovative travelogue *The Pirate Queen: In Search of Grace O'Malley and Other Legendary Women of the Sea*, in which Barbara Sjoholm set out to follow the footsteps of women seafarers in Northern Europe.

Collingridge, Vanessa

Boudica: The Life of Britain's Legendary Warrior Queen. Woodstock, NY: Overlook Press, 2006. 390pp. ISBN 9781585677788.

In the first century C.E., Rome was extending her empire across Europe and into England. The Romans were welcomed by many of the English rulers, including a certain King Prasutagus—but his wife Boudica was not so genial to the Romans, not after they raped her two daughters following Prasutagus's death. This is the magnificent story of the woman who fought back, told with Collingridge's flair for detailed historical narrative. By rallying her peoples to deflect the invaders, Boudica managed to sack three Roman-occupied cities before succumbing to defeat—and even this heroic last stand, as Collingridge shows, has became the stuff of legend. Read this to learn about the early Roman influence in Britain, the warrior queen who refused to kowtow to the invaders, and the legends that have followed in her wake ever since.

> **Subjects:** Boudica • Rulers • Royalty • Leadership • Warriors • War • Politics • Labor • History • Ancient History • Dark Ages • First Century • Military History • Women's History • Social History • England • Europe • Biography

> **Now Try:** For another look at the lasting impact of the Queen of the Iceni, turn to *Boudica: Iron Age Warrior Queen*, by Richard Hingley and Christina Unwin. As in Collingridge's biography, this book examines Boudica's role both as a military leader and as an enduring part of the British mythos. Then take a closer look at Boudica's revolt in Graham Webster's *Boudica: The British Revolt Against Rome A.D. 60*; this quick read is concise but packed with details about Boudica's military campaigns. Fiction lovers will also want to try Manda Scott's *Boudica Quadrilogy*, a series of historical novels that brings the queen and her turbulent times to life. The first in the series is *Boudica: Dreaming the Eagle*, we follow Boudica as she comes of age as a warrior.

Fraser, Antonia

Marie Antoinette: The Journey. New York: N.A. Talese/Doubleday, 2001. 512pp. ISBN 9780385489485.

Ah, Marie Antoinette: she's the strumpet queen who told her starving subjects to eat cake—or at any rate, that's how her indignant biographers remembered her in the wake of her death. But as best-selling novelist and historian Fraser shows, the story is not so simple. In this enlightening, balanced biography, Fraser plucks out the nuances of Marie Antoinette's complicated, difficult life, showing how she was, at least in part, a victim of circumstance. With rich details that bring to life eighteenth-century France and the colorful characters of the upper nobility, Fraser gives context to Marie Antoinette's political shortcomings. Her errors were egregious, but her miserable marriage and complete lack of guidance worked against her; read this captivating narrative to rediscover the woman who was both a terrible politician and a surprisingly likeable person.

Subjects: Marie Antoinette • Royalty • Politics • Labor • History • Social History • Women's History • Eighteenth Century • France • Europe • Biography

Now Try: Like Fraser, Carolly Erickson paints a more sympathetic picture of Marie Antoinette than most in *To the Scaffold: The Life of Marie Antoinette.* Fraser's fans will enjoy this readable, engaging account of her childhood and ill-fated life as queen, replete with fascinating details of the royal lifestyle in eighteenth-century France. Likewise, Evelyne Lever has more pity than contempt for the queen in *Marie Antoinette: The Last Queen of France;* translated from the French, this engrossing biography relies on primary documents and keen historical research to shine light on Marie Antoinette's misguided decisions as queen. Fiction lovers will also want to try *The Hidden Diary of Marie Antoinette: A Novel,* a vivid portrait of a privileged but lonely woman. Author Carolly Erickson, drawing on her experience as a historical biographer, includes period details and historical references that bring Marie's France to life.

Fraser, Antonia

Mary, Queen of Scots. New York: Delacorte Press, 1969 (2001). 613pp. ISBN 9780385311298.

Fans who missed the first biography of best-selling historian and novelist Fraser will be delighted to discover this excellent account of Mary, the bitter rival of Queen Elizabeth I. Though she wrote it early in her career, all the hallmarks of Fraser's excellent writing are present: the narrative is gripping, the details are fascinating, the setting is fully realized. Travel back to the year 1542, when the death of James V propelled a six-day-old female to the Scottish throne. Follow this infant ruler, first through her childhood in France, then to her teenaged ascension to the throne of France by marriage, then to her contentious return to Scotland, where she struggled to maintain her Catholic identity in a strongly Protestant country—and then explore the final tragic episode of her life, when she was beheaded at the command of her own cousin Elizabeth.

Subjects: Mary, Queen of Scots • Rulers • Royalty • Leadership • Politics • Labor • Christianity • Religion • History • Women's History • Social History • Sixteenth Century • France • Scotland • England • Europe • Biography

Now Try: Focus now on the period of Mary's life for which she is best remembered, the years of her reign in Scotland, in J. A. Guy's *Queen of Scots: The True*

Life of Mary Stuart. Unabashedly sympathetic to the queen, this fascinating biography convincingly shows her to have been a competent ruler and skillful politician, a boon to Scotland, who was unfairly reviled in the wake of her death; with excellent scholarship and eminently readable prose, this is sure to appeal to Fraser's fans. And don't miss best-selling biographer Alison Weir's *Mary, Queen of Scots, and the Murder of Lord Darnley*, in which Weir argues that Mary was innocent of her husband's murder—that, in fact, she would have been a good ruler had it not been for her exceedingly poor taste in men. Finally, even readers who normally avoid fiction will want to consider *Mary Queen of Scotland and the Isles: A Novel.* Meticulously researched by historical biographer Margaret George, this sweeping novel vividly re-creates the political and social environment of its tragic heroine.

Frieda, Leonie

Catherine de Medici: Renaissance Queen of France. New York: Fourth Estate, 2003. 440pp. ISBN 9780060744922.

Catherine de Medici has not been treated kindly by history, as Frieda bluntly states in her introduction: "To many she is the very incarnation of evil." But in this carefully researched biography, based in part on letters written by Catherine herself, Frieda reveals Catherine to be a far more complicated figure than the one-dimensional poisoner that popular history would have us remember. Born in Italy in 1519, this wealthy young woman married into French royalty in her teens, only to find herself playing second fiddle to her husband Henri's mistress. But when Henri died, Catherine found herself in a position of enormous power, responsible not only for mothering the future kings of France but for presiding over the country's religious battles. In this engaging account of the queen's political maneuverings, Frieda argues that Catherine, though certainly a shrewd politician, had France's best interests at heart.

> **Subjects:** de Medici, Catherine • Rulers • Royalty • Leadership • Politics • Labor • Christianity • Religion • Motherhood • History • Women's History • Social History • Sixteenth Century • Italy • France • Europe • Biography

> **Now Try:** Like Frieda, R. J. Knecht argues that the Queen of France was simply doing the best she could in his book *Catherine De' Medici.* Many similar themes are covered in this biography, but read it in particular for the further insight into the religious turmoil of sixteenth-century France; though more academic in tone than Frieda's book, it illuminates Catherine's leadership and politics, and especially her role—or lack thereof—in the infamous St. Bartholomew's Day massacre. Readers may also enjoy learning about another de Medici woman, Isabella, in Caroline P. Murphy's *Murder of a Medici Princess.* Like Frieda's book about Catherine, Murphy's biography draws on scrupulous research to portray the life (and gruesome death) of a sixteenth-century noblewoman.

Grant, Michael

Cleopatra. Edison, NJ: Castle Books, 1972 (2004). 301pp. ISBN 9780785818281.

And now let us introduce Cleopatra, one of history's great . . . linguists? Yes, actually: Cleopatra was a talented multilinguist, shows renowned classical historian Grant, and also the author of works on such disparate topics as alchemy and agriculture. Discover Cleopatra as you've never seen her before, a brilliant woman of diverse talents who managed her strategic affairs both inside and outside the bedroom. In four chronological sections—"Cleopatra's First Twenty-One Years," "Cleopatra and Caesar," "Cleopatra and Antony," and "Cleopatra against Rome"—Grant takes us through Cleopatra's remarkable and tragic life as the

ruler of Egypt in the first century B.C.E. In an academic but accessible style, Grant illuminates Cleopatra's stunning intellect and political triumphs, ending with her death by asp and the crumbling of her empire.

> **Subjects:** Cleopatra • Rulers • Royalty • Leadership • Politics • Labor • History • Classical History • Ancient History • First Century B.C.E. • Women's History • Social History • Greece • Roman Empire • Europe • Africa • Egypt • Biography

> **Now Try:** Given the enduring charm of Cleopatra some two thousand years after her death, it is no surprise that many good biographies await the eager reader. Perhaps turn to *Cleopatra*, by Ernle Dusgate Selby Bradford, who writes with a rigorous but accessible scholarly approach that will appeal to Grant's fans. Like Grant, Bradford shows the queen of Egypt as a fully developed woman with a keen sense of military strategy, not just a pretty face who was in the right political place at the right time. Fiction readers will also want to try *The Memoirs of Cleopatra: A Novel*, by biographer and historical novelist Margaret George. Teeming with historical details and delivered with George's flair for storytelling, this epic tale presents a compelling, unforgettable portrait of Cleopatra.

Liss, Peggy K.

Isabel the Queen: Life and Times. New York: Oxford University Press, 1992 (2004). 398pp. ISBN 9780195073560.

You learned about Queen Isabel (a.k.a. Isabella) in grade school, of course: she and her husband, King Ferdinand (a.k.a. Fernando) were the ones with enough foresight in the 1490s to finance that plucky explorer, Christopher Columbus. Good people all around, right? Not so fast. Isabel's patronage of Columbus heralded the era of European exploration and conquest, of slaughter and enslavement in the New World. And we can find plenty of evidence of Isabel's character right on her home turf: she was a loving wife and mother, yes, and a devout Catholic—but her religious devotion, paired with the enormous power she wielded, led to devastating consequences for the Jews and Muslims in Spain. Liss presents a serious, scholarly biography of the Queen of Spain, but readers willing to undertake the academic prose will find themselves rewarded with a meticulously researched portrait of a powerful woman whose influence was both far-reaching and violent.

> **Subjects:** Isabella of Castile • Rulers • Royalty • Leadership • Religion • Christianity • Violence • Marriage • Mothers • Relationships • History • Women's History • Social History • History of Religion • Medieval History • Fifteenth Century • Spain • Europe • Biography

> **Now Try:** When Isabel waged her battles against the non-Catholics of Spain, she precipitated the demise of a vibrant, intellectual culture. Read about this community in *The Ornament of the World: How Muslims, Jews and Christians Created a Culture of Tolerance in Medieval Spain*, by Maria Rosa Menocal. Alternately, readers can find a more apologetic interpretation of Isabel with Nancy Rubin Stuart's *Isabella of Castile: The First Renaissance Queen*. Liss does not attempt to discount Isabel's persecution of Spain's non-Catholics, but she does emphasize the more positive aspects of the Queen's life, including her patronage of the arts, her successful unification of the various kingdoms with Spain, and her devotion as a mother.

Mankiller, Wilma Pearl, and Michael Wallis

Mankiller: A Chief and Her People. New York: St. Martin's Press, 1993. 310pp. ISBN 9780312098681.

The eleven-year-old Wilma was perfectly happy in Oklahoma, but in the 1950s, the United States government uprooted her Cherokee family to San Francisco, where poverty and racism shaped her existence. Yet this racism led to her growing awareness of her identity as a Native American: she became an activist and, in 1985, she became the principal chief of the Cherokee Nation. In part, this is the story of her amazing life, both as a public leader and as a private woman who overcame a terrible car accident and a kidney transplant to become the first woman chief of the Cherokees; it is also a story of the Cherokee people themselves, filled with their history and native myths. This engrossing read is satisfying both as an autobiography and as a social history of the Cherokee Nation.

Subjects: Rulers • Leadership • Activism • Native Americans • Race • History • Women's History • Social History • American History • America • Twentieth Century • Autobiography

Now Try: Continue with *Every Day Is a Good Day: Reflections of Contemporary Indigenous Women*, in which Mankiller collects essays by nineteen native women. Covering such diverse topics as spirituality, identity, community, and land conservation, these pieces eloquently speak to Native American identity from the perspectives of a variety of women, from doctors to artists to teachers.

Rounding, Virginia

Catherine the Great: Love, Sex, and Power. New York: St. Martin's Press, 2007. 566pp. ISBN 9780312328870.

In 1729, a German princess of minor nobility was born, a little girl named Sophie Frederica Auguste—but you probably know her better as Catherine the Great, the woman who ruled Russia for thirty-four years. She arrived in Russia as a teenage bride to Peter, the tsar-to-be—but when he ascended the throne, the woman now known as Catherine pulled off a coup with a little help from a lover. In this engrossing biography, based on memoirs, letters, and other contemporary documents, you'll see the human side of Catherine II, the empress who reigned longer than any other tsar. Scholar Rounding focuses here not on politics or government as much as on Catherine's personal life, on her roles as mother, grandmother, art enthusiast—and, yes, as voracious lover to a series of desirable men.

Subjects: Catherine the Great • Rulers • Royalty • Leadership • Relationships • Mothers • Grandmothers • Art • History • Women's History • Social History • Eighteenth Century • Russia • Europe • Biography

Now Try: Discover Catherine in her own words in *The Memoirs of Catherine the Great,* by Catherine, Empress of Russia. Look for the translation by Markus Cruse and Hilde Hoogenboom, in which Catherine recalls her early years and considers the prickly subject about the rather suspicious death of her husband Peter. Then turn to Isabel De Madariaga's *Catherine the Great: A Short History,* for a nice companion to Rounding's biography; whereas Rounding primarily emphasizes Catherine's personal life, this book fleshes out Catherine's politics and governance. Catherine enthusiasts will also want to read Henri Troyat's *Catherine the Great.* Though he writes with a far more scholarly, stately tone than does Rounding, Troyat is a formidable biographer who skillfully crafts a narrative of Catherine's personality and politics. And for a much lighter read, try *Jewels of the Tsars: The Romanovs and Imperial Russia,* by Prince Michael of Greece. Starting with Catherine and ending with the last reigning Romanov, Nicholas II, this gorgeous book uses portraits and photographs to document the regalia and the jewels of the Russian nobility.

Seagrave, Sterling, and Peggy Seagrave

Dragon Lady: The Life and Legend of the Last Empress of China. New York: Knopf, 1992. 601pp. ISBN 9780679402305.

"We do not even know her name," observe husband-and-wife team Sterling and Peggy Seagrave. Born in 1835 in China, this pretty young girl was chosen at the age of sixteen to become a concubine to Emperor Hsien-Feng. We would not remember this woman of humble origins had she not given birth to a son—for she alone among the emperor's wives and concubines produced a male heir. Renamed Tsu Hsi, she became the dowager empress upon the emperor's death in 1861, and continued to rule for nearly fifty years. History has not been kind to the empress, remembering her as an ambitious and devious power monger—but as the Seagraves argue, her bad reputation stems from the malicious slander of her enemies. In this engaging, meticulously researched biography, the authors reinterpret this fascinating woman, exposing the half-truths and lies that have sullied her memory. Read this not only to gain a new understanding of Tsu Hsi but to visit China in the waning years of the imperial dynasty.

> **Subjects:** Tsu Hsi • Rulers • Royalty • Leadership • Politics • Labor • History • Women's History • Social History • Nineteenth Century • China • Asia • Biography

> **Now Try:** Frustratingly few biographies of Tsu Hsi have been written, but readers willing to try a fictionalized account of her life will be delighted with Anchee Min's *Empress Orchid*. Like the Seagraves, Min paints a sympathetic portrait of the empress, fleshing her out into a multifaceted figure. Exhaustively researched and replete with vivid details, this is a historically accurate representation of Tsu Hsi and the political climate of China in the nineteenth century. Follow with the sequel, *The Last Empress*.

Strachey, Lytton

Queen Victoria. New York: Harcourt, Brace and Company, 1921 (2006). 273pp. ISBN 142183085X.

Though first published in 1921, this remarkable biography of Queen Victoria has endured, influencing the public's perception of the nineteenth-century queen of England both at the time of its publication and in the generations since. Having come of age during Victoria's reign, author Strachey's familiarity with his subject gives the book an intimate feel; rather than restricting his biography to dry facts and recitations of history, Strachey fleshes out the character of the queen, illuminating her personality with stories of her friendships and relationships. Follow the story of her life, from her childhood through her ascension to the throne in 1837 at age eighteen, through her marriage to Prince Albert and her reign of sixty-three years—the longest reign of any British monarch before or since. Meet a very human Victoria, one with a famous temper and a great sense of affection for her friends, family, subjects, and country.

> **Subjects:** Victoria • Rulers • Royalty • Leadership • Politics • Labor • Marriage • Friendships • History • Women's History • Social History • Nineteenth Century • England • Europe • Biography

Now Try: For a more recent general biography of the queen, turn to historian Walter L. Arnstein's *Queen Victoria*; with meticulous scholarship and an engaging prose style, this excellent account is a succinct survey of Victoria's life, with attention given both to the individual and the nineteenth-century England in which she lived. See also *Queen Victoria: A Personal History*, in which historian Christopher Hibbert pays special attention to the queen as wife, mother, and friend. And readers wishing to know more about the Victorian Age may wish to try John Plunkett's examination of a slice of social history, *Queen Victoria: First Media Monarch*. With fascinating illustrations and vivid historical details, the book considers the relationship between the monarchy and the public in the Victorian Age.

Waller, Maureen

Sovereign Ladies: The Six Reigning Queens of England. New York: St. Martin's Press, 2007. 554pp. ISBN 9780312338015.

In the long line of the English monarchy, going all the way back to Egbert in the 800s, only six women have ruled as sovereigns: Mary I, Elizabeth I, Mary II, Anne, Victoria, and Elizabeth II. In this captivating collective biography, author Waller considers them all, fleshing out their life stories and personalities within the contexts of their various milieus. Thoroughly researched and eminently readable, the book examines not only the lives and reigns of the queens, but also the thorny questions of gender that attended each queen's reign. The illuminating biographies and the focus on the tensions between womanhood and monarchy make this a fascinating exploration of both history and sexual politics.

Subjects: Mary I • Elizabeth I • Mary II • Anne • Victoria • Elizabeth II • Rulers • Royalty • Leadership • Politics • Labor • Gender • History • Women's History • Social History • England • Europe • Biography • Collection

Now Try: You've read about the women who ruled in their own name; now read about the other women of power in England's history in *Wives of the Kings of England: From Hanover to Windsor*, by Mark Hichens. In this succinct survey, you'll meet the royal consorts to the kings during the past three centuries; read this to find out about their lives, their marriages, and their influence upon their husbands.

Weir, Alison

Eleanor of Aquitaine: A Life. New York: Ballantine Books, 2000. 441pp. ISBN 9780345405401.

Consummate biographer Alison Weir here turns her deft hand to Eleanor of Aquitaine, the twelfth-century queen consort to Louis VII of France and, later, to Henry II of England. We know Eleanor thanks to her enduring presence in myths and popular culture; she is even featured as a character in Shakespeare's play *King John*. In this meticulously researched biography, Weir draws from these myths and from the few existing primary sources, gently correcting misperceptions of the woman whose legend is far larger than life. We meet the real Eleanor of Aquitaine, who—as the wife of two powerful kings and the mother of Richard the Lionheart—wielded tremendous influence during a time when most women were powerless. And we learn about the turbulent Europe in which Eleanor lived; Weir's rigorous scholarship and eye for historical detail brings medieval Europe to life, fleshing out the politics and the feudal systems of the day. Accessible and compulsively readable, this is an exemplary biography of Eleanor and an excellent study of medieval Europe.

Subjects: Eleanor of Aquitaine • Royalty • Politics • Labor • History • Marriage • Mothers • Relationships • Medieval History • Twelfth Century • Women's History • Social History • France • England • Europe • Biography

Now Try: Can't get enough of Eleanor? Turn to another stellar biography of the twelfth-century queen in *Eleanor of Aquitaine and the Four Kings*, by Amy R. Kelly. Like Weir, Kelly draws on primary sources to paint a captivating picture of the queen, skillfully placing her politics and power in the context of a tumultuous Europe of the Middle Ages. Fiction readers will also devour *The Book of Eleanor: A Novel of Eleanor of Aquitaine*. With accurate historical details and a flair for pacing and story, author Pamela Kaufman paints a portrait of an intelligent, spirited Eleanor.

Weir, Alison

The Life of Elizabeth I. New York: Ballantine, 1998. 532pp. ISBN 9780345405333.

In 1558, Mary I of England—that is, Bloody Mary—died without an heir, opening the throne to her twenty-five-year-old half-sister Elizabeth. Of course, most folks at the time assumed that she would cede her power to a king, but Elizabeth famously decided not to marry. This remarkable choice to forsake marriage, at a time when women yielded power to men as a matter of course, is the subject of much discussion in this excellent study of Elizabeth I. Best-selling biographer Weir considers the personal relationships of the Virgin Queen—with her friends, her advisors, her cousin Mary, and her possible lover, the Earl of Leicester—as well as the public image and the political and religious decisions made by the woman who reigned for forty-five years. Bringing Tudor England to life with rich details and keen historical research, *The Life of Elizabeth I* is a fascinating overview of the woman whose reign brought peace and prosperity to England.

Subjects: Elizabeth I • Rulers • Royalty • Leadership • Politics • Friendships • Relationships • Labor • Christianity • Religion • History • Women's History • Social History • Sixteenth Century • England • Europe • Biography

Now Try: Pair Weir's biography of Elizabeth with Anne Somerset's biography, *Elizabeth I*. Whereas Weir focuses on Elizabeth's personal life and relationships, Somerset examines the queen's political and governing choices, placing the religious conflicts, the wars, and the political intrigues of the day into context; enjoyable to read and thoroughly researched, it makes for an excellent complement to the more personal side of Elizabeth seen in Weir's book. Then, for those who wonder if the Virgin Queen really was a virgin, turn to Sarah Gristwood's *Elizabeth & Leicester: Power, Passion, and Politics*; though we will never know the exact relationship shared by these two remarkable figures, what we *do* know is fascinating; read this to learn more about Elizabeth and to discover one of history's more colorful characters, the Earl of Leicester.

Weir, Alison

Queen Isabella: Treachery, Adultery, and Murder in Medieval England. New York: Ballantine Books, 2005. 487pp. ISBN 9780345453198.

In the year 1308, at the ripe old age of twelve, a princess named Isabella was whisked from her home in France to marry Edward II of England. The bisexual Edward paid rather more attention to his lovers than to his pretty young wife; small wonder, then, that Isabella and her own lover, Roger Mortimer, led a rebellion to place Isabella's son on the throne and to murder Edward with a red-hot iron (though Roger Mortimer did not enjoy the victory for very long, as Isabella had *him* killed off, too). But is the story really as straightforward as that? Was Isabella really the conniving murderer that history would have us believe? With her characteristic flair for historical setting and narrative, Weir tells the story of Isabella's fascinating life, offering alternative viewpoints to her wicked image; she was hungry for power, yes, but she may not have been as malicious as the history lessons have taught us.

Subjects: Isabella of France • Royalty • Politics • Labor • Marriage • Relationships • Violence • History • Women's History • Social History • Medieval History • Fourteenth Century • England • France • Europe • Biography

Now Try: Like Weir, P. C. Doherty sifts through the half-truths and myths surrounding Isabella to try to find out what really happened in England in the fourteenth century. In *Isabella and the Strange Death of Edward II*, Doherty explores the complicated relationships that Isabella shared with Edward and Mortimer, offering a scintillating account of the intrigues, conspiracies, and plots that led to the deaths of Isabella's husband and lover. Edith Felber's spirited historical novel *Queen of Shadows: A Novel of Isabella, Wife of King Edward II* will also please readers with its rich period details as the queen seeks revenge against her unfaithful husband.

Autobiography and Memoirs

An autobiography is a person's recollection of her entire life, while a memoir is a recollection of parts of her life. In women's autobiography and memoir, the focus is on women's lives.

Surprisingly, these are two of the more difficult genres to define—or at least to distinguish. At first glance, it seems easy: an autobiography is a person's recollection of her entire life, while a memoir is a recollection of parts of her life. Certainly this is a good working definition, but it gets very unwieldy very quickly, because *most* Women's Nonfiction titles contain at least some elements of memoir. Furthermore, most memoirs and autobiographies can easily fit under several headings. Should Sue Monk Kidd's *Dance of the Dissident Daughter* go here, or under "Spiritual Growth and Meditation," or under "Feminism"? Does one look for Nobel Peace Prize winner Wangari Maathai's memoir *Unbowed* here, or under "Global Perspectives," or under "Activism and Social Issues," or under "Leadership and Politics"? For our purposes here, my definition is narrow and, I confess, somewhat arbitrary. A great number of women have written about their lives, and you will find their stories peppered throughout this book; what you will find in this section is a very selective sampling of women who have written not only about their lives, but about women's issues, in a very deliberate way.

Angelou, Maya

I Know Why the Caged Bird Sings. New York: Random House, 1970. 281pp. ISBN 9780375507892.

Maya Angelou, a tremendous force in the American Civil Rights movement of the 1960s, wears many hats: among other things, she is a poet, a professor, an actress—and, as we see in the enduring classic *I Know Why the Caged Bird Sings*, she is a voraciously talented autobiographical writer. Hers is an emotionally difficult story to read, but her painful experience growing up as an African American girl in a racist and sexist America is essential reading for anyone who wants to understand the bitter climate of the country in the 1930s and '40s. Trauma is the hallmark of the first seventeen years of Angelou's life: she is raped by her mother's boyfriend; she goes mute when she feels guilt after her rapist is murdered; she endures an unplanned, out-of-wedlock pregnancy; and throughout, she struggles against the twin specters of racism and sexism. This is a grim book, yes, but beautifully written, with examples of love and hope that shine in spite of everything.

Subjects: Coming of Age • African Americans • Race • Sexual Discrimination • Relationships • Daughters • Granddaughters • Rape • Sexuality • History • American History • Women's History • America • Young Adult • Autobiography

Now Try: *I Know Why the Caged Bird Sings* is but the first of Angelou's six-part autobiographical series. Continue reading about her life in her second autobiography, *Gather Together in My Name*. Picking up where the first book left off, we find a seventeen-year-old Angelou, struggling at various odd jobs to provide for her infant son. Told in Angelou's characteristically beautiful, evocative prose, this book is less bleak than *I Know Why the Caged Bird Sings*, though difficult events and disappointing romantic relationships do crop up throughout. Then turn to the writings of Alice Walker, a prominent African American woman writer who, like Angelou, infuses her experiences into her writings. Any of Walker's nonfiction or fiction will appeal to Angelou's fans, but perhaps start with the epistolary novel *The Color Purple*, about a black woman who overcomes physical and psychological violence in Georgia in the 1930s.

Boyd, Helen

My Husband Betty: Love, Sex, and Life with a Crossdresser. New York: Thunder Mouth Press, 2003. 285pp. ISBN 9781560255154.

"A woman in a man's shirt is sexy, assumed to be straight, perfectly normal, and well adjusted," writes Helen Boyd, "while a man in a woman's negligee is assumed to be gay, sexually deviant, or comic." In an attempt to dispel stereotypes about male-to-female transgendered people, Boyd presents this insightful examination of transgender identity. As the wife of a cross-dressing husband, she is more than familiar with the subject, and she weaves her own experience into the narrative, along with the stories of other transgendered people she interviewed. This memoir provides an excellent overview of transgenderism, supported with discussions about related topics such as gender, sexual orientation, sexuality, and relationships.

Subjects: Crossdressing • Transgender • Gender • Queer Sexuality • Sexuality • Relationships • Marriage • America • Memoir

Now Try: Follow up with Boyd's sequel, *She's Not the Man I Married: My Life with a Transgender Husband*; this time, the relationship stakes are even higher, as Boyd's husband spends increasingly more time cross-dressing, and as he begins to contemplate the idea of undergoing a transsexual operation. Readers may also enjoy the practical advice in Peggy J. Rudd's *My Husband Wears My Clothes: Crossdressing from the Perspective of a Wife*; written for the lovers and spouses of transgender people, this is a thorough guide to the thorny questions of gender and identity faced by people in transgender relationships.

Brownmiller, Susan

In Our Time: Memoir of a Revolution. New York: Dial Press, 1999. 360pp. ISBN 9780385314862.

When a thirty-something journalist named Susan Brownmiller attended a consciousness-raising meeting in 1968, her conversion was instantaneous: a feminist was born. As a key player in the women's movement in the years that followed—after all, it was she who penned the famous treatise *Against Our Will: Men, Women, and Rape*—she was in the thick of women's history, advocating for such diverse causes as equal wages, reproductive choice, and ending domestic violence. This is her memoir, a fascinating glimpse into her own activities as a feminist and a broader look at the overall history and impact of the women's movement in America.

Subjects: Feminism • Sexual Discrimination • History • Women's History • Social History • American History • Twentieth Century • America • Memoir

Now Try: If you haven't read the book that made Brownmiller famous, go grab a copy of *Against Our Will: Men, Women, and Rape*. Now a classic feminist text, this is the book that catapulted Brownmiller into the limelight of the women's movement when it was first published in 1975. It is a disturbing, eye-opening examination of the psychology and sociology of rape, of the power and control that rapists wield and the treatment of rape in the eyes of the law. Then continue to examine rape from a feminist perspective with *I Never Called It Rape: The Ms. Report on Recognizing, Fighting, and Surviving Date and Acquaintance Rape*. Journalist Robin Warshaw presents a disturbing portrait of societal attitudes toward rape, while offering practical advice on fighting the problem.

Cole, Joni B., Rebecca Joffrey, and B. K. Rakhra, eds.

This Day: Diaries from American Women. Hillsboro, OR: Beyond Words, 2003. 286pp. ISBN 9781582701028.

What's the average day like for an American woman? Seems there's no such thing, as we see in this wonderful collection of diary entries from women across America. In *This Day*, you'll find a snapshot of life as seen from the perspective of a variety of women, from all sorts of backgrounds, states, races, and walks of life. "Retired Church Secretary Who Spoils Her Grandkids and Dog" comes to us from Rockford, Illinois; "Caregiver to Husband with Lou Gehrig's Disease" comes from Parker, Colorado; and "President of the National Organization for Women" comes from Washington, D.C. Some of the women are famous, some you've never heard of, but all of the diary entries—whether mundane or exciting, familiar or unusual—work together to form a fascinating mosaic portrait of the lives of women in America.

Subjects: Diary • America • Memoir • Collection

Now Try: Editors Cole, Joffrey, and Rakhra know a good thing when they see it. Turn now to their follow-up book, *This Day in the Life: Diaries from Women Across America*. Once again, the collection features the diary entries of a single day from the viewpoint of women across the country, women famous and unknown, rich and poor, old and young, busy and bored. And for more snippets of daily life, try *The Norton Book of Women's Lives*, edited by Phyllis Rose. This time the focus is on famous women, with luminaries such as Joan Didion and Billie Holiday offering their perspectives on a wide range of experiences.

Conway, Jill K., ed.

Written by Herself: An Anthology. New York: Vintage Books, 1992. 672pp. ISBN 9780679736332.

Autobiography enthusiasts will be delighted to discover this anthology of American women's writing, edited by Conway, who is herself an autobiographer. In this magnificent collection, you'll meet twenty-five women from a variety of backgrounds: There are artists, scientists, activists, and slaves; there are contemporary women and women from the past; there are women from a variety of races, educational levels, and social classes. Some of the writers, such as Maya Angelou and Gloria Steinem, will be familiar to readers, whereas others will be unknown, but in each case, the writing is strong and powerful; read this to hear the voices of American women as they reflect on their lives and experiences.

> **Subjects:** Autobiography • Activism • Labor • America • Anthology • Collection

> **Now Try:** *Written by Herself* contains writings by women from the United States; now get perspectives from women around the globe in another anthology edited by Kerr, *Written by Herself, Volume II: Women's Memoirs from Britain, Africa, Asia, and the United States.* As in the first volume, you'll meet women from a variety of settings and eras who have made a difference. Some names, such as Isak Dinesen, are easily recognizable, but in most cases, readers will enjoy discovering new and unfamiliar stories of women around the world.

Kanafani, Deborah

Unveiled: A Woman's Journey through Politics, Love, and Obedience. London: Simon & Schuster, 2008. 255pp. ISBN 9780743291835.

To a Lebanese-American woman with a keen interest in Arab issues and politics, the dashing Palestinian diplomat Marwan Kanafani seemed a perfect match for twenty-something Deborah. But when their marriage dissolved and Deborah tried to regain custody of their two children, the realities of sexual discrimination and patriarchy in the Middle East threatened her maternal rights. This riveting memoir tells the story of Kanafani's experiences as a stranger in a strange land, with a cast of high-ranking friends and enemies playing a role in her battle for custody. Read this both for the story of one woman's family drama and for the insight into Middle Eastern culture from the perspective of an American woman.

> **Subjects:** Gender • Sexual Discrimination • Politics • Palestine • Middle East • Asia • Memoir

> **Now Try:** Those readers who enjoyed seeing the Middle East through Kanafani's American eyes will enjoy *Kabul Beauty School: An American Woman Goes behind the Veil.* Author Deborah Rodriguez had traveled to Afghanistan intending to work as a nurse's aide, but she wound up opening a beauty school instead. This is the memoir of her experience teaching hairdressing in Kabul, brought to life with a cast of her Afghan women beauty students.

Kidd, Sue Monk

The Dance of the Dissident Daughter: A Woman's Journey from Christian Tradition to the Sacred Feminine. San Francisco: HarperSanFrancisco, 1996. 238pp. ISBN 9780060645885.

Perhaps you know Sue Monk Kidd for her best-selling novels, *The Secret Life of Bees* and *The Mermaid Chair*; possibly you even remember her Christian spiritual nonfiction writings from early in her career. Now discover *The Dance of the Dissident Daughter*, the remarkable story of her spiritual journey from Southern Baptist Christianity to a pagan approach, one that embraces the feminine and dispenses with traditional patriarchal paradigms. Readers who only know Kidd through her fiction will be delighted to recognize the same powerful storytelling and evocative prose that distinguishes her novels in this compelling, deeply personal story of paradise lost and faith rediscovered.

Subjects: Paganism • Religion • Christianity • Spirituality • Feminism • America • Memoir

Now Try: Readers intrigued by Kidd's discoveries of the sacred feminine will find more food for thought in Judith Duerk's classic *Circle of Stones: Woman's Journey to Herself*. Like Kidd, Duerk does not coerce readers into accepting any particular dogma; rather, she encourages readers to use dreams, images, and symbols to shape their spiritual understandings and to embrace the potential for feminine enlightenment within them; straightforward but profound, elegant but accessible, this is a mystical, powerful guidebook for women who want to discover their own spiritual power.

Maathai, Wangari

Unbowed: A Memoir. New York: Alfred A. Knopf, 2006. 314pp. ISBN 9780307-263483.

Where does one begin describing the accomplishments of Wangari Maathai? Born in 1940, she was the first African woman to win the Nobel Peace Prize; she was the first woman in East and Central Africa to earn a Ph.D.; she was the first woman in her region to become an associate professor; she presently serves in Parliament as Kenya's deputy minister in Ministry for Environment and Natural Resources. Perhaps most important, she founded the Green Belt Movement, a grassroots eco-feminist movement in which women in Kenya plant trees to better their environment. In this accessible, captivating memoir, you'll meet this amazing woman, who was named by *Time* magazine as one of the one hundred most influential people in the world.

Subjects: Activism • Feminism • Leadership • Politics • Labor • Sexual Discrimination • Nobel Peace Prize • Peace • Biology • Kenya • Africa • Twentieth Century • Memoir

Now Try: As founder of the Green Belt Movement, Maathai was awarded the Nobel Peace Prize "for her contribution to sustainable development, democracy, and peace." Learn more about the movement in *The Green Belt Movement: Sharing the Approach and the Experience* (made from 100% recycled materials, of course) in which Maathai describes why she started the movement and how the movement works.

Reid, Constance

Slacks and Calluses: Our Summer in a Bomber Factory. Washington, DC: Smithsonian Institution Press, 1944 (1999). 181pp. ISBN 9781560983873.

In 1943, America was embroiled in World War II. With so many of the nation's able-bodied men serving overseas, gender roles on the home front were undergoing a stunning transformation: to keep the momentum of the war effort in full swing, women were being asked to perform jobs that had traditionally been the domain of men. And thus it was that two school teachers, Constance Reid and Clara Marie Allen, spent their summer vacations building bombers. "We were the kind of girls who knew nothing about airplanes except that they had wings and they flew," explains Reid. "When one flew overhead we waited until somebody said 'That's a Liberator!' Then we looked into the sky and echoed wisely, 'Yes, it is, isn't it?'" But they were fast learners: by the end of the summer they were performing sophisticated technological work on bombers—and they were learning the social consequences of wearing pants instead of skirts. First published in 1944, this memoir is still fresh and funny, enjoyable both as a history lesson and as a thumping good read in its own right.

> **Subjects:** Labor • History • History of Labor • Women's History • Social History • American History • War • World War II • Twentieth Century • America • Memoir • Humor • Quick Read

> **Now Try:** During World War II, not every woman became a Rosie the Riveter à la Reid and Allen. Discover the variety of ways in which women endured the war in *Since You Went Away: World War II Letters from American Women on the Home Front*, by Judy Barrett Litoff and David C. Smith. This stunning collection of wartime letters brings to life the daily struggles and sacrifices faced by American women while their loved ones served overseas.

Steinem, Gloria

Outrageous Acts and Everyday Rebellions. New York: Holt, Rinehart, and Winston, 1983 (1995). 370pp. ISBN 9780030632365.

Gloria Steinem is an icon of American feminism; you've surely heard her name, but if you've never read any of her writings, you're in for a treat. This marvelous collection of twenty-eight short essays serves as an excellent introduction to her activist politics. With writing as fresh and relevant as when the book was first published in 1983, you'll discover Steinem's insightful, cogent thinking on such topics as menstruation, transsexuality, and politics—and of course, you'll find the hysterically funny essay "I Was a Playboy Bunny," about the time Steinem went undercover and worked for Playboy to gather information about the women's working conditions. Sometimes satirical, sometimes angry, sometimes sad, these essays showcase Steinem's talent as a major thinker of twentieth-century feminism.

> **Subjects:** Feminism • Second-wave Feminism • Activism • Sexual Discrimination • America • Memoir • Essays • Collection

> **Now Try:** Pair Steinem's memoir with Patricia Cronin Marcello's *Gloria Steinem: A Biography*. Whereas much of the focus of *Outrageous Acts* was on politics and feminism in America at large, this biography digs deeper into Steinem's personal life, illuminating her childhood, her relationship with her mother, and her college years. This is perfect for those who want to know about the background of the woman who would go on to become one of America's leading feminists.

Wicklund, Susan

This Common Secret: My Journey as an Abortion Doctor. New York: Public Affairs, 2007. 268pp. ISBN 9781586484804.

In 1976, Susan Wicklund—young, confused, and unintentionally pregnant—suffered a horrific abortion experience in which the doctor callously drugged her into submission, completely disregarding her tears and her questions. Wicklund carried the memory with her when she began medical school, and, when she herself became an abortion provider, she determined to offer sympathetic, supportive abortions. This is her memoir of her years as an abortion doctor, characterized by her conviction that no woman should abort until she is certain about her decision. Filled with stories that demonstrate the emotional nature of abortion, this is not the ranting of a crazed zealot but rather the thoughtful, insightful reminiscence of a woman who understands the need for abortion, as well as the need for counseling and education prior to abortion. Despite the threats that Wicklund has received throughout her years as an abortion doctor, she is committed to pro-choice politics, which she eloquently discusses in this compelling memoir.

Subjects: Abortion • Doctors • Health • Sexual Health • Pro-Choice • America • Memoir

Now Try: Hear more pro-choice stories from real people who have dealt with the difficult realities of abortion in two further books. In *The Choices We Made: Twenty-Five Women and Men Speak Out about Abortion*, editor Angela Bonavoglia collects stories from twenty-five people, including Kathy Najimy and Ursula K. Le Guin, that speak out in favor of the right of women to choose abortion. Then turn to *Behind Every Choice Is a Story*, in which Gloria Feldt, the president of Planned Parenthood, shares the stories of women who have had abortions—in the process fleshing them out into real people, not just statistics.

Global Voices

Global voices refers to the biographies of women from around the world, particularly outside of North America.

North American audiences are devouring books about people from distant lands. In part this is due to the two wars being fought by the United States, one in Iraq, the other in Afghanistan; Americans want to know more about the people in these foreign countries. Unsurprisingly, stories about Middle Eastern women are especially popular, but books about women in all parts of the world have a strong following. Read these books to learn about the customs, values, and social norms in other countries; some of them will be drastically different, while others will be surprisingly universal.

Aung San Suu Kyi and Alan Clements

The Voice of Hope. New York: Seven Stories Press, 1997 (2008). 301pp. ISBN 9781583228456.

Most people in the West knew little about Myanmar and even less about its government until Cyclone Nargis devastated the Southeast Asian country in 2008, at which time the whole world watched in horror as the military junta refused to let foreigners deliver humanitarian aid. But the people of Myanmar (formerly known as Burma) have lived under the junta since the 1960s—and Aung San Suu Kyi has dared oppose it. For her leadership of the democratic opposition to Myanmar's oppressive government, she received the Nobel Peace Prize; she was also placed under house arrest. Comprising a series of engrossing conversations between Aung San Suu Kyi and Alan Clements, *The Voice of Hope* illuminates the activist's humanitarian philosophies as well as her deep commitment to Buddhist spirituality.

Subjects: Nobel Peace Prize • Peace • Activism • Politics • Buddhism • Religion • Spirituality • Myanmar • Asia • Memoir

Now Try: Continue learning about the life and politics of Aung San Suu Kyi's *Freedom from Fear: And Other Writings*. Collecting various essays, speeches, and other pieces, the book illuminates the history and political climate of Myanmar and shows how Aung San Suu Kyi has struggled to resist the country's totalitarian regime. Read this to gain insight into her personal life, her public activism, and the country she continues to fight for. Then learn more about the oppression caused by the junta in Myanmar with *Burma: The State of Myanmar*, in which David I. Steinberg paints a disturbing portrait of the politics, culture, and society of contemporary Myanmar.

Chang, Jung

Wild Swans: Three Daughters of China. New York: Simon & Schuster, 1991 (2003). 524pp. ISBN 9780671685461.

This epic family story begins starkly—"At the age of fifteen my grandmother became the concubine of a warlord general"—and it does not relent for another five hundred pages. Absolutely gripping in its style and story, this powerful family history tells the story of three Chinese women: the author, her mother Bao Qin, and her grandmother Yu-fang. Experience the dynamic, tragic history of China in the twentieth century—the Communist Revolution, the Japanese occupation, the tyranny of Chairman Mao—through the eyes of these three women, as they and the people they love grapple with hardships such as foot-binding, death, slavery, and insanity. This is an eye-opening account of life in China during several decades of tumultuous political upheaval, made poignant and personal by the excellent rendering of the three heroines.

Subjects: Relationships • Mothers • Daughters • Grandmothers • Granddaughters • Marriage • History • Women's History • Politics • War • Violence • Twentieth Century • China • Asia • Memoir • Biography

Now Try: Learn more about Mao in *Mao: The Unknown Story*; this time Jung Chang does not talk about her family but rather about the tyrant's policies on a societal level. And, though it does not have the epic scope of *Wild Swans*, Nien Cheng's book *Life and Death in Shanghai* will appeal to readers who want to know more about what life was like in China during the Cultural Revolution. Brutally honest in tone, this is the memoir of an innocent victim of Mao's brutal policies. Learn how one woman's comfortable life was destroyed when she was falsely imprisoned in solitary confinement for six years; her keen political insights, as well as the heartbreaking grace with which she writes about the people she loves, will resonate with fans of *Wild Swans*. Finally, consider trying Mo Yan's vivid, violent epic novel of Chinese life in the twentieth century, *Big Breasts and Wide Hips*. This powerful story of survival speaks to the harsh realities of being a woman in China.

Hiratsuka, Raicho

In the Beginning, Woman Was the Sun: The Autobiography of a Japanese Feminist.
Weatherhead Books on Asia. New York: Columbia University Press, 2006. 335pp.
ISBN 9780231138123.

Here in the West, when we think of early-twentieth-century feminism, people
such as Margaret Sanger spring to mind; now learn about first-wave feminism in
the East with the autobiography of Raicho Hiratsuka (alternately known as
Hiratsuka Raicho, as family names come first in Japanese). Born in 1886,
Hiratsuka grew up to become Japan's most influential feminist. In her lifetime, she
founded the Japan Federation of Women's Organizations; the New Women's Association, dedicated to women's suffrage; and *Seito*, a women's literary journal of
lasting impact. In this captivating autobiography, painstakingly translated from
the Japanese by Teruko Craig, discover the remarkable achievements of this feminist foremother and gain insight into her childhood and personal life.

Subjects: Feminism • Activism • History • Women's History • Nineteenth Century •
Twentieth Century • Japan • Asia • Autobiography

Now Try: Now meet another Japanese feminist in *The Only Woman in the Room: A Memoir.* Born in 1924 in Vienna to a father who was a Russian Jew, Beate Gordon seems an
unlikely person to embrace Japanese feminism—but when her family moved to Japan,
she saw firsthand the discrimination that Japanese women faced. Read this fascinating
memoir to discover a woman who has devoted a lifetime to feminist causes both inside
and outside Japan.

Labzina, Anna Evdokimovna, Gary Marker, and Rachel May

Days of a Russian Noblewoman: The Memories of Anna Labzina, 1758–1821.
DeKalb: Northern Illinois University Press, 2001. 170pp. ISBN 9780875802770.

You've probably never heard of Anna Evdokimovna Labzina, née Yakoleva—and
in a way, that's good: this is not the story of one of the celebrated Russian elite, but
rather the ordinary story of an ordinary woman—though to be sure, her two husbands' circles did occasionally include some notable figures, including Grigorii
Potemkin and Catherine the Great. The real strength of the book, however, comes
from the glimpse it gives into domestic life in a Russia long since past. Through
two separate documents, a memoir and a diary, we learn how a little girl born in
1756 to a family of minor nobility grew, was thrown into an arranged marriage
with a philandering man, and how she outlived him to marry a man of her own
choosing. Though Labzina's stylized nineteenth-century prose takes some getting
used to, it is well worth the effort to discover the fascinating look at one woman's
perspective on marriage, family, and identity in tsarist Russia.

Subjects: History • Marriage • Women's History • Eighteenth Century • Nineteenth
Century • Russia • Europe • Memoir • Diary • Quick Read

Now Try: Now hear from other Russian women in the remarkable collection *Russia
through Women's Eyes: Autobiographies from Tsarist Russia*, edited by Toby W. Clyman
and Judith Vowles; with eleven writings by nineteenth-century Russian women, this
book shines light on issues such as family, education, and national identity. See also *The
Life of a Russian Woman Doctor: A Siberian Memoir, 1869–1954*, written by Anna
Nikolaevna Bek and edited by Anne Dickason Rassweiler. Told in diary format, this is
the remarkable story of Dr. Bek, a young woman who in 1894 resolved to become a doctor after witnessing her mother's death.

Latifa, and Chékéba Hachemi

My Forbidden Face: Growing Up under the Taliban: A Young Woman's Story. New York: Hyperion, 2001. 210pp. ISBN 9780786869015.

In 1996, Latifa (not her real name) was a normal sixteen-year-old girl, busy with going to school, watching movies, and listening to music—and then the Taliban came. Suddenly, the Kabul that Latifa knew and loved was gone, transformed into a city of nightmares. No longer could she leave the house unless escorted by a close male relative, and even then she had to cover her face and arms with a chadri; failure to obey could result in stoning. With vivid, disturbing details and a compulsively readable prose style, this memoir paints a horrific picture of Afghan women's lives under the Taliban; haunting and all-too-realistic, Latifa's is a story you won't forget.

Subjects: Coming of Age • Sexual Discrimination • Islam • Religion • Afghanistan • Middle East • Asia • Memoir • Young Adult • Quick Read

Now Try: Latifa speaks to us as a victim of the Taliban's oppressive rule; now experience the effect of the Taliban through the eyes of a visitor, the Spanish journalist Anna Tortajada. Determined to see for herself what the Taliban was doing, Tortajada traveled in 2000 to Pakistan and Afghanistan. In *The Silenced Cry: One Woman's Diary of a Journey to Afghanistan,* we see how Taliban law denied women everything from health care to education to normal everyday jobs. Compellingly written, this eye-opening account gives context to Latifa's story by illuminating the terrible restrictions suffered by women both inside and outside Kabul.

Masuda, Sayo

Autobiography of a Geisha. New York: Columbia University Press, 2003. 185pp. ISBN 9780231129503.

Perhaps you're familiar with the fictionalized narrative of the geisha experience in Arthur Golden's *Memoirs of a Geisha.* Now turn to *Autobiography of a Geisha,* written not by a Western man with a vivid imagination but by Sayo Masuda, who at the age of twelve was sold to a geisha house for a paltry sum. If you're expecting glamour and romance, think again: Masuda's life as a geisha is marked by violence and despair. She is abused both physically and verbally; she suffers from depression and attempts to kill herself; and even when she does escape the geisha lifestyle, she finds herself struggling to survive in World War II Japan. The narrator's candid, intimate voice, translated from the Japanese by G. G. Rowley, makes this a compelling, albeit grim, read.

Subjects: Geishas • Labor • Sexual Exploitation • Violence • Sexuality • Relationships • History • Women's History • Social History • Twentieth Century • Japan • Asia • Autobiography • Quick Read

Now Try: For another autobiography of a Japanese geisha, turn to *Geisha of Gion: The Memoir of Mineko Iwasaki,* written by Mineko Iwasaki and translated by Rande Brown Ouchi. Fans of Arthur Golden's *Memoirs of a Geisha* may be interested to know that he interviewed Iwasaki as background research for his novel; Iwasaki, however, was outraged at Golden's depiction of geisha life. To set the record straight, she published *Geisha of Gion,* her memoir of her time as a geisha in the second half of the twentieth century.

Menchú, Rigoberta, and Elisabeth Burgos-Debray

I, Rigoberta Menchú: An Indian Woman in Guatemala. London: Verso, 1984 (1994). 251pp. ISBN 9780860910831.

Rigoberta Menchú's life has been marked by death and violence. Her brother was tortured to death by the military; her father was burned alive when he participated in a political demonstration; her mother was kidnapped, raped, and murdered for her activism. Their crime? They wanted better living conditions for themselves and for other indigenous peoples of Guatemala. But despite the horrific violence done to her family, Menchú persevered, devoting her life to improving the lives of native Guatemalans and winning the 1992 Nobel Peace Prize for "her work for social justice and ethno-cultural reconciliation based on respect for the rights of indigenous peoples." In this stunning autobiography, you'll learn not only about Menchú's tragic life and activism, but also about the cultural and religious lifestyles of Guatemalan Native Americans.

> **Subjects:** Native Americans • Latinas • Race • Nobel Peace Prize • Peace • Violence • Activism • Religion • Spirituality • Guatemala • Autobiography

> **Now Try:** Ever since Menchú published her autobiography, and especially in the wake of her winning the Nobel Peace Prize, questions as to the book's authenticity have lingered. Was Menchú truly illiterate and uneducated? Does she stretch the truth to make her story more compelling? Well, yes, concludes anthropologist David Stoll in *Rigoberta Menchú and the Story of All Poor Guatemalans*, though her creative liberties in no way diminish the crimes of the Guatemalan army. In an era when many memoirists and autobiographers deviate from the truth, consciously or unconsciously, this is a fascinating study, one that calls some of Menchú's claims into question but which does not, in Stoll's opinion, invalidate or undermine her Nobel Peace Prize.

Nafisi, Azar

Reading Lolita in Tehran: A Memoir in Books. New York: Random House, 2003. 356pp. ISBN 9780375504907.

In 1995, fed up with the Ayatollah's oppressive influence in the University of Tehran, English professor Nafisi resigned—but not without secretly taking seven female students with her. In the private sanctuary of her own home, Nafisi conducted literature classes, teaching classic—and forbidden—texts such as *Pride and Prejudice*, *The Great Gatsby*, and, of course, *Lolita*. Nafisi's memoir, then, is both literary criticism and social criticism; we delve into the rich messages of the novels and into the difficult lives of the women who suffer under Iran's Islamic Republic. Beautifully written, this is a moving story of courage, activism, and the power of literature.

> **Subjects:** Literature • Education • Activism • Relationships • Sexual Discrimination • Islam • Religion • War • Iran • Middle East • Asia • Memoir

> **Now Try:** Jump back in time now with *Daughter of Persia: A Woman's Journey from Her Father's Harem through the Islamic Revolution*, by Sattareh Farman-Farmaian and Dona Munker. Farman-Farmaian was not an activist in the sense that Nafisi was—she deliberately tried to avoid attracting government ire—and yet, like Nafisi, she saw higher education as a means of improving the lives of Iranian students, and in 1958, she founded the Tehran School of Social Work. This is an excellent complement to *Reading Lolita in Tehran*, not only because it tells the story of another Iranian woman committed to social justice but because it gives historical context to the decades that preceded the Ayatollah's rise to power.

Nemat, Marina

Prisoner of Tehran: A Memoir. New York: Free Press, 2007. 306pp. ISBN 9781416537427.

It is 1982. Though the Islamic Revolution has turned Iran into a repressive Islamic state, a sixteen-year-old Christian girl named Marina Nemat nonetheless dares to protest the quality of her education by leading a strike in her high school, for which she is arrested, tortured, and sentenced to die. At the last minute she is saved, but the price is dear: to have her sentence reduced from execution to life in jail, her "savior" Ali demands that she convert to Islam, forsake her boyfriend, and marry him, instead. With no other choice, Nemat consents to Ali's coercion, but it is only after he is assassinated that she is released from prison. This is a harrowing, vivid memoir of one woman's political imprisonment and her lingering psychological scars; the ending is ultimately positive, but be forewarned: you'll need a box of tissues to reach the happy ending.

Subjects: Violence • Politics • Islam • Christianity • Religion • Activism • Iran • Middle East • Asia • Memoir

Now Try: For another eye-opening story of a woman who fought back against the Islamic Revolution, turn to Shirin Ebadi's *Iran Awakening: A Memoir of Revolution and Hope*. At the time the Ayatollah Khomeini took power, Ebadi was the most prominent female jurist in Iran; a year later, she was out of a job. Learn how she became a human rights lawyer and how she was jailed at the same prison that held Nemat captive in this remarkable memoir of activism and dissent.

Ramphele, Mamphela

Across Boundaries: The Journey of a South African Woman Leader. New York: Feminist Press at the City University of New York, 1997. 244pp. ISBN 9781558611658.

Born in 1947 with the dual disadvantages of being both black and female in South Africa's apartheid system, Mamphela Ramphele's life is marked by triumph and tragedy alike. She is both a medical doctor and a Ph.D. of anthropology; she is the first black woman to hold the vice chancellorship at the University of Cape Town; she is a lifelong activist who worked to bring health care to South Africans who were suffering under apartheid. But she has suffered for her successes: in the 1970s, the apartheid government banished her to a remote corner of the country, and it was during her exile that the father of her child, fellow activist Steve Biko, was tortured and murdered. Read about Ramphele's remarkable story in her autobiography, told in her engaging, descriptive prose.

Subjects: Activism • Doctors • Health Care • Leadership • Education • Politics • Race • Gender • Apartheid • Violence • Relationships • Mothers • History • Women's History • Social History • South Africa • Africa • Autobiography

Now Try: During her college years, Ramphele's activism and politics were greatly influenced by anti-apartheid activist Steve Biko. Learn more about the man who was her colleague, her political ally, her lover, and her child's father in Donald Woods's *Biko*, a biography that illuminates not only Biko but the apartheid system that he and Ramphele fought.

Satrapi, Marjane

Embroideries. New York: Pantheon Books, 2005. 100pp. ISBN 9780375423055.

You may already be familiar with Satrapi thanks to the two-part memoir of her girlhood, *Persepolis* (annotated below), but even if you've never encountered her before, you're in for a treat with this lovely gem of a book. The setting is simple: a group of Iranian women—Satrapi as a young woman, some of her female relatives, and their friends—are gathered for tea and company. What unfolds through their various stories is a glimpse into women's lives in the Middle East in the latter part of the twentieth century: through the course of their conversations, they discuss issues such as marriage, faith, family, love, and—of course—sex. Satrapi's straightforward black-and-white illustration style makes this an accessible graphic novel, even for those readers who are hesitant to read books in a graphic format.

> **Subjects:** Gender • Race • Islam • Religion • Relationships • Sexual Health • Sexual Discrimination • Politics • Iran • Middle East • Asia • Graphic Novel • Memoir • Quick Read

> **Now Try:** For more insight into the lives of Iranian women, turn to the perspective offered by Jane Howard, who as the wife of a diplomat, lived in Iran for several years. In her book *Inside Iran: Women's Lives*, Howard balances her Western viewpoint with plentiful tales about the women she met, providing insight into the role of gender under Islamic law in the everyday lives of Iranian women in the late 1990s.

Satrapi, Marjane

Persepolis. New York: Pantheon Books, 2003. 153pp. ISBN 9780375422300.

Born in 1969 to two Iranian Marxists, young Marjane Satrapi's first years were happy and blissfully normal, populated with loving family members and good friends. But in 1979, the Islamic Revolution rocked the country, and shortly thereafter Iran went to war with Iraq. In this captivating memoir, the tumultuous changes of the time—cultural, social, religious, political—form the backdrop for Satrapi's story, in which the innocence of her youth gives way to the violent political upheavals that threaten her family members and her way of life. With stark black-and-white illustrations, this graphic novel vividly portrays the coming of age of a young woman amidst the frenzied climate of Iran in the early 1980s.

> **Subjects:** Coming of Age • Islam • Iran • Middle East • Asia • Twentieth Century • Graphic Novel • Memoir • Quick Read • Young Adult

> **Now Try:** *Persepolis* ends with a fourteen-year-old Satrapi leaving Iran to attend high school in Vienna, a heartbreaking scene in which she takes leave of her parents. Don't let this tearful goodbye be your last encounter with Marjane; instead, continue following her story in the sequel, *Persepolis 2: The Story of a Return*, in which our young heroine completes her high school education in Austria before returning to Iran for college; many new characters, including a few boyfriends and a husband, propel the story of Marjane's transformation from teenager to young woman. Then turn to *Journey from the Land of No: A Girlhood Caught in Revolutionary Iran*. In 1979, a precocious and talented twelve-year-old, Roya Hakakian, was living a happy life with her family in Tehran; though they were Jews in a largely Islamic country, they got along well with their neighbors, with no threat of religious persecution. Then comes the Islamic Revolution, and everything changes: Iran is plunged into war, and Roya finds herself losing her freedoms, both as a Jew and as a young woman. Told in evocative, lyrical prose, this is a fast-paced, powerful memoir of coming-of-age amid violence and strife, where being a female Jew threatened not only Hakakian's freedoms but her very life.

Women Warriors

Here are stories of women who served in the military in various capacities, including espionage and combat.

In a world where wars have traditionally been fought by men, the voices of women speak with a special clarity. The titles in this section represent the perspectives of women from the past and the present, from America and abroad, who have served in times of war. Readers interested in women warriors will also want to refer to Chapter 4: Women's History, Chapter 7: Women at Work, and Chapter 8: Women and Society.

Bandel, Betty, and Sylvia J. Bugbee

An Officer and a Lady: The World War II Letters of Lt. Col. Betty Bandel, Women's Army Corps. Hanover, NH: University Press of New England, 2004. 222pp. ISBN 9781584653776.

In 1942, just a few months after the Japanese had attacked Pearl Harbor, Betty Bandel decided to join the new Women's Army Auxiliary Corps (later known as the Women's Army Corps, or WAC). Shortly thereafter she found herself in basic training and, before long, she and a select few other women were being primed for leadership in the Officer Candidate School. This is the story of Bandel's rise to lieutenant colonel, told through letters that she wrote and received during her time in the WAC. In her sparkling, clever, engaging prose, Bandel offers a glimpse into a fascinating slice of military history by revealing the powerful new role of women in the military in World War II.

> **Subjects:** Bandel, Betty • Warriors • History • Military History • Women's History • Labor • Twentieth Century • America • World War II • Letters • Memoir
>
> **Now Try:** For a somewhat different perspective, turn to *One Woman's War: Letters Home from the Women's Army Corps, 1944–1946*, by Anne Bosanko Green. Unlike Bandel, Green did not serve as an officer but as a surgical technician. Fans of Bandel's book will appreciate Green's candid letter-writing style, and they will enjoy reading about the contrasting experiences of Bandel's role as an officer and Green's role as a lower-ranking servicewoman.

Carl, Ann

A WASP among Eagles: A Woman Military Test Pilot in World War II. Washington, DC: Smithsonian Institution Press, 1999. 132pp. ISBN 97815-60988427.

During World War II, the WASPs—the Women Airforce Service Pilots—comprised an extraordinary group of women, aviators who served on the home front by testing repaired military planes and flying them to airfields. In this page-turning memoir, you'll meet Ann Carl, a WASP who made aviation history as the first woman to fly a jet. Read about her daring adventures as a test pilot for experimental aircraft and get a glimpse into the work done by the WASPs—work that was undervalued at the time and that, even today, is too often ignored by history books.

> **Subjects:** Aviation • Labor • Adventure • Sexual Discrimination • World War II • History • Military History • American History • Social History • Twentieth Century • War • Violence • America • Memoir • Quick Read

> **Now Try:** Next meet another WASP, Marion Stegeman Hodgson, in *Winning My Wings: A Woman Airforce Service Pilot in World War II*. Told in the form of letters to a Marine pilot, the book recounts the action and adventure of WASP service: the terror of learning to fly, the sorrow over pilots killed in crashes, the joy of soaring the skies. Like Carl's memoir, this book illuminates the largely forgotten services performed by women aviators on the home front in World War II.

Edmonds, S. Emma E.

Memoirs of a Soldier, Nurse, and Spy: A Woman's Adventures in the Union Army. Boston: De Wolfe, Fiske, 1864 (2000). 266pp. ISBN 9780875805849.

In 1861, Franklin Thompson joined the Union Army, where he served as a soldier, a male nurse, and a spy; his disguise as an Irish washerwoman was especially effective because, in fact, Mr. Thompson was actually a woman named Sarah Emma Edmonds. Raised by a father who wanted a son rather than a daughter, Edmonds had spent years trying to act like man, and thus she was able to fool everyone when she joined the army. While she was certainly not the only woman to disguise her sex to fight in the Civil War, she was the only one bold enough to publish her story after the fact. First published in 1864, this is the account of Edmonds's two years in the army, remarkable not only for its stirring adventures but for the incredible disguise that Edmonds was able to maintain.

> **Subjects:** Warriors • Nurses • Espionage • Labor • Adventure • War • Violence • History • Military History • Women's History • Civil War • Nineteenth Century • America • Memoir

> **Now Try:** Continue learning about the fascinating Mr. Thompson/Ms. Edmonds in *The Mysterious Private Thompson: The Double Life of Sarah Emma Edmonds, Civil War Soldier*. In this biography, Laura Leedy Gansler fleshes out Edmonds's story, giving us more insight into her relationships with her abusive father and filling in the blanks about her post-service life. Learn how Edmonds married, raised two children, and became the only woman to claim a Civil War pension.

Wakeman, Sarah Rosetta, and Lauren M. Cook

An Uncommon Soldier: The Civil War Letters of Sarah Rosetta Wakeman, Alias Private Lyons Wakeman, 153rd Regiment, New York State Volunteers. Pasadena, MD: The Minerva Center, 1994. 110pp. ISBN 9780963489517.

Whereas Sarah Emma Edmonds published a memoir of her time disguised as a man in the Union Army (see the previous annotation for *Memoirs of a Soldier, Nurse, and Spy*), Sarah Rosetta Wakeman never had a chance to write a book about her military service; she died of dysentery before the war finished. What we have instead is a collection of her letters home to her family back in New York. Meet Sarah Wakeman, also known as Private Lyons Wakeman, a woman who served admirably as a soldier and died without the secret of her sex becoming known. Wakeman's simple, unpolished prose allows her voice to shine as she recounts her experiences, and the book's illustrations—including a photo of a very masculine-looking Sarah—give context to her two years of service in the Union Army.

Subjects: Warriors • Labor • Adventure • War • Violence • Gender • History • Military History • Women's History • Civil War • Nineteenth Century • America • Letters • Memoir • Collection • Quick Read

Now Try: In 1876, a sensational autobiography was published, a book that rattled any number of social norms. *The Woman in Battle: A Narrative of the Exploits, Adventures, and Travels of Madame Loreta Janeta Velazquez* was written by a bisexual, cross-dressing Cuban woman who had fought for the Confederacy disguised as Lieutenant Harry T. Buford. Be forewarned: the book's authenticity has been disputed in academic circles, but readers willing to try a book that may contain some (or possibly a lot of) fiction will be delighted with the daring exploits of the gender-bending Velazquez.

Xie, Bingying, Lily Chia Brissman, and Barry Brissman

A Woman Soldier's Own Story: The Autobiography of Xie Bingying. New York: Columbia University Press, 2001. 281pp. ISBN 9780231122504.

Born in 1906, Xie Bingying (or Bingying Xie, the Westernized version of her name), was a feminist well ahead of her time. Most little girls born into rural China in the early twentieth century passively accepted their gender roles, but not Xie: she fought against foot-binding, the marriage her parents arranged for her, the unquestioning obedience expected of her—she even went on a hunger strike to persuade her parents to give her the same educational opportunities as her brothers received. While Xie did not always get her way—her feet *were* bound, and the arranged marriage did take place, though it lasted only long enough to give her an infant daughter—she always persevered, transforming from a precious child activist to a lifelong adult social reformer and feminist. In this magnificent autobiography, first published in two parts in 1936 and 1948 and translated by her daughter and son-in-law, you'll discover the remarkable story of Xie's early life, from her childhood years to her time as an adult in the military.

Subjects: Warriors • War • Violence • Activism • Feminism • Politics • Labor • Gender • Sexual Discrimination • History • Women's History • Military History • Social History • Twentieth Century • China • Asia • Autobiography

Now Try: Jump forward in time to the late 1980s and discover "Words on the Night Breeze," a Chinese radio show in which women called in to talk about their lives. In *The Good Women of China: Hidden Voices*, written by the show's host, Xinran, discover the problems endured by Chinese women at the tail end of the twentieth century; though written decades after *A Woman Soldier's Own Story*, the stories of sexual discrimination and rigid gender roles endured by the women in Xinran's book are disturbingly similar to the injustices that Bingying fought against decades earlier.

Women in the Margins

Titles included in "Women in the Margins" tell the stories of women who exist outside the mainstream—in terms of sexual identity, racial and cultural identity, or religious identity.

"Women in the Margins" is about women who exist outside the mainstream. They are women, of course, so their sex alone is enough to identify them as Other; but their identities are additionally shaped by experiences and backgrounds that set them apart. Books in the "Queer Identity" section speak to the experience of defying what Adrienne Rich describes as "compulsory heterosexuality."

The "Racial and Cultural Identity" subsection features books by American women whose race, ethnicity, or national origin places them outside of the dominant white culture—with one exception; as a Native American in the early seventeenth century, Pocahontas was very much in the dominant culture, though the racial dynamics of America were about to change drastically.

Not all of the women in "Religious Identity" are marginalized by their religious identities, per se. It was perfectly normal for medieval women to devote their lives to Christianity, for instance, but Margery Kempe took a most unusual step when she told her husband that she would no longer sleep with him. Some of the women in these books practice faiths that are popular in their countries, while others do not; their stories are included here because they offer unusual insight into the intersection of religion, faith, gender, and women's issues.

Queer Identity

The "Queer Identity" section gathers titles in which minority sexual orientation plays a prominent role in the lives of the writers.

While books written by and about bisexuals, transsexuals, and lesbians can be found throughout this text, the "Queer Identity" section gathers titles in which minority sexual orientation plays a prominent role in the lives of the writers. Read these for the character-driven stories or to explore the realities of sexual identity politics. And for more books about women with queer identities, turn to the "Queer Romantic Relationships" section of Chapter 2.

Bechdel, Alison

Fun Home: A Family Tragicomic. Boston: Houghton Mifflin, 2006. 232pp. ISBN 9780618477944.

Did Alison Bechdel's father kill himself? We'll never know for sure, though we can be certain that he was unhappy: he was a gay man trapped in a heterosexual marriage. His troubled life and tragic death constitute the book's chief focus, but *Fun Home* is also a memoir of Bechdel's own childhood, coming of age, and lesbian coming-out. With frequent allusions to art, literature, and poetry, this is a sophisticated, cerebral book that considers very deep themes of sexuality, sexual orientation, family, and death, rendered in gorgeous illustrations by Bechdel's talented hand.

Subjects: Lesbians • Queer Sexuality • Coming of Age • Memoir • America • Graphic Novel

Now Try: Meet Bechdel as an adult in *The Indelible Alison Bechdel: Confessions, Comix, and Miscellaneous Dykes to Watch Out For*, a lovely collection of miscellanea that work together to create a scattershot memoir. Much lighter in tone than *Fun Home*, the book includes cartoon strips, single-panel gems, and mini-essays, some of which are strictly autobiographical, some of which are more fictionalized. Art and musings from throughout Bechdel's life, from her earliest years through her professional career, give insight into Bechdel's experiences as a lesbian, a political commentator, and cartoonist.

Blum, Louise A.

You're Not from Around Here, Are You?: A Lesbian in Small-Town America. Madison: University of Wisconsin Press, 2001. 271pp. ISBN 9780299170905.

This would be a garden-variety memoir of life and love in America—there is romance, a house to purchase, a pregnancy—but there's one noticeable detail that makes this story a little bit different: the two main characters are lesbians. Author Blum, a poet, novelist, and college professor, here turns her gift for lovely prose and lucid storytelling to the experience of her pregnancy in a small (and often small-minded) town in Pennsylvania. As with many memoirs written by lesbian mothers, this covers some familiar themes, such as undergoing artificial insemination and grappling with the changes that a pregnancy brings to any romantic relationship; unlike many lesbian memoirs, however, this story is not set in a progressive city but in a traditional small town. Read this for a glimpse into the unique trials faced by a same-sex couple in a town that is slow to embrace change, and to meet the remarkable women who face their challenges with wit and grace.

Subjects: Lesbian Sexuality • Queer Sexuality • Sexuality • Mothers • Relationships • Fertility • Pregnancy • Birth • America • Memoir

Now Try: In Blum's memoir we hear primarily from the perspective of the biological mother, the author herself; what if the story had been written by the nonbiological mother, Connie? Now hear from lesbian mothers who *don't* give birth to their children in *Confessions of the Other Mother: Nonbiological Lesbian Moms Tell All.* Edited by Harlyn Aizley, this anthology gives voices to the women who, though they have no biological relation to their children, are nonetheless mothers in every sense of the word; learn how they both struggle and thrive in their relationships in these heartfelt, thought-provoking essays.

King, Florence

Confessions of a Failed Southern Lady. New York: St. Martin's Press/Marek, 1985. 278pp. ISBN 9780312162153.

"I will say one thing in my own favor," writes King, in perhaps the most famous line from her book, "no matter which sex I went to bed with, I never smoked on the street." If that isn't the definition of a lady, what is? Southern Literature meets the lesbian memoir in this wickedly funny autobiography of a rambunctious young woman who comes of age in the mid-twentieth-century American South. There's a mother whose vocabulary consists primarily of choice swear words, a British-born father who seems hopelessly out of place, a grandmother determined to make a proper southern lady out of her granddaughter—and then there's the granddaughter herself, the delightfully witty King. Follow her from her childhood in Virginia through her various sexual escapades with men in high school through her dawning awareness of her lesbian orientation in college in Mississippi. By turns laugh-out-loud funny and reflective, the story captures the difficulties of exploring one's sexuality in the southern states of yesteryear.

> **Subjects:** Lesbian Sexuality • Bisexuality • Queer Sexuality • Sexuality • Dating • Relationships • Daughters • Granddaughters • Coming of Age • History • Women's History • Twentieth Century • America • Humor • Autobiography

> **Now Try:** If you can't get enough of King's acerbic commentary, turn to her book *Reflections in a Jaundiced Eye*. This time, she focuses less on her own life story (though don't worry, she still includes plenty of personal anecdotes) and more on the American way of life, with biting commentary that ridicules everything from celebrities she doesn't like to peculiar American social habits, all with her trademark southern humor. Readers who enjoy King's wit will also want to try *We're Just Like You, Only Prettier: Confessions of a Tarnished Southern Belle*, in which Celia Rivenbark offers a side-splitting commentary on southern life.

McCloskey, Deirdre N.

Crossing: A Memoir. Chicago: University of Chicago Press, 1999. 266pp. ISBN 9780226556680.

For decades, academic economist Donald McCloskey had been dressing in women's clothing, but in his fifties, he realized that cross-dressing was not enough to satisfy his psychological needs: he needed to become a woman not just in spirit but in body. This fascinating memoir tells of his biological transformation from man to woman, from Donald to Deirdre. Be forewarned that this is a painful story: Deirdre's two children cannot accept their father's change; Deirdre's wife insists on a divorce; Deirdre's sister tries to have her sibling declared insane to prevent the surgeries—and, perhaps most painful for the reader, Deirdre is so very self-absorbed that she cannot seem to understand why the people close to her struggle, unsuccessfully, to accept her transformation. But this is nonetheless a captivating story of one man's journey to womanhood, filled with thought-provoking questions on the nature of gender, sex, and identity.

> **Subjects:** Cross-dressing • Transgender • Transsexuality • Gender • Psychology • Biology • Queer Sexuality • Sexuality • Marriage • Children • Relationships • America • Memoir

> **Now Try:** The parallels are striking: like McCloskey, Jennifer Finney Boylan lived for years as a man, worked as an academic, enjoyed a satisfying marriage, and fathered two children. But Boylan's story is happier than McCloskey's; though her wife and children find their father's transformation difficult to accept, they do persevere, and the family stays intact. Read the enjoyable, insightful memoir *She's Not There: A Life in Two Genders* to discover Boylan's journey from James to Jennifer.

Meaker, Marijane

Highsmith: A Romance of the 1950's, a Memoir. San Francisco: Cleis Press, 2003. 207pp. ISBN 9781573441711.

In the early 1950s, Patricia Highsmith was a dark-haired beauty, just beginning a career as a writer of psychological thrillers. Marijane Meaker was a tawny-haired beauty, also about to embark on a lifelong writing career. And for two wild years, both writers were lovers, taking the literature scene of New York City by storm. This is Meaker's memoir of their affair, told in her fast-paced, gripping, artfully crafted style; it is also a biography of Highsmith, a fascinating but oftentimes unlikable character. The overall tone is bittersweet—the 1950s romance ultimately dissolves, and a reunion in the 1990s reveals Highsmith to have become a bitter woman and a callous anti-Semite—but the characters and setting are fascinating, and the romance, though doomed, is brilliant while it lasts.

> **Subjects:** Highsmith, Patricia • Lesbian Sexuality • Bisexuality • Romance • Writing • History • American History • Twentieth Century • America • Memoir • Biography

> **Now Try:** Whereas Meaker focuses on a brief slice of Highsmith's life, author Andrew Wilson considers her entire story in *Beautiful Shadow: A Life of Patricia Highsmith*. This thoughtful biography, based in part on Highsmith's journals, reveals a complicated, difficult, and profoundly unhappy woman and considers her influence on crime fiction and on gay and lesbian fiction. And those who have never read a Highsmith novel may wish to start with *The Price of Salt*, written under her pseudonym, Claire Morgan; first published in 1951, the book is part suspense and part lesbian romance, a serious contrast to the underground lesbian pulp novels of the day.

Richards, Renée, and John Ames

No Way Renée: The Second Half of My Notorious Life. New York: Simon & Schuster, 2007. 302pp. ISBN 9780743290135.

> Because there are so few memoirs written by transsexuals, each one is, by definition, unusual; what makes Richards's exceptionally uncommon is that, at age seventy-two, she has lived about half her life as a male, half as a female. Prior to her sex-reassignment surgery in 1975, she was Richard Raskind—a successful amateur tennis player, a leading surgeon, a husband, and a father. This fascinating memoir touches on that history so as to give the reader context, but the primary focus is on Richards's life as Renée, a biological woman. In her candid, engaging style, she tells of her divorce, her romances, her relationship with her son, and her struggles to reclaim her career both on the tennis court and in the operating room. Read to discover Richards's unusual life story and to contemplate her thought-provoking perspectives on gender and sexuality.

> **Subjects:** Transsexuality • Gender • Marriage • Children • Relationships • America • Memoir

> **Now Try:** Even before Richards underwent her sex-reassignment surgery in the 1970s, Christine Jorgensen paved the way in the 1950s by becoming one of the first people to undergo a sex change. Read how George William became Christine in Richard F. Docter's *Becoming a Woman: A Biography of Christine Jorgensen*. With his thorough research and readable style, Docter looks at Jorgensen before and after surgery, revealing not only her personal life but the history and politics of transsexuality.

Racial and Cultural Identity

> Women whose race or cultural heritage is outside the mainstream play central roles in the titles in this section.

With twenty-one entries, the "Racial and Cultural Identity" section covers more books than any other section in this text. The abundance of good books in this area stems from the important roles played by race and culture in each of our lives. No amount of assimilation, cultural homogeneity, or mainstream influence can change the color of our skins or the heritage of our families. While most of these books offer fascinating character portraits, their biggest appeal is in the questions they raise. Read these to explore thought-provoking questions about race, culture, and identity and to see how women of various races find their places within society at large.

Allen, Paula Gunn

Pocahontas: Medicine Woman, Spy, Entrepreneur, Diplomat. San Francisco: HarperSanFrancisco, 2003. 350pp. ISBN 9780060536879.

> If you only vaguely remember Pocahontas from your high school history class, or if your image of her has been shaped by popular culture, then you owe it to yourself to revisit her in this remarkable biography. Allen, one of the foremost writers of Native American history and thought (see, for instance, her landmark title *The Sacred Hoop*, annotated in Chapter 2), dismisses the typical interpretation of Pocahontas as a doe-eyed naïf, recasting her as a self-assured young woman with an astute spiritual and intellectual acumen, one who assumed various roles to bridge the gap between her Powhatan people and the new English settlers who came to Jamestown in 1607. Allen places Pocahontas within the context of her own native traditions and within the larger setting of transcontinental politics at the dawn of the seventeenth century, using vivid prose and thoughtful observations to show her as a fully realized Native American and person, not just a plaything of European invaders.

> **Subjects:** Pocahontas • Native Americans • Race • Politics • Spirituality • History • Women's History • American History • Sixteenth Century • America • Biography

> **Now Try:** An excellent companion to Allen's study of Pocahontas is Helen C. Rountree's *Pocahontas, Powhatan, Opechancanough: Three Indian Lives Changed by Jamestown*. Like Allen, Rountree is a leading Native American scholar, determined to present the native perspective in her writings; in this collective biography, she shines further light on Pocahontas, as well as on two other key Powhatan players in the story of Jamestown's settlement, Opechancanough and Powhatan himself. Fans of Allen's book will appreciate the emphasis on Native American history and the thought-provoking examination of the merging of two cultures. Then look at the broad picture of early English influence in America with *Love and Hate in Jamestown: John Smith, Pocahontas, and the Start of a New Nation*. Pocahontas plays a significant role, but journalist David A. Price extends the scope of his captivating narrative to consider the impact of the entire Jamestown colony.

Arana, Marie

American Chica: Two Worlds, One Childhood. New York: Dial Press, 2001. 309pp. ISBN 9780385319621.

> "There is a fundamental rift between North and South America," writes *Washington Post Book World* editor Arana, "a flaw so deep it is tectonic." She is speaking of geology, yes, but also of cultures. It is a subject she knows well: as the daughter of an American mother and a Peruvian father, she grew up straddling two worlds, two cultures, two identities. This is the story of Arana's conflicted childhood on two continents, as well as the story of the fiery marriage between her two passionate but mismatched parents. With melodic prose and a keen eye for detail, Arana

brings life to Peru and America in the 1950s and '60s as she grows into a young woman whose national identity spans two continents.

> **Subjects:** Coming of Age • Latinas • Race • Relationships • Marriage • Peru • America • Global Perspectives • Twentieth Century • Memoir • Young Adult

> **Now Try:** Journey again to Peru, but this time through the eyes of an Italian child. In *Gringa Latina: A Woman of Two Worlds*, Gabriella De Ferrari tells the story of her complicated identity: she was born and raised in Peru, but she grew up with the transplanted culture of her two Italian parents. Carefully crafted settings and a graceful prose style will appeal to fans of *American Chica*, as will the themes of culture and national identity.

Boyd, Loree

Spirit Moves: The Story of Six Generations of Native Women. Novato, CA: New World Library, 1996. 436pp. ISBN 9781880032596.

Loree Boyd, a Cree/Blackfoot Metis Native American, tells the stories of six generations of women in this loving tribute to one family. Arranged in three sections devoted to the perspectives of grandmother Anne, mother Silversong, and the author herself, the book shares the life stories of these women and the foremothers they remember. Themes of gender, race, and spirituality carry the family story from 1886 through the dawn of the twenty-first century, resulting in an epic that is sometimes tragic, sometimes joyful, and ultimately inspiring as it reveals the women's struggles with, and triumphs over, racism and sexism.

> **Subjects:** Native Americans • Gender • Race • Spirituality • Women's History • History • Nineteenth Century • Twentieth Century • Canada • Biography • Memoir

> **Now Try:** For more inspiring stories of Native American women, turn to *Sifters: Native American Women's Lives*, edited by historian Theda Perdue. Though more academic in approach, fans of *Spirit Moves* will enjoy learning about the lives of various native women, including well-known figures such as Sacagawea and Pocahontas as well as less familiar women from the past and present.

Brave Bird, Mary, and Richard Erdoes

Lakota Woman. New York: Grove Weidenfeld, 1990. 263pp. ISBN 9780802-111012.

"I had my first baby during a firefight, with the bullets crashing through one wall and coming out through the other," writes Mary Brave Bird on the first page of her breathtaking book, and the gripping narrative never relents: with vivid language and an un-put-downable plot, she tells the story of her youth and early adulthood as a Sioux woman. It is an emotionally difficult story to read: born into poverty and educated at a school where the nuns beat the Indian students, she was raped at the age of fourteen and fired upon at the Battle of Wounded Knee. Darkly humorous ("In 1975 the feds put the muzzles of their M-16s against my head, threatening to blow me away. It's hard being an Indian woman.") and brutally honest, the book recounts not only the painful episodes of Mary Brave Bird's life but also the good parts: she finds love with an activist and community with the American Indian Movement. This is both a stunning autobiography and an eye-opening look into Native American traditions, values, religions, and ways of life.

Subjects: Coming of Age • Native Americans • Race • Violence • Rape • Politics • Spirituality • Religion • Marriage • Mothers • Relationships • History • Women's History • American History • Twentieth Century • America • Autobiography • Young Adult

Now Try: Find out what happened to Mary Brave Bird in her sequel, *Ohitika Woman*. Be warned: this book is every bit as disturbing and painful as the first autobiography. Alcoholism, abuse, divorce, and drugs each play a vicious part—but despite her many serious struggles, Brave Bird offers a message of hope. Feminism, activism, and Native American pride shine through, making this book a blend of pain and promise, of sorrow and hope. Readers interested in knowing more about Lakota history will also want to try Susan Bordeaux Bettelyoun's *With My Own Eyes: A Lakota Woman Tells Her People's History*. Read this account of nineteenth-century life for the heartfelt story of one woman's experiences, and to give historical context to the events of Mary Brave Bird's life.

Bundles, A'Lelia Perry

On Her Own Ground: The Life and Times of Madam C.J. Walker. New York: Scribner, 2001. 415pp. ISBN 9780684825823.

Born just two years after the Civil War ended, a poor Louisiana black girl named Sarah Breedlove hardly seemed destined for success, yet by the time she transformed as an adult into Madame C. J. Walker, she was fabulously rich. We may be thankful that she began losing her hair in the 1890s, because this cosmetic affliction motivated her to develop her own line of hair care products for black women. What started as a private experiment with ointments turned into a pioneering industry, propelled by Walker's business savvy and strategic marketing. Bolstered by her financial success, Walker went on to become an activist for racial justice and social equality in the early twentieth century. Read about this remarkable woman in this engaging biography, written by Walker's own great-great-granddaughter, the journalist A'Lelia Perry Bundles.

Subjects: Walker, Madam C. J. • Entrepreneurs • Business • Labor • Cosmetics • Beauty • Appearance • African Americans • Race • Activism • History • Women's History • Social History • American History • History of Business • Nineteenth Century • Twentieth Century • America • Biography

Now Try: Learn more about the mysterious Madam Walker in another fascinating biography, Beverly Lowry's *Her Dream of Dreams: The Rise and Triumph of Madam C. J. Walker*. Very little is known about Walker's personal life, but Lowry supplements what we do know of her story with meticulous research, fleshing out the personality and private life of the entrepreneur and civil rights activist. Then meet another black entrepreneur, Madam Walker's contemporary A. G. Gaston. Born into poverty in 1892, Gaston achieved extraordinary success as a businessman, despite a racially inhospitable culture. Read his remarkable story in *Black Titan: A. G. Gaston and the Making of a Black American Millionaire*, by Carol Jenkins and Elizabeth Gardner Hines.

Erdrich, Heid E., and Laura Tohe, eds.

Sister Nations: Native American Women Writers on Community. St. Paul: Minnesota Historical Society Press, 2002. 230pp. ISBN 9780873514279.

Nonfiction fans who appreciate good fiction short stories and poems won't want to miss this lovely anthology, which brings together the writing of forty-nine Native American women from various backgrounds and tribes. Representing a range of emotions and experiences, this is an exemplary collection, with uniformly strong writing on themes such as race, family, and gender. Don't be nervous, nonfiction readers: there are plenty of real-life essays and stories within these pages, along with a short biography of each author, and additional information about the tribe or nation from which she hails.

> **Subjects:** Native Americans • America • Biography • Essays • Anthology • Collection

> **Now Try:** Those who took pleasure from the fiction within *Sister Nations* will enjoy the collection edited by prolific Native American author Paula Gunn Allen, *Spider Woman's Granddaughters: Traditional Tales and Contemporary Writing by Native American Women*. In this haunting anthology, seventeen native women present stories—some old, some new—that cover themes of love, loss, politics, and identity.

Fernandez Barrios, Flor

Blessed by Thunder: Memoir of a Cuban Girlhood. Seattle, WA: Seal Press, 1999. 243pp. ISBN 9781580050210.

Author Barrios was born while a hurricane raged in Cabaiguán, Cuba, just a few years before Castro came to power—and yet this dramatic entry into the world was only a portent of the drama that little Flor would face as she grew up in communist Cuba. With vivid, lyrical prose, Barrios recounts her troubled childhood: the political nightmares that rocked her family, the labor camp where she was forced to pick tobacco and sugar cane, the eventual exile/escape to the United States. Read this not only for a glimpse into the history of Cuba but for the tender story of the author's spiritual connections with her family both during and after the harrowing trials of her childhood.

> **Subjects:** Coming of Age • Children • Spirituality • Race • Class • Latinas • Politics • History • Twentieth Century • Cuba • Caribbean • Memoir • Young Adult

> **Now Try:** Hop across the Caribbean to meet Esmeralda Santiago in her memoir *When I Was Puerto Rican*. Discover the Puerto Rico of the 1950s, where Santiago lived in poverty with her parents and siblings, moving at the age of thirteen to a hostile, unwelcoming Brooklyn. Fans of *Blessed by Thunder* will enjoy Santiago's vivid details and evocative descriptions of her native country and her harsh new home in America, and they will be inspired by her eventual triumph over poverty and discrimination.

Frank, Anne, Otto Frank, Mirjam Pressler, and Susan Massotty

The Diary of a Young Girl: The Definitive Edition. New York: Doubleday, 1995. 340pp. ISBN 9780385473781.

You're probably already familiar with Anne Frank's diary; it is one of the most celebrated works of the twentieth century, studied by schoolchildren around the globe. But if you have somehow missed reading it—or if you have never read it for your own pleasure, outside the walls of the classroom—then by all means do find a copy of this extraordinary document. (Any version will suffice, though this particular edition incorporates material omitted from previous editions, especially with regards to Anne's growing sexual awareness.) A gifted writer, Frank started the diary on her thirteenth birthday in 1942 and chronicled two dark and dangerous years, during which she, her immediate family, and four others lived in hiding from the Nazis in cramped quarters. Understandably, the brutal effect of the Holocaust on Frank and her fellow Jews is apparent throughout the diary (and bear in mind that she stopped writing in it before the final horrible chapter of their lives, when they were betrayed and sent to their deaths) and yet, despite the inconceivably difficult circumstances in which Frank came of age, this is ultimately an optimistic, positive book. Read this not only to deepen your understanding of Holocaust history but to share in Frank's thoughts on family, religion, romance, and ethics as she grows into a young woman.

> **Subjects:** Judaism • Religion • Coming of Age • War • Violence • Relationships • Sexuality • Spirituality • History • World War II • Netherlands • Twentieth Century • Diary • Memoir • Young Adult

> **Now Try:** Complement your reading of Frank's diary with *Anne Frank, Beyond the Diary: A Photographic Remembrance*, by Ruud van der Rol and Rian Verhoeven. Filled with photographs and insightful historical and political commentary, this accessible book gives context to the diary, rooting Frank's story within the larger story of the Holocaust.

Furiya, Linda

Bento Box in the Heartland: My Japanese Girlhood in Whitebread America. Emeryville, CA: Seal Press, 2006. 307pp. ISBN 9781580051910.

"I expected a classic elementary school lunch of a bologna, cheese, and Miracle Whip sandwich and a bag of Durkee's potato sticks," recalls Linda Furiya, thinking back to the first time she brought a packed lunch to school, "but all I saw were three round rice balls wrapped in waxed paper. Mom had made me an *obento*, a Japanese-style boxed meal. I snapped the lid shut before the other girls caught a glimpse of what was inside. . . . My *obento* lunches were a glaring reminder of the ethnic differences between my peers and me." Growing up in the 1960s as the only Japanese student in her Indiana town, Furiya was profoundly embarrassed at how her family's food set her apart—and yet she loved the taste of green tea, of miso soup, of tofu with ginger. In this enjoyable memoir, Furiya uses vivid details and sensuous descriptions of food to narrate the tensions between her Japanese roots and her new American identity as she comes of age. And for those readers eager to taste the Japanese cuisine that shaped her life, Furiya includes recipes at the end of each chapter.

> **Subjects:** Food • Recipes • Coming of Age • Asian Americans • America • Twentieth Century • Memoir • Young Adult

> **Now Try:** Though she grew up two decades later than Linda Furiya, Bich Minh Nguyen could surely relate; as a Vietnamese immigrant living in Michigan, she felt out of place in her school and town. In *Stealing Buddha's Dinner: A Memoir*, she recalls how her love of Vietnamese cuisine conflicted with her desire to fit in by eating American foods.

Golden, Marita

Don't Play in the Sun: One Woman's Journey through the Color Complex. New York: Doubleday, 2004. 195pp. ISBN 9780385507868.

There's racism, but then again there's racism. Discrimination on the basis of skin color is not a simple matter of black and white, as it were; as novelist Marita Golden explains, the particular shade of a black person's skin influences discrimination, even among black people themselves. As a child, Golden was ashamed of her dark skin, a message hammered home by society, by classmates, even by her own mother, who advised her daughter to avoid playing in the sun; it was not until she was an adult that she came to appreciate the beauty of her own dark skin.

Part memoir and part sociological study of the color complex in the media, popular culture, and society, this is a thought-provoking, disturbing narrative.

Subjects: African Americans • Race • Appearance • Body Image • Media • Sociology • America • Memoir • Quick Read

Now Try: Continue studying the color complex with Margaret L. Hunter's thought-provoking book *Race, Gender, and the Politics of Skin Tone*. Offering both a historical overview and a shrewd analysis of contemporary issues, the book examines the politics of skin color in African American and Mexican American communities while emphasizing the experiences of women. And fans of *Don't Play in the Sun* who want to know more about the author will enjoy *Migrations of the Heart: An Autobiography*, in which Golden discusses her childhood, her college education, her marriage—and most significantly, her move to Nigeria. In Africa she develops a powerful new understanding of race and skin color—but she also develops an ugly understanding of the traditional gender roles expected of "dutiful" wives.

Golden, Marita, and Susan Richards Shreve, eds.

Skin Deep: Black Women & White Women Write about Race. New York: Nan A. Talese, 1995. 309pp. ISBN 9780385474092.

Black women and white women tackle race head-on in this thought-provoking collection of essays and stories by leading scholars, writers, and activists. Twenty writers consider race in various contexts, from friendships to families, from relationships to careers, but reader be warned: the questions they raise do not have easy answers. With contributions from such luminaries as Naomi Wolf, Joyce Carol Oates, Toni Morrison, and Eudora Welty, this collection sparkles for its unusually high caliber of scholarship and thought; it is not to be missed by anyone who cares about race and sex in modern society.

Subjects: Race • Gender • African Americans • Feminism • Third-wave Feminism • America • Essays • Anthology • Collection • Memoir

Now Try: Continue thinking about race in *Skin Deep: How Race and Complexion Matter in the "Color-Blind" Era*, edited by Cedric Herring, Verna Keith, and Hayward Derrick Horton. A variety of races—including black, white, Latino, and biracial identities—are discussed in this collection of eye-opening essays by scholars who take a serious look at how race continues to play a role in contemporary society.

Hart, Elva Treviño

Barefoot Heart: Stories of a Migrant Child. Tempe, AZ: Bilingual Press/ Editorial Bilingüe, 1999. 236pp. ISBN 9780927534819.

"My whole childhood, I never had a bed." With the very first sentence of her book, Hart's memoir plunges into the gritty reality of her youth. As one of six siblings born to two migrant workers in mid-twentieth-century America, Hart spent her early years toiling in the fields, struggling day in and day out—not only to put food on the table but also to carve out a slice of the American dream. With a lovely, lilting style and a gift for evoking the farms and fields of her childhood, Hart unflinchingly recalls the racial discrimination faced by her family as they slowly but surely made progress toward a better life.

Subjects: Latinas • Race • Agriculture • Labor • Relationships • America • Twentieth Century • Memoir • Young Adult

Now Try: It may not be as gritty as *Barefoot Heart,* but readers wishing for another Chicana perspective from the mid-twentieth-century will enjoy *Farmworker's Daughter: Growing Up Mexican in America.* This is the story of Rose Castillo Guilbault, who moved with her divorced mother from Mexico to an agricultural community in America in the 1960s. With vivid descriptions of the era and a keen awareness of race, discrimination, and identity, Guilbault paints a portrait of her rocky coming of age; her new life in America is not as harsh as Hart's, but her perceptive insights into the Chicana experience will speak to Hart's fans.

Herrera Mulligan, Michelle, and Robyn Moreno, eds.

Border-Line Personalities: A New Generation of Latinas Dish on Sex, Sass, and Cultural Shifting. New York: Rayo, 2004. 299pp. ISBN 9780060580766.

Is there such a thing as a universal Latina experience? In a word, no: the wealth of perspectives and backgrounds presented in this excellent anthology quickly dispatch that notion. And yet there is a shared theme among the writings of these modern Latina women, a theme of struggle and change as old ways clash with new. In sections on family, romance, identity, and growth, these essayists contemplate what it means to be a Latina in contemporary America. Each woman's experience is different, but in each case the honesty and thoughtfulness of the essays will give readers insight into the various ways that women are shaping and reshaping their Latina identities in the United States today.

Subjects: Latinas • Race • Gender • Family • Relationships • Twenty-first Century • America • Memoir • Essays • Anthology • Collection

Now Try: Learn more about the experiences of Latinas in America in another excellent anthology, *Latina: Women's Voices from the Borderlands*, edited by Lillian Castillo-Speed. Incorporating fiction alongside essays and memoirs, this book contains a vibrant mix of Latina writings about such topics as race, racism, gender, and national identity.

hooks, bell

Bone Black: Memories of Girlhood. New York: Henry Holt, 1996. 183pp. ISBN 9780805041453.

In 1952, a poor black family in Kentucky welcomed its newest family member, a little girl named Gloria Jean Watkins—or, as she is known these days, bell hooks. hooks, famous now for her activism as a black feminist scholar, turns here to the story of her childhood, when books were her best friends and poetry was her outlet. In short, provocative vignettes, we discover the racism and sexism that shaped the young hooks, the influences that would eventually lead to her activism as an adult. Written in hooks's gorgeous, lyrical prose, this is a powerful memoir of a black girl's coming of age in the racially tense mid-twentieth-century American South.

Subjects: Coming of Age • African Americans • Race • Class • History • Women's History • American History • Social History • Twentieth Century • America • Memoir • Quick Read • Young Adult

Now Try: Continue now with the sequel, *Wounds of Passion: A Writing Life*. Here we meet a slightly older hooks as she enters college and begins a tumultuous fifteen-year-affair with a poet. Like *Bone Black*, this is an emotional, beautifully written memoir, filled with pain and passion, race and sex, anger and romance. Readers who enjoy hooks's insight into race may also enjoy *Child of the Jungle: The True Story of a Girl Caught between Two Worlds*. Author Sabine Kuegler is white, but her perspective on race and identity is remarkable, thanks to her childhood in tribal New Guinea. Read this memoir for the story of the author's unusual upbringing, and to contemplate the broader issues of race, culture, and conflicting civilizations.

Jacobs, Harriet A.

Incidents in the Life of a Slave Girl: Written by Herself. Boston: Published for the Author, 1861. Mineola, NY: Dover, 2001. 167pp. ISBN 0486419312.

"I was born a slave," Harriet Jacobs writes in the first line of her autobiography, "but I never knew it till six years of happy childhood had passed away." And even when she did learn of her enslaved status, she still lived a relatively pleasant life with a white owner who taught her to read. But when her mistress died, the real tragedy began: Jacobs was sold to Dr. Flint, and her life became pure misery. In short, straightforward chapters, Jacobs recalls her servitude in the physician's household and the doctor's repeated predatory sexual advances. Out of desperation, Jacobs conceived two children with a white man from the community, hoping to dissuade Dr. Flint—but even then, his lechery continued unabated. It was only after several unsuccessful attempts at escape that Jacobs managed to leave his clutches, though it would be misleading to suggest that she found freedom; instead, she lived in secrecy in tiny, cramped quarters for seven years, managing not to go insane only by reading her Bible and catching occasional glimpses of her children through cracks in the wall. The story ultimately ends happily when a white woman purchases Jacobs's freedom, but the long years of suffering before escaping slavery make for a harrowing account. As one of the first slave narratives written, and one of the only ones penned by a woman, this is a remarkable document, essential for anyone interested in African-American history, women's history, or American history.

> **Subjects:** Slavery • Race • African Americans • Coming of Age • Granddaughters • Mothers • Children • Labor • Sexual Exploitation • Religion • Christianity • History • Women's History • American History • Nineteenth Century • America • Autobiography • Quick Read

> **Now Try:** For more firsthand accounts of nineteenth-century slaves, turn to the stories collected in *Six Women's Slave Narratives* (no editor is credited for this 1988 collection, but the ISBN is 9780195052626). Learn about the experiences of six women slaves and ex-slaves as they recount their life stories both before and after the Civil War; though none of them are as well known as Jacobs, their stories are compelling, providing a glimpse into the unique trials endured by women that is too often missing from other slave narratives. Then consider the horrors of slavery with *A Mercy*, a novel by Pulitzer Prize–winning author Toni Morrison. Populated by strong women characters, the book explores such topics as the destruction of black families and the enslavement of Native Americans.

Kingston, Maxine Hong

The Woman Warrior: Memoirs of a Girlhood among Ghosts. New York: Knopf, 1976. 209pp. ISBN 9780394400679.

Growing up in California in the 1940s, Kingston and her family were surrounded by ghosts—that is, people who weren't Chinese. Born in America to a Chinese family, Kingston grappled with race issues from an early age, turning to traditional Chinese folktales and myths to nurture her Asian identity in a society that was hostile to outsiders. But these same stories that cultivated her racial identity taught difficult lessons about gender: women, and especially girls, were lesser beings; it took extraordinary strength and ability for a woman to distinguish herself. In her lyrical, beautiful style, Kingston reflects on the rich, powerful, complicated stories of her childhood and the themes of race and gender that characterized her coming of age in America.

> **Subjects:** Coming of Age • Asian Americans • Race • Gender • Sexual Discrimination • Twentieth Century • America • Memoir

> **Now Try:** *The Woman Warrior* was Kingston's first book; now continue with her second memoir, *China Men*, about three generations of Chinese men in America. Again, Kingston deftly weaves myth, legend, and memoir to consider gender and race in the lives of her family members; told in her evocative storytelling style, the book's focus on masculinity offers a thought-provoking contrast to the themes of womanhood considered in *The Woman Warrior*. Readers who enjoy fiction will also want to try the works of Amy Tan. Start with her first novel, *The Joy Luck Club*, about American women who come to understand their ancestry by listening to the stories of their Chinese mothers.

Lee, Mary Paik, and Sucheng Chan

Quiet Odyssey: A Pioneer Korean Woman in America. Seattle: University of Washington Press, 1990. 201pp. ISBN 9780295969466.

Having immigrated to America in 1905, when Lee was five years old, the Paik family members were among the very first Koreans in the United States, though they did not become pioneers willingly; rather, they moved to escape Japanese oppression in their homeland. But life in America presented a whole new set of challenges: whereas before the Paik family had been well-off members of the racial majority, in the new country they were outsiders. Mary Paik Lee, née Paik Kuang Sun, encountered racism at a young age, and throughout her childhood, the family was desperately poor, as her father could only find low-paying, grueling jobs. In part, this is the story of one family's struggles with race and class in an unwelcoming new land; but it is also a story of triumph, because Lee lived to see her adopted society's racist attitudes evolve as the decades passed. With plentiful photographs and three appendixes to give context, this is an engrossing glimpse into Asian American history, told through the eyes of a remarkable woman.

> **Subjects:** Asian Americans • Race • Class • History • American History • Social History • Twentieth Century • America • Autobiography • Quick Read

> **Now Try:** For another story of a Korean family in America, turn to *Home Was the Land of Morning Calm: A Saga of a Korean-American Family*. Like Lee, K. Connie Kang was a daughter in a Korean family that was forced to flee their homeland after the Japanese invaded, though it took them many years to reach America. Fans of *Quiet Odyssey* will enjoy Kang's insightful writing about race, culture, identity, and family, told in a lyrical, captivating style.

Mills, Kay

This Little Light of Mine: The Life of Fannie Lou Hamer. New York: Dutton, 1993. 390pp. ISBN 9780525935018.

Born to Mississippi sharecroppers in 1917, Fannie Lou Hamer knew first-hand what it was like to be black and poor in the American South. Day-to-day living was a struggle, and the African Americans of the Deep South were politically disempowered: though technically they were en-franchised, in reality few blacks had voting rights. But with the rise of the Civil Rights movement in the 1960s, Hamer found her voice, literally: her powerful singing voice became a tool of the movement, inspiring others to fight racial discrimination. In this accessible, thoroughly researched biog-raphy, learn how a poorly educated woman became a key leader in the Civil Rights movement, fighting on behalf of poor people and blacks both in Mississippi and on the national stage at the Democratic conventions of 1964 and 1968.

> **Subjects:** African Americans • Race • Class • Activism • Politics • Labor • History • Women's History • Social History • American History • Twentieth Century • America • Biography

> **Now Try:** Continue learning about Hamer's impact on the Civil Rights move-ment in another excellent biography, *For Freedom's Sake: The Life of Fannie Lou Hamer.* Historian Chana Kai Lee focuses on Hamer's political activities and the intersection of race, class, and gender in the early Civil Rights movement, while exploring the personal life experiences—such as involuntary steriliza-tion—that drove Hamer to become an activist. And readers wanting to know more about the civil rights movement will enjoy Steven Kasher's *The Civil Rights Movement: A Photographic History, 1954–68.* The book's narrative offers an overview of the movement, gorgeously illustrated by some of the most stunning images of the era.

Nam, Vickie, ed.

YELL-Oh Girls! Emerging Voices Explore Culture, Identity, and Growing Up Asian American. New York: Quill, 2001. 297pp. ISBN 9780060959449.

In this vibrant collection of essays, poems, and stories, editor Nam brings together the voices of young women who speak about what it means to be young, Asian, and female in the United States. With writers who trace their backgrounds to such places as Hawaii, China, Southeast Asia, and India, the collection presents a variety of perspectives, from not only the young women themselves but also a select few established adult Asian women writers. In themed sections such as "Family Ties" and "Finding My Voice," the contributors cover such topics as dating, body image, food, and racism in their quest to explore female Asian-American identity.

> **Subjects:** Asian Americans • Race • Gender • Coming of Age • America • Memoir • Essays • Anthology • Collection • Young Adult

> **Now Try:** Though the ages of the writers in *Leaving Deep Water: Asian American Women at the Crossroads of Two Cultures* span the decades, fans of *YELL-Oh Girls!* will find much to love in this anthology. Edited by Claire S. Chow, the book brings together writings by Asian-American writers from a variety of national backgrounds as they discuss race, sex, and everyday topics such as careers and family; the candid experiences and compelling writing will appeal to those who liked the refreshing voices in *YELL-Oh Girls!* And for a historical perspective, try

Asian/Pacific Islander American Women: A Historical Anthology, edited by Shirley Hune and Gail M. Nomura. In this collection of scholarly essays, you'll examine the issues and experiences of Asian women past and present as they have immigrated to America (or, as with Hawaii, as they have been *assimilated* by America). Fans of *YELL-Oh Girls!* will appreciate the attention to such topics as race, culture, and community.

Võ Linda Trinh, and Marian Sciachitano, eds.

Asian American Women: The Frontiers Reader. Lincoln: University of Nebraska Press, 2004. 369pp. ISBN 9780803296275.

"The chapters in this collection," explain editors Võ and Sciachitano, "give voice to the complexities of our lived experiences and struggles both within the United States and in the transnational spaces many of us occupy. These voices remind us that long ago we broke our silences, and there is no going back." Fifteen essays continue to break this silence in this magnificent collection that speaks to the complicated realities of Asian American women's lives. These writings are accessible to the lay reader, speaking eloquently on such topics as immigration, national identity, and class and labor.

> **Subjects:** Asian Americans • Gender • Race • Sexual Discrimination • Feminism • Third-wave Feminism • Activism • America • Global Perspectives • Memoir • Essays • Anthology • Collection

> **Now Try:** The silence surrounding Asian American women's lives continues to be broken in two remarkable books by the Asian Women United of California, *Making Waves: An Anthology of Writings by and about Asian American Women* and *Making More Waves: New Writing by Asian American Women*. Both anthologies bring together the fiction, poetry, and nonfiction writings of Asian American women, shedding light on their experiences as they grapple with such topics as race, activism, labor, and injustices both historical and contemporary.

Zook, Kristal Brent, ed.

Black Women's Lives: Stories of Pain and Power. New York: Nation Books, 2006. 263pp. ISBN 9781560257905.

Too often, the stories of black women remain silent, overshadowed by the stories of black men and by the cacophony of mainstream America. To fight against this silence, journalist Zook traveled around the country to interview ten African American women, including a filmmaker in California, a principal in Georgia, a farmer in Vermont, and an inmate in Washington. With her compassionate perspective and engaging prose, Zook devotes a chapter to each woman, revealing the struggles and successes of their individual lives. Some of the stories are heartening, some discouraging, but in all cases the women's voices shine through, giving the reader candid insight into the experiences of ten black women in America.

> **Subjects:** African Americans • Gender • Race • Sexual Discrimination • Activism • America • Biography • Collection

> **Now Try:** Those who loved the accessible tone, compelling profiles, and candid stories of *Black Women's Lives* will enjoy reading about the experiences of African American women in *Sister Gumbo: Spicy Vignettes from Black Women on Life, Sex and Relationships*, edited by Ursula Inga Kindred and Mirranda Guerin-Williams. Based on interviews with African American women throughout the country, the book offers a glimpse into the everyday lives of black women; sex and relationships constitute a significant part of the discussion, but other topics are addressed too, such as spirituality and self-image.

Religious Identity

1

Here are books that tell the stories of women whose lives have been profoundly shaped by their religious beliefs.

A variety of religions are represented in the "Religious Identity" section, but all of the women have one thing in common: their lives have been profoundly shaped by their religious faiths. Some of the women practice their faiths without fear of persecution, as does Barbara Brown Taylor in *Leaving Church*; others, such as Anne Hutchinson, practice in the face of persecution, as we see in Eve LaPlante's *American Jezebel: The Uncommon Life of Anne Hutchinson, the Woman Who Defied the Puritans*. Read these books to be inspired and to learn more about a particular religion (even if it is your own). Readers interested in religious and spiritual themes will also want to refer to Chapter 2, which contains a section on "Spiritual Growth and Meditation," along with sections on several different religions.

2

3

Curott, Phyllis W.

4

Book of Shadows: A Modern Woman's Journey into the Wisdom of Witchcraft and the Magic of the Goddess. New York: Broadway Books, 1998. 302pp. ISBN 9780767900546.

Phyllis Curott was in her final year of law school when she began to experience psychic visions, precognitive flashes, and peculiar dreams of goddesses—though at first she was reluctant to have her cards read, as a pagan friend of hers suggested. But when she did open up to the possibilities of magic, she discovered the ancient religion of Wicca. Now a high priestess (but still a practicing lawyer!), Curott has written the memoir of her spiritual journey, an intimate look at how goddess worship has transformed her life. Included in the text are spells, rituals, and other various resources for practicing Wicca, making this both a compelling narrative and a useful how-to guide for novice Wiccans.

5

6

Subjects: Wicca • Paganism • Witches • Goddesses • Memoir • America • How-to

Now Try: Continue with Curott's follow-up, *The Love Spell: An Erotic Memoir of Spiritual Awakening*. As the subtitle suggests, this is a spicy story, filled with plenty of steamy scenes that ensue when Curott casts a love spell. But this is not just a simple romance; this is a cautionary tale, too, because we learn that even the best spells can't force a romance to work. Readers looking for additional stories of witches may also wish to try *A Witch Like Me: The Spiritual Journeys of Today's Pagan Practitioners*, in which Sirona Knight collects the biographies of thirteen different Wiccans.

7

Ehrlich, Elizabeth

8

Miriam's Kitchen: A Memoir. New York: Viking, 1997. 370pp. ISBN 9780670869084.

Author Ehrlich had always been something of a casual Jew, but that was before she met her mother-in-law Miriam. Over the course of countless hours spent as a guest in Miriam's kitchen, Ehrlich experienced a spiritual transformation, spurred by the marvelous food and by Miriam's own courageous life story. Upon learning that her mother-in-law had survived imprisonment in a Holocaust concentration camp, Ehrlich found herself awakening to the richness of Jewish spirituality; she eventually resolved to make her own kitchen kosher and to teach her children about their Jewish heritage. Told in Ehrlich's lovely, evocative prose, this is a contemplative memoir of spiritual discovery, family bonding, and food, filled with kosher recipes for readers to try in their own kitchens.

> **Subjects:** Judaism • Religion • Spirituality • Food • Recipes • Relationships • Marriage • Children • Mothers • Grandmothers • Memoir

> **Now Try:** For another food memoir that lovingly speaks to the power of family and community, turn to *The Language of Baklava*, in which Diana Abu-Jaber recalls memories of her family and her struggle to find her identity as the child of an American mother and a Jordanian father. Though without the religious dimension of *Miriam's Kitchen*, fans of Ehrlich will enjoy Abu-Jaber's loving stories of her family, her depictions of dual cultures, and her reminiscences of the importance of food—and, of course, readers who are handy in the kitchen will be eager to try the recipes for Jordanian cuisine.

Gehrke-White, Donna

The Face behind the Veil: The Extraordinary Lives of Muslim Women in America. New York: Citadel Press, 2006. 299pp. ISBN 9780806527215.

"Even with anti-Muslim sentiment running higher in the United States than ever before," writes journalist Gehrke-White, women are staying strong in the Muslim faiths: "they wear their veils despite catcalls; they attend mosque despite being segregated from men. . . . I set out to find out why this is so, and who these women are." The result of Gehrke-White's investigation is this fascinating collective biography comprising fifty short profiles of Muslim-American women. Arranged in five parts, including "The New Traditionalists" and "The Converts," you'll discover the intersection of faith, gender, and national identity in the lives of American Muslim women in chapters such as "Zarinah: An Islamic-Style High School Queen" and "Dr. Armena Haq: A Stethoscope and a Hijab."

> **Subjects:** Islam • Religion • Gender • America • Biography

> **Now Try:** Learn more about American women's Islamic identity in two further books. *Daughters of Another Path: Experiences of American Women Choosing Islam* was written by Carol Anderson Anway after her daughter converted from Christianity to Islam. This is partly a memoir of the lessons Anway learned, and partly a collection of more than fifty stories of women who became Muslims, arranged in chapters such as "Forsaking the Previous Path: Reactions of Relatives" and "The Daughters Speak Out: What Muslim Converts Would Like Us to Know." Then turn to Carolyn Moxley Rouse's *Engaged Surrender: African American Women and Islam*; though it is a denser, more academic work than *Islam Our Choice*, readers will enjoy the thought-provoking insight into the intersection of race and religion experienced by African American Muslim women.

Kempe, Margery, and John Skinner

The Book of Margery Kempe: A New Translation. New York: Image Books/Doubleday, 1998. 343pp. ISBN 9780385490375.

After having borne fourteen children, Margery Kempe surprised her husband by informing him that, henceforward, she was going to abstain from sexual relations. Why would this happily married woman—the owner of a brewery, no less—make such a startling announcement? She got it straight from God. In this

remarkable spiritual account, considered by many to be the first known autobiography written in English, an illiterate medieval woman dictated her journey toward God, beginning with the vision of Christ that catalyzed her conversion and set her on the path to Christianity, peppered with numerous physical pilgrimages along the way. Any edition will suffice, though this translation in particular arranges Kempe's story in a readable, chronological fashion, perfect for following the story of her spiritual triumphs and struggles.

Subjects: Christianity • Religion • Spirituality • Marriage • Mothers • Relationships • Travel • History • Women's History • History of Religion • Medieval History • Fourteenth Century • Fifteenth Century • Autobiography

Now Try: While Kempe wrote what may have been the first autobiography in the English language, a mystic named Julian of Norwich may have been the very first woman to write a book in English. This anchoress was, in fact, one of the many people Kempe met on her religious pilgrimages, a holy woman who had had a series of stunning religious visions. Read about these visions in her writings, variously titled *Showings* or *Revelations of Divine Love*.

Klapheck, Elisa, and Toby Axelrod

Fraulein Rabbiner Jonas: The Story of the First Woman Rabbi. San Francisco: Jossey-Bass, 2004. 220pp. ISBN 9780787969875.

In 1935, Regina Jonas was ordained as the world's first woman rabbi—and shortly thereafter, everyone promptly forgot about her. To be sure, the Second World War and the Holocaust were consuming international attention, though author Klapheck speculates that certain patriarchal mind-sets may have been happy to let her slip into obscurity. But, no matter why Rabbi Jonas was neglected in decades past, her story has been restored to its rightful place with this insightful biography. With precise, straightforward language translated by Toby Axelrod, Klapheck tells the story of Jonas's tremendous struggle to become ordained, her arduous work as a rabbi in Germany in the 1930s, her brief romance, and her death in Auschwitz in 1944 at the age of forty-two. Appended to this remarkable biography is Jonas's inspiring treatise, "Can Women Serve as Rabbis?" —which answers, emphatically, that women certainly can.

Subjects: Jonas, Regina • Rabbis • Clergy • Judaism • Religion • History • History of Religion • Women's History • World War II • Twentieth Century • Germany • Europe • Biography • Quick Read

Now Try: Regina Jones was the first woman rabbi; now read about another first in *Lesbian Rabbis: The First Generation*, by Rebecca T. Alpert, Ellen Sue Levi Elwell, and Shirley Idelson. Though more academic in tone than Klapheck's book, this collection of essays by eighteen lesbian rabbis will appeal to fans of *Fraulein Rabbiner Jonas* for its frank discussion of the tensions between traditional Judaism and groundbreaking new approaches; the struggles and triumphs of these women will strike a chord with readers who were moved by Rabbi Jonas's experiences.

LaPlante, Eve

American Jezebel: The Uncommon Life of Anne Hutchinson, the Woman Who Defied the Puritans. San Francisco: HarperSanFrancisco, 2004. 312pp. ISBN 9780060562335.

> Anne Hutchinson liked to hold a weekly bible-study meeting for women at her house, where she would interpret scripture and contemplate on its meaning. And why not? She believed that God could speak to people at any place, at any time, that religious insight could be gained both inside and outside the walls of a church. Nothing about her attitude would raise an eyebrow today—but in the early seventeenth century, the Puritan community was scandalized. At best, she was a heretic; at worst, she was a witch, controlled by Satan and intent on corrupting the community. Discover the remarkable life of this independent thinker in *American Jezebel*, a thoroughly researched biography that illuminates Hutchinson's life story, from her birth in England to her trial on the charge of antinomianism (that is, believing that faith alone is sufficient for salvation) in Massachusetts to her banishment to Rhode Island—where, free to practice her religion as she saw fit, she founded a colony.
>
> > **Subjects:** Hutchinson, Anne • Politics • Religion • Christianity • Sexual Discrimination • History • Women's History • American History • History of Religion • Seventeenth Century • England • America • Biography
> >
> > **Now Try:** Focus now on the religious climate of Massachusetts in the 1630s in *The Times and Trials of Anne Hutchinson: Puritans Divided*. Drawing on primary documents, historian Michael P. Winship fleshes out the rigorous religious laws that defined the Puritan lifestyle and breathes life into the key players at Hutchinson's two trials, making this a fascinating, in-depth examination of Hutchinson's legal and religious battles.

Pechilis, Karen, ed.

The Graceful Guru: Hindu Female Gurus in India and the United States. New York: Oxford University Press, 2004. 260pp. ISBN 9780195145373.

> According to stereotype, gurus are wizened old men sitting in lotus position at the top of isolated mountains, but as we see in *The Graceful Guru*, that stereotype needs some rethinking. In this collection of scholarly essays, we meet ten women who have embraced the role of guru, traditionally reserved for men. This collective biography shows how Hindu women are becoming gurus—teachers, spiritual leaders, embodiments of the divine—both in India and the United States, while including a wealth of contextual analysis on gender and religion. The book is aimed at a scholarly audience, but it is accessible for the lay reader who wants to understand the contemporary move toward the inclusion of women in the guru sphere.
>
> > **Subjects:** Hinduism • Religion • Spirituality • Gender • India • America • Essays • Biography • Collection
> >
> > **Now Try:** Two additional books illuminate the lives of women in India who are embracing spiritual roles traditionally reserved for men. In *Women in Ochre Robes: Gendering Hindu Renunciation*, Meena Khandelwal considers women Hindu ascetics and the role of gender in renunciation, the act of giving up worldly concerns to live a spiritual life. In *Daughters of the Goddess: The Women Saints of India*, Linda Johnsen looks at six living Hindu saints, women who embody the feminine Divine.

Pederson, Rena

The Lost Apostle: Searching for the Truth about Junia. San Francisco: Jossey-Bass, 2006. 278pp. ISBN 9780787984434.

Are you familiar with the name Junias? If not, don't worry; even avid readers of the Christian Bible can be pardoned for forgetting him, since he is only mentioned in one tiny verse in Romans. He would be easy to ignore, except it turns out that he was actually a she: Junias was really a woman named Junia, and she was the only female apostle. The gender confusion arose from the political goals of scribes and early church fathers; rather than admit that a woman held such an esteemed position, they found it convenient to turn her into a man. In this captivating account of gender politics in the early Christian church, journalist Pederson considers not only Junia but other significant women in church history, too, including Mary Magdalene; what she finds is a pattern of exclusion and discrimination that worked against women. Read this to discover the lives of Junia and other women who have been neglected and marginalized for too long.

Subjects: Junia • Apostles • Christianity • Religion • Sexual Discrimination • History • History of Religion • Women's History • Ancient History • First Century • Middle East • Asia • Biography

Now Try: Pederson is a journalist, not a biblical scholar, meaning that her book is accessible for the average person; readers wanting a more scholarly approach to Junia's identity, however, will enjoy Eldon Jay Epp's *Junia: The First Woman Apostle*. Like Pederson, Epp investigates the motivations for the textual change from Junia to Junias by digging into the politics of the early church. As would be expected of the president of the Society of Biblical Literature, Epp's research is meticulous and thorough, but his insightful arguments and fascinating subject matter make this an enjoyable read, even for those without a strong background in biblical scholarship. Then jump forward in time to meet another unusual Christian, Luisa de Carvajal. Born in 1568, this Spanish woman risked her life and freedom to spread Catholicism in Protestant England. Read about her exploits in *The She-Apostle: The Extraordinary Life and Death of Luisa de Carvajal* by Glyn Redworth.

Schaeffer, Kurtis R.

Himalayan Hermitess: The Life of a Tibetan Buddhist Nun. New York: Oxford University Press, 2004. 220pp. ISBN 9780195152982.

Born in 1675 in Tibet, Orgyan Chokyi knew from a young age that the ordinary life was not for her; rather, she wanted to devote her life to spiritual study as a Buddhist nun. We know this because, in direct contradiction of her master's orders, she recorded her entire life story, penning the very first autobiography by a Tibetan woman. In *Himalayan Hermitess*, Schaeffer skillfully translates Chokyi's story, allowing us to see how she became a nun and a hermitess, bolstered by her spiritual visions and interactions with the divine. Schaeffer also provides a thorough introduction to the history of Buddhism in Tibet, along with thoughtful commentary on the place of Chokyi's autobiography in the religious literary tradition.

Subjects: Chokyi, Orgyan • Nuns • Buddhism • Religion • Gender • Solitude • History • History of Religion • Women's History • Sixteenth Century • Seventeenth Century • Tibet • Asia • Autobiography

Now Try: For even earlier writings of women Buddhists, turn to *First Buddhist Women: Poems and Stories of Awakening*, by Susan Murcott. Like Schaeffer, Murcott provides context and analysis for each of her translations, making this a fascinating, informative glimpse into the spiritual lives of early Buddhist women, who range from teachers and wives to prostitutes and courtesans.

Spink, Kathryn

Mother Teresa: A Complete Authorized Biography. San Francisco: HarperSanFrancisco, 1997. 306pp. ISBN 9780062508256.

Beatified at the time of her death and quite possibly on her way to sainthood, Blessed Teresa of Calcutta was one of the best-known Christians of the twentieth century or, for that matter, in all of history. As a nun, she devoted her life to ministering to the sick and the destitute; her tremendous commitment to charity and good works made her an international celebrity—though, as biographer Spink shows, Mother Teresa was not interested in personal glory. Far from it: her goal was to serve Christ, not to become a household name. She was an intensely private person, but Spink has done an admirable job of parsing out details of Mother Teresa's life, from her childhood in Yugoslavia to her service in the country with which she will forever be associated, India. In this engaging biography, written with Mother Teresa's input and blessing, learn about the religious passion that drove this winner of the Nobel Peace Prize.

> **Subjects:** Mother Teresa • Nuns • Nobel Peace Prize • Peace • Activism • Christianity • Religion • Yugoslavia • India • Twentieth Century • Biography

> **Now Try:** Mother Teresa wrote prodigiously; any of her books will be of interest to readers wanting to know more about her thoughts, but perhaps start with *Mother Teresa: Come Be My Light: The Private Writings of the "Saint of Calcutta."* Edited by Catholic priest Brian Kolodiejchuk, a personal friend of Mother Teresa, the book collects letters written by Mother Teresa that illuminate her religious beliefs and internal spiritual struggles. Then explore the lives of women saints throughout history with Sarah Gallick's *The Big Book of Women Saints*, a collective biography of more than four hundred Catholic women.

Taylor, Barbara Brown

Leaving Church: A Memoir of Faith. San Francisco: HarperSanFrancisco, 2006. 234pp. ISBN 9780060771744.

For twenty years, Barbara Brown Taylor served as an Episcopal priest. It was a job she loved, and one she excelled at: she was named by Baylor University as one of the twelve most effective English-speaking preachers. But her convictions about her faith and her calling, so certain when she was first ordained, slowly began to crumble. At first, the geography cure seemed to work, when a move from Atlanta to a tiny rural town revitalized her ministry, but eventually Taylor realized that the best way for her to serve God was to leave the priesthood. Beautifully written, this is a poignant, deeply personal memoir of one woman's crisis of faith and eventual renewal.

> **Subjects:** Religion • Christianity • Labor • America • Memoir

> **Now Try:** For another entrancing memoir of evolving faith, turn to *Grace: A Memoir*. Mary Cartledgehayes didn't enter the Methodist ministry until she reached middle age, though when she finally took the plunge, it was with the same zest and zeal that characterized all of her choices in life. Like Taylor, Cartledgehayes eventually left her job, though not her faith. *Grace* is a bit edgier in tone and style than *Leaving Church*, but Taylor's fans will enjoy meeting another charismatic, intelligent spiritual thinker.

Turpin, Joanne

Women in Church History: 21 Stories for 21 Centuries. Cincinnati, OH: St. Anthony Messenger Press, 2007. 232pp. ISBN 9780867167764.

You know all about the church fathers, the patriarchs who have shaped doctrine, thought, and practice throughout the history of Christianity. But what about the church mothers? In this lovely collective biography, Joanne Turpin shines light on the remarkable stories of twenty-one women, one for each century of the church's history. Many of the names will be new to readers, but each woman profiled deserves to be known, not only for her contributions to the church and her inspiring faith but for her unique and fascinating life story. With plenty of historical and religious context and a short prayer at the end of each chapter, this is an enlightening survey of Christian women throughout the ages.

Subjects: Christianity • Religion • History • History of Religion • Women's History • Global Perspectives • Biography • Collection

Now Try: Joanne Turpin wrote about the lives of women in church history; now read about spiritual women in their own voices in *Invincible Spirits: A Thousand Years of Women's Spiritual Writings*, edited by Felicity Leng. Though views from more than just the Christian faith are presented here, fans of *Women in Church History* who enjoy reading about religious and spiritual women, regardless of faith, will be pleased with this excellent collection. Arranged thematically into chapters such as "Love and Fulfillment" and "Faith and Renewal," the book features well-known writers such as Julian of Norwich and Emily Dickinson alongside lesser-known names—but whether famous or not, the authors each present writings that are intellectually thought-provoking and spiritually inspiring.

Willis, Janice Dean

Dreaming Me: From Baptist to Buddhist, One Woman's Spiritual Journey. New York: Riverhead Books, 2002. 321pp. ISBN 9781573229098.

Having grown up in racially tense Alabama in the 1950s, Janice Dean Willis was an angry young black woman by the time the Civil Rights movement kicked into high gear. The violent, high-energy, high-impact methods of the Black Panthers appealed to her—but that was before she went to Asia. Traveling briefly to India during her college years and then to Nepal for an extended stay, Willis discovered the nonviolence philosophy of Buddhism. Thus began her journey toward a new religion, a new sense of identity, and a new way of understanding race. Follow her path of spiritual awakening through her travels, her studies, her Buddhist practice in this enchanting, beautifully written memoir.

Subjects: Buddhism • Religion • Spirituality • African Americans • Race • India • Nepal • Asia • America • Memoir

Now Try: Now meet Faith Adiélé, another African American Buddhist woman, in her delightful memoir *Meeting Faith: The Forest Journals of a Black Buddhist Nun*. While on a year's hiatus in Tibet, she became intrigued with Buddhism, eventually becoming not just a Buddhist but a Buddhist *nun*. Her enjoyable writing style and her keen observations on religion and race will resonate with fans of *Dreaming Me*.

Consider Starting With . . .

The titles below are some of the most popular, enduring Life Stories of Women's Nonfiction:

Curie, Eve. *Madame Curie: A Biography.*

Frank, Anne. *The Diary of a Young Girl.*

Fraser, Antonia. *Mary, Queen of Scots.*

Nafisi, Azar. *Reading Lolita in Tehran: A Memoir in Books.*

Pernoud, Régine. *Joan of Arc: Her Story.*

Weir, Alison. *Eleanor of Aquitaine: A Life.*

Fiction Read-Alikes

- **Brown, Rita Mae.** Nowadays, Rita Mae Brown is probably best known for her cozy *Mrs. Murphy Mysteries*, coauthored with her cat, Sneaky Pie Brown—so you may be surprised to discover her first novel, *Rubyfruit Jungle.* First published to absolutely no acclaim in 1973, this semi-autobiographical story of a feisty lesbian making her way in the world became an underground success thanks to word of mouth; fortunately, it's easy to find a copy these days. Many of Brown's other books will also appeal, especially stand-alone titles such as *Southern Discomfort*, about an unusual romance in early-twentieth century Alabama.

- **Chopin, Kate.** A classic feminist novella first published in 1899, *The Awakening* tells the story of a financially comfortable but spiritually unhappy woman, Edna Pontellier, who slowly comes to understand that marriage and motherhood are preventing her from living a creative, fulfilling life.

- **Diamant, Anita.** She gets barely a mention in the Book of Genesis, but Dinah is fully realized as a daughter, a wife, a widow, a midwife, and a child of God in *The Red Tent*, a lyrical historical novel that weaves biblical tales with Diamant's vivid reconstruction of ancient women's lives. Strong female leads star in her other two novels to date, *Good Harbor* and *The Last Days of Dogtown*.

- **Golden, Arthur.** Based partly on his interviews with Sayo Masuda, author of *Autobiography of a Geisha*, Arthur Golden's *Memoirs of a Geisha* elegantly imagines the life of Chiyo, a poor fisherman's daughter who becomes a leading geisha in the 1930s and '40s.

- **Hwang, David Henry.** Based on a true story, *M. Butterfly* is a provocative play about Rene Gallimard, a Frenchman who discovers that Song Liling, the beautiful Chinese woman with whom he carried on a multiyear affair, is actually a man. Themes of race, sex, sexuality, gender, and the clash between East and West make this a brilliant, disturbing read.

- **McCrumb, Sharyn.** With her compelling characters and richly drawn Appalachian setting, any of the novels in McCrumb's <u>Ballad</u> series will appeal to readers who want to immerse themselves in different worlds. Perhaps start with *The Ballad of*

Frankie Silver, in which modern-day mystery blends with the true story of Frankie Silver, who was sent to her death in 1833, the first woman ever hanged for murder in North Carolina.

- **Oke, Janette.** Oke writes heartwarming Christian fiction with a strong sense of place, usually featuring young women protagonists. Try starting with the novel that heralded the inspirational Christian genre, *Love Comes Softly*. Published in 1979, Oke's first novel introduces us to pioneer woman Marty Claridge, who must explore and develop her faith if she is to survive personal heartache on the rugged frontier.

- **Peters, Julie Ann.** Meet Regan, a perfectly normal teenage girl, and her brother Liam, who wants to be a perfectly normal teenage girl. *Luna* is about a person who is female in all but physiology; this unusual coming-of-age story raises questions (though does not necessarily provide answers) about gender, sexuality, and identity. Any of Peters's novels will appeal to readers who want to think about issues of sexual identity; perhaps continue with *Keeping You a Secret*, about a young woman's painful journey toward a lesbian identity.

- **Rhys, Jean.** If you loved Mr. Rochester in Charlotte Brontë's classic novel *Jane Eyre*, perhaps you shouldn't read *Wide Sargasso Sea*. This feminist re-interpretation tells us the story of Rochester's secret wife, the madwoman in the attic, who was a lovely, sane young woman until her brutish husband drove her mad. Continue with Rhys's other novels, all of which feature nuanced female characters who must find their place in society.

- **Salzman, Mark.** Questions of religious faith and Christian identity are at the core of *Lying Awake*, an evocative, thought-provoking novel about Sister John of the Cross, a nun who experiences euphoric religious visions, but at a terrible cost: she suffers from epileptic seizures, and she must decide whether to treat her medical condition at the risk of losing her faith. Salzman's fiction and nonfiction alike will appeal to readers who savor literary prose and memorable characters.

- **Tan, Amy.** In her character-driven novels, Tan examines the relationships between Chinese women, among themselves and with society as a whole. Start with *The Joy Luck Club*, a beautifully written novel that explores mothers and daughters, generational conflict, and the tensions between two radically different cultures.

- **Tyree, Omar.** Themes of race, class, morality, and sexuality shine throughout the novels of Omar Tyree. Perhaps start with *Flyy Girl*, about Tracy Ellison, a smart and beautiful young black woman who must negotiate the complicated terrain of drugs, sexual awakening, and African American culture as she comes of age in Philadelphia in the 1980s.

- **Walker, Alice.** One of the most acclaimed authors writing today, Alice Walker crafts novels that feature deep themes, gorgeous prose, and unforgettable characters. Her masterpiece, *The Color Purple*, is an epistolary novel told primarily from the perspective of Celie, a black woman in the

American South in the early twentieth century. Addressing her letters first to God, then to her sister in Africa, Celie slowly overcomes tragedy—rape, forced marriage, the death of her child—to grow in her faith, to discover sexual happiness, to start her own business, and to develop into a powerful, independent woman.

Chapter 2

Personal Growth

Definition

> "Personal growth" as a subcategory of Women's Nonfiction comprises books that support and guide readers in endeavors of self-improvement, particularly in their relationships, including spiritual ones.

Personal growth can be interpreted broadly, and one might wonder whether *any* book could fall under its purview: characters in narrative literature almost always experience some type of personal development, and even books that are strictly instructional in nature are intended to develop the reader's knowledge of a particular topic. For our purposes, however, "personal growth" as a subcategory of Women's Nonfiction comprises those books that support and guide readers in endeavors of self-improvement, particularly in their relationships, including spiritual ones.

Why not title this chapter "Relationships," then? The shortcoming of the word "relationships" is that, at first glance, it only suggests three types of human relationships: those of family, those of friendship, and those of romance. The broader term "personal growth" allows for a more creative interpretation of relationships, permitting books on psychology and religion to enter the fold.

Many of the titles in the personal growth genre are pure narratives; for instance, Rebecca Walker's memoir *Baby Love: Choosing Motherhood after a Lifetime of Ambivalence* tells the story of her decision to become a mother, replete with reflections on motherhood, pregnancy, and emotional growth. Likewise, Meredith Hall's moving *Without a Map* tells of how she was forced to give up a child for adoption and how the reverberations of her personal tragedy continued to echo throughout her adult life. Other titles, however, blend how-to instructions with storytelling; thus we get a wild mix of succulent stories and spot-on advice in Joan Price's delightful *Better Than I Ever Expected: Straight Talk about Sex after Sixty*. Yet other titles offer short meditations, intended to be read and savored in small doses, rather than devoured in one sitting; such is the case with the lovely book *Meditation Secrets for Women: Discovering Your Passion, Pleasure, and Inner Peace*, by Camille Maurine and Lorin Roche.

Appeal

Personal growth books are those that inspire thought and reflection about relationships; by offering stories, advice, and food for thought, they guide readers toward contemplating the relationships in their own lives. Some of the titles do this very explicitly; Rachel Greenwald's *Find a Husband after 35 Using What I Learned at Harvard Business School: A Simple 15-Step Action Program* is designed to help middle-aged and senior women take stock of their own lives and to play up their strengths. Other books provoke thought by example rather than by instruction; readers who have absolutely no intention of adopting will nonetheless find themselves contemplating the experience of AIDS orphans when they read Melissa Fay Greene's *There Is No Me without You*.

Character is a primary appeal factor in personal growth books. Well-developed characters allow us as readers to relate to their experiences and to care about their relationships, even when those experiences are far outside our own point of reference; thus readers who have never suffered from infertility problems become attached to Peggy Orenstein as she tries to conceive a baby in *Waiting for Daisy*. Likewise, the appeal factors that indicate good storytelling—an appropriate pace, an engaging story line, interesting details, enjoyable prose—can make or break a book in the personal growth genre.

In books that do not depend on a sustained cover-to-cover narrative—that is, how-to guides and books of meditations—writing style plays a critical role. Thus readers seeking information about the experience of Buddhist women in America will want to turn to *Women Practicing Buddhism: American Experiences*, edited by Peter N. Gregory and Susanne Mrozik, if they want to immerse themselves in academic contemplation; readers who prefer a more conversational tone, on the other hand, will prefer Geri Larkin's chatty guide to everyday Buddhism, *Plant Seed, Pull Weed*.

Organization

The first section, "Psychology," contains arguably the most personal of all the personal growth books; these are the books that explore and explain women's relationships with their own minds. The titles in this category look at the biology and psychology of women's brains, and seek to understand the science behind the ways that women relate to themselves, to each other, and to men.

The second section, "Celebrating Women," features books that pay tribute to women's minds, bodies, and experiences. It is followed by the third section, "Relationships," with books that celebrate or explore women's relationships with siblings, parents, children, relatives, and friends. The "Straight Romantic Relationships" section includes books that discuss romance of the heterosexual variety, while "Queer Romantic Relationships" includes books that discuss romance of the same-sex variety. And then there is the section "The Single Woman," with books that do *not* discuss romance—or at any rate, books that show that singlehood is a fine alternative to romance.

The "Motherhood" category comes next; books about mothers and their children are included, of course, along with titles that examine the role of motherhood in society. Two additional sections round out the Motherhood section, "Fertility and

Adoption" and "Pregnancy, Childbirth, and Nursing." Both sections feature narratives and memoirs, along with how-to guides.

The final section, "Spiritual Growth and Meditation," features books that will appeal to women of any religious or spiritual inclination. Some of the titles contain books of meditation and prayers, though without preference for any particular religious tradition; other titles examine the role of the feminine divine in the past and in the present. Six sections follow, each with titles specific to one of the world's five main religions—Christianity, Judaism, Islam, Buddhism, and Hinduism—or to Paganism and goddess worship.

Psychology

Titles in this section focus on the mental and emotional lives of women.

Books on women's psychology can be surprisingly controversial. Whenever someone claims insight into why women behave the way they do, someone else will object—and to be sure, this is an understandable response: There is no universal psychology of women; even if most women think and act in a particular way, there will be plenty of others to prove the exception.

What makes psychology particularly volatile, however, is the debate of nature versus nurture. Even committed feminists disagree about whether gender is hardwired into our brains—and if gender *is* assumed to be a biological and psychological function of sex, there is no agreement whatsoever about the extent to which environment and society play mitigating factors. Each title in this subgenre presents a unique viewpoint; whether readers ultimately agree or disagree with a particular title, however, each book presents food for thought, to be embraced or dismissed according to the reader's own perspective—and according to how convincingly the authors make their case.

Belenky, Mary Field, et al.

Women's Ways of Knowing: The Development of Self, Voice, and Mind.
New York: Basic Books, 1986 (1997). 256pp. ISBN 9780465092123.

> How do we know what we know? Humans have pondered this question for millennia, but until the publication of *Women's Ways of Knowing*, most psychologists who tried to find answers had used men as their subjects. In this groundbreaking book, now a classic of psychology and Women's Studies, the authors sought to determine whether there were differences between the ways women and men learned. Based on interviews with 135 female college students, *Women's Ways of Knowing* argues that women do learn differently than men in areas such as subjective knowledge and procedural knowledge. Though written in an academic, occasionally dense

style, this is imperative reading for anyone who wants to understand the psychology of gendered thinking.

Subjects: Psychology • Gender • Feminism • Education

Now Try: Ten years after their collaborative effort shook the world of academia, the authors of *Women's Ways of Knowing* responded with a follow-up title, *Knowledge, Difference, and Power: Essays Inspired by Women's Ways of Knowing*. With contributions from other scholars as well as their own essays, the authors expand on their original theory and defend it against criticisms. This is a welcome sequel for those who were inspired by the original volume.

Brizendine, Louann

The Female Brain. New York: Morgan Road Books, 2006. 279pp. ISBN 978076-7920100.

Coming down firmly on the side of nature in the nature-versus-nurture debate is *The Female Brain*, a wide-ranging look at the neurobehavioral functions of women's brains. Clinical psychiatrist Brizendine examines the innate biology of the female brain, from molecules to hormones, neural structure to genetics. In the course of looking at the female brain through the entire course of life, from birth through adulthood through menopause and beyond, she posits that female brains are, in some ways, different from male brains. These biological differences, Brizendine argues, lead to behavioral differences between the sexes; for instance, infant girls are better able to gaze at faces. With an accessible style and plenty of anecdotes to illustrate the scientific points, the book provides food for thought for anyone curious about inherent differences between the brains of men and women.

Subjects: Psychology • Gender • Biology • Feminism

Now Try: Another champion of nature over nurture in the debate over gender differences is *Brain Sex: The Real Difference between Men and Women*, by Anne Moir and David Jessel. With an engaging, readable style, the book examines the inner workings of brain structures and hormones, offering a thought-provoking hypothesis for behavior differences between the sexes. *Brain Sex* is older than *The Female Brain*, but its clear explanation of biology, as well as its detailed examination of the implications for interactions in real life, make it a relevant companion read.

Estés, Clarissa Pinkola

Women Who Run with the Wolves: Myths and Stories of the Wild Woman Archetype. New York: Ballantine Books, 1992 (2003). 520pp. ISBN 9780345377449.

In seeking to fill the roles that modern life demands, women too often ignore their primal instincts, argues Jungian scholar Estés. To help them reclaim these neglected feelings, Estés discusses the role of women in a wealth of fables, stories, and legends from around the world. By analyzing the psychological underpinnings of the stories, Estés helps readers identify the passions that can help them become wild women. The writing is informed by excellent psychological scholarship but is easily accessible for the lay reader.

Subjects: Psychology • Gender • Feminism

Now Try: Like Estés, Jean Shinoda Bolen wants women to get in touch with the instincts that lurk within. In *Goddesses in Everywoman: A New Psychology of Women*, Bolen uses a framework of seven goddesses to help women identify and understand their inherent personality types. Readers interested in gender and psychology may also want to try *Iron John: A Book about Men*, in which Robert Bly uses myths and fairy tales to describe the inner workings of men.

Fels, Anna

Necessary Dreams: Ambition in Women's Changing Lives. New York: Pantheon Books, 2004. 297pp. ISBN 9780679442448.

Women have more access to higher education and career advancement than ever before—so why do they still feel guilty when they strive to advance their careers? The problem, explains psychiatrist Fels, is that women don't enjoy the same praise for their ambition that men traditionally receive. Even today, ambitious women struggle for acceptance; social peers may question whether ambitious women are devoted to their families and children, while husbands may feel threatened. Yet *Necessary Dreams* argues that ambition is a desirable, positive force in women's lives; this is a clarion call for society to readjust its thinking, to begin supporting ambition in women just as it has always supported it in men.

> **Subjects:** Psychology • Gender • Feminism • Sociology • Labor • Work–Life Balance

> **Now Try:** Like Fels, clinical psychologist Debra Condren recognizes that ambition in women is a trait to be cultivated and encouraged. In *am-BITCH-ous*, she argues that women can and should strive for career success. But she is more than just a cheerleader for women with aspirations; her book contains a wealth of suggestions, tips, and plans for women to use—not only to advance their own careers but also to help others understand why ambition in women is a praiseworthy attribute.

Gilligan, Carol

In a Different Voice: Psychological Theory and Women's Development. Cambridge, MA: Harvard University Press, 1982 (2000). 184pp. ISBN 9780674445437.

When it was first published in 1982, *In a Different Voice* shook up all the established scholarship on gender and development; to this day it remains an incredibly influential work in both psychology and Women's Studies. Psychologist Gilligan examines the moral development of young girls, arguing that society shapes them differently than it shapes boys. She swiftly dispatches the notion that girls' moral development is inferior, showing instead that it is simply different: girls, for instance, are taught to be less aggressive and to value relationships more. In so doing, she applies a feminist critique to frameworks of psychology that neglect or disdain the female perspective. The text is sophisticated and cerebral, but it is essential for those wanting to understand moral development and feminism.

> **Subjects:** Psychology • Gender • Feminism • Quick Read

> **Now Try:** Discover more about gender differences in development in another classic of feminist psychology, *Toward a New Psychology of Women*. Like Gilligan, author Jean Baker Miller argues that the psychology of women is not inferior to that of men, only different. With careful analysis and thought-provoking observations, she places concepts such as domination, vulnerability, and cooperation into a gendered context. Though it was first published decades ago, the book still provides insight into the psychology of women and their role in society.

Hines, Melissa

Brain Gender. Oxford: Oxford University Press, 2004. 307pp. ISBN 9780195084108.

What causes behavioral differences between the sexes, nature or nurture? Of the many impassioned books that speak to both sides of the debate, *Brain Gender* stands out for its neutral, unbiased approach. With impeccable research and a commitment to uncovering the facts, author Hines looks at the neuroscience and the biology of the human brain in males and females. Her fascinating examination of sex differences—from hormones to behaviors to preferences in sexual orientations—raises a host of questions; while not all of those questions are answered, the thoughtful, scholarly information is accessible enough that readers will be able to begin forming their own educated opinions.

> **Subjects:** Psychology • Gender • Biology • Feminism
>
> **Now Try:** Those who love reading about science and the biology of sex may be delighted to discover *The X in Sex: How the X Chromosome Controls Our Lives*. With dry British wit, David Bainbridge demystifies the sex chromosomes in this accessible quick-read. Though less contentious than *Brain Gender*, Bainbridge's magnificent defense of female chromosomes appeals to those seeking more information about the scientific and biological differences between the sexes.

Lawler, Jennifer

Punch! Why Women Participate in Violent Sports. Terre Haute, IN: Wish, 2002. 152pp. ISBN 9781930546509.

Boxing, hockey, wrestling—not so long ago, these sports were the sole province of men, but with the advent of Title IX and a gradual shift in popular perceptions, more and more women have embraced violent contact sports. In this enlightening, perceptive book, author Lawler draws on research with athletes and coaches to consider women and their participation in violent sports. Interspersing the research with her own perspective as a black belt in tae kwon do, Lawler crafts a text that examines the history of women in violent sports and the psychology of practicing women athletes, as well as the conflicting feminist responses to this recent phenomenon.

> **Subjects:** Sports • Athletes • Violence • Exercise • History • Sports History • Social History • Women's History • Twentieth Century • Sociology • Feminism • Quick Read
>
> **Now Try:** Sports don't get more violent than boxing, and as *Punch!* explained, women are in the thick of it. Learn about the women who have embraced this high-contact, highly competitive sport in *Women Boxers: The New Warriors,* a visually stunning tribute by Delilah Montoya, María Teresa Márquez, and C. Ondine Chavoya. Readers who simply want visual proof of women's participation in the ring will be richly rewarded with the shocking photographs of women boxers, while those seeking a deeper understanding of women's attraction to the violence of the sport will appreciate the insightful introductory chapter, which explores the history and psychology of women's relationship with boxing. See also Leah Hager Cohen's *Without Apology: Girls, Women, and the Desire to Fight,* the true story of a boxing champion and the inner-city girls she coached; the riveting story and Cohen's analysis of women and violence make this a thought-provoking read.

Legato, Marianne J., and Laura Tucker

Why Men Never Remember and Women Never Forget. Emmaus, PA: Rodale, 2005. 248pp. ISBN 9781579548971.

Legato, a professor of clinical medicine and the founder of the Partnership for Gender-Specific Medicine, draws on current research to demystify the differences between women and men. She explores the biology of the brain and examines the psychological and behavioral ramifications in our everyday lives. But this is far more than a science book; Legato does not merely expose the differences between the sexes, but proposes suggestions to help people better cope with them. With clear, intelligent writing, the author helps readers understand sex differences in various stages of life—from infancy through childhood through marriage—while showing how to apply this understanding to our relationships with the other sex.

Subjects: Psychology • Gender • Biology • How-to

Now Try: Those who like the accessible, informed tone of Legato's science writing should turn to *Sex on the Brain: The Biological Differences between Men and Women*. Pulitzer Prize winner Deborah Blum combines her incisive journalistic skills with her conversational, personable writing style to synthesize research about men, women, and their relationships to one another. No topic goes untouched: from hormones to relationships, monogamy to gender, sexual orientation to lust, Blum presents the science behind sex differences, making this a stimulating, thought-provoking read.

Schulz, Mona Lisa

The New Feminine Brain: Developing Your Intuitive Genius. New York: Free Press, 2006. 464pp. ISBN 9780743243070.

Neuroscientist Schulz explores the hardwiring of women's brains in this accessible, practical book. She discusses complicated issues of biology in an understandable way, though her focus is not as much on the science of difference as on the implications for women. Women who ignore the feminine qualities of their brains risk bad moods, anxiety, and depression; instead, they should embrace their intuitive qualities to find happiness and emotional stability. Quizzes, exercises, and a ten-step program help readers to understand and develop their own intuitive potential.

Subjects: Psychology • Gender • Biology • How-to

Now Try: For another empowering book that affirms the positive qualities of women's brains, turn to *What Happy Women Know: How New Findings in Positive Psychology Can Change Women's Lives for the Better*, by Dan Baker, Cathy Greenberg, and Ina L. Yalof. Negative qualities such as perfectionism or a lack of self-esteem can plague women, but the authors show that women have a host of positive qualities to draw on. Practical steps and compassionate advice help women develop their happiness by using strengths they already have.

Celebrating Women

In this section, we feature books about the spirit, beauty, and extraordinary accomplishments of women.

The "Celebrating Women" section features books that are the antidote to every sexist comment you've ever been subjected to. Have you ever been told that you can't do something because you're a girl (or a woman)? Have you ever been made to feel that your sexual organs are dirty? Do you ever feel ugly or useless or timid? Restore your spirits with books that celebrate us as women, warts and all. Some titles, such as Rivka Solomon's *That Takes Ovaries!*, are of the feisty grrrrl-power bent; others, such as Frances Borzello's *Seeing Ourselves: Women's Self-Portraits*, are more contemplative in tone. Whether quirky or profound, radical or subtle, these are books that will make you proud to be a woman. Be sure to also look at the "Emotional Wellness" section of Chapter 3.

Alvrez, Alicia

The Ladies' Room Reader: The Ultimate Women's Trivia Book. Berkeley, CA: Conari Press, 2000. 306pp. ISBN 9781573245616.

So which do you prefer, sex or shopping? If you'd rather skip the sex, you're in good company; 57 percent of women would rather hit the stores—though when they're at those stores, they're not going to reach for the items on the bottom shelves: "We hate stuff we have to bend over for, not because we aren't willing to bend, but because we are afraid of getting bumped into from behind." These and other fascinating facts comprise the quirky *Ladies' Room Reader*, a fun glimpse into women's thoughts and behaviors both now and in the past. Read this to brush up on your women's trivia in topics varying from female bodies to celebrities to sexual habits.

Subjects: Trivia • Sociology • History • Social History • Quick Read

Now Try: Hungry for more trivia? How about this: cities with major league baseball teams boast a divorce rate that is 23 percent lower than in cities without. Continue gulping up trivia in Alvrez's follow-up, *The Ladies' Room Reader Revisited: A Curious Compendium of Fascinating Female Facts.* Think your skills are good enough as they are? Quick! Who was featured on a postage stamp, Abigail Adams, Betty Ford, or Dolley Madison? Find out in *The Ladies' Room Reader Quiz Book: 1,000 Questions and Answers about Women and the Things They Love*, by Leslie Gilbert Elman. Then try a women's trivia book with a practical slant, Francesca Beauman's *Everything but the Kitchen Sink: What Every Modern Woman Needs to Know.* In chapters as varied as "Women in Malawi," "Personal Advertisements" and "How to Eat a Pineapple," Beauman relates facts ranging from the useful (use vinegar as an eco-friendly cleaning product) to the truly bizarre (the phrase "Would you like to dance?" is translated into nineteen languages).

Angier, Natalie

Woman: An Intimate Geography. Boston: Houghton Mifflin, 1999. 398pp. ISBN 9780395691304.

It's hard to describe *Woman: An Intimate Geography*. To call it a biology book is technically true, but that label doesn't even begin to reflect the scope or majesty of this lovely tribute to women's bodies. Perhaps we should instead call it epic poetry: with her lyrical, gorgeous writing style, Angier's prose reads more like a luxurious, delicious poem than a traditional science text. Call it what you will, the book is a captivating study of the female human. In chapters such as "The Well-Tempered Clavier: On the Evolution of the Clitoris" and "Holy Water: Breast Milk," Angier delves into the physical characteristics of women's bodies, illuminating territory that you thought you already knew.

Subjects: Biology • Science

Now Try: No one writes like Natalie Angier, but readers wishing to know more about the science of women's bodies will be delighted with two other captivating biology books. In her classic *The Descent of Woman*, Elaine Morgan considers the role of women in evolution, arguing that women's bodies played a crucial role in the development of the species. And in *The Naked Woman: A Study of the Female Body*, Desmond Morris—the same scientist who wrote the influential book *The Naked Ape*—looks at the female body in minute detail; there are chapters on breasts and genitals, of course, but also on feet, cheeks, ears, even eyebrows.

Bickman, Connie

Tribe of Women: A Photojournalist Chronicles the Lives of Her Sisters around the Globe. Novato, CA: New World Library, 2001. 139pp. ISBN 9781577311300.

At the age of forty, Connie Bickman packed her camera and went on a journey around the world. In every country she visited, from Peru to Egypt, Turkey to Tanzania, Belize to Nepal, she snapped pictures of women and girls. More than ten years and thirty thousand photos later, she recorded her travels in this breathtaking photo journal. Experience the daily lives and activities of women and girls in Bickman's gorgeous color photos, eloquently supported by Bickman's engaging travel narrative. These dazzling images form a tribute to women's lives and experiences in cultures and countries around the globe.

> **Subjects:** Art • Global Perspectives • Travel • Memoir • Quick Read

> **Now Try:** Readers eager for more photos of women throughout the world will want to indulge in *Mother, Daughter, Sister, Bride: Rituals of Womanhood*, by Joanne Bubolz Eicher and Lisa Ling. Published by National Geographic, this stunning collection of images showcases women from a variety of cultures as they participate in rituals such as marriages and birthday celebrations.

Blackledge, Catherine

The Story of V: A Natural History of Female Sexuality. New Brunswick, NJ: Rutgers University Press, 2004. 322pp. ISBN 9780813534558.

"Why," asks scientist Blackledge, "if female genitalia embody arguably the most important job on the planet—creating, supporting, and giving birth to offspring—[is] there so little clear, accurate, and consistent information available?" To remedy this dearth of information, Blackledge wrote *The Story of V*, a meticulously researched history of the vagina. Drawing on such diverse fields as art, biology, zoology, and myth, Blackledge paints a portrait of the various understandings and interpretations of the vagina around the globe, from ancient history through the present, concluding with a resounding defense of the power and purpose of the female orgasm. Thoughtfully written, this is an eye-opening look at an organ that is supremely important but which so few people understand.

> **Subjects:** Vaginas • Sexuality • History • Women's History • Social History • History of Science • History of Medicine • Biology

> **Now Try:** Focus now on more recent sexual history with the remarkable book *The Technology of Orgasm: "Hysteria," the Vibrator, and Women's Sexual Satisfaction*. Author Rachel Maines unveils the origins of the vibrator, a device originally developed as a time-saving device for physicians who were tired of treating women's so-called hysteria with manual massage. Then turn to *O: The Intimate History of the Orgasm*, in which Jonathan Margolis draws on fields such as anthropology, biology, and religion to unveil the social history of women's and men's orgasms.

Borzello, Frances

Seeing Ourselves: Women's Self-Portraits. New York: Harry N. Abrams, 1998. 224pp. ISBN 9780810941885.

Throughout the history of art, men have created portraits of women (especially *nude* women, for some reason). But what of women artists? How do they see themselves? In this magnificent history of art and society, art historian Borzello contemplates that question by examining five centuries' worth of self-portraits by women artists. With illustrations of nearly 250 paintings and photographs, this is a lavishly illustrated exploration of women's changing perceptions of themselves, thoroughly supported by Borzello's insightful art criticism and social and historical analysis. Both entertaining and informative, this is essential reading for those interested in art and women's history.

Subjects: Art • Artists • History • Art History • Women's History • Social History • Sixteenth Century • Seventeenth Century • Eighteenth Century • Nineteenth Century • Twentieth Century

Now Try: You'll find more of Borzello's thoughtful commentary on women's self-portraits in an essay in Liz Rideal's *Mirror, Mirror: Self-Portraits by Women Artists*, a stunning collection of art reproductions. Bolstered by contextual essays written by art scholars, the book features the self-portraiture of women artists from the seventeenth century to the present; paintings and photos are included, of course, but so, too, are other media, including ceramics and woodcuts. Other books of interest are Jordi Vigue's *Great Women Masters of Art*, a collective biography featuring reproductions of art by eighty-four women painters, and Julian Bell's *500 Self-Portraits*, collecting a dazzling array of self-portraits by women as well as men.

Ensler, Eve

The Vagina Monologues. New York: Villard, 2001. 185pp. ISBN 9780375756986.

It began simply enough, with Eve Ensler chatting with her friends about sex. Then, sensing the potential of the topic, Ensler more formally interviewed two hundred women about their vaginas. Lo and behold, *The Vagina Monologues* was born. From its genesis as a stage play, *The Vagina Monologues* has become an international feminist activist movement, a triumphant declaration that celebrates women and praises the vagina. Catch it as a stage production if you can, and savor it word-for-word here in the book version. Indulge in all that vaginas have to offer—the politics, the magic, the empowerment, the eroticism—in the book's chapters on topics ranging from birth to sexuality, from violence to feminism.

Subjects: Vaginas • Feminism • Third-wave Feminism • Activism • Quick Read

Now Try: Ensler does it again, this time with the whole female form. If you loved her reflections on vaginas in *The Vagina Monologues*, you'll clamor for her contemplation of breasts, thighs, tummies, and more in *The Good Body*. Featuring the perspectives of various women on body image, beauty, dieting, and self-loathing/self-loving, this is another empowering, thought-provoking commentary on women's relationships with their own bodies. Then contemplate body image with a work of fiction, Carolyn Mackler's marvelous book *The Earth, My Butt and Other Big Round Things*. This time the focus is not on vaginas but on the whole body, as protagonist Virginia Shreves learns to love her overweight body in spite of the negative messages she hears from her parents, her friends, and the media.

Guzman, Sandra

The Latina's Bible: The Nueva Latina's Guide to Love, Spirituality, Family, and La Vida. New York: Three Rivers Press, 2002. 323pp. ISBN 9780609806968.

Women seeking advice and affirmation for the unique experience of being Latina in the United States need look no further than this comprehensive guide, in which Puerto Rican Guzman tackles a dizzying number of topics, from love and marriage to career success to body image and health. In her candid, conversational style, Guzman looks at race head-on, covering such thorny questions as what it means to date white men and how to meld with the dominant American culture without losing one's identity. Filled with quirky sidebars, statistics, and profiles of successful Latina women in America, this is a joyous celebration of everything Latina and an indispensable guide to living the Latina life to the fullest.

Subjects: Latinas • Race • Lifestyle • Body Image • Health • Relationships • Spirituality • Dating • Marriage • America • How-to

Now Try: Readers looking for further inspiring stories of the Latina experience will enjoy *The Book of Latina Women: 150 Vidas of Passion, Strength, and Success,* by Sylvia Mendoza. In highlighting the successes of Latinas from the past and in the present, this empowering collective biography celebrates women both famous and lesser known, showing how they overcame racism and sexism to achieve success in the United States and across the globe.

Leibovitz, Annie, and Susan Sontag

Women. New York: Random House, 1999. 239pp. ISBN 9780375500206.

You may already be familiar with Annie Leibovitz; she has been the photographer behind the lens for countless celebrity shots in *Rolling Stone*, *Vogue*, and *Vanity Fair*, and she has published several collections of her photography. Now she turns her attention to American women from a variety of backgrounds: there's a coal miner, and there is Elizabeth Taylor; there is a schoolteacher, and there is Toni Morrison; there is a battered woman, and there is Martha Stewart. The book is introduced by a provocative essay on women and photography by Susan Sontag, followed by more than two hundred stunning portraits of American women, uninterrupted by text. Dip into the book randomly, or luxuriate for hours over the photos, or gulp it down straight through, from cover to cover; no matter how you approach it, this is a gorgeous collection of portraits, a tribute to women from all walks of life.

Subjects: Art • America • Collection • Quick Read

Now Try: For more photos of American women, turn to *A Day in the Life of the American Woman: How We See Ourselves*, by Sharon J. Wohlmuth, Carol Saline, and Dawn Sheggeby. The lovely photos of women from different races, backgrounds, and cultures shows them going about their ordinary lives—at work, at home, at play, alone and with family and friends. Then, for photos of women in America and abroad, try *Woman: A Celebration*, in which Peter Fetterman collects historical and contemporary photos of women around the globe.

Muscio, Inga

Cunt: A Declaration of Independence. Seattle: Seal Press, 1998 (2002). 277pp. ISBN 9781580050753.

Not everyone has yet heard the good news: "Cunt" is no longer a bad word. Says who? Says the delightful radical lesbian feminist Inga Muscio, who's on a one-woman crusade to reclaim the word, rather in the same way that Eve Ensler has made it okay to say "vagina" in public. Why, asks Muscio, should a word that refers to the glorious, beautiful genitals of a woman be used as an insult? With this refreshing perspective as a framework, we are treated to a cunt-lovin' treatise on cunts as body parts, "cunt" as a word of power, cunts as the essential defining element of liberated women. Part memoir and part feminist theory, this is heady, radical, third-wave feminism at its edgiest, related with passion, anger, and verve.

> **Subjects:** Cunts • Vaginas • Feminism • Third-wave Feminism • Sexuality • Lesbian Sexuality • Queer Sexuality • Memoir

> **Now Try:** The only person who writes like Inga Muscio is, well, Inga Muscio. Fortunately for her fans, she's written a follow-up to *Cunt*, titled *Autobiography of a Blue-Eyed Devil: My Life and Times in a Racist, Imperialist Society.* With her trademark hard-hitting style and her uncanny ability to ask prickly questions about society, Muscio here turns to the subject of history, exposing the extent to which white patriarchy has informed our collective understanding of the past.

Solomon, Rivka, ed.

That Takes Ovaries!: Bold Females and Their Brazen Acts. New York: Three Rivers Press, 2002. 230pp. ISBN 9780609806593.

In this quirky, sassy, empowering collection of essays, a variety of women from different races, classes, and backgrounds share stories of courage and chutzpah. As the title itself suggests, the stories within are sometimes irreverent, sometimes funny, and always feminist. The contributors—most of whom will be unfamiliar to readers—write about episodes when they faced down difficult situations; there is Kathleen, who scolded an intruder in her home and shamed him into walking away, and Tess, who decided she would wear a skin-revealing tank top over her large body, onlookers be damned. Hard-hitting and vibrant, these brief essays celebrate women as they step out of their comfort zones.

> **Subjects:** Feminism • Third-wave Feminism • Activism • Adventure • Essays • Anthology • Collection • Young Adult • Quick Read

> **Now Try:** For more stories of brave women, turn to *Women of Courage: Inspiring Stories from the Women Who Lived Them*, edited by Katherine Martin. Like *That Takes Ovaries!*, this is an inspiring collection of writings by women who have faced life's challenges with fortitude and determination; powerful and thought-provoking, it is a celebration of the inner strength and courage of ordinary women.

Relationships

Here you will find books about the connections and associations between women and their family members and friends.

Relationships are ubiquitous within Women's Nonfiction—and, for that matter, within the broader realms of nonfiction and even fiction. If a book has any characters, whatsoever, you may be assured that relationships exist. To narrow the subgenre down to a manageable scope, only books that deal explicitly with women's relationships with family, friends, and significant others are included here. Some of the books, such as Ellen Perry Berkeley's *At Grandmother's Table* are celebratory in nature, while others, such as Susan Shapiro Barash's *Tripping the Prom Queen,* are more investigative. Still others, such as *Daughters and Mothers,* by Dorothy Firman and Julie Firman, are how-to guides to instruct us in improving our relationships.

Apter, T. E.

The Sister Knot: Why We Fight, Why We're Jealous, and Why We'll Love Each Other No Matter What. New York: Norton, 2007. 308pp. ISBN 9780393060584.

Sisterly love is a complicated thing, as psychologist author Apter finds in her thought-provoking study of the relationships between sisters. Chapters such as "Protection and Resentment" and "Success and Insecurity: When One Sister Outshines the Other" show that the range of emotions and actions between sisters covers a broad spectrum: sometimes they can be unspeakably cruel to one another, while at other times their shared empathy can be more rewarding than any other relationship. Though the prose is somewhat scholarly in tone, the text sparkles with excerpts from the interviews of seventy-six sisters the author conducted as part of her research.

Subjects: Sisters • Relationships • Rivalry

Now Try: Marcia Millman, also a psychologist, studies the intricacies of sisters' relationships in *The Perfect Sister: What Draws Us Together, What Drives Us Apart*; with its focus on nurturing and healing, this engaging read is especially helpful for those women who have troubled relationships with their sisters. Also helpful for those women who want to grow closer to their sisters is *My Sister, My Self: Understanding the Sibling Relationship That Shapes Our Lives, Our Loves, and Ourselves*, in which author Vikki Stark offers a how-to guide to help sisters understand and improve their relationships.

Barash, Susan Shapiro

Tripping the Prom Queen: The Truth about Women and Rivalry. New York: St. Martin's Press, 2006. 274pp. ISBN 9780312342319.

"Few women," writes Barash in her introduction, "want to acknowledge the presence of envy, jealousy, and competition in their lives." But whether they admit it or not, posits Barash, many women do enter into intense rivalries with other women. Based on interviews with five hundred women and supported with ample evidence from pop culture, the book exposes a reality of jealousy and competition in women's relationships, in chapters such as "Snow Queens and Soccer Moms: Envy over Children" and "Working Girls and Bossy Women: Envy on the Job." Those who view women's relationships through rose-tinted glasses will be in for a surprise; those who suspect that women's relationships often revolve around fierce competition will find confirmation in this thought-provoking, readable study.

Subjects: Rivalry • Relationships

Now Try: Those who liked the mix of quotes, personal reflection, academic scholarship, and references to pop culture in *Tripping the Prom Queen* will be delighted with *Catfight: Rivalries among Women—From Diets to Dating, from the Boardroom to the Delivery Room*. In this intelligent, thought-provoking study, Leora Tanenbaum explores the societal factors that lead women to compete with one another in various settings, from romantic relationships to physical appearance to personal politics.

Beanland, Ame Mahler, and Emily Miles Terry, eds.

It's a Chick Thing: Celebrating the Wild Side of Women's Friendships. Berkeley, CA: Conari Press, 2000. 189pp. ISBN 9781573241960.

Female bonding has never been so much fun. Not for the tame or the timid, this feisty collection of essays is a celebration of women whose friendships thrive on adventure and thrill-seeking. In chapters such as "Cheeky Chicks" and "Chicks in Charge," meet women with attitude—some who are famous, some who might just be your next-door neighbor. With humor and chutzpah, the various contributors recount some of their zanier exploits with their best gal pals, from riding in women's motorcycle gangs to crashing celebrity parties. And for those readers who want to inject some spirit into their own female friendships, lists such as "Chick Reads" and "Chick Flicks" highlight some easy ideas for adding zest to their relationships.

Subjects: Friendships • Relationships • Quick Read

Now Try: For a slightly tamer read, turn to *The Secret Language of Girlfriends: Talking Loudly, Laughing Wildly, and Making the Most of Our Most Important Friendships,* by Karen Neuburger. The best moments of female friendships—from crazy hijinks to everyday encounters—shine in this spirited tribute to girlfriends. Inspiring and empowering, the book affirms the unique qualities of women's friendships and rejoices in the ways that women interact with their girlfriends. And for a spunky, sassy look at the joys of female friendship, don't miss *The Girlfriends' Bible,* by Cathy Hamilton, the creator of the Boyfriend-in-a-Box. Each page delivers a verse, Bible-style, of advice and inspiration for girlfriends.

Berkeley, Ellen Perry, ed.

At Grandmother's Table: Women Write about Food, Life and the Enduring Bond between Grandmothers and Granddaughters. Minneapolis, MN: Fairview Press, 2000. 298pp. ISBN 9781577490968.

In this poignant collection of essays and recipes, sixty-seven women remember the relationships they had with their grandmothers. Each contributor recalls times from her childhood, honoring not only the grandmother she loved but also the special bond forged over the food her grandmother prepared. The grandmothers —and the writers themselves—come from a variety of countries, backgrounds, and cooking traditions. Rich, sensual descriptions of ingredients and cooking evoke the joys of bonding over food, while fond memories offer tribute to the relationship between granddaughters and grandmothers; readers who are cooks themselves will be pleased with the recipes that accompany each essay.

Subjects: Grandmothers • Granddaughters • Relationships • Food • Recipes • Essays

Now Try: Though it does not emphasize cooking, *Chicken Soup for the Grandma's Soul: Stories to Honor and Celebrate the Ageless Love of Grandmothers*, by Jack Canfield, is a good choice for those who loved *At Grandmother's Table*. Like all the titles in the <u>Chicken Soup</u> series, the book collects tender, inspiring essays that warm the heart. Then continue the celebration of grandmothers by reading the magnificent book *Grandmothers*, a collection of photo-essays by journalist Lauren Cowen and photographer Jayne Wexler, in which twenty-three grandmothers and their grandchildren are profiled with moving prose and beautiful photos.

Firman, Dorothy, and Julie Firman

Daughters and Mothers: Making It Work. Deerfield Beach, FL: Health Communications, 2003. 300pp. ISBN 9780757301247.

Mother and daughter Dorothy Firman and Julie Firman, both psychotherapists, know that it takes work for adult women to maintain good relationships with their mothers. In this guide for improving relationships between mothers and daughters, the authors draw on their own personal experiences, as well as those of their patients, to examine mother–daughter relationships. The book illuminates the causes of conflict while offering advice for women who want to fix problems in their relations with their mothers or daughters. Anecdotes, quizzes, and writing exercises make this an accessible, practical guide for women at any stage of life.

Subjects: Daughters • Mothers • Children • Relationships • How-to

Now Try: Communication expert Deborah Tannen, best known for her insight into problems between the sexes, turns her focus to mothers and their adult daughters in *You're Wearing That?: Understanding Mothers and Daughters in Conversation*. Filled with examples of real conversations, the book explores the different perspectives that mothers and daughters hold in their interactions; Tannen's thought-provoking analysis will help readers understand how they communicate, or fail to communicate, with their own mothers and daughters. Try also *I'm Not Mad, I Just Hate You!: A New Understanding of Mother-Daughter Conflict*, in which Roni Cohen-Sandler and Michelle Silver offer practical advice for improving relationships between teenage daughters and their mothers.

Moore, Suzanne

Girlfriends Are the Best Friends of All: A Tribute to Laughter, Secrets, Girl Talk, Chocolate, Shopping—and Everything Else Women Share. Boulder, CO: Blue Mountain Press. 64pp. ISBN 9780883968598.

This slim volume may not look like much, but this breezy read packs a lot of substance into its sixty-four pages. With a tone that ranges from tender to sassy, author Moore devotes the first part of the book to celebrating female friendships, with sections such as "Top Ten Things Only Women Understand" and "Girlfriends Just Know." The second part is a practical how-to guide with suggestions for activities for women and their friends, including "Start a Book Club" and "Have a Beauty Night." This gem is filled with inspiration and advice for every woman who values her girlfriends.

Subjects: Friendships • Relationships • How-to • Quick Read

Now Try: Those who love the inspirational celebration of female friendships and practical advice in *Girlfriends Are the Best Friends of All* will love *Girlfriends: Invisible Bonds, Enduring Ties*. With compassion and insight, Carmen Renee Berry and Tamara Traeder present stories of women's friendships in every stage of life, and the final section helps girlfriends strengthen their relationships with ideas for parties and bonding. Then celebrate female friendship with *Sisterhood of the Traveling Pants*, Ann Brashares's novel of friendship, growth, and healing among four young women.

Pryor, Liz

What Did I Do Wrong?: When Women Don't Tell Each Other the Friendship Is Over. New York: Free Press, 2006. 193pp. ISBN 9780743286312.

Losing a friendship is awful; losing a friendship without knowing why is even worse. *What Did I Do Wrong?* is a compassionate, sensitive exploration of the pain that comes when close female friendships are inexplicably ended. Based on interviews with women who have been dumped by their best friends as well as the author's own experiences, this readable, personal book helps make sense of the devastating ways that women sometimes treat each other when a friendship is over. Practical suggestions for coping, including a section on writing cathartic letters to former friends, make this a valuable tool for any woman who has lost a best friend, whether she was the one to end the relationship or not.

Subjects: Friendships • Relationships • How-to • Quick Read

Now Try: Sometimes the best way to cope with pain is to read about others who have suffered in similar ways. In *The Friend Who Got Away: Twenty Women's True Life Tales of Friendships That Blew Up, Burned Out or Faded Away*, editors Jenny Offill and Elissa Schappell present a collection of essays by women who have endured the loss of female friendships. These thoughtful, emotional stories will soothe readers who are struggling to cope with their own losses, while validating the pain and heartbreak they have experienced.

Saline, Carol, and Sharon J. Wohlmuth

Mothers & Daughters. New York: Doubleday, 1997. 127pp. ISBN 9780385481250.

The magic of the bond between mothers and daughters shines here in thirty-seven short photo-essays, based on interviews with women from all walks of life—most of whom will be unfamiliar to readers, though a few well-known women, such as Margaret Atwood and Cathy Guisewite, are included. In lovingly crafted profiles, journalist Saline and photographer Wohlmuth illuminate the emotions shared by women in a variety of mother–daughter relationships: Some of the essays present traditional relationships, while others explore nontraditional examples, including adopted children and lesbian mothers. The sensitive, touching prose and the gorgeous photos make *Mothers & Daughters* a book to savor and treasure.

Subjects: Mothers • Daughters • Children • Relationships • Quick Read • Essays • Collection

Now Try: The perfect companion to *Mothers & Daughters* is *Daughters and Mothers*, also a collection of photo-essays. Journalist Lauren Cowen and photographer Jayne Wexler interviewed twenty-nine sets of mothers and daughters, including some well-known subjects such as congresswoman Pat Schroeder, to create a moving tribute to the mother–daughter relationship. And readers who love heart-warming stories of mothers and daughters will enjoy the tender essays in *Chicken Soup for the Mother & Daughter Soul: Stories to Warm the Heart and Honor the Relationship*, by Jack Canfield.

Saline, Carol, and Sharon J. Wohlmuth

Sisters. Philadelphia: Running Press, 1994 (2004). 135pp. ISBN 978156-1384501.

Ace team Saline and Wohlmuth (see the previous annotation for their *Mothers & Daughters*) unite here to create a beautiful tribute to sisters. Collecting thirty-six profiles of two or more sets of sisters, the book pairs short essays by journalist Saline with images by photographer Wohlmuth. Some of the names, such as civil rights icon Coretta Scott King and model Christy Turlington, will be more familiar, while others will be new, but in each case the lovely prose and beautiful photographs combine to create a stunning portrait of sisterhood. Try to get the second, tenth-anniversary edition, which features follow-up stories for thirteen of the sets of sisters originally profiled in the first edition.

Subjects: Sisters • Relationships • Quick Read • Essays • Collection

Now Try: Though they do not feature photographs, the books of the beloved *Chicken Soup for the Soul* series are perfect for readers who enjoy poignant, heart-warming stories of relationships. For more beautiful writing on the bond that sisters share, turn to two volumes of the series, *Chicken Soup for the Sister's Soul* and *Chicken Soup for the Sister's Soul 2*, edited by Jack Canfield.

Sheehy, Sandy

Connecting: The Enduring Power of Female Friendship. New York: William Morrow, 2000. 394pp. ISBN 9780380974306.

Women who have close female friends know that they have something special; women without close female friends know they're missing something. An obvious truth, perhaps, but there is nothing banal about *Connecting*, a beautifully written celebration of female friendship through the various stages of life. With lovely prose and a compassionate voice, journalist Sheehy examines the different stages of female friendship and looks at the different forms the friendship can take, including "companions in crisis," "nurturing friends," and "mentors and protégés." Not only does the book rejoice in the various facets of friendship, but it also considers ways to make those friendships endure and offers suggestions for how to handle the problems that inevitably surface.

Subjects: Friendships • Relationships • How-to

Now Try: Like Sandy Sheehy, author Joy Carol knows that women's relationships—whether with friends, mothers, or sisters—are worth fighting for, even when things go wrong. In *The Fabric of Friendship: Celebrating the Joys, Mending the Tears in Women's Relationships*, she reflects on the beauty of women's friendships, while acknowledging that sometimes things don't work out. The book offers solutions for improving friendships and catharsis for friendships that have broken. And for a lovely portrait of the friendships of women (and a few men), turn to *Best Friends*, in which photographer Sharon J. Wohlmuth and essayist Carol Saline vividly capture the beauty of friendships amongst people both famous and unknown.

Vassel, Rachel, and Derek Blanks

Daughters of Men: Portraits of African-American Women and Their Fathers. New York: Amistad, an imprint of HarperCollins, 2007. 170pp. ISBN 9780061350351.

This stunning collection of photo-essays is a proud tribute to successful African American women and the fathers who have supported them. Each profile highlights a high-profile woman, including celebrities such as singer Beyoncé and actress Sanaa Lathan—but though each woman has a successful career, the focus is not on *her*, but rather on the relationship she shares with her father and the role he played in helping her achieve success. Beautiful photographs and inspiring, heart-warming stories work together to rejoice in the special bond between black women and their fathers.

Subjects: Fathers • Daughters • Children • Relationships • African Americans • Race • Essays • Collection • Quick Read

Now Try: Now look at the bond between fathers and children among ordinary black people. Though some of the subjects of *Pop: A Celebration of Black Fatherhood* are well known, most of the people in these photo-essays are regular folks who could easily live next door. In fifty-one profiles, author Carol Ross presents touching, tender words from black fathers alongside beautiful photographs that celebrate the relationships between men and their children.

Straight Romantic Relationships

The "Straight Romantic Relationships" section features books about women's romantic involvement with men.

Instructional guides abound; try starting with *How to Succeed with Men*, written by David Copeland and Ron Louis, who have obligingly demystified the inner workings of men's brains. Or try one of the many other types of books in the section; Marilyn Yalom's book *A History of the Wife* makes for fascinating reading, while Colleen Curren's *Altared* offers a sampling of essays about weddings.

Arons, Katie, and Jacqueline Shannon

Sexy at Any Size: The Real Woman's Guide to Dating and Romance. New York: Simon & Schuster, 1999. 173pp. ISBN 9780684854151.

Large women, rejoice: *Sexy at Any Size* is for every reader who recognizes that big is beautiful. Rather than pushing women to lose weight, the book offers affirmation that desirable women come in plus sizes, and teaches readers how to use their size as an advantage in the dating field. With a breezy, conversational style, the authors offer tips on dating for larger women, covering such topics as how to meet men, where to travel to meet men who appreciate bigger women, and how to develop a fashion style that complements larger body types. Empowering and positive, this is a welcome antidote to dieting books and dating guides that emphasize slim.

Subjects: Dating • Relationships • Sexuality • Body Image • Weight • Health • Sexual Health • How-to • Quick Read

Now Try: Now move on to the remarkable book *Big Big Love: A Sourcebook on Sex for People of Size and Those Who Love Them.* Hanne Blank has written a book for women and men that both celebrates and examines sex for large people. Informative and thought-provoking, this is a comprehensive guide for accepting the joys of sex among larger body types, covering everything from sex toys to sexual health, queer sex to arousal and desire. Then turn to Jennifer Weiner's insightful novel *Good in Bed,* about an overweight woman who comes to realize that she deserves better than her lousy boyfriend.

bandele, asha

The Prisoner's Wife: A Memoir. New York: Scribner, 1999. 219pp. ISBN 9780684850733.

By many accounts, asha bandele had a blessed life: a college-educated young African American woman from a good family, she was moving beyond an unfulfilling former marriage and growing in her identity as a poet. It was her poetry, in fact, that led her to her destiny in the one area of happiness that her life lacked: romance. While reading her poetry to a group of inmates, bandele met Rashid, a man serving time for second-degree murder. *The Prisoner's Wife* is the unlikeliest of love stories, tracing the romance between bandele and Rashid through their initial tentative attraction, their growing love, and their eventual marriage—even while he was still behind bars. bandele's gift for poetic language recalls the bittersweet emotions, the struggles, and the triumph of joy in unexpected circumstances in this moving narrative.

> **Subjects:** Incarceration • Dating • Marriage • Relationships • African Americans • Race • America • Memoir
>
> **Now Try:** Though different in tone and approach, Bridget Kinsella's *Visiting Life: Women Doing Time on the Outside* makes for a fascinating companion to *The Prisoner's Wife.* Like bandele, Kinsella never expected to find romance behind bars, yet this literary agent found herself falling for a writer, never mind that he was sentenced to life without parole for murder. *Visiting Life* is a memoir that details Kinsella's difficult romance, as well as a sociological examination of the lovers and family members who must adjust when the men they love go to prison.

Carlin, Patricia, and Michael Miller

How to Tell If Your Boyfriend Is the Antichrist: (And If He Is, Should You Break Up with Him?) Philadelphia: Quirk Books, 2007. 112pp. ISBN 9781594741401.

Face it, all of us have wondered, during the course of a romantic relationship: Is the person I'm dating the Antichrist? Or if we haven't asked ourselves that question, it's high time we did, according to writer Carlin and illustrator Miller. (If he's the Antichrist, he wants to torture your soul for eternity—"so unless you're into that sort of thing, break up now.") In this pseudo how-to guide, readers are treated to seventy-three irreverent, wildly funny chapters that help determine if a particular boyfriend is, for instance, "An Extraterrestrial," "A Total Bastard," "Actually Twins," or "Suffering from Amnesia." The snarky humor and droll illustrations make this a wickedly funny pick-me-up for anyone with questions about her boyfriend.

Subjects: Dating • Relationships • Humor • How-to • Quick Read

Now Try: Never mind if your boyfriend really is the Antichrist; it could be worse, explains Justin Racz in *50 Boyfriends Worse than Yours*. With shameless stereotyping of bad boyfriend types such as "One Position Peter" and side-splitting illustrations, the humor will leave readers in hysterics. For more laughs, try the signature humor of the sequin-sporting Sweet Potato Queens in *The Sweet Potato Queens' Book of Love*, in which Jill Conner Browne treats readers to recipes and guidance in finding love; chapters such as "Men Who May Need Killing, Quite Frankly" will be especially useful to those who have conclusively determined that they're dating the Antichrist.

Copeland, David, and Ron Louis

How to Succeed with Men. Paramus, NJ: Reward Books, 2000. 450pp. ISBN 9780130145093.

Copeland and Louis have a knack for understanding the male of the human species, as evidenced by the first sentence of their book: "Men are trouble." In straightforward, sympathetic language, they acknowledge the various problems that men bring to the dating game—and they help women who want to date men in spite of those problems. Chapters such as "The Eight Signs That He Is Ready for the Commitment Conversation" and "The Seven Keys to Keeping a Long-Term Relationship Happy, Exciting, and Hot" provide concrete tips for women at every stage of the relationship, from the predating action plan to long-term commitment and marriage. Anecdotes, quizzes, and practical advice make this a thorough, useful guide for finding, dating, and keeping men.

Subjects: Dating • Relationships • How-to

Now Try: Leave it to a hairdresser to unravel the mysteries of dating. After honing her skills at dispensing dating advice while styling hair, Felicia Rose Adler wrote *Master Dating: How to Meet & Attract Quality Men!*, brimming with keen insights based on real-life examples. With a positive, inspiring approach and a conversational writing style, *Master Dating* offers useful solutions to guide women as they embark on the dating journey.

Corral, Jill, and Lisa Miya-Jervis, eds.

Young Wives' Tales: New Adventures in Love and Partnership. Seattle, WA: Seal Press, 2001. 287pp. ISBN 9781580050500.

In this collection of thirty stellar essays, the institution of marriage gets a thorough critical examination. The essayists, all women in their twenties and thirties, consider their current and former long-term romantic commitments from a myriad of angles. The women come from a variety of racial, cultural, and sexual backgrounds, a diversity reflected in the relationships they discuss: traditional heterosexual marriages are included, but so, too, are lesbian relationships, polyamorous relationships, and long-term but unmarried relationships. Hard questions about commitment, with no easy answers, make *Young Wives' Tales* a thought-provoking and stimulating tour through the joys and struggles of romance.

Subjects: Marriage • Relationships • Feminism • Essays • Anthology • Collection

Now Try: Daniel Jones, editor of the "Modern Love" column of the *New York Times*, has culled fifty of the best stories into one satisfying collection, *Modern Love: 50 True and Extraordinary Tales of Desire, Deceit, and Devotion*. Though less feminist in tone than *Young Wives' Tales*, the intelligent writing and impressive scope will appeal to readers as they explore the triumphs, tragedies, and oddities of contemporary romance.

Curran, Colleen, ed.

Altared: Bridezillas, Bewilderment, Big Love, Breakups, and What Women Really Think about Contemporary Weddings. New York: Vintage Books, 2007. 368pp. ISBN 9780307277633.

Weddings are supposed to be magical affairs, the crowning event in a woman's life—but as the twenty-seven writers in this anthology show, it takes a lot of work to pull off a wedding (and even then, it might not be perfect). Readers who are planning their own weddings or who have gone through weddings of their own will wince, laugh, cry, and sympathize with the bride writers as they relate their experiences in launching marital bliss: there are events to plan, logistical nightmares to fix, relatives to please, and staggering amounts of money to fret over. Covering a range of emotions, types of marriages, and even outcomes (not everyone goes through with the wedding plans, after all), this collection offers an in-depth look at the joys and struggles of planning for, and participating in, the wedding day.

Subjects: Marriage • Essays • Anthology • Collection

Now Try: As the essayists in *Altared* so artfully explain, weddings and marriage are not necessarily as joyful as we would like them to be. In *The Conscious Bride: Women Unveil Their True Feelings about Getting Hitched*, psychologist Sheryl Paul examines the various factors that lead to stress and disillusionment for new brides and brides-to-be. Based on interviews with married women and Paul's own experience as a bridal counselor, *The Conscious Bride* helps women understand the complicated, conflicting emotions they feel as they journey into marriage.

Dillow, Linda, and Lorraine Pintus

Gift-Wrapped by God: Secret Answers to the Question, "Why Wait?" Colorado Springs, CO: WaterBrook Press, 2002. 227pp. ISBN 9781578565856.

Women are bombarded with messages from society encouraging them to have sex. In magazines, on television, in conversations with friends—no matter where they turn, the societal pressure to have sex is intense. Unmarried women of a Christian faith who prefer to wait until marriage to have sex can find it incredibly difficult to resist the pressure; sometimes they begin to question the wisdom of waiting, and sometimes they decide to capitulate by engaging in sex outside of marriage. Based in scripture and Christian theology, *Gift-Wrapped by God* presents a case for waiting till marriage, but it does far more than preach: with sympathy and common sense, the authors offer practical advice and real-life stories to help women wait until marriage, whether they are virgins or whether they are rededicating themselves to sexual chastity.

Subjects: Chastity • Sexuality • Dating • Relationships • Christianity • Religion • How-to

Now Try: Directed at both women and men, Lauren F. Winner's book *Real Sex: The Naked Truth about Chastity* continues the discussion about maintaining sexual purity prior to marriage. Winner asks hard questions about the value of chastity and answers them with theologically sound guidance from the Christian Bible. She honestly addresses the societal pressures that face unmarried Christians and acknowledges the difficulty of resisting sex. With an accessible style that examines the history and purpose of chastity, *Real Sex* is a standout among the many books that encourage Christians to wait until marriage before having sex.

Feldhahn, Shaunti Christine

For Women Only: What You Need to Know about the Inner Lives of Men. Sisters, OR: Multnomah, 2004. 189pp. ISBN 9781590523179.

Author Feldhahn has managed to penetrate the interior workings of men's brains, thanks to hundreds of interviews she conducted with men from all walks of life. With chapters such as "The Truth about the Way You Look: Why What's on the Outside Matters to Him on the Inside," the book deconstructs the struggles, emotions, and inner thoughts of men, using accessible language that interprets the male psyche in a way that speaks to women readers. Feldhahn writes from a Christian perspective, though readers of other faiths will find much to mull over in this thought-provoking guide to understanding and accommodating gender differences with husbands and other men in our lives.

Subjects: Gender • Marriage • Relationships • Communication • Christianity • Religion • How-to • Quick Read

Now Try: *Why Marriages Succeed or Fail: And How You Can Make Yours Last*, though without a religious perspective, should appeal to fans of *For Women Only*. Using his research of real-life married couples, psychologist John Gottman presents convincing evidence for what works, and what doesn't work, in married relationships. His practical advice, concrete tips, and insightful sociological analysis will help married couples understand their communication differences and work toward improving their marriages.

Greenwald, Rachel

Find a Husband after 35 Using What I Learned at Harvard Business School: A Simple 15-Step Action Program. New York: Ballantine Books, 2003. 322pp. ISBN 9780345466259.

While many how-to books are content to offer general advice, Harvard MBA Greenwald takes things to the next level with her rock-solid fifteen-step approach. Drawing on her marketing expertise, Greenwald presents a business model for landing a husband, replete with performance reviews, budgeting, and branding —there's even a chapter devoted to the exit strategy. Practical tips relating to appearance, lifestyle, and where to meet men will help women get married in as little as two years. With a straightforward, no-nonsense style, the sensible advice and detailed plan will help single women in their thirties and beyond meet the bottom line by finding a good husband.

Subjects: Dating • Relationships • Midlife • How-to

Now Try: A perfect complement to *Finding a Husband after 35* is Helena Hacker Rosenberg's *How to Get Married after 35: A User's Guide to Getting to the Altar*. Whereas Greenwald presented a business plan to follow, Rosenberg emphasizes introspection. Though she does offer solid advice for finding a husband, the real strength of the book is its focus on personal analysis; with sensitivity and common sense, *How to Get Married after 35* helps women understand and adjust their own perspectives to increase their chances of marriage.

Price, Joan

Better than I Ever Expected: Straight Talk about Sex after Sixty. Emeryville, CA: Seal Press, 2006. 269pp. ISBN 9781580051521.

Push that stereotype of the virginal old maid right out of your head: senior women are more than capable of enjoying happy sex lives. After menopause, of course, a few adjustments may be necessary—and *Better than I Ever Expected* covers them all. For every woman of a certain age, whether she is looking to spice up a long-term relationship, playing the dating game, or finding sexual pleasure all on her own, this engagingly written how-to guide covers sexual health and satisfaction in all its glory. In an honest, empowering tone, author Price shares stories of sexually satisfied senior women while offering practical advice on achieving happy, healthy sex in the golden years.

Subjects: Sexuality • Seniors • Health • Sexual Health • How-to

Now Try: If you need more evidence that women of a certain age can enjoy a good sex life, turn to the memoir *Prime: Adventures and Advice on Sex, Love, and the Sensual Years.* Pepper Schwartz—who is, ironically, a relationship adviser—finds herself single after twenty-three years of marriage. With humor and insight, she recounts the midlife dating adventures and mishaps of a confessedly hormonal woman; there is no happily-ever-after romantic ending with a Mr. Right, but don't worry, there are plenty of steamy sex scenes with a series of enchanting Mr. Wrongs.

Rinehart, Paula

Sex and the Soul of a Woman: The Reality of Love & Romance in an Age of Casual Sex. Grand Rapids, MI: Zondervan, 2004. 191pp. ISBN 978031-0252207.

Maintaining sexual purity before marriage is incredibly difficult, acknowledges author Rinehart, and many women fail. But rather than condemn women who have had sex before marriage, Rinehart offers sympathy and guidance for those who want to renew their commitment to sexual purity. Without offering harsh judgments, she examines the reasons for avoiding casual sex and for holding out for marriage. In a compassionate, accessible style that employs a practical and useful interpretation of scripture, Rinehart helps Christian women—both those who are virgins and those who have had sex—commit, or recommit, themselves to chastity.

Subjects: Chastity • Sexuality • Dating • Relationships • Christianity • Religion • How-to • Quick Read

Now Try: Read more from Paula Rinehart in *Choices: Finding God's Way in Dating, Sex, Singleness, and Marriage,* coauthored with her husband, Stacy Rinehart. With chapters such as "Going against the Grain of Your Culture" and "Celibacy in a Sexy World," *Choices* candidly addresses the difficulty of staying chaste and offers guidance in maintaining sexual purity before marriage, while providing additional insight into choosing dating and marriage partners in the context of a Christian lifestyle. Then turn to the candid advice of *The Invisible Bond: How to Break Free from Your Sexual Past,* by abstinence educator Barbara Wilson. Written for Christian women, the book examines the psychological causes of the shame caused by sexual indiscretions and offers realistic measures to overcome that shame.

Spindel, Janis

How to Date Men: Dating Secrets from America's Top Matchmaker. New York: Plume, 2007. 249pp. ISBN 9780452288676.

For all those who've wished there were a manual for navigating the dating field, there's good news: author Spindel, of Janis Spindel Serious Matchmaking, Inc., has written a sensible, accessible, straightforward guide that makes sense of the ins and outs of dating. Chapters such as "The Rendezvous Strategy: The First Phone Call" and "He's Just As Nervous As You Are: Meeting Each Other's Families" takes readers through all stages of dating, from the initial stages of the first encounter through moving in together and planning for marriage. With a light-hearted style, simple quizzes, and down-to-earth reminders ("Not every man is going to be interested in you, no matter how beautiful, smart, or successful you are"), *How to Date Men* is a fresh, useful guide for novice daters and veteran romancers alike.

Subjects: Dating • Relationships • How-to

Now Try: Those who enjoyed the lighthearted style and sensible advice in *How to Date Men* will find much to love in *Men Are Like Fish: What Every Woman Needs to Know about Catching a Man*. With quotes, cartoons, and gentle good humor, Steve Nakamoto uses a fishing metaphor to make sense of the dating game, with chapters such as "Fishing Lessons: Improve Your Chances with Preparation" and "The Bait: Make Your Attraction More Powerful." The book's practical advice and insightful perspective will help demystify the dating process for women who are seeking a mate and for those who wonder what to do once they reel in a boyfriend.

Whitman, Stacy, and Wynne Whitman

Shacking Up: The Smart Girl's Guide to Living in Sin without Getting Burned. New York: Broadway Books, 2003. 303pp. ISBN 9780767910408.

Moving in together, stress journalist Stacy Whitman and her attorney sister Wynne Whitman, is not for everyone, and it shouldn't be attempted without some foresight; "we wouldn't want you to lease the car only to find out it's a lemon." *Shacking Up* is the perfect how-to guide for helping women decide if, when, and how to move in with their boyfriends before marriage. With a sassy conversational style, the book presents advice gleaned from interviews with cohabitating couples, along with practical tips and quizzes. Covering everything from shared finances to legal considerations to the gravitation toward marriage, this is a fun approach to the serious concerns that face women as they contemplate romantic cohabitation.

Subjects: Cohabitation • Dating • Lifestyle • How-to

Now Try: While the Whitman sisters present cohabitation as a temporary (if possibly long-term) condition, leading to either marriage or a breakup, Dorian Solot and Marshall Miller consider those who intend to commit to one another without pursuing marriage in *Unmarried to Each Other: The Essential Guide to Living Together as an Unmarried Couple*. The book is an excellent guide for unmarried cohabitating couples seeking legal and social acceptance, whether they are heterosexual or nontraditional partners. See also *Money without Matrimony: The Unmarried Couple's Guide to Financial Security*, in which Sheryl Garrett and Debra A. Neiman help unmarried couples navigate the complex world of shared finances; this informative how-to guide covers topics such as child-raising, estate planning, and taxes for cohabitating partners.

Yalom, Marilyn

A History of the Wife. New York: HarperCollins, 2001. 441pp. ISBN 9780060193386.

Marilyn Yalom has a gift for presenting academic information in an engaging, compulsively readable style. Her scholarship is rigorous, but her inclusion of primary documents and cultural references, presented in accessible language, turns this social history into a fascinating narrative. Yalom's ambitious subject is the history of the wife in society, starting with wives in classical antiquity and continuing through the millennia to wives in the modern milieu. Changing perspectives on wives and marriage, including concepts of adultery, procreation, religion, and independence, are examined throughout history and across the globe. Fans of social history, religious history, and feminism will particularly enjoy this examination of the social contexts that defined and shaped women and wives throughout the ages.

Subjects: Marriage • Relationships • History • Social History • Women's History • History of Religion

Now Try: A natural companion to *A History of the Wife* is Stephanie Coontz's book *Marriage, a History: From Obedience to Intimacy, or How Love Conquered Marriage.* The focus here is not so much on the role of women as wives, but rather on the role of marriage in society. With insightful analysis, Coontz shows how the motivations for marriage—including money, power, children (and, recently, love)—have changed from ancient times to the present day. Compelling prose and an enjoyable writing style make this a fun and informative slice of social history.

Zackheim, Victoria, ed.

The Other Woman: Twenty-one Wives, Lovers, and Others Talk Openly about Sex, Deception, Love, and Betrayal. New York: Warner Books, 2007. 276pp. ISBN 9780446580229.

Twenty-one women from a variety of ages, backgrounds, and sexual orientations try to make sense of romantic betrayal in this painful, poignant, compassionate anthology of essays about a taboo topic: infidelity. With perspectives from both those who have been betrayed and those who have done the betraying, this remarkable anthology explores the feelings that go hand-in-hand with infidelity: pain, anguish, dark humor—even, occasionally, freedom. Uniformly excellent writing from such authors as Jane Smiley and Pam Houston make this a compelling, if sometimes heart-wrenching, collection of stories.

Subjects: Infidelity • Sexuality • Marriage • Relationships • Essays • Anthology • Collection

Now Try: For another collection of insightful musings on romance gone awry, turn to *The Honeymoon's Over: True Stories of Love, Marriage, and Divorce*, edited by Andrea Chapin and Sally Wofford-Girand. Not every essay focuses on infidelity—indeed, some contributors write about romantic success—but each is tinged with sadness and an acknowledgment of the difficulties of romance. Try also *Mr. Wrong: Real-Life Stories about the Men We Used to Love*, in which editor Harriet Brown collects essays about the one who—fortunately—got away. Some of the pieces are lighthearted and flippant, while others explore the despair and pain of ruined romance.

Queer Romantic Relationships

Women loving women provides the focus to titles in this section.

"Queer" was once a derogatory slur, and certainly can still be used as such. But the term has been reclaimed by sexual minorities to such an extent that one can now even pursue a degree in Queer Studies. For ease of speaking and writing, this is a huge relief; we can replace the cumbersome phrase "sexual minorities" and the alphabet-soup jumble "GLBTQ" with an efficient, catchall term for anyone who is not strictly heterosexual. Read below for titles about queer relationships of all stripes. And for more books about the queer experience, see the "Queer Identity" section in Chapter 1.

Elder, Lindsey, ed.

Early Embraces: True-Life Stories of Women Describing Their First Lesbian Experience. Los Angeles: Alyson, 1996. 190pp. ISBN 9781555833541.

In this lovely collection of essays, editor Lindsey Elder brings together women who recall their first same-sex encounters. Because the stories describe budding lesbian experiences, they are imbued with a sense of innocence and discovery that is so often lacking in romantic nonfiction. Tender, honest, and poignant, some of the stories are funny, some exhilarating, some bittersweet, but in all cases they speak to those special moments in lesbian women's lives when they first encountered the romantic love of another woman.

Subjects: Lesbian Sexuality • Queer Sexuality • Sexuality • Dating • Relationships • Essays • Anthology • Collection • Young Adult • Quick Read

Now Try: Editor Lindsey Elder knows a good thing when she sees it; continue with the essays of first lesbian encounters in *Early Embraces II* and *Early Embraces III*. Then, for a slightly different perspective, turn to Elder's compilation *Beginnings: Lesbians Talk about the First Time They Met Their Long-Term Partner*; this time the focus is not on first love but on first *lasting* love. And for a fictional treatment of a lesbian's coming out, try M. E. Kerr's lovely novel *Deliver Us from Evie*, about a courageous young woman in a small Midwestern town.

Larkin, Joan

A Woman Like That: Lesbian and Bisexual Writers Tell Their Coming Out Stories. New York: Avon Books, 1999. 326pp. ISBN 9780380976980.

An impressive range of emotions is reflected in this anthology of thirty-one essays by lesbian and bisexual women. From pride to humiliation, pleasure to sorrow, anxiety to liberation, the book explores the depth and scope of human feeling that attends the coming-out experience. For some, coming out happened as a sudden epiphany; for others it was a gradual process; but for all of the writers, coming out was a profound and significant step in their quest for sexual identity. With American writers from a variety of ages, races, and economic backgrounds, this collection is a compelling tribute to the social, romantic, and familial dynamics of coming out.

Subjects: Lesbian Sexuality • Bisexuality • Queer Sexuality • Essays • Anthology • Collection

Now Try: Read more about the coming-out experience in *Testimonies: Lesbian and Bisexual Coming-out Stories*, edited by Sarah Holmes and Jenn Tust. In these moving, passionate essays, more than twenty women writers from a variety of backgrounds share the hope, heartbreak, confusion, and joy of announcing their sexual identities to themselves and to the world. And those who enjoy reading about "first time" experiences might like the essays collected in *My Little Red Book*, edited by Rachel Kauder-Nalebuff. In this case, the "first time" refers to the onset of menstruation, with writers such as Meg Cabot, Joyce Maynard, and Gloria Steinem recalling their first periods.

Orndorff, Kata, ed.

Bi Lives: Bisexual Women Tell Their Stories. Tucson, AZ: See Sharp Press, 1999. 251pp. ISBN 9781884365096.

In *Bi Lives*, editor Orndorff collects eighteen interviews with eighteen bi-sexual women to create a remarkable, eye-opening book. Ranging in age from twenty-one to fifty-seven, the women come from diverse back-grounds, races, and classes. The women take a variety of approaches to re-lationships: some are single, some are monogamous, some are dating men, or women, or both. Their perspectives are varied, but no matter their particular point of view, in each case the women's insights shed new light on what it means to be a bisexual woman.

Subjects: Bisexuality • Queer Sexuality • Sexuality • Relationships

Now Try: Though published in 1991, *Bi Any Other Name: Bisexual People Speak Out* is still a relevant read today, and an excellent companion to *Bi Lives*. Ed-ited by Loraine Hutchins and Lani Kaahumanu, it collects stories of bisexual men and women into sections such as "Community" and "Politics," showcasing their thoughts and struggles as they seek to forge their identity in an unforgiving world. And for a look at bisexuality from a social sciences per-spective, try *A History of Bisexuality*, in which Steven Angelides take a scholarly approach to understanding the role of bisexuality within the larger picture of sexuality.

Sacks, Rhona

The Art of Meeting Women. A Guide for Gay Women: How to Meet the Women You Want to Meet. Brooklyn, NY: Slope Books, 1998 (2001). 192pp. ISBN 9780966069808.

It's not easy for women to meet women—but with this empowering how-to book, it gets a little bit easier. Practical advice on where to meet queer women, how to initiate and maintain contact, and how to sustain happy relationships make this a helpful guide for any lesbian or bisexual on the dating scene. But perhaps most valuable is the advice on how women can improve their outlooks so that all of the details fall into place; the two chapters on insecurity and self-esteem, in particular, will give women the boost of confidence they need to increase their chances of success and to weather rejection.

Subjects: Dating • Relationships • Lesbian Sexuality • Queer Sexuality • How-to • Quick Read

Now Try: Add a little humor to the quest for lesbian dating with *Is It a Date or Just Coffee?: The Gay Girl's Guide to Dating, Sex, and Romance*. With sass and wit, author Mo Brownsey's how-to guide covers dating, sex, relationships—even breakups—with chapters such as "Polyamory (Or, When One Is Not Enough)" and "Top Ten Things You Don't Want to Hear on a First Date." Bisexual women will also want to try *The Bisexual's Guide to the Universe: Quips, Tips, and Lists for Those Who Go Both Ways*, by Nicole Kristal and Mickey Skee. Light-hearted and irreverent, the book blends practical advice with quirky trivia as it explores bisexual dating, sex, and life-styles.

Stendhal, Renate

True Secrets of Lesbian Desire: Keeping Sex Alive in Long-Term Relationships. Berkeley, CA: North Atlantic Books, 2003. 199pp. ISBN 9781556434754.

"It's easy to say 'Couples need to communicate better!'" acknowledges relationship counselor Stendhal, but not so easy to do, especially when it comes to topics of sex and desire. Even long-term partners may be shy or embarrassed to broach the subject—but they more than anyone need to be able to speak freely: without good communication, these couples risk sexual stagnation. When long-term partners communicate openly, however, their sex lives becomes more meaningful and more satisfying than the sex lives of people in short-term relationships. Stendhal, herself a lesbian, teaches long-term lesbian couples how to communicate and helps them reignite their sexual passions. This is a thoughtful, sensitive how-to guide, written from an empowering feminist perspective.

> **Subjects:** Communication • Sexuality • Lesbian Sexuality • Queer Sexuality • Relationships • Feminism • How-to • Quick Read

> **Now Try:** Though written for heterosexual couples, *Confessions of a True Romantic: The Secrets of a Sizzling Relationship from America's Romance Coach* has solid advice and suggestions for improving communication that will appeal to fans of *True Secrets of Lesbian Desire*. Author Gregory J. P. Godek, a relationship counselor, includes checklists, exercises, and a "relationship report card" to help long-term couples strengthen their sexual, romantic, and emotional bonds.

Stevens, Tracey, and Katherine Wunder

How to Be a Happy Lesbian: A Coming Out Guide. Asheville, NC: Amazing Dreams, 2002. 188pp. ISBN 9780971962804.

Despite its subtitle, this useful little book is far more than just a coming-out guide. To be sure, there is plenty here for the woman who is coming out as a lesbian, with information on such topics as coming out to one's family and learning to cope with the outside world. But this is an excellent choice for lesbians, no matter how long they've been out; sections such as "Handy Items for Safer Sex," "Lesbian Fiction and Film," and "How to Find Other Lesbians with Similar Interests" make this a comprehensive resource on living a happy lesbian lifestyle, told in a fun, accessible, well-organized style.

> **Subjects:** Lesbian Sexuality • Queer Sexuality • Sexuality • Dating • Relationships • How-to • Quick Read

> **Now Try:** Another fun read about finding happiness as a lesbian is *So You Want to Be a Lesbian?: A Guide for Amateurs and Professionals*, by Liz Tracey and Sydney Pokorny. With quizzes, tips, and a wealth of resources, this is an excellent guide for women who want to embrace their lesbian identities. And those looking for a more detailed discussion of coming out should turn to *Outing Yourself: How to Come Out as Lesbian or Gay to Your Family, Friends, and Coworkers*, in which author Michelangelo Signorile offers guid-

ance to the lifelong process of coming out in section such as "Outing Yourself to Yourself," "Outing Yourself to Other Gay People," and "Coming Out Every Day."

Strock, Carren

Married Women Who Love Women. New York: Doubleday, 1998 (2008). 228pp. ISBN 9780385488259.

Twenty-five years into her marriage with a loving husband, author Strock realized that she was in love with her female best friend. In part, this book is her memoir of her dawning awareness of her sexual orientation and her struggle to understand her new identity within the context of her marriage—a marriage that, incidentally, is still going strong. But this book is also a study of the larger picture of women whose sexual orientations change after marriage. Based on Strock's interviews with more than one hundred married women who discovered that they loved other women, the book reveals the complexities of a complicated topic, showing that sexual orientation is rarely a simple thing.

Subjects: Lesbian Sexuality • Bisexuality • Queer Sexuality • Marriage • Relationships • Midlife • Memoir

Now Try: Though more academic in tone than Strock's book, readers wishing to know more about women who discovered their love for women after getting married will enjoy Karol L. Jensen's *Lesbian Epiphanies: Women Coming Out in Later Life.* Drawing on interviews with women who came out during their marriages, the book explores the social and psychological issues faced by married women whose sexual orientations have changed.

The Single Woman

Here you will find stories about women on their own, living their lives without a committed, lifelong partner.

"The Single Woman" section features two types of books. Some are by women who don't have stable romantic relationships and who are perfectly fine with that, thanks very much. The others are by women who would prefer to be involved with someone but are not. Ranging from humorous to resigned, joyful to irritated, there are a wide variety of perspectives represented in this group of independent women.

Browne, Jill Conner

The Sweet Potato Queens' Field Guide to Men: Every Man I Love Is Either Married, Gay, or Dead. New York: Three Rivers Press, 2004. 241pp. ISBN 9781400049684.

Ladies, if you haven't yet encountered the Sweet Potato Queens, you're in for a treat. Dressing themselves in lurid colors, too much makeup, and a jaw-dropping combination of feathers, rhinestones, and sequins, these southern belles pack attitude and sass into every one of their books. In their *Field Guide to Men,* designated author Browne brings the Queens' side-splitting southern humor and brassy style to the topic of the unfortunate species known as men. Wickedly funny stereotypes of spuds—er, men—such as the overweight "Pud Spud" and the elusive good catch, the "Stud Spud," detail the dating options and approaches available to single women. And if women, understandably, choose to forgo relationships with men, they can spend their time instead making the mouth-watering, artery-clogging recipes in the book.

> **Subjects:** Solitude • Dating • Recipes • Humor

> **Now Try:** Keep the laughs coming with the quintessentially Southern humor of *Somebody Is Going to Die if Lilly Beth Doesn't Catch That Bouquet: The Official Southern Ladies' Guide to Hosting the Perfect Wedding*, by Gayden Metcalfe and Charlotte Hays. Though the focus is on nuptials rather than singlehood, the irreverent attitude and sassy style will appeal to fans of the Sweet Potato Queens—and those who enjoyed the recipes in *Field Guide to Men* will find plenty of delectable food ideas, whether they're hosting a wedding or not.

DePaulo, Bella M.

Singled Out: How Singles Are Stereotyped, Stigmatized, and Ignored, and Still Live Happily Ever After. New York: St. Martin's Press, 2006. 325pp. ISBN 9780312340810.

Single women and men alike will rejoice in this unapologetic analysis of the single lifestyle. With insight and verve, author DePaulo systematically deconstructs the myths of singledom, including "You Are Miserable and Lonely and Your Life Is Tragic" and "Like a Child, You Are Self-Centered and Immature and Your Time Isn't Worth Anything Since You Have Nothing to Do But Play." Snarky, snappy, and refreshingly bitter, *Singled Out* is an academic but eminently readable analysis of the discrimination and stereotypes that face single people. Readers will find confirmation that marriage isn't all it's cracked up to be and that single people are perfectly capable of being happy.

> **Subjects:** Solitude • Mental Health

> **Now Try:** For a look at single life as it relates to women in particular, turn to Ellen Kay Trimberger's book *The New Single Woman*. Trimberger, a professor of Women's and Gender studies, studied twenty-seven single women and learned that they found happiness in life without having a romantic partner. Though the scholarly tone is not as catchy as the style in DePaulo's book, the solid evidence and intelligent analysis will give readers affirmation that solitude is a viable path to personal satisfaction.

Ganahl, Jane

Naked on the Page: The Misadventures of My Unmarried Midlife. New York: Viking, 2007. 310pp. ISBN 9780670038244.

"Where art thou, astrologically perfect, sexually compatible man of my future?" asks *San Francisco Chronicle* writer Ganahl near the beginning of her book. This rollicking memoir details Ganahl's attempts to answer that question over the course of her forty-ninth year. With lots of friends, a great daughter, and an exciting, lucrative career, she's ready to embrace the final missing ingredient in her life, romance—but what she ends up embracing is a series of awful matches. In some memoirists' hands this would be tragic, but Ganahl's knack for humor turns her luckless dating into laugh-out-loud comedy, while her reflections on middle age round out her engaging life story.

Subjects: Solitude • Midlife • Dating • America • Humor • Memoir

Now Try: For another upbeat, positive memoir of a single older woman, turn to Barbara Feldon's *Living Alone & Loving It: A Guide to Relishing the Solo Life*. After her divorce, Feldon felt depressed and scared of being single, but she eventually came to realize the pleasure and happiness of being an independent single woman. Her story is inspiring, and her practical advice, gleaned from her own experience, will help readers develop healthy attitudes and sensible strategies for reveling in solitude.

Ganahl, Jane, ed.

Single Woman of a Certain Age: 29 Women Writers on the Unmarried Midlife—Romantic Escapades, Heavy Petting, Empty Nests, Shifting Shapes, and Serene Independence. Maui, HI: Inner Ocean, 2005. 242pp. ISBN 9781930722583.

It's one thing to be single when you're eighteen, with the whole of your life on the horizon; it's another to be single in midlife, when the dating scene has changed. In this collection of twenty-nine witty, insightful essays, some women decide to skip the dating scene entirely, preferring to find happiness (and sexual satisfaction!) in the single life; other women gamely plunge into romantic forays, with the middle-age issues of grown children, menopause, and single incomes adding complexity to a dating landscape where all the rules seem to have changed. Generally positive in tone, though with a healthy dose of bitterness thrown in, these essays illuminate the good and the bad of being an independent woman at midlife.

Subjects: Solitude • Midlife • Dating • Lifestyle • Essays • Anthology • Collection

Now Try: *Flying Solo: Single Women in Midlife* is partly self-help book and partly a celebration of solitude in middle age. With chapters such as "Men: The Icing, Not the Cake" and "Midlife's Gifts to Single Women," authors Carol M. Anderson, Susan Stewart, and Sona Dimidjian act as cheerleaders for women who find themselves unmarried in their forties and beyond. Based on a study of eighty-seven unmarried, middle-aged women, this book affirms the joys of independent living and offers insightful, solid advice for making the most of solitude. And singles of any age who want to find sexual satisfaction will find ample instruction in Betty Dodson's *Sex for One: The Joy of Selfloving*.

Lewis, Karen Gail

With or Without a Man: Single Women Taking Control of Their Lives. Palo Alto, CA: Bull, 2001. 246pp. ISBN 9780923521509.

So you don't have a man in your life: maybe it's not your ideal situation, explains author Lewis, but that's no reason to be unhappy; you just have to approach things a little differently. In this affirming how-to guide, she offers candid advice on finding emotional and sexual fulfillment in solitude. Chapters such as "Hope for Horniness—Facing Your Sexual Feelings" and "Preparing for Old Age" give practical tips for coping with singleness, while abundant quizzes and questions for reflection will help women understand their own perspectives. Empowering and positive, the book will help women make positive changes to their thoughts and lifestyles, priming them to lead happier lives whether or not romance comes calling.

Subjects: Solitude • Sexual Health • Mental Health • Health • Lifestyle • How-to

Now Try: Both men and women will appreciate Judy Ford's book *The Art of Being Satisfied, Fulfilled and Independent*. Filled with practical advice and a no-nonsense attitude, Ford exhorts people to stop regretting the single life and to revel in the joys of independent living. Based on her own experiences with widowhood and divorce and on stories from other singles, Ford convincingly shows readers how to reenvision solitude as a desirable and beneficial lifestyle.

Mapes, Diane, ed.

Single State of the Union: Single Women Speak Out on Life, Love, and the Pursuit of Happiness. Emeryville, CA: Seal Press, 2007. 277pp. ISBN 9781580052023.

In this satisfying compilation of essays, a variety of women—some single and young, some widowed, some divorced, even some who have left singlehood behind—write about the single life in all its manifestations. Some of the essays look at fun topics, such as Rachel Kramer Bussel's "A Work in Progress: Inside the Mind (and Bed) of a Single Sex Columnist"; other contributions are more serious, as with single mother Margaret Smith's "Doctor, Donor, Desperado." Readers hungry for thoughtful insight into single womanhood will find a variety of perspectives and emotions, ranging from joyous to resigned, feisty to reflective.

Subjects: Solitude • Mental Health • Essays • Anthology • Collection

Now Try: For more insight into the variety of ways in which women approach singlehood, turn to *The Improvised Woman: Single Women Reinventing Single Life*. Author Marcelle Clements interviewed dozens of single women to discover their perspectives on solitude; their views on everything from children to sex to old age make this a thought-provoking examination of the many paths women take toward searching for—and usually achieving —happiness.

Marshall, Jennifer A.

Now and Not Yet: Making Sense of Single Life in the Twenty-First Century. Colorado Springs, CO: Multnomah Books, 2007. 198pp. ISBN 9781590526491.

It's a fact of life: some women in their twenties, thirties, and even beyond are single, despite their heartfelt desire to get married. Author Marshall, herself an unmarried woman, sympathizes with the frustration—but rather than wallow in self-pity, she advises her readers to make the most of the single life. Written from a Christian perspective and with a solid basis in scripture, she shows that solitude can serve God's plan. Though *Now and Not Yet* honestly addresses the difficulties of being single, including the necessity of delaying motherhood, the overall tone is positive in its advice to stop fretting over marriage and to start embracing life, and God's will, in the here and now.

Subjects: Solitude • Christianity • Religion • Spirituality • Twenty-first Century • Quick Read

Now Try: Like Marshall, author Lori Smith is a Christian woman who remains single, despite her desires to the contrary. In her book *The Single Truth: Challenging the Misconceptions of Singleness with God's Consuming Truth*, she discusses her journey toward acceptance, while frankly acknowledging the challenges of being alone. Her thoughtful study of scripture shows that, personal desires notwithstanding, the path to happiness is to accept God's plan for our lives. Seek further affirmation of the unintended single life in *Revelations of a Single Woman: Loving the Life I Didn't Expect*, by Connally Gilliam; this bright, candid, and moving memoir shows one woman's journey toward accepting God's will for her life.

Stewart, Jerusha

The Single Girl's Manifesta: Living in a Stupendously Superior Single State of Mind. Naperville, IL: Sourcebooks Casablanca, 2005. 260pp. ISBN 9781402205033.

> Single has never seemed so sweet. For all women who are romantically unattached, dating, or in a relationship—anyone who is not actually married—this is the perfect how-to guide for relishing the single lifestyle. With a hip, fresh tone, author Stewart guides readers through four steps of embracing your singledom, with chapters such as "Technically, You're Single If That's How You File Your Taxes, Right?" and "Individual Upkeep: Oil Changes, House Payments, and Dinner for One." Based on her interviews with satisfied singles, Stewart has crafted an edgy, empowering guide to the happy single life, featuring fun quizzes, practical advice, and useful resources.
>
> **Subjects:** Solitude • Dating • Mental Health • Lifestyle • Humor • How-to
>
> **Now Try:** For more quirky, vibrant advice on living up the single life, turn to Sue Ostler's *Get On with It!: How to be Sassy, Successful & Single*. Featuring anecdotes from savvy singles, tips and advice, and useful lists, this is every woman's guide to injecting zest into the single life. And for those who know that singledom is an enviable state of being, turn to *Even God Is Single (So Stop Giving Me a Hard Time)* by Karen Salmansohn. Funny and fresh, this indispensable handbook offers twenty-six retorts to the inevitable doubters who can't believe that single women can be happy women.

Motherhood

> Women as parents is the common theme of the titles in this section.

Motherhood, as Erma Bombeck wryly notes, is the second-oldest profession (see the first annotation in this section); it is a role that nearly all women adopt during their lifetimes, and as such, there is a wealth of literature written about it, and to choose from. Some of the books, such as *Breeder*, present the reflections of mothers; others, such as *The Hip Mama Survival Guide*, offer encouragement and advice to any woman who has ever wondered why her child didn't come with an instruction manual. Still other titles focus on the role of motherhood in society, rather than on the memoirs or experiences of individual women; Susan Maushart's book *The Mask of Motherhood*, for instance, asks hard questions about the realities faced by modern mothers in America. Readers may also wish to peruse the "Working Mothers" section of Chapter 8, "Women and Society," featuring books about the interplay between motherhood and career.

Bombeck, Erma

Motherhood: The Second Oldest Profession. New York: McGraw-Hill, 1983. 177pp. ISBN 9780070064546.

> Though written in the early 1980s, *Motherhood* is still as funny today as it ever was. As in all of her books, humor columnist Erma Bombeck expertly blends comedy and poignancy in *Motherhood*, giving zest to the experiences of everyday life. A mother of three and a prolific writer, Bombeck has a wealth of background to draw on ("I once spent more time writing a note of instructions to a babysitter than I did on my first book"). With humor that is gentle but not bland, universal but not generic, this is a timeless read, perfect for anyone who wants a laugh about the trials of motherhood.
>
> > **Subjects:** Mothers • Children • Humor • America • Memoir • Quick Read
> >
> > **Now Try:** Like Bombeck, Elizabeth Soutter Schwarzer knows that motherhood must be appreciated with a healthy dose of humor. In *Motherhood Is Not for Wimps: No Answers, Just Stories*, Schwarzer delivers short essays (such as "Tutus, Boogers, & Quesadillas: A Day in the Life") that will leave readers rolling with laughter. But the book is not just about comedy; occasionally tender and poignant, the story is both a humorous look at raising children and a moving tribute to the sheer joy of motherhood.

Buchanan, Andrea J., ed.

It's a Boy: Women Writers on Raising Sons. Emeryville, CA: Seal Press, 2005. 251pp. ISBN 9781580051453.

> In this tender collection of essays, thirty women share their reflections on raising sons. A stellar collection of authors, including such luminaries as Jodi Picoult and Caroline Leavitt, explore the joys and trials unique to mothering boys. Covering topics such as masculinity, circumcision, bullying, and wishing for a daughter but getting a boy instead, the anthology presents stories that represent a wide emotional range, from heartwarming to nerve-wracking, humorous to heartbreaking. With compelling stories and impressive insight, the contributors show that mothering a son is a challenging and rewarding experience, markedly different from mothering a daughter.
>
> > **Subjects:** Mothers • Sons • Children • Gender • Essays • Anthology • Collection
> >
> > **Now Try:** For another high-quality collection of women's thoughts on mothering sons, turn to *Between Mothers and Sons: Women Writers Talk about Having Sons and Raising Men*, edited by Patricia Stevens. As in *It's a Boy*, the contributors contemplate the difficulties of raising sons and celebrate the unique bond that women and their sons share. Some of the essays are light and humorous, while others will move the reader with their profoundly touching stories. Then try Ann F. Caron's thoughtful book *Strong Mothers, Strong Sons: Raising the Next Generation of Men*, filled with practical advice on raising sons.

Buchanan, Andrea J., ed.

It's a Girl: Women Writers on Raising Daughters. Emeryville, CA: Seal Press, 2006. 247pp. ISBN 9781580051477.

> Following her collection *It's a Boy* (see previous annotation), editor Buchanan turns to the other side of motherhood with this anthology of essays about raising girls. Featuring writing by such authors as Jacquelyn Mitchard and Joyce Maynard, these stories reveal the breadth of experiences involved in having

daughters. Themes of gender and femininity recur throughout, as the mothers reflect on societal norms (the color pink seems inescapable) and the desire to raise strong daughters (should we teach them to be feminists?). Some of the essays are light and funny, while others—such as the story of confronting a daughter's eating disorder—will leave the reader thinking.

> **Subjects:** Mothers • Daughters • Children • Gender • Essays • Anthology • Collection
>
> **Now Try:** Now put the mother–daughter relationship into historical context with *Mothers and Daughters in the Twentieth Century: A Literary Anthology*, edited by Heather Von Prondzynski. This vibrant collection of essays, poems, and fiction stories showcases a dazzling roster of famous women writers across the globe, including Margaret Atwood, Jean Rhys, and Amy Tan. Gain insight into the complicated bond between mothers and daughters with perspectives that cover a range of emotions, cultural backgrounds, and time periods.

Figes, Kate, and Jean Zimmerman

Life after Birth: What Even Your Friends Won't Tell You about Motherhood. New York: St. Martin's Press, 2001. 263pp. ISBN 9780312261924.

Upon the birth of a child, the societal expectation is that the new mother will be overjoyed. Indeed, author Figes was ecstatic about becoming a new mother—but, as with so many other women, the ecstasy was tempered by a host of negative feelings. Drawing on her own experiences and on research and interviews, Figes examines the scope of emotions that mothers face during pregnancy, birth, and early motherhood. Her compassionate treatment of such taboo topics as postpartum depression and overwhelming exhaustion legitimize the unpleasant aspects of motherhood that many women are ashamed to admit. Readable and informative, *Life after Birth* is an excellent resource for new mothers as they face changes in their health and relationships.

> **Subjects:** Mothers • Birth • Pregnancy • Mental Health • Sexual Health • Health • Romantic Relationships • Friendships • Relationships
>
> **Now Try:** Women bewildered by the wild range of emotions brought on by new motherhood will find affirmation in Nina Barrett's *I Wish Someone Had Told Me: A Realistic Guide to Early Motherhood*. Drawing on interviews with women who have struggled to adjust to motherhood, the book offers support and succor for this emotional time; sympathetic and nonjudgmental in tone, the book relieves the pressure of achieving the impossible societal ideals of new motherhood.

Gore, Ariel

The Hip Mama Survival Guide. New York: Hyperion, 1998. 270pp. ISBN 9780786882328.

Gore, editor of the magazine *Hip Mama*, delivers a refreshingly candid how-to guide for motherhood. This is the manual that covers it all, from preconception to birthing (see Chapter 2, "Childbirth Sucks") to raising children in a world where any number of things can go wrong. Sections such as "You Can Nurse, Even after a Nipple Piercing" will speak to the target audience of Generation X mothers, while more serious sections, such as "Avoiding Evil Judges and Hard-Ass Attorneys" address ways to cope if the parents split up. Funny, informative, and fun, this is an empowering Third-Wave feminist approach to motherhood.

> **Subjects:** Mothers • Children • Pregnancy • Birth • Feminism • How-to

> **Now Try:** Continue with the semi-sequel to *The Hip Mama Survival Guide,* Gore's memoir *The Mother Trip: Hip Mama's Guide to Staying Sane in the Chaos of Motherhood*. Though not a guide in the step-by-step sense, the book offers a wonderful model of modern motherhood; women seeking inspiration will find much to aspire to in Gore's experiences. Her feminist musings on motherhood and society, along with her frank recounting of her own triumphs and missteps in being a parent, make for a powerful, candid tribute to motherhood in today's world.

Gore, Ariel, and Bee Lavender, eds.

Breeder: Real-Life Stories from the New Generation of Mothers. Seattle: Seal Press, 2001. 268pp. ISBN 9781580050517.

Gore and Lavender, editors of the magazine *Hip Mama*, bring together stories that give a new spin on motherhood. Edgy, fresh, even shocking, the writers in this collection speak from the uncharted territory of Generation X motherhood. A variety of women—single mothers, lesbian mothers, teenage mothers—talk about everything from becoming a parent (through natural birth, assisted reproductive technologies, or adoption) to providing for their children (yes, stripping is a legitimate career choice) to the anxiety and fear that overwhelm mothers when their children are sick. For every young mother who has worried that she doesn't fit the norm, this collection proudly shows that there *is* no norm when it comes to modern motherhood.

> **Subjects:** Mothers • Children • Class • Essays • Anthology • Collection

> **Now Try:** Hear more voices from the new breed of mothers in *Mothers Who Think: Tales of Real-life Parenthood*, edited by Camille Peri and Kate Moses. As in *Breeder*, this collection showcases a variety of nontraditional approaches to motherhood, with essays that range from quirky to hilarious to deeply profound. Then try the memoir *The Big Rumpus: A Mother's Tale from the Trenches*, in which Ayun Halliday encapsulates the essence of today's hip mama. Zany, distracted, and devoted to her hellions—er, children—Halliday perfectly captures the craziness and the joy of raising kids in a frenetic urban setting.

Maushart, Susan

The Mask of Motherhood: How Becoming a Mother Changes Everything and Why We Pretend It Doesn't. New York: New Press, 1999. 266pp. ISBN 9781565844834.

In today's society, explains author Maushart, the concept of motherhood is couched in myths that are "not simply inaccurate, or ill-informed, but downright disabling. . . . Is it any wonder that the transition to motherhood among American women is increasingly associated with the onset of a full-scale identity crisis?" To counter the abundance of misinformation plaguing mothers, Maushart eloquently discusses motherhood as it really is, uncovering the sometimes dismal realities of pregnancy, breastfeeding, career/life juggling, and other topics that can cause women to feel guilt. *The Mask of Motherhood* is by no means a tirade against child-raising; rather it is an honest examination of the struggles of motherhood, an affirmation for women who have discovered the emotional toll that motherhood brings.

Subjects: Mothers • Mental Health

Now Try: Like Maushart, veteran social science writer Naomi Wolf understands that motherhood brings emotional difficulties right along with the emotional highs. In *Misconceptions: Truth, Lies, and the Unexpected on the Journey to Motherhood*, she turns her engaging prose to the unpleasant side of motherhood. Thought-provoking and intelligently written, *Misconceptions* exposes both the external problems new mothers face, such as the difficulty of getting good information when trying to find doctors, and the internal turmoil, including the pain of separation when mothers return to work.

Newman, Catherine

Waiting for Birdy: A Year of Frantic Tedium, Neurotic Angst, and the Wild Magic of Growing a Family. New York: Penguin Books, 2005. 261pp. ISBN 9780143034773.

When her first child is two-and-a-half years old, Catherine Newman becomes pregnant with her second child. This situation is not exactly unprecedented in the history of humankind, and yet Newman manages to tell the story of her second pregnancy in a way that is fresh and magical. Journey through the joys, anxieties, and anticipation of pregnancy with the mother, father, and brother-to-be as they anticipate, and finally meet, Birdy. This quirky humor on every page ("I didn't understand that having a baby would be like falling in love, but like falling in love on a bad acid trip") blends with the tender warmth of maternal love in this unexpectedly compelling memoir.

Subjects: Pregnancy • Birth • Mothers • Children • Humor • Memoir

Now Try: With the abundance of parenting memoirs available, many come across as banal or derivative—but the uber-talented writer Anne Lamott, like Newman, achieves excellence in her book *Operating Instructions: A Journal of My Son's First Year*. Beginning with her unexpected pregnancy and covering her first year of motherhood, Lamott infuses humor and grace into her story of becoming a single mother in her mid-thirties. Themes of religion, friendship, life—even death, when a friend is diagnosed with a terminal illness—make for a rich tapestry as Lamott embraces her son's first year.

Spencer, Paula

Momfidence!: An Oreo Never Killed Anybody and Other Secrets of Happier Parenting. New York: Three Rivers Press, 2006. 272pp. ISBN 978030-7337429.

Given the myriad of signals about how to raise children, how is a mother supposed to keep up with it all? She isn't, explains author Spencer, the columnist behind the "Momfidence" column in *Woman's Day*. There's no way mothers can do it all, and more important, there's no need to. With her sensible advice and reassuring tone, Spencer puts the pressures of modern motherhood into perspective, showing that it's okay to err occasionally and that women don't need to treat motherhood as a competitive sport. This is a breath of fresh air, a welcome antidote to the unnecessary guilt that women feel if they realize that they aren't the perfect mother—because, frankly, no one is.

Subjects: Mothers • Children • Mental Health • How-to

Now Try: Looking for more reassurance that you don't have to be the perfect mother? Look no further than *The Three-Martini Playdate: A Practical Guide to Happy Parenting*. With humor and common sense, Christie Mellor uses chapters such as "Child Labor: Not Just for the Third World!" and "'Children's Music': Why?" to put modern parenting into wickedly funny perspective. For a more serious approach to maintaining mental health as a mother, try *Even June Cleaver Would Forget the Juice Box: Cut Yourself Some Slack (and Still Raise Great Kids) in the Age of Extreme Parenting*. In this how-to guide, author Ann Dunnewold shows that perfect parenting is an unhealthy and unrealistic ideal, while offering positive, concrete steps for readers to improve their emotions and their outlook.

Walker, Rebecca

Baby Love: Choosing Motherhood after a Lifetime of Ambivalence. New York: Riverhead Books, 2007. 210pp. ISBN 9781594489433.

How does a bisexual, biracial, famous Third-Wave feminist decide to become a mother? It is no easy thing. Acutely aware of society's conflicting messages about career and identity versus motherhood, Walker struggled with the choice to reproduce before conceiving a child with her male partner. On one level, this is a memoir of Walker's personal journey through pregnancy and motherhood, including her tumultuous relationship with her own mother, Alice Walker; on another, it is a reflection on the larger societal issues of motherhood and all it entails, including topics such as health care and reproductive options. The book's lyrical prose and wrenching honesty illuminate the complicated, conflicting nature of motherhood in a way that will leave readers thinking.

Subjects: Pregnancy • Birth • Mothers • Children • Feminism • America • Memoir

Now Try: Learn more about Rebecca Walker in her earlier book *Black, White and Jewish: Autobiography of a Shifting Self*. In this memoir of shaping an identity as a child, teen, and young woman, discover the racial, religious, and feminist themes that converged to create the multifaceted woman who ultimately chose motherhood in *Baby Love*. This is an especially good choice for those readers who want more information about the difficult relationship with her mother that recurs in *Baby Love*; with its focus on Walker's home life in her younger years, *Black, White and Jewish* fleshes out both the writer and her famous mother.

Warner, Judith

Perfect Madness: Motherhood in the Age of Anxiety. New York: Riverhead Books, 2005. 327pp. ISBN 9781573223041.

Modern motherhood, writes journalist Warner, carries with it "this feeling—this widespread, choking cocktail of guilt and anxiety and resentment and regret . . . [It is] poisoning motherhood for American women today." *Perfect Madness* is an examination of this poison, a beautifully written but disturbing examination of the societal pressures that mothers today face. Difficult topics, from the trend for mothers to regiment their children's lives to the insufficient support for motherhood in current American policy, will provide readers with a thought-provoking, unsettling insight into motherhood as it is practiced today.

Subjects: Mothers • Mental Health • Feminism

Now Try: Less weighty in approach but every bit as thoughtful as *Perfect Madness* is *The Mommy Myth: The Idealization of Motherhood and How It Has Undermined All Women*. Authors Susan J. Douglas and Meredith W. Michaels mercilessly examine the image of the mother in thirty years' worth of popular media. Snarky but sensible, bitter but insightful, *The Mommy Myth* is a scathingly honest critique of motherhood as it appears in print, television, radio, and film.

Wilder-Taylor, Stefanie

Sippy Cups Are Not for Chardonnay, and Other Things I Had to Learn as a New Mom. New York: Simon Spotlight Entertainment, 2006. 218pp. ISBN 9781416-915065.

Forget your notions of motherhood as tender, warm, and gentle. In this wild ride of a memoir, Wilder-Taylor replaces saccharine sentiment with scathingly funny commentary. With essays short enough to keep the attention of distracted new mothers, the author reflects on being pregnant, trying to nurse, and discovering the joys of motherhood through the first part of her daughter's life. Irreverent humor, plentiful cursing, and a keen appreciation for the absurd make this a hysterically funny examination of one woman's successes and blunders, the perfect antidote for books that pressure women to be the perfect mother.

> **Subjects:** Mothers • Children • Pregnancy • Birth • Humor • America • Memoir • Essays • Collection

> **Now Try:** Wilder-Taylor isn't the only new mother who understands the comedy of child-raising. In her book *Smotherhood: Wickedly Funny Confessions from the Early Years*, Amanda Lamb applies her biting sense of humor to the story of her struggles to balance parenthood, career, marriage, and sanity. Raucous and witty, this hilarious memoir pokes fun at the absurdities of motherhood while affirming the joys that children bring.

Wolk, Claudine

It Gets Easier! And Other Lies We Tell New Mothers. New Buck Press, 2008. 200pp. ISBN 9780979767647.

"I could not believe this was motherhood," Wolk realized, shortly after the birth of her son, "misery and crying and being enslaved to a demanding infant." Years later, with the benefit of experience on her side, she decided to commit the lessons she learned to paper. The result is *It Gets Easier!*, a breezy how-to guide brimming with information gleaned from Wolk's own experiences, as well as from her interviews with other successful mothers. Chatty, quirky, and funny, the book is filled with sensible advice and practical tips to help women navigate pregnancy, childbirth, and early motherhood.

> **Subjects:** Motherhood • Humor • How-to • Quick Read

> **Now Try:** If *It Gets Easier!* left you wiping away tears from laughing so hard, don't miss the humor in *I Was a Really Good Mom before I Had Kids: Reinventing Modern Motherhood*. Based on their interviews with more than one hundred mothers, authors Trisha Ashworth and Amy Nobile present tips on keeping sane during motherhood, with chapters such as "Oh My God, I Don't Want to Color Right Now." Then, for a memoir that speaks to the bewilderment of new motherhood, turn to Andrea J. Buchanan's *Mother Shock: Loving Every (Other) Minute of It*. Honest and compelling, Buchanan's triumphs and stumbles as she negotiates the uncharted territory of child-raising will resonate with women who felt overwhelmed during early motherhood.

Fertility and Adoption

Biological, emotional, and social issues surrounding women's ability to conceive and bear children provide the focus for some of the titles in this section, while the social and emotional issues surrounding adoption provide focus for others.

In the "Fertility and Adoption" section, you'll discover the voices of women who have struggled with infertility, who have chosen to adopt, or both; and you'll hear from women who have themselves given up children for adoption. You'll also find how-to guides to help women overcome infertility and to steer would-be mothers through the process of adopting.

Clunis, D. Merilee, and G. Dorsey Green

The Lesbian Parenting Book: A Guide to Creating Families and Raising Children. Seattle, WA: Seal Press, 1995 (2004). 378pp. ISBN 9781878067685.

As psychologists and lesbians with families of their own, Clunis and Green are excellent guides on this comprehensive tour of lesbian parenting. No stage is left uncovered: they take readers from the initial steps in getting a baby (Should you adopt? Foster a child? Find a way to conceive?) through all the stages of child development, with chapters such as "On the Road to Adulthood: Ten to Fourteen Years" offering detailed information on each phase of growth. With its mix of excellent parenting advice and suggestions for dealing with the unique challenges of being a lesbian mother, the book will help women raise happy, healthy children in a world that still marginalizes lesbian mothers and their children.

Subjects: Mothers • Children • Lesbian Sexuality • Fertility • Adoption • How-to

Now Try: Whether lesbian or not, single women who are considering adoption as a route to motherhood should try Lee Varon's *On Your Own: The Complete Guide to Adopting as a Single Parent*. Bolstered with practical advice and thought-provoking exercises, this is a comprehensive guide to deciding whether to adopt and how to go about it; even lesbian women who have committed partners will find the book's focus on nontraditional adoptions to be useful. For a lighter read, try *Love Makes a Family: Portraits of Lesbian, Gay, Bisexual, and Transgender Parents and Their Families*, by Gigi Kaeser and Peggy Gillespie. Though not a how-to guide, fans of *The Lesbian Parenting Book* will find affirmation for nontraditional families in the gorgeous photos and moving interviews in this celebratory collection of photo-essays.

Greene, Melissa Fay

There Is No Me without You: One Woman's Odyssey to Rescue Her Country's Children. New York: Bloomsbury (USA), 2007. 472pp. ISBN 9781596912939.

Though still grieving from the deaths of her husband and daughter, Haregewoin Teferra agreed to take in a child who had been orphaned by AIDS. Then she took in another, and another—and soon, one woman's home in Ethiopia had transformed into an orphanage for children whose families had been destroyed by AIDS. With beautiful, captivating prose, author Greene tells the story of Teferra's mission to rescue as many children as possible, deftly interweaving the social and political threads of AIDS into the narrative. This profoundly moving story of courage and activism is also the story of Greene herself, the adoptive mother of two children from Teferra's orphanage.

Subjects: Teferra, Haregewoin • Adoption • Children • AIDS • Activism • Labor • Health • Ethiopia • Africa • Global Perspectives • Biography • Memoir

Now Try: Turn now to the painful but inspiring story of AIDS orphan Kevin Sumba. While on a journey to Africa to document HIV and AIDS, filmmaker Miles Roston met Sumba, a child living alone in the wake of his parents' deaths. Five years later, Roston searched out the teenaged Sumba again, and this time they flew back to the United States to try to find answers to AIDS from people in power. Read Roston's riveting account of Sumba's story and their quest to make a difference *Taking Away the Distance: A Young Orphan's Journey and the AIDS Epidemic in Africa.*

Hall, Meredith

Without a Map: A Memoir. Boston: Beacon Press, 2007. 221pp. ISBN 978080-7072738.

It is 1965. Sixteen-year-old Meredy Hall falls for a boy and, being sexually naïve, she unwittingly conceives a child. She is kicked out of high school, kicked out of her mother's home, sent to live with her father, and forced to give up her baby. The loss casts a shadow on her life; as she grows into adulthood, she shuns the familiar and escapes overseas, moving in loneliness from one country to another. Much later, having returned to America, she receives a phone call out of the blue: her son wants to make contact. Lyrically written, this is a profoundly moving story of the pain of forced adoption and the power and healing of reconciliation.

Subjects: Adoption • Mothers • Solitude • America • Memoir

Now Try: Meredy Hall was but one victim of societal ostracism and forced adoption in the mid-twentieth century. Learn about the one and a half million girls whose babies were taken from them in *The Girls Who Went Away: The Hidden History of Women Who Surrendered Children for Adoption in the Decades before Roe v. Wade.* Author Ann Fessler interviewed more than a hundred women who were forced to surrender their children in the 1950s, '60s, and '70s; their painful stories paint a heartbreaking portrait in this disturbing oral history.

Margolis, Cindy, Kathy Kanable, and Snunit Ben-Ozer

Having a Baby—When the Old-fashioned Way Isn't Working: Hope and Help for Everyone Facing Infertility. New York: Penguin Group, 2008. 224pp. ISBN 9780399533853.

Perhaps you already knew Cindy Margolis as a celebrity model. Meet her again in her new role, as spokeswoman for Resolve: The National Infertility Association, and as author of this guidebook for any woman who is struggling to conceive a child. In part, this is the story of Margolis herself, who conquered her infertility with in vitro fertilization. But the true strength of the book is in the wealth of information and support it offers to infertile women; covering everything from medical technologies to financial costs to adoption, this is a comprehensive guidebook for women and couples who want to become parents, delivered with compassion and honesty.

Subjects: Fertility • Adoption • Health • Mothers • Children • Memoir • How-to

Now Try: Pair *Having a Baby* with Toni Weschler's remarkable *Taking Charge of Your Fertility: The Definitive Guide to Natural Birth Control, Pregnancy Achievement, and Reproductive Health*. The high-quality information will help women better understand their bodies and recognize signs of fertility in their menstrual cycles; a charting system will help women see the fertility patterns that can help lead to conception. Then explore the medical technologies of conception with *What to Do When You Can't Get Pregnant: The Complete Guide to All the Technologies for Couples Facing Fertility Problems*. Using straightforward, accessible language, authors Daniel A. Potter and Jennifer S. Hanin first explain the medical problems in both women and men that can prevent them from conceiving; then they demystify the variety of medical options for overcoming infertility.

Newman, Janis Cooke

The Russian Word for Snow: A True Story of Adoption. New York: St. Martin's Press, 2001. 232pp. ISBN 9780312252144.

Various attempts to prime her body for conception weren't working, and Janis Newman was already in her forties. Pregnancy seemed less and less likely—and then she and her husband saw video footage of a baby Russian boy who captured their hearts. This is the story of their six-month ordeal to adopt Alex as they struggle with bureaucrats, interminable paperwork, and the cultural disadvantages of being foreigners in Russia. Compellingly written, this memoir captures the sorrow of infertility, the anxiety of international adoption, and the ultimate joy of bringing home a child to love.

Subjects: Adoption • Mothers • Children • Russia • Memoir

Now Try: A natural companion to *The Russian Word for Snow* is Margaret L. Schwartz's book *The Pumpkin Patch: A Single Woman's International Adoption Journey*. In relating her quest to adopt from Ukraine, Schwartz's memoir covers many of the same struggles of international adoption that Newman and her husband faced—but in this case, the story comes from the perspective of a single mother, and she adopts not one child, but two.

Orenstein, Peggy

Waiting for Daisy: A Tale of Two Continents, Three Religions, Five Infertility Doctors, an Oscar, an Atomic Bomb, a Romantic Night, and One Woman's Quest to Become a Mother. New York: Bloomsbury, 2007. 228pp. ISBN 9781596910171.

Critically acclaimed, best-selling feminist writer Orenstein may already be familiar to readers from her writing in the *New York Times Magazine* and her illuminating study *Schoolgirls: Young Women, Self-Esteem and the Confidence Gap*. In *Waiting for Daisy*, she turns her remarkable gift for prose to a deeply personal topic, her battle with—and eventual victory over—infertility. Grounded in her feminist perspective and related in her refreshing, witty style, Orenstein shares her transformation from a deliberately childless career woman to a woman stubbornly determined to become a mother, despite being in her mid-thirties and having only one ovary. Readers will agonize with Orenstein through her years of difficult infertility treatments and heartbreaking miscarriages; then they will rejoice as Orenstein finally conceives and carries Daisy to term.

Subjects: Fertility • Mothers • Children • Feminism • Humor • America • Memoir

Now Try: The doctors told Julia Indichova that it was medically impossible for her to conceive a child—but like Orenstein, she was absolutely dogged in her determination to beat the odds. *Inconceivable: A Woman's Triumph over Despair and Statistics* is the memoir of Indichova's battle with infertility and her triumphant pregnancy;

though her approach to infertility is different from Orenstein's, with a focus on natural rather than technological treatments, her engaging prose and her remarkable courage will resonate with fans of *Waiting for Daisy*.

Pregnancy, Childbirth, and Nursing

Titles in this section cover issues surrounding conception and birth.

In the "Pregnancy, Childbirth, and Nursing" section, you'll learn how to conceive children, even when the, er, traditional approach isn't an option; and you'll learn how to get through pregnancy and childbirth, through both the examples related by women's memoirs and the advice offered in how-to guides.

Askowitz, Andrea

My Miserable, Lonely, Lesbian Pregnancy. San Francisco, CA: Cleis Press, 2008. 248pp. ISBN 9781573443159.

Most folks get pregnant the old-fashioned way, but that plan presented a hitch for Andrea Askowitz; being a lesbian is not generally conducive for introducing sperm to egg. But she wanted a baby, and she finally conceived, thanks to a fertility donor—and immediately she found herself in pregnancy hell. This is the darkly funny memoir of nine months of hormone swings, hideous underwear, and bodily aches and pains, told in Askowitz's acerbic, acidic tone. She is grouchy, she is bitchy, she is whiny, and she is laugh-out-loud funny because of it. Read this for a hilarious accounting of one lesbian's foray into nine cranky months of childbearing.

> **Subjects:** Pregnancy • Fertility • Mothers • Relationships • Lesbian Sexuality • America • Humor • Memoir
>
> **Now Try:** Now read about gay pregnancy from the male side of things in *The Kid: What Happened after My Boyfriend and I Decided to Go Get Pregnant: An Adoption Story*. Neither Dan Savage nor his partner Terry could bear a child (obviously), so instead the would-be parents chose to adopt. Savage is hysterically funny in this memoir, arguably even funnier than in his syndicated sex advice column "Savage Love." Askowitz's fans will love his droll sense of humor and the male perspective on getting with child in a nontraditional way.

Block, Jennifer

Pushed: The Painful Truth about Childbirth and Modern Maternity Care. Cambridge, MA: Da Capo Lifelong, 2007. 316pp. ISBN 9780738210735.

More than ever before, the process of childbirth in the United States is characterized by rote procedural medical practices. The majority of births are induced or hastened with drugs, and almost a third of deliveries occur by cesarean. In *Pushed*, feminist writer Block, an editor of the seminal women's health book *Our Bodies, Ourselves*, questions whether the widespread heavy-handedness of invasive medicine in labor is truly necessary. While recognizing that many births do require serious medical intervention, Block decries the trend toward routine

C-sections and labor-inducing drugs, arguing instead for a return to natural vaginal birth as the preferred norm.

Subjects: Birth • Pregnancy • Health • Health Care • Feminism

Now Try: Perinatologist Marsden Wagner, for fifteen years the director of Women's and Children Health for the World Health Organization, agrees with Block that American mothers are too often subjected to unnecessary medical intervention. In *Born in the USA: How a Broken Maternity System Must Be Fixed to Put Women and Children First*, Wagner exposes how the political and financial interests of medical practitioners and insurance companies have replaced the interests of mothers. With clear, passionate writing, he persuasively argues for options that will permit and encourage women to be able to choose natural birth.

Cohen, Marisa

Deliver This!: Make the Childbirth Choice That's Right for You—No Matter What Everyone Else Thinks. Emeryville, CA: Seal Press, 2006. 279pp. ISBN 9781580051538.

When it comes to delivering babies, mothers-to-be face a dizzying number of options—and no matter what they pick, somebody is going to disapprove. If women opt for a cesarean section with plenty of painkillers, they'll be criticized for shirking on the "real" experience of labor; if they hire a doula to help with home delivery, they'll be criticized for risking the baby's health in the event of an emergency. Enough with the judgments, says Marisa Cohen; women have the right to choose whichever delivery style they want—and in *Deliver This!*, she offers the information they need to make the best choice. Bolstered by the stories of women who have chosen a variety of ways to bring their babies into the world, this engaging book sheds light on labor choices that are mainstream, alternative, and a bit of both.

Subjects: Birth • Pregnancy • Health • Health Care • How-to

Now Try: For a more in-depth examination of the medical procedures of birth, turn to *The Thinking Woman's Guide to a Better Birth*. Unlike Cohen, Henci Goer freely criticizes the overuse of medical processes such as the cesarean section and the episiotomy. Fans of *Deliver This!* who want more details about their birth options, however, will appreciate the voluminous research and remarkable insight in this survey of hospital delivery options.

Davis, Elizabeth

Heart and Hands: A Midwife's Guide to Pregnancy & Birth. Berkeley, CA: Celestial Arts, 1987 (2004). 229pp. ISBN 9780890874943.

A perennial favorite among midwifery books is *Heart and Hands: A Midwife's Guide to Pregnancy & Birth*. In this richly informative guide, midwife author Elizabeth Davis covers the entire birthing experience, from prenatal care to labor to postpartum care. Photographs, drawings, and stories of mothers supplement the detailed information, presented in clear, accessible prose. The book is targeted toward midwives, but expectant mothers can read it to learn about their own bodies and pregnancies; furthermore, each chapter includes a "For Parents" section, written specifically to help expectant mothers and fathers understand natural birthing.

Subjects: Birth • Pregnancy • Health • Health Care • Mothers • Labor • How-to

Now Try: Readers interested in natural birthing but nervous about trying it themselves should turn to *Childbirth without Fear: The Principles and Practice of Natural Childbirth*, by Grantly Dick-Read. Though first published in 1959, the principles in this frequently updated guide are still relevant today. The book presents an honest discussion of the pain, tension, and fear of childbirth, while offering practical advice for reducing the pain of delivery, even for mothers who forgo pain medication during labor.

Gaskin, Ina May

Ina May's Guide to Childbirth. New York: Bantam Books, 2003. 348pp. ISBN 9780553381153.

Gaskin, president of the Midwives Alliance of North America, presents readers with a remarkable book about natural birth. In part this is a how-to guide, a detailed examination presented in ordinary language that explains the physical birthing process; expectant mothers will especially appreciate the ideas for reducing and controlling pain during delivery. But this is not just a medical text; the guide uses anecdotes and personal stories to give voice to women who have delivered birth naturally, making the book an emotional exploration of childbirth as well as a practical discussion of labor.

Subjects: Birth • Pregnancy • Health • Health Care • Mothers • How-to

Now Try: Now get an ever deeper understanding of the midwife experience with Gaskin's book *Spiritual Midwifery*. An enduring classic among books on natural birth, this how-to guide demystifies the birthing process for expectant mothers and midwives alike, with an emphasis on the spiritual essence of labor. Fans of *Spiritual Midwifery* will find more stories of mothers and their natural births to supplement the detailed health information.

Giles, Fiona

Fresh Milk: The Secret Life of Breasts. New York: Simon & Schuster, 2003. 267pp. ISBN 9780743211475.

There is no other book quite like *Fresh Milk*. The subject, breast-feeding, is a topic with which many women will be familiar—at least until they discover Giles's fascinating book, which examines breast-feeding in fascinating new ways. With her frank observations and engaging prose, Giles draws on her own experience and a questionnaire to look at breast-feeding in modern society, tackling topics that are weird (nursing pornography), sensitive (the sexual sensations of nursing), even bizarre (there's a recipe for ice cream made from breast milk). Essays and fictionalized accounts from other writers bolster Giles's exploration of a deeply personal topic in the context of society at large.

Subjects: Breast-feeding • Essays

Now Try: Read more about nursing in *The Breastfeeding Cafe: Mothers Share the Joys, Challenges, and Secrets of Nursing*, a collection of thought-provoking essays from a variety of women. Editor Barbara L. Behrmann arranges the contributions thematically to showcase the breadth of emotional experiences inherent to breast-feeding, ranging from intimate to frustrating to empowering. Then, for a light, entertaining account of one woman's breast-feeding experience, turn to *How My Breasts Saved the World: Misadventures of a Nursing Mother*, Lisa

Wood Shapiro's memoir of her struggles with nursing and her determination to make it work.

Holloway, Kris, and John Bidwell

Monique and the Mango Rains: Two Years with a Midwife in Mali. Long Grove, IL: Waveland Press, 2007. 212pp. ISBN 9781577664352.

At the age of twenty-two, American Kris Holloway traveled to a tiny village in Mali to serve as a Peace Corps volunteer. There she met Monique, the young midwife who was single-handedly struggling to deliver babies, despite her limited education and woefully inadequate health resources. With her lovely prose and keen eye for detail, Holloway describes the remarkable Monique and her inspiring battle to improve the lives of women and children in a patriarchal, deeply traditional society. Readers will find themselves transported to a West Africa where infant mortality is high, where women don't know about birth control, and where one person's activism truly makes a difference.

Subjects: Doctors • Health Care • Birth • Pregnancy • Mothers • Activism • Labor • Travel • Mali • Africa • Memoir

Now Try: Jump across the globe from Mali to an Amish community in Pennsylvania in *A Midwife's Story*, a memoir by midwife Penny Armstrong. Because of the striking similarities and differences between the two settings, this is a thoughtful companion to *Monique and the Mango Rains*: like Monique, Armstrong works in a setting that is vastly different from the modern American hospital, where technology and medical advances are absent—yet Armstrong's memoir shows natural home birth in a positive light, whereas Monique's experience shows the desperate need for Mali women to have different options.

Huggins, Kathleen

The Nursing Mother's Companion. Boston: Harvard Common Press, 1999 (2005). 284pp. ISBN 9781558321519.

In this comprehensive, clearly written guide, registered nurse Huggins covers everything women need to know for breast-feeding their children. Detailed instructions for every stage of breast-feeding are presented in chronological order, from prenatal planning to the first week to the first two months and beyond. Huggins addresses common problems and difficulties with nursing and includes a wealth of information on such topics as breast pumps, mother and baby separation, drug interactions, and safety. Quick-reference survival guides, specific to the age of the baby, make this a convenient book to refer to, though any reader who wants to know about the complete ins and outs of the breast-feeding experience will enjoy reading the book from cover to cover.

Subjects: Breast-feeding • How-to

Now Try: For additional perspectives on nursing, try two other excellent how-to guides. From the La Leche League International comes *The Womanly Art of Breastfeeding*, in which authors Judy Torgus and Gwen Gotsch offer detailed, step-by-step instructions on the nursing experience, covering everything from clothing for the mother to dealing with colicky babies to involving the father. Then turn to *Breastfeeding Made Simple: Seven Natural Laws for Nursing Mothers*, by Nancy Mohrbacher and Kathleen A. Kendall-Tackett; in straightforward, accessible language, this guide presents seven laws, such as "Law 4: More Breastfeeding at First Means More Milk Later," that give context to the big picture of nursing.

Menelli, Sheri, ed.

Journey into Motherhood: Inspirational Stories of Natural Birth. Carlsbad, CA: White Heart, 2005. 351pp. ISBN 9780974785325.

In a culture where childbirth is so very often characterized by heavy medication, invasive procedures, and cesarean sections—oftentimes when they are medically unnecessary—the voices of women who have delivered their children naturally are a breath of fresh air. In this collection of thought-provoking stories, forty-eight women share a variety of experiences. Some of them give birth at home, some in a hospital; some use doulas or midwives, or even go through the whole experience completely alone; some use the water birth technique, some use self-hypnosis. Honest and empowering, these stories rejoice in the beauty of natural birth and introduce readers to the wide array of natural birthing alternatives.

Subjects: Birth • Mothers • Essays • Anthology • Collection

Now Try: Readers eager for more stories of natural birth will be delighted with reading *Adventures in Natural Childbirth: Tales from Women on the Joys, Fears, Pleasures, and Pains of Giving Birth Naturally*, edited by Janet Schwegel. Arranged by type of caregiver (midwife, doctor, doula, or unassisted), these essays celebrate the range of emotions, good and bad alike, that attend childbirth. Women wishing to pursue natural birth for themselves will appreciate the insightful advice that introduces each section.

Murkoff, Heidi Eisenberg, Arlene Eisenberg, and Sandee Eisenberg Hathaway

What to Expect When You're Expecting. New York: Workman, 2002 (2008). 597pp. ISBN 9780761125495.

Love it or hate it, *What to Expect When You're Expecting* is inescapable, a mainstay among the many, many books written for pregnant women. The book's biggest strength is the very same aspect that repels some readers: it gives absolutely thorough information on pregnancy. For some people, the comprehensive approach is invaluable; for others, the detailed discussion of possible complications will provoke excessive anxiety. Whether *What to Expect* gives too much information or just the right amount is a matter of personal opinion; what is indisputable is that the book offers detailed information in plain language on every step of pregnancy, from preconception and conception through nine months of pregnancy and delivery.

Subjects: Pregnancy • Birth • Health • Health Care • Mothers • How-to

Now Try: If *What to Expect* covers pregnancy from A to Z, why bother reading anything else? Much of the same information is covered in *The Mother of All Pregnancy Books,* but author Ann Douglas adopts a more optimistic tone, using humor and common sense to give perspective to pregnancy. Try also Laura Riley's *Pregnancy: The Ultimate Week-by-Week Pregnancy Guide,* which shows the growth of the fetus through every week of its development; this detailed examination of the baby's development can help expectant mothers synthesize the wealth of information in *What to Expect.*

Sloan, Louise

Knock Yourself Up: No Man? No Problem!: A Tell-all Guide to Becoming a Single Mom. New York: Avery, 2007. 284pp. ISBN 9781583332863.

"We [single mothers] . . . believe we have a lot to offer as moms," writes lesbian single mother Sloan. "About the only thing we [don't] have to offer our kids is a guy named Dad." Working on the assumption that single moms can provide for the needs of their children, Sloan presents a stellar how-to guide for women who want to have children but who don't have the choice to do it the traditional way (see Chapter 2, "Buying Dad: How to Make the Most Natural Thing in the World Unnatural"). From the messy practicalities of conception (see Chapter 3, "Trysts with the Turkey Baster") to financial and social considerations for the single mother and child, the book draws on Sloan's experience and on the stories of other single moms to present the whole experience of single motherhood by choice. Humorous and engagingly written, the book frankly acknowledges that single motherhood is a difficult option and that not every woman should choose it, but for those who do, this memoir-cum-guide shows that it can be done, and done successfully.

Subjects: Fertility • Pregnancy • Birth • Solitude • Health Care • Mothers • Children • Humor • How-to • Memoir

Now Try: For a somewhat different perspective on single motherhood, turn to *The Single Woman's Guide to a Happy Pregnancy*. Unlike Sloan, author Mari Gallion directs her book toward mothers who may not have deliberately chosen single motherhood. Whether a conception is planned or not, however, this empowering, positive how-to guide will help women as they journey through single pregnancy, with advice on everything from meditation to paternal child support to baby showers.

Spiritual Growth and Meditation

> Books in the "Spiritual Growth and Meditation" section center on the inner lives of women, and their religious beliefs and practices.

Women have been writing about their spiritual growth for millennia; just turn to Mary Ford-Grabowsky's lovely anthology *Sacred Voices: Essential Women's Wisdom through the Ages* for evidence. The books in this section represent some of the finest examples of spiritual and religious writing in print. Some of the books, especially in the sections specific to a particular religion, advocate for a specific theological point of view; others, such as Pythia Peay's *Soul Sisters*, do not endorse a particular dogma but rather embrace the feminine divine, regardless of religion or spiritual tradition. Yet other books present meditations that speak to the unique spiritual experiences of women.

Six sections are devoted to titles that endorse six religions: Christianity, Judaism, Islam, Buddhism, Hinduism, and Paganism/goddess worship. Because Christianity has historically been a dominant force in the West, and because many books on Judaism, Islam, Buddhism, and Hinduism are written in a tongue other than English, there are far more books on Christian women's experiences than on women's experiences in other religions available to the English-speaking American reader. Nonetheless, I have tried to present a fairly balanced selection of books, both in terms of the number of titles discussed and the relative quality of those titles.

Allen, Paula Gunn

The Sacred Hoop: Recovering the Feminine in American Indian Traditions. Boston: Beacon Press, 1986 (1992). 311pp. ISBN 9780807046005.

Native American traditions, argues Laguna Indian Allen, are essentially feminine and matriarchal; they are rooted in feminine values, and they honor women and womanhood. In this academic but extremely accessible collection of essays, Allen expounds on this idea of the feminine in American Indian ways of life through several recurring themes; one such theme, for instance, is that "traditional tribal lifestyles are more often gynocratic than not, and they are never patriarchal." Deftly blending concepts of feminism, gender, and Native American identity, *The Sacred Hoop* presents a thoughtful, and thought-provoking, means of interpreting and embracing the power of the feminine in the context of tribal history and traditions.

> **Subjects:** Native Americans • Gender • Race • Feminism • America • Essays • Collection

> **Now Try:** Allen has written several books about gender and Native American identity, any of which will appeal to fans of *The Sacred Hoop*; perhaps try *Grandmothers of the Light: A Medicine Woman's Sourcebook*, in which Allen retells twenty-one stories of Native American goddesses. Readers may also enjoy the writings of another Laguna woman, Leslie Silko; her book *Yellow Woman and a Beauty of the Spirit: Essays on Native American Life Today* explores themes of race, racism, and Native American identity; its title essay in particular will appeal to Allen's fans for its focus on the feminine.

Bolen, Jean Shinoda

Crossing to Avalon: A Woman's Midlife Quest for the Sacred Feminine. New York: HarperSanFrancisco, 1994 (2004). 303pp. ISBN 9780062501127.

To heal herself from a midlife crisis, psychiatry professor Bolen traveled to Europe on a pilgrimage to sacred sites. With beautiful, thoughtful prose, she evokes the spiritual and historical contexts of holy destinations such as Chartres and Glastonbury. But this is far more than a mere travelogue; beyond the physical journey, this lyrical memoir describes Bolen's spiritual journey as she reconnects with the feminine elements of spirituality within religious traditions. Her spiritual awakening and her insight into the sacred feminine aspects of the divine make for a moving, thought-provoking memoir.

> **Subjects:** Spirituality • Goddesses • Religion • History • History of Religion • Social History • Feminism • Midlife • Travel • France • Scotland • England • Britain • Europe • Memoir

> **Now Try:** For another moving account of one woman's spiritual journey, turn to *On Pilgrimage: A Time to Seek*, by Jennifer Lash, née Jini Fiennes. After undergoing treatment for cancer, lapsed Catholic Lash was not sure exactly what she was looking for, but she knew she wanted to explore faith as an option for physical and emotional healing—so, with no particular goal in mind, she set

out upon a holy pilgrimage through France and Spain. Her spiritual discoveries, recounted in her lovely prose, will stir readers who enjoyed *Crossing to Avalon.*

Borysenko, Joan

Inner Peace for Busy Women: Balancing Work, Family, and Your Inner Life. Carlsbad, CA: Hay House, 2003. 179pp. ISBN 9781401901226.

It's a fact: the overwhelming majority of women lead busy lives, and that's not going to change any time in the near future. Between children, career, relationships, and all the various tasks that life throws our way each day, we are always active, always on the go. The trick to dealing with this busyness, explains Borysenko, is not to try to make it go away—which would be impossible, anyway—but to learn to find calm in all aspects of life, no matter how chaotic things get. In this compassionate, engaging guide, chapters such as "Do You Really Need That Lizard? Creating Financial Freedom" and "Mothers and Daughters: Forgiveness and Grace" teach women how to adjust their perspectives and to embrace the peaceful state of mind, not just temporarily but for an entire lifetime.

Subjects: Work–Life Balance • Mental Health • How-to • Quick Read

Now Try: Pair *Inner Peace for Busy Women* with the lovely book *The Courage to Be Yourself: A Woman's Guide to Emotional Strength and Self-Esteem.* Like Borysenko, author Sue Patton Thoele encourages women to attend to their spiritual and emotional needs, guiding them through the steps to achieve peace in a busy lifestyle; you'll learn to identify obstacles, recognize and face fear, and heal from spiritual, physical, and practical problems.

Casey, Karen

Each Day a New Beginning: Daily Meditations for Women. Center City, MN: Hazelden, 1982 (2006). 400pp. ISBN 9780866835015.

In this lovely, exquisitely written book, Karen Casey collects 365 meditations, one for each day of the year. At the beginning of each day's entry is an inspirational quote from a woman; these words of wisdom come from a variety of savvy ladies, many of whom readers will recognize, such as Judy Chicago, Anne Morrow Lindbergh, and Helen Keller. Then follows a short reflection piece to help readers place the day's theme in context, concluding with a brief affirmation. The book may be followed chronologically throughout the year, or readers may use the subject index to point them to topics such as compassion, goals, or memory. Though the book is written specifically to help women who are healing from pain and addiction, the powerful words will provide motivation to all readers, regardless of their particular circumstances.

Subjects: Meditations • Prayer • Spirituality • Mental Health • Collection

Now Try: The natural follow-up read is the sequel *A Woman's Spirit: More Meditations from the Author of Each Day a New Beginning.* Casey once again compiles daily meditations, one for each day of the year, replete with affirmations and quotations from wise women. Try also *Believing in Myself: Self Esteem Daily Meditations for Healing and Building Self-esteem;* though Earnest Larsen's book is not targeted to women in particular, the daily meditations, inspiring quotes, and powerful affirmations will appeal to fans of Karen Casey.

Eisler, Riane Tennenhaus

The Chalice and the Blade: Our History, Our Future. Cambridge, MA: Harper & Row, 1987 (1998). 261pp. ISBN 9780062502872.

A classic text of both religious history and women's history, *The Chalice and the Blade* is essential reading for anyone curious about the role of women in the history of Western religion. Under Eisler's thoughtful guidance, travel back to a time in our distant past when society was different, when matriarchy was the way of life, when goddesses enjoyed their rightful place in the religious pantheon—when the patriarchal norms of violence and dominance, so prevalent today, were tempered by the feminine respect for community and equality. With an astonishing command of scholarship in such diverse areas as religion, archaeology, and art, Eisler envisions history in a whole new way, convincingly creating a portrait of society that embraced the feminine—and showing that a return to a feminine society is within our grasp.

> **Subjects:** Paganism • Religion • History • Prehistory • Ancient History • Dark Ages • History of Religion • Women's History • Social History • Goddesses • Feminism • Gender • Archaeology • Europe
>
> **Now Try:** Complement Eisler's historical interpretation with the thought-provoking book *When God Was a Woman*. With impeccable scholarship, author Merlin Stone shows how patriarchal forces slowly but surely obliterated the feminine from religious life, warping society away from a matriarchal tradition into the male-dominated patterns that we know today. Then turn to *Free to Believe: Liberating Images of God for Women*, in which Mary Crist Brown restores the feminine to religious imagery, not just in historical context but in a way that is applicable for modern readers.

Ford-Grabowsky, Mary, ed.

Sacred Voices: Essential Women's Wisdom through the Ages. San Francisco: HarperSanFrancisco, 2002. 358pp. ISBN 9780062517029.

Across the globe and as long as there has been pen and paper (or papyrus, or parchment, or vellum), women have been recording their religious thought and experiences. In this magnificent anthology of essays, short fiction, and poems, editor Ford-Grabowsky collects religious and spiritual writings from more than 150 women, along with a short biographical overview of each writer's life. A breathtaking array of perspectives is represented, from mainstream world traditions to alternative religions, from the ancient East to the modern West. Readers will recognize some voices, such as Hypatia and Margery Kempe, while others will be unknown to readers; but whether familiar or new, contemporary or historical, the pieces work together to present a remarkable tapestry of women's religious thoughts from around world and throughout the ages.

> **Subjects:** Religion • Spirituality • History • History of Religion • Women's History • Global Perspectives • Biography • Prayer • Essays • Anthology • Collection
>
> **Now Try:** Continue to discover the voices of women in religion with *Wise Women: Over Two Thousand Years of Spiritual Writing by Women*, edited by Susan Neunzig Cahill. With nearly one hundred writings, including essays, poems, and fiction, this anthology is a natural companion to *Sacred Voices*. Arranged

by faith and chronology, the writings reflect the religious and spiritual experiences of women from a wide background of faiths, countries, and contexts, from the ancient Middle East to the contemporary West.

Gates, Janice

Yogini: The Power of Women in Yoga. San Rafael, CA: Mandala, 2006. 160pp. ISBN 9781932771886.

Through most of the thousands of years that yoga has been practiced, the vast majority of yogis have been men, but in modern times, an estimated ninety percent of students are women. The purpose of *Yogini* is twofold: to honor the growing number of women yoga teachers and to teach women how to integrate yoga into their daily lives. With beautiful photos and inspiring essays, the book documents the influence of women instructors and shows women how to become aware of the feminine elements of yoga in their spiritual and physical practices.

> **Subjects:** Yoga • Spirituality • Gender • Meditation • Exercise • Health • Mental Health • Biography • Essays • Collection • Quick Read

> **Now Try:** Apply the lessons learned in *Yogini* with the guidance offered in *A Woman's Book of Yoga: Embracing Our Natural Life Cycles.* Authors Machelle M. Seibel, a gynecologist, and Hari Kaur Khalsa, a yogi, have written a guide to using yoga to improve health in the various aspects of women's lives, including menstruation, menopause, and pregnancy. Combining spiritual and physical advice, the book's focus on meditation, breathing, and asanas offers practical advice for incorporating yoga into a holistic health approach.

Gimbutas, Marija

The Language of the Goddess: Unearthing the Hidden Symbols of Western Civilization. London: Thames & Hudson, 2001. 388pp. ISBN 9780500282496.

In this painstakingly researched examination of ancient civilizations, archeology professor Gimbutas restores the feminine divine to its rightful place in the history of early Western religion. With impressive scholarship that draws from such fields as myth, art, and cultural history, Gimbutas convincingly demonstrates that, before Western society transformed into its current patriarchal way of life, people in prehistoric Europe worshipped goddesses and honored the feminine elements of religion. Plentiful illustrations of ancient symbols and artifacts support the book's interpretation of feminine influences in ancient lifestyles in areas such as birth, death, and regeneration. Written for an academic audience but accessible for the lay reader, the book offers a thought-provoking vision of the influence of the goddess in past millennia.

> **Subjects:** Art • History • Art History • Archaeology • Prehistory • Ancient History • Paganism • Religion • History of Religion • Women's History • Social History • Goddesses • Feminism • Europe

> **Now Try:** Now move beyond Europe to discover goddesses across the globe in *The Great Cosmic Mother: Rediscovering the Religion of the Earth,* by Monica Sjoo and Barbara Mor. Lavishly illustrated, this reference book illuminates the influence of goddesses and matriarchal cultures in ancient times in civilizations across the planet. Fans of *The Language of the Goddess* will appreciate the book's accessible prose and impressive scholarship in disciplines including art, history, and archaeology.

Khalsa, Hari Kaur

A Woman's Book of Meditation: Discovering the Power of a Peaceful Mind. New York: Avery, 2006. 184pp. ISBN 9781583332535.

Not sure how to meditate? You're not alone. Let yoga instructor Hari Kaur Khalsa teach you how in this step-by-step guide. Though not a yoga guide per se, the book draws on yoga principles to cover all the basics of meditation, including breath control, postures, and visualization techniques. Then, with a basic understanding of meditation, even beginners can start to practice the thirty-nine meditations in the book, such as "Meditation for Intuition and Conquering Fear" and "Meditation for the Blossoming of Your True Self." Chosen specifically with women practitioners in mind, the selection of meditations will help women channel their energies, develop their spiritualities, and cope with the problems they face in their daily lives.

> **Subjects:** Meditation • Prayer • Spirituality • Mental Health • Yoga • How-to • Collection • Quick Read

> **Now Try:** Turn now to any or all of the meditation books by Sue Patton Thoele: *The Woman's Book of Courage: Meditations for Empowerment & Peace of Mind*; *The Woman's Book of Soul: Meditations for Courage, Confidence, and Spirit*; and *The Woman's Book of Confidence: Meditations for Strength and Inspiration*. Though each has a different theme, all three titles will be welcome complements to *A Woman's Book of Meditation*. Each title features thoughtful daily meditations and pithy quotes, designed to inspire women to pause and reflect as part of each day's routine.

Maurine, Camille, and Lorin Roche

Meditation Secrets for Women: Discovering Your Passion, Pleasure, and Inner Peace. San Francisco: HarperSanFrancisco, 2001. 292pp. ISBN 9780-062516978.

Celibate male monks on isolated mountaintops have one set of rules for meditation; modern women with busy lives have a completely different set of rules, set forth here in an empowering, inspiring how-to guide by wife-and-husband team Maurine and Roche. Instead of dulling their senses and dampening their perceptions, women should rejuvenate themselves by embracing the range of their emotions through whatever technique works; if it's sitting in lotus position, fine; if it's strolling through an art gallery, that's fine, too. Happy, worried, playful, fearful, sexy—whatever a woman is feeling, there is a meditation in the book to help her channel the energy into a positive, restorative spiritual experience. Supplemented with practical advice, real-life stories, and thought-provoking questions, the meditations will help women tap into their feminine spiritual strengths and celebrate the freedom and peace that meditation brings.

> **Subjects:** Meditation • Prayer • Spirituality • Mental Health • How-to

> **Now Try:** Women seeking to improve their spiritual and emotional happiness will love the practical and empowering advice in *The Woman's Comfort Book: A Self-Nurturing Guide for Restoring Balance in Your Life*, by Jennifer Louden. Though not a meditation book per se, the marvelous variety of activities—such as creating a comfort journal, taking a long bath, even hiding under

the covers—fits nicely into the broad definition of meditation championed in *Meditation Secrets for Women*. Practical advice, blissfully indulgent activities, and creative ideas blend together in this lovely guide to taking care of oneself.

McCauley, Lucy, Amy Greimann Carlson, and Jennifer Leo, eds.

A Woman's Path: Women's Best Spiritual Travel Writing. San Francisco: Travelers' Tales, 2000. 256pp. ISBN 9781885211484.

Physical travel meets spiritual travel in this remarkable collection of thirty-two essays by women writers, including such well-known names as Anne Lamott and Maya Angelou. In these eye-opening, thought-provoking pieces, the writers travel to countries and cities around the globe, sometimes on a deliberate spiritual pilgrimage, sometimes with no expectation of the spiritual experience awaiting them. Some of the destinations, such as India and Japan, are natural candidates for spiritual growth; other destinations, such as Poland, the Bahamas, and even New York City, may seem unlikely settings for spiritual encounters. Expected or unexpected, the spiritual experiences in locations near and far will appeal to fans of both spiritual writing and travel writing.

Subjects: Spirituality • Travel • Essays • Anthology • Collection

Now Try: Readers inspired by *A Woman's Path* to make their own spiritual travels may enjoy *Go Girl: Finding Adventure Wherever Your Travels Lead*, though it has a Christian bent not found in *A Woman's Path*. Mixing stories of historical and contemporary spiritual women travelers along with her own travel experiences, author Marlee LeDai encourages women to discover the spiritual possibilities of travel, while including helpful how-to tips and practical advice.

Peay, Pythia

Soul Sisters: The Five Divine Qualities of a Woman's Soul. New York: J.P. Tarcher/Putnam, 2002. 241pp. ISBN 9781585421626.

"All across the country, all across the world, women are picking up the discarded threads of patriarchal religions and reweaving new myths, rituals, and traditions for themselves," writes journalist Peay. "The focus has shifted away from an exclusively male god to a cosmos that includes a goddess, too." In this guidebook, Peay helps readers reclaim the feminine qualities of the divine, no matter what spiritual or religious tradition they may come from. With exercises, meditations, and quotes from a variety of spiritual women, the book shows how to embrace the five feminine traits of spirituality—courage, faith, beauty, love, and magic—and to apply them to their own spiritual paths.

Subjects: Spirituality • Gender • Religion • Meditation • Prayer • How-to

Now Try: Like Peay, author Joan Borysenko understands that women are approaching God in ways that diverge from traditional patriarchal religious traditions. In *A Woman's Journey to God: Finding the Feminine Path*, she speaks to all women, regardless of their spiritual background, showing that a feminine form of worship can work within their own religious frameworks. Drawing on examples of spiritual women in history as well as her own experiences, Borysenko offers insight and inspiration for women who want to embrace the feminine in their spiritual and religious practices.

Schaef, Anne Wilson

Meditations for Women Who Do Too Much. San Francisco: Harper & Row, 1990 (2004). 380pp. ISBN 9780062548665.

For all those women who know they'd like to meditate but who can never seem to find the time, *Meditations for Women Who Do Too Much* is just what the doctor ordered. Though the book does not, alas, add more hours to the day, it *does* put the hours into perspective, showing that making time for oneself should always be on the schedule. With one meditation for each day of the year, each entry follows a three-part structure to guide readers toward rest and relaxation: at the beginning there is a quote, followed by a short, thought-provoking meditation, concluding with a brief affirmation. A thematic index can point the reader directly toward a particular topic, such as "Hanging in There," "Multi-Tasking," and "Crazy, Feeling." Written with a warm, gently humorous approach, the book serves up sanity and restoration on a daily basis.

> **Subjects:** Meditation • Prayer • Spirituality • Lifestyle • Mental Health • Collection
>
> **Now Try:** For a lovely companion read, turn to *The Woman's Retreat Book: A Guide to Restoring, Rediscovering, and Reawakening Your True Self—in a Moment, an Hour, a Day, or a Weekend.* Author Jennifer Louden understands how difficult it is to carve out time for oneself— but she also understands how important it is for women to nurture their own needs. Whether you're looking for a physical retreat or just a few minutes of personal solitude, the book dispenses practical advice and creative ideas to show readers how to create a sanctuary, any where and any place.

Scruggs, Afi

Beyond Stitch and Bitch: Reflections on Knitting and Life. Hillsboro, OR: Beyond Words, 2004. 139pp. ISBN 9781582701035.

In this collection of lovingly crafted thought pieces, knitter Scruggs shines a light on the spiritual qualities of knitting. With a warm, melodious style, she reflects on the quiet joy of the act of knitting, a process that lulls her into a meditative state of mind. Even those readers who don't knit will appreciate her tender treatment of such knitting experiences as giving hand-crafted pieces as gifts. Knitters will be pleased to find knitting patterns throughout; even novices will be able to try their hands at knitting by following the photographs and how-to instructions.

> **Subjects:** Knitting • Spirituality • Meditation • Mental Health • Essays • Collection • Quick Read
>
> **Now Try:** Now that you've read *Beyond Stitch and Bitch*, you may want to see the book referred to in the title, Debbie Stoller's *Stitch 'N Bitch: The Knitter's Handbook*; the patterns and how-to sections are excellent, though be warned that it is a sassier, snarkier read. Then, for more reflections on the joys of knitting, turn to two additional books: *KnitLit: Sweaters and Their Stories and Other Writing about Knitting*, edited by Linda Roghaar and Molly Wolf, and *Knitting Yarns and Spinning Tales: A Knitter's Stash of Wit and Wisdom*, edited by Kari A. Cornell. Each book is a collection of essays about the pleasures of knitting, written with a warmth and charm that will remind readers of Scruggs's book.

Sharma, Arvind, and Katherine K. Young, eds.

Her Voice, Her Faith: Women Speak on World Religions. Boulder, CO: Westview Press, 2002. 327pp. ISBN 9780813365916.

In this excellent collection of essays, eight women scholars speak on the role of women in eight faiths: Hinduism, Buddhism, Confucianism, Taoism, Judaism, Christianity, Islam, and Wicca. In each piece, the writers incorporate their own experiences into a broader picture that explores the historic and contemporary participation of women in religion. Though scholarly in approach, the authors are careful to write in a style accessible to the lay reader, making this collection an excellent and illuminating introduction to the ways women have been influenced by the various scriptures, canons, dogmas, and practices of major religions around the world.

Subjects: Religion • Gender • Feminism • History • History of Religion • Women's History • Essays • Anthology • Collection

Now Try: *Her Voice, Her Faith* examines the general role of women in religion; now explore the role of women in religion through the voices of individual believers. In *WomanPrayers: Prayers by Women throughout History and around the World*, editor Mary Ford-Grabowsky collects religious prayers from well over one hundred women. With its emphasis on the feminine religious experience, the historical and contemporary perspectives will give context to the changing perspectives and roles of women in the faiths discussed in *Her Voice, Her Faith*, as well as from alternative traditions.

Walker, Barbara G.

The Woman's Encyclopedia of Myths and Secrets. San Francisco: Harper & Row, 1983 (1995). 1124pp. ISBN 9780062509253.

A classic text of women's studies, *The Woman's Encyclopedia of Myths and Secrets* is absolutely indispensable reading for anyone interested in the role of women and religion. Though intended as a reference text, Walker's engaging writing style makes the book appropriate for cover-to-cover reading. Granted, reading the whole text does take some time; with well over a thousand pages, this is a comprehensive work with a magnificent scope, covering the role of women in religion, myth, and legend since the dawn of time and across the globe. Discover famous goddesses, women saints, female fertility symbols, and obscure feminine traditions in this remarkable tribute to the reach of women in the history of religion.

Subjects: Religion • History • History of Religion • Women's History • Social History • Spirituality • Gender • Feminism • Encyclopedia

Now Try: The natural companion to *The Woman's Encyclopedia of Myths and Secrets* is *The Woman's Dictionary of Symbols and Sacred Objects*, also by Walker. Again, the scope is breathtaking: there are 753 articles on religious and spiritual symbols and objects, replete with 636 illustrations. Arranged by topics such as "Deities' Signs," "Body Parts," and "Fruit and Foodstuffs," the book examines the feminine context of sacred objects from religious traditions across time and throughout the world.

Christian Perspectives

The "Christian Perspectives" section showcases a small sampling of the many, many books written for Christian women audiences.

Books discussed here include devotionals, memoirs, biographies, and biblical analyses, some written from a conservative or fundamentalist perspective, others written from a more liberal bent. Readers looking for a "safe" first choice—one that does not promote any particular dogma or denomination—may wish to start with Jacqueline E. Lapsley's *Whispering the Word*, an empowering analysis of women from the Old Testament. Readers will also want to explore the "Religious Identity" section of Chapter 1.

Clairmont, Patsy, et al.

The Women of Faith Daily Devotional. Grand Rapids, MI: Zondervan, 2002. 391pp. ISBN 9780310240693.

From the pen of six Christian women authors comes this lovely collection of daily devotional readings. Each month has a theme—January, for instance, is "Hope," and August is "Humor"—and each day's entry has a three-part structure to help women bring focus to their lives. Each entry starts with a quote from the Bible, followed by a short devotional for meditation and thought; wrapping up each day is a short affirmative prayer. Based firmly in Christian theology, the writings help place the issues that women face in their lives in a context of daily faith and renewal.

> **Subjects:** Christianity • Religion • Devotional • Prayer • Meditations • Collection

> **Now Try:** Those who like a daily dose of Christian devotional reading will enjoy *The One Year Book of Devotions for Women*, by Jill Briscoe. Each day's entry features a quote from the Bible, a suggestion for biblical reading, and a brief thought piece on its meaning for women's lives. Then, for a book that approaches devotionals from a somewhat different perspective, turn to Lisa Harper's book *What the Bible Is All about for Women: A Devotional Reading for Every Book of the Bible*. This is not a day-by-day guide but rather a book-by-book guide; Harper discusses each book of the Bible, showing how scripture can apply to women's issues in their daily lives.

Hosier, Helen Kooiman

100 Christian Women Who Changed the Twentieth Century. Grand Rapids, MI: F.H. Revell, 2000. 379pp. ISBN 9780800757281.

In this engagingly written collective biography, author Hosier shines light on the lives of one hundred women who made a remarkable difference in the twentieth century. Arranged in eight broad themes, including "Bible Study Ministry, Education" and "Business, Politics, Social Change," the profiles cover women from around the globe. Some of the names, such as Flannery O'Connor and Kathie Lee Gifford, will be familiar to readers; but whether the women are known or unknown, the discussion of their good works and the role that Christian faith played in their lives will be inspiring to readers.

> **Subjects:** Christianity • Religion • History • History of Religion • Women's History • Global Perspectives • Biography • Collection

> **Now Try:** For further inspiring stories of a wide variety of Christian women, including Abigail Adams, Condoleezza Rice, and Florence Nightingale, readers should turn to *Sisterhood of Faith: 365 Life-Changing Stories about Women Who Made a Difference*, by Shirley Brosius. Presented in the format of a daily devotional, each entry starts with a line from scripture, followed by a brief profile of

a Christian woman in three parts: her service, her message, and her story; concluding each entry is a thought-provoking response that encourages readers to reflect on their own lives.

Jensen, Jane Richardson, and Patricia Harris-Watkins

She Who Prays: A Woman's Interfaith Prayer Book. Harrisburg, PA: Morehouse, 2005. 212pp. ISBN 9780819221131.

A stellar collection of perspectives from religious and spiritual traditions around the world, *She Who Prays* is written for Christian women who know that faith comes in many forms. Arranged both for timeframe (there are daily, weekly, and seasonal prayers) and for theme (such as "Prayers for Hearth and Home and Beyond"), this book collects prayers that honor and celebrate women and their experiences. The authors swiftly dispatch unnecessary patriarchal influences, deliberately avoiding sex-based references unless they are relevant; God, for instance, is not referred to as "the Father." Though written for a Christian audience, the book calls on prayers from other faiths as appropriate; this inclusive approach will be upsetting for some readers, but those who enjoy alternative ways to celebrate Christian faith will find much to love.

> **Subjects:** Prayer • Christianity • Religion • Spirituality • Feminism • Global Perspectives • Collection • Quick Read

> **Now Try:** For more interfaith inspiration, turn to *God Has No Religion: Blending Traditions for Prayer*, by Frances Sheridan Goulart. With sensitivity toward language and gender, the book collects prayers for a variety of occasions and themes, such as "Prayers for Peace and Justice" and "Prayers for the Earth and the Animals." Inclusive in tone and broad in scope, these prayers are intended to satisfy people of all faiths, regardless of their particular religions.

Juana Inés de la Cruz, Margaret Sayers Peden, and Ilan Stavans

Poems, Protest, and a Dream: Selected Writings. New York: Penguin Books, 1997 (2005). 248pp. ISBN 9780140447033.

Born in the mid-seventeenth century, Sor Juana was a feminist before her time and a Christian whose religious writings still reverberate with readers today. In this magnificent selection of some of Sor Juana's finest writings, readers will find the "Response to the Illustrious Poetess Sor Filotea de la Cruz," an essay in which Sor Juana draws on her impressive theological background to defend the right of women to be educated. Also included in this edition are some of Sor Juana's poems and a scene from one of her plays, as well as an introduction to Sor Juana's milieu by scholar Stavans. Read the original Spanish side-by-side with translator Peden's English interpretations to discover the profound spiritual, religious, and feminist thinking of a brilliant Christian woman.

> **Subjects:** Christianity • Religion • Feminism • History • Seventeenth Century • Mexico • Collection

> **Now Try:** Those who enjoyed the poems in *Poems, Protest, and a Dream* can turn now to the bilingual edition of *Sor Juana's Love Poems*, also known as *Poemas de Amor*, though with a less overtly religious theme than in some of her writings, this collection showcases Sor Juana's intense spirituality within the context of her romantic poetry. Then turn to *Sor Juana, or, The Traps of Faith*, a fascinating biography by Octavio Paz that will help readers understand the life of the woman responsible for such enduring spiritual literature.

Lamott, Anne

Traveling Mercies: Some Thoughts on Faith. New York: Pantheon Books, 1999. 275pp. ISBN 9780679442400.

Author Anne Lamott is a multitalented writer, as evidenced by her novels and nonfiction on a variety of subjects—but she is arguably at her best when she writes about her faith. Having dealt with alcoholism, drug abuse, and single motherhood, she is an unlikely advocate of religious faith, and yet it is precisely these experiences that make her story so compelling; despite a difficult life, Lamott emerges as a zealous Christian, albeit one with a keen irreverent streak. Discover her captivating prose, her witty humor, and her affirming, inspiring Christian faith in her essays in *Traveling Mercies*, about her long journey from despair to Christianity.

Subjects: Christianity • Religion • Humor • Essays • America • Memoir

Now Try: Part of Lamott's appeal is that, despite making a great deal of mistakes in life, she maintains her faith and her spirituality. Now meet another person who has kept his faith during adverse circumstances, Brennan Manning. In *The Ragamuffin Gospel: Good News for the Bedraggled, Beat-Up, and Burnt Out*, Manning shows readers that even people who've made mistakes can look forward to grace and redemption. Then continue with Lamott's two sequels about faith. *Plan B: Further Thoughts on Faith* presents a middle-aged Anne, still preserving in her faith and trying to keep her sanity through her son's teenaged years. *Grace (Eventually): Thoughts on Faith,* her most recent (but hopefully not last!) book on faith, is replete with her usual array of diverse topics ranging from the personal to the political to the divine.

Lapsley, Jacqueline E.

Whispering the Word: Hearing Women's Stories in the Old Testament. Louisville, KY: Westminster John Knox Press, 2005. 154pp. ISBN 9780664224356.

In *Whispering the Word*, religion professor Lapsley deftly blends feminist scholarship with scriptural analysis to consider four stories about women in the Old Testament. "If we pay attention," she explains, "if we listen for a sometimes soft voice, God encounters us in these stories." Lapsley's interpretation of these stories—featuring such characters as Rachel, Naomi, and Moses' mother and sister—offers an empowering, positive approach to understanding the women of the Bible. With her nuanced textual analysis and her accessible writing style, she crafts a narrative that is appropriate for scholars and general readers alike.

Subjects: History • Judaism • Christianity • Feminism • Religion • Women's History • History of Religion • Ancient History • Classical History • Middle East • Asia • Quick Read

Now Try: For another insightful feminist analysis of women's stories in the Old Testament, turn to Lillian R. Klein's *From Deborah to Esther: Sexual Politics in the Hebrew Bible.* In this thought-provoking analysis of scripture, Klein considers gender and womanhood by examining the stories of such women as Hannah, Bathsheba, and the wife of Job. Then turn to Orson Scott Card's *Women of Genesis* series, featuring novelizations of the lives of Old Testament women; first in the series is *Sarah.*

L'Engle, Madeleine, and Carole F. Chase

Glimpses of Grace: Daily Thoughts and Reflections. San Francisco: HarperSanFrancisco, 1996. 368pp. ISBN 9780060652807.

Though best remembered for her magnificent young adult science fiction book *A Wrinkle in Time*, L'Engle produced a wealth of fiction and nonfiction for adults, some of it essentially secular, some of it deeply religious. *Glimpses of Grace* is a remarkable sampling of L'Engle's Christian writing, selected by editor Chase from among the many pieces in the L'Engle oeuvre. Presented as a collection of daily meditations, each entry illuminates L'Engle's compassionate, intelligent approach to the Christian faith. The beautiful, lyrical writing will inspire readers as they follow their own spiritual paths each day.

Subjects: Christianity • Religion • Spirituality • Meditation • Collection

Now Try: Readers eager to read more of L'Engle's Christian writings have many choices; a good place to continue is with *Bright Evening Star: Mystery of the Incarnation*. In part, this is a spiritual memoir, filled with examples from L'Engle's own life—but beyond that, this is a thought-provoking study that explores the indecipherable mystery of the incarnation of God into the person of Jesus; no simple answers are given, but L'Engle's insight into theology will give readers plenty of food for thought. L'Engle also infuses her fiction with Christian themes; try, for instance, *A Live Coal in the Sea*, about an Episcopalian priest married to an astronomer.

Pagels, Elaine H.

Adam, Eve, and the Serpent. New York: Random House, 1988. 189pp. ISBN 9780394521404.

Because she writes about controversial subjects, Elaine Pagels tends to command a strong reaction: her interpretations are alternately revered and reviled by her audience. In *Adam, Eve, and the Serpent*, this expert in the history of early Christianity considers the development of sexual values within the first centuries of the Christian church. Christianity had the potential to become a religion of sexual liberation and equality between the sexes, argues Pagels, but political maneuverings of people such as Augustine led to a different reality; the creation story, in particular, resulted in a sexually repressive worldview that devalued women. This is a thought-provoking historical analysis that illuminates contemporary Christian sexual values.

Subjects: Sexuality • Sexual Discrimination • Christianity • Religion • History • History of Religion • Ancient History • Classical History • Quick Read

Now Try: If you enjoyed Pagels's treatment of the delicate topic of sexuality, you may enjoy the book that first brought her to fame (or to infamy, depending on your perspective). In *The Gnostic Gospels*, she discusses Gnosticism, an alternate form of Christianity that ultimately ceded to Christian orthodoxy as we know it in the first years of the Church. The Gnostics, explains Pagels, took a more egalitarian view toward women, sexuality, and the feminine divine. Readers interested in early church history will also enjoy *Misquoting Jesus: The Story behind Who Changed the Bible and Why*, in which Bart D. Ehrman describes the process by which sacred texts were selected, edited, censored, and publicized.

Jewish Perspectives

In the "Jewish Perspectives" section, you'll find books written to address the spiritual identities of Jewish women.

Some titles in this section, such as E. M. Broner's *Bringing Home the Light*, offer guidance for practice rituals that celebrate Jewish womanhood; others are more exploratory in nature, such as Danya Ruttenberg's *Yentl's Revenge*, a collection of essays about the confluence of Judaism and feminism. And for more books about Jewish women, see the "Religious Identity" section of Chapter 1.

Adelman, Penina V., ed.

Praise Her Works: Conversations with Biblical Women. Philadelphia: The Jewish Publication Society, 2005. 228pp. ISBN 9780827608238.

In the course of researching rituals for her daughter's bat mitzvah, Adelman, a scholar of Judaism and Women's Studies, came across an obscure medieval text, the Midrash ha-Gadol. Inspired by its references to twenty-two biblical women, Adelman assembled a group of Jewish women writers to bring their stories to life. Each character—including familiar names such as Rebekah and Sarah as well as lesser-known figures such as the woman identified only as "Widow from Tzarephath"—stars in her own chapter, in which the various authors present the pertinent passages from the Midrash along with their own insightful commentaries on the biblical women. Read this for an exploration into Jewish women's history and for the thought-provoking commentary on women's issues, then and now.

Subjects: Judaism • Religion • Essays • Collection

Now Try: Continue discovering the lives of women in the Bible in *Sisters at Sinai: New Tales of Biblical Women*. With engaging prose and profound spiritual insight, author Jill Hammer vividly reimagines stories of ancient Jewish women, blending scant textual evidence with her own creative reinterpretations to breathe fresh life into the stories of twenty-four women such as the wife of Lot and Queen Vashti.

Broner, E. M.

Bringing Home the Light: A Jewish Woman's Handbook of Rituals. San Francisco: Council Oak Books, 1999. 225pp. ISBN 9781571780843.

In this thought-provoking guidebook, rooted firmly in sacred Jewish texts and Jewish theology, author Broner collects dozens of rituals that celebrate the feminine in Judaism. Arranged seasonally, some of the rituals are gender-specific, such as "Menses: Blood Songs" and "Women at the Wall," while other transcend gender, such as "Losing Friends, Great Grievings." The rituals include commentary, ingredients, instructions, and reflections from Broner's own experience as a Jewish woman. With thoughtful, elegant prose, Broner shows women how to rejoice in the feminine, and feminist, aspects of Jewish celebration and ritual.

Subjects: Judaism • Religion • Feminism • How-to

Now Try: For more Jewish celebrations that honor the feminine, turn to Penina V. Adelman's book *Miriam's Well: Rituals for Jewish Women around the Year*, which includes female-centric rituals for themes ranging from virginity to infertility to honoring foremothers. As in *Bringing Home the Light*, the rituals are arranged seasonally and supplemented with insightful commentary and sacred stories.

Frankel, Ellen

Five Books of Miriam: A Woman's Commentary on the Torah. New York: G. P. Putnam, 1996. 354pp. ISBN 9780399141959.

The role of women in the Torah is given new life in this remarkable interpretation by Jewish scholar and storyteller Frankel. Rather than applying a dry academic lens to the sacred texts, Frankel employs the voices of the women who appeared in those texts; thus we hear directly from such women as Eve, Sarah, Dinah, and Lilith. In the examination of the book of Genesis, for instance, Leah, Esther, and Miriam all chime in about the creation of human beings: "The Hebrew language is a gendered tongue," explains Leah, while Esther discusses how the Torah "strains against these grammatical limits." This creative approach fleshes out the experience of the women in the Bible while interpreting the sacred texts in a way that re-envisions women's issues in a fresh new way.

Subjects: Judaism • Religion • Feminism

Now Try: For a more scholarly, methodical approach to the Torah, turn to *The Torah: A Women's Commentary*, edited by Tamara Cohn Eskenazi and Andrea L. Weiss. A refreshing supplement to previous commentaries that only partially consider the role of women in the Bible, this magnificent piece of scholarship applies a close lens to the text while illuminating contemporary issues as they apply to Jewish women today.

Ruttenberg, Danya, ed.

Yentl's Revenge: The Next Wave of Jewish Feminism. Seattle, WA: Seal Press, 2001. 230pp. ISBN 9781580050579.

In this excellent anthology of writings by young Jewish feminists, editor Ruttenberg collects twenty essays that speak to the complicated marriage of Judaism and modern feminism. The contributors discuss a wide variety of themes: A. C. Hall reflects on tradition in "The Nice Jewish Boy"; Dina Hornreich contemplates identity in "I Was a Cliché"; Jennifer Bleyer discusses the peculiar blend of Jewish Orthodoxy and hard-core feminism in "From Riot Grrl to Yeshiva Girl, or How I Became My Own Damn Rabbi." Edgy or reflective, traditional or hip, resolutely Jewish or spiritually confused—no matter her perspective, each writer brings insight and candor to the multifaceted question of modern Jewish feminism.

Subjects: Judaism • Religion • Feminism • Essays • Anthology • Collection

Now Try: For more thought-provoking analysis of feminism and Judaism, turn to *She Who Dwells Within: A Feminist Vision of a Renewed Judaism*, by rabbi Lynn Gottlieb. With engaging prose and nuanced arguments, Gottlieb brings together history, scripture, and modern insight to envision a more feminist approach to Judaism. Then, for an inspiring look at feminism throughout the history of Judaism, turn to *Defiant Muse: Hebrew Feminist Poems from Antiquity to the Present*, by Shirley Kaufman et al.; arranged

chronologically, this remarkable collection of poems, presented in both Hebrew and English, reveals how feminist thought has influenced Jewish poets
throughout the ages.

Women of Reform Judaism (U.S.)

A Gift of Prayer: The Spirituality of Jewish Women. New York: Women of
Reform Judaism/UAHC Press, 2001. 79pp. ISBN 9780807408070.

A Gift of Prayer is a moving collection of more than forty Jewish spiritual
writings, including prayers, poems, and meditations. Composed by
women rabbis and by members of Women of Reform Judaism, The Federation of Temple Sisterhoods, these beautiful writings are arranged topi-
cally, in chapters such as "For Thanks and Blessing," "For the Sabbath,"
and "Talking to God." Though only seventy-nine pages long, the inspiring texts, accompanied by lovely illustrations by Jewish artists, make the
book a wholly satisfying, spiritually nourishing read.

Subjects: Judaism • Religion • Prayer • Meditation • Spirituality • Anthology
• Collection • Quick Read

Now Try: Now seek further inspiration from Jewish women of the past. In
Seyder Tkhines: The Forgotten Book of Common Prayer for Jewish Women, author
Devra Kay uncovers the largely forgotten Jewish women's prayers of the seventeenth century, while providing insightful historical commentary. Then
turn to *Voices of the Matriarchs: Listening to the Prayers of Early Modern Jewish
Women,* in which author Chava Weissler unearths forgotten prayers to examine the history of Jewish women in the seventeenth, eighteenth, and nineteenth centuries.

Muslim Perspectives

The "Muslim Perspectives" section features books that speak to
women who follow the beliefs and practices of Islam.

Some titles here speak directly to the experience of Muslim women in
modern America, while others take a more global or historical approach. Readers will also want to peruse two sections in Chapter 1 that include books about
Muslim women, "Global Voices" and "Religious Identity."

Ahmed, Leila

Women and Gender in Islam: Historical Roots of a Modern Debate. New
Haven, CT: Yale University Press, 1992. 296pp. ISBN 9780300049428.

The role of women in Islam has a long, complicated, multifaceted history,
as seen in this fascinating social history from Muslim feminist Leila
Ahmed. With thought-provoking insights and an engaging tone, she examines the history of the religion, from the pre-Islamic Middle East
through medieval Iraq through contemporary Egypt. Ahmed unflinchingly criticizes the sexual oppression that has occurred in the name of Islam, while at the same time she fleshes out the social milieu that
precipitated those oppressions. Though scholarly in tone and approach,

the book is accessible for lay readers, even those with no background in Islam or Women's Studies.

Subjects: Islam • Religion • History • History of Religion • Women's History • Social History • Sexual Discrimination • Feminism

Now Try: For an alternative historical analysis of women in Islam's history, turn to *My Soul Is a Woman: The Feminine in Islam*. Distancing herself from traditional feminist criticism, author Annemarie Schimmel presents a reverent, thoughtful analysis of the religion in this carefully researched book. Drawing on passages from the Qur'an, stories of Muslim women in history, and centuries of religious writings, Schimmel shows that Islam has a long tradition of celebrating women; this reflective approach makes for an excellent companion to the more critical *Women and Gender in Islam*.

Haddad, Yvonne Yazbeck, Jane I. Smith, and Kathleen M. Moore

Muslim Women in America: The Challenge of Islamic Identity Today. New York: Oxford University Press, 2006. 190pp. ISBN 9780195177831.

In the contemporary West, Muslim women "must contend not only with the rising level of anti-Islamic sentiment," explain scholars Haddad, Smith, and Moore, "but also with the increasingly popular belief that Islam treats women, at best, as second-class citizens." Does Islam really oppress American Muslim women? How do Muslim women reconcile their religion and beliefs with mainstream American culture? With candor and insight, *Muslim Women in America* addresses these and other questions central to the shifting identities of American Muslim women. In chapters such as "Persistent Stereotypes" and "Claiming Public Space," the authors present a scholarly but accessible discussion of the ways in which race, religion, and sex influence the experience of Muslim women in America today.

Subjects: Islam • Gender • Religion • Race • Stereotypes • Sexual Discrimination • America • Quick Read

Now Try: Now learn about the experience of American Muslim women in *Voices of Resistance: Muslim Women on War, Faith and Sexuality*, edited by Sarah Husain. With a variety of pieces such as essays, letters, poetry, and artwork, this anthology brings together a diverse array of perspectives on what it means to be a modern Muslim woman in the West. In the same vein, try *Shattering the Stereotypes: Muslim Women Speak Out*, in which editor Fawzia Afzal-Khan collects essays, fiction, art, and poetry by a variety of Muslim women whose breadth of experience defies simplistic categorization.

Helminski, Camille Adams, ed.

Women of Sufism: A Hidden Treasure: Writings and Stories of Mystic Poets, Scholars & Saints. Boston: Shambhala, 2003. 308pp. ISBN 9781570629679.

The women of Sufism come to life in this lovely anthology of writings, some of which are written by Sufi women, some of which are written by men *about* Sufi women. With a variety of historical documents—including poems, prayers, songs, and visions—the book uncovers the lives of Sufi women from around the globe and throughout the centuries, from the time of Muhammad through the present day. Scholar Helminksi presents a thoughtful biographical overview of each woman, whether she is the author or the subject of the writings; this historical and religious context, combined with the primary documents, makes for a fine survey of women in Sufism throughout the ages.

Subjects: Sufism • Islam • Religion • Spirituality • History • History of Religion • Women's History • Global Perspectives • Biography • Anthology • Collection

Now Try: Learn more about the history of women in Sufism in *Early Sufi Women: Dhikr An-Niswa Al-Muta 'Abbidat as Sufiyyat*, a medieval text by Muhammad ibn al-Husayn Sulami about eighty-four Sufi women who lived between the eighth and eleventh centuries. In this modern edition, Rkia Elaroui Cornell places English translations side by side with the original Sufi texts, allowing readers to discover a remarkable contemporary account of the foremothers of Sufism.

Wadud, Amina

Qur'an and Woman: Rereading the Sacred Text from a Woman's Perspective. New York: Oxford University Press, 1993 (1999). 118pp. ISBN 9780195128369.

For centuries, the Qur'an has been written, transcribed, and interpreted by men. Now, in this remarkable reinterpretation, author Wadud approaches the sacred text from a feminine, and feminist, perspective. In chapters such as "Distinctive Female Characters in the Qur'an" and "Male Authority," Wadud rediscovers the sacred writings, convincingly demonstrating the egalitarian nature of the Qur'an. With insight and clarity, she reconsiders traditional notions of sex, language, and gender roles, making this a thought-provoking read for anyone interested in understanding the place of women in Islam.

Subjects: Islam • Religion • Feminism • Gender • Quick Read

Now Try: The natural companion to *Qur'an and Woman* is *"Believing Women" in Islam: Unreading Patriarchal Interpretations of the Qur'an.* Like Wadud, author Asma Barlas interprets the Qur'an from a feminist perspective, arguing that it treats men and women equally and that sexual discrimination in Islam stems not from the Qur'an itself but rather from distorted patriarchal readings. Read this engaging study for the sophisticated analysis of sexism in Islam's history and for the refreshing feminist interpretation of the Qur'an.

Buddhist Perspectives

In the "Buddhist Perspectives" section, you'll discover books that speak to the unique spiritual needs of women who follow the spiritual teachings of Guatama Buddha.

Some of the titles here are instructional guides, while others are more reflective. For additional books about women's experiences with Buddhism, see also the "Religious Identity" section of Chapter 1.

Boucher, Sandy

Opening the Lotus: A Woman's Guide to Buddhism. Boston: Beacon Press. 194pp. ISBN 9780807073148.

In this beautifully written book, author Boucher, a sixty-something lesbian, discusses her experience with Buddhism. With lyrical prose and thoughtful reflections, she recalls her spiritual journey toward an understanding of the feminine qualities of the religion, offering her experience as inspiration for other women seeking the feminine in Buddhism. A discussion of the basics of Buddhism, complete with helpful meditation techniques, makes this a powerful how-to guide to the religion, while chapters on the history, practice, and teachings of Buddhism in relation to women make this a thought-provoking examination of gender and Buddhism.

Subjects: Buddhism • Religion • Spirituality • Meditation • Gender • Feminism • Seniors • Lesbian Sexuality • Queer Sexuality • Memoir • How-to • Quick Read

Now Try: Readers seeking further insight into the feminine potential of Buddhism will find much to love in Christina Feldman's *Woman Awake: Women Practicing Buddhism*. In simple, engaging prose, this how-to guide presents a framework for envisioning the feminine spirituality of Buddhism by offering meditations on such topics as inner empowerment; readers new to Buddhism and meditation will appreciate the guidelines for meditation and the clear, insightful writing.

Gregory, Peter N., and Susanne Mrozik, eds.

Women Practicing Buddhism: American Experiences. Boston: Wisdom, 2008. 239pp. ISBN 9780861715398.

In 2005, Smith College hosted a conference titled "Women Practicing Buddhism: American Experiences," an acknowledgment of the growing number of women in the United States who are turning to Buddhism as an alternative to Western religions. Editors Gregory and Mrozik have compiled essays that were presented at the conference in this eye-opening collection of writings by a variety of contributors, including nuns, writers, and teachers. Though generally academic in style, the writings are accessible and relevant to the lay reader, with topics including race, class, and power as they relate to women's Buddhism in America.

Subjects: Buddhism • Religion • America • Essays • Anthology • Collection

Now Try: Before Sandy Boucher wrote her Buddhist memoir/how-to guide *Opening the Lotus* (annotated above), she edited *Turning the Wheel: American Women Creating the New Buddhism*, an anthology of writings that contemplate the intersection of feminism and Buddhism in America. Readers who enjoyed the diverse range of topics and perspectives in *Women Practicing Buddhism* will enjoy the thoughtful—and thought-provoking—contemplations of spirituality and gender as they relate to women in America today.

Larkin, Geri

Plant Seed, Pull Weed: Nurturing the Garden of Your Life. San Francisco: HarperOne, 2008. 208pp. ISBN 9780061349041.

Gardening books are not exactly difficult to find in the library or at the bookstore; with so many to choose from, why should readers turn to *Plant Seed, Pull Weed*? The thorough explanation of how to plan, plant, and sustain a garden makes this a good choice for novice gardeners—but this is far, far more than a simple guide for planning a garden. Author Geri Larking, a Buddhist priest, uses the garden as a metaphor for living a better life. Based in Buddhist teachings but relevant for anyone seeking spiritual sustenance, the book's accessible, enjoyable prose shows readers how to use the act of gardening as a springboard to spiritual and emotional wellness.

Subjects: Gardening • Buddhism • Religion • How-to

Now Try: If the gardening metaphor of *Plant Seed, Pull Weed* spoke to your spiritual sensibilities, don't miss *The Chocolate Cake Sutra: Ingredients for a Sweet Life*, also by Geri

Larkin. This time Larkin compares spiritual development to food, likening the ingredients of the kitchen to the ingredients for spiritual wellness. With thoughtful reflections and candid advice, Larkin shows readers how to nurture their spirits—and yes, there is a recipe for chocolate cake. Fans of Larkin will also enjoy the compassionate wisdom of *Making a Change for Good: A Guide to Compassionate Self-Discipline*. Zen teacher Cheri Huber's engaging style will help readers nurture the spirit by focusing on the positive.

Tisdale, Sallie

Women of the Way: Discovering 2,500 Years of Buddhist Wisdom. San Francisco: HarperSanFrancisco, 2006. 299pp. ISBN 9780060598167.

As a faithful Buddhist and a dedicated feminist, Sallie Tisdale was troubled by the underrepresentation of women in the Buddhist religious tradition. To compensate for their exclusion, she wrote *Women of the Way*, a delightfully creative reinterpretation of the sutras that form the sacred texts of the religion. Informed by historical research and spiritual reverence, Tisdale applies an inventive feminist approach in retelling the stories of women in Buddhist literature, fleshing out their stories and restoring them to prominence. Lyrical and lovely, the book illuminates the rich tradition of women in the history of Buddhism, rescuing them from oblivion.

Subjects: Buddhism • Religion • Feminism • History • History of Religion • Women's History • Global Perspectives • Biography

Now Try: Turn now to *Buddhist Women on the Edge: Contemporary Perspectives from the Western Frontier*, edited by Marianne Dresser. In this collection of essays, readers will find more examples of women in Buddhism, in both the past and present. Inspiring and thought-provoking, these pieces highlight the influence of women in Buddhism, while reflecting on women's issues in contemporary Buddhist practice.

Hindu Perspectives

> The "Hindu Perspectives" section explores the role of Hinduism in women's lives.

Linda Johnsen's *The Living Goddess* discusses the long tradition of goddess worship in Hinduism, as does David R. Kinsley's *Hindu Goddesses*, while *Encountering Kali*, edited by Rachel Fell McDermott and Jeffrey John Kripal, considers the most famous Hindu goddess of all. Readers will find additional titles about women and Hinduism in the "Religious Identity" section of Chapter 1, "Life Stories."

Johnsen, Linda

The Living Goddess: Reclaiming the Tradition of the Mother of the Universe. Saint Paul, MN: Yes International, 1999. 185pp. ISBN 9780936663234.

Goddess worship in the West is regarded as an oddity, a peculiar alternative to mainstream religions; in contrast, author Johnsen explains, India has sustained and celebrated goddess worship for millennia. In this inspiring and remarkable social history, Johnsen explores the various goddesses in Hindu beliefs and examines India's long tradition of honoring the feminine elements of spirituality; Kali, of course, gets a thorough discussion, but so do other goddesses who will be less familiar to Western readers. Drawing on stories, folklore, sacred texts, and other historical and religious sources, the book uses engaging scholarship and engrossing prose to place goddess worship in India into historic and contemporary context.

Subjects: Hinduism • Religion • History of Religion • Goddesses • India • Quick Read

Now Try: Now discover the feminine potential of Hinduism as it is practiced today. In *The Path of the Mother*, Savitri L. Bess writes about twentieth-century women gurus such as Ammachi and Amma, weaving their biographies with stories of goddess worship and examples of Hindu feminine spirituality. Practical advice on meditation, chanting, and forming a spiritual connection with goddesses will help readers develop their own feminine approach to Hinduism and goddess worship.

Kinsley, David R.

Hindu Goddesses: Visions of the Divine Feminine in the Hindu Religious Tradition. Berkeley: University of California Press, 1986 (1997). 281pp. ISBN 9780520053939.

The rich pantheon of goddesses in the Hindu religion comes to life in this excellent encyclopedic resource. Prominent individual deities such as Kali and Sita are included, as well as goddesses such as the Mahadevi that transcend individual identity; lesser-known village goddesses are discussed, too, along with the idea of India as a goddess. Scholar Kinsley provides historical context for each goddess, along with an overview of the myths, characteristics, and types of worship associated with her. Though *Hindu Goddesses* is intended as a reference text, readers may read it as a cover-to-cover narrative to understand the breadth of influence of the various goddesses in the tradition of Hindu worship.

Subjects: Goddesses • Hinduism • Religion • History of Religion

Now Try: Learn more about the power of goddesses in Hinduism in *Devi: Goddesses of India*, edited by John Stratton Hawley and Donna Marie Wulff. Collecting twelve essays about twelve goddesses, each of whom have ties to the great goddess Devi, the book illuminates various attributes and roles of the goddesses, including death, grace, consort, and mother.

McDermott, Rachel Fell, and Jeffrey John Kripal, eds.

Encountering Kali: In the Margins, at the Center, in the West. Berkeley: University of California Press, 2003. 321pp. ISBN 9780520232396.

As a goddess, Kali is associated with a multitude of roles, often contradictory: she is destroyer, mother, consort; she is sometimes black, sometimes blue, sometimes red; her maw drips with blood, and her necklace is made of severed heads. So powerful is her image that, even in the Judeo-Christian West, Kali is becoming a familiar name. In *Encountering Kali*, a variety of scholars seek to demystify Kali and to understand how she is changing as she becomes integrated into Western cultures. The essays are scholarly in tone, but the writing is accessible for lay readers, providing thought-provoking analysis of the mythology, worship, and interpretation of Kali.

Subjects: Kali • Goddesses • Hinduism • Religion • Anthology • Collection

Now Try: Discover more about Kali in two additional books. In *Kali: The Feminine Force*, author Ajit Mookerjee treats readers to photographs and paintings of Kali, giving a visual, visceral dimension to the book's discussion of the goddess's feminine power and influence. Then find further illustrations and thought-provoking discussion in *Kali: The Black Goddess of Dakshineswar*, in which author Elizabeth U. Harding explores the nature and history of Kali and the Dakshineswar Kali Temple where she is worshipped.

Pagan Perspectives and Goddess Worship

In the "Pagan Perspectives and Goddess Worship" section, you'll find books written about or for women who are nonreligious or pantheistic in their beliefs—some with a Wicca focus, others with no particular religious perspective.

Start with the tremendously influential book by Starhawk, *The Spiral Dance*, and be sure to take a look at the "Religious Identity" section of Chapter 1 for additional titles by pagan women.

Budapest, Zsuzsanna Emese

The Holy Book of Women's Mysteries. Berkeley, CA: Wingbow Press, 1989 (2007). 308pp. ISBN 9780914728672.

A modern classic of women's pagan texts, *The Holy Book of Women's Mysteries* is a must-read for anyone curious about the intersection of feminism and spirituality. With engaging prose and keen insight, witch author Budapest covers a wealth of topics for contemporary pagans, with chapters ranging from "Feminist Witchcraft" to "Women's Holidays in the Dianic Tradition" to "Shamanism throughout Herstory." On one level, this is a thought-provoking examination of the personal and political in women's pagan worship; on another, this is an eminently practical how-to guide, replete with spells, rituals, and resources for finding the ingredients and tools necessary to practice paganism.

> **Subjects:** Paganism • Wicca • Religion • Spirituality • Goddesses • Feminism • How-to
>
> **Now Try:** Delve deeper into the feminist avenues of paganism in *Rebirth of the Goddess: Finding Meaning in Feminist Spirituality*, by feminist scholar Carol P. Christ. In this reflective analysis, Christ draws on her own experience and on her extensive research into goddess religions to illuminate the history and practice of goddess worship; though somewhat more academic than *The Holy Book of Women's Mysteries*, the book's nuanced exploration of feminine spirituality will appeal to those who enjoyed Budapest's book.

Monaghan, Patricia

Goddess Companion: Daily Meditations on the Goddess. St. Paul, MN: Llewellyn, 1999. 398pp. ISBN 9781567184631.

Discover mystical writings and religious reflections that span time and space in this beautiful tribute to goddesses everywhere. Prayers, songs, and other spiritual writings from cultures and religious traditions around the globe are assembled here in a daily meditation format. Each day's entry starts with a short piece of spiritual writing that honors a goddess or goddesses, followed by a thoughtful meditation on understanding and applying the sacred feminine in daily life. Readers may approach the book in chronological order, or they may select readings from one of three indexes: the Culture Index (for instance, Egyptian or Germanic); the Subject Index (for instance, Creativity or Fertility); and, of course, the Goddess Index, with listings for deities and religious women such as Isis, Lucia, and Circe.

Subjects: Paganism • Meditation • Goddesses • Spirituality • Religion • Anthology • Collection

Now Try: Continue discovering the power of spiritual writings about goddesses in Sirona Knight's *Goddess Bless!: Divine Affirmations, Prayers, and Blessings*. In chapters that offer affirmations, prayers, and blessings on themes such as love and daily living, readers will find tributes to more than one hundred goddesses such as Anu, Aphrodite, and Ezili.

Morrison, Dorothy

Everyday Magic: Spells & Rituals for Modern Living. Saint Paul, MN: Llewellyn, 1998. 320pp. ISBN 9781567184693.

"Almost anyone can work a spell," writes Wiccan Morrison, "and you don't have to be a genius to obtain successful results." In the first part of this straightforward how-to guide, she introduces readers to the ingredients and tools necessary for casting spells, in chapters such as "Magical Boosters" and "The Gifts of Nature." Then, in the second part of the book, Morrison presents a lengthy grimoire of spells for a wide variety of topics, from business success to eloquence to stinging insects. Maintaining that magic can and should have a place in modern life, she offers practical advice for novices and veterans alike.

Subjects: Spells • Wicca • Paganism • Religion • How-to

Now Try: For more practical spells, turn to two other books by Morrison, *Everyday Moon Magic: Spells & Rituals for Abundant Living* and *Everyday Sun Magic: Spells & Rituals for Radiant Living*. As in *Everyday Magic*, Morrison includes spells to be used for a variety of purposes, along with a discussion of the astrological influences that the moon and the sun have upon the practice of magic. Supplement Morrison's books with *A Witches' Bible: The Complete Witches' Handbook*, a guide to rites, spells, ingredients, and more, by Janet and Stewart Farrar.

Starhawk

The Spiral Dance: A Rebirth of the Ancient Religion of the Great Goddess. San Francisco: Harper & Row, 1979 (1999). 218pp. ISBN 9780060675356.

A seminal work among texts of paganism and women's spirituality, *The Spiral Dance* comes to us from Starhawk, a feminist activist, educator, and witch. With luminous writing and profound spiritual insights, Starhawk introduces readers to a feminist approach to witchcraft, drawing on history and stories as well as her own experiences and worldviews. But this is not just a theoretical discussion of feminine spirituality: the book is also a useful guide for practicing pagans, filled with exercises, charms, spells, and other spiritual rituals to use for such purposes as winning in court, combating loneliness, and honoring the waxing moon.

Subjects: Paganism • Wicca • Religion • Feminism • Spells • Meditation • How-to

Now Try: The influence of *The Spiral Dance* has been tremendous; it is responsible in no small part for the surge of interest in Wicca and paganism in the United States in the past few decades. Learn more about the movement toward paganism in another influential book, *Drawing Down the Moon: Witches, Druids, Goddess-Worshippers, and Other Pagans in America*, in which Margot Adler examines the history and contemporary influence of the modern neo-pagan movement in the United States.

Consider Starting With . . .

A small sampling of some of the most beloved Personal Growth titles are listed here:

Angier, Natalie. *Woman: An Intimate Geography.*

Browne, Jill Conner. *The Sweet Potato Queens' Field Guide to Men: Every Man I Love Is Either Married, Gay, or Dead.*

Eisler, Riane Tennenhaus. *The Chalice and the Blade: Our History, Our Future.*

Ensler, Eve. *The Vagina Monologues.*

Gaskin, Ina May. *Ina May's Guide to Childbirth.*

Lamott, Anne. *Traveling Mercies: Some Thoughts on Faith.*

Newman, Catherine. *Waiting for Birdy: A Year of Frantic Tedium, Neurotic Angst, and the Wild Magic of Growing a Family.*

Fiction Read-Alikes

- **Bohjalian, Chris.** The birthing mother was already dead when the midwife, Sybil Danville, performed an emergency C-section. Or was she? In *Midwives,* a novel of murky morality, childbirth, and midwifery, Sybil's teenage daughter struggles to grasp the medical issues and politics of home birth. Then try Bohjalian's other novels, all of which feature richly drawn characters who must grapple with difficult situations. In *Trans-Sister Radio*, for instance, Allie must examine her romantic feelings after her boyfriend undergoes a sex-change operation.

- **Brontë, Charlotte.** Ultimately, the classic novel *Jane Eyre* is a romance, but the happily-ever-after ending is a long time in coming. First, Jane must grow into her own as an independent woman, learning to trust her own spiritual, religious, and moral convictions before she can find love with the enigmatic Mr. Rochester. Or, for a more traditional romance, try Brontë's lesser-known novel *Vilette.*

- **Dickey, Eric Jerome.** The narrator may be a man, but the heart of *Genevieve* is the novel's title character. Heavy themes of race, marriage, sexuality, fidelity, and family swirl around the compelling, mysterious Genevieve Forbes, a successful businesswoman with a dark past. Each of Dickey's novels feature complicated relationships among richly drawn characters; a good follow-up is *The Other Woman*, a psychologically intense story about a woman who discovers her husband's infidelity.

- **Gibbons, Kaye.** Any of Gibbons's novels will please readers for their nuanced characters. Try her debut, *Ellen Foster*, about a young girl who learns that family transcends biological relations. And in the beautifully written *Divining Women*, set in North Carolina in 1918, a pregnant Maureen is living in terror at the hands of her abusive, psychologically domineering husband; it is only when her relative Mary offers her nurturing friendship and support that Maureen can find the strength to stand up to her spouse.

- **Kidd, Sue Monk.** Kidd's first novel, *The Secret Life of Bees*, stars a teenaged girl named Lily whose sense of self revolves around her nanny, her distant father, and her long-dead mother. Likewise, Kidd's subsequent novel *The Mermaid Chair* features relationships of all sorts—with family, with lovers, with the land, with the self—as the middle-aged Jessie Sullivan, temporarily freed from her obligations as wife and mother, begins to reflect on her personal happiness.

- **Picoult, Jodi.** Fans of Personal Growth might try any of the books by uber-popular novelist Jodi Picoult, beloved for her hard-hitting look at difficult problems in women's lives. Perhaps start with *Keeping Faith*, which tackles themes of marriage, fidelity, romance, motherhood, and religion.

- **Rice, Luanne.** *Follow the Stars Home* sure doesn't seem like a romance, not at first, considering that Mr. Right leaves his wife upon discovering that their unborn child will have serious health problems. But flash forward ten years: single mom Dianne is doing an admirable job of caring for her disabled daughter Julia; her heart is going out to a troubled young woman; and she is poised to discover romance again. This is a novel of the many types of love, of the healing power of relationships. Themes of family and friendship are important in all of Rice's books; continue with *The Edge of Winter*, about healing broken family relationships and starting new romances.

- **Shreve, Anita.** How well do we ever know our lovers? In *The Pilot's Wife*, Kathryn receives the news that every pilot's spouse dreads: her husband has been killed in a plane crash. In the wake of his death, Kathryn discovers shocking news about his hidden double-life, news that forces her to consider the meaning of marriage, love, and happiness. All of Shreve's novels have magnificent characters and thought-provoking themes; another good bet is *The Weight of Water*, about love and fidelity.

- **Smith, Lee.** Set in post–Civil War North Carolina, *On Agate Hill* shouldn't be read without a box of tissues nearby. It is a story of love found and lost, of infidelity and death, of hopes dashed—but readers prepared to undertake the emotional roller-coaster will be moved by the novel's beautiful tribute to the power of relationships, as seen in the story of the protagonist, the richly drawn Molly Petree. Smith's other novels will please readers, too; for a much lighter read, try *The Last Girls*, about four women who reunite after decades spent apart.

- **Sparks, Nicholas.** Fans of the wildly popular Nicholas Sparks know that he tugs at the heartstrings without mercy. Any of his novels would be good for those who enjoy Personal Growth books; perhaps start with *A Bend in the Road*, which does eventually deliver a happy ending, but not without first exploring themes of murder, betrayal, infertility, and single parenthood.

- **Zane.** Themes of sex, race, sex, friendship, sex, family, and sex—with a little sex thrown in—form the basis of Zane's raunchy, earthy *Shame on It All*. Go on some wild adventures, both in and out of the bedroom, with three African American sisters as they grow in their relationships with each other, with their friends, and with a series of attractive men. Or focus on marital relationships with *Addicted*, about a woman whose passions threaten to destroy her life.

1

2

3

4

5

6

7

8

Chapter 3

Health, Wellness, and Beauty

Definition

In this chapter, you'll find books about keeping the female body beautiful and healthy.

Publishing in the areas of women's health, wellness, and beauty is huge. For evidence, just glance around the next time you're waiting in line at the grocery store. Advice to women about health (especially concerning diet), emotional wellness, and physical beauty screams from the magazine covers. Of these topics, writing about beauty is especially prevalent, with publications devoted to every conceivable element of glamour, from skin to hair to nails to topics that would have raised an eyebrow even ten years ago; who knew there could be a reading audience for the different types of bikini waxes?

At first glance it may seem easy to define the category of women's health, wellness, and beauty books. Any book that helps women improve or maintain health, or that helps them understand or practice beauty, is fair game. The problem is that some books may be healthy for one person but not for another. A weight-loss book, provided it recommends healthy practices, is appropriate for someone who needs to lose weight; it is poison for someone suffering from anorexia. Then there are broader, more abstract questions to consider. Are weight-loss books good because they help women achieve healthy weights? Yes, sometimes. Are weight-loss books bad because they reflect our society's obsession with thinness? Yes, sometimes.

The same quandaries apply to many beauty books. Is it appropriate to include them in the same chapter that addresses women's wellness? Sometimes a little makeup can lift a woman's spirits and improve her body image. But too much focus on beauty can be psychologically devastating, as Cheri K. Erdman argues in *Nothing to Lose: A Guide to Sane Living in a Larger Body*.

For the purposes of this chapter, a variety of books are discussed, from those that specifically address the potential pitfalls of too much attention to appearance, to those that celebrate women's beauty. The annotations make clear the focus of each book, allowing the reader to choose for herself what fits her needs.

Appeal

The most striking appeal of books about women's health, wellness, and beauty is the personal connection. The great majority of these books are deliberately written to strike a personal chord with the reader. We turn to these books to read about other women in similar circumstances, to see ourselves mirrored from the pages. Whether the circumstances are commonplace—"How do other women with frizzy hair manage their curls?"—or profound—"How have other women coped with cancer?"—the books endeavor to offer guidance in a personal, meaningful way.

Quality information is a compelling draw for many of the health books, especially the ones concerned with disease. One of those books is Kathy Kastan's *From the Heart: A Woman's Guide to Living Well with Heart Disease*, which offers practical advice for women living with the number one cause of death in America. Sometimes the information is of a very personal nature, and a book can help the reader anonymously find answers to questions that might be too embarrassing to ask of a doctor or bookseller; *For Women Only: A Revolutionary Guide to Overcoming Sexual Dysfunction and Reclaiming Your Sex Life*, by Jennifer Berman, Laura Berman, and Elisabeth Bumiller, helps women learn about sexual satisfaction.

Another draw of these books is the element of emotional support. Marisa Acocella Marchetto's *Cancer Vixen* is not a medical text but a heartfelt memoir of one woman's battle with breast cancer—an excellent choice for women with any sort of cancer. Offering emotional support on another important topic is Gloria Steinem's *Revolution from Within: A Book of Self-Esteem*, about nurturing one's mental health.

But many of these books offer more than the emotional support of personal stories; in many cases, they are filled with practical advice. Nearly all of the books about diet and appearance have step-by-step instructions, such as Shalini Vadhera's *Passport to Beauty: Secrets and Tips from around the World for Becoming a Global Goddess*, filled with advice on creating natural cosmetics with products from the grocery store. Likewise, the Boston Women's Health Book Collective classic *Our Bodies, Ourselves* offers practical health advice for women. And a pleasantly surprising number of books in women's health, beauty, and wellness simultaneously offer all of the appeals: personal connection, quality information, emotional support, and practical advice.

Organization

The first section, "Physical Health, Diet, and Exercise," features general health books for women, along with a subsection called "Sports and Fitness." Next up is the "Body Image" section, with books about the impact of society on the way women view their own bodies. This is followed by the "Cancer and Disease" category, including books about various types of cancer, physical disease, and mental illnesses. Under this section are two subsections; "Eating Disorders" covers eating disorders such as bulimia and anorexia, while "Addiction" discusses substance abuse. Then we have "Sexual Health and Satisfaction," with books about women's sexual happiness and physical health, plus a subsection titled "Menstruation and Menopause."

In the next section, "Emotional Wellness," you'll find an eclectic variety of titles, all designed to help women improve their emotional well-being; the "Midlife and Aging" subsection has books for women of a certain age, while "Recovery from Trauma" speaks to the emotional needs of women recovering from traumatic experiences such as rape and miscarriage. Finally, the "Beauty, Fashion, and Appearance" section features books about fashion, style, and beauty, as well as a section specifically devoted to cosmetics.

Physical Health and Diet

Here are guides to eating well, feeling better, and keeping your body in great shape.

If you're like most women, you've read your fair share of diet books, health books, magazine articles, and doctor's office pamphlets that implore you to lose weight and get in shape. Many of these books are utter tripe; they are written by companies looking to make a buck off of women's low self-esteem, or they are well-intentioned guides that simply don't speak to readers' individual backgrounds. The titles annotated here have been carefully chosen for their quality and for their recognition that different women have different bodies and, therefore, different needs.

Boston Women's Health Book Collective

Our Bodies, Ourselves: A New Edition for a New Era. New York: Simon & Schuster, 2005. 832pp. ISBN 9780743256117.

First published in 1970 as a feminist reaction to health books that ignored or neglected women's needs, *Our Bodies, Ourselves* is an enduring classic, a treasure trove of information about all aspects of women's health. Written in clear, accessible language, the book has a dual purpose. First, as one would expect, the book offers information about women's health in sections such as "Taking Care of Ourselves" and "Relationships and Sexuality." What makes this an especially valuable health book, however, is the book's second purpose, to make readers aware of the inequities in women's health care that still persist in the medical establishment, even today. With a feminist, activist slant that encourages women to take charge of their own health and to advocate for better treatment from their doctors, this is an empowering, educational book, indispensable for any woman's bookshelf.

Subjects: Health • Feminism • Activism • Body Image • Diet • Exercise • Mental Health • Relationships • Sexuality • Health Care • Sexual Health • Menstruation • Pregnancy • Birth • Fertility • Midlife • Seniors

Now try: The marvelous Dr. Christiane Northrup continues the discussion of women's health in *Women's Bodies, Women's Wisdom: Creating Physical and Emotional Health and Healing*. As in *Our Bodies, Ourselves*, Northrup encourages women to take control of their health and health care, although hers is a more holistic approach, one that places women's physical health within the context of their everyday lives; the emotional and spiritual emphasis makes it an excellent companion to the more straightforward *Our Bodies, Ourselves*. And don't miss *Dr. Nieca Goldberg's Complete Guide to Women's Health*, in which Dr. Nieca Goldberg offers frank, accessible advice on women's unique health needs, from age-old health issues such as pregnancy and menopause to more recent issues such as cosmetic surgery and Botox.

Delaney, Lisa

Secrets of a Former Fat Girl: How to Lose Two, Four (or More!) Dress Sizes, and Find Yourself along the Way. New York: Hudson Street Press, 2007. 246pp. ISBN 9781594630330.

Note: This is not a diet book. And that is precisely why it is so very effective. Journalist Delaney writes not about dieting but about motivation, about changing one's attitude and self-image. She is well-suited to dispense advice: as a woman who dropped seventy pounds and has kept off the weight for decades, she understands what works and what doesn't. Attempting a particular diet will yield only temporary results; reworking an entire outlook can result in permanent changes. With concrete advice and Delaney's seven secrets of weight loss, this is a practical, accessible guide geared toward women who are sick of dieting and who want something better to help them lose weight.

Subjects: Weight • Body Image • Mental Health • Health • How-to

Now Try: Like Delaney, Janice Taylor understands that diets usually disappoint, that something different is necessary to lose weight and to keep it off. In *Our Lady of Weight Loss: Miraculous and Motivational Musings from the Patron Saint of Permanent Fat Removal*, she offers a unique approach to reenvisioning food, based on her own experience in losing fifty pounds; she encourages readers to redirect their food cravings into art, crafts, and other creative outlets. Or try reading *The Skinny: How to Fit into Your Little Black Dress Forever: The Eat-What-You-Want Way to Lose Weight and Keep It Off*, by Melissa Clark and Robin Aronson. Though this is a diet book, it nicely compliments *Secrets of a Former Fat Girl*, because it does not advocate any particular type of diet or food plan; rather, the authors teach readers new ways to think about food and eating, emphasizing a positive and empowering approach to weight loss.

Forsythe, Cassandra E.

Women's Health Perfect Body Diet: The Ultimate Weight Loss and Workout Plan to Drop Stubborn Pounds and Get Fit for Life. New York: Rodale, 2008. 356pp. ISBN 9781594867903.

Unless you live in a cave, you know that dieting and exercise books marketed at women are everywhere. Each one clamors for attention, claiming that it offers a unique approach to weight loss and health. What makes *Women's Health Perfect Body Diet* any different from the others? For one thing, it's actually three books in one; after you do a quick measurement to determine whether you're shaped like a pear, an apple, or an avocado, you follow the diet and exercise plans written for your specific fruit shape. And another reason why this is a superior book: it's actually fun to read. With a chatty tone, frequent doses of humor, and plentiful anecdotes from women who are trying to get in shape, author Forsythe manages to make dieting and exercise both enjoyable and informative.

Subjects: Weight • Dieting • Exercise • Health • Humor • How-to

Now Try: Remember what fruit shape you are? Geralyn Coopersmith takes the fruit metaphor even further, helping women identify their bodies as one of six different shapes in *Fit and Female: The Perfect Fitness and Nutrition Game Plan for Your Unique Body Type*. With a readable, accessible style, she presents exercises and diet plans that are tailored to readers' individual shapes. Read this in conjunction with *Women's Health Perfect Body Diet* to find a health plan that matches your particular needs.

Fulda, Jennette

Half-Assed: A Weight-loss Memoir. Berkeley, CA: Seal Press, 2008. 300pp. ISBN 9781580052337.

At the tender age of twenty-three, Jennette Fulda was morbidly obese. At the tender age of twenty-four, she was still morbidly obese—372 pounds, to be exact. For a full year, she had realized that she needed to lose weight, thanks to a wake-up call in the form of gallbladder surgery, but still she did nothing. That inertia is part of what makes this such a worthwhile read: Fulda is a flawed person, one who suffers from the same lapses and mistakes as the rest of us—and despite that, she still managed to drop 186 pounds. This is the inspiring story of a young woman who found it within herself to change her eating habits and to begin exercising—first by walking, then by adding other activities such as weight-lifting and running. Funny, frank, and compulsively readable, this memoir will speak to anyone who has ever struggled to lose weight.

> **Subjects:** Weight • Dieting • Exercise • Body Image • Health • America • Memoir • Young Adult
>
> **Now Try:** For another chronicle of the trials of losing weight, turn to *The Weight-Loss Diaries*. Like Fulda, author Courtney Rubin uses humor and an engaging prose style to detail the screw-ups and setbacks she endured on her journey through two years of losing weight. Or try *Confessions of a Carb Queen: The Lies You Tell Others & the Lies You Tell Yourself: A Memoir*, by Susan Blech and Caroline Bock. This is the story of Susan Blech and her struggle to slim down from 468 pounds; with honesty and sensitivity, she offers a detailed discussion of the mental and emotional rigors she went through to lose two hundred pounds.

Guiliano, Mireille

French Women Don't Get Fat. New York: Knopf, 2005. 263pp. ISBN 9781400042128.

Mireille Guiliano, the CEO of the French champagne house Cliquot, here answers a question that mystifies Americans: How is it that French women eat and drink whatever they like without gaining weight? Their diets are filled with cheeses, croissants, red wine, and other calorie-laden foods, and yet French obesity rates are far lower than in America. The secrets to their slim figures are surprisingly simple. You don't have to bother with a gym, for instance, if you walk frequently; you can indulge in rich foods if you mind your portion size; and if you learn to luxuriate in food, savoring every deliberate bite, you'll stop cramming in meals, a practice that invariably leads to overeating. As much a guide to emotional happiness and food sensibility as a diet and exercise guide, this charming book encourages us to rethink our attitudes toward food—but don't worry, there are plenty of delectable recipes to get you started on the French path.

Subjects: Food • Dieting • Exercise • Health • Mental Health • Recipes • How-to

Now Try: You learned the principles of cultivating your inner French woman in Guiliano's first book; now dig deeper in her follow-up, *French Women for All Seasons: A Year of Secrets, Recipes & Pleasure*. Emphasizing moderation in all things, Guiliano presents even more recipes, along with tips on everything from entertaining to dressing fashionably to aging with style. Then try a book written in response to *French Women Don't Get Fat*, Naomi Moriyama's *Japanese Women Don't Get Old or Fat: Secrets of My Mother's Tokyo Kitchen*, featuring Japanese recipes for healthful—and youthful—living.

Sparrowe, Linda, and Patricia Walden

The Woman's Book of Yoga and Health: A Lifelong Guide to Wellness. Boston: Shambhala, 2002. 363pp. ISBN 9781570624704.

Yoga has been around for about five thousand years, give or take—but for most of its history, it has been practiced by men. In this excellent guide, yogis Sparrowe and Walden consider yoga with women's unique needs in mind. With a focus on *asanas*, the physical postures of yoga, the book focuses on different stages of women's lives—pregnancy, menopause, menstruation—and on relieving specific problems such as stress, depression, and headaches. With clear, easy-to-understand descriptions of poses and detailed explanations of benefits and contraindications, the photos and text make this how-to guide suitable for beginners and advanced practitioners alike.

Subjects: Yoga • Exercise • Health • How-to

Now Try: Supplement the physical poses of *The Woman's Book of Yoga and Health* with *Yoga: A Gem for Women*. Written by Geeta S. Iyengar, the daughter of world-renowned yogi B. K. S. Iyengar, this excellent book explores the theory and practice not only of active poses but of breathing, meditation, and restoration, all written with special attention to the changing needs of women as they go through the various stages of life.

Sports and Fitness

Athletic activities are featured in the titles in this section.

For the most part, the books discussed in this section are instructional guides, although each of the titles are enjoyable for their discussion of women, sports, and exercise. Read them to brush up on your skills or to learn more about topics such as tennis, sailing, and bodybuilding. Sports fans will also want to see the section titled "Women Athletes" in Chapter 7.

Antoun, Rob

Women's Tennis Tactics. Champaign, IL: Human Kinetics, 2007. 211pp. ISBN 9780736065726.

Rob Antoun, a veteran coach of women's tennis, has created a detailed guide that is suitable for beginning through advanced players. His insight and advice are excellent, and the diagrams and step-by-step instructions are straightforward and easy to follow. With chapters such as "Tactical Returning" and "Playing the Baseline," the book's primary audience will be tennis players, although anyone interested in learning more about the sport will enjoy the author's observations on the art of tennis playing as it relates to women.

Subjects: Tennis • Sports • Athletes • Exercise • How-to

Now Try: Even if you don't play the sport, you can still dive into the fascinating world of women's tennis with *Venus Envy: A Sensational Season inside the Women's Tennis Tour.* The word "sensational" in the subtitle is no exaggeration: dysfunction, intrigue, rivalries, and sexual escapades abound. Author L. Jon Wertheim, a writer with *Sports Illustrated*, offers a glimpse into the behind-the-scenes drama of professional women's tennis that will captivate players and fans alike.

Colgate, Doris

Sailing. A Ragged Mountain Press Woman's Guide. Camden, ME: Ragged Mountain Press, 1999. 174pp. ISBN 9780070067202.

As president of the National Women's Sailing Association, Doris Colgate knows what she's talking about when it comes to sailing. *Sailing* is chock full of advice for anyone who wants to sail, including chapters devoted to getting started, sailing smart, and using the wind. Of special interest to women readers is Colgate's emphasis on the feminine qualities of sailing; a willingness to communicate and a keen desire to understand, for instance, make women natural candidates for sailing. A generous helping of anecdotes and advice from women sailors illuminates women's sailing issues such as clothing, fitness, and relationships.

Subjects: Sailing • Sports • Nature • Adventure • Travel • How-to • Quick Read

Now Try: Written especially for women who find themselves as the co-owners of their husbands' boats, *It's Your Boat Too: A Woman's Guide to Greater Enjoyment on the Water* takes the perspective that, if your spouse is going to have fun on a boat, you may as well learn, too. With lots of practical advice and suggestions, author Suzanne Giesemann explains the basics of sailing, while striving to empower women to develop the confidence they need to enjoy sailing. Look for additional guidance in Maria Russell's book *The Best Tips from Women Abroad*, featuring advice on sailing from women, for women.

Fair, Lorrie, and Mark Gola

Fair Game: A Complete Book of Soccer for Women. Chicago: Contemporary Books, 2003. 182pp. ISBN 9780071426893.

Lorrie Fair is more than qualified to write an instructional book about soccer. She plays for the U.S. women's national team, she won three national titles with the University of North Carolina, and she was on the women's World Cup team. In this tremendously informative guide, she shares her own insights and experiences as she lays out the rules of soccer. With plentiful photos, sidebars, and quotes from other women soccer players, she discusses techniques, strategies, and psychological tricks to improve one's game. The book is intended for soccer players, though anyone with an interest in women's sports will enjoy reading about Fair's perspective on the game.

Subjects: Soccer • Sports • Athletes • Exercise • How-to • Quick Read

Now Try: Whereas *Fair Game* emphasizes instruction, *Women's Soccer: The Passionate Game* is pure celebration. Even if you've never kicked a soccer ball in your life, you'll appreciate the beautiful photos and quirky bits of trivia in this tribute to the role of women in soccer. Written by Barbara Stewart and Helen Stoumbos, the book includes history, stats, interviews, and anecdotes that will delight fans of women's soccer.

Hall, Adrienne

Backpacking. A Ragged Mountain Press Woman's Guide. Camden, ME: Ragged Mountain Press, 1998. 160pp. ISBN 9780070260276.

Good for both the novice and experienced backpacker, *Backpacking* is a thorough how-to guide written with women in mind. Generously peppered with anecdotes, inspirations, and tips from veteran women backpackers, the book offers detailed, practical advice on undertaking backpacking adventures that last anywhere from one night to several months, replete with checklists of what to bring and recommended exercises for getting into shape. What makes *Backpacking* especially attractive is its attention to subjects that matter to women, such as menstruation, gear designed for women's bodies, and child care.

Subjects: Backpacking • Nature • Exercise • Adventure • Travel • How-to • Quick Read

Now Try: If you're excited by the thought of backpacking but not quite ready to sacrifice all the comforts of life, turn to Bobbi Hoadley's book *Babes in the Woods: The Woman's Guide to Eating Well, Sleeping Well, and Having Fun in the Backcountry*. Whether you're backpacking, hiking, camping, or plain old picnicking, this is your guide for enjoying the great outdoors while retaining some vestige of civilization. Hoadley covers topics such as hygiene, clothing, cooking, and exercising, all written to appeal to women who yearn for outdoor adventures that retain at least some creature comforts.

Sandoz, Joli, and Joby Winans, eds.

Whatever It Takes: Women on Women's Sport. New York: Farrar, Straus and Giroux, 1999. 323pp. ISBN 9780374525972.

Whatever It Takes collects fifty-six powerful essays about sports written by a variety of women, many of whom will seem surprising choices; who would have thought of essayist Annie Dillard as an athlete? The editors' decision to solicit contributions from notable authors as well as recognized sports heroes, however, was an inspired choice: the writing throughout the anthology is magnificent, and the treatment of sports as a subject is compelling. A wide variety of sports is covered, ranging from traditional women's sports such as horseback riding and softball to decidedly untraditional sports such as squash and wrestling. Superior writing and captivating stories make this a joyous celebration of women in sports.

Subjects: Sports • Athletes • Exercise • Essays • Anthology • Collection

Now Try: Fiction lovers will want to read *A Whole Other Ball Game: Women's Literature on Women's Sport*, also edited by Sandoz, in which another stellar cast of writers turns to women in sports, this time with short stories and poems. And be sure not to miss *Game Face: What Does a Female Athlete Look Like?*, edited by Jane Gottesman and Geoffrey Biddle. This beautiful collection of black-and-white photographs celebrates women in sports, from celebrity sports stars to amateur enthusiasts.

Schoenfeld, Brad

Sculpting Her Body Perfect. Champaign, IL: Human Kinetics, 2000 (2008). 226pp. ISBN 9780736001540.

> Brad Schoenfeld is the next best thing to having your own personal trainer. This fitness expert has packed his advice and experience into an excellent instructional guide that women can use at home or at the gym. Good for the novice and the advanced body builder alike, the book offers 118 exercises designed to tone, to shape, and to take off excess pounds in chapters such as "Hourglass Back," "Shapely Shoulders," and "Sexy Chest." Filled with illustrations, photographs, detailed instructions, and anecdotes from women bodybuilders, this is an accessible, easy-to-understand guide written with women's unique needs in mind.

> **Subjects:** Exercise • How-to

> **Now Try:** Perhaps anaerobic exercise isn't your cup of tea, or maybe you'd like to supplement the intensive, focused exercises suggested in Schoenfeld's book. In that case, try *Fitness through Aerobics*, by Jan Galen Bishop. With clear instructions and illustrations, the book provides a variety of exercises and routines that readers can use to improve their cardiovascular health and overall fitness.

Body Image

> Books about body image focus on perceptions we as women have about the way we look or appear to others.

The "Body Image" section discusses some of the most emotionally charged titles in this entire text. This is not a neutral topic. All women have an opinion about their bodies—and unfortunately, those opinions tend to be negative. Height, weight, skin color, race, complexion, hair, and shape are just some of the contentious topics discussed here. Books such as Susan Bordo's *Unbearable Weight*, about societal norms of beauty, may make you cry; others, like Nancy Amanda Redd's *Body Drama*, will have you cheering yourself for your beautiful body. Readers will also enjoy the section in Chapter 4 titled "Women's Bodies and Sexuality Throughout History" and the positive body images in the "Celebrating Women" section of Chapter 2.

Bordo, Susan

Unbearable Weight: Feminism, Western Culture, and the Body. Berkeley: University of California Press, 1993. 361pp. ISBN 9780520079793.

> You'll never look at female bodies the same way again after reading Bordo's insightful analysis of women's bodies and body image in the West. In a series of essays such as "Hunger as Ideology" and "Anorexia Nervosa: Psychopathology as the Crystallization of Culture," Bordo applies her feminist perspective to the peculiar, perverse, and pervasive

norms of women's bodies, especially with regard to size, shape, and weight. Be forewarned, the prose is academic and dense, and some readers may be turned off by the book's own unbearable weight. Readers willing to tackle the scholarly jargon, however, will be rewarded with a fine piece of feminist thought, replete with thought-provoking commentary on Western beauty ideals.

Subjects: Beauty • Body Image • Appearance • Weight • Gender • Feminism • Essays • Collection

Now Try: For further serious feminist writing about societal ideals of women's bodies, turn to the anthology *The Politics of Women's Bodies: Sexuality, Appearance, and Behavior*, edited by Rose Weitz. Although not every essay is as weighty as Bordo's writing, the various contributors apply keen scholarship to their pieces about body image and sexuality. Those readers who would like a break from heavy academic writing will enjoy *Body Outlaws: Rewriting the Rules of Beauty and Body Image*, edited by Ophira Edut. (Interestingly, this book was formerly known as *Adios, Barbie!* until Mattel threatened to sue.) Though much lighter in tone and style than *Unbearable Weight*, readers will enjoy the excellent writing and thought-provoking insights into body image presented in this engaging collection of essays.

Craig, Maxine Leeds

Ain't I a Beauty Queen?: Black Women, Beauty, and the Politics of Race. Oxford: Oxford University Press, 2002. 198pp. ISBN 9780195142679.

"Each day of their lives," writes sociologist Craig, "black women rearticulate the meaning of black racial identity as they position themselves in relation to culturally available images of black womanhood." It is this intersection between racial identity and racial imagery that forms the basis of Craig's thought-provoking study. Drawing on primary historical documents and interviews with black women, Craig's scholarship examines the changing roles of black women's beauty and racial identity in American history. With writing that is academic but accessible, *Ain't I a Beauty Queen?* invites readers to consider themes of African American appearance as it has been historically depicted both in the mainstream press and in minority publications.

Subjects: Beauty • Body Image • Appearance • Media • African Americans • Race • Gender • Class • History • Women's History • Social History • American History • Twentieth Century • America • Quick Read

Now Try: With the historical context of *Ain't I a Beauty Queen?* in mind, turn now to *Hair Matters: Beauty, Power, and Black Women's Consciousness*, in which author Ingrid Banks interviews more than fifty black women to unveil the meaning of their hair in terms of race, sex, class, and beauty. Then, for a more lighthearted read, turn to the fun facts in *Hair Story: Untangling the Roots of Black Hair in America*, by Ayana D. Byrd and Lori L. Tharps. With plentiful illustrations and examples from pop culture, this social history reveals the beauty and meaning of the hair of black women and black men in America.

Erdman, Cheri K.

Nothing to Lose: A Guide to Sane Living in a Larger Body. San Francisco: HarperSanFrancisco, 1995. 189pp. ISBN 9780062512536.

Erdman's premise is simple but wonderfully refreshing: big is beautiful, no matter what society says. Of course, considering the prevalence of anti-fat bias in the media, it can be very difficult for women to overcome years of messages to the contrary, but that's where Erdman steps in. Drawing on personal experiences and stories from other large women, she shows readers how to improve their self-images and how to see the beauty of larger sizes. She encourages women to stay healthy, of course, but she cautions against diets or exercising for the purpose of weight loss, urging readers instead to simply eat healthy foods and to exercise for the pleasure of it. Engaging and empowering, *Nothing to Lose* offers positive, practical steps for women to learn to love their bodies, no matter the size.

Subjects: Weight • Body Image • Appearance • Health • Mental Health • How-to • Quick Read

Now Try: For more of Erdman's inspiring approach to improving body image, turn to *Live Large! Affirmations for Living the Life You Want in the Body You Already Have*. Arranged in the form of short meditations, each page presents a thoughtful paragraph, an affirmation, and a "size-wise" action. Then try *Bountiful Women: Large Women's Secrets for Living the Life They Desire*, in which psychologist Bonnie Bernell presents strategies to help large women cope in a small-minded world.

Etcoff, Nancy L.

Survival of the Prettiest: The Science of Beauty. New York: Doubleday, 1999. 325pp. ISBN 9780385478540.

Psychologist author Etcoff, of the Harvard Medical School, tackles a commonly held belief in this readable book: beauty is not just a social construct, after all. Instead, Etcoff says, there are biological and psychological forces that work to nurture and elevate beauty. Drawing on scientific research and cultural comparisons, Etcoff convincingly argues that beauty is an evolutionary survival trait, not just a lucrative creation of the media and society. Clear prose, frequent wit, and persuasive examples make this a good choice for any woman interested in beauty, and for lovers of compelling social science.

Subjects: Beauty • Appearance • Science • Psychology • Biology • Sociology

Now Try: Steve Jeffries expands on Etcoff's argument that beauty is a survival trait in *Appearance Is Everything: The Hidden Truth Regarding Your Appearance Discrimination*. Success in life is largely dependent on physical beauty, says Jeffries, and lack of success can often be traced to lack of physical beauty. Solid social science research and a readable style make this a compelling book, though it is disturbing to realize how much we let appearance influence our judgments, despite our best intentions. This is an eye-opener for anyone who is unconvinced of the power and influence of physical appearance.

Kuczynski, Alex

Beauty Junkies. New York: Doubleday, 2006. 290pp. ISBN 9780385508537.

Americans are enjoying a love affair with cosmetic surgery, explains *New York Times* writer Kuczynski, and surgeons are happy to satisfy their desires. Cosmetic surgery is typically fast and profitable for the doctors, and the patients love the improvements they get from Botox, liposuction, nose jobs, breast augmentations, and a host of other procedures. Or at least, they love the improvements until something goes wrong, as Kuczynski herself discovered after a treatment to her upper lip didn't go as planned.

With engaging prose, Kuczynski explores the cosmetic surgery industry, offering a fascinating look at why Americans shell out billions of dollars—and risk serious physical health complications—in the pursuit of beauty.

>   **Subjects:** Cosmetic Surgery • Beauty • Appearance • Body Image

>   **Now Try:** Virginia L. Blum continues the discussion of society's obsession with cosmetic surgery in *Flesh Wounds: The Culture of Cosmetic Surgery*. Like Kuczynski, she speaks from personal experience going under the knife, offering her own story and her thoughtful cultural insights into questions of beauty, beauty image, and identity. Then, for a deeper knowledge of how our present obsessions with surgical beauty improvements came to be, turn to *Venus Envy: A History of Cosmetic Surgery*, in which Elizabeth Haiken explores the tensions between doctors' goals and patients' demands in the twentieth century.

Martin, Courtney E.

Perfect Girls, Starving Daughters: The Frightening New Normalcy of Hating Your Body. New York: Free Press, 2007. 330pp. ISBN 9780743287968.

Young women have always been concerned about their appearance, but the cult of perfection is reaching frightening new heights. In this profoundly disturbing investigation into body image and beauty, writer and activist Martin draws on more than a hundred interviews with girls between the ages of nine and nineteen to paint an ugly and disturbing portrait of modern beauty ideals. Young women are obsessed with achieving the perfect body: they think incessantly about their weight and appearance, frequently to the point where they develop life-threatening eating disorders. With beautiful writing and a keen sense of compassion, Martin reveals the shocking, pervasive trend among young women toward hating their bodies.

>   **Subjects:** Body Image • Beauty • Appearance • Eating Disorders • Health • Mental Health • Feminism • Young Adult

>   **Now Try:** Author Leslie Goldman, herself a recovered anorexic, adds further insight into the unpleasant body ideals of modern America in *Locker Room Diaries: The Naked Truth about Women, Body Image, and Re-imagining the "Perfect" Body*. Turning to her own familiar haunt, the women's locker room of her local gym, she interviewed her fellow exercise junkies to reveal their attitudes toward body image and appearance; the results, unsurprisingly, show that women of all ages are obsessed with getting thinner. Then enter the harrowing near-future dystopia of Kit Reed's *Thinner Than Thou*, a science fiction novel in which dieting has replaced religion and obesity is a crime.

Molinary, Rosie

Hijas Americanas: Beauty, Body Image, and Growing Up Latina. Emeryville, CA: Seal Press, 2007. 327pp. ISBN 9781580051897.

Having grown up as the only Puerto Rican girl in her school, author Molinary appreciates from personal experience how difficult it can be to maintain dual identities as a Latina in the United States. The tension between these conflicting cultures forms the basis of *Hijas Americanas*, an eye-opening exploration of what it means to be a Latina girl in America. Based on Molinary's interviews with eighty Latinas, her own experiences, and on the survey results submitted by 500 Latinas, the book illuminates the stereotypes and the realities that Latina girls grapple with, covering such themes as beauty, prejudice, and depictions of Latinas in the media.

>   **Subjects:** Beauty • Body Image • Latinas • Race • Stereotypes • America • Young Adult

Now Try: Though more academic in approach than *Hijas Americanas*, the book *From Bananas to Buttocks: The Latina Body in Popular Film and Culture* makes for a good companion read. Edited by Myra Mendible, this collection of essays brings together writings of scholars from a wide variety of backgrounds as they contemplate the representation of Latinas such as Jennifer Lopez and Salma Hayek in the popular media. The academic investigations in the collection help give context to the frustrations voiced by the young Latinas in *Hijas Americanas*.

Redd, Nancy Amanda

Body Drama. New York: Gotham, 2008. 271pp. ISBN 9781592403264.

If there's anyone qualified to write about body image, Nancy Redd is it: she graduated with honors from Harvard with a degree in Women's Studies . . . and then she won the Miss America swimsuit competition. In this fantastic book, Redd shows us that real women have real bodies: some of us are skinny, some of us are fat; some of us have acne, some of us have out-of-control body hair; some of us have bum luck with our fingernails, and some of us have breasts that we'd love, if only they were bigger, or smaller, or perkier. This is a health book for women and girls, with accessible information on topics mundane and serious, but it is unlike any other health book you've seen before: there are hundreds of photos of naked, normal, un-airbrushed women—and the centerpiece? Why, it's a full-color spread of twenty-four glorious vulvas in all their natural beauty. Though aimed at teen girls and twenty-somethings, this empowering book will be a delight for women of any age who want sound medical advice and a healthy body image.

Subjects: Body Image • Appearance • Health • Mental Health • Feminism • Young Adult

Now Try: If you found yourself delighted to see pictures of real, normal, perfectly ordinary vaginas in *Body Drama*, then you owe it to yourself to get—what else?—vaginal coloring books. You'll probably have to spring for them at a bookstore, since libraries typically don't carry coloring books (and since they *really* don't carry copies of *genital* coloring books). But the price will be worth it. Find some crayons and markers and have a blast with *Cunt Coloring Book: Drawings*, by Tee Corinne, and *The Big Coloring Book of Vaginas*, by Morgan Hastings. As with *Body Drama*, these books serve to remind readers that women's body parts are beautiful, that air-brushed photos of porn stars do *not* represent reality.

Shanker, Wendy

The Fat Girl's Guide to Life. New York: Bloomsbury, 2004. 274pp. ISBN 9781582344287.

"If you ever want to make people visibly uncomfortable," advises journalist Shanker, "just say the f-word out loud." She is referring, of course, to the word "fat"—and in this snarky, sassy, snappy book, she re-envisions the word in a wonderful new light. With refreshing honesty and a zippy wit, this memoir describes the years Shanker spent trying to lose weight, and her eventual realization that fat is a perfectly fine way to be. Emphasizing the importance of health over the societal imperative of thinness,

Shanker shares her own journey toward fat acceptance, along with her biting commentary on the way that society perceives fat.

Subjects: Weight • Health • Body Image • Beauty • Appearance • Gender • Mental Health • Feminism • Third-wave Feminism • Humor • Memoir

Now Try: For an excellent collection of writings about what it means to be fat in America, turn to *Scoot Over, Skinny: The Fat Nonfiction Anthology*, edited by Donna Jarrell and Ira Sukrungruang. The contributors—including women and men, fat people and those who love them—relate their own experiences with being fat, sharing insights on the prejudices faced by fat people and the pervasive, persistent ways that society reviles people of size.

Vincent, Norah

Self-Made Man: One Woman's Journey into Manhood and Back Again. New York: Viking, 2006. 290pp. ISBN 9780670034666.

Most women who venture into a man's world do so metaphorically. Norah Vincent did so literally when she modified her appearance to include a crew cut, men's clothing, and a convincing five-o'clock shadow. For over a year she lived as "Ned," immersing herself in masculine strongholds such as monasteries, strip clubs, and bowling alleys. Her goal was to see if she could pass for a man, even in the tricky realm of dating. The result is a fascinating piece of investigative journalism, strengthened with Vincent's insights into gender from her most unusual perspective.

Subjects: Body Image • Transgender • Gender • Sociology • America

Now Try: Norah Vincent infiltrates the secrets of sex and gender; now try authors who go undercover to explore race and class. In his 1959 classic *Black Like Me*, John Howard Griffin darkens his skin and discovers the painful truths of racial discrimination in the deep South. And in her controversial, compelling reporting in *Nickel and Dimed: On (Not) Getting by in America*, Barbara Ehrenreich goes undercover to see if she can survive in low-wage occupations such as cleaning houses, waiting on tables, and working at Wal-Mart.

Wann, Marilyn

Fat! So?: Because You Don't Have to Apologize for Your Size! Berkeley, CA: Ten Speed Press, 1998. 207pp. ISBN 9780898159950.

"Most Americans would rather get hit by a truck than get fat," writes the going-on-three-hundred-pound Wann. "Amputation of a leg is preferable. Some would rather die." Enough with the fat hatred, says Wann: it's time to place our priorities where they belong, on healthiness. What matters is that you eat well and exercise; and if you still happen to be fat, it doesn't matter, because you'll be healthy. Chock full of quotes, tips, pictures of beautiful fat women—even a dress-up Venus of Willendorf—this fun, sassy book emphasizes health and shows that fat is a beautiful way to be.

Subjects: Weight • Health • Body Image • Beauty • Appearance • Mental Health • Humor • Quick Read

Now Try: Energize yourself with two fat-positive memoirs by two famous ladies of bountiful size. In *Wake Up, I'm Fat!*, Emmy-winning actress Camryn Manheim, of the television show *The Practice*, shares the story of her success in show business, replete with jibes at the people who were too blinded by her size to see her talent. In *Skinny Women Are Evil: Notes of a Big Girl in a Small-minded World*, comedian/actress Mo'Nique, of the television show *The Parkers*, gleefully bashes skinny women while offering a stirring tribute to the beauty of fat.

Wolf, Naomi

The Beauty Myth: How Images of Beauty Are Used against Women. New York: William Morrow, 1991 (2007). 348pp. ISBN 9780688085100.

> A classic in the field of women's studies, Wolf's book is still as relevant and thought-provoking as when it was published in 1991. Feminist Wolf examines the societal pressures on women to be beautiful, pressures that are, if anything, even more prevalent today. She examines these damaging influences in several different spheres of life, including the workplace, the bedroom, and the cosmetic surgeon's office. Accessible and insightful, *The Beauty Myth* is recommended not just for feminists but for anyone uncomfortable with the beauty objectification of women.
>
> > **Subjects:** Beauty • Appearance • Media • Body Image • Sociology • Feminism
> >
> > **Now Try:** Meet Jean Kilbourne, another spitfire feminist who's had it up to here with unhealthy images of women in the media. In her book *Deadly Persuasion: Why Women and Girls Must Fight the Addictive Power of Advertising*, she makes a convincing and disturbing case for the dangers of advertisements marketed toward girls and women, showing that the pervasive and insidious effects of advertising can negatively affect their physical health, their emotional health, and their relationships.

Cancer and Disease

> Various ailments and unhealthy conditions, and how women have dealt with them, provide focus to the stories in this section.

The books in this section include personal survival memoirs—such as Susanna Kaysen's unforgettable *Girl, Interrupted*, about living with mental illness—as well as books that include practical advice on coping with illness, such as Kathy Kastan's *From the Heart: A Woman's Guide to Living Well with Heart Disease*. They speak not only to women who have suffered from disease, but to those who wish to understand a particular disease.

Carr, Kris

Crazy Sexy Cancer Tips. Guilford, CT: Skirt!, 2007. 203pp. ISBN 978159-9212319.

> "Sexy" and "cancer:" we don't typically put those two words next to each other, but this isn't your typical book. When Kris Carr was diagnosed with cancer at the age of thirty-one, she had the presence of mind to document her treatment and recovery with photographs and words. The first part of this book is her memoir—but then we go on to meet other young women as they battle cancer. Vibrant and flashy, the quirky photos and personal testimonies show these cancer survivors as beautiful, bold women. With

chapters such as "Holy Shit! I Have Cancer, Now What?" and "Bald Is Beautiful and Other Facts about Femininity and Fashion," the book offers tips and inspiring stories of coping with cancer; it is marketed toward a younger crowd, but women of any age will welcome the book's message about staying sexy in spirit, even in the face of cancer.

Subjects: Cancer • Body Image • Mental Health • Health • Humor • Memoir • Biography • Quick Read

Now Try: Though without the spicy language and snarkiness of *Crazy Sexy Cancer Tips*, Laura Jensen Walker's *Thanks for the Mammogram!: Fighting Cancer with Faith, Hope, and a Healthy Dose of Laughter* is every bit as funny. Like Kris Carr, Walker was only in her thirties when she was diagnosed with cancer. With chapters such as "Beauty and the Breast" and "How to Lose Thirty Pounds in Thirty Days: The Chemo Diet Way," this hysterically funny memoir tells the story of how one young woman depended on humor and religious faith to triumph over cancer.

Delinsky, Barbara

Uplift: Secrets from the Sisterhood of Breast Cancer Survivors. New York: Pocket Books, 2001. 293pp. ISBN 9780743431361.

Perhaps you're already familiar with Barbara Delinsky from having read her thought-provoking novels; now meet her in a very personal way in *Uplift*. Here Delinsky shares her own experiences in surviving breast cancer, along with the stories of more than three hundred other survivors. In chapters such as "Radiation: Soaking Up the Rays" and "Chemo and Hair: Mane Matters," you'll find anecdotes, tips, and reflections from strong women who have successfully fought back against breast cancer. Read this for practical ideas on coping with breast cancer or simply to find inspiration and encouragement from other women who have been there.

Subjects: Breast Cancer • Cancer • Health

Now Try: For more inspiring stories of women who have triumphed over breast cancer, turn to the wonderful book *B.O.O.B.S.: A Bunch of Outrageous Breast-Cancer Survivors Tell Their Stories of Courage, Hope, & Healing*, edited by Ann Kempner Fisher. Featuring women from a variety of backgrounds, this collection of essays is a testament to the courage of ten women survivors; it will empower and encourage anyone who is battling with cancer herself. Readers who enjoy poetry will wish to turn to *The Cancer Poetry Project: Poems by Cancer Patients and Those Who Love Them*, edited by Karin B. Miller.

Drescher, Fran

Cancer Schmancer. New York: Warner Books, 2002. 236pp. ISBN 9780446530194.

With all the attention given to breast cancer, it can be hard to find books about the other cancers that affect women. Thankfully, celebrity Fran Drescher, of the television series *The Nanny*, chose to write about her experience with uterine cancer. With her straightforward prose and liberal doses of comedy, Drescher turns a difficult battle with cancer into a readable, optimistic story. At times the narrative events are painful: there is a frustrating series of doctor visits with nothing but incorrect diagnoses, and there is even a chapter on the loss of Drescher's beloved dog. But with the support of family and friends, and the ultimate remission of the cancer, this is an uplifting account of dealing with cancer. The fascinating and peculiar perils of celebrity life add to the book's appeal.

Subjects: Uterine Cancer • Cancer • Health • Relationships • America • Memoir

Now Try: For another celebrity memoir of cancer, try *No Time to Die: Living with Ovarian Cancer*, by Liz Tilberis, who was editor of the magazine *Harper's Bazaar*. In this case the disease is ovarian cancer, the unwelcome cousin to Drescher's uterine cancer. With humor and honesty, the book chronicles the author's diagnosis, chemotherapy, bone-marrow transplant, and remission (though be aware that, several years after the book's publication, Tilberis lost her battle with cancer). Readers who liked Drescher's portrayal of celebrity life will enjoy Tilberis's glimpses into the world of fashion and publishing.

Jamison, Kay R.

An Unquiet Mind: A Memoir of Moods and Madness. London: Picador, 1997. 224pp. ISBN 9780330346511.

As a professor of psychiatry at the Johns Hopkins School of Medicine, Dr. Kay Jamison knew all about manic depression; after all, she'd cowritten the classic text on the subject, *Manic-Depressive Illness*. But hers was far more than a clinical understanding of the disease; having suffered from manic-depression since adolescence, she had firsthand knowledge of the highs and the lows, the stunning periods of creativity and the debilitating episodes of depression. With clarity, candor, and vivid detail, she recalls her years of struggling with the disease, her attempted suicide, and her eventual decision to medicate her illness, even at the risk of losing her creative powers.

Subjects: Manic Depression • Mental Health • Health • America • Memoir

Now Try: If you think Jamison had it bad, wait till you meet Marya Hornbacher. Like Jamison, she suffered from manic depression—and also alcoholism, drug abuse, self-mutilation, anorexia, and bulimia. Read about her struggles and cautious recovery in *Madness: A Bipolar Life*. Then, for a memoir of another mental illness, paranoid schizophrenia, turn to the compelling memoir *The Center Cannot Hold: My Journey through Madness*, in which Elyn R. Saks details her horrific battle with mental illness and the drugs that both helped and hurt her.

Kastan, Kathy

From the Heart: A Woman's Guide to Living Well with Heart Disease. Cambridge, MA: Da Capo Lifelong, 2007. 263pp. ISBN 9780738210933.

Informative, accessible, and inspiring, *From the Heart* offers practical advice and compassionate support for women living with heart disease, the leading cause of death in women. As the president of WomenHeart: The National Coalition for Women with Heart Disease, Kastan is eminently qualified to write about the subject, but she does not focus on technical medical details. Instead she uses her background as a therapist to pen a guide to emotional wellness in the face of heart disease, drawing on her own experience and the personal stories of other women who have coped with the illness. Down-to-earth advice and meaningful suggestions make this an invaluable, practical resource for any woman with heart disease.

Subjects: Heart Disease • Mental Health • Health • How-to

Now Try: A wonderful complement to Kastan's guide is *Women Are Not Small Men: Life-Saving Strategies for Preventing and Healing Heart Disease in Women*, by cardiologist Nieca Goldberg. A wealth of practical advice and step-by-step suggestions makes this book every bit as useful as Kastan's, but it emphasizes an understanding of medical causes and treatments, whereas Kastan's book emphasizes the emotional aspects of health. This is a good suggestion for women who liked the practical advice in Kastan's book but who want more of a medical focus for preventing and living with heart disease.

Kaysen, Susanna

Girl, Interrupted. New York: Turtle Bay Books, 1993. 168pp. ISBN 978067-9423669.

"It was a spring day, the sort that gives people hope: all soft winds and delicate smells of warm earth. Suicide weather." What sort of mind could write something so very bizarre, so very disturbing? The mind of Susanna Kaysen, that's who, and no wonder: though she wrote her memoir nearly thirty years after the fact, she was still affected by her time at McLean Hospital. In 1967, she had semi-voluntarily committed herself to the psychiatric hospital, where she was to spend two years being treated for borderline personality disorder—though whether the diagnosis was ultimately correct is disconcertingly unclear to both Kaysen and the reader. Through a series of short vignettes, delivered in Kaysen's brilliant, evocative style, we get a glimpse into the mind of a teenage girl who is lucid, observant, intelligent, and possibly—but not certainly—insane.

> **Subjects:** Borderline Personality Disorder • Mental Health • Health • America • Young Adult • Memoir • Quick Read

> **Now Try:** Kaysen may or may not have had borderline personality disorder; Rachel Reiland definitely did. In *Get Me Out of Here: My Recovery from Borderline Personality Disorder*, we meet a married accountant and mother of three with a troubled existence: in addition to her suicide attempts and violent outbursts, she suffered from substance abuse and anorexia. An eventual diagnosis of borderline personality disorder made sense of her behavior; in this captivating memoir, we see how she struggled with her disease and how, ultimately, she recovered. Then, for another stunning memoir of mental illness, turn to *The Quiet Room: A Journey Out of the Torment of Madness*, by Lori Schiller and Amanda Bennett. This time the disease is schizoaffective disorder, but fans of *Girl, Interrupted* will savor Schiller's provocative descriptions of the terrors of mental illness.

Lucas, Geralyn

Why I Wore Lipstick to My Mastectomy. New York: St. Martin's Press, 2004. 208pp. ISBN 9780312334451.

At only twenty-seven years of age, Geralyn Lucas was diagnosed with breast cancer. Undergoing a mastectomy seemed like the overwhelmingly sensible thing to do—except, well, it would mean giving up a breast, and Lucas didn't know what to do: "This was one part of the diagnosis that no one would discuss with me: what it means to have one boob in a boob-obsessed universe." In this candid, fast-paced, breezy memoir, Lucas recounts her diagnosis, surgery, chemotherapy, and recovery, but this is more than a typical survivor's memoir; with her insightful reflections on cancer, beauty, and body image, this is both an empowering story of survival and a thought-provoking contemplation on how disease affects our understanding of self.

> **Subjects:** Breast Cancer • Cancer • Body Image • Appearance • Memoir • America • Quick Read

> **Now Try:** Unlike Geralyn Lucas, Jessica Queller was not diagnosed with breast cancer at an early age, but her situation was grim nonetheless. Her mother had fended off breast cancer, only to die from ovarian cancer at age fifty-eight, and Queller herself

tested positive for the BRCA gene mutation, meaning that she was extremely likely to develop breast cancer and ovarian cancer. Those who enjoyed Lucas's reflections on body image and beauty will be drawn in by Queller's thoughts as she contemplates, and ultimately chooses, a preventative double mastectomy in *Pretty Is What Changes: Impossible Choices, the Breast Cancer Gene, and How I Defied My Destiny*.

Marchetto, Marisa Acocella

Cancer Vixen: A True Story. New York: Knopf, 2006. 211pp. ISBN 9780307263575X.

She's in her early forties, she has the world's best fiancé, she has shoes enough for a small nation, and she has the ultra-cool job of drawing cartoons for *The New Yorker*. Then Marisa discovers a lump in her breast. Told in graphic novel form, *Cancer Vixen* is the story of one woman's diagnosis, treatment, and remission from breast cancer. Though at times sobering and even heartbreaking, this sassy example of real-life Chick Lit is a pick-me-upper for anyone who has ever suffered from cancer (and even those who haven't). Fashion, beauty, and drama in Manhattan—expertly rendered in Machetto's vivid colors—coexist with deeper subjects of marriage, death, and infertility, making this memoir both refreshingly lighthearted and surprisingly profound.

Subjects: Breast Cancer • Cancer • Health • Chick Lit • Dating • Relationships • Marriage • Fashion • America • Graphic Novel • Memoir • Quick Read

Now Try: Graphic novels boast a thriving number of memoirs and personal stories, including several remarkable cancer stories. In *Cancer Made Me a Shallower Person: A Memoir in Comics*, Miriam Engelberg tells a story similar to Marchetto's, complete with diagnosis, treatment, and recovery from breast cancer. The humor is darker and the art is bleaker, but the power and honesty will resonate with Marchetto fans. Other good bets include *Mom's Cancer*, in which author Brian Fies focuses on the effects of the disease on the immediate family, and *Our Cancer Year*, by husband-and-wife team Harvey Pekar and Joyce Brabner about cancer, marriage, and life.

Eating Disorders

Eating disorders involve unhealthy psychological patterns that cause one to eat or refuse to eat—such as anorexia nervosa, bulimia, and binge eating.

The "Eating Disorders" section features books about the eating disorders that affect young women—and older women, too, as we learn in *The Body Myth*, by Margo Maine and Joe Kelly. Memoirs comprise a big part of this section—try starting with Marya Hornbacher's *Wasted*—though books with a broader focus are here, too, such as the unsettling photo-essay *Thin*, by Lauren Greenfield, David B. Herzog, and Michael Strober.

Benson, Lorri Antosz, and Taryn Leigh Benson

Distorted: How a Mother and Daughter Unraveled the Truth, the Lies, and the Realities of an Eating Disorder. Deerfield Beach, FL: Health Communications, 2008. 230pp. ISBN 9780757305948.

Life was pretty much perfect. Steve and Lorri Benson shared a happy marriage; their finances were sound; their three daughters were thriving in school—and then Lorri discovered her oldest child, a high school sophomore, in the act of purging. In this cowritten memoir, both mother and daughter share their perspectives on the nightmare of Taryn's eating disorder. You'll meet Taryn, an overachieving teenager who hates her body and hates her self, and you'll meet Lorri, a mother plagued with self-doubt as she watches her child's health weaken. There is ultimately a happy ending, with Taryn in active recovery, but the journey there is painful for mother, child, and family. Read this for insight into the way that eating disorders affect both individuals and the people who love them.

> **Subjects:** Eating Disorders • Bulimia • Body Image • Health • Mental Health • Mothers • Daughters • Relationships • America • Memoir • Young Adult

> **Now Try:** For another moving memoir of triumph over eating disorders, turn to *Inner Hunger: A Young Woman's Struggle through Anorexia and Bulimia*. At age fourteen, Marianne Apostolides developed anorexia and then bulimia to lose weight and become more popular. Her heartfelt, powerful descriptions of her diseases and her recovery, along with her reflections on how her illnesses affected her relationships with her family, will resonate with fans of *Distorted*.

Bullitt-Jonas, Margaret

Holy Hunger: A Memoir of Desire. New York: A. A. Knopf, 1999. 253pp. ISBN 9780375400940.

It's an all-too-familiar story: Bullitt-Jonas's family seemed perfect to outsiders, but their overachieving lifestyle had devastating effects. The father was an alcoholic, the mother was chronically depressed, and the daughter, struggling with her difficult relationship with her parents, turned to food. Painfully honest and deeply disturbing, this memoir recalls Bullitt-Jonas's years of overeating and the dysfunctional home atmosphere that exacerbated her addiction. This fast-paced read is understandably grim in tone, though it concludes on a positive note: between her Christian faith and her attendance at Overeaters Anonymous meetings, she is able to recover from her addiction.

> **Subjects:** Eating Disorders • Overeating Disorder • Spirituality • Christianity • Religion • Body Image • Health • Mental Health • Relationships • America • Memoir • Young Adult

> **Now Try:** For another candid memoir of overeating, turn to *It Was Food vs. Me—and I Won* by Nancy Goodman. Though lighter in tone than *Holy Hunger*, fans of Bullitt-Jonas will appreciate Goodman's nuanced understanding of the psychological problems that cause eating disorders and her honesty in recounting her own struggles. Then, for readers who want an accessible medical explanation of the biology and psychology behind overeating, turn to the compassionate discussion and practical advice of *Why Can't I Stop Eating?: Recognizing, Understanding, and Overcoming Food Addiction* by Debbie Danowski and Pedro Lazaro.

Greenfield, Lauren, David B. Herzog, and Michael Strober

Thin. San Francisco: Chronicle Books, 2006. 191pp. ISBN 9780811856331.

If it weren't for the pleasant setting, you might think you were looking at victims of widespread famine or war. But no: the extraordinarily thin women captured in Greenfield's photographs are patients at the Renfew Center, an institution for those who suffer from eating disorders. In this shocking photo-essay, you'll meet twenty teenaged girls and women who have wasted away to practically nothing. The vivid photos are supplemented with thoughtful interviews and excerpts from the women's journals, making this a visceral, powerful glimpse into the mental and physical terrors of eating disorders.

> **Subjects:** Eating Disorders • Anorexia • Body Image • Health • Mental Health • Young Adult • Quick Read

> **Now Try:** If the journal excerpts of *Thin* helped you better understand the perspectives of women with eating disorders, try Morgan Menzie's *Diary of an Anorexic Girl.* This collection of thoughts, prayers, poems, and eating schedules, told from the perspective of Menzie's fictionalized alter-ego, takes us into the mind of a woman who drops to eighty-nine pounds before beginning to recover from anorexia.

Hornbacher, Marya

Wasted: A Memoir of Anorexia and Bulimia. New York: HarperCollins, 1998. 298pp. ISBN 9780060187392.

"Don't eat," Hornbacher's inner voice hissed. "I'm not going to let you eat. I'll let you go as soon as you're thin, I swear I will. Everything will be okay when you're thin." But this duplicitous inner voice was lying: "She never let me go," acknowledges Hornbacher. "And I've never quite been able to wriggle my way free." Powerful, personal, and frightening, this is Hornbacher's record of her anorexia and bulimia—the seductive lure of purging, the times spent in hospitals, the horrifying drop to fifty-two pounds, when doctors gave her a week to live. This is an eye-opening account of the mental and physical distortions of eating disorders, but reader be warned: Though Hornbacher is much healthier by the end of the book, she is still struggling to break completely free of the grip of her diseases.

> **Subjects:** Eating Disorders • Anorexia • Bulimia • Body Image • Health • Mental Health • America • Memoir

> **Now Try:** It is perhaps inaccurate to describe a book about anorexia as upbeat, but *Stick Figure: A Diary of My Former Self* is downright cheerful compared with *Wasted*; readers looking for a more promising antidote to the grim realities of Hornbacher's story would do well to turn to this memoir by Lori Gottlieb. Make no mistake, this narrative takes some unpleasant turns as the author's body dwindles away, but she eventually recognizes her disease for what it is and embarks on a full recovery.

Liu, Aimee

Solitaire: A Narrative. New York: Harper & Row, 1979. 215pp. ISBN 9780060-126520.

It's a common refrain: the ambitious daughter of high-achieving parents, in her quest to be the perfect child, develops an obsession with her weight. In Liu's case, that obsession took the form of anorexia. Though this is an older title, published in 1979 when Liu was only twenty-five, the book remains popular because of its relevant, insightful message. Told in novelist Liu's lovely prose style, the memoir offers a visceral account of living with anorexia at a time when few people knew about the disease or understood its dangers.

> **Subjects:** Eating Disorders • Anorexia • Body Image • Health • Mental Health • America • Memoir

> **Now Try:** Now jump forward nearly thirty years and read Liu's sequel, *Gaining: The Truth about Life after Eating Disorders.* As in *Solitaire,* we once again peer into Liu's life, watching as she relapses in middle age before recovering once again from her eating disorders. But this is more than just a memoir: we also meet other recovering anorexics and bulimics of various ages, races, and even sexes in this well-researched examination of the lingering effects of eating disorders. Then continue learning about the sociological impact of eating disorders in *Regaining Your Self: Breaking Free from the Eating Disorder Identity: A Bold New Approach* by Ira M. Sacker and Sheila Buff. Solid medical research, anecdotes and stories from those with eating disorders, and practical advice make this a valuable companion to Liu's books.

Maine, Margo, and Joe Kelly

The Body Myth: Adult Women and the Pressure to Be Perfect. Hoboken, NJ: John Wiley, 2005. 279pp. ISBN 9780471691587.

It's only teen girls and adolescents who get eating disorders, right? Not so fast. As clinical psychologist Maine shows, women in their thirties, forties, and beyond are feeling increased pressure to maintain the "perfect body." In their anxiety over body image, many begin to take drastic measures with their food, embarking on unhealthy diets and developing disordered eating habits. Maine thoroughly explores this grim new reality, but she also offers hope for women with poor body images, whether or not they suffer from eating disorders. With anecdotes, compassionate advice, and practical steps for improving physical and mental health, this is an excellent guide to overcoming negative body images and harmful eating habits.

> **Subjects:** Eating Disorders • Body Image • Health • Mental Health • Psychology • Health Care • How-to

> **Now Try:** For more of Maine's insightful discussion of body image, turn to *Body Wars: Making Peace with Women's Bodies: An Activist's Guide.* Covering a whole slew of topics—including obesity, dieting, cosmetic surgery, and advertising—she takes popular culture to task by soundly criticizing society's unrealistic beauty ideals, while offering specific steps for fighting against the unhealthy images that surround us. And for further suggestions on improving one's body image, turn to the compassionate wisdom of *Bodylove: Learning to Like Our Looks—and Ourselves,* by Rita Jackaway Freedman.

Addiction

Addiction involves an unhealthy relationship with a substance or activity—in these titles, alcohol and drugs.

With books about drug addiction and alcoholism, the "Addiction" section offers somber food for thought. Ease yourself into these important but painful books with the lightest of the bunch, Emily Flake's wryly humorous graphic novel *These Things Ain't Gonna Smoke Themselves*. Or plunge directly into one of the nightmarish stories of addiction with Caroline Knapp's *Drinking: A Love Story*.

Flake, Emily

These Things Ain't Gonna Smoke Themselves: A Letter to a Very Bad Habit. New York: Bloomsbury, 2007. 112pp. ISBN 9781596913288.

People who smoke will relate to Emily Flake's memoir. People who have never smoked will better understand the appeal of smoking. People who are trying to quit won't know whether to laugh or cry. And if you are a former smoker—well, I hate to say it, but maybe it's best if you avoid this book altogether. Emily Flake can't decide whether her book is a love letter or a hate letter to smoking. She bitterly describes the terrible physical and societal problems of smoking, but she also describes, with formidable clarity, the forbidden pleasure of a cigarette. With very dark humor and edgy illustrations, this short graphic novel is the stark testimony of a woman who knows she's addicted but who doesn't know if she wants to be free.

Subjects: Smoking • Drugs • Addiction • Humor • Memoir • Graphic Novel • Quick Read

Now Try: Andrew Wicks, the hero of *Too Cool to Be Forgotten*, differs from Emily Flake in one very significant way: he definitely wants to quit smoking, as we learn when he seeks help from a hypnotist. But the perils and pleasures of smoking still loom large in this fiction graphic novel; like Flake's book, it will speak to smokers and nonsmokers alike. Flake's fans will also enjoy the narrative and illustrations of the book's talented author/artist Alex Robinson.

Holden, Kate

In My Skin: A Memoir. New York: Arcade, 2006. 285pp. ISBN 978158-0052184.

She was a nice girl from a loving family, a college graduate with a stable job and a comfortable lifestyle. Then, on a whim, Kate Holden stepped out of character and tried heroin. From that first hit, she was hooked. In seemingly no time, she lost her friends, her apartment, and her job—and without a job, she had no way to pay for her addiction. In desperation, she turned to prostitution, first by turning tricks on the street, then by seeking employment at brothel houses. In this harrowing but lyrically written memoir, Holden recounts the nightmare of drug addiction, the stark reality of sex work, and the long, painful road to recovery.

Subjects: Addiction • Drugs • Prostitution • Labor • Relationships • Australia • Memoir

Now Try: Holden's story, though grim, ultimately ends on a note of hope; readers willing to read a story of addiction with a tragic ending should try *Terry: My Daughter's Life-and-Death Struggle with Alcoholism*, by George S. McGovern. Like Holden, Terry McGovern came from a good family; her father George, after all, ran for president in 1972. But as George McGovern shows, a good family wasn't enough; despite rehab, family support, intensive counseling, and several years of sobriety, alcoholism eventually claimed Terry's life. This is a sad but compelling story, a heartfelt look at the dangers of alcohol addiction.

Knapp, Caroline

Drinking: A Love Story. New York: Dial Press, 1996. 258pp. ISBN 978038-5315517.

Journalist Knapp is brutally, wrenchingly honest in her memoir of addiction: "I drank when I was happy and I drank when I was anxious and I drank when I was bored and I drank when I was depressed, which was often." Her drinking ruined everything—her relationships, her physical health, her mental health—and yet she did not realize she was an alcoholic. It took years for her to move past her denial and to seek help, which she found in Alcoholics Anonymous. This is a painful memoir in all ways (on top of everything else, Knapp battled with anorexia), but it is ultimately a story of recovery. Those who have never suffered from alcoholism will have their eyes opened by Knapp's descriptive writing; those who do suffer from alcoholism will find inspiration.

Subjects: Alcoholism • Drugs • Addiction • Eating Disorders • America • Memoir

Now Try: Knapp found succor in Pete Hamill's memoir *A Drinking Life*, and those who enjoyed *Drinking* will appreciate it, too: Hamill artfully describes the joys and the sorrows of the alcoholism that nearly destroyed his life—and, as in Knapp's book, readers will be inspired when the author finally recovers. Likewise, Augusten Burroughs ultimately beats his alcoholism in *Dry*, though the road there is twisted and bizarre. Burroughs relies on dark humor far more than Knapp does, but those who appreciate Knapp's vivid descriptions and lucid prose will be drawn to *Dry*.

Wurtzel, Elizabeth

More, Now, Again: A Memoir of Addiction. New York: Simon & Schuster, 2002. 333pp. ISBN 9780743223300.

"Even if you keep a record," writes Wurtzel, "it is still difficult—no, impossible—to say when it went from casual use to a bad habit to a problem to abuse to addiction." She is certainly in a position to say, having tried everything from acid to ecstasy to heroine. She was able to control her drug use, mostly, but she developed an addiction to cocaine and to the prescription drug Ritalin, and the addictions slowly began to corrupt the seemingly charmed life of the best-selling author of *Prozac Nation*. Written with gut-wrenching honesty, this is the story of Wurtzel's numerous attempts to come clean, delivered in an edgy, eminently readable style.

Subjects: Drugs • Addiction • America • Memoir

Now Try: Wurtzel paints a startling portrait of the two drugs that controlled her life, Ritalin and cocaine; now learn more about them from a scientific background. Leslie L. Iversen's *Speed, Ecstasy, Ritalin: The Science of Amphetamines* provides medical and sociological contexts for understanding the drugs; the frequent use of anecdotes and case studies will appeal to those who liked the personal voice in Wurtzel's book. Likewise, Dominic Streatfeild includes stories and anecdotes from cocaine users in *Cocaine: An*

Unauthorized Biography, an excellent sociological and historical survey of the drug. Finally, those who enjoyed the pain and honesty of Wurtzel's style will want to read her first memoir, *Prozac Nation: Young and Depressed in America*, about the severe depression she suffered as a young woman.

Zailckas, Koren

Smashed: Story of a Drunken Girlhood. New York: Viking, 2005. 342pp. ISBN 9780670033768.

"Like most women, I remember my first drink in tender minutiae," writes Zailckas. "I am fourteen, which is the norm these days, when the mean age of the first drink for girls is less than thirteen years old." Immediately she is hooked. Nothing stops her—hangovers, blackouts, a stomach-pumping at the emergency room, date rape—nothing interferes with her decade-long affair with alcohol. This is a scary story, but the most unsettling aspect is Zailckas's contention that young women's drinking is a severe problem at the societal level. She interweaves her personal narrative with research and statistics that convincingly attest to a nationwide problem. Readers will be troubled by Zailckas's conclusions, though they will be heartened by her personal recovery.

Subjects: Alcoholism • Drugs • Addiction • Gender • America • Memoir • Young Adult

Now Try: Like Zailckas, Janice Erlbaum spent her adolescence in a haze, though her experience was rather more dramatic. In *Girlbomb: A Halfway Homeless Memoir*, she describes her difficult home life (she lives for a while in a shelter to escape her stepfather), her alcohol and drug abuse, and her frequent, casual sexual encounters. Fans of *Smashed* will enjoy Erlbaum's captivating writing style, and will applaud her eventual recovery. Fans of *Smashed* will also enjoy the lucid descriptions of addiction and substance abuse in Susanna Sonnenberg's book *Her Last Death: A Memoir*. This time the drug user is not the author but her mother; nonetheless, the alcoholism, drug use, and casual sex in the house affected Sonnenberg's childhood in tragic, terrible ways.

Sexual Health and Satisfaction

Desires, thoughts, and physical manifestations related to women's sexuality provide the focus to titles in this section.

In a time and age when sex is everywhere—on the radio, on television shows, in magazine articles, in books—it's amazing how much we still don't know about our own bodies. The books in this subgenre seek to dispel the myths and correct the misunderstandings about sex. You'll find answers to questions biological and physiological (Which parts do what? How does orgasm work? How does one cope with sexually transmitted diseases?) and answers to questions about sexual pleasure (Can single women have happy sex lives? How about older women? How can lesbians improve their sexual encounters?).

Berman, Jennifer, Laura Berman, and Elisabeth Bumiller

For Women Only: A Revolutionary Guide to Overcoming Sexual Dysfunction and Reclaiming Your Sex Life. New York: Henry Holt, 2001. 269pp. ISBN 97808-05078831.

Many women, explain sisters Jennifer and Laura Berman, are ashamed to talk about their sexual problems, while others have internalized the idea that sexual dysfunction is normal. But in this empowering guide, urologist Jennifer and sex therapist Laura show that sexual health is every bit as important as other types of health, and that a variety of treatments are available for sexual problems. Written in clear, compassionate language, the doctors help women understand the biological and psychological causes of sexual dysfunction, while explaining treatments such as medication, therapy, and exercise. Accessible and informative, this is an excellent, positive approach to improving the sex lives of women and their partners.

> **Subjects:** Sexual Health • Health • Sexuality • Biology • Psychology • Mental Health • Health Care • How-to

> **Now Try:** For more intelligent, down-to-earth advice on improving sexual health, turn to *I'm Not in the Mood: What Every Woman Should Know about Improving Her Libido*, in which physician Judith Reichman discusses hormonal problems and other causes that can result in a decreased libido. Then, to understand sexual problems in a larger scope, try Hilda Hutcherson's *What Your Mother Never Told You about S.E.X.* Working on the assumption that many women's sex lives are unfulfilling simply because they don't have the information they need, gynecologist Hutcherson presents a wonderful overview of everything sexual—anatomy, eroticism, biological problems—in this grown-up's guide to Sex Ed.

Bouchéz, Colette

The V Zone: A Woman's Guide to Intimate Health Care. New York: Simon & Schuster, 2001. 256pp. ISBN 9780684870977.

Everything you ever wanted to know about sexual health but were too timid to ask is explained in glorious detail in this comprehensive guide. With clear, accessible language, medical journalist Bouchéz covers topics ranging from urinary tract infections to mysterious bumps to sexual diseases. But this is not just for women who have noticed something amiss; with its thorough explanations, supportive illustrations, and frequent sidebars, this is every woman's guide to understanding her sexual organs and sexual health. Use this book not only for answers to medical problems, but for general knowledge about maintaining sexual wellness.

> **Subjects:** Health • Sexual Health • Health Care • How-to

> **Now Try:** Pair *The V Zone* with another accessible medical book, *A Woman's Guide to Sexual Health*, by Mary Jane Minkin and Carol V. Wright. Naturally, this title discusses some of the same topics covered in Bouchéz's book, such as sexually transmitted diseases and infections, but it also covers related women's health issues such as menstruation, fertility, and contraception.

Chalker, Rebecca

The Clitoral Truth: The Secret World at Your Fingertips. New York: Seven Stories Press, 2000. 256pp. ISBN 9781583220382.

Women's sexual responses, writes feminist activist Chalker, have long been "dismissed, undervalued, unexplored, or misunderstood." Seeking to correct the myths and misinformation, Chalker presents this lovely guide to the clitoris, the surprisingly complex organ that features not just the glans (with four times as many nerve endings as the glans of the penis) but the shaft, the hood, and a host of other intricate body parts that many women (to say nothing of men!) don't really know about. With detailed illustrations and straightforward language, *The Clitoral Truth* demystifies the biology of the only body part of females *or* males that exists solely to provide pleasure. Also included is a chapter called "Beyond Intercourse: New Erotic Possibilities," a practical discussion of how women and their lovers can explore the potential of sexual pleasure.

Subjects: Clitorises • Sexuality • Sexual Health • Health • Biology • How-to

Now Try: No lover? No problem! Betty Dodson's *Sex for One: The Joy of Selfloving* shows how people of either sex can experience sexual pleasure by themselves, whether or not they have sexual partners. The helpful illustrations and candid, positive discussion will appeal to fans of the sex-positive messages in *The Clitoral Truth.*

Dillow, Linda, and Lorraine Pintus

Intimate Issues: Conversations Woman to Woman: 21 Questions Women Ask about Sex. Colorado Springs, CO: Water Brook Press, 1999. 274pp. ISBN 978157-8561490.

Conflicting messages about sex and sexuality bombard us every day, making it difficult for Christian women to know what God does and does not sanction in the bedroom. To alleviate the confusion, Christian authors Dollow and Pintus asked 1,000 women what they wanted to know about sexual relations between husbands and wives. The twenty-one most frequently asked questions form the chapter headings of the book: "What Do I Do When I Don't Want to Do It?" is one, and "What's Not Okay in Bed?" is another. With a solid grounding in scripture, the authors present thoughtful, faith-based guidance for Christian women who want to be both godly and sensuous.

Subjects: Christianity • Religion • Sexuality • Marriage

Now Try: Women and men alike who want more information about the Christian approach to sexuality will do well to turn to the perennially popular book *Intended for Pleasure,* by Ed Wheat and Gaye Wheat. Covering such diverse topics as lovemaking techniques, orgasm, impotency, and sex for seniors, this is a comprehensive guide to all things sexual for married Christian couples, written with a firm basis in scripture.

Eden, Dawn

The Thrill of the Chaste: Finding Fulfillment While Keeping Your Clothes On. Nashville, TN: W Publishing Group, 2006. 212pp. ISBN 9780849913112.

Columnist and blogger Dawn Eden is no stranger to sexuality; she is not a virgin, and she didn't become a Christian until she was in her thirties. It is precisely this background that makes her argument for chastity compelling: as someone who developed her views as an adult *after* living a sexually promiscuous lifestyle, her point of view strikes the reader as heartfelt and legitimate, cultivated with the benefit of perspective and age. Drawing on Christian theology and her own experiences with sex and renewed chastity, Eden eloquently makes a case for sexual purity as the most satisfying option for singles, while offering practical advice to help single readers maintain or recommit to chastity.

Subjects: Sexuality • Dating • Relationships • Christianity • Religion • How-to

Now Try: Readers who like the honest voice and spiritual sensibility of *The Thrill of the Chaste* may enjoy the book *Soul Virgins: Redefining Single Sexuality*, by Douglas Rosenau and Michael Todd Wilson. With a basis in Christian scripture, *Soul Virgins* helps singles understand sex within the context of spiritual and religious fulfillment, while practical suggestions help readers learn how to enjoy physical and spiritual sexuality without compromising their sexual purity.

Hite, Shere

The Hite Report: A Nationwide Study on Female Sexuality. New York: Macmillan, 1976 (2000). 438pp. ISBN 9780025518513.

When it was first published in 1976, the *Hite Report* made a big splash, and to this day it continues to have an enormous impact on the public's understanding of female sexuality. Based on the responses from 3,000 surveys taken by women all across America, the report reveals women's attitudes toward sexuality in all its facets, with sections on such topics as intercourse, masturbation, lesbians, and older women. At the time of its original publication, the most startling finding concerned women's preference for clitoral stimulation, rather than vaginal penetration—and while this is no longer shocking news, the report is still relevant today for its clear, straightforward examination of women's sexualities.

Subjects: Sexuality • Gender • America

Now Try: The natural follow-up, of course, is *The Hite Report on Male Sexuality*. Based on 7,000 survey responses, this report considers sexuality from the point of view of men, covering such topics as fidelity, masturbation as a complement to partner sex, and men's feelings about women's bodies. Then turn to Hite's predecessor, the pioneering sex researcher Alfred Kinsey, whose in-person interviews with men and women about their sexual lives turned into two books, *Sexual Behavior in the Human Male* (1948) and *Sexual Behavior in the Human Female* (1953). Although Kinsey died in 1956, the Kinsey Institute continues his work; see, for instance, *The Kinsey Institute New Report on Sex: What You Must Know to Be Sexually Literate* (1990), by June Machover Reinisch, Ruth Beasley, and Debra Kent.

Hutcherson, Hilda

Pleasure: A Woman's Guide to Getting the Sex You Want, Need, and Deserve. New York: Putnam, 2006. 316pp. ISBN 9780399153044.

"Your best friend can tell you her surefire secret to sensual bliss, but it may not work for you at all," writes gynecologist Hutcherson, a sex columnist for *Essence* and *Glamour* magazines. "You could try to replicate the steamiest scene in the sexiest movie and find that it just feels ridiculous when it's you and your husband, instead of two young movie stars." There are many, many different paths to sexual pleasure, and this excellent guide does a remarkable job of exploring them. Chapters such as "Your Body: Female Sexual Awareness," "Knowing Yourself: Discovering What Feels Good," and "The Pleasures of Cunnilingus" explain the intricacies of sexual pleasure, while offering practical (and fun!) suggestions for getting the most out of your sex life.

Subjects: Sexuality • Sexual Health • Health • How-to

Now Try: Looking for more ways to spice up your sex life? Learn from the experiences of ordinary women in *Women Who Love Sex: Ordinary Women Describe Their Paths to Pleasure, Intimacy, and Ecstasy*. Culling the responses from her interviews with hundreds of women, sex therapist Gina Ogden presents an honest, empowering look at women's sexual happiness, covering not just the mechanics of sexual activity but also the emotional and spiritual conditions that contribute to women's sexual pleasure.

Lavinthal, Andrea, Jessica Rozler, and Cindy Luu

The Hookup Handbook: A Single Girl's Guide to Living It Up. New York: Simon Spotlight Entertainment, 2005. 232pp. ISBN 9780689876462.

This is not our mothers' dating scene. Long gone are the days of formal courtship, and even casual dating seems to be going the way of the dodo. For career-minded twenty-something singles, the new norm is the hookup, the no-strings-attached sexual encounter that might (but probably won't) lead to a relationship. With chapters such as "Drink Till He's Cute: The Fall-Down-Drunk Hookup," "The Best Bud Tryst: When Platonic Turns Erotic," and "Your Own Personal Hookup Contract: Break This and There Will Be Hell to Pay," the authors describe this new dating terrain, offering practical advice with a healthy helping of jaded cynicism. Edgy, witty, and wry, *The Hookup Handbook* covers everything you need to know about the modern relationship scene.

Subjects: Sexuality • Sexual Health • Health • Relationships • Dating • Humor • How-to • Quick Read

Now Try: Continue learning about the complicated terrain of the hookup scene in *The Happy Hook-Up: A Single Girl's Guide to Casual Sex*, by Alexa Joy Sherman and Nicole Tocantins. With a hip tone and some very sensible advice, the authors offer serious guidance (see Chapter 2, "Herpes and Scabies and Crabs, Oh My!") along with more lighthearted takes on negotiating the world of casual sex. Then take a more sobering look at the hook-up phenomenon with Kathleen Bogle's *Hooking Up: Sex, Dating, and Relationships on Campus*. Sociologist Bogle does not moralize or preach, but she does take an even-handed approach to her study of hooking up among college students, revealing trends both good and bad.

Livoti, Carol, and Elizabeth Topp

Vaginas: An Owner's Manual. New York: Thunder's Mouth Press, 2004. 267pp. ISBN 9781568582955.

Despite the title, this wonderful health book discusses far more than vaginas. Gynecologist Livoti and her daughter Topp present a thorough exploration of women's sexual organs, along with a host of related topics, from menstruation to sex, sexually transmitted diseases to abortion, menopause to medical complications. Anecdotes and personal asides liven up the text without interfering with the book's primary purpose: to deliver a thorough overview of women's sexual health. With plain, straightforward language, the authors elegantly explain the mysteries of women's bodies, making this an indispensable, accessible guide.

Subjects: Vaginas • Sexual Health • Health • Biology • How-to

Now Try: It's more lighthearted in tone than *Vaginas*, but Lisa Sussman's *Brazilian Waxes, Lazy Ovaries & Outrageous Orgasms: Embarrassing Questions and Sassy Answers on Women's Sexual Health* is a welcome supplement. Once again, the topic is women's sexual health, but in this case the material tends more toward the curious than the serious; learn, for instance, how long it takes women to reach orgasm with a vibrator, and find out if size really does matter.

Newman, Felice

The Whole Lesbian Sex Book: A Passionate Guide for All of Us. San Francisco: Cleis Press, 2004. 376pp. ISBN 9781573441995.

The Whole Lesbian Sex Book is exactly that: a sex manual for lesbians of every stripe. This is for those who are strictly lesbian, bisexual, or transgendered; for those who enjoy the extreme S&M play and those who like vanilla oral sex; for those who like sex toys, those who prefer group sex, those who are single, those who really aren't quite sure what they like. No matter what your persuasion (literally: even straight men can glean a lot from this book), this is a comprehensive guide to women's sexual pleasure, relayed in accessible language and with an emphasis on both safety and fun.

Subjects: Lesbian Sexuality • Sexuality • Sexual Health • Health • How-to

Now Try: Pair *The Whole Lesbian Sex Book* with a complementary read, *The Lesbian Sex Book: A Guide for Women Who Love Women*, by Wendy Caster and Rachel Kramer Bussel. Brimming with how-to advice and fascinating trivia and history, this can be treated as a reference (topics are conveniently arranged from A to Z) or as a cover-to-cover narrative read that gracefully covers the breadth of lesbian sexualities.

Rose, Tricia

Longing to Tell: Black Women Talk about Sexuality and Intimacy. New York: Farrar, Straus and Giroux, 2003. 453pp. ISBN 9780374190613.

Stereotypes of the sexual black woman abound in the media; there's the asexual mammy, for instance, and the hypersexed hip-hop woman. Forming a stark contrast to these caricatures are the stories found in *Longing to Tell*, a collection of twenty mini-histories culled from hundreds of interviews conducted by scholar Rose. Candid, vivid, and intimate, the women's voices speak to their own experiences with sex, sexuality, and relationships. Themes of African American identity and the intersection of race and sex underpin the women's stories, making this an eye-opening look at the issues that really matter to black women. Representing a cross-section of economic and lifestyle backgrounds, the women paint a vibrant, emotional portrait of the joys, sorrows, and realities of sex and love that comprise black women's experiences.

Subjects: Sexuality • Sexual Health • Relationships • Gender • African Americans • Race • Sociology • Collection

Now Try: Black women looking for fiction that affirms their sexual experiences have been reading Zane's novels and short stories for years; now, with *Dear G-Spot: Straight Talk about Sex and Love*, Zane ventures into nonfiction to discuss the realities of sex for women, black or otherwise. With absolutely frank, in-your-face honesty, Zane answers letters from her readers, delivering practical advice on all topics sexual, from monogamy to oral sex to satisfaction.

Sheehy, Gail

Sex and the Seasoned Woman: Pursuing the Passionate Life. New York: Random House, 2006. 354pp. ISBN 9781400062638.

Vanity Fair editor and best-selling author Gail Sheehy here turns her talented hand to the subject of sex in midlife and beyond, a stage that she calls "second adulthood." Drawing on interviews with more than one hundred women, Sheehy identifies various approaches to sex and passion: Some women are fully embracing romance, dating, and sex; some are resigned to an unfulfilling sex life, whether they are married or single; some have a low libido and have lost their youthful interest in sex. Most, though, whether in long-term relationships, newly single, or lifelong independents, are keen on enjoying their sex lives—and for those whose passion has dwindled because of hormonal changes, there's good news: recent advances in sexual health care now make it possible to combat the ravages of menopause. This is an eye-opening look at the ways in which women in their prime are taking control of their sexual happiness.

Subjects: Sexuality • Health • Sexual Health • Relationships • Midlife • Seniors

Now Try: If you're looking for further evidence that good sex is still possible once midlife hits, turn to *Over the Hill and between the Sheets: Sex, Love, and Lust in Middle Age*, edited by Gail Belsky. In this collection of essays from women and men over forty, the writers share the joys and struggles of sex, sexuality, and relationships as the body ages.

Menstruation and Menopause

> The books in this section focus on physical processes related to women's fertility cycles.

Do you remember hiding in the bathroom with a box of tampons, trying to interpret the indecipherable diagram on the package insert? Here's hoping you've learned more about menstruation since then—but even if you've become an expert, you'll discover new things in the "Menstruation and Menopause" section. How-to guides as well as sociological perspectives on menstruation and menopause offer food for thought along with medical wisdom.

Boston Women's Health Book Collective

Our Bodies, Ourselves: Menopause. New York: Simon & Schuster, 2006. 350pp. ISBN 9780743274876.

Since 1970, the Boston Women's Health Book Collective has been continuously updating and revising its landmark women's health book, *Our Bodies, Ourselves*; now we have a book from them devoted entirely to menopause. This accessible, empowering guide covers every aspect of menopause, with chapters ranging from "Hot Flashes, Night Sweats, and Sleep Disturbances" to "Emotional Well-Being and Managing Stress" to "Vulvovaginal Changes." As with the original *Our Bodies, Ourselves*, the book discusses more than just physical and mental health, with chapters on the politics of health care and the pro-feminist ways in which women can seek better care during menopause.

Subjects: Menopause • Health • Sexual Health • Health Care • Feminism

Now Try: Complement the information in *Our Bodies, Ourselves: Menopause* with *Is It Hot in Here? Or Is It Me?: The Complete Guide to Menopause,* by Pat Wingert and Barbara Kantrowitz. With plentiful illustrations, charts, and informative tidbits, this is another accessible and informative guide to everything menopause, from specific medical problems to the larger picture of lifestyle changes. Try also *Healthy Transitions: A Woman's Guide to Perimenopause, Menopause & Beyond,* by Neil Shulman and Edmund S. Kim; engaging and informative, the book's additional focus on perimenopause will be welcomed by women who have not yet entered full-fledged menopause.

Francina, Suza

Yoga and the Wisdom of Menopause: A Guide to Physical, Emotional, and Spiritual Health at Midlife and Beyond. Deerfield Beach, FL: Health Communications, 2003. 269pp. ISBN 9780757300653.

As women enter menopause, their bodies undergo a host of physical, psychological, physiological, and spiritual changes—which is exactly why they should consider yoga, explains yoga instructor Francina: "Among the many benefits that set yoga apart from other forms of exercise is the effect yoga postures and breathing practices have not only on the muscles and bones of your body, but also on your organs and glands." In chapters such as "Key Poses to Help Balance Your Hormones" and "Practicing Yoga to Reduce Breast Cancer Risk," Francina guides readers through yoga poses that work in harmony with menopause and the senior years. The poses are explained with clear instructions and helpful illustrations, and anecdotes from yoginis of a certain age give the narrative a lively, conversational feel.

Subjects: Menopause • Yoga • Exercise • Health • Mental Health • Spirituality • Midlife • Seniors • How-to

Now Try: Looking for a supplement to your yoga practice? Try reading Maggie Spilner's *Walk Your Way through Menopause: 14 Programs to Get in Shape, Boost Your Mood, and Recharge Your Sex Life No Matter What Your Current Fitness Level.* With both low- and high-impact walking workouts, the book offers exercise routines designed with the menopausal woman in mind.

Houppert, Karen

The Curse: Confronting the Last Unmentionable Taboo: Menstruation. New York: Farrar, Straus and Giroux, 1999. 263pp. ISBN 9780374273668.

Think twice the next time you reach for a tampon. A whole industry is making a profit around the notion that menstruation is unsanitary, unhygienic, and unmentionable in polite company—and whether or not you agree with those characterizations, you should know that tampons with traces of the carcinogen dioxin are disturbingly common, the result of a lack of government oversight. But this is not just a diatribe on the commercialization of menstruation and the health risks of sanitary products; Houppert's wide-ranging study is a look at menstruation in all its glory, with examples drawn from myth to popular culture to the bible. Read this both to understand society's attitudes about menstruation and to gain insight into an industry that plays a key role in the life of nearly every woman of childbearing age.

Subjects: Menstruation • Business • Health • Health Care • Sexual Health • Sociology • Feminism • History • Women's History • Social History

Now Try: Though *The Wise Wound: Eve's Curse and Everywoman* does not scrutinize tampons with Houppert's critical eye, readers who enjoyed *The Curse* will enjoy this sociological look at the history of menstruation. Authors Penelope Shuttle and Peter Redgrove draw on biology, psychology, myth, and popular culture to argue that menstruation is not a curse but a blessing; scholarly in tone but accessibly written, this inspiring feminist study encourages women to reclaim the power and privilege of their periods.

Northrup, Christiane

The Wisdom of Menopause: Creating Physical and Emotional Health and Healing During the Change. New York: Bantam Books, 2001 (2007). 589pp. ISBN 9780553-801217.

"The conventional view of menopause as a scary transition heralding 'the beginning of the end' couldn't be father from the truth," writes the fabulous Dr. Christiane Northrup, author of such bestselling women's health books as *Women's Bodies, Women's Wisdom*. Speaking not only as a medical doctor with a keen spiritual awareness but also as a woman who has herself gone through menopause, Northrup offers a comprehensive guide to making the most of menopause. There are chapters on hormone replacement and diet, of course, but also on emotional wellness, body image, relationships, and other topics related to the hormonal changes of menopause. Northrup's accessible, engaging discussions of health and health care, bolstered by examples from her own life, make this an invaluable and enjoyable guide to thriving during midlife and beyond.

Subjects: Menopause • Health • Health Care • Sexual Health • Mental Health • How-to

Now Try: Readers who enjoy Northrup's candid, conversational style may wish to turn to medical columnist Colette Bouchéz. In *Your Perfectly Pampered Menopause: Health, Beauty, and Lifestyle Advice for the Best Years of Your Life*, Bouchéz covers the ins and outs of menopause, addressing issues ranging from sexual health to hot flashes to weight gain during menopause.

Posner, Trisha

This Is Not Your Mother's Menopause: One Woman's Natural Journey through Change. New York: Villard Books, 2000. 153pp. ISBN 9780375503986.

For millions of women, the onset of menopause heralds the way for hormone replacement therapy, but when her gynecologist advised her to take estrogen supplements, Trisha Posner hesitated. Hormone replacement therapy could fight osteoporosis, heart disease, and a lowered metabolism—but it also carried with it an increased risk for breast cancer, a prevalent disease among the women of Posner's family. This is the memoir of Posner's journey to find an alternative to hormone replacement, and though it is not a medical text proper, Posner's engaging discussion of her success with diet, exercise, and nutritional supplements will be inspiring to women who want a natural way to cope with menopause.

Subjects: Menopause • Health • Health Care • Biology • Food • Exercise • Drugs • Midlife • Memoir • Quick Read

Now Try: With its mix of wholesome recipes and empowering essays by menopausal women, Gabriele Kushi's *Embracing Menopause Naturally: Stories, Portraits, and Recipes* is an excellent companion to *This Is Not Your Mother's Menopause*. Try also *Managing Menopause Naturally: Before, During, and Forever*, in which Dr. Emily Kane discusses symptoms of menopause, ways to prevent disease, and supplements to take for dealing with menopause naturally.

Emotional Wellness

The inner feelings and emotional health of women take center stage in titles here.

Feeling glum? Cheer up with books from the "Emotional Wellness" section. Some of the books focus on improving self-esteem (see Gloria Steinem's *Revolution from Within*); some speak to specific groups, such as black women (try Jenyne M. Raines's *Beautylicious!*); and some, like Susan Anderson's *Porn for Women*, are guaranteed to brighten any woman's day.

Anderson, Susan

Porn for Women. San Francisco: Chronicle Books, 2007. 89pp. ISBN 9780811855518. 9781599212227.

The cover art says it all: we see a picture of a strapping young man pushing a vacuum cleaner. Open the book, and you'll see other photos of attractive men doing the unthinkable. One fellow wants to skip the NFL playoffs to go to the crafts fair; another forbids you to empty the litter box, insisting that he be the one to scoop out the kitty's poop; yet another begs your pardon while he stops the car to ask for directions. Shamelessly pandering to stereotypes, this mock photo shoot will leave you cackling. (I speak from experience; take this to work and your female colleagues will erupt into hysterics— though, puzzlingly, male colleagues might not be as receptive.) The book takes only a few minutes to read, but it will brighten your whole day.

Subjects: Stereotypes • Gender • Humor • Quick Read

Now Try: For another dose of snarky humor, turn to *PMS [Problems Men Started]*, by Nikki Hardin and Caitilin McPhillips. Collecting columns of the same name from the feminist magazine *skirt!*, this quick read will leave you laughing over those puzzling and irritating bastions of male influence such as golf, wet t-shirt contests, and—shudder —the Speedo. Fun and quirky, this is a great book to giggle over with your girlfriends.

Gilman, Susan Jane

Kiss My Tiara: How to Rule the World as a Smartmouth Goddess. New York: Warner Books, 2001. 205pp. ISBN 9780446675772.

> "It used to be, if we gals wanted to look like a model, all we had to do was be born with extraordinary genes, grow to five-foot ten, subsist on lettuce, and maybe develop a coke habit," writes author Gilman. "Now, it seems, we've also got to have our looks 'enhanced' by an underpaid production assistant with a fifty-thousand-gigabyte hard drive." Gilman doesn't have much use for airbrushed supermodels—or for pay inequity, sexism, aerobics classes, right-wing Republicans, or anything that prevents women from living their lives to the fullest. With wickedly funny chapters such as "We Don't Shape History by Shaping Our Thighs" and "Every Idiot We Date Is One Less Idiot We Risk Marrying," Gilman takes a fresh look at women's issues, showing her readers that powerful women are happy women.

> **Subjects:** Lifestyle • Feminism • Humor • Quick Read

> **Now Try:** If you liked Gilman's snarky, sensible approach to women's issues, do yourself a favor and find *The Modern Goddess' Guide to Life: How to Be Absolutely Divine on a Daily Basis* (first sentence: "I believe we were put on this planet for two reasons: to have great sex and to help other people."). With humor and sass, Francesca De Grandis presents games and quizzes that show women how to celebrate their fabulous inner goddesses.

Kirsch, Melissa

The Girl's Guide to Absolutely Everything. New York: Workman, 2006. 477pp. ISBN 9780761142133.

> *The Girl's Guide to Absolutely Everything* is exactly that, a guide to darn near everything. There's a chapter on finances (learn to invest!), a chapter on fashion (learn which type of bra you need), a chapter on friends (pick your traveling companions wisely!)—in short, a chapter on all the various subjects that young women need to know about. With her laugh-out-loud style and sassy sensibility, journalist Kirsch has created a fabulous resource for women in their twenties and thirties. Filled with checklists, sidebars, illustrations, and quotes, this is a one-stop shop for everything a girl needs to know; refer to it for specific questions, or enjoy it cover-to-cover for a sinfully entertaining read.

> **Subjects:** Lifestyle • Humor • How-to

> **Now Try:** Pair *The Girl's Guide to Absolutely Everything* with another excellent read, *The Modern Girl's Guide to Life.* Jane Buckingham's engaging, entertaining style will appeal to readers who want to learn more about topics ranging from etiquette to buying a home to asking for a raise. Likewise, readers will enjoy the helpful tips and chatty tone of *The Go-Girl Guide: Surviving Your 20s with Savvy, Soul, and Style,* by Julia Bourland.

Raines, Jenyne M.

Beautylicious!: The Black Girl's Guide to the Fabulous Life. New York: Harlem Moon/Broadway Books, 2004. 200pp. ISBN 9780767911108.

Jenyne Raines, a former beauty editor with *Essence* magazine, gets straight to the point: "You put the *bomb* in *bombshell*. Your looks are smoldering, your personality is dynamic, and the total you is, well, *kaboom!*" The problem, of course, is that not every woman realizes how great she really is. In this chatty, engaging guide, Raines helps black women recognize their best qualities, while offering practical guidance in areas such as fashion, beauty, health, and dating. Filled with inspiring quotes and spot-on advice, this empowering book offers valuable tips for all women, with special attention given to the unique needs of black women.

> **Subjects:** Lifestyle • African Americans • Race • How-to • Quick Read
>
> **Now Try:** Continue now with *The BAP Handbook: The Official Guide to the Black American Princess*, by Kalyn Johnson et al. Filled with sassy insights and honest discussions on everything from black hair and college to marriage and exercise, this is a thorough, accessible how-to guide for living life to the fullest.

Steinem, Gloria

Revolution from Within: A Book of Self-Esteem. Boston: Little, Brown, 1992. 377pp. ISBN 9780316812405.

Gloria Steinem, one of the driving forces of Second- and Third-Wave feminism, here redirects her attention from large social issues toward personal happiness. With her deeply insightful observations and characteristic flair for elegant prose, Steinem considers the importance of self-esteem and the various ways it can be nurtured. Drawing on her own experiences and on the examples of others, she offers readers a variety of thoughtful approaches toward understanding and embracing the self, concluding with two very useful appendices on meditation and bibliotherapy. Written with women in mind but suitable for men, this compassionate, empowering book is a gentle guide for improving self-esteem.

> **Subjects:** Psychology • Mental Health • Meditation • How-to • Memoir
>
> **Now Try:** Continue boosting your self-esteem with the lovely *Succulent Wild Woman: Dancing with Your Wonder-Full Self!*, in which author Sark encourages women to overcome their fears and obstacles by nurturing their creative, outrageous selves. Then turn to the inspiring, courageous stories of women who have battled demons both internal and external in the anthology *Roar Softly and Carry a Great Lipstick: 28 Women Writers on Life, Sex, and Survival*, edited by Autumn Stephens.

Midlife and Aging

> The "Midlife and Aging" section celebrates women as they reach middle age and seniority.

In choosing which books to read, consider the mood you're in. Do you want snarky and sassy? Nora Ephron's *I Feel Bad about My Neck* is for you. Do you want a bold, motivational approach? Try *Not Your Mother's Midlife*, by Nancy Alspaugh and

Marilyn Kentz. Read any or all of these to meet women who have aged with grace and style.

Alspaugh, Nancy, and Marilyn Kentz

Not Your Mother's Midlife: A Ten-Step Guide to Fearless Aging. Kansas City, MO: Andrews McMeel, 2003. 215pp. ISBN 9780740735240.

"No amount of lying, silicone, or Botox will change the fact that underneath it all you are still forty-five or fifty-five or sixty-five," write Aslpaugh and Kentz—and that's just fine, because midlife is a time to be celebrated. Don't believe it? With the exercises, quotes, anecdotes, and visualizations presented in this elegant guide, even skeptics will stop resenting middle age and begin embracing its possibilities. In chapters such as "Awaken to the Muse" and "Don't Just Vent . . . Reinvent," you'll find practical tips to help build your confidence and brighten your attitude as you journey into the prime of your life.

> **Subjects:** Midlife • Mental Health • How-to
>
> **Now Try:** Now turn to any or all of four books by Cathleen Rountree: *Coming into Our Fullness: On Women Turning Forty*; *On Women Turning 50: Celebrating Mid-Life Discoveries*; *On Women Turning 60: Embracing the Age of Fulfillment*; and *On Women Turning 70: Honoring the Voices of Wisdom*. (The younger set may also enjoy her book *On Women Turning 30: Making Choices, Finding Meaning*.) Each title is a photo-journalistic celebration of women of a certain age, with profiles, photos, and words from successful women, famous and ordinary, who are embracing their ages with zest and enthusiasm.

Bolen, Jean Shinoda

Crones Don't Whine: Concentrated Wisdom for Juicy Women. Boston: Conari Press, 2003. 116pp. ISBN 9781573249126.

"I am proposing that it is time to reclaim and redefine 'crone' from the word pile of disparaging names to call older women," writes psychiatrist Bolen, "and to make becoming a 'crone' a crowning inner achievement of the third phase of life." In this lovely celebration of women of a certain age, Bolen shows how to appreciate and cultivate the crone lifestyle. Her warm advice, delivered in such chapters as "Crones Laugh Together," "Crones Listen to Their Bodies," and, of course, "Crones Don't Whine," offers an empowering, refreshing approach to making the most of the golden years.

> **Subjects:** Seniors • Psychology • Spirituality • Mental Health • How-to • Quick Read
>
> **Now Try:** For another positive, liberating take on senior women, turn to *The Next Fifty Years: A Guide for Women at Mid-Life and Beyond*, by Pamela D. Blair. In a series of short, pithy, engaging essays, Blair dispels negative stereotypes about aging and offers her own positive perspective on the beauty of the senior years. Fans of *Crones Don't Whine* will especially enjoy Blair's sensible advice and practical how-to tips on embracing all that the senior lifestyle has to offer.

Cunningham, Michael, and Connie Briscoe

Jewels: 50 Phenomenal Black Women Over 50. New York: Little, Brown, 2007. 213pp. ISBN 9780316113045.

Master photographer Michael Cunningham teams up with novelist Connie Briscoe to create an enchanting tribute to black women of a certain age. In this lovely photo-essay, you'll meet fifty successful black women, ranging from artists and poets to activists and mothers. Some of the subjects, such as Nikki Giovanni and Marion Wright Edelman, will be familiar to readers, while many others will be new; famous or otherwise, the women share their perspectives on race, sex, maturity, and life. Read *Jewels* straight through from cover to cover, or indulge in one gorgeous photo at a time.

Subjects: Seniors • Midlife • African Americans • Race • Biography • Quick Read

Now Try: Continue learning from the voices of maturity in *Life's Spices from Seasoned Sistahs: A Collection of Life Stories from Mature Women of Color*, in which editor Vicki L. Ward brings together the stories, poems, and essays of senior women from a variety of races and ethnicities. Readers may also be interested in *Tomorrow Begins Today: African American Women as We Age*, by Cheryl D. Woodruff; though its emphasis is on practical advice rather than artistic presentation, fans of *Jewels* will appreciate the life stories and wise advice of the middle-aged and senior black women in the book.

Ephron, Nora

I Feel Bad about My Neck: And Other Thoughts on Being a Woman. New York: Knopf, 2006. 137pp. ISBN 9780307264558.

Never mind all those cheerful books about aging; writer Nora Ephron has a much snarkier perspective, thank you very much: "Every so often I read a book about age, and whoever's writing it says it's great to be old. It's great to be wise and sage and mellow; it's great to be at the point where you understand just what matters in life. I can't stand people who say things like this." In this wickedly funny collection of essays on aging, Ephron reveals the pitfalls of growing old: she can never find her reading glasses, she has to devote more and more time to maintaining her appearance, and—of course—there is her traitor neck, which one day decided to stop being attractive, and now there is nothing she can do about it. Whether you're young or old, you'll find yourself snickering at Ephron's droll wit and deliciously jaded perspective on life.

Subjects: Seniors • Humor • America • Essays • Collection • Quick Read

Now Try: Hear the voice of another woman confronting the truth about aging in Anne Kreamer's *Going Gray: What I Learned about Beauty, Sex, Work, Motherhood, Authenticity, and Everything Else That Really Matters*. At forty-nine years of age, Kreamer decided to stop dying her hair to see what life would be like with a gray coiffure. The result is this engaging, enjoyable contemplation on beauty, age, and society. And don't miss *For Keeps: Women Tell the Truth about Their Bodies, Growing Older, and Acceptance*, in which editor Victoria Zackheim collects twenty-seven essays on the vagaries of aging in a female body.

Levine, Suzanne

Inventing the Rest of Our Lives: Women in Second Adulthood. New York: Viking, 2005. 260pp. ISBN 9780670033119.

"Second Adulthood is the unprecedented and productive time that our generation is encountering as we pass the dreaded landmark of a fiftieth birthday," writes

Levine, a former editor with *Ms.* magazine. "The next twenty-five years can be a second chance—to do it better, to do it differently, to do it wiser." And in this empowering study, she shows readers how, with chapters such as "You're Not Who You Were, Only Older" and "Health, Beauty, and What You Cannot Change." Based on her interviews with fifty inspiring women and drawing from current medical research, Levine presents an honest assessment of the senior years and provides motivating examples of how to make the most of second adulthood.

Subjects: Midlife • Seniors • Mental Health

Now Try: Like Levine, author Karen Baar recognizes that modern women are embracing midlife and seniority with zest. In *For My Next Act . . .: Women Scripting Life after Fifty*, Baar presents examples of women who have used their older years to as an opportunity to redefine their passions and identities. Both thought-provoking and inspiring, the book elegantly deconstructs the negative stereotypes about women in their fifties and beyond.

Tenneson, Joyce

Wise Women: A Celebration of Their Insights, Courage, and Beauty. Boston: Little, Brown, 2002. 143pp. ISBN 9780821228012.

The magnificent photo-essay *Wise Women* celebrates American women aged sixty-five to one hundred through a series of short profiles (and if your reaction is anything like mine, the book will bring tears to your eyes). The profile of each woman consists of a stunning portrait by photographer Tenneson alongside a brief quote from the subject. You'll meet famous women, such as Angela Lansbury, as well as women who might not be celebrities but who have done remarkable things, such as Dr. Johnetta Cole, the first black female president of Spelman College. Though it is only 143 pages long, you could spend all day luxuriating in this inspiring homage to women in their old age.

Subjects: Seniors • America • Collection • Quick Read

Now Try: For more lovely photos of women of a certain age, turn to *Fearless Women: Midlife Portraits*, by Nancy Alspaugh, Marilyn Kentz, and Mary Ann Halpin. The concept is brilliant: to emphasize their fearlessness of aging, each of the fifty women in the book holds a sword. The women are in their forties, fifties, and sixties, younger than their sisters in *Wise Women*, but fans of Tenneson's book will love the gorgeous portraiture and the empowering approach to aging.

Recovery from Trauma

Here are books about how women are affected by and deal with profound emotional or physical abuses and shocks.

Even if you have never suffered from a traumatic event, the books in the "Recovery from Trauma" section are guaranteed to strike a chord. And if you have suffered from trauma, then the books may be very difficult to read, as each author below has a gift for describing her experiences. Readers who feel able to read about traumas such as incest, female genital mutilation, and miscarriage will want to try some of the memoirs and thought-pieces, such as Amy Kuebelbeck's *Waiting with Gabriel*. Readers looking for more practical advice on recovering from trauma will want to try a how-to guide, such as Karen A. Duncan's *Healing from the Trauma of Childhood Sexual Abuse*.

De Puy, Candace, and Dana Dovitch

The Healing Choice: Your Guide to Emotional Recovery after an Abortion. New York: Simon & Schuster, 1997. 237pp. ISBN 9780684831961.

"The journey toward resolving post-abortion pain," write therapists De Puy and Dovitch, "begins with your awareness that the decision you made to end your unwanted pregnancy was a choice that altered the course of your life." Written with compassion and sensitivity, this guide is for any woman who has suffered emotionally after an abortion, no matter what her reasons for terminating the pregnancy. In sections such as "The Healing Realm of Solitude," "Making Guilt Constructive," and "Recognizing Abortion as a Loss," this nonjudgmental guide helps women cope with and understand their pain. It is not written from a religious perspective, though there is a chapter devoted to spirituality and religion. Filled with stories from post-abortive women, exercises to help readers understand their emotions, thought-provoking quotes, and a list of recommended reading and organizations that women can turn to for support, this is an excellent guide to acknowledging and resolving the emotional trauma brought on by abortion.

> **Subjects:** Mental Health • Abortion • Health • How-to

> **Now Try:** Pair the practical advice of *The Healing Choice* with the stories of *Experiencing Abortion: A Weaving of Women's Words*, by Eve Kushner. Based on interviews with post-abortive women, the book offers profiles of women from a variety of ages and backgrounds, arranged into chapters such as "Coping with Stress and Regaining Control" and "Lifting the Veil of Denial." The book has no particular political agenda, other than to give voice to women who too often have no chance to speak about their experiences with abortion.

Duncan, Karen A.

Healing from the Trauma of Childhood Sexual Abuse: The Journey for Women. Westport, CT: Praeger, 2004. 244pp. ISBN 9780275980849.

"A woman is not responsible for how [childhood sexual abuse] affected her, just as she is not responsible for the perpetrator abusing her," writes psychologist Duncan. "The responsibility a woman can take is for her own healing." With compassion and grace, Duncan demonstrates how women can begin this healing journey by exploring the different stages of recovery; there is a chapter called "Remembering the Trauma," for instance, and one titled "Ending the Pretense." Blending practical advice with stories of women who have survived childhood sexual abuse, this is a powerful guidebook to recovery.

> **Subjects:** Incest • Sexual Exploitation • Violence • Mental Health • Health • Psychology • How-to

> **Now Try:** Another excellent guide to recovering from sexual abuse is E. Sue Blume's *Secret Survivors: Uncovering Incest and Its Aftereffects in Women*. The clearly written book discusses the many negative effects of incest, while offering support and guidance to women who are recovering from sexual abuse. Readers should also turn to *The Sexual*

Healing Journey: A Guide for Survivors of Sexual Abuse, in which Wendy Maltz helps women and men alike to recover from sexual abuse and to nurture healthy sexual attitudes.

Faldet, Rachel, and Karen Fitton, eds.

Our Stories of Miscarriage: Healing with Words. Minneapolis, MN: Fairview Press, 1997. 200pp. ISBN 9781577490333.

"Some people do not understand having a miscarriage means losing a baby, rather than losing a bunch of tissue," writes Amy Desherlia, one of forty-six women and four men to contribute essays, stories, and poems to *Our Stories of Miscarriage*. For those who have never suffered a miscarriage, this compassionate, sensitive collection provides insight into the tragedy faced by the mothers and fathers; for those who have endured one or more miscarriages, the book offers solace and support from others who have been in the same place. Sorrowful but beautiful, heart-wrenching but sympathetic, the book is a powerful, touching acknowledgment of the grief of miscarriage and the hope of recovery.

> **Subjects:** Miscarriage • Mental Health • Health • Essays • Anthology • Collection • Quick Read

> **Now Try:** For another painful but cathartic book about miscarriage, turn to *Miscarriage, Women Sharing from the Heart*. Authors Marie Allen and Shelly Marks, both of whom have suffered miscarriages, examine the process of grieving, bereavement, and recovery, interspersing their compassionate discussion with the stories of more than one hundred mothers and fathers who have miscarried.

Gross, Jessica Berger, ed.

About What Was Lost: 20 Writers on Miscarriage, Healing, and Hope. New York: Penguin, 2007. 266pp. ISBN 9780452287990.

Nearly one quarter of all pregnancies end in miscarriage, and yet the topic is rarely discussed. In *About What Was Lost*, editor Jessica Berger Gross gives twenty women a chance to break the silence by writing about their pregnancy losses. With eloquence and sensitivity, authors such as Pam Houston, Joyce Maynard, and Susanna Sonnenberg address the heartache that inevitably comes with miscarriage, whether the pregnancy was planned, unexpected, or even unwanted. Intimate and personal, powerful and graceful, the essays speak to the sorrow of miscarriage and the hope of healing.

> **Subjects:** Miscarriage • Mental Health • Health • Essays • Anthology • Collection

> **Now Try:** Another supportive, caring guide to coping with pregnancy loss is *A Piece of My Heart: Living through the Grief of Miscarriage, Stillbirth, or Infant Death*. Written by Molly Fumia, who lost her own infant son shortly after his birth, this book gives grieving parents permission to remember their loss while offering solid advice on healing. Interspersed with quotes from Elie Wiesel, this is a spiritually moving, compassionate exploration of coping with grief and recovering from the pain.

Harrison, Kathryn

The Kiss. New York: Random House, 1997. 207pp. ISBN 9780679449997.

If you've read the novels of Kathryn Harrison, you're already familiar with her evocative, captivating prose—but given the subject of her memoir, you may come to wish that she were not nearly so gifted a writer. This is the story of the author's four-year affair with her father, a man who had disappeared from his daughter's life when she was only six months old. Kathryn was reunited with him after twenty years had passed, during which time he had remarried, fathered other children, and entered the ministry; in other words, he hardly seemed like the sort of person who would initiate a sexual relationship with his own daughter. *The Kiss* is deeply disturbing, but Harrison's vivid descriptions of her relationships—with her father, with her mother, with her grandparents—make for a compelling story, and readers will be rewarded with Harrison's eventual escape from her father.

> **Subjects:** Incest • Daughters • Fathers • Relationships • America • Memoir • Quick Read
>
> **Now Try:** For another painful but beautifully written memoir of incest, turn to *Because I Remember Terror, Father, I Remember You*. From the ages of four through eighteen, author Sue William Silverman was sexually molested by her father, a prominent government official. This is the story of the trauma Silverman endured during and after her father's abuse; it is a harrowing story, though ultimately there is a happy ending as the author recovers with the help of her husband and her therapist.

Jessop, Carolyn, and Laura Palmer

Escape. New York: Broadway Books, 2007. 413pp. ISBN 9780767927567.

When she was eighteen years old, Carolyn Jessop became the fourth wife of a man nearly twice her age. She didn't ask for the marriage, but her opinion didn't matter in the eyes of the Fundamentalist Church of Jesus Christ of Latter Day Saints (FLDS), the sect whose followers broke away from mainstream Mormonism so that their men could practice polygamy. Every aspect of Jessop's life was controlled by her psychologically abusive husband—when and if she would have sex with him, how her children would be raised, how the money she earned from teaching would be spent. Jessop wanted to leave, but not at the risk of losing her children—but seventeen years into the marriage, she managed to escape with all eight of them. Disturbing, vivid, and evocative, this page-turning memoir shows us how one woman managed to single-handedly defy the insular world of the FLDS community.

> **Subjects:** Fundamentalist Church of Jesus Christ of Latter Day Saints • Religion • Sexual Exploitation • Violence • Marriage • Polygamy • Mothers • Children • Relationships • America • Young Adult • Memoir
>
> **Now Try:** Now meet another woman who defied the FLDS in *Stolen Innocence: My Story of Growing Up in a Polygamous Sect, Becoming a Teenage Bride, and Breaking Free of Warren Jeffs*. Despite her protests, author Elissa Wall was forced into marriage at the age of fourteen, a traumatic, loveless nightmare that she endured for four years. But she managed to escape, and more: it was partly on the basis of Wall's moving courtroom testimony that the former leader of the FLDS church, Warren Jeffs, is now serving time for his crimes against young women. Readers interested in learning about the complicated history of marriage in the Mormon Church will want to discover the two compelling stories related in David Ebershoff's novel *The 19th Wife*. The first story, set in the year 1875, concerns a figure from history named Ann Eliza, a disgraced wife of Brigham

Young; the second story, entirely fictional, tells of a young gay man who reluctantly revisits his Mormon past when his mother stands accused of murder.

Kluger-Bell, Kim

Unspeakable Losses: Understanding the Experience of Pregnancy Loss, Miscarriage, and Abortion. New York: W.W. Norton, 1998. 170pp. ISBN 9780393045727.

"There is hardly a life untouched by a pregnancy loss, and yet each one seems so unknowable and unknown," writes psychotherapist Kluger-Bell, who has herself suffered a miscarriage. "We seem to have no words to name our experiences of these losses. Or perhaps we turn away in an attempt to avoid a confrontation with one of life's darkest and cruelest twists, a life ended before it begins." Kluger-Bell has written this compassionate, sensitive book for the women in the United States each year whose pregnancies end in stillbirth or miscarriage (6.5 million women) or abortion (1.5 million women). Blending her own experience as a therapist with stories of women who have suffered pregnancy losses, Kluger-Bell creates a dialogue about a topic that is too often taboo, shedding light on the grief suffered by women and their families and offering practical advice on beginning the healing process.

> **Subjects:** Miscarriage • Abortion • Pregnancy • Psychology • Quick Read
>
> **Now Try:** Turn now to two other books written to help grieving parents through the trauma of pregnancy loss and infant death. In *Empty Cradle, Broken Heart: Surviving the Death of Your Baby*, Deborah L. Davis encourages parents to grieve and remember their child, while suggesting ways to recover from the pain. And in *Empty Arms: Coping after Miscarriage, Stillbirth and Infant Death*, Sherokee Ilse and Arlene Appelbaum help parents deal with their grief, both at the time of their baby's death and in the years afterward. Readers will also find solace in *An Exact Replica of a Figment of My Imagination: A Memoir*, in which Elizabeth McCracken works through the anguish of losing a child at birth.

Korn, Fadumo, and Sabine Eichhorst

Born in the Big Rains: A Memoir of Somalia and Survival. New York: Feminist Press at the City University of New York, 2006. 185pp. ISBN 9781558615311.

Be forewarned: this is not an easy book to read. With evocative, lush, poetic prose, Korn's memoir is almost too vivid in some places. The description of her circumcision at seven years of age ("Hands touched my body everywhere, a horde of hands, pressing, tearing, pulling") is graphic and visceral, and the subsequent medical complications are horrific. Yet readers willing to enter Korn's world will be rewarded with a gorgeously rendered story that plunges us into the Somali way of life. This is a disturbing and violent book, yes, but it is also a hopeful book, a triumphant story of one woman's emotional recovery from genital mutilation and her transformation into a champion of women's rights.

> **Subjects:** Female Genital Mutilation • Violence • Sexual Exploitation • Health • Activism • Somalia • Africa • Memoir • Quick Read
>
> **Now Try:** Unlike Korn, whose culture encouraged her to look forward to circumcision, Fauziya Kassindja never wanted to undergo the procedure, thanks

to the enlightened views of her father. Tragically, he died, and Kassindja was scheduled to be circumcised. Hours before the operation, she escaped her native Togo and fled to the United States, only to face two years of imprisonment; read about her harrowing story and her ultimate victory in *Do They Hear You When You Cry?* Then, for another heartbreaking memoir, turn to *Desert Flower: The Extraordinary Journey of a Desert Nomad*. With vivid, evocative language, Waris Dirie describes her Somali childhood, her circumcision, and her journey to become a human rights ambassador with the United Nations.

Kuebelbeck, Amy

Waiting with Gabriel: A Story of Cherishing a Baby's Brief Life. Chicago: Loyola Press, 2003. 174pp. ISBN 9780829416039.

"'You have a beautiful baby,' the ultrasound technician said quietly. She was studying the flickering images on her screen, staring intently at the shadows of the tiny heart. I think she had already seen that our baby was going to die." These three sentences form the first paragraph of Amy Kuebelbeck's heart-wrenching memoir of her doomed pregnancy. It was during her second trimester that she learned that her undelivered son, Gabriel, suffered from hypoplastic left heart syndrome: essentially, her baby had only half of a heart. While in the womb his mother's placenta would sustain him, but upon delivery, he would have days, at the most, to live; in fact, Gabriel only survived a few hours after he was born. But the impact he had upon the lives of his mother, father, and two sisters was tremendous, as we see in this beautiful, poignant tribute to an infant who changed his family forever. This is a story of religious faith and spirituality, of living through and recovering from pain.

> **Subjects:** Pregnancy • Birth • Christianity • Religion • Spirituality • America • Memoir • Quick Read

> **Now Try:** The details are different, but those who were touched by *Waiting with Gabriel* won't want to miss *Losing Malcolm: A Mother's Journey through Grief*. Author Carol Henderson was expecting a perfectly healthy baby boy, but when he was only three days old, he was diagnosed with a serious heart defect, and two surgeries were unable to save his life. This is a tear-jerking story of loss and eventual recovery, told in Henderson's graceful, lovely style.

Mai, Mukhtar, Marie-Thérèse Cuny, and Linda Coverdale

In the Name of Honor: A Memoir. New York: Atria Books, 2006. 172pp. ISBN 9781416532286.

In a remote village in Pakistan, a twelve-year-old boy stood accused of *zina-bil-jabar*, of sexual relations outside marriage. Recognizing it as a fabricated charge, the boy's sister, Mukhtar Mai, went to speak to the village council in his defense. The council decided to mete out justice by extracting honor from the boy's family in the most horrific way: Mukhtar was sentenced to be gang-raped, and so she was dragged to a nearby stable, where four men proceeded to brutally rape her. To these men, says the illiterate Mai through the pen of translator Cuny, "a woman is simply an object of possession, honor, or revenge. They marry or rape them according to their conception of tribal pride. They know that a woman humiliated in that way has no other recourse except suicide." Suicide certainly tempted Mai, but she found the courage to fight back by suing the council. The supreme court of Pakistan judged in her favor, and Mai used the money to establish a girls' school in her village. Given the nature of the subject, the book is dark and disturbing at times, but ultimately this is an inspiring story of a woman who found the strength to survive and to make something good come out of a horrible perversion of justice.

> **Subjects:** Rape • Violence • Sexual Exploitation • Law • Activism • Pakistan • Memoir • Quick Read

> **Now Try:** At first glance, Ayaan Hirsi Ali might seem an odd suggestion for those who like Mukhtar Mai. Mai spent her childhood in Pakistan and was gang-raped; Ali spent her childhood in Somalia and was genitally mutilated. But both women grew up to become women's rights activists, and both women eloquently speak out against the misogyny of traditional Muslim societies. Read Ali's *Infidel* memoir to discover how she sought a better life for herself and how she, like Mai, opened the world's eyes to violence against Muslim women.

Massé, Sydna, and Joan Phillips

Her Choice to Heal. Colorado Springs, CO: Chariot Victor, 1998. 122pp. ISBN 9781564767349.

While some women can recover quickly from the emotional and physical stress of having an abortion, many others take a long time to heal, and some never heal at all. Still others find that their true suffering begins months or even years after their abortions. Authors Massé and Phillips understand what it's like, having both undergone abortions themselves. With utter compassion and sensitivity, they offer clear guidance for Christian women who want to begin the healing process. Filled with personal stories from post-abortive women, passages from scripture, and blank pages for women to write down their reflections, this graceful guidebook helps women turn to their Christian faiths to overcome their guilty feelings about abortion.

> **Subjects:** Abortion • Christianity • Religion • Mental Health • How-to • Quick Read

> **Now Try:** Psychotherapist Theresa Karminski Burke, founder of Rachel's Vineyard, a ministry for post-abortive women, and post-abortion expert David C. Reardon team up to write *Forbidden Grief: The Unspoken Pain of Abortion*, an excellent companion to *Her Choice to Heal*. Recognizing that post-abortive women rarely have a chance to acknowledge and deal with their grief, the authors offer a sensitive study of the trauma faced by women after their abortions; the book affirms the pain that women suffer, and offers ways to help them heal.

Sebold, Alice

Lucky. New York: Scribner, 1999. 254pp. ISBN 9780684857824. 9780517706831.

From the very first page of her memoir, novelist Alice Sebold reels her reader in and doesn't let go. Witness the book's first three sentences: "In the tunnel where I was raped, a tunnel that was once an underground entry to an amphitheater, a place where actors burst forth from underneath the seats of a crowd, a girl had been murdered and dismembered. I was told this story by the police. In comparison, they said, I was lucky." Caveat reader: this is a violent book. There is violence in the rape and beating of the author, of course, but there is emotional violence in her recovery as she struggles to reevaluate her relationships with family and friends, and as she fights to have her attacker brought to justice. An unforgettable book, *Lucky* is both deeply disturbing and ultimately inspiring for its story of triumph and recovery.

Subjects: Rape • Violence • America • Memoir

Now Try: For another vivid memoir of rape and its devastating effects, turn to Nancy Venable Raine's *After Silence: Rape and My Journey Back*. Like Sebold, Raine writes with a powerful, compelling style, detailing her attack and her long struggle to recover with candor and insight. See also *Telling: A Memoir of Rape and Recovery*, in which Patricia Weaver Francisco recalls her rape, her shaky recovery, and her realization that her pain could not be endured in silence.

Walls, Jeannette

The Glass Castle: A Memoir. New York: Scribner, 2005. 288pp. ISBN 9780743-247535.

For years, little Jeannette's life didn't seem traumatic. Granted, her first memory was of being burned alive (this is what happens when three-year-olds cook on the stove), and it's true that her family was often desperately hungry, and it must be admitted that her father got moody, even violent, when he drank. But life seemed like one big adventure, what with moving to new places every few months and meeting new people and studying astronomy and math with her father, who was brilliant when he wasn't passed out drunk. Growing into her teen years, however, Walls lost her optimism as her faith in her parents dwindled. The family was dirt poor, literally; without indoor plumbing, they couldn't afford to bathe. Walls ate one "meal" a day by scrounging for other students' discarded leftovers in the bathroom trash cans of her high school. And extended family members and local townspeople began to take sexual liberties with Walls and her siblings; life wasn't so rosy, after all. Words can't begin to do justice to *The Glass Castle*, a memoir absolutely unlike any other. It is the story of a childhood that is both adventurous and tragic, fascinating and appalling, related in the eloquent, vivid words of journalist Walls.

Subjects: Coming of Age • Class • Daughters • Sisters • Relationships • America • Young Adult • Memoir

Now Try: For another popular coming-of-age story in the so-bizarre-it-must-be-true category, turn to *Running with Scissors: A Memoir*, by Augusten Burroughs. When his mother decided she would rather be a poet than a parent, Burroughs was sent to live with the family psychiatrist, an unorthodox man with a houseful of strange children. Some of the family's peculiarities are lighthearted, as when the children chop a hole in the roof to let in the sunshine; some of the peculiarities are horrifying, as when teenaged Burroughs enters into an affair with a man twenty years his senior, the eldest son of the psychiatrist—who, incidentally, sanctions the affair. Though without the focus on class found in *The Glass Castle*, fans of Walls will appreciate the dark humor of a most abnormal childhood.

Beauty, Fashion, and Appearance

Here you'll find books about how women should look and dress.

You'll find books on the whole gamut of women's beauty here: there are books about handbags, books about shoes, books about clothes, books about the history of fashion. How-to guides such as *Sam Saboura's Real Style* sit alongside fascinating social histories such as *A History of the Breast*, by Marilyn Yalom.

Antoine-Dariaux, Geneviève

A Guide to Elegance: For Every Woman Who Wants to Be Well and Properly Dressed on All Occasions. New York: William Morrow, an imprint of HarperCollins, 1964 (2004). 224pp. ISBN 9780060757342.

The French—let's go ahead and admit it—the French are just more stylish than the rest of us. And so it is the French we turn to for the very best of fashion advice, as we see here with Mme. Geneviève Antoine-Dariaux's timeless classic *A Guide to Elegance*. First published in 1964, this fashion guide has endured because of its irreproachable advice and charming style ("I cannot restrain myself from expressing the dismay I feel when I see a woman carry an alligator handbag with a dressy ensemble merely because she has paid an enormous sum of money for it. Alligator is strictly for sports or travel, shoes as well as bags, and this respected reptile should be permitted to retire every evening at 5 P.M."). Covering every fashion topic conceivable, from grooming and wardrobes to cosmetics and glasses, this is a lovely fashion guide with a classic feel.

> **Subjects:** Fashion • Clothing • Appearance • How-to

> **Now Try:** None of Antoine-Dariaux's advice will do one whit of good, alas, if the woman who follows it does not have the personality to support her fashion. Fortunately we have another classic guide, first published in 1938, to help us navigate the complicated rules of etiquette. *Better than Beauty: A Guide to Charm*, by Helen Valentine, Alice Thompson, and Emery I. Gondor, offers advice on everything from tone of voice to eating in public to choosing which topics are appropriate for conversation.

Brown, Bobbi, and Marie Clare Katigbak-Sillick

Living Beauty. New York: Springboard Press, 2007. 207pp. ISBN 9780821258347.

Cosmetics guru and celebrity makeup artist Bobbi Brown, herself a fifty-something woman, here presents a beauty guide for women of a certain age. The book emphasizes cosmetics, of course, offering detailed instructions on when and how to use makeup, but it also discusses related issues such as clothing, hair, and diet and exercise. Gorgeous photos accompany the advice in chapters such as "The Makeup-Only Face Lift: Surgery-Free Ways to Wipe away the Years" and "The Real Fountain of Youth: Eat Well and Break a Sweat," making this an excellent guide to looking great in the golden years.

> **Subjects:** Fashion • Appearance • Cosmetics • Midlife • Seniors • How-to • Quick Read

> **Now Try:** Looking for more beauty and lifestyle tips for middle-aged and senior women? Turn to *The Grown-Up Girl's Guide to Style: A Maintenance Bible for Fashion, Beauty, and More*, in which fashion reporter Christine Schwab reveals

the secrets of fashion, makeup, and healthy living. Read this for Schwab's spot-on advice and to revel in the gorgeous photos of beautiful older women.

Brown, Bobbi, and Sally Wadyka

Bobbi Brown Beauty Evolution: A Guide to a Lifetime of Beauty. New York: HarperCollins, 2002. 211pp. ISBN 9780060088811.

Bobbi Brown, cosmetics genius and makeup artist to the stars, here presents another wonderful book about beauty. (She has written several titles; see the annotation above for *Living Beauty*, for instance.) This is a wonderful, thorough guide to maintaining beauty, covering topics ranging from cosmetics and skin care to plastic surgery and staying beautiful through cancer. Brown has chapters devoted to different ages, skin tones, and styles, written in her clear prose and supported with tons of color photos. Read it cover-to-cover to get a comprehensive introduction to beauty cultivation and maintenance, then refer back as necessary for a refresher and for new style ideas.

> **Subjects:** Fashion • Appearance • Cosmetics • How-to • Quick Read

> **Now Try:** Pair Bobbi Brown's book with a book from the editorial director of *Elle*, Rona Berg. *Beauty: The New Basics* gives the low-down on everything from basic upkeep and cosmetics to skin care and hair color. Filled with color photos, sidebars, illustrations, and fun trivia, the book is an informative, entertaining guide to everything a woman needs to know about beauty.

Cunningham, Michael

Queens: Portraits of Black Women and Their Fabulous Hair. New York: Doubleday, 2005. 199pp. ISBN 9780385514620.

Michael Cunningham has an eye for beauty and the talent to capture it on film. In this lovely photo-essay, he collects fifty photos of black women sporting a dizzying number of hairdos: bald and bleached, braids and afros, natural and dreadlocked, pulled-back and free-falling, short and long. Supporting the gorgeous portraiture are quotes and anecdotes that shine light on black women's thoughts on race, beauty, body image, and identity. *Queens* can serve as a coffee-table book to inspire conversation, or as a cover-to-cover read that illuminates the role of hair in the lives of black women.

> **Subjects:** Hair • Appearance • Body Image • African Americans • Race • Collection • Quick Read

> **Now Try:** Looking for more about black women's hair? Editors Juliette Harris and Pamela Johnson have culled essays and stories that speak to black women's relationships with their hair in *Tenderheaded: A Comb-Bending Collection of Hair Stories*, in which frequent photos and images illustrate the words of such writers as Angela Y. Davis and Toni Morrison. Then catch Michael Cunningham's first book, *Crowns: Portraits of Black Women in Church Hats*. Once again, he captures the beauty of black women with his magnificent photography; this time, though, the emphasis is not on hair but on church hats. Revel in the variety of shapes, sizes, styles, and attitudes expressed by these beautiful accessories, and savor the quotes on beauty, fashion, and faith offered by black women.

Finney, Kathryn

How to Be a Budget Fashionista: The Ultimate Guide to Looking Fabulous for Less. New York: Ballantine Books, 2006. 222pp. ISBN 9780812975161.

What will it be this week, buying groceries or buying a new pair of jeans? Here's some good news: after reading *How to Be a Budget Fashionista*, you won't have to choose. Kathryn Finney teaches you all you need to know about finding the best clothes for the best price—and while she's at it, she tells you what to look for in garments and accessories to develop a wardrobe with style. Filled with insider tips—how to sniff out sales, how to ferret out high-end items in second-hand stores, which Web sites to visit—this is a wonderfully useful book, delivered in Finney's fun, catchy writing style.

Subjects: Fashion • Clothing • Appearance • Finances • How-to

Now Try: Discover more secrets of fashion style in *The Lucky Shopping Manual: Building and Improving Your Wardrobe Piece by Piece*. With their quirky, sassy style, Kim France and Andrea Linett cover everything you need to know about clothes, from finding the best bargains, buying the basics, and knowing where you can cut corners and where you should pony up the cash.

Johnson, Anna

Handbags: The Power of the Purse. New York: Workman, 2002. 486pp. ISBN 9780-761123774.

Handbags: they're the one accessory that most women can't leave home without. Fortunately, this indispensable item comes in a dizzying array of manifestations, ensuring that even the choosiest women can find something to suit their tastes and needs. For just a sampling of the many varieties of purse possibilities, take a gander at the nine hundred color photographs contained in this visual feast of a book. In chapters such as "Class Acts, Elegant Icons" and "Novelty & Caprice: Handbag Humor," you'll discover a cornucopia of handbag images, each one supplemented with a brief text passage to explain its origin or meaning. Skim through the book quickly or luxuriate over the gorgeous photos; either way, this is a sensual and satisfying tribute to the purse.

Subjects: Purses • Fashion • Appearance • Quick Read

Now Try: Though it does not have as many photos as Johnson's book, *Handbags: What Every Woman Should Know* nonetheless contains a wealth of illustrations for readers who can't get enough of purses. Written by veteran fashion-book author Stephanie Pedersen, this charming read considers the history of purses throughout the centuries and around the world. It's a fun, quick read, filled with interesting facts and handbag trivia.

Koda, Harold

Extreme Beauty: The Body Transformed. New York: Metropolitan Museum of Art, 2001. 168pp. ISBN 9781588390141.

When it comes to women's bodies (and to a lesser extent, to men's bodies), people throughout history have found no shortage of creative clothing to manipulate, exaggerate, distort, embellish, and otherwise transform human flesh. Examine this history of fashion in glorious, full-color detail in the breathtaking *Extreme Beauty*, the companion book to a Metropolitan Museum of Art exhibit of the same name. The book's five sections (Neck and Shoulders, Chest, Waist, Hips, and Feet) explore fashions past and present from around the world, from the coils worn around the necks of Burmese women to the stilettos on the feet of Western women to the bound feet of Chinese women. Photography, sculpture, paintings, and other magnificent illustrations chronicle the extremes of fashion, ably supported by Koda's intriguing narrative about the social and historical implications of beauty ideals around the world and across the ages.

Subjects: Fashion • Appearance • Art • History • Art History • Women's History • Social History • Global Perspectives • Quick Read

Now Try: Those who love the blend of art and fashion history in *Extreme Beauty* simply must get their hands on a copy of *The Collection of the Kyoto Costume Institute: A History from the 18th to the 20th Century*, by Akiko Fukai and Tamami Suoh. Filled with color photos of pieces in the collection of the Kyoto Costume Institute, this gorgeous book presents a history of three hundred years of fashion; the emphasis is on women's apparel, though men's clothing and accessories are also included.

Krupp, Charla

How Not to Look Old: Fast and Effortless Ways to Look 10 Years Younger, 10 Pounds Lighter, 10 Times Better. New York: Springboard Press, 2008. 224pp. ISBN 9780446581141.

Are your wrinkles getting you down? Do your jeans look horribly old-lady? Or worse—are you trying to stuff your mature body into midriff-baring jeans that were designed for a twenty-year-old? Stop making the fashion mistakes of old age and start looking younger by following the excellent advice of Charla Krupp, style expert of the *Today Show*. Whether you're looking for quick fixes (think cosmetics, hair highlights, new shoes) or more expensive solutions (think Botox, dental surgery, sexy new eyeglasses), you'll find the advice you need in this attractive, visually satisfying book, dispensed with Krupp's sensible, tell-it-like-it-is style.

Subjects: Fashion • Appearance • Cosmetics • Midlife • Seniors • How-to

Now Try: Pair Krupp's excellent advice with the tips in *Forever Cool: How to Achieve Ageless, Youthful and Modern Personal Style*. With humor and sass, Sherrie Mathieson helps the fifty-plus age group find the clothes and accessories they need to look good. You'll find advice for men as well as for women, along with a valuable section on how to shop smarter.

Mulvey, Kate, and Melissa Richards

Decades of Beauty. New York: Checkmark Books, 1998. 205pp. ISBN 97808-16039203.

A century of beauty trends comes to life in this magnificent photo history of fashion. Presented on a decade-by-decade chronological basis, the book examines every aspect of women's beauty, from clothing and accessories to cosmetics and hair care. The narrative text focuses on the historical context of the evolving beauty ideals, while the gorgeous photos illustrate the changing trends in all their magnificent glory. Treat *Decades of Beauty* as a visually-satisfying coffee-table book, or read it from cover to cover to immerse yourself in the history of a hundred years of beauty.

Subjects: Fashion • Appearance • Clothing • Cosmetics • Body Image • History • Women's History • Social History • Nineteenth Century • Twentieth Century • Quick Read

Now Try: Readers especially interested in beauty ideals during the second half of the twentieth century would do well to turn to *Fifty Years of Fashion: New Look to Now*. Written by Valerie Steele of the Fashion Institute of Technology, this lavishly illustrated book presents a fascinating social history of five decades of fashion trends, from zoot suits to hot pants.

Pedersen, Stephanie

Bra: A Thousand Years of Style, Support and Seduction. Newton Abbot, UK: David & Charles, 2004. 128pp. ISBN 9780715320679.

Ah, the bra, that garment of so many purposes. It supports, it lifts; it squeezes, it pinches; it flattens, it plumps, and—if done right—it enchants the beholder. "The bra is perhaps the most powerful element of a woman's wardrobe," observes journalist Pedersen. "What other item of clothing inspires such devotion, yearning, admiration, frustration, and delight?" In this breezy, quirky survey of the modern bra and its numerous predecessors, sections such as "Medieval Misery" and "Bras of the Big Screen" take us through the history of this indispensable garment. Lavishly illustrated with photos and illustrations, this is both a lovely coffee-table book and succinct overview of the item that has shaped women's breasts through the ages.

> **Subjects:** Bras • Clothing • Fashion • Appearance • Body Image • History • Women's History • Social History • Quick Read

> **Now Try:** *Uplift: The Bra in America*, by Jane Farrell-Beck and Colleen Gau, is not the quick read that Pedersen's book is, nor does it boast the plentiful illustrations, but readers wishing to dig a little deeper into the story of the bra will be delighted with this social history. In this engaging and insightful study, you'll follow the evolution of the bra in America, from its genesis in the 1860s as an alternative to the corset to its essential role in the wardrobe of modern women athletes.

Pedersen, Stephanie

Shoes: What Every Woman Should Know. Newton Abbot, UK: David & Charles, 2005. 128pp. ISBN 9780715322345.

Having discovered a winning formula for fashion writing in her book *Bra* (see the preceding annotation), author Stephanie Pedersen returns with another scintillating garment history. This time, the subject is shoes, and the history spans 10,000 years, give or take. From the earliest moccasins to the stunning stiletto, from the platform to the pump, this is a fun, fact-filled overview of the history of the glorious shoe. With an engaging prose style and plentiful illustrations of shoes in all their dazzling varieties, this celebration of footwear is both educational and lovely to look at.

> **Subjects:** Shoes • Clothing • Fashion • Appearance • Body Image • History • Women's History • Social History • Quick Read

> **Now Try:** Continue indulging your shoe mania with Linda O'Keeffe's book *Shoes: A Celebration of Pumps, Sandals, Slippers & More*. Like Pedersen's book, this is a quick, captivating look at the history of shoes, filled with footwear tidbits and factoids and lavishly illustrated with color photos.

Saboura, Sam, and L. G. Mansfield

Sam Saboura's Real Style: Style Secrets for Real Women with Real Bodies. New York: Clarkson Potter, 2005. 191pp. ISBN 9781400097715.

Sam Saboura, host of the television show *Extreme Makeover*, has done a wonderful service for those of us who don't happen to be fashion models. (Full disclosure: I am not a fashion model.) Whether you're tall or short, flat-chested or busty, full-figured or slender—or some magnificent combination of them all—Saboura shows you how to make the most of whatever body type you have in this marvelous guide to style. Get insider information on choosing the right clothes, making the most of a tailor, and accentuating your shape with the right underwear. Fun, informative, and brimming with charts, pictures, tips, and sidebars, this refreshing guide will help you transform your style, your wardrobe, and your image.

> **Subjects:** Fashion • Appearance • How-to • Quick Read

> **Now Try:** Like Sam Saboura, Kendall Farr recognizes that women come in different shapes and sizes. In *The Pocket Stylist: Behind-the-Scenes Expertise from a Fashion Pro on Creating Your Own Unique Look,* she helps readers with everything they need to know about fashion, from finding the right bra size and choosing the right underwear to selecting the best pieces for a wardrobe and making the most of a tailor.

Seligson, Susan

Stacked: A 32DDD Reports from the Front. New York: Bloomsbury, 2007. 229pp. ISBN 9781596911178.

Is there any body part with such universal appeal as the breast? From the pirate's dream (that is, a sunken chest—get it?) to the 300,000 American women who undergo breast augmentation surgery *each year*, the breast fascinates us, literally from the time we are born. In this wickedly funny investigation, Susan Seligson explores breasts in a variety of settings: we are treated, for instance, to a study of breast slang, a behind-the-scenes look at a pornography magazine, and a visit to a surgeon's office during a routine breast augmentation. (I may add, from deeply personal experience, that the chapter on bra-fitting and bra-buying is *extremely* valuable.) Fast-paced, witty, and eminently readable, this is a captivating sociological look at the breast in America today.

> **Subjects:** Breasts • Appearance • Body Image • Sociology • America • Humor

> **Now Try:** If you found yourself captivated by the information unearthed by Susan Seligson, continue learning about breasts in *Boobs: A Guide to Your Girls.* Author Elisabeth Squires treats us to a wonderful array of facts and, er, figures about the breast, in chapters such as "Cut and Paste: Surgical Answers to Breast Dilemmas" and "The More Mature Breast: Saggy, Yet Sexy & Sassy." Partly a guide to caring for and relishing your breasts, and partly a trove of breast lore, this is a quirky, informative, superbly enjoyable read. And if witty, engaging investigative reporting into unusual topics is your thing, turn to any of Mary Roach's books: *Stiff: The Curious Lives of Human Cadavers; Spook: Science Tackles the Afterlife;* and *Bonk: The Curious Coupling of Science and Sex.*

Steele, Valerie

The Corset: A Cultural History. New Haven, CT: Yale University Press, 2001. 199pp. ISBN 9780300090710.

Most of us, if we bother to think of corsets at all, think of them with a sense of relief: thank goodness we don't have to wear *those* anymore. Lacing one's midriff in such inhospitable materials as whalebone and steel was indeed an uncomfortable, even dangerous, form of women's fashion for four centuries. But the corset carried with it a glamorous, erotic image, one that still fascinates even today, as we learn in this engrossing social history. Author Steele, the chief curator at the Museum at the Fashion Institute of Technology, treats us to an overview of the corset in history, bolstering her enjoyable prose with illustrations of corsets past and present.

Subjects: Corsets • Clothing • Fashion • Appearance • Body Image • Sociology • History • Women's History • Social History • Quick Read

Now Try: Continue learning about the corset and its fashion heir, the bra, in Béatrice Fontanel's *Support and Seduction: The History of Corsets and Bras.* As in Steele's book, this cultural study considers the garments that women have used to lift, shape, smooth, and—occasionally—mangle their bodies, from ancient times through the present; an engaging prose style and numerous illustrations and photos make this a thoroughly enjoyable read.

Thomas, Angela

Do You Think I'm Beautiful?: The Question Every Woman Asks. Nashville, TN: Thomas Nelson, 2003. 215pp. ISBN 9780785263555.

"Oh, I *want* to be Cinderella," admits Angela Thomas. "I want to be the most beautiful woman at the ball, but I've never been bold enough to think of myself as her. Maybe the lessons of junior high linger. Maybe I've been conditioned by my environment. Maybe I'm just a coward." But with middle age encroaching, Thomas began to take a hard look at her self-image and came to some startling conclusions. It doesn't matter what the other kids at school thought, she realized, or what your husband thinks, or even what you think of yourself: what matters is what God thinks—and simply put, God thinks you're beautiful. In this lovely, honest, affirming book, Thomas draws on biblical scripture and personal anecdotes to invite Christian women to see themselves as God sees them, as beautiful human beings.

Subjects: Appearance • Christianity • Religion

Now Try: Readers who were inspired by Thomas's Christian approach to beauty will find more food for thought in Nancy Stafford's *Beauty by the Book.* Drawing on scripture, personal experience, and her own insightful observations, Stafford helps women to recognize the beauty that God sees in them. Then try *Wanting to Be Her: Body Image Secrets Victoria Won't Tell You*, in which Michelle Graham exposes the impossible beauty standards of contemporary society, offering instead a body image based on a relationship with God.

Yalom, Marilyn

A History of the Breast. New York: Alfred A. Knopf, 1997. 331pp. ISBN 978067-9434597x.

"On the one hand, breasts are associated with the transformation from girlhood to womanhood, sexual pleasure, and nursing," writes gender scholar Yalom. "On the other, they are increasingly associated with cancer and death." Indeed, the breast has a variety of meanings, mythologies, and symbolisms—and in this sweeping social history, Yalom attempts to examine them all. With her engaging tone and fascinating subject matter,

Yalom considers the breast across the ages, from prehistoric figurines found in modern-day Turkey to breast-obsessed medieval painters to contemporary nipple piercings. Supported with myriad illustrations, photos, and art reproductions, this is a compelling social history of the changing attitudes toward the breast in Western society.

Subjects: Breasts • Body Image • Appearance • History • Women's History • Social History • Global Perspectives

Now Try: Learn more about society's fascination with the female breast in Carolyn Latteier's *Breasts: The Women's Perspective on an American Obsession*. Though with a more current emphasis than the historical approach in Yalom's book, readers will enjoy the insight into such varied topics as breast-feeding, sexuality, body image, and evolution. And readers looking for more social histories of body parts will naturally want to try *A Mind of Its Own: A Cultural History of the Penis*, by David M. Friedman.

Cosmetics

Makeup and other products and practices intended to enhance beauty are covered by titles in this section.

As you might expect, the "Cosmetics" section includes plenty of practical cosmetic advice, but there's more here than just instructional guidance. Learn about the social and business history of the cosmetic industry in *Hope in a Jar*, by Kathy Lee Peiss, or let celebrity makeup artist Kevyn Aucoin dazzle you with his cosmetic art in *Face Forward*.

Aucoin, Kevyn

Face Forward. Boston: Little, Brown, 2000. 195pp. ISBN 9780316286442.

Uber-talented celebrity makeup artist Kevyn Aucoin, author of several books on cosmetics, here presents a book with an intriguing concept: to demonstrate the transformative potential of makeup, he applies his skill to celebrities by turning them into . . . other celebrities. Thus Tina Turner becomes Cleopatra, Liza Minelli becomes Marilyn Monroe, and Gwenyth Paltrow—you'll have to see it to believe it—becomes James Dean. This visually stunning book is a remarkable showcase of Aucoin's talent, with plenty of dishy commentary on the celebrities he transforms, but it is also a guide to makeup for us mortals, with step-by-step instructions delivered in Aucoin's enthusiastic, empowering style.

Subjects: Cosmetics • Fashion • Appearance • How-to • Quick Read

Now Try: For more advice on applying cosmetics in fantastic new ways, turn to Aucoin's *Making Faces*. With detailed instructions and background explanations for the reasoning behind every technique, this is an accessible guide to making your makeup work for you. Plentiful photos of celebrities and ordinary folks demonstrate how to apply Aucoin's techniques and show what the fantastic final results look like.

Begoun, Paula

The Beauty Bible: The Ultimate Guide to Smart Beauty. Seattle, WA: Beginning Press, 1997 (2002). 510pp. ISBN 9781877988295.

The subtitle of this excellent book is no exaggeration: *The Beauty Bible* really is the ultimate guide to all of the cosmetics, practices, and products associated with beauty. Writing in her engaging, informative style, makeup expert Begoun covers a dizzying array of topics, from combating puffy eyes and caring for cuticles to opting for collagen injections and exfoliating sun-damaged skin. Chapters such as "Skin Care Basics for Everyone," "Makeup Application Step by Step," and "Miracles, Frauds, & Facts" offer a comprehensive overview of everything there is to know about creating and maintaining perfect beauty; read it cover-to-cover for a thorough education, or refer to it as needed for clear, succinct advice.

> **Subjects:** Cosmetics • Fashion • Appearance • How-to

> **Now Try:** For more expert beauty advice, turn to two other books by Begoun, *Don't Go to the Cosmetics Counter without Me: A Unique Guide to Over 35,000 Products, Plus the Latest Skin-Care Research* and *Don't Go Shopping for Hair Care Products without Me: Over 4,000 Brand Name Products Reviewed, Plus the Latest Hair Care Information*. In each book, Begoun gives readers savvy advice on which products to avoid and which products are worth their price.

Carmindy

The 5-Minute Face: The Quick and Easy Makeup Guide for Every Woman. New York: Regan, 2007. 192pp. ISBN 9780061238260.

Learn the secrets of fast, easy makeup from an artist who's seen it all; as the makeup host of the television show *What Not to Wear* and a frequent contributor to such magazines as *Vogue* and *Cosmopolitan*, Carmindy knows her stuff. Working from an approach that emphasizes natural beauty, Carmindy demonstrates the tricks to achieving a perfectly made-up face in the space of a few minutes. Her clear advice, supported with a wealth of color photos, makes for an accessible and practical makeup guide for finding the right cosmetics and knowing when and how to apply them.

> **Subjects:** Cosmetics • Fashion • Appearance • How-to • Quick Read

> **Now Try:** Looking for more simple makeup tricks? Turn to *Makeup Makeovers: Expert Secrets for Stunning Transformations*, written by celebrity makeup artist Robert Jones. With excellent makeup advice, detailed how-to instructions, and jaw-dropping before-and-after photos, this is a visually satisfying insider's guide to minimizing flaws and enhancing natural beauty.

Pallingston, Jessica

Lipstick. New York: St. Martin's Press, 1999. 228pp. ISBN 9780312199142.

If you've never given a second thought to that little tube of color you apply to your lips each morning, think again. Lipstick, as we learn in this delightful social history, has a long history—a history of about five thousand years, in fact, judging from the first known example of lipstick unearthed in ancient Ur. Read Pallingston's chatty, witty survey to find out how women in various cultures around the world and across the centuries have created and applied this beloved cosmetic. But this is not just a history book: there are useful how-to sections on dealing with salespeople, applying lipstick for the best effect, choosing the right color, and creating lipstick in your own home.

Subjects: Lipstick • Cosmetics • Fashion • Appearance • History • Women's History • Social History • How-to

Now Try: For a fun companion read, turn to *Read My Lips: A Cultural History of Lipstick*, by Meg Cohen Ragas and Karen Kozlowski. As with Pallingston's book, this quick read gives a nice overview of the lipstick in history, showing how people in different cultures used natural ingredients to color their lips. What makes this book particularly inviting is the collection of photos of women, past and present, sporting their lovely lipsticked lips.

Peiss, Kathy Lee

Hope in a Jar: The Making of America's Beauty Culture. New York: Metropolitan Books, 1998. 334pp. ISBN 9780805055504.

We've come a long way from the time when the recommended cosmetic treatment for skin diseases was "the warm urine of a little boy." In this meticulously researched book, Peiss takes us through the fascinating history of cosmetics in American culture, tracing the changes in their popularity and appearance over the centuries. Peiss focuses in particular on the origins of the cosmetic industry, offering profiles of the pioneering entrepreneurs such as Madame C. J. Walker and Elizabeth Arden. Especially interesting is the book's discussion about the influence of race in cosmetics; in a society where lighter skin was widely perceived as aesthetically superior, women of color had to be creative to find cosmetics that suited their own beauty needs. Engagingly written, this is a thought-provoking history of makeup, race, and entrepreneurship in America.

Subjects: Cosmetics • Fashion • Appearance • Body Image • Business • Entrepreneurs • Labor • Race • Sociology • History • Women's History • Social History • History of Business • History of Labor • American History • America • Biography

Now Try: Another engrossing study of the history of beauty is Teresa Riordan's wonderful *Inventing Beauty: A History of the Innovations That Have Made Us Beautiful*. This time, the scope of the book is worldwide, and everything related to beauty—not just cosmetics—is fair game. From the inflatable bra to deodorant, wrinkle creams to facials, discover the variety of ingenious (and sometimes alarming) ways that women have altered their appearance throughout history and across the globe.

Vadhera, Shalini

Passport to Beauty: Secrets and Tips from around the World for Becoming a Global Goddess. New York: St. Martin's Griffin, 2006. 240pp. ISBN 9780312349622.

With all the books on cosmetics and beauty tips available, to say nothing of the many magazine articles and Web sites, it can be hard to choose one. Vadhera's book is a good pick because it offers a wide variety of natural choices, all of which can be tried at home after a jaunt to the local grocery store. A big part of the book's fun comes from the international scope; makeup artist Vadhera digs up beauty tips from every continent except Antarctica, though she is careful to only endorse products that American women will easily be able to purchase. Affordable, readily available, natural products (such as spices, teas, and oils) are emphasized.

Subjects: Cosmetics • Appearance • Travel • Global Perspectives

Now Try: Though without the globe-trotting theme of Vadhera's book, *Earthly Bodies & Heavenly Hair: Natural and Healthy Personal Care for Every Body* is a good complement to *Passport to Beauty*. Author Dina Falconi includes hundreds of recipes for the care of skin, hair, mouth, and more, all of which can be made with natural products readily available from most grocery stores. The recipes are simple enough for beginners and contain only ingredients that are natural and safe for the body. Thorough explanations of the uses and properties of the ingredients make for informative and practical reading.

Consider Starting With . . .

The following list offers some of the most popular and enjoyable Health, Wellness, and Beauty titles:

Boston Women's Health Book Collective. *Our Bodies, Ourselves: A New Edition for a New Era.*

Guiliano, Mireille. *French Women Don't Get Fat.*

Harrison, Kathryn. *The Kiss.*

Kaysen, Susanna. *Girl, Interrupted.*

Walls, Jeannette. *The Glass Castle: A Memoir.*

Wolf, Naomi. *The Beauty Myth: How Images of Beauty Are Used against Women.*

Fiction Read-Alikes

- **Anderson, Laurie Halse.** Why doesn't freshman Melinda Sordino say anything? It's tough being a social pariah—the other kids hate her because she called the cops at a party last summer—but the real reason for her silence is far darker: she was raped. *Speak* is a novel of violence, loneliness, and eventual recovery from sexual trauma. You'll discover compelling young women in Anderson's other novels, too; try *Catalyst*, about a girl whose mental health is destabilized by the death of her mother and the rejection letter from the only college she wants to attend.

- **Delinsky, Barbara.** If you liked Delinsky's *Uplift: Secrets from the Sisterhood of Breast Cancer Survivors*, turn to her novels, featuring strong women who undergo spiritual and emotional journeys. *Coast Road* is a good place to start: Jack was a lousy husband, but when his ex-wife falls into a coma, he rushes to her side. Topics such as illness, parenting, miscarriage, breast cancer, and romance make this a rich, thought-provoking read.

- **Keyes, Marian.** Cocaine? Yes. Alcohol? All the time. Addicted? Of course not! Or at least, Rachel doesn't think she has a problem until she winds up in the hospital. *Rachel's Holiday* is about a young woman who reluctantly enrolls in a drug rehab clinic, where she realizes she needs to make some hard changes—but despite the heavy themes, this is a light, witty, fast-paced story. Keyes has a gift for dealing with serious issues while maintaining a positive tone; meet some of her other fascinating characters in books such as

Angels, about a woman who loses her job and her marriage, and *Lucy Sullivan Is Getting Married*, about depression, alcoholism, and the pursuit of romance.

- **King, Stephen.** Forget your preconceived notions of Stephen King as a horror novelist. Though certain supernatural and horrific elements are present, *Rose Madder* is the story of woman's escape from a violent marriage and her change from a meek, miserable abused wife to a strong, independent woman. King is a master of character development, and many of his other novels will appeal to readers who want strong women who overcome adversity; another good bet is *The Shining*, about a woman who must defend herself and her child when her husband succumbs to madness.

- **Mackler, Carolyn.** Life is tough: sophomore Virginia Shreves is fat, her brother raped a woman, and her parents are completely self-absorbed. *The Earth, My Butt, and Other Big Round Things* tackles some intense issues— body image, eating disorders, health, rape, recovery—but don't worry. Virginia ultimately comes to terms with loving her own body, loving herself, and learning to be healthy both physically and mentally. Continue discovering strong young women in Mackler's other novels, such as *Vegan Virgin Valentine*, about an overachieving teenager who begins to question her priorities.

- **McCall Smith, Alexander.** Meet the most enjoyable sleuth since Miss Marple in *The No. 1 Ladies' Detective Agency*, the first title in the series of the same name. Precious Ramotswe, a middle-aged black woman of considerable physical girth, is Botswana's only (but therefore best) female detective; read this series not so much for the mysteries but for Mma Ramotswe's insight into human nature, and for the fully realized African setting.

- **McKinley, Robin.** What better way to contemplate beauty and body image than in the classic fairy tale "Beauty and the Beast"? In *Beauty*, a retelling of the familiar story, the title character is actually sort of plain; it is only as she grows to love the beast that she begins to understand what beauty—both internal and external—really is. McKinley has written several fairy-tale adaptations, all of which gently urge the reader to reconsider traditional ideas about the role of women; perhaps follow *Beauty* with a darker novel, *Deerskin*, which recasts an obscure fairy tale about a princess who is raped by her father.

- **Morrison, Toni.** In 1941 Ohio, eleven-year-old Pecola Breedlove seizes on an obsession: though she sees herself as ugly, she thinks that everything would be better if only she had blue eyes. *The Bluest Eye* is a deeply unsettling look at race, beauty, body image, violence, and madness; though it is Morrison's first novel, it shines with her beautiful prose, complex characters, and profound social insights. Readers who like to read about the ability of women to survive in the face of violence will enjoy Morrison's other novels, too; perhaps continue with the story of Sethe, an escaped slave, in the haunting novel *Beloved*.

- **Weisberger, Lauren.** As the former assistant to the editor of *Vogue*, Weisberger knows all about high fashion. Discover clothes, cosmetics, accessories, and beauty ideals of the high-pressure fashion industry in *The Devil Wears Prada*, a staple of Chick Lit, or try any of her other books to meet women who grapple with careers, relationships, and family—all while being very fashionably dressed.

Chapter 4

Women's History

The key to understanding women's history is in accepting—painful though it may be—that it is the history of the majority of the human race.

—Gerda Lerner

Definition

History books are those that explore the actions of human beings throughout time. Women's history focuses on the lives of women, and often particularly on social history.

Before we define Women's History, let's start by defining *history* proper. This should be easy, right? History books are those that explore the actions of human beings throughout time. It's as simple as that.

Except it isn't.

Let's try an experiment. Tell me what you think of as you read these phrases: the history of Germans; the history of American pioneers; the history of Muslims; the history of scientists. Are you thinking of the history of German women, of pioneer women, of Muslim women, of scientist women? Or do you unintentionally think of men? If you're like most people, your default image of any group of people is one of men, unless the group of people in question is typically populated by women: the history of prostitutes or the history of nurses, for instance, will jolt us into remembering women.

History, as they say, is written by the victors, and the victors have almost always been men. Historical records tend to be written by and about men. Politicians, military leaders, explorers, conquerors, philosophers—those individuals whose stories we depend on to flesh out our understanding of the past—are primarily men. Thus the history that we learn in school is shaped by the things that mattered to those men: political history and military history dominate our studies.

Social history is far less common in classrooms—and to be fair, it is far more diffi-cult for historians to find records about the common man—er, woman. It is primarily through diaries, journals, and letters that we hear the voices of ordinary women, and these are the very documents that are most likely to be lost or discarded, if indeed they are written at all; throughout most of history, there was no need to educate women. Who needs literacy when your only duty in life is to raise children and run the house? The documents that are easier for historians to find—newspapers, statutes, important political tracts—have been written almost exclusively by men, about men.

But in the 1970s, second-wave feminism shook up the hallowed halls of academia. For the first time, scholars began in earnest to ask questions about the ordinary folks in history, the poor people, the minority people, the women. What were their daily lives like? What clothes did they wear? How was labor distributed between the sexes? How did women raise their children, what foods did they prepare, what recreational activi-ties did they pursue? Suddenly, the value of "trivial" primary documents—from oral histories and slave narratives to women's magazines and personal diaries—became very, very important. So, too, did the value of archaeology take on new importance. Even in societies where most women (and most men, for that matter) could not deliber-ately record their histories, the skilled archeologist could nonetheless uncover the acci-dental record of their lives by examining the evidence of their homes, their graves, even their very bodies.

It is still unfortunately true that contemporary history books tend to gloss over women's history. Yes, it is imperative to understand the political and military history of the world; yes, it is harder to find evidence of women's history. But though it takes more diligence to uncover the story of women in the past, their history is every bit as important as that of men. Token attempts to highlight an individual woman here or there do not speak to the larger issue: to understand human history, we must viscerally understand women's history.

Appeal

We love to read Women's History books because, darn it, they tell us the stories that no one bothered to teach us in our history classes. We had to learn all about the im-portant military campaigns of the American Civil War, and which general was on whose side, and which states seceded when. This would have been a lot easier to swal-low if we'd known about the women who spied for their armies, or the women who dressed in drag and took up arms, or the women who, um, entertained the male sol-diers. (Read all about them in Mary Elizabeth Massey's *Women in the Civil War*.)

We read Women's History because it is *our* history. Most of us will never rule countries (though you have to admit, the Byzantine women did it with style; see Judith Herrin's *Women in Purple*). It's pretty safe to say that none of us are part of an all-female society that kills off men after exploiting them for reproductive purposes (but if this de-scribes you, please turn to Lyn Webster Wilde's *On the Trail of the Women Warriors*). And while I can't claim to control the elite men of society with my sexual charms and irresistible conversational skills (modesty prevents me from making such an asser-tion), I was nonetheless fascinated by Katie Hickman's *Courtesans: Money, Sex, and Fame in the Nineteenth Century*.

So most of us will never be government leaders or military heroes or national celebrities, but like our mothers before us, we marry, we raise children, we prepare food, we practice our faiths. Like pioneer Anne Ellis, who recorded her memoir in *The Life of an Ordinary Woman*, we are normal people who worry about relationships and money and illness. We love discovering the characters who make history come alive, as we see in Vicki León's fabulous <u>Uppity Women</u> books; we love exploring their fascinating stories, as we see in Zahi A. Hawass's *Silent Images: Women in Pharaonic Egypt*. We read for the rich details that transport us to different settings, as with Jenny Jochens's *Women in Old Norse Society*; we read for inspiration (you'll likely want to take over the world after reading Autumn Stephens's *Wild Women*) and for sobering reminders of where our foremothers have been (see Anne Llewellyn Barstow's disturbing *Witchcraze*). With their attention to place, era, and setting, the books in this chapter explore the shared history of women—but readers who hunger for even more women's history will find further reading ideas elsewhere in this book, especially in Chapter 1: "Life Stories," and in Chapter 5: "Adventure and Travel."

Organization

The major sections are arranged chronologically, with "Women throughout the Ages," "Ancient and Classical Eras," "Dark and Middle Ages," "Renaissance and Enlightenment," "Nineteenth Century," and "Twentieth Century and Beyond." I have made efforts to include histories about women from a variety of nations and ethnicities in each of these categories. Additionally, there are seven thematic sections in the chapter: "Women's Bodies and Sexuality throughout History," "Women throughout American History," "Religious Life in Antiquity," "Colonial and Revolutionary America," "The American Old West," "The American Civil War," and "Women and War in the Twentieth Century."

Women throughout the Ages

Here you will find stories about how particular women shaped and were shaped by their historical eras.

Historians and scholars normally specialize in one discrete time period, but sometimes they broaden the scope to look at themes or subjects over the course of centuries or millennia. This is a good starting place for readers who want to look at the big picture of women's history. Those new to women's history can find general overviews—try Vicki León's engaging, accessible <u>Uppity Women</u> series—while aficionados of women's history can learn new things from in-depth treatments by topic—as with E. J. W. Barber's *Women's Work: The*

First 20,000 Years: Women, Cloth, and Society in Early Times—or by geography—as with Julia Tuñón's *Women in Mexico: A Past Unveiled*.

Barber, E. J. W.

Women's Work: The First 20,000 Years: Women, Cloth, and Society in Early Times. New York: Norton, 1994. 334pp. ISBN 9780393035063.

And here we have a captivating book on . . . textiles? Surely a book on cloth is going to be—there's no nice way to say this—boring, right? Not so fast! The story of cloth is really the story of women, as archeologist Barber explains in her preface: "The reader will find in these pages glimpses of real women of all sorts—peasants, entrepreneurs, queens, slaves, honest souls, and crooks—good and bad, high and low." With her remarkably entertaining writing style and brilliant ability to glean insight into women's lives through the study of fabric, Barber treats the reader to a fascinating portrait of women's lives in the murky depths of prehistory; this is suitable for both scholars and for casual readers, whether or not they realized they had an interest in prehistoric textiles.

Subjects: Clothing • Labor • Archaeology • History • Women's History • Prehistory • Ancient History

Now Try: For an excellent, physically beautiful companion read, turn to *World Textiles: A Visual Guide to Traditional Techniques* by John Gillow and Bryan Sentance. With nearly eight hundred photos, this is a lovely, informative survey of the history of textiles around the globe; though it does not have Barber's emphasis on gender, readers will enjoy the gorgeous illustrations and the insightful discussion of the role of cloth in human history.

Fraser, Antonia

The Warrior Queens. New York: Vintage Books, 1990 (New York: Anchor Books, 2004). 383pp. ISBN 9780679728160.

Fraser, an accomplished biographer and detective novelist, is a master at presenting historical fact in an engrossing format. In *The Warrior Queens*, she turns her deft hand to a special subset of women soldiers, women who not only participated in war but who actually led armies. Beginning with Boadacia, the queen who tried to defend Britain against the invading Romans in 60 C.E., and ending with recent women rulers such as Margaret Thatcher, Fraser presents a series of biographies about women's lives, leadership, and battles. Famous personages such as Catherine the Great and lesser-known leaders such as Queen Jinga of Angola are discussed in this scholarly but lively work.

Subjects: Warriors • History • Military History • War • Violence • Leadership • Labor • Global Perspectives • Biography • Collection

Now Try: Hungering for more information about leading warrior women? You'll find them in the collective biography *Hell Hath No Fury: True Stories of Women at War from Antiquity to Iraq*, alongside women who served from less exalted positions, including spies, reporters, and combatants. With a readable, entertaining style, co-authors Rosalind Miles and Robin Cross present profiles of women warriors throughout history, some famous, some obscure. And those who enjoyed Fraser's detailed, insightful writing in *The Warrior Queens* may be pleasantly surprised to discover her detective novels. Try starting with *Quiet as a Nun*, the first in a series featuring television reporter-cum-amateur sleuth Jemima Shore, in which the heroine investigates the murder of an heiress.

A History of Women in the West. Cambridge, MA: Belknap Press of Harvard University Press.

The five volumes of *History of Women in the West* do not pretend to present a comprehensive overview of European women's history. Instead, each volume offers a fascinating selection of essays about women's experiences, from Aline Rousselle's "Body Politics in Ancient Rome" (in Volume 1) to Elisja Schulte van Kessel's "Virgins and Mothers between Heaven and Earth" (in Volume 3) to Luisa Passerini's "The Ambivalent Image of Women in Mass Culture" (in Volume 5). Because the essays are written by various contributors, some are more accessible than others, but with the great variety of topics—such as law, religion, marriage, science, gender, and class— there is something here for every reader.

Schmitt Pantel, Pauline, ed. *A History of Women in the West, Vol. 1: From Ancient Goddess to Christian Saints.* 2000. 600pp. ISBN 9780674403697.

Klapisch-Zuber, Christiane, ed. *A History of Women in the West, Vol. 2: Silences of the Middle Ages.* 2000. 592pp. ISBN 9780674403680.

Davis, Natalie Zemon and Arlette Farge, eds. *A History of Women in the West, Vol. 3: Renaissance and Enlightenment Paradoxes.* 2000. 592pp. ISBN 9780674403680.

Fraisse, Genevieve and Michelle Perrot, eds. *A History of Women in the West, Vol. 4: Emerging Feminism from Revolution to World War.* 2000. 652pp. ISBN 9780674403666.

Thébaud, Francoise, ed. *A History of Women in the West, Vol. 5: Toward a Cultural Identity in the Twentieth Century.* 2000. 728pp. ISBN 9780674403659.

Subjects: History • Women's History • Ancient History • Classical History • Dark Ages • Medieval History • Sixteenth Century • Seventeenth Century • Eighteenth Century • Nineteenth Century • Twentieth Century • Feminism • Greece • Roman Empire • Europe • Essays

Now Try: Though her scholarly tone takes some getting used to, Gisela Bock is worth reading because of her succinct, insightful analysis of European women's history since the Middle Ages. In her *Women in European History*, she explores themes of gender, politics, and society, identifying how and why social norms changed, and synthesizing the various trends that occurred at different times in different corners of the continent. Bock's book, with its linear, cohesive approach to history, helps give context to the many disparate topics discussed in the volumes of *History of Women in the West*.

Jones, Constance

1001 Things Everyone Should Know about Women's History. New York: Doubleday, 1998. 294pp. ISBN 9780385476737.

If you have even the faintest interest in women's history, you need to know about Cleopatra, obviously, and Joan of Arc, and the Equal Rights Amendment and feminism. But Constance Jones thinks you should also know about Aretha Franklin and Mata Hari, eating disorders and the Kinsey Report, pinup girls, and secretaries. In this utterly compelling overview of women in world history, Jones provides one thousand and one snapshots of women and women's issues throughout time and across the globe. Blending quirky curiosities with momentous historical events, the book is both entertaining and informative, perfect for those who want a popular survey of women's world history.

Subjects: History • Women's History • Global Perspectives • Young Adult

Now Try: For an excellent companion read, turn to *The 100 Most Influential Women of All Time: A Ranking Past and Present*, in which Deborah G. Felder collects brief profiles of one hundred women who have made a difference. Unsurprisingly, there are plenty of politicians, leaders, and activists here (Eleanor Roosevelt is number one), but those who enjoyed the inclusion of celebrities and pop culture in *1001 Things Everyone Should Know about Women's History* will be delighted to see such names as Coco Chanel (number 51), Frida Kahlo (number 78), and Billie Holliday (number 90) populating the list.

Jones, David E.

Women Warriors: A History. Washington, DC: Brassey's, 1997 (Dulles, VA: Potomac Books, 2005). 279pp. ISBN 9781574881066.

Historically speaking, the inclusion of American women in the military is a recent phenomenon—but as *Women Warriors* shows, women throughout the world have been going to war since ancient times. The Amazons and Joan of Arc will be familiar to readers, but the strength of this wide-ranging history is the attention to lesser-known warriors such as Juliana D'Acosta, the eighteenth-century "Warrior Nanny" from Portugal who rode an elephant into battle, and Nguyen Thi Ba, the Vietnamese innkeeper who poisoned more than two hundred French invaders in 1907. Numerous anecdotes and fascinating facts, relayed in Jones's captivating prose, make this an informative read of truly global scope.

Subjects: Warriors • History • Military History • War • Violence • Labor • Global Perspectives

Now Try: Fewer warriors are considered in *Battle Cries and Lullabies: Women in War from Prehistory to the Present* than in *Women Warriors*, but what author Linda Grant De Pauw lacks in scope she makes up for in depth. With a carefully researched, chronological approach, De Pauw examines the nitty-gritty details of women's warring over time and across the globe, discussing issues such as prevailing social norms, dressing (and cross-dressing), and sexual relationships with fellow soldiers. A variety of women, wars, and social and historical contexts are examined at length in this expansive history.

León, Vicki

Uppity Women series. Berkeley, CA: Conari Press.

For fun, informative, entertaining writing about women's history, there is no finer choice than Vicki León. Infused with León's engaging, irreverent sense of humor, the Uppity Women series offers a thoroughly researched, wonderfully entertaining overview of sassy women throughout the ages. Each book features short biographies, bolstered by tidbits and factoids that flesh out the social and cultural climates of the women's lives. These are quick reads, meticulously researched but utterly readable, suitable for casual readers and serious students alike.

Uppity Women of Ancient Times. 1995. 243pp. ISBN 9781573240109.

Uppity Women of Medieval Times. 1997. 247pp. ISBN 9781573240390.

Uppity Women of the Renaissance. 1999. 308pp. ISBN 9781573241274.

Uppity Women of the New World. 2001. 314pp. ISBN 9781573241878.

Subjects: History • Women's History • Social History • Ancient History • Classical History • Dark Ages • Medieval History • Fourteenth Century • Fifteenth Century • Sixteenth Century • Seventeenth Century • Eighteenth Century • Nineteenth Century • Middle East • Egypt • Africa • Greece • Roman Empire • Europe • Asia • North America • South America • Australia • New Zealand • Global Perspectives • Humor • Biography • Young Adult • Quick Read

Now Try: If you love the way León makes history come alive, turn to her book *Working IX to V: Orgy Planners, Funeral Clowns, and Other Prized Professions of the Ancient World.* With her signature humor and snappy style, she introduces us to the regular working stiffs of antiquity, from politicians and priestesses to lawyers and professional virgins. Fans of the Uppity Women series may also enjoy *From Pocahontas to Power Suits: Everything You Need to Know about Women's History in America.* Its chronological focus is narrower than the scope of León's series, and author Kay Mills is somewhat more serious in tone than the lighthearted León, but readers will nonetheless enjoy the quirky, accessible approach to women's history.

Miles, Rosalind

Who Cooked the Last Supper?: The Women's History of the World. New York: Three Rivers Press, 2001. 342pp. ISBN 9780609806951.

"Man the Hunter, man the toolmaker, man the lord of creation stalks the primeval savannah in solitary splendor through every known version of the origin of our species," writes Rosalind Miles. "In reality, however, woman was quietly getting on with the task of securing a future for humanity—for it was her labor, her skills, her biology that held the key to the destiny of the race." Women usually get the short end of the stick in history texts, but Miles does her best to compensate in this witty, thought-provoking social history. In chapters such as "The Rights of Woman," "The Great Goddess," and—ahem—"The Rise of the Phallus," Miles shows how individuals (famous and otherwise) and groups of women contributed to the progress and development of human society throughout history and across the globe.

Subjects: History • Women's History • Social History • Global Perspectives • Humor

Now Try: Pair *Who Cooked the Last Supper?* with another excellent history, *The Subordinated Sex: A History of Attitudes toward Women*, by Vern L. Bullough, Brenda K. Shelton, and Sarah Slavin. By surveying men's attitudes toward women from prehistoric times to the present, this book makes an excellent companion to Miles's study and underscores the sexism and barriers that have trivialized women's roles throughout history.

Pendle, Karin, ed.

Women & Music: A History. Bloomington: Indiana University Press, 1991 (2001). 358pp. ISBN 9780253343215.

"Why is a feminine quality in music only laudable if the composer is a man?" asks musicologist Karin Pendle in her preface. "Is music by women excluded from study because it is deemed to be of inferior quality in comparison with music by men? What counts as quality anyway?" In seeking to address these and other feminist questions, Pendle has compiled an excellent collection of scholarly essays about women in music. Chapters cover a diverse array of topics, from Ann N. Michelini's "Women and Music in Ancient Greece and Rome" to Robert Whitney Templeman's "Women in the World of Music: Latin America, Native America, and the African Diaspora." With a global scope that covers women's music from ancient times to the present, from indigenous music to classical Western pieces to jazz, this is a fascinating, comprehensive study of women's participation in music throughout the ages.

> **Subjects:** Music • Musicians • Labor • History • Women's History • Music History • Global Perspectives

> **Now Try:** Now learn about the history of women in music through a wealth of primary sources in *Women in Music: An Anthology of Source Readings from the Middle Ages to the Present*, edited by Carol Neuls-Bates. Collecting such diverse texts as diaries, poems, and letters, the anthology gives voice to women composers, educators, and performers, while scholarly essays give context to the documents.

Restoring Women to History series. Bloomington: Indiana University Press.

The Restoring Women to History series comprises four concise, superbly researched books of women's history. Each volume examines women's lives from ancient times to the present, emphasizing their experiences in the context of their specific cultures. Addressing political, religious, social, and cultural concerns, these engaging studies offer a scholarly but accessible overview of women's histories in various parts of the world. Each book is a succinct, fast read, so there's no need to feel intimidated at the thought of reading the entire series, though those wishing to study a particular region will wish to start with the volume that focuses on their specific interest.

Berger, Iris, and E. Frances White. *Women in Sub-Saharan Africa: Restoring Women to History.* 1999. 169pp. ISBN 9780253334763.

Nashat, Guity, and Judith E. Tucker. *Women in the Middle East and North Africa: Restoring Women to History.* 1999. 160pp. ISBN 9780253334787.

Navarro, Marysa, Virginia Sánchez Korrol, and Kecia Ali. *Women in Latin America and the Caribbean: Restoring Women to History.* 1999. 128pp. ISBN 9780253213075.

Ramusack, Barbara N., and Sharon L. Sievers. *Women in Asia: Restoring Women to History.* 1999. 266pp. ISBN 9780253334817.

> **Subjects:** History • Women's History • Social History • Latinas • Middle East • Africa • Caribbean • Mexico • South America • Asia • Global Perspectives

> **Now Try:** Another excellent scholarly analysis of women in world history is the three-volume *Women's History in Global Perspective*, edited by Bonnie G. Smith. Read the first volume for an overview and comparison of women's history throughout time and across the globe, and to synthesize the lessons learned in the four volumes of the Restoring Women to History series. Then plunge into Smith's second and third volumes for essays with a more regional focus.

Schwarz-Bart, Simone, and André Schwarz-Bart

In Praise of Black Women. 3 vols. Madison: The University of Wisconsin Press, 2001. 956pp. ISBN 9780299172503 (v.1), 9780299172602 (v.2), and 9780299172701 (v.3).

Travel through the centuries and across the world with *In Praise of Black Women*, an ambitious, wide-ranging collective biography of black women. Three volumes have already been written (*Ancient African Queens*, *Heroines of the Slavery Era*, and *Modern African Women*), and a fourth volume, *Modern Women of the Diaspora*, is forthcoming. You'll meet women such as Amina Kulibali, who founded the Gabu dynasty; Phyllis Wheatley, the American slave and poet; and Miriam Makeba, the South African singer. Engagingly written and supported with ample illustrations, this is a remarkable celebration of black women throughout time and around the globe.

> **Subjects:** History • Women's History • Social History • Race • African Americans • Africa • Caribbean • South America • America • Global Perspectives • Biography
>
> **Now Try:** Now learn more about African women's experiences by reading *Women Writing Africa*. Discover the lives of African women in their own words in the three volumes of the book: *The Southern Region*, by M. J. Daymond et al; *West Africa and the Sahel*, by Esi Sutherland-Addy and Aminata Diaw; and *The Eastern Region*, by Amandina Lihamba et al. (Also watch for *The Northern Region*, forthcoming.) See also *Women in Sub-Saharan Africa: Restoring Women to History*, by Iris Berger and E. Frances White; part of the excellent Restoring Women to History series (see the previous annotation), this scholarly but accessible study explores African women's lives from ancient times through the present.

Tuñón, Julia

Women in Mexico: A Past Unveiled. Translations from Latin America series. Austin: University of Texas Press, Institute of Latin American Studies, 1999. 144pp. ISBN 9780292781603.

There are serious gaps in our collective knowledge of the history of Mexican women, acknowledges scholar Tuñón: "We know that women have been present, that they are a historical subject, and that their absence from historical sources does not imply their absence from the process through which the country has been built. The problem is how to fill these gaps." In this vivid history of women in Mexico, Tuñón goes a long way toward filling those holes. In chapters such as "Mexican Women in the Nineteenth Century: Idols of Bronze or Inspiration of the Home?" and "Women in New Spain: The End of One World and the Shaping of Another," Tuñón considers Mexican women's lives from precolonial times through the twentieth century. Thought-provoking and unapologetically feminist, this is a scholarly but readable study of the role of gender in Mexican society.

> **Subjects:** History • Women's History • Latinas • Gender • Feminism • Mexico • Quick Read
>
> **Now Try:** Focus now on a slice of Mexican women's history by turning to *The Women's Revolution in Mexico, 1910–1953*, edited by S. E. Mitchell and Patience A. Schell. Featuring both scholarly essays and primary historical documents, the book reconsiders the Mexican Revolution through the eyes and experiences of women in the public and private spheres. Though the historical scope is more focused than in *Women in Mexico*, readers will appreciate the insightful observations on gender and Mexican society.

Women's Bodies and Sexuality throughout History

The books in this section focus on women's sexual and reproductive roles throughout history.

To summarize the "Women's Bodies and Sexuality Throughout History" section in a genteel fashion, we may say that these are the books that explore women's physical and reproductive roles across the ages. Alternately, we can skip the pleasantries: these are the sex books! Whether your interests are academic, salacious, or a bit of both, you'll find something here to pique your curiosity.

Herman, Eleanor

Sex with Kings: 500 Years of Adultery, Power, Rivalry, and Revenge. New York: Morrow, 2004. 287pp. ISBN 9780060585433.

If you've ever caught yourself guilty scanning the tabloid headlines for the latest royal scandal—or if you've boldly purchased the tabloid for your own salacious pleasure reading, onlookers be damned—then this is the book for you. This is the glorious history of the royal mistress in Europe, from medieval times through our present-day Camilla Parker-Bowles, with stops in between for such dashing ladies as Madame de Pompadour. Mistresses, we learn, served not just as sexual playthings but as companions, political sounding boards, and, not infrequently, mothers. Witty and absorbing, this is the history you wish they'd taught you in school.

> **Subjects:** Sexuality • Relationships • Politics • Rulers • Royalty • History • Women's History • Social History • Europe • Biography • Collection

> **Now Try:** Naturally, you'll want to turn to Herman's sequel, *Sex with the Queen: 900 Years of Vile Kings, Virile Lovers, and Passionate Politics*. Learn how queens have satisfied their yearnings with courtiers, military heroes, and various men-about-court for centuries of European history. Another un-put-downable read is *A Treasury of Royal Scandals: The Shocking True Stories of History's Wickedest, Weirdest, Most Wanton Kings, Queens, Tsars, Popes, and Emperors*, in which Michael Farquhar exposes a delightful number of high-profile scandals; sinfully fascinating sexual exploits are covered, of course, but so, too, are other delicious intrigues involving power-hungry maniacs and hedonistic revelers.

Marks, Lara

Sexual Chemistry: A History of the Contraceptive Pill. New Haven, CT: Yale University Press, 2001. 372pp. ISBN 9780300089431.

In Western nations, oral contraception has become ubiquitous, to the point where it is known simply as "the Pill." What we take for granted today, however, has a long and complicated history, as seen in this fascinating history of chemistry, medicine, and women's issues in the twentieth century, both in America and across the globe. Drawing on extensive research and interviews with women who were involved with the development of the Pill in its early stages, historian Marks presents an eminently readable account of the scientific development of oral contraception, deftly weaving in the political themes of race, religion, class, and nationality that affected—and continue to affect—its use and distribution.

Subjects: Birth Control • Sexual Health • History • Chemistry • Science • History of Medicine • History of Science • Women's History • Social History • Twentieth Century • Global Perspectives

Now Try: Continue learning about the fascinating history of oral contraception in *On the Pill: A Social History of Oral Contraceptives, 1950–1970*, in which Elizabeth Siegel Watkins looks at the Pill's influence through two decades of American history. Part social history and part history of medicine, this quick read examines the contentious issues such as safety and feminism that surrounded the Pill in the years after it first became widely available to American women.

Prioleau, Elizabeth Stevens

Seductress: Women Who Ravished the World and Their Lost Art of Love. New York: Viking, 2003. 366pp. ISBN 9780670031665.

"The seductress…. She's the blond bimbette in a string bikini; the stacked vamp in Spandex; the Chanel-suited nymphobitch of Sullivan & Cromwell; the servile artist's muse and maidservant," writes scholar Prioleau. "But we've got it wrong." In this delightful romp through history, Prioleau redefines the seductress: she's not just a pretty face—and in fact, she may not be pretty at all; rather, she is a woman of character, charisma, and personality. Armed with this refreshing new take on women's sexiness, Prioleau brings to life seductresses across the centuries, from Aphrodite to Mary Magdalene to Eleanor of Aquitaine. Fun, feisty, and empowering, *Seductress* pays tribute to the vixens of the past and encourages us to follow their examples.

Subjects: Sexuality • History • Women's History • Social History • Feminism • Global Perspectives • Biography • Collection

Now Try: Pair *Seductress* with another engrossing social history, Jane Billinghurst's *Temptress: From the Original Bad Girls to Women on Top*. With lavish illustrations from paintings, film, and photography, *Temptress* is a visual feast of seductive women throughout history. Billinghurst's strong feminist scholarship in disciplines such as art and literature makes this both a thought-provoking academic read and a beautiful visual compendium of temptresses past and present.

Riddle, John M.

Contraception and Abortion from the Ancient World to the Renaissance. Cambridge, MA: Harvard University Press, 1992. 341pp. ISBN 9780674-168756.

Scholars generally believe that people did not have access to reliable contraception until the eighteenth century, but in this thoroughly researched social history, historian Riddle convincingly argues that ancient and medieval women had a working knowledge of effective contraception and abortion. For evidence, he considers the low fertility rates of ancient and medieval societies, as well as references to contraceptives and abortion drugs within historical medical books. Though scholarly in approach, this is an accessible, thought-provoking read that offers a glimpse into the vegetables and herbs that women used as birth control in the distant past.

Subjects: Abortion • Birth Control • Sexual Health • History • Women's History • Social History • History of Medicine • History of Science • Ancient History • Classical History • Dark Ages • Medieval History • Sixteenth Century • Seventeenth Century • Health • Sexual Health • Europe

Now Try: After Riddle wrote *Contraception and Abortion*, he was left with a burning question: if ancient and medieval peoples had knowledge of contraceptives, what happened to it? Why was the knowledge lost to their descendants? He studies those questions in *Eve's Herbs: A History of Contraception and Abortion in the West*, finding that the practice of contraception and abortion became criminalized over the centuries and that the women who maintained the knowledge were often accused of witchcraft. This is an excellent look at the early social, religious, and political influences that threatened women's reproductive choices in medieval and Renaissance Europe. See also Andrea Tone's book *Devices and Desires: A History of Contraceptives in America*, which considers the limited (and usually illegal) contraceptive options available to American women before the twentieth century and the gradual shift in policy toward effective, legalized birth control.

Solinger, Rickie

Pregnancy and Power: A Short History of Reproductive Politics in America. New York: New York University Press, 2005. 303pp. ISBN 9780814798270.

The personal is inextricable from the political in this eye-opening history of women's reproduction in the United States. Starting with the founding of America in 1776 and continuing chronologically through the present, historian Solinger examines the complicated, fascinating, and oftentimes ugly history of the politics surrounding women's bodies. Abortion is discussed, of course, but so are other topics such as forced sterility, forced adoption, and forced pregnancy and childbearing. Expertly drawing together issues of race, class, and nationality, Solinger paints a broad picture of reproductive politics in America in this engaging, thought-provoking social history.

Subjects: Birth Control • Abortion • Politics • Race • Class • History • Women's History • Social History • History of Medicine • History of Science • American History • Eighteenth Century • Nineteenth Century • Twentieth Century • Health • Sexual Health • America

Now Try: An excellent companion read for *Pregnancy and Power* is Linda Gordon's book *The Moral Property of Women: A History of Birth Control Politics in America*. This social history details the struggles, triumphs, and controversies surrounding reproduction and birth control in America in the nineteenth and twentieth centuries. See also *Roe v. Wade: The Abortion Rights Controversy in American History*, in which N. E. H. Hull and Peter Charles Hoffer consider the legal history behind the criminalization and subsequent legalization of abortion in America; the writing is scholarly but accessible, perfect for the reader who wants to understand the court decisions and public policies that have affected the rights, or lack of rights, of women to choose abortion in the past two hundred years.

Yoshimi, Yoshiaki

Comfort Women: Sexual Slavery in the Japanese Military during World War II. New York: Columbia University Press, 2002. 253pp. ISBN 9780231120333.

Japanese scholar Yoshimi was the first historian to prove conclusively that the Japanese military orchestrated the procurement and exploitation of comfort women during World War II. In this disturbing work of social and military history, Yoshimi draws on primary documents, diaries, and memoirs to expose the horrific story of the 200,000 comfort women who were enslaved as sexual servants—systematically forced to suffer the sexual and violent caprices of Japanese soldiers during the Second World War. Yoshimi's research remains controversial in Japan, where certain parties would prefer to believe that the comfort women chose to be sexually exploited—or, at the very least, that the military did not condone their exploitation. Read this eye-opening book to discover one of the most influential works of history at work in the world today and to understand the fierce debate currently raging in Japan over the correct interpretation of history.

Subjects: Comfort Women • Rape • Violence • Sexual Exploitation • History • Military History • Social History • Women's History • World War II • Twentieth Century • Japan • Asia

Now Try: Now turn to the painful stories of comfort women as told by the women themselves in two books, *The Comfort Women: Japan's Brutal Regime of Enforced Prostitution in the Second World War*, by George L. Hicks, and *True Stories of the Korean Comfort Women*, by Keith Howard. Both books give voice to the survivors of the "comfort stations" of World War II, allowing their terrible, humiliating experiences to speak for themselves.

Women throughout American History

A particular focus on women in American history distinguishes the titles in this section.

Books in the "Women throughout American History" section look at the experiences of women since the founding of the United States in 1776—and in some cases, even before the country was born, as with *A Thousand Years over a Hot Stove* by Laura Schenone. These books emphasize themes and subjects as they explore the social milieus of times past.

Collins, Gail

America's Women: Four Hundred Years of Dolls, Drudges, Helpmates, and Heroines. New York: William Morrow, 2003. 556pp. ISBN 9780060185107.

You may recognize Gail Collins from her work with the *New York Times*; she was the first woman to become editor of that illustrious journal's editorial page, and now she writes an insightful, wickedly funny column in those pages. In *America's Women*, she turns her trademark humor and intelligent observations to the history of women in America. Arranged chronologically in chapters such as "Daily Life in the Colonies: Housekeeping, Children, and Sex" and "The Gilded Age: Stunts, Shorthand, and Study Clubs," the book illuminates the lives of American women through four centuries. Collins does an admirable job of presenting the stories of racial minorities, poor women, and others whose histories can be difficult to unearth, making this an expansive, informative, and eminently entertaining work of social history.

Subjects: History • Women's History • American History • Social History • Seventeenth Century • Eighteenth Century • Nineteenth Century • Twentieth Century • America

Now Try: Like Gail Collins, Kay Bailey Hutchison recognizes the importance of the obscure and famous alike in her collective biography *Leading Ladies: American Trailblazers*. As the first woman from Texas ever elected to the U.S. Senate, Hutchison knows leadership material when she sees it. Arranged thematically into chapters such as "The Good Fight: Women in the Military" and "A Dream of the Future: Women's Suffrage and Civil Rights," the book delivers fascinating stories of women throughout American history.

Kerber, Linda K., and Jane Sherron De Hart, eds.

Women's America: Refocusing the Past. New York: Oxford University Press, 1982 (2004). 478pp. ISBN 9780195029826.

Four centuries of American women's history come alive in this superb anthology of primary and secondary sources. Engaging essays from scholars, such as Susan J. Douglas's "Why the Shirelles Mattered: Girl Groups on the Cusp of a Feminist Awakening," give context to a wealth of historical documents, including writings by Sarah and Angelina Grimké, Margaret Sanger, and a slave known only as Rose, as well as legal documents such as the Comstock Law and Title IX. Intended for students and scholars but thoroughly suitable for popular audiences, this engaging book is a fascinating, informative survey of American women's history.

Subjects: History • Women's History • American History • Social History • Seventeenth Century • Eighteenth Century • Nineteenth Century • Twentieth Century • America • Essays • Anthology • Collection

Now Try: If you enjoyed the wealth of primary sources in *Women's America*, continue with *Through Women's Eyes: An American History with Documents*, by Ellen Carol DuBois and Lynn Dumenil. This excellent overview of American women's history presents a wealth of written and visual primary and secondary sources—including letters, maps, photographs, and illustrations—supported by an accessible discussion of the experiences of women in American history.

Kessler-Harris, Alice

Out to Work: A History of Wage-Earning Women in the United States. New York: Oxford University Press, 1982 (2003). 400pp. ISBN 9780195030242.

A classic of labor history and women's history, *Out to Work* tells the fascinating story of women's work in the United States, from colonial times to the present. With exhaustive research and stellar scholarship, historian Kessler-Harris presents a picture of the changing roles of women's work in America, illuminating how social concepts of family, race, and class through the various social milieus informed women's participation in labor. Engagingly written and thought-provoking, this social history shines light on the breadth of women's labor in America, simultaneously celebrating the contributions of women and decrying the American tradition of marginalizing women into low-paying or "feminine" jobs.

Subjects: Labor • Class • History • Women's History • History of Labor • Social History • Seventeenth Century • Eighteenth Century • Nineteenth Century • Twentieth Century • American History • America

Now Try: Turn now to a remarkable anthology edited by Rosalyn Fraad Baxandall, Linda Gordon, and Susan Reverby, *America's Working Women: A Documentary History 1600 to the Present*. Collecting a wealth of primary documents such as letters, journal entries, and poetry by and about working women, the book covers four hundred years of women's labor in the United States. Then, for an examination of American women's labor in modern times, turn to the essays in *The Sex of Class: Women Transforming American Labor*, edited by Dorothy Sue Cobble, in which a variety of scholars consider such topics as class, sexual orientation, and globalism in contemporary America.

Lerner, Gerda

Black Women in White America: A Documentary History. New York: Pantheon Books, 1972 (1992). 630pp. ISBN 9780394475400.

In this magnificent work of social history, the story of African American women in the United States comes to life through a wealth of primary sources. In sections such as "From Service Jobs to the Factory," "The Rape of Black Women as a Weapon of Terror," and "On the Road to Freedom," the book presents documents that speak to the long history of oppression, discrimination, struggle, and triumph that has characterized black women's experiences in America from slave times through the present. Most of the documents come from the pen of black women, though a few—most notably the bills of sale for slaves—come from other perspectives. Although presented as disparate pieces rather than a continuous narrative, *Black Women in White America* can be read straight through, from cover to cover, for a riveting overview of black women's history.

> **Subjects:** Race • African Americans • Gender • Sexual Discrimination • History • Women's History • Social History • Nineteenth Century • Twentieth Century • America

> **Now Try:** Continue learning about the history of black women in America with *The Book of African American Women: 150 Crusaders, Creators, and Uplifters*. With smart, succinct prose, Tonya Bolden profiles the lives of black women who have made a difference in American history, starting in 1619 and continuing through the present day. Some of the women in this collective biography will be recognizable, but many others will have stories and experiences that bring the reader new, unfamiliar chapters in black women's history.

Lerner, Gerda

The Majority Finds Its Past: Placing Women in History. New York: Oxford University Press, 1979 (2005). 217pp. ISBN 9780195025972.

"Women's History challenges the androcentric assumptions of traditional history and assumes that the role of women in historical events—or the absence of women from them—must properly be illuminated and discussed in each and every case," writes Gerda Lerner, one of the most respected and influential scholars in the field of women's history. In this remarkable collection of essays written over the course of Lerner's career, Lerner discusses not only the role of women in American history, but also the act of studying women's history. Thus this thought-provoking book serves both as an overview of women in American history and as a critical contemplation of the goals and purposes of women's history scholars.

> **Subjects:** History • Women's History • Social History • American History • America • Essays

Now Try: Continue exploring American women's history in the excellent book *Born for Liberty: A History of Women in America*. Feminist scholar Sara M. Evans presents a lively, thoroughly researched history of American women in both the private and public spheres. Evans considers the experiences of groups from a variety of backgrounds, races, and classes, making this a comprehensive, inclusive survey of the history of women in America.

Schenone, Laura

A Thousand Years over a Hot Stove: A History of American Women Told Through Food, Recipes, and Remembrances. New York: W. W. Norton, 2003. 412pp. ISBN 9780393016710.

History has never tasted so good. Discover the history of American women, going all the way back to the centuries before European conquests, through the foods they have cooked. Like it or not, women in America as elsewhere have traditionally been the ones to prepare and serve food, and so it is within a framework of food that Laura Schenone shapes her mesmerizing history. With anecdotes, illustrations, and interesting tidbits of food history, Schenone explores the influence of food on society in various times, cultures, and ethnic groups. Interspersed throughout the narrative are recipes that readers may try at home, such as Pine Nut Soup, Blueberry Cream Salad, and Corn Custard.

Subjects: Food • Recipes • Labor • History • History of Labor • Women's History • Social History • American History • America

Now Try: Meet ninety-nine wild women from throughout time and across the globe in *Wild Women in the Kitchen: 101 Rambunctious Recipes & 99 Tasty Tales*, by chefs extraordinaire Nicole Alper and Lynette Rohrer. All sorts of women are included in this collection of mini-biographies and recipes, from Ayn Rand to Catherine de Medici, Marie Antoinette to Golda Meir, Frida Kahlo to Cleopatra. Each profile features a brief description of the woman's life, with emphasis on what made her extraordinary; then, on the following page, there's a recipe that relates in some way to her heritage, time period, or preferred foods.

Ancient and Classical Eras

The "Ancient and Classical Eras" section contains books about women's lives in ancient Greece and Rome, as well as other settings in the ancient world.

Try Anthony Barrett's *Agrippina* for a fascinating character study, or Lyn Webster Wilde's historical investigation *On the Trail of the Women Warriors: The Amazons in Myth and History*. Other geographical locations are covered, too, as in *Silent Images: Women in Pharaonic Egypt*, by Zahi A. Hawass.

Barrett, Anthony

Agrippina: Sex, Power, and Politics in the Early Empire. New Haven, CT: Yale University Press, 1996. 330pp. ISBN 9780300065985.

Agrippina has not been treated kindly by history—but, as classics historian Barrett argues, that's because she was not treated kindly by her contemporaries, who could not gracefully accept the idea of a powerful woman. With a keen understanding of archaeological and historical research, Barrett convincingly debunks the unflattering stories associated with her: Agrippina most likely did not, for instance, murder her husband Claudius, nor did she sleep with her son Nero, nor did she sleep with her brother Caligula. Read this scholarly but engaging biography to discover the woman whose greatest crime was to be politically ambitious in a first-century society that resented female power.

> **Subjects:** Agrippina • Politics • Relationships • History • Women's History • Ancient History • Classical History • First Century • Roman Empire • Europe • Biography
>
> **Now Try:** Meet Agrippina's great-grandmother in another intriguing biography by Barrett, *Livia: First Lady of Imperial Rome*. Like her descendent, Livia was a powerful woman, the wife of the first Roman emperor, Caesar Augusta—and as with Agrippina, her power did not rest well with her enemies. Barrett defends Livia against her accusers and fleshes out her personal and political interests in this thoroughly researched history. And for a change of pace, try Jo Graham's novel *Black Ships*, a retelling of the *Aeneid* from the perspective of a slave woman who survived the fall of Troy.

Bruhns, Karen Olsen, and Karen E. Stothert

Women in Ancient America. Norman: University of Oklahoma Press, 1999. 343pp. ISBN 9780585196602.

"If men are knowable in the archaeological record, women must be knowable as well," write scholars Bruhns and Stothert. It's a simple but powerful premise, one that invites a gendered approach to ancient history. In this meticulously researched study of women in the pre-Columbian Americas, Bruhns and Stothert revisit the androcentric models that have dominated archeology, painting a fascinating picture of the lives of ancient Native American women. By drawing on the scientific archaeological record and by interpreting the art of ancient peoples, the authors illuminate the lifestyles of women, considering such topics as religion, agriculture, and gender roles. The text is scholarly but accessible, bolstered by a wealth of illustrations depicting figurines, bowls, mummies, even floor plans of ancient buildings.

> **Subjects:** Archeology • Art • Native Americans • Gender • History • Women's History • Prehistory • Ancient History • South America
>
> **Now Try:** Focus now on the lives of Mexican women in *Indian Women of Early Mexico*, edited by Susan Schroeder, Stephanie Gail Wood, and Robert Stephen Haskett. The scholarly essays in this collection consider both precolonial and colonial women, shedding light on such topics as housework, marriage, class, and labor among native Mexican peoples.

Hamel, Debra

Trying Neaira: The True Story of a Courtesan's Scandalous Life in Ancient Greece. New Haven, CT: Yale University Press, 2003. 200pp. ISBN 9780300094312.

Neaira thought she had it made: having escaped her life as a sex slave in a brothel, she was in a happy, long-term relationship with Stephanos, the father of her children. Unfortunately, Stephanos had made a bitter enemy, Apollodoros, who sought to destroy him by taking Neaira to court. The charge? Apollodoros claimed that, in contradiction of Athenian law, Stephanos and Neaira were living as husband and wife. In this engrossing social history, Hamel takes us to fourth-century B.C.E. Greece, illuminating the life story of Neaira and fleshing out the social, cultural, and legal customs of classical Athens.

Subjects: Neaira • Courtesans • Sexual Exploitation • Marriage • Relationships • History • Women's History • Social History • Ancient History • Classical History • Fourth Century B.C.E. • Greece • Europe • Biography • Quick Read

Now Try: If Neaira's trial has you hungry to learn more about the legal status of women in the ancient world, turn to Eva Cantarella's book *Pandora's Daughters: The Role and Status of Women in Greek and Roman Antiquity*. With a scholarly approach but written for a general audience, the book draws on both literary and legal documents to consider the legal standing of women in ancient Greece and Rome.

Hawass, Zahi A.

Silent Images: Women in Pharaonic Egypt. New York: Harry N. Abrams, 2000. 207pp. ISBN 9780810944787.

Who isn't familiar with the lovely visage of Nefertiti, the proud and beautiful queen of Egypt? Her face symbolizes our concept of femininity in ancient Egypt—but, as famed Egyptologist Hawass reveals, Nefertiti was the exception, not the rule. In this magnificently illustrated study of ancient Egyptian art and architecture, Hawass looks beyond the celebrated queens and goddesses to consider gender norms among ordinary women. Drawing on paintings, sculptures, temple reliefs, and other relics, Hawass paints a nuanced picture of women's daily lives, liberally sprinkling his historical narrative with photos from his own excavations.

Subjects: Art • Archeology • History • Art History • Women's History • Ancient History • Classical History • Egypt • Africa

Now Try: Continue exploring the lives of ancient Egyptian women in *Mistress of the House, Mistress of Heaven: Women in Ancient Egypt* by Anne K. Capel and Glenn Markoe. This gorgeous book matches insightful, accessible essays with full-color reproductions of Egyptian art—including statues, paintings, jewelry, and figurines—to illuminate the daily lives of Egyptian women, from queens and slaves to priestesses and goddesses. Then try Michelle Moran's novel *Nefertiti*, which brings the powerful queen to life against a backdrop of a fully realized ancient Egypt.

Meyers, Carol L.

Discovering Eve: Ancient Israelite Women in Context. New York: Oxford University Press, 1988. 238pp. ISBN 9780195049343.

If we only consider the Hebrew Bible, there's not very much to go on to help us understand the lives of ancient Israelite women. The Bible's primary characters are men; the few women who do get included tend to be exceptional; and, after all, the sacred texts were written by men, not women. In *Discovering Eve*, religious scholar Meyers aims to set the record straight. She revisits the Bible, applying a skillful linguistic approach to reinterpret the role of women, and she considers archeological evidence to understand the lives of ordinary Israelite women. This is a masterful, convincingly argued piece of scholarship, written in an academic style but accessible for the general reader.

Subjects: Archeology • History • Women's History • Social History • Ancient History • Classical History • Israel • Middle East • Asia

Now Try: In *Discovering Eve*, Meyers explored the daily lives of ancient Israelite women; now focus on their religious lives in Meyers's *Households and Holiness: The Religious Culture of Israelite Women*. Once again, Meyers delivers her insights with clear prose and stellar scholarship, fleshing out the diversity of religious beliefs and practices among Israelite women in antiquity.

Pomeroy, Sarah B.

Goddesses, Whores, Wives, and Slaves: Women in Classical Antiquity. New York: Schocken Books, 1975 (1995). 265pp. ISBN 9780805235623.

Prior to Sarah B. Pomeroy's work, classical scholarship often ignored or trivialized ancient women's lives, and feminist studies within the field were almost unheard of. But the year 1975 saw the publication of *Goddess, Whores, Wives, and Slaves*, a pioneering book that almost single-handedly ushered in a new, feminist approach to the study of ancient civilizations. In its pages Pomeroy paints a compelling portrait of women's daily lives in the Roman Empire, covering such various topics as class, religion, politics, and marriage. Thoroughly researched and accessibly written, this is an enduring social history of ancient women's lives, a classic of Classics.

Subjects: History • Women's History • Social History • Ancient History • Classical History • Greece • Egypt • Roman Empire • Europe • Africa

Now Try: A marvelous companion to *Goddess, Whores, Wives, and Slaves* is *Women's Life in Greece and Rome: A Source Book in Translation*, by Mary R. Lefkowitz and Maureen B. Fant. As with Pomeroy's study, the book shines light on various aspects of women's lives—marriage and adultery, motherhood and sterility, money and property—but in this case, primary documents comprise the bulk of the text; you'll discover the roles of women in society straight from the mouths of women and men alike. And no one with even the faintest interest in ancient European women's history will want to miss *Women in the Classical World: Image and Text*, by Elaine Fantham et al. This stunning study of ancient women's lives, liberally supported with primary documents and reproductions of art, sheds light on a number of facets of daily life in antiquity, including birth control, adultery, clothing, and religious beliefs.

Wilde, Lyn Webster

On the Trail of the Women Warriors: The Amazons in Myth and History. New York: Thomas Dunne Books, 2000. 213pp. ISBN 9780312262136.

Like most of us, author Wilde knew a little bit about the Amazons, mainly from myths and legends. (And from *Xena, Warrior Princess*.) But her mild curiosity turned into an obsession to discover whether they had really existed or not: "This quest has taken me through the dustiest depths of libraries, into the brilliant but cluttered minds of academics, through the realms of feminism both inspirational and ideological, into the world of sorcerers, psychologists, and magicians"—and, for the record, into Ukraine, the site of a Greek colony in the distant past. Utterly compelling in both subject and style, this book is the remarkable account of Wilde's quest to separate fact from fiction in our understanding of the Amazons.

Subjects: Amazons • Warriors • Archeology • History • Women's History • Ancient History • Classical History • Ukraine • Europe

Now Try: Wilde isn't the only person obsessed with the Amazons. Meet Jeannine Davis-Kimball, an archeologist has who unearthed the remains of women warriors in Europe and Asia. In her book *Warrior Women: An Archaeologist's Search for History's Hidden Heroines*, co-authored with Mona Behan, Davis-Kimball recounts her archeological digs. She offers an accessible and fascinating examination of the evidence, offering a thought-provoking discussion about the possibility of the Amazons' existence.

Religious Life in Antiquity

The religious and spiritual lives of women in ancient times provides the focus on titles in this section.

Religion played a huge role in the lives of the ancients, as we see in "Religious Life in Antiquity." Jewish women, Egyptian goddesses, Greek priestesses, and women in the upstart Christian religion all had their roles. Readers wishing to discover more about women's religious history will also want to see the sections on the various religious perspectives in Chapter 2.

Connelly, Joan Breton

Portrait of a Priestess: Women and Ritual in Ancient Greece. Princeton, NJ: Princeton University Press, 2007. 415pp. ISBN 9780691127460.

Priestesses in ancient Greece, it turns out, had it pretty good: while the other women were running households, serving as slaves, and generally being denied the legal rights that men enjoyed, priestesses were being treated with a high degree of respect. In this enjoyable, accessible social history, art historian and archeologist Connelly considers the day-to-day concerns and practices of priestesses—their clothes, their rituals, their training—and places their roles within the context of society at large. Based on such sources as archeological evidence, art, and literature, this is a fascinating glimpse into religious history, supported with more than one hundred illustrations.

> **Subjects:** Priestesses • Paganism • Religion • History • History of Religion • Women's History • Social History • Ancient History • Classical History • Greece • Europe

> **Now Try:** Learn more about the role of religion in the lives of ancient Greek women in two other social histories. In *Citizen Bacchae: Women's Ritual Practice in Ancient Greece*, Barbara E. Goff looks at how religious ritual influenced the lives of women from a variety of backgrounds, not just priestesses. And in *Girls and Women in Classical Greek Religion*, Matthew Dillon examines the meanings and purposes of the various rites that women and girls performed.

Frymer-Kensky, Tikva Simone

Reading the Women of the Bible. New York: Schocken Books, 2002. 449pp. ISBN 9780805241211.

If you thought you knew the women of the Bible, you'll need to think again. In this engrossing feminist interpretation of the Hebrew Bible, scholar Frymer-Kensky considers women such as Sarah, Ruth, and Jezebel, along with obscure and anonymous figures, grouping them loosely into four main categories: victors, victims, virgins, and women with voice. What she finds is that though women's roles were generally subordinate to men's, they were not considered to be inferior. Her insightful, empowering reading of women in the ancient texts is fresh and bold, a welcome antidote to biblical readings that marginalize and trivialize women's roles.

> **Subjects:** Judaism • Christianity • Religion • History of Religion • Women's History • Ancient History • Feminism • Middle East • Asia

> **Now Try:** For another feminist approach to the women of the Bible, turn to *Helpmates, Harlots, and Heroes: Women's Stories in the Hebrew Bible* by Alice Ogden Bellis. Working within a feminist and Womanist framework, Bellis considers women such as Ruth, Esther, and Eve, showing them to be powerful, strong figures who made their mark in a patriarchal world.

King, Karen L.

The Gospel of Mary of Magdala: Jesus and the First Woman Apostle. Santa Rosa, CA: Polebridge Press, 2003. 230pp. ISBN 9780944344583.

"Few people today are acquainted with the Gospel of Mary," acknowledges ecclesiastical historian King. Small wonder: it had disappeared for more than fifteen centuries, and when it was rediscovered, only an estimated half of the original text remained—and even that was in a Coptic translation. Yet the part of this second-century document the has survived is fascinating: it shows a Mary of Magdala who was an apostle on par with the others—an apostle who, in fact, received a direct vision from Jesus, to the consternation of a jealous Peter. King's seriously scholarly analysis is necessarily dense and at times difficult to read, but it is worth the effort to discover the voice of Mary Magdalene (no, she *wasn't* a prostitute) and her spiritual teachings about prophecy and the soul.

> **Subjects:** Magdalene, Mary • Apostles • Christianity • Religion • Spirituality • History • History of Religion • Women's History • Ancient History • Second Century • Middle East • Asia

> **Now Try:** If Mary of Magdala was such an important figure, the author of her very own gospel, then why was she never recognized as an apostle? In *Mary Magdalene, the First Apostle: The Struggle for Authority*, Ann Graham Brock investigates that question, exploring the politics and history of the early Christian church and exposing the early sexual discrimination that prevented Mary from being acknowledged as an apostle. Then try *Mary, Called Magdalene*, Margaret George's captivating novelization of Mary's life.

Kraemer, Ross Shepard

Her Share of the Blessings: Women's Religions among Pagans, Jews, and Christians in the Greco-Roman World. New York: Oxford University Press, 1992. 275pp. ISBN 9780195066869.

Until recently, writes religious scholar Kraemer, "bastions of male scholars rarely even thought about the study of women. Behind their disinterest, which was largely shared by the small number of women scholars, lay the insidious, significant, and unarticulated assumption that human religion and human history were identical with men's religion and men's history." In this magnificent study of women's religious practices in antiquity, Kraemer skillfully dispatches that assumption. With her clear prose and insightful analysis, Kraemer examines the roles, rituals, and beliefs of ancient women pagans, Jews, and Christians, articulating the social contexts and gender norms that both nurtured and restricted their religious activities. This is a thoroughly researched, engagingly written piece of history, suitable for scholars and general readers alike.

Subjects: Religion • Paganism • Judaism • Christianity • History • History of Religion • Women's History • Social History • Ancient History • Classical History • Greece • Roman Empire

Now Try: In *Her Share of the Blessings*, Kraemer offers a compelling interpretation of ancient women's religious lives; in *Women's Religions in the Greco-Roman World: A Sourcebook*, Kraemer presents us with primary documents that allow us to understand women's religious lives from the perspectives of the ancients themselves. Arranged into sections such as "Observances, Rituals, and Festivals" and "Religious Office," the book collects contemporary writings about women's religious beliefs and practices, penned by women and men alike.

Lesko, Barbara S.

The Great Goddesses of Egypt. Norman: University of Oklahoma Press, 1999. 319pp. ISBN 9780585116808.

"Too many of the seriously researched works on Egyptian goddesses remain beyond the reach of most readers, in scholarly series or European journals or monographs of small circulation, and are readily available to only the most determined researcher," observes historian Lesko. Fortunately, she has written *The Great Goddesses of Egypt*, a skillful synthesis of the existing scholarship augmented by her own insightful observations. Lesko examines the qualities, powers, and myths associated with Isis, Hathor, and five other goddesses of ancient Egypt, while illuminating the lives and religious beliefs of the people who worshipped them.

Subjects: Goddesses • Religion • History • History of Religion • Women's History • Social History • Ancient History • Classical History • Egypt • Africa

Now Try: Readers interested in the religious lives of the ancient Egyptians will find a treasure trove of information in *The Complete Gods and Goddesses of Ancient Egypt*, by Richard H. Wilkinson. This exhaustive study covers all of the deities of Egypt in clear, comprehensible prose; those who enjoyed Lesko's book will appreciate the detailed descriptions of the gods and goddesses, as well as the discussion of worshippers' rituals and beliefs.

Dark and Middle Ages

Here are books about women's lives in Europe during the times referred to as medieval—that is, approximately between 500 and 1500 C.E.

Historical sources about women from the medieval era are scant, but the books in the "Dark and Middle Ages" section dig deep to tell the stories of women's lives. For a broad geographical overview, read the words of medieval women collected in

Marcelle Thiébaux's anthology *The Writings of Medieval Women*, or focus on a particular region, as with *Women in Old Norse Society*, by Jenny Jochens.

Hambly, Gavin, ed.

Women in the Medieval Islamic World: Power, Patronage, and Piety. New York: St. Martin's Press, 1998. 566pp. ISBN 9780312210571.

Piecing together the story of Muslim women in recent times can be a challenge for a historian; piecing together the story of Muslim women in medieval times is extraordinarily difficult: records are scarce, and contemporary scholars usually placed little value on women's experiences. But editor Hambly has assembled twenty essays by scholars who, with only meager sources to work with, have nonetheless illuminated the lives of women in the Islamic world in the Middle Ages. Some of the women were famous in their times; some were not; some were fictional heroines of literature. The scholarly writing of the collection is dense at times, but it is well worth the read to discover a history that has largely been forgotten.

> **Subjects:** Islam • Religion • History • Women's History • Social History • Medieval History • Middle East • Asia • Essays • Collection • Anthology

> **Now Try:** Quite contrary to the official record and popular perception, Fatima Mernissi argues that women have actually led Muslim states, going all the way back to the year 622. In her fascinating investigation, *The Forgotten Queens of Islam*, she uncovers fifteen Muslim women, either monarchs or consorts, who ruled in the medieval world. Then, to continue studying Muslim women's history beyond the Middle Ages, try *Women in Middle Eastern History: Shifting Boundaries in Sex and Gender.* Edited by Nikki R. Keddie and Beth Baron, this collection of scholarly essays focuses on women's history and gender and their intersections with such themes as religion, law, patriarchy, and marriage.

Herrin, Judith

Women in Purple: Rulers of Medieval Byzantium. Princeton, NJ: Princeton University Press, 2001. 304pp. ISBN 9780691095004.

When Emperor Leo IV died in the year 780, his wife Irene became the first empress of the Byzantine Empire. (She may well have poisoned dear old Leo, but that's a story for another time.) Under her leadership, and quite contrary to precedent, she defended the legitimacy of icons in Christian worship, which were widely perceived to be sinful symbols of idolatry. This defense of art would make a fascinating story unto itself—but wait! There's more! Irene's son Constantine VI died without male heirs, meaning that Irene's granddaughters Euphrosyne and Theodora became empresses in their own turn—and, like their grandmother, they, too, ruled with authority and power, sanctioning the role of the controversial icon in the church. Read this fascinating, compelling collective biography to learn about three remarkable women and the religious and social climate of Byzantium in the Dark Ages.

> **Subjects:** Irene • Euphrosyne • Theodora • Rulers • Politics • Art • Religion • Christianity • History • History of Religion • Women's History • Dark Ages • Medieval History • Eighth Century • Ninth Century • Byzantium • Europe • Biography • Collection

Now Try: Now learn more about the lives of women in the Byzantine Empire in Carolyn L. Connor's *Women of Byzantium*. You'll meet the empresses again, of course, but you'll also discover the lives of ordinary women. Fans of *Women in Purple* will appreciate the book's engaging prose style and the emphasis on religion and art. Then immerse yourself in eleventh-century Byzantium with Julia Kristeva's gorgeous novel *Murder in Byzantium*, a literary mystery that dances between the present and the medieval past.

Jochens, Jenny

Women in Old Norse Society. Ithaca, NY: Cornell University Press, 1995. 266pp. ISBN 9780801431654.

It's not easy to find English-language histories of Norse women, let alone histories of *medieval* Norse women; fortunately, scholar Jenny Jochens has provided us with the engrossing, magnificently researched *Women in Old Norse Society*. Drawing on Old Norse literature and legal documents, she paints a picture of women's lives in medieval Iceland and Norway, both during pagan times and after the advent of Christianity. She addresses an impressive number of topics, from marriage and childbirth to pastimes and labor, resulting in a fascinating account of women's experiences in the Old Norse world.

Subjects: History • Women's History • Social History • Religion • History of Religion • Paganism • Christianity • Dark Ages • Medieval History • Iceland • Norway • Europe

Now Try: "Vikings are irredeemably male in the popular imagination," writes Judith Jesch, but after reading her excellent book *Women in the Viking Age*, you'll be pleasantly educated about the other half of the population. With its focus on medieval Scandinavian woman, it is an excellent companion to *Women in Old Norse Society*; this is a scholarly but thoroughly accessible account that draws on literature, mythology, and historical evidence to make for an engaging read. See also the biography *The Far Traveler: Voyages of a Viking Woman*, in which Nancy Marie Brown uncovers the story of Gudrid, a medieval woman who made a habit of traversing the North Atlantic.

Shahar, Shulamith

The Fourth Estate: A History of Women in the Middle Ages. London: Methuen, 1983 (2003). 351pp. ISBN 9780416354102.

"There has never been a book about the 'History of men in the Middle Ages,' nor is it likely that there will ever be one," writes historian Shahar. By default, studies of medieval history are studies of medieval *men's* history, unless the historian takes special care to root out the scant resources relating to women. Fortunately, Shahar has done just that with *The Fourth Estate*, perhaps the most important single volume ever written about medieval European women. Based on exhaustive research, this engaging, thought-provoking history considers women in a variety of roles—as townspeople, as nuns, as wives, as peasants—to create a fascinating portrait of medieval women's lives in Europe.

Subjects: History • Women's History • Social History • Medieval History • Europe

Now Try: Shahar vividly describes women's lives in medieval Europe; now supplement this historical overview with a portrait of one woman's life in Ann Baer's novel *Down the Common*. Grounded in solid historical research, this narrative features a medieval English peasant named Marion. Fans of *The Fourth Estate* will recognize Marion's experiences as she copes with issues such as child raising, pregnancy, social standing, and death and illness.

Thiébaux, Marcelle, ed.

The Writings of Medieval Women: An Anthology. New York: Garland, 1987 (1994). 536pp. ISBN 9780815313922.

> "The writings of medieval women contribute generously to our understanding of women's lives and history, to their centuries, and to all of medieval literature," writes scholar Thiébaux in her introduction. This anthology, then, presents not just a sampling of women's writing, but also an extraordinary glimpse into the thoughts, customs, conventions, and social concerns of women in the Middle Ages. Some of the writers, such as Marie de France and Hildegard of Bingen, may be familiar to readers, while others, such as Amalasuintha of Italy and Baudonivia of Poitiers, have largely been forgotten by history. Thiébaux skillfully introduces each document to flesh out the context of each writer's time and culture, making this a valuable resource for anyone interested in the lives of medieval European women.

> > **Subjects:** History • Women's History • Dark Ages • Medieval History • Global Perspectives • Anthology • Collection

> > **Now Try:** Continue indulging in the writings of medieval European women in Carolyne Larrington's *Women and Writing in Medieval Europe: A Sourcebook.* Featuring primary documents and Larrington's clear analysis, the book is arranged thematically into chapters such as "Love, Sex, and Friendship" and "Motherhood and Work." Readers may also enjoy *Women's Lives in Medieval Europe: A Sourcebook*, in which Emilie Amt presents women's writings and other primary sources to illuminate medieval women's lives in relation to such areas as law, religion, and social class.

Renaissance and Enlightenment

> Books in the "Renaissance and Enlightenment" section discuss the turbulent social upheavals that swept through Europe in the sixteenth, seventeenth, and eighteenth centuries.

For a general overview of how these changes affected women, try Margaret L. King's *Women of the Renaissance*, or focus on a particular theme, as with Caroline Weber's fascinating *Queen of Fashion: What Marie Antoinette Wore to the Revolution*.

Barstow, Anne Llewellyn

Witchcraze: A New History of the European Witch Hunts. San Francisco: Pandora, 1994. 255pp. ISBN 9780062500496.

> The witch hunts of sixteenth- and seventeenth-century Europe must be interpreted as a widespread epidemic of violence against women, argues historian Barstow in this disturbing but fascinating history: "An analysis of violence ... exposes the sexual terror and brutality at the heart of the witch hunts, a topic too little discussed." In framing her study against the

backdrop of a societal misogyny, she shows how the witch hunts were motivated by the hatred of women's bodies, the fear of their sexualities, and the resentment of their intellects. Insightful and thought-provoking, this feminist analysis of the violence done against women in the name of religion shows how the persecution of witches contributed to the oppression of women in society at large.

Subjects: Witches • Violence • Gender • Sexual Discrimination • Religion • Christianity • History • Women's History • History of Religion • Sixteenth Century • Seventeenth Century • Europe

Now Try: Readers wishing to learn more about the witch craze in Europe would do well to turn to *The Witch-Hunt in Early Modern Europe* by Brian P. Levack. Though without the overarching feminist themes of *Witchcraze*, it nonetheless scrutinizes the politics, cultural attitudes, and sexual mores that led to the victimization of (primarily) women as witches. Read this for an excellent survey of the witch hunts and for an in-depth look at the historical beliefs about witches and witchcraft.

King, Margaret L.

Women of the Renaissance. Women in Culture and Society series. Chicago: University of Chicago Press, 1991. 333pp. ISBN 9780226436173.

There's only been one edition of this 1991 book, but don't let that keep you from discovering King's text; it is perhaps the single-best general history of Western women during the Renaissance. Drawing on a variety of meticulously researched sources, King considers the experiences of European women in three sections, "Women in Families," "Women in the Church," and "Women in High Society." She explores their daily lives, as well as their place within the larger context of Renaissance history. This is an engaging study, perfect for scholars but quite suitable for casual readers.

Subjects: History • Women's History • Social History • Medieval History • Fourteenth Century • Fifteenth Century • Sixteenth Century • Seventeenth Century • Europe

Now Try: Supplement King's history of Renaissance women with two collective biographies. *Extraordinary Women of the Medieval and Renaissance World: A Biographical Dictionary* by Carole Levin et. al. illuminates the lives of remarkable women across the globe; readers will enjoy the captivating, informative introduction to seventy women from the Middle Ages and the Renaissance whose names have largely been forgotten. Then look to the magnificent Antonia Fraser. She is best known for her royal biographies, but she turns her talented hand to women from all walks of life in her ironically titled book *The Weaker Vessel*. Discover a host of seventeenth-century women—courtesans and ladies of the court, actresses and businesswomen, witches and nuns—in this captivating social history.

Moore, Lucy

Liberty: The Lives and Times of Six Women in Revolutionary France. New York: HarperCollins, 2007. 464pp. ISBN 9780060825263.

Liberty! Equality! ... Sorority? Oh yes, indeed: the French Revolution of the eighteenth century was not orchestrated and implemented by men, not entirely anyway. For instance, there was Germaine de Staël, who helped write the 1791 constitution, and there was the scantily clad Thérésia de Fontenay, who helped bring down Robespierre. In this splendidly written history, you'll meet six women who took active roles in the French Revolution, despite fierce resistance from their male counterparts (who were, apparently, interested in liberty and equality for *men*). This is a captivating collective biography that restores six remarkable women to history while painting a crisp narrative of the French Revolution.

Subjects: Activism • War • Violence • History • Women's History • Social History • Eighteenth Century • France • Europe • Biography • Collection

Now Try: Now step back in time about a century, give or take, to read *Love and Louis XIV: The Women in the Life of the Sun King*. The era and climate is different, but fans of *Liberty* will enjoy discovering the lives of an earlier generation of politically influential French women, delivered to us from the pen of none other than the uber-talented, uber-popular historian Antonia Fraser.

Vickery, Amanda

The Gentleman's Daughter: Women's Lives in Georgian England. New Haven, CT: Yale University Press, 1998. 436pp. ISBN 9780300075311.

In *The Gentleman's Daughter*, historian Vickery explores neither the nobility nor the poor, but the middle class, those women who "described themselves as 'polite,' 'civil,' 'genteel,' 'well-bred,' and 'polished.'" Drawing on the letters, diaries, and account books written by these genteel ladies, Vickery presents a richly detailed portrait of their lives, considering such diverse topics as pregnancy, vulgarity, courtship, and home economics. Written for an academic audience but fully accessible for general readers, this is an informative, thought-provoking look at women's daily lives in eighteenth-century England.

Subjects: History • Women's History • Social History • Eighteenth Century • England • Europe

Now Try: Concentrate now on an aspect of Georgian women's lives that you may well have never even considered: travel. In Brian Dolan's *Ladies of the Grand Tour: British Women in Pursuit of Enlightenment and Adventure in Eighteenth-Century Europe*, you'll meet eighteenth-century Englishwomen who traveled to the continent for any number of reasons—to seek adventure, to discover new ways of thinking, to escape from an unpleasant home, to carry on sordid affairs away from the prying eyes of neighbors and family. Those who enjoyed *The Gentleman's Daughter* will appreciate Dolan's reliance on women's letters and diaries, as well as his entertaining writing style.

Weber, Caroline

Queen of Fashion: What Marie Antoinette Wore to the Revolution. New York: Henry Holt, 2006. 412pp. ISBN 9780805079494.

"In charting Marie Antoinette's fateful course from the gilded halls of Versailles to the blood-splashed steps of the guillotine, historians rarely emphasize the tremendous importance that her public attached to what she was wearing at each step along the way," writes scholar Weber, but "a thorough reexamination of Marie Antoinette's biography reveals the startling consistency and force with which her costumes triggered severe sociopolitical disorder." This, then, is the history of eighteenth-century France as you've never read it before, a history seen through the lens of Marie Antoinette's provocative—literally—fashion statements. But it is also a biography of the queen herself, a fascinating new examination of her personality and politics interpreted through her deliberate clothing choices.

Subjects: Marie Antoinette • Fashion • Appearance • Royalty • History • Social History • Women's History • Eighteenth Century • France • Europe • Biography

Now Try: Hungering for more fashion? Turn to Valerie Steele's magnificent book *Paris Fashion: A Cultural History*. Explore the history of France from the fourteenth century through the present day in this engrossing study of fashion trends. Fans of *Queens of Fashion* will enjoy Steele's engaging style and her insightful examination of the influence of fashion on art, politics, and French society.

Colonial and Revolutionary America

Women's lives in the early days of European settlement of the Americas provides the focus of these titles.

Witches and wars, conquerors and colonizers—these were tumultuous times in the New World and the new United States, as we see in the books of "Colonial and Revolutionary America." These books excel in teasing out the causes and effects of the sweeping social changes that forever altered the lives of the native and immigrant women of North America.

Berkin, Carol

Revolutionary Mothers: Women in the Struggle for America's Independence. New York: Knopf, 2005. 194pp. ISBN 9781400041633.

Besides a few big names—Abigail Adams, Betsy Ross, Martha Washington—it's all too easy to forget about women in the American Revolution. Fortunately, American history professor Berkin has written the superb *Revolutionary Mothers*, which considers not only specific figures who played key parts but also the broader roles of women as a group: wives, for instance, maintained their homes in the absence of men; camp followers provided the armies with food, clean laundry, and sexual distraction; some women even took up arms and participated in combat. Meticulously researched and engagingly written, the book provides insight into the wartime activities of a variety of women—rich and poor, Loyalist and Revolutionary, black, white, and Native American—who shaped the tenor of the American Revolution as surely as the men did.

Subjects: History • Women's History • American History • Social History • Eighteenth Century • America • Quick Read

Now Try: Readers hungry for more information about the lives of ordinary women during the American Revolution will do well to turn to *Liberty's Daughters: The Revolutionary Experience of American Women, 1750–1800*. In the first part of the book, historian Mary Beth Norton sets the stage by exploring the lifestyles of American women prior to the Revolution; in the second part, she deftly examines the cultural changes that swept through the country during and after the war. Fans of *Revolutionary Mothers* will appreciate Norton's crisp writing and attention to themes such as political activity, class, and race. Then try Suzanne Adair's book *The Blacksmith's Daughter*, a historical novel featuring a cast of women who lived during the Revolutionary War.

Hill, Frances

A Delusion of Satan: The Full Story of the Salem Witch Trials. New York: Doubleday, 1995 (2002). 269pp. ISBN 9780385472555.

Frances Hill wastes no time plunging into her chilling narrative. Witness the first two sentences of the first chapter: "Almost thirty died. Well over a hundred languished for months in cramped, dark, stinking prisons, hungry and thirsty, never moving from the walls they were chained to, unsure if they would ever go free." One almost wishes that Hill were not an accomplished novelist and journalist: her storytelling is all too believable, her setting far too vivid. Brace yourself for a haunting journey back to the 1600s, when the Puritan town of Salem, Massachusetts, was seized by witch-hunting hysteria. This is both a thought-provoking history of the Salem witch trials and a disturbing study of human psychology, backed by Hill's superb scholarship and keen observations.

> **Subjects:** Witches • Violence • Psychology • History • Women's History • American History • Seventeenth Century • America

> **Now Try:** Those wishing to further understand the terror of the witch trials can once again depend on Frances Hill. In *The Salem Witch Trials Reader*, she presents a wealth of court records and testimonies from the trials, allowing readers to examine the historical primary sources for themselves. And, as in *A Delusion of Satan*, Hill again offers her own insightful interpretation, giving context to the documents from the witch trials. Readers will also want to turn to Arthur Miller's classic play *The Crucible*, a harrowing interpretation of the madness in Salem.

Norton, Mary Beth

Founding Mothers & Fathers: Gendered Power and the Forming of American Society. New York: Knopf, 1996. 496pp. ISBN 9780679429654.

Go back to a time when men were men and women were women, except when they weren't. Gender roles among the American colonists may have been rigid, but there were plenty of people willing to break the rules, as Norton shows in this fascinating social history. You may already know about Anne Hutchinson, excommunicated in part for daring to lead a women's Bible study group in her home, but did you know about Thomas Hall, who could sew as well as a woman and dressed the part? (Just call him Thomasine, like his neighbors did.) Based on court cases and other contemporary documents, this is a scholarly but thoroughly accessible account of gender norms in white American society in the seventeenth century.

> **Subjects:** Gender • History • Women's History • American History • Social History • Seventeenth Century • America

> **Now Try:** Continue learning about women in colonial times by turning to Carol Berkin's excellent *First Generations: Women in Colonial America*. Based on a wealth of historical documents such as legal records and diaries, Berkin examines the lives and gender roles of women—black, white, and Native American—in sixteenth- and seventeenth-century America. This is an engrossing portrait of daily life that covers a wealth of topics, from agriculture and household management to marriage and motherhood.

Perdue, Theda

Cherokee Women: Gender and Culture Change, 1700–1835. <u>Indians of the Southeast series</u>. Lincoln: University of Nebraska Press, 1998. 252pp. ISBN 9780803237162.

"Native women emerge from the historical shadows only if we approach their study on two levels," writes historian Perdue. "We must pay attention to how women and men related to each other within their own societies, and we must look at ways in which those relations became part of the larger debate over Indians and Indian policy." It is with this framework that Perdue constructs her remarkable social history of Cherokee women. With writing that is scholarly yet accessible to the lay reader, she argues persuasively for a new interpretation of history, one that sees Cherokee women as influential figures in their nation's history, equally as important as native men in their contributions to their society. Deftly researched and thought-provoking, the book examines the role of gender in Cherokee society and sheds light on the power that women wielded in their everyday lives.

Subjects: Native Americans • Gender • Race • History • Social History • Women's History • American History • Eighteenth Century • Nineteenth Century • America

Now Try: Learn more about the history of Cherokee women in *Weaving New Worlds: Southeastern Cherokee Women and Their Basketry*, by Sarah H. Hill. This is a book about basketry, yes, but also about the much bigger picture of the lives and responsibilities of Cherokee women over three centuries; the magnificent research, combined with Hill's insightful analysis of historical gender roles within Cherokee culture, will appeal to fans of *Cherokee Women*.

Roberts, Cokie

Founding Mothers: The Women Who Raised Our Nation. New York: William Morrow, 2004. 359pp. ISBN 9780060090258.

Every student raised in America knows about the Founding Fathers: they fought off the British, they signed the Declaration of Independence, they wrote the Constitution. But what of the Founding Mothers? Veteran news journalist Cokie Roberts sets about answering that question in her eminently readable social history of the wives, mothers, and daughters of the Founding Fathers. The recognizable names—Abigail Adams, Martha Washington—are included, of course, but so too are lesser-known women such as Eliza Pinckney and Mercy Otis Warren. Drawing on such sources as diaries, letters, and even recipes, this lively history allows us to see the American Revolution through the eyes of the women, permitting us to worry about pregnancy and cooking and maintaining a house along with the battles and campaigns for which the war is famous.

Subjects: History • Women's History • American History • Social History • Eighteenth Century • America

Now Try: If you enjoyed the many excerpts of women's writing that Roberts included in *Founding Mothers*, just wait till you indulge in the wonderful collection of documents in *Women's Voices, Women's Lives: Documents in Early American History*, edited by Carol Berkin and Leslie Horowitz. There's a little of everything here—diaries, newspapers, court proceedings, fiction, and more—all of it chosen to illuminate the experiences of American women in the seventeenth and eighteenth centuries. Whereas *Founding Mothers* focused primarily on well-to-do white women, this collection also features writing by and about women from a variety of races and social classes.

Socolow, Susan Migden

The Women of Colonial Latin America. <u>New Approaches to the Americas series</u>. Cambridge, UK: Cambridge University Press, 2000. 237pp. ISBN 9780521470520.

In the Spanish and Portuguese settlements of colonial America, explains author Socolow, it was sex—more than race, more than social class—that determined a person's identity and social standing, and women suffered for it: "By law and tradition, men held the lion's share of power in government, religion, and society.... A man, particularly a father, was supreme within his family." *The Women of Colonial Latin America* seeks to understand the lives that these subjugated women lived, though Socolow takes care not to present them as victims. Readers will enjoy Socolow's insightful discussion of gender, race, and politics, and their influence on women in the New World during the colonial years.

Subjects: History • Women's History • Latinas • American History • Social History • Fifteenth Century • Sixteenth Century • Seventeenth Century • Eighteenth Century • Nineteenth Century • Latin America • Caribbean • America

Now Try: Experience the tumultuous climate of the Latin American New World through the eyes of Malinche, the woman who was slave, lover, and interpreter for conquistador Hernán Cortés. In Laura Esquivel's sultry, beautifully written novel *Malinche*, we travel to the troubled setting of Mexico in the sixteenth century, when the invasion of the Spanish introduced a lifestyle that clashed, violently, with the native culture. Richly detailed and firmly grounded in accurate history, Esquivel's treatment of Malinche's compelling life story will seduce readers who enjoy studying the history of colonial Latin American women.

Nineteenth Century

> Books in the "Nineteenth Century" section speak to the irrevocable changes that occurred at all levels of society, all across the globe, in the 1800s.

Serfdom was abolished in Russia in 1861, but Barbara Alpern Engel shows us that life did not get easier for women in *Between the Fields and the City*. The American experiment in democracy was well under way, yet the blight of slavery continued, as we see in Dorothy Sterling's *We Are Your Sisters*. Read these books for a sense of the political, social, and economic upheavals that affected women in the nineteenth century.

Engel, Barbara Alpern

Between the Fields and the City: Women, Work, and Family in Russia, 1861–1914. Cambridge, UK: Cambridge University Press, 1994. 254pp. ISBN 9780521442367.

After the abolition of serfdom in Russia in 1861, peasant women found themselves faced with an entirely new option: they could leave the agricultural lifestyles they had always known to take their chances in the cities. Leaving their country homes was liberating for many; they abandoned deeply patriarchal traditions, limited opportunities, and restrictive gender norms; some even abandoned husbands. But life in the city was sometimes just as bad: wages were meager, workdays were long, sexual harassment and discrimination were rampant. Drawing on a wealth of primary documents and archival resources, Engel, one of the foremost scholars of Russian history, presents an eye-opening account of the new Russian woman of the late nineteenth and early twentieth centuries, bolstering her study with plentiful images, maps, and tables; even readers with no background in Russian history will find this an accessible narrative.

Subjects: Labor • Relationships • Gender • Class • History • Women's History • Nineteenth Century • Twentieth Century • Russia • Europe

Now Try: In *Between the Fields and the City*, Engel considered the peasants who migrated to the cities; now she turns to women radicals, activists, and feminists in *Mothers and Daughters: Women of the Intelligentsia in Nineteenth Century Russia*. Once again, Engel applies her insightful historical analysis and crisp writing style to her subject, illuminating the lives of nineteenth-century Russian women who rebelled against traditional patriarchy to carve out their niche in society. Then read about a Russian woman with a most unusual career choice in *Angel of Vengeance: The "Girl Assassin," the Governor of St. Petersburg, and Russia's Revolutionary World*. With engrossing details and excellent research, Ana Siljak tells the story of Vera Zasulich, who in 1878 assassinated a governor—and lived to tell about it.

Hickman, Katie

Courtesans: Money, Sex, and Fame in the Nineteenth Century. New York: Morrow, 2003. 363pp. ISBN 9780066209555.

Back in the day, writes Katie Hickman, English courtesans were "important people…. These were highly cultured women; rich, famous and, most remarkably, independent females in an era in which this was almost an impossibility." These were no streetwalkers, but influential women who used their charms—their intelligence, their personalities, their good company, their sexual abilities—to derive social and financial power from the elite. Meet five of these English courtesans in Hickman's deliciously entertaining narrative, a detailed portrait of high society that blends gossipy tidbits with serious scholarship; engrossing and witty, this collective biography offers an intriguing glimpse into a slice of nineteenth-century social history.

Subjects: Courtesans • Relationships • Business • Labor • History • Women's History • Social History • Nineteenth Century • England • Europe • Biography • Collection

Now Try: Hop across the channel to see how the English courtesans' sisters in France were living in *Grandes Horizontales: The Lives and Legends of Four Nineteenth-Century Courtesans*. In this intriguing collective biography, Virginia Rounding explores the stories of four Parisian courtesans, deftly exploring the sexual and financial politics of their lives. Readers will also enjoy *Memoirs of a Courtesan in Nineteenth-Century Paris*, by Céleste Vénard de Chabrillan, comtesse. First published in 1854, the same details that scandalized mid-nineteenth-century readers will enchant modern readers as they gain a rare glimpse into the life and business dealings of a courtesan from a bygone era.

Plante, Ellen M.

Women at Home in Victorian America: A Social History. New York: Facts on File, 1997. 242pp. ISBN 9780816033928.

By the time a middle-class girl of the nineteenth century reached the ripe old age of sixteen, writes journalist Plante, she would be seriously preparing for marriage, at which point her main duty was to provide "a cheerful, loving and comfortable home for her husband and the children she would soon have—an oasis of peace and morality in a bustling, noisy and rapidly industrializing society." Discover how American women made their homes "cheerful, loving and comfortable" in this engrossing social history, which draws on a wealth of primary sources, including women's letters and diaries, *Godey's Lady's Book,* and the popular writings of the Beecher sisters. In her lucid, thoroughly readable style, Plante covers everything domestic, from knitting and home decoration to courtship and old age.

> **Subjects:** History • Women's History • Social History • American History • Nineteenth Century • America

> **Now Try:** Hop across the Atlantic to see how America's sisters in London lived their lives in *Victorian London's Middle-Class Housewife: What She Did All Day.* With her clear, enjoyable writing style, historian Yaffa Draznin paints a detailed portrait of nineteenth-century women's daily lives in the city, examining such topics as money management, fashion choices, religious and charitable activities, and housekeeping.

Stephens, Autumn

Wild Women: Crusaders, Curmudgeons, and Completely Corsetless Ladies in the Otherwise Virtuous Victorian Era. Berkeley, CA: Conari Press, 1992. 249pp. ISBN 9780943233369.

While most of the women in nineteenth-century America were busy being proper and ladylike, a few adventurous rebels decided to buck social norms for their own purposes. You'll be familiar with some of them, of course, such as Annie Oakley and Emily Dickinson, but you may be surprised to discover headstrong ladies such as bandit cowgirl Pearl Hart and Nevada prostitute Julia Bulette. With chapters including "Flamboyant Flirts and Lascivious Libertines," "Hatchet Queens and Pistol Packers," and "Scandalous Socialites and Hellraising Heiresses," this wonderfully entertaining collective biography celebrates the spirit of independent, powerful American women in the nineteenth century.

> **Subjects:** History • Women's History • American History • Social History • Nineteenth Century • America • Biography • Collection • Young Adult

> **Now Try:** Though a bit more scholarly in tone than *Wild Women,* Catherine Clinton's book *The Other Civil War: American Women in the Nineteenth Century* is a thoroughly readable companion piece that gives historical context to the lives of the women discussed in Stephens's book. Clinton draws a fascinating picture of the social and political climate of the nineteenth century, exploring the struggles of women to overcome sexual repression and fleshing out the lives of the individuals who fought to improve women's lives.

Sterling, Dorothy, ed.

We Are Your Sisters: Black Women in the Nineteenth Century. New York: W. W. Norton, 1984 (1997). 535pp. ISBN 9780393017281.

"To be a black woman in nineteenth-century America was to live in the double jeopardy of belonging to the 'inferior' sex of an 'inferior' race," writes editor Sterling. "Yet two million slave and two hundred thousand free women of that time possessed a tenacity of spirit, a gift of endurance, a steadfastness of aspiration that helped a whole population to survive." In this wonderful collection of primary documents, you'll discover these women in their own words. Drawing from diaries, letters, newspaper accounts, autobiographies, and transcripts of historical interviews, Sterling brings together the voices of women from all walks of life, from the poorest slaves to educated freedwomen. Read their moving testimonies to explore a variety of topics—including labor, marriage, rape, and abolition—through the eyes of nineteenth-century African American women.

Subjects: African Americans • Race • History • Women's History • Social History • American History • Nineteenth Century • America

Now Try: To hear more voices of black women in America's history, turn to *Written by Herself: Literary Production by African American Women, 1746–1892*, in which editor Frances Smith Foster gives literary and historical context to the writings of slaves, activists, and other African American women writers.

The American Old West

Lives of women in the American West during the latter half of the nineteenth century are explored in the books in this section.

Prostitutes and pioneers, cowgirls and mail-order brides—these are the colorful characters we meet in "The American Old West." Emphasizing both character and setting, these books vividly depict the hardships and adventures of the women who sought their fortunes in the expanding American frontier.

Ellis, Anne

The Life of an Ordinary Woman. Boston: Houghton Mifflin, 1929 (1999). 300pp. ISBN 9780395957837.

First published in 1929, the memoir of Anne Ellis is deceptively titled. It is true that she was ordinary according to some measures: she was a poor pioneer woman in the hardscrabble frontier in the late nineteenth century, a woman who worked hard in an unforgiving climate where death, sickness, and exhaustion were frequent companions. By another reckoning, however, Ellis was far from ordinary: she faced the hard knocks of life with determination, sensibility, and a healthy dose of wry humor, managing to survive the harsh Colorado existence with her sanity and perspective intact. Evocative and candid, this is a fine piece of Western literature, told in Ellis's engaging, straightforward style.

Subjects: History • Women's History • American History • Nineteenth Century • American Old West • America • Memoir

Now Try: Continue learning about Ellis in her follow-up book, *'Plain Anne Ellis'; More about the Life of an Ordinary Woman.* Learn how the widowed Ellis worked as a cook, installed telephone lines, and successfully campaigned for County Treasurer, all while raising her children as a single mother. As in her first book, Ellis relates her memoir with her enjoyable style and frank depictions of day-to-day life. Readers who enjoy Ellis's subtle humor and frank narrative style will also want to try *Nothing to Do but Stay*, in which author Carrie Young recalls her mother's determination to eke out an existence in early twentieth-century North Dakota.

Enss, Chris

Pistol Packin' Madams: True Stories of Notorious Women of the Old West. Guilford, CT: TwoDot, 2006. 93pp. ISBN 9780762737758.

In the rough and gritty world of the Old West, there weren't many career options available to pioneer women; fortunately, the oldest profession of all presented a profitable business opportunity for a few creative entrepreneurs. Meet Mattie Silks, the red light queen of Denver, Tessie Wall, a favorite of the Barbary Coast, and eleven other career-minded women in this wickedly entertaining collective biography. Chris Enss relates their stories in a chatty, lighthearted style, presenting a sampling of shrewd businesswomen who weren't afraid to shoot a gun to defend their brothels.

Subjects: Prostitutes • Entrepreneurs • Business • Labor • History • American Old West • Women's History • American History • Social History • Nineteenth Century • America • Biography • Collection • Young Adult • Quick Read

Now Try: Though it does not have the same gossip-column breeziness of *Pistol Packin' Madams*, Anne Seagraves's *Soiled Doves: Prostitution in the Early West* will nonetheless appeal to fans of Chris Enss. With a flair for the dramatic and a sense for spicy storytelling, Seagraves introduces us to a variety of young women who sold their bodies to earn a living.

Holmes, Kenneth L., ed.

Best of Covered Wagon Women. Norman: University of Oklahoma Press, 2008. 304pp. ISBN 9780806139142.

As editor of the <u>Covered Wagon Women</u> series, historian Holmes is intimately familiar with a wealth of writing by women pioneers. In *Best of Covered Wagon Women,* he selects the very best entries from the eleven-volume series, giving them context with his clear historical analysis. You'll meet eight nineteenth-century pioneer women through the words of their letters and their diaries; some of the writers were clearly educated, whereas others employed creative, organic spellings and turns of phrase, but in each case they convey a sense of the adventures and struggles of the pioneering life in the American Old West.

Subjects: American Old West • History • Women's History • Social History • American History • Nineteenth Century • America • Diary • Letters • Anthology • Collection

Now Try: For a somewhat lighter read about women in the Old West, turn to *Hearts West: True Stories of Mail Order Brides on the Frontier*. By weaving her own lively historical interpretation with excerpts of letters, journals, newspapers, and other primary sources, author Chris Enss creates an absorbing portrait of women who, unwilling to venture into the frontier alone, found a ticket to the West by relieving eligible pioneer bachelors of their loneliness.

LeCompte, Mary Lou

Cowgirls of the Rodeo: Pioneer Professional Athletes. Sport and Society series. Urbana: University of Illinois Press, 1993 (2000). 252pp. ISBN 9780252020292.

When professional rodeo was established as a sport in America in 1882, there was no room for sexism. Women who worked on ranches were just as sturdy and athletic as their male counterparts, and so they participated as professional cowgirls almost from the inception of the sport. In this dazzling history of rodeo in the American West, author LeCompte studies a century of cowgirls, from their wild beginnings in the late-nineteenth-century frontier to the golden age of women's rodeo in the 1920s to the gritty competitions of modern times. This well-researched, scholarly social history is a delightful, illuminating read, supported with plenty of photographs and cultural analysis.

> **Subjects:** Cowgirls • Rodeo • Sports • Athletes • Exercise • History • Sports History • Social History • Women's History • Nineteenth Century • Twentieth Century • American History • Violence • American Old West • America

> **Now Try:** Cowgirl culture comes alive in the glorious portraiture of *Rodeo Girl*. Author/photographer Lisa Eisner has captured 140 gorgeous photos, in color and black-and-white, that document a group of young women, each hoping to be the next Miss Rodeo America. The vivid, dramatic images from the world of rodeo draw attention not only to the high-energy scenes of competition at fevered pitch, but also to the quiet, reflective, behind-the-scenes moments.

Morgan, Lael

Good Time Girls of the Alaska-Yukon Gold Rush. Fairbanks, AK: Epicenter Press, 1998. 351pp. ISBN 9780945397632.

Alaska is much farther north than the region we typically think of as the Old West, but as historian Morgan deftly shows, Alaskan women employed themselves in the same fashion as their sisters in warmer climes. Good jobs in the gold rush were hard to come by, so many women took to entertaining the male miners. Part narrative history, part collective biography, *Good Time Girls* introduces us to the lifestyles and experiences of prostitutes, showgirls, and determined social climbers. Morgan transforms her historical research into an engrossing read, supplemented with photographs, excellent for scholars and general readers alike.

> **Subjects:** Prostitutes • Entrepreneurs • Business • Labor • History • American Old West • Women's History • American History • Social History • Nineteenth Century • America • Biography • Collection

> **Now Try:** Readers willing to read a more scholarly study of prostitution in the Old West will be delighted with Jan MacKell's *Brothels, Bordellos & Bad Girls: Prostitution in Colorado, 1860–1930*. Drawing on a wealth of historical sources, MacKell presents a detailed, captivating survey of prostitution, painting a portrait of the grim realities—alcoholism, abuse, health problems—faced by sex workers in the hardscrabble frontier.

Peavy, Linda S., and Ursula Smith

Pioneer Women: The Lives of Women on the Frontier. New York: Smithmark, 1996. 144pp. ISBN 9780831772208.

It's not a lengthy book, but you may find yourself lingering over the pages of *Pioneer Women*. Black-and-white photographs depict the reality of life in the inhospitable American West of the nineteenth century, while the authors' words give context to the stark images. The photographs alone make the book worthwhile, but readers looking for an intelligent discussion of life on the frontier will enjoy the narrative. Discover the lives of pioneer women of different races, classes, and backgrounds, explored though a wealth of different topics, from pregnancy and childbirth to homesteading and cooking.

Subjects: History • Women's History • Social History • American History • Nineteenth Century • American Old West • America • Quick Read

Now Try: For more photos of women's lives in the Old West, turn to *Women of the West*, by Cathy Luchetti and Carol Olwell. Bolstered by excerpts of diaries, letters, and memoirs of pioneer women, the photos offer a glimpse of what life on the frontier was really like. Then take an in-depth view of frontier life through the eyes of one woman with *Letters of a Woman Homesteader*, by Elinore Pruitt Stewart. In the early twentieth century, Stewart took a job at a ranch in Wyoming; her vivid recollection of her experience will illuminate the setting, the hardships, and the pleasures of life in the Old West.

The American Civil War

Here you'll find the stories of women during the War between the States in the mid-nineteenth century.

Like no other conflict, the War between the States continues to fascinate Americans—but too often the stories of women are relegated to footnotes. The books of the "American Civil War" section restore women to the historical narrative; even avowed Civil War buffs will find new material here. Nurses, war widows, and women soldiers in drag are but some of the remarkable characters you'll meet. And readers looking for additional stories of women and war will want to turn to the "Women Warriors" section of Chapter 1, the "Espionage and War" section of Chapter 5, the "Women in the Military" section of Chapter 7, and the "War, Violence, and Peace" section of Chapter 8.

Hall, Richard

Women on the Civil War Battlefront. Modern War Studies. Lawrence: University Press of Kansas, 2006. 397pp. ISBN 9780700614370.

Richard Hall is not the first Civil War historian to write about the women who served in the Civil War (see, for instance, *All the Daring of the Soldier*, annotated next), but he is the first to write about women Civil War combatants on such a large scale—because, as he convincingly explains, his research suggests that more women served than anyone has ever before suspected. Through exhaustive examination of countless historical documents, Hall has unearthed evidence that at least one thousand—possibly *several* thousand—women served on both sides of the war. Filled with examples of women soldiers and propelled by insightful analysis, *Women on the Civil War Battlefront* offers a scholarly introduction to women who have, until now, been lost to history.

Subjects: Warriors • Civil War • Gender • Sexual Discrimination • War • Violence • Labor • History • Military History • American History • Nineteenth Century • America

Now Try: Although far fewer women are discussed in *They Fought Like Demons: Women Soldiers in the Civil War* than in Hall's book, it is a superb choice for readers who want to know more about the women who went into battle. Authors DeAnne Blanton and Lauren M. Cook examine the women who went undercover to join the armies as well as the battles in which they served. With excellent scholarship and insight, the book considers the women's motivations for going into combat and details the struggles they endured to remain incognito.

Leonard, Elizabeth D.

All the Daring of the Soldier: Women of the Civil War Armies. New York: W. W. Norton, 1999 (New York: Penguin Books, 2001). 368pp. ISBN 9780393047127.

Have you ever heard of Franklin Thompson, the Civil War soldier who fought courageously at Fredericksburg? Perhaps you'd recognized him by his real name, Sarah Emma Edmonds. Plenty of women dressed in drag to be able to join in combat during the Civil War, while others took slightly more conventional routes to get at the action, serving as spies, as nurses, even as mascots. Learn about their surprising stories in *All the Daring of the Soldier*, an informative history that draws on historical documents to uncover the tales of women in the thick of the Civil War.

Subjects: Warriors • Civil War • Gender • Sexual Discrimination • War • Violence • Labor • History • Military History • American History • Nineteenth Century • America

Now Try: A good companion read is Bonnie Tsui's *She Went to the Field: Women Soldiers of the Civil War*. Readers wishing to know more about the women discussed in Leonard's book will find additional information about them here, along with material about women not covered in *All the Daring of the Soldier*; the author's painstaking research provides plenty of solid historical detail for anyone curious about the women who served in the Civil War and the extraordinary measures they took for the privilege of participating.

Massey, Mary Elizabeth

Women in the Civil War. Lincoln: University of Nebraska Press, 1994. 371pp. ISBN 9780803282131.

In the first part of the nineteenth century, explains historian Massey, most women deferred to the sensibilities of their husbands and fathers, eschewing political activism in favor of developing their domestic spheres. There was no reason for the status quo to change, barring a sweeping social movement that might "arouse their emotions, permit them to work with and not against their men, remove them mentally and physically from their narrow domestic world, and challenge them to perform great new tasks and assume new responsibilities." Cue the American Civil War: we so often remember this conflict as a piece of bloody military history, as a political struggle over race, money, and states' rights, but that view presents only part of the picture. By studying the wartime mantles claimed by women—as nurses, as feminists, as spies, as abolitionists—Massey illuminates the social history of the Civil War, showing how the conflict opened some new doors for American women.

> **Subjects:** War • Civil War • History • Women's History • Social History • American History • Nineteenth Century • America

> **Now Try:** Continue studying the roles of American women during the Civil War by turning to Webb B. Garrison's *Amazing Women of the Civil War*. In this captivating collective biography, Webb brings to life the stories of spies, activists, army wives, nurses, and other remarkable women, some of whom—Harriet Tubman, Louisa May Alcott, Dorothea Dix—will be familiar, and others who will be new to readers. Then, for a compelling novel of one woman's fight to survive in the Civil War, turn to Charles Frazier's *Cold Mountain*, starring a woman who must learn to fend for herself when all of the men leave for battle.

Schultz, Jane E.

Women at the Front: Hospital Workers in Civil War America. Civil War America. Chapel Hill: University of North Carolina Press, 2004. 360pp. ISBN 9780807828670.

> During the bloody War between the States, women from both the Confederacy and the Union furthered the cause by taking jobs in hospitals. Many served as nurses, while others worked as laundresses, custodians, and seamstresses. Readers will recognize the names of a few of these women—Dorothea Dix, Louisa May Alcott, Harriet Tubman—but most of the twenty thousand women relief workers never achieved fame. Historian Schultz has done an impressive job of unearthing the role of these women not only during the Civil War but afterward, when they sought their pensions to varying degrees of success. This engaging book illuminates a group of people often overlooked by Civil War buffs, and it raises thought-provoking questions about race, gender, and social standing during a time of tremendous societal upheaval.

> **Subjects:** Nurses • Health Care • Civil War • War • Violence • Labor • History • History of Medicine • Social History • American History • Nineteenth Century • America

> **Now Try:** Explore the world of the relief workers described by Schultz in Gordon Dammann and Alfred J. Bollet's *Images of Civil War Medicine: A Photographic History*. Some 250 photographs show the facilities and medical tools of the 1860s, along with the workers who used them. Readers may also wish to try *The Colors of Courage: Gettysburg's Hidden History: Immigrants, Women, and African-Americans in the Civil War's Defining Battle*, by Margaret S. Creighton. This insightful piece of scholarship considers the immigrant warriors who fought at Gettysburg, as well as the women and African American civilians who played a role in the battle and its aftermath.

Young, Elizabeth

Disarming the Nation: Women's Writing and the American Civil War. Women in Culture and Society. Chicago: University of Chicago Press, 1999. 389pp. ISBN 9780226960876.

> "The literature of the Civil War regularly underscores and capitalizes on the generative power of masculinity.... In the land of the self-made man, the story of national self-division—like the birth of a nation—apparently

needs no mothers," observes literature scholar Young, with tongue firmly in cheek. In this fascinating blend of literary criticism and social history, she examines how the writings of six women in the nineteenth and twentieth centuries shaped, and continue to shape, our understanding of the Civil War. Some of the authors, such as Harriet Beecher Stowe and Louisa May Alcott, will be familiar names; others, such as Loreta Velazquez—who managed to serve in the war by dressing in drag—may be new. With a scholarly but eminently accessible voice, Young applies a feminist literary approach to the texts of the women writers, showing how their works have influenced perceptions of the Civil War.

> **Subjects:** Writing • War • Civil War • History • Women's History • Social History • American History • Nineteenth Century • Twentieth Century • America
>
> **Now Try:** Elizabeth Young examined how women's writing shaped our perceptions of the Civil War. In *Blood & Irony: Southern White Women's Narratives of the Civil War, 1861–1937*, Sarah E. Gardner takes a similar approach, showing how the postwar American South was defined and interpreted by such authors as Margaret Mitchell and Katherine Anne Porter.

Twentieth Century and Beyond

Titles in this section represent the diversity of women's lives in the last century.

The "Twentieth Century and Beyond" section features a wide array of books, with something for everyone. Interested in a particular region? Try *African Women: A Modern History* by Catherine Coquery-Vidrovitch. Want to learn about a niche interest? Ann Ferrar's *Hear Me Roar: Women, Motorcycles, and the Rapture of the Road* should do, or perhaps *Can She Bake a Cherry Pie?: American Women and the Kitchen in the Twentieth Century* by Mary Drake McFeely. Or maybe social history intrigues you; try starting with *Flapper* by Joshua Zeitz.

Bloch, Avital H., and Lauri Umansky, eds.

Impossible to Hold: Women and Culture in the 1960's. New York: New York University Press, 2005. 342pp. ISBN 9780814799093.

The 1960s come alive in this excellent collection of essays about women and culture. In chapters such as Avital H. Bloch's "Joan Baez: A Singer and Activist" and Julia L. Foulkes's "Ambassadors with Hips: Katherine Dunham, Pearl Primus, and the Allure of Africa in the Black Arts movement," the book explores the women of the 1960s, some familiar (think Yoko Ono and Diana Ross) and some forgotten. Written from a scholarly but accessible perspective, the collection considers the pop culture of the era, as well as the budding sense of activism and feminism amongst women in the 1960s.

> **Subjects:** History • Women's History • Social History • American History • Feminism • Activism • Twentieth Century • America • Essays • Anthology • Collection
>
> **Now Try:** Now explore the history of both the 1950s and the 1960s in Catherine Gourley's *Gidgets and Women Warriors: Perceptions of Women in the 1950s and 1960s*. Lavishly illustrated with photos from the era, the book considers American society's

changing attitudes towards women's issues and the dawning of feminism; the book is less scholarly in tone than *Impossible to Hold*, but readers will appreciate the keen insights into the culture and climate of women's issues in the wake of World War II.

Cook, Sharon A., Lorna R. McLean, and Kate O'Rourke, eds.

Framing Our Past: Canadian Women's History in the Twentieth Century. Montreal: McGill-Queen's University Press, 2001. 495pp. ISBN 9780773-521728.

If it is possible to capture the breadth, depth, and scope of the lives of twentieth-century Canadian women in one book, then *Framing Our Past* is it. A dizzying number of topics are covered, both in the private sphere (leisure activities, religious practices, fashion, housework) and in the public sphere (political activities, social movements, spending habits). With a readable, jargon-free style, the authors consider various women's roles—as mothers, as businesswomen, as wives, as leaders—by drawing on standard primary documents such as diaries and letters, as well as objects such as posters, art, and dressmaking patterns. Gorgeously and profusely illustrated, this is an extremely accessible overview of twentieth-century Canadian women's history.

> **Subjects:** History • Women's History • Social History • Canada • Twentieth Century
>
> **Now Try:** Whereas *Framing Our Past* focuses on Canadian women's history in the twentieth century, *Rethinking Canada: The Promise of Women's History* considers history going all the way back to colonial times. Edited by Veronica Jane Strong-Boag and Anita Clair Fellman, this is a collection of scholarly but accessible essays on a variety of topics, including race, immigration, marriage, and violence.

Coquery-Vidrovitch, Catherine

African Women: A Modern History. Social Change in Global Perspective. Boulder, CO: WestviewPress, 1997. 308pp. ISBN 9780813323602.

As the nineteenth century gave way to the twentieth, African women's lives were still essentially similar to the lives of their foremothers: they married, they had children, they worked the land. But with the advent of colonialism and modernization, sweeping changes reshaped the social norms, both in the country and the cities. In this meticulously researched study of the experiences of sub-Saharan African women from the late nineteenth century to the present, historian Coquery-Vidrovitch considers a variety of themes, from labor and education to marriage and sexuality to politics and art. This is an articulate, insightful exploration of the diversity of African women's experiences, written for a scholarly audience but accessible for general readers and supported with maps, illustrations, and photos.

> **Subjects:** History • Women's History • Social History • Nineteenth Century • Twentieth Century • Africa
>
> **Now Try:** Focus now on a slice of twentieth-century African women's history in Wunyabari O. Maloba's *African Women in Revolution*, a scholarly but clearly written study of African women's participation in seven revolutionary move-

ments since World War II. Fans of Coquery-Vidrovitch's work will appreciate the feminist attention to gender, daily life, and politics in this exploration of women's struggles for national and personal liberation.

Faderman, Lillian

Odd Girls and Twilight Lovers: A History of Lesbian Life in Twentieth-Century America. Between Men—Between Women. New York: Columbia University Press, 1991. 373pp. ISBN 9780231074889.

The glorious, complicated, tragic, and triumphant history of lesbians in America comes alive in this fascinating, engaging social history. Starting with the euphemistic "romantic friendships" that were acknowledged in the late nineteenth century, scholar Faderman shows how same-sex romantic relationships between women evolved in the public eye, taking the reader through such eras as the Roaring Twenties, the radical sixties, and the cautiously open nineties, when lesbian participation in mainstream society started to become a legitimate possibility. Drawing on primary sources such as newspaper articles, books, and films, Faderman presents a thorough—and thoroughly researched—history of one hundred years of American lesbian life, complete with discussions about race, class, and feminism.

> **Subjects:** Lesbian Sexuality • Queer Sexuality • Sexuality • History • Social History • Women's History • American History • Twentieth Century • Feminism • America

> **Now Try:** Learn more about the history of lesbian women, and gay men, too, in *Out of the Past: Gay and Lesbian History from 1869 to the Present*. With meticulous research and an accessible tone, journalist Neil Miller paints a wide-reaching portrait of the politics and social history of queer movements and queer individuals, bolstered by numerous examples of primary source materials.

Ferrar, Ann

Hear Me Roar: Women, Motorcycles, and the Rapture of the Road. New York: Crown Trade Paperbacks, 1996 (North Conway, NH: Whitehorse Press, 2000). 211pp. ISBN 9780517881729.

In this history book of a most unusual subject, Ann Ferrar studies a century of women motorcyclists. With an empowering, pro-woman attitude, Ferrar considers the intrepid women who chose to forsake social norms in favor of the freedom of the road. Loaded with photographs and quotes from women motorcyclists, this is a celebration of everyone from the pioneering drivers of the early 1900s to the drag-racing Harley riders in the present day. Following this spirited discussion is a substantial how-to section for women motorcyclists, including chapters about motorcycle safety and motorcycle selection.

> **Subjects:** Motorcycling • Adventure • History • Twentieth Century • America • How-to • Quick Read

> **Now Try:** If Ferrar piqued your curiosity about early women motorcyclists, consider Susie Hollern's lovely photo history, *Women and Motorcycling: The Early Years*. Vintage black-and-white photos of women and their motorcycles offer glimpses into early twentieth-century history, while vignettes illuminate the lives of the riders. For further examination of contemporary women cyclists, turn to *Bike Lust: Harleys, Women, and American Society*, in which author Barbara Joans uses interviews and personal observations to profile the various sub-sub-cultures of American women bikers, including the Biker Chicks and the Lady Passengers.

Inness, Sherrie A., ed.

Disco Divas: Women and Popular Culture in the 1970s. Philadelphia: University of Pennsylvania Press, 2003. 232pp. ISBN 9780812237078.

1

> Propelled by women's liberation and second-wave feminism, pop culture responded, at least in part, by gaining a feminist consciousness. Remember the television show *Charlie's Angles*? Those babelicious starlets weren't just eye candy—they were empowered, independent women thriving as detectives. In this excellent collection of essays, various scholars revisit the 1970s to explore the impact of feminism on pop culture, and vice versa; see, for instance, "'Who's That Lady?' *Ebony* Magazine and Black Professional Women," by Toni C. King, and "Hysterical Scream or Rebel Yell? The Politics of Teen-Idol Fandom," by Ilana Nash. This is a vibrant, thought-provoking exploration of feminism in the 1970s as seen through the lens of the media and popular culture.

2

> **Subjects:** Feminism • Second-wave Feminism • Media • History • Women's History • Social History • American History • Twentieth Century • America • Essays • Anthology • Collection

3

> **Now Try:** It's a much lighter read, but if you enjoyed *Disco Divas*, you won't want to miss Catherine Gourley's *Ms. and the Material Girls: Perceptions of Women from the 1970s through the 1990s*. In this fast-paced but thoroughly researched social history, Gourley examines three decades of popular culture and media—magazines, movies, television broadcasts, music—to reveal the feminist sensibilities of the times.

4

López Springfield, Consuelo, ed.

Daughters of Caliban: Caribbean Women in the Twentieth Century. Bloomington: Indiana University Press, 1997. 316pp. ISBN 9780253332493.

5

> In *Daughters of Caliban*, women's studies scholar López Springfield brings together essays that consider a century of Caribbean women's experiences. Scholars from a variety of fields—anthropology, health, literature, law—bring their perspectives to a wealth of topics in essays such as "The Power to Heal: Haitian Women in Vodou" by Karen McCarthy Brown and "Menstrual Taboos, Witchcraft Babies, and Social Relations: Women's Health Traditions in Rural Jamaica" by Elisa J. Sobo. As this is written for a scholarly audience, general readers may find that the academic style takes some getting used to, but their efforts will be rewarded with insightful, thought-provoking discussions of race, class, colonialism, and other themes that have informed Caribbean women's lives in the twentieth century.

6

> **Subjects:** Latinas • Caribbean • Feminism • History • Women's History • Twentieth Century • Essays

7

> **Now Try:** Readers wishing to know more about the experiences of Caribbean women will find an excellent companion in *Women & Change in the Caribbean: A Pan-Caribbean Perspective*, edited by Janet Henshall Momsen. Drawing on their experience in such fields as agriculture, economics, and feminism, the contributing scholars explore the lives of contemporary Caribbean women by considering a variety of topics, from politics and gender roles to labor and marriage.

8

Mabe, Catherine

Roller Derby: The History and All-Girl Revival of the Greatest Sport on Wheels. Denver, CO: Speck Press, 2006. 159pp. ISBN 9781933108117.

If you thought roller derby was dead, think again. Women are strapping on their skates and donning their protective gear to race around the track. This is a competitive, surprisingly rigorous sport, as seen in the vivid, high-impact photos that dominate the book. Author Mabe presents an overview of roller derby, beginning with its origins in the 1930s and continuing through the revival on modern-day racetracks. Vignettes and quotes from players accompany the gorgeous photos and illustrations, making this an excellent introduction to the pro-woman, girl-power nature of this spectacular sport. An explanation of rules and slang describes the intricate knowledge necessary for any roller-derby enthusiast.

Subjects: Roller Derby • Athletes • Sports • Adventure • History • Social History • Twentieth Century • Twenty-first Century • America • Quick Read

Now Try: For a more detailed examination of roller derby, turn to author Melissa Joulwan—known as "Melicious" on the track—one of the women directly responsible for the present-day revival of roller derby. A founding member of the Texas Rollergirls, she is a champion racer, perfectly suited for telling the story of modern roller-derby racing in *Rollergirl: Totally True Tales from the Track.* She includes a generous sampling of derby-girl profiles, anecdotes, and quotations, as well as an insightful look at her own transformation from naïve nerdy girl to full-fledged sport enthusiast. And for a companion read that is very strange, but strangely enjoyable, try Toni Carr's *Knockdown Knits: 30 Projects from the Roller Derby Track,* featuring knitting patterns inspired by roller derby.

McFeely, Mary Drake

Can She Bake a Cherry Pie?: American Women and the Kitchen in the Twentieth Century. Amherst: University of Massachusetts Press, 2000. 194pp. ISBN 9781558-492509.

Forgive a personal aside, but I cannot cook—and I cannot count the number of times this shortcoming has called into question my gender or my womanhood. Thus I completely agree with the premise of this marvelous book, that despite the developments of the twentieth century—microwaves, processed foods, Wonder Bread—women have been, and continue to be, judged on their skills in the kitchen. With a captivating, frequently witty writing style, scholar McFeely explores the changing nature of the kitchen throughout the twentieth century, from the days when women truly prepared (and often grew) their own food to modern times, when the ability to prepare food—though no longer imperative—persists as a token of womanhood. Written from a delightfully feminist perspective, the book offers a thought-provoking discussion of gender and an intriguing glimpse into a slice of American women's social history.

Subjects: Food • Labor • Gender • Feminism • History • Women's History • Social History • American History • Twentieth Century • America • Quick Read

Now Try: Dive deeper into the history of women's cooking with *Perfection Salad: Women and Cooking at the Turn of the Century.* In this engrossing social history, journalist Laura Shapiro takes us back to the late nineteenth and early twentieth centuries, showing how women fought to ease their burdens in the kitchen by relying on quick, easy, processed (and oftentimes tasteless) foods. Fans of McFeely's writing will enjoy Shapiro's captivating style and feminist observations.

Ruíz, Vicki

From Out of the Shadows: Mexican Women in Twentieth-Century America. New York: Oxford University Press, 1998. 240pp. ISBN 9780195114836.

"As farm workers, flappers, labor activists, barrio volunteers, civic leaders, and feminists, Mexican women have made history," writes historian Ruíz. "Their stories, however, have remained in the shadows." To counter the neglect of Mexican women in American history, Ruíz presents this powerful, meticulously researched study of Chicanas in the twentieth century. In such chapters as "With Pickets, Baskets, and Ballots" and "La Nueva Chicana: Women and the Movement," she explores the experiences of Mexican women, applying her nuanced insights to the big themes—race, class, and gender—as well as topics such as community and activism. Written from a Chicanisma feminist perspective, this is a scholarly but accessible exploration of the lives of Mexican American women in the twentieth century.

> **Subjects:** Latinas • Race • Class • Gender • Chicanisma • Feminism • History • Women's History • Social History • American History • Twentieth Century • America
>
> **Now Try:** Ruíz examines the experiences of Mexican American women—Chicanas—in the twentieth century; now consider the experiences of American women who hail from all of Latin America in Hedda Garza's *Latinas: Hispanic Women in the United States.* Elegantly and accessibly written, this study illuminates the impact of Mexican, Central American, and South American women in the United States in the nineteenth and twentieth centuries, examining individual activists as well as general social changes.

Zeitz, Joshua

Flapper: A Madcap Story of Sex, Style, Celebrity, and the Women Who Made America Modern. New York: Crown, 2006. 338pp. ISBN 978140-0080533.

Oh, those flappers: The bobbed hair! The sassy attitudes! The cigarettes, the booze, the steamy sensuality! Permit historian Joshua Zeitz to take you back to the Roaring Twenties in this unputdownable social history. All your favorite flappers are here, from Zelda Fitzgerald to Coco Chanel to the dishy Louise Brooks. Both a collective biography and a history of the fashion, attitudes, and sexual norms of the 1920s, this is history at its scintillating finest, based on excellent scholarship and relayed in an utterly captivating style; it is appropriate both for serious scholars and for anyone interested in these femmes fatales.

> **Subjects:** Flappers • Fashion • History • Women's History • Social History • Twentieth Century • America • Biography • Collection
>
> **Now Try:** For another captivating scholarly examination of the 1920s, turn to *The Damned and the Beautiful: American Youth in the 1920's* by Paula S. Fass. In this engrossing, thoroughly researched social history, Fass considers the youth culture of the era by examining such topics as politics, leisure activities, and sexual mores. Then, for a lighter companion read, turn to Ellie Laubner's *Fashions of the Roaring '20s.* In this entertaining, informative book, Lauber explores and depicts the beauty ideals of the era, supplementing her narrative with a wealth of period photos and illustrations. And fiction lovers, of course, will

want to read the quintessential novel of American decadence by the quintessential author the 1920s, F. Scott Fitzgerald's *The Great Gatsby*.

Women and War in the Twentieth Century

> Whether they served as combatants or not, women across the globe were affected, directly or indirectly, by the wars of the twentieth century.

Some of the stories in this section are character-driven, as we see in the harrowing book *Zlata's Diary: A Child's Life in Sarajevo* by Zlata Filipović. Others have a more sociological perspective, as with *Clipped Wings: The Rise and Fall of the Women Airforce Service Pilots (WASPS) of World War II* by Molly Merryman. Some of them will break your heart, while others will amaze you with forgotten tales of courage and independence. Readers interested in women and war will also want to see the "Women Warriors" section of Chapter 1, the "Espionage and War" section of Chapter 5, the "Women in the Military" section of Chapter 7, and the "War, Violence, and Peace" section of Chapter 8.

Filipović, Zlata

Zlata's Diary: A Child's Life in Sarajevo. New York: Viking, 1994. 200pp. ISBN 9780670857241.

Meet Filipović, a bright young girl whose diary reads like that of any eleven-year-old girl, at least at the beginning; it is filled with references to music and books and movies. But Filipović's childhood innocence ends abruptly when Sarajevo erupts into ethnic war. Covering two years between 1991 and 1993, this is the story of a young woman whose very life is threatened by the violence of war: food is scarce, electricity is a memory, her house burns down, and bombs fall incessantly. Understandably, the diary is unbearably grim at times, but it is a compelling read, a powerful look at the effects of war through the eyes of a child—and, fortunately, it does offer a happy ending for Filipović and her family.

Subjects: War • Violence • Coming of Age • History • Women's History • Twentieth Century • Bosnia and Herzegovina • Europe • Diary • Young Adult • Quick Read

Now Try: For another powerful, disturbing story of the Bosnian war, turn to *The Stone Fields: An Epitaph for the Living*. American anthropologist Courtney Angela Brkic visited Bosnia twice in the 1990s, first with the United Nations and then with Physicians for Human Rights. In this bleak memoir, Brkic draws on interviews with war survivors and on her experience excavating a mass grave to paint a picture of a ravaged Bosnia. Then turn to *This Was Not Our War: Bosnian Women Reclaiming the Peace*, in which author Swanee Hunt draws on interviews with twenty-six women survivors to illustrate the horrors suffered by ordinary people during the conflict.

Gavin, Lettie

American Women in World War I: They Also Served. Boulder, CO: University Press of Colorado, 1997 (2006). 295pp. ISBN 9780870818257.

Though they were not yet allowed to serve in combat, more than forty thousand women donned uniforms to serve in noncombatant roles in World War I. Drawing on personal interviews and source material such as memoirs and diaries, author Lettie Gavin constructs an impressive history of the role of American women, arranged according to the units in which they served. With photographs, statistics, and compelling anecdotes, *American Women in World War I* restores the women to their rightful place in history, while revealing the discrimination that plagued them and the sexist attitudes that prevented them from receiving the treatment they deserved in the war's aftermath.

> **Subjects:** Warriors • World War I • Sexual Discrimination • War • Violence • Labor • History • Military History • American History • Social History • Twentieth Century • America

> **Now Try:** While women in America were relegated to noncombatant roles in World War I, women in Russia were allowed to serve in combat for the first time. Read the fascinating story of these six thousand soldiers in Laurie S. Stoff's *They Fought for the Motherland: Russia's Women Soldiers in World War I and the Revolution.* The book is scholarly in tone, but readers will be captivated by the numerous accounts of individual women, the examination of women's combat units, and the analysis of the uniquely Russian social norms at work during World War I.

Kelsey, Marion

Victory Harvest: Diary of a Canadian in the Women's Land Army, 1940–1944. Montreal: McGill-Queen's University Press, 1997. 227pp. ISBN 9780773516632.

When Marion Kelsey's husband joined the Canadian Army, he was sent overseas to England to serve in World War II. Kelsey followed shortly thereafter, expecting only to visit him, not to join the war effort herself—but soon she had joined the Women's Land Army, a stint that would last four years. With honest, sometimes naïve words, Kelsey's diary reveals one woman's struggle to cope with a world war while far away from home. Kelsey's observations of war, her growth as a person and servicewoman, and her unflagging homesickness for Canada make this a unique, touching perspective on World War II.

> **Subjects:** Warriors • Violence • Labor • History • Military History • War • World War II • Twentieth Century • Britain • Canada • Diary • Autobiography

> **Now Try:** *Victory Harvest* offers a glimpse of what it meant to be a Canadian, a woman, and a soldier. Now learn more about Canadian servicewomen in *A History of Women in the Canadian Military*, by Barbara Dundas. Read about the courageous women who fought unofficially during colonial times, the nurses who served in the World Wars, and the modern women who serve in full combat capacity. Generously illustrated, this text is the most comprehensive resource available on the subject of the women who have served throughout Canada's history.

Merryman, Molly

Clipped Wings: The Rise and Fall of the Women Airforce Service Pilots (WASPS) of World War II. New York: New York University Press, 1998. 239pp. ISBN 9780585330778.

> In World War II, the WASPS—Women Airforce Service Pilots—made history by being the first American women to fly military planes. Their success was remarkable, considering the rampant sexism of the era, discussed here in heartbreaking detail: the WASP pilots were not accorded military rank or given veterans' benefits, and in 1944 their pioneering group was disbanded. Based on historic documents and interviews with former WASPS, *Clipped Wings* presents the bittersweet history of the courageous women who flew in World War II, their dazzling successes in the skies, and their struggles against sexual discrimination.
>
> **Subjects:** Warriors • Aviation • Labor • Sexual Discrimination • War • Violence • World War II • History • Military History • American History • Social History • Twentieth Century • America
>
> **Now Try:** America wasn't the only country employing women pilots in World War II. In *Those Wonderful Women in Their Flying Machines: The Unknown Heroines of World War Two*, author Sally Van Wagenen Keil discusses not only the WASPS of America but the Air Transport Auxiliary of England. Her engaging style brings life to the successes on both sides of the Atlantic and sheds further light on the demoralizing sexism of the era. See also *Women Pilots of World War II*, written by WASP veteran Jean Hascall Cole. The oral histories of thirty-five airwomen, all members of the same graduating WASP class, recall the drama and adventure of flying in the pilots' own words.

Pennington, Reina, and John Erickson

Wings, Women, and War: Soviet Airwomen in World War II Combat. Modern War Studies. Lawrence: University Press of Kansas, 2001 (2007). 304pp. ISBN 9780700611454.

> Just as the Soviet Union was the first modern state to allow women into combat in World War I, it was the first to allow women to fly in its air force in World War II. Women served alongside male pilots and even in their own all-female units. In this meticulously researched history, author Pennington presents the story of these airwomen as they served on the Eastern Front. The chilling tales of their exploits and bravery make this a compelling narrative, while details of the organization and history of the all-female units will delight military enthusiasts.
>
> **Subjects:** Aviation • Warriors • World War II • War • Violence • Labor • History • Military History • Social History • Twentieth Century • Soviet Union • Russia
>
> **Now Try:** Get deeper into the lives of the Soviet airwomen of World War II by reading *Night Witches: The Untold Story of Soviet Women in Combat* by Bruce Myles. The author's extensive interviews with the veterans allows their voices to shine, and the heroism of their actions propels the book from one daring feat to the next. Then try Amy Goodpaster Strebe's *Flying for Her Country: The American and Soviet Women Military Pilots of World War II*. The book's scholarship provides a solid overview of the pioneering pilot women of World War II, while providing a fascinating juxtaposition of two very different groups of airwomen.

Walker, Keith

A Piece of My Heart: The Stories of 26 American Women Who Served in Vietnam. Novato, CA: Presidio Press, 1985 (1997). 350pp. ISBN 978089-1416173.

> In *A Piece of My Heart*, twenty-six women recall their harrowing experiences at the heart of the Vietnam War. Based on the author's interviews with Army nurses, Red Cross volunteers, radio operators, and others, this oral history is a moving tribute to the women who served in Vietnam and a candid testament to the war's lasting effects. The women recall a panoply of topics, from operating in tense conditions to surviving under fire to interacting with the locals. Vivid images and honest voices make this a powerful collection of stories, not one for the faint of heart.
>
> > **Subjects:** Warriors • War • Violence • Labor • History • Military History • Vietnam War • American History • Twentieth Century • Vietnam • Asia
> >
> > **Now Try:** Hear more women's stories from Vietnam in Olga Gruhzit-Hoyt's *A Time Remembered: American Women in the Vietnam War*. Each chapter profiles a different woman, examining her rationale for entering the conflict, her experiences in Vietnam, and the lasting effects of service on her life afterward. The stories of a variety of nurses, Red Cross volunteers, and other servicewomen are explored here with sympathy and candor; their experiences are both informative and riveting.

Yellin, Emily

Our Mothers' War: American Women at Home and at the Front During World War II. New York: Free Press, 2004. 447pp. ISBN 9780743245142.

> While going through the attic after her mother's death, Emily Yellin found letters her mother had written while serving in the Red Cross in World War II. Researching *Our Mothers' War* was, in effect, like "[riffling] through the memories stored in the attics of other women's lives from World War II. And sure enough, I found gems waiting there … some smooth, some rough, some sparkling, some worn down—but all precious gems that have hardly ever been appraised or even displayed before." These rarely seen gems constitute the basis of Yellin's fascinating scholarship, which takes us into the lives of a wide variety of American women—wives and WASPs, volunteers and nurses, white women, African American women, Japanese American women—as they experienced World War II.
>
> > **Subjects:** World War II • War • History • Women's History • American History • Twentieth Century • America
> >
> > **Now Try:** For another thoughtful narrative about the lives of women during World War II, turn to Brenda Ralph Lewis's *Women at War: The Women of World War II—at Home, at Work, on the Front Line*. Like Yellin, Lewis liberally sprinkles her study with the words of the women who experienced the war, along with period photos and illustrations. Those who enjoyed *Our Mothers' War* will appreciate Yellin's clear writing and her attention to women from a variety of backgrounds. And for a fictionalized treatment of World War II, try Michael Ondaatje's evocative novel *The English Patient*. Set in Italy, it features a compelling cast of characters, including a nurse named Hana who cares for a man who was horribly injured in the war.

Consider Starting With . . .

Begin learning about Women's History with some of the most accessible, popular titles, listed here:

Collins, Gail. *America's Women: Four Hundred Years of Dolls, Drudges, Helpmates, and Heroines.*

Hill, Frances. *A Delusion of Satan: The Full Story of the Salem Witch Trials.*

León, Vicki. The *Uppity Women* books, beginning with *Uppity Women of Ancient Times.*

Miles, Rosalind. *Who Cooked the Last Supper?: The Women's History of the World.*

Pomeroy, Sarah B. *Goddesses, Whores, Wives, and Slaves: Women in Classical Antiquity.*

Roberts, Cokie. *Founding Mothers: The Women Who Raised Our Nation.*

Fiction Read-Alikes

- **Bradley, Marion Zimmer.** The familiar story of King Arthur is dramatically retold from the perspective of women in *The Mists of Avalon*, an epic fantasy novel that re-creates the religious, political, and social settings of the Dark Ages in England, replete with themes of feminism, goddess worship, gender inequity. Continue exploring these themes in *Fall of Atlantis*, the second book in the Avalon series.

- **Butler, Octavia.** Even readers who typically avoid Science Fiction will be enchanted with *Kindred*, in which Dana, a modern black woman, is repeatedly called back in time to the nineteenth century; there, she must face the awful choice of either fighting against slavery or saving the life of a slaveholder—because, like it or not, this brute of a man is her ancestor; if he dies without producing an heir, Dana's own existence will be negated.

- **McCullough, Colleen.** Readers who love reading about life in the ancient world will enjoy many of McCullough's novels. Start perhaps with *Antony and Cleopatra*, which tells the story of the doomed lovers against a vivid backdrop of a politically tumultuous Rome. Or try some of McCullough's historical novels in other settings; *The Thorn Birds*, a family saga of twentieth-century life in the Australian Outback, is a perennial favorite.

- **Mitchell, Margaret.** The beloved *Gone with the Wind* is a timeless classic, a story of love, marriage, betrayal, and death, all set against the backdrop of the Civil War and its immediate aftermath; it is at once a war story, a romance, and an homage to the Antebellum South.

- **Sherwood, Frances.** Frances Sherwood has a gift for drawing the reader into historical settings. In *The Book of Splendour*, you'll travel to seventeenth-century Prague, where the Jewish community lives in fear of a pogrom. There are dashes of fantasy mixed here, most notably with the golem created by Rabbi Loew to protect the Jews, but at essence this is a wonderfully realized history filled with the exciting figures of the time—Johannes Keppler, Emperor Rudolph II, John Dee, and Edward Kelley— seen from the perspective of a young married Jewish woman, Rochel Werner, who finds herself falling in love with the golem. Or try *Vindication*, a novelization of the life of eighteenth-century feminist Mary Wollstonecraft.

- **Twain, Mark.** Meet Joan of Arc through the eyes of one of her biggest fans, none other than the American literary giant Mark Twain. In his novel *Personal Recollections of Joan of Arc*, told from the point of view of her fictional friend Louis de Contes, Twain deftly weaves historical research with his imaginative genius to flesh out the saint's childhood, visions, military campaigns, and martyrdom in medieval France.

- **Undset, Sigrid.** Sigrid Undset's *Kristin Lavransdatter* trilogy is historical fiction at its finest. Based on impeccable historical research, and crafted with the utmost care—Undset refused to use any words that were not in use at the time the series took place—this is the story of a woman in fourteenth-century Norway, filled with heavy themes of religion, love, marriage, and motherhood. Start with *The Wreath*, and be sure to get the editions translated by Tiina Nunnally.

- **Wharton, Edith.** With vivid details and a gorgeous prose style, Wharton's novels follow the lives of women in nineteenth- and twentieth-century America. Discover the lifestyles of the upper class in 1870s New York in *The Age of Innocence*, a tragic romance of star-crossed lovers stymied by the insurmountable social mores and conventions of the time, or try *The House of Mirth*, about a woman who cannot follow the rigid caste rules of high society in the early twentieth century.

Chapter 5

Adventure and Travel

The last thing I wanted was infinite security, and to be the place an arrow shoots off from. I wanted change and excitement and to shoot off in all directions myself, like the colored arrows from a Fourth of July rocket.

—Sylvia Plath

This chapter covers the twin themes of Adventure and Travel. These are two areas that traditionally have been beyond the reach of women—or have they? The books you'll find in this chapter prove that women can be as adventurous and well-traveled as men. Because the titles in these two sections differ somewhat from each other in characteristics and appeal, their definitions and appeal descriptions are handled separately.

Organization

Adventure stories in a variety of settings, from oceans to jungles to the North and South Poles, constitute the first section, which is followed by "Adventures in History" and "Espionage and War." Next up is the travel section, followed by "Travel History" and "Where to Go and How to Get There."

Adventure

Definition of Adventure

Tales of daring and excitement comprise the genre of adventure, and here are the true stories women have to tell.

The Adventure genre is a diplomat in the world of books. It draws together readers from diverse backgrounds and reading interests, offering something for everybody. Nonfiction readers whose chief interests lie in other genres, such as science writing or investigative reporting or historical writing, are drawn to the genre-blending qualities of adventure stories. Even dedicated fans of fiction can be tempted into reading nonfiction with the right adventure title; the exciting events and swift pacing of adventure books can lull readers into thinking they're reading a novel. Likewise, adventure books can attract readers to Women's Nonfiction; anyone who thinks that women's history is boring is in for a pleasant surprise.

Adventure books are, by definition, plot-driven. The plot can take any number of themes—survival and intrigue, espionage and war, nature and intrigue—but whatever the focus, the plot is sure to compel readers with action and excitement, almost always delivered with a fast sense of pacing. The books are further driven by the setting, with exotic locales and historical eras contributing to the atmospheric tension.

The best adventure books are also character-driven—and in Women's Nonfiction adventure books, those characters are women. Sometimes those women deliberately seek their thrills, as did the expedition of mountain-climbing women in *Annapurna: A Woman's Place*, by Arlene Blum. Other times adventure comes to women unbidden; Jerri Nielsen never dreamed that she would be battling breast cancer at the South Pole, as we discover in her survival memoir *Ice Bound*. But whether the women purposefully hunt for adventure or not, we come to care about them, and we race through the pages to find out how they fared.

Appeal of Adventure

We read Adventure books to get our pulses racing. Authors of adventure stories deliberately tell tales with gripping plots, delivered with a fast pace and a keen sense of atmosphere, be it thrilling or suspenseful or bleak. We also read adventure books to discover lands and times that are vastly different from our own. Margaret Lowman introduces us to the steamy environs of the heights of the jungle in *Life at the Treetops*, and Elizabeth M. Norman plunges us into Indonesia in World War II with *We Band of Angels*.

And women's adventure books offer a sense of empowerment. Exciting stories and exotic locales can be found throughout the adventure genre, but women's adventure books deliver inspiring, girl-power moments. When we think of explorers and adventurers, we too often think of men; women's adventure books remind us that women are every bit as resourceful, intrepid, and courageous as their male counterparts.

It might not be wise to read adventure books in public. Involuntary exclamations of "You tell 'em, sister!" and "You go, girl!" might draw some strange looks. But that's the price of reading about women's adventures; the exciting stories of these authors will draw you in. If you would rather avoid the vicarious thrill of scaling Everest, then don't read Stacy Allison's *Beyond the Limits*, and if you'd rather not learn what it's like to row yourself across the Atlantic, then by all means stay away from Maud Fontenoy's *Across the Savage Sea*.

Alcorn, Susan

We're in the Mountains, Not over the Hills: Tales and Tips from Seasoned Women Backpackers. Oakland, CA: Shepherd Canyon Books, 2003. 260pp. ISBN 978093-6034027.

The thirty-some senior women interviewed in *We're in the Mountains* can tell you that age is no excuse to give up mountain climbing. Any reader, regardless of age or sex, can take inspiration from their hiking stories, told in a readable, conversational style. But these are not just cozy feel-good essays: these women face the same grueling adventures and rigorous challenges that confront hikers of any age, including enraged wildlife, perilous temperatures, and daring rescues. Read this both for the motivational stories and the practical advice and tips for hiking in the golden years.

> **Subjects:** Mountain Climbing • Backpacking • Exercise • Seniors • Nature • Adventure • Travel • How-to

> **Now Try:** Few people have the stamina, health, and courage to hike the entire Appalachian Trail. At age fifty-nine, Leslie Mass decided to see if she was one of them. In her memoir, *In Beauty May She Walk: Hiking the Appalachian Trail at 60*, Mass describes the physical and mental challenges of hiking the trail from beginning to end, with special emphasis on the trials unique to women and seniors.

Allison, Stacy, and Peter Carlin

Beyond the Limits: A Woman's Triumph on Everest. Boston: Little, Brown, and Co., 1993 (Seattle, WA: Milestone Books, 1999). 282pp. ISBN 9781883697822.

> With conversational, accessible prose, *Beyond the Limits* invites readers into the life of Stacy Allison, the first American woman to climb Mount Everest. Unsurprisingly, this is a book filled with adventure and derring-do, as Allison goes into compelling detail about the perils and inevitable tragedies of scaling the world's tallest mountain. But it is also a book of introspection and insight, fleshed out with Allison's unflinching discussion of her own personal obstacles. In Allison's hands, the challenges of extreme mountain climbing are just as significant as the challenges of leaving an abusive marriage.

> **Subjects:** Mountain Climbing • Everest • Exercise • Nature • Adventure • Travel • Relationships • Nepal • Tibet • China • Asia • Memoir

> **Now Try:** For more stories of women overcoming challenges, turn to the collection of essays in *Leading Out: Women Climbers Reaching for the Top* (titled in the second edition as *Mountaineering Stories of Adventurous Women*). Not all of the writers face the same serious personal issues as Allison, and not all of the physical obstacles are as daunting as Everest, but the spirit and inspiration of these women mountain climbers will resonate with those who enjoyed *Beyond the Limits*. At times suspenseful and always engaging in style, a collection of essays compiled by Rachel Da Silva, *Leading Out*, honors the struggles and bravado of women who seek their adventures from the tops of mountains.

Arnesen, Liv, Ann Bancroft, and Cheryl Dahle

No Horizon Is So Far: Two Women and Their Extraordinary Journey across Antarctica. Cambridge, MA: Da Capo Press, 2003. 365pp. ISBN 978073-8207940.

> One day Ann Bancroft, a schoolteacher from Minnesota, contacted another schoolteacher, Liv Arnesen—a woman she'd never met—to propose a joint trek, on foot, across the Antarctic. It's not as crazy as it sounds: both women had prior experience exploring the continent, and both agreed

that it would be a great way to engage students. So, armed with food, supplies, skis, laptops, and really heavy sledges, they set out in the year 2000 to become the first women to traverse Antarctica. Frostbite, injuries, brutal temperatures, and blizzards all threatened the explorers, but, as this riveting account shows, they ultimately prevailed.

Subjects: Adventure • Antarctica • Nature • Memoir • Young Adult

Now Try: At least Arnesen and Bancroft had each other for company on their expedition; Pam Flowers had no one to talk to on her 2,500 mile journey across the North American Arctic. Or rather, she had eight someones to talk to—it's just that sled dogs don't make great conversationalists. The dogs were essential for the journey—not only for transportation and navigation but for preserving their human's sanity. Read about this incredible adventure in *Alone across the Arctic: One Woman's Epic Journey by Dog Team*, co-written by children's book author Ann Dixon.

Blum, Arlene

Annapurna: A Woman's Place. San Francisco: Sierra Club Books, 1980 (1998). 256pp. ISBN 9780871562364.

In 1978, Arlene Blum led a group of thirteen women from various countries to the top of Annapurna, the world's tenth-highest mountain. With descriptive, evocative prose, Blum recounts the compelling story of the first expedition of women to scale the Himalayan mountain. While the book certainly contains the nail-biting elements you'd expect from a narrative about a radical mountaineering expedition—avalanches, unbelievably cold temperatures, dangerous interpersonal conflicts—it also focuses on the friendships, teamwork, and logistics involved in planning and executing an unprecedented adventure. Dramatic events make this a real page-turner, while the successful triumph over nature's most brutal obstacles makes it an inspiring read.

Subjects: Mountain Climbing • Annapurna • Adventure • Exercise • Nature • Travel • Nepal • Asia

Now Try: If you've read Jon Krakauer's *Into Thin Air*, you know about the ill-fated expedition to Mount Everest in 1996. The team made it to the top, only to be devastated by a blizzard the next day. Among the survivors was Lene Gammelgaard, author of *Climbing High: A Woman's Account of Surviving the Everest Tragedy*. Like Blum, she packs her story with suspense and action, while fleshing out the adventures and tragedies with very human, personal descriptions of the personalities and idiosyncrasies of the mountaineers.

Bové, Jennifer, ed.

A Mile in Her Boots: Women Who Work in the Wild. Palo Alto, CA: Solas House, 2006. 288pp. ISBN 9781932361377.

Anthologist Bové puts the "field" in "field biologist." With her experience in spending time outdoors, both in work and at play, she was eminently qualified to select the thirty-three stories of women whose work takes them outdoors. Though the contributors' professions take them on a variety of different adventures—including fighting fires, fishing for salmon, and hunting for fugitives—the stories are similar in several satisfying ways: each is a brief, riveting examination of careers in the great outdoors, told in an accessible style by the women who work there.

Subjects: Nature • Labor • Adventure • Global Perspectives • Essays • Collection • Anthology

Now Try: Though written in 1980, Anne LaBastille's *Women and Wilderness* is still popular and relevant today. The book comprises profiles of fifteen professional outdoorswomen, including scientists and explorers, as well as a discussion of the facets of modern life that keep most women separated from the outdoors—facets that have worsened significantly in the decades since the book was first written.

Fontenoy, Maud

Across the Savage Sea: The First Woman to Row across the North Atlantic. New York: Arcade Pub, 2005. 149pp. ISBN 9781559707626.

Maud Fontenoy could have chosen to row across the North Atlantic from east-to-west, but that was a little too easy, and besides, it had already been done. Instead she opted for the more frustrating winds and currents of the west-to-east route, becoming the first woman to accomplish the voyage. For four months in 2003, she lived on a twenty-four foot boat, surviving on dehydrated food and desalinated water and propelling herself the old-fashioned way, with a pair of oars. The beauty of Fontenoy's prose and the incessant dangers of her journey make this a gripping, page-turning read.

Subjects: Rowing • Adventure • Atlantic Ocean • Nature • Memoir • Young Adult • Quick Read

Now Try: As soon as she was done conquering the Atlantic, Fontenoy turned right around and conquered the Pacific. *Challenging the Pacific: The First Woman to Row the Kon-Tiki Route* describes her expedition, undertaken two years after the Atlantic adventure. Here's hoping we'll see a book about her most recent trip around the Antarctic. Then, for another ocean adventure, turn to *Titanic Adventure: One Woman's True Life Voyage Down to the Legendary Ocean Liner*, by Jennifer Carter. There's no super-human rowing this time, but readers looking for thrills will find plenty here, as Carter describes the expedition she led to salvage the artifacts from the doomed ship.

Greenlaw, Linda

The Hungry Ocean: A Swordboat Captain's Journey. New York: Hyperion, 1999. 265pp. ISBN 9780786864515.

Linda Greenlaw is gritty, resourceful, courageous, and matter-of-fact—and no wonder, as she is the world's only female captain of a swordfish boat. She is also a gifted writer, as we see in *The Hungry Ocean*, her chronicle of one month at sea. Greenlaw and her fishermen have a successful fishing expedition, but not without their share of adventure. The accommodations on the boat are meager, the weather is a continuous threat, on-the-fly health care must suffice for injuries and illness, and infighting among the crew whittles away at everyone's sanity. It's hard to say which is more fascinating, the glimpse into life on a fishing boat or the captivating narrator herself.

Subjects: Fishing • Adventure • Nature • Atlantic Ocean • Memoir

Now Try: Perhaps you remember Greenlaw as a character from *The Perfect Storm: A True Story of Men against the Sea*, by Sebastian Junger. If you haven't read it yet, then brace yourself for a compelling but tragic true story. The good news is that Greenlaw survives a hurricane in 1991; the bad news is that she's the last person to talk to the crew of a boat that did not survive. Or, for much lighter fare, turn to Greenlaw's second book, *The Lobster Chronicles: Life on a Very Small Island*. Readers curious to know more about fishing and boating will find plenty here, alongside Greenlaw's descriptions of her eccentric island neighbors.

Henry, Pat

By the Grace of the Sea: A Woman's Solo Odyssey around the World. Camden, ME: International Marine/McGraw-Hill, 2003. 353pp. ISBN 9780071355278.

Her ex-husband was a louse, her business was bankrupt, her checking account was dwindling, and her self-esteem was plumbing new depths. In a bold move to escape the pressures of normal life and to restore her sense of well-being, the forty-eight-year-old Pat Henry set sail from Acapulco, Mexico—and she didn't come back for another eight years. Told in diary form, this is the story of the oldest woman to circumnavigate the globe. Naturally, the memoir is filled with episodes of adventure and danger, but it also includes more reflective moments. Especially interesting is Henry's growing skill as an artist; during her solo journey, she became good enough at painting coastal scenes that she was able to finance her travels by selling her watercolors. This is perfect reading for the armchair traveler, alternately thrilling and inspiring.

> **Subjects:** Sailing • Travel • Adventure • Solitude • Mental Health • Midlife • Seniors • Art • Artists • Global Perspectives • Diary • Memoir

> **Now Try:** Henry was the oldest woman to sail solo around the world; now meet the youngest, Tania Aebi, in her memoir *Maiden Voyage*. Armed with only the barest knowledge of sailing but a whole lot of courage, this eighteen-year-old woman successfully accepted a challenge from her father to sail the globe. Adventures aplenty pepper her narrative, along with more contemplative passages of spiritual discovery as Aebi comes of age.

Lowman, Margaret

Life in the Treetops: Adventures of a Woman in Field Biology. New Haven, CT: Yale University Press, 1999. 219pp. ISBN 9780300078183.

Margaret Lowman climbs trees for a living. She is a tropical botanist, a scientist who studies the ecosystems of the canopies in jungles around the world. The difficulties of scaling the trees—be it with ropes, cranes, pulleys, or hot air balloons—are all in a day's work for her. So too are confrontations with wildlife, battles with blazing temperatures, and exposure to tropical diseases—and that's to say nothing of the more mundane battles of trying to keep a house and raise kids while trying to succeed in a male-dominated career. Read this for Lowman's captivating account of her daily adventures in the treetops, and for an insider's account of field research in action.

> **Subjects:** Botany • Biology • Science • Labor • Adventure • Nature • Global Perspectives • Memoir

> **Now Try:** Like Lowman, Kathleen Crane is a woman scientist in a male-dominated field who works in fascinating but inhospitable environs around the globe. This time, though, the setting is the water. Crane is an oceanographer whose job has led her to study everything from underwater volcanoes to naval ships to the *Titanic*. Read about her scientific discoveries, her adventures, and her battles with institutional sexism in *Sea Legs: Tales of a Woman Oceanographer*.

McCauley, Lucy, ed.

Women in the Wild: True Stories of Adventure and Connection. Travelers' Tales Guides. San Francisco, CA: Travelers' Tales, 1998 (2004). 307pp. ISBN 9781932361063.

Communing with the great outdoors can take place in distant locales—as when Joanna Greenfield visits Kenya and Israel in "Hyena"—or in the more familiar United States, as seen in Lynne Cox's "The Pelican." Whether foreign or domestic, ordinary or exotic, every essay in McCauley's collection examines the relationship between women and nature. Some of the stories are exhilarating, while others are more introspective, but with perceptive writing by a variety of talented authors, including Annie Dillard, Alice Walker, and Jane Goodall, this anthology speaks to those seeking adventure both externally and internally.

Subjects: Nature • Adventure • Travel • Exercise • Global Perspectives • Essays • Collection • Anthology

Now Try: Another excellent anthology of women's writing about the outdoors comes to us from the editors of the Adventura series. *Gifts of the Wild: A Woman's Book of Adventure* contains essays about women's adventures in the wilderness. At home and across the world, in deserts, oceans, rivers, and mountains—even in the wilderness of urban America—these women explore the breadth of experiences to be found out of doors. Many of the essays emphasize the spiritual nature of outdoor adventuring, which should appeal to readers of *Women in the Wild*.

Nielsen, Jerri, and Maryanne Vollers

Ice Bound: A Doctor's Incredible Battle for Survival at the South Pole. New York: Talk Miramax Books/Hyperion, 2001. 362pp. ISBN 978078-6866847.

Dr. Jerri Nielsen was the only physician for a group scientists stationed in the Antarctic. Between her responsibilities as a doctor and the harsh natural environment, her life was already adventurous—and then she discovered the lump in her breast. A self-administered biopsy revealed it to be cancerous, but rescue was out of the question, because she was located in an area that was only accessible during the summer months. Nielsen's account of her makeshift chemotherapy is riveting, while her descriptions of the natural beauty of Antarctica are both graceful and haunting.

Subjects: Doctors • Breast Cancer • Cancer • Health Care • Adventure • Nature • Antarctica • Memoir

Now Try: For another account of emergency, self-administered medicine, turn to the nail-biting story in Aron Ralston's memoir *Between a Rock and a Hard Place*. Ralston was an experienced hiker, but a freak accident caused a boulder to pin his arm against a cliff wall. For six days Ralston was trapped, and he knew that he would die unless he took drastic action—and so he decided to cut off his arm with the only tool he had available, a cheap knife. This is a gritty, unforgettable story of survival.

Rogers, Susan Fox, ed.

Going Alone: Women's Adventures in the Wild. Emeryville, CA: Seal Press, 2004. 256pp. ISBN 9781580051064.

Most of us never experience the types of radical adventures described in Rogers's anthology. Tracking sharks, following moose, snowshoeing across mountain ranges—for most folks, these stories are the stuff of dreams. Amazingly, the contributors in this collection not only took part in these adventures, but they did it unassisted. Each essay recounts the various authors' spellbinding interactions with life in the rough without anybody to turn to. The captivating, sometimes harrowing escapades of these lone-wolf women make for edge-of-your-seat storytelling, while the reflections and inspirations of the adventurers offer plenty of food for thought.

> **Subjects:** Nature • Adventure • Travel • Exercise • Solitude • Global Perspectives • Essays • Collection • Anthology

> **Now Try:** Rogers has edited several travel anthologies, all of them deeply satisfying. Similar to *Going Alone* is *Solo: On Her Own Adventure*, another collection of essays written by rugged-individual outdoorswomen. Another good choice is her collection *Two in the Wild*; this time, the essays center on women who seek their thrills in pairs. Then turn to a book by one of the contributors to *Going Alone*, adventurer Sherry Simpson. In *The Accidental Explorer*, she recounts her experiences in hiking and backpacking (and nearly drowning) in her home state, Alaska.

Winters, Kelly

Walking Home: A Woman's Pilgrimage on the Appalachian Trail. Los Angeles: Alyson Books, 2001. 333pp. ISBN 9781555836580.

Kelly Winters had always wanted to hike the Appalachian Trail; a breakup with a boyfriend gave her just the motivation she needed to tackle two thousand miles of mountains from Georgia to Maine. Rich details whisk the reader to the trail: there are aching joints, relentless rain showers, unwelcome wildlife encounters, and quirky fellow hikers. The strength of this book, however, is not the physical journey but the emotional discovery and contemplation. Themes of feminism and empowerment are the perfect backdrop for the unexpected romantic affair that unfolds when Winters meets another woman hiker.

> **Subjects:** Backpacking • Hiking • Adventure • Exercise • Travel • Appalachian Trail • Relationships • Lesbian Sexuality • Bisexuality • Queer Sexuality • America • Memoir

> **Now Try:** In her own way, Adrienne Hall discovered a relationship while hiking the Appalachian Trail. Unlike Winters, Hall had the advantage of hiking the entire trail with her romantic partner, but hers was an emotional journey nonetheless; in *A Journey North: One Woman's Story of Hiking the Appalachian Trail*, the boyfriend is merely that: a boyfriend, one whose faults are thrown into sharp relief as they hike the trail together. But their shared adventure, replete with vivid descriptions of the glories and vagaries of long-term backpacking, turns into a sophisticated emotional journey, culminating with a mountaintop marriage proposal.

Adventures in History

Here are women's adventure tales taken from the pages of history.

If you slept through your history classes in high school, it's because your teacher forgot to include the books from the "Adventures in History" section. Pirates and robbers, aviators and mountain climbers, escaped convicts and mad scientists (all women, of course) populate these stories of survival and intrigue from times gone by. And don't forget to turn to Chapter 4, "Women's History" for other tales of derring-do from the past.

Cordingly, David

Seafaring Women: Adventures of Pirate Queens, Female Stowaways, and Sailors' Wives. **(Previously published as** *Women Sailors and Sailors' Women: An Untold Maritime History.***)** New York: Random House Trade Paperbacks, 2007. 286pp. ISBN 9780375758720.

As a veteran maritime museum curator, David Cordingly is familiar with the full breadth and scope of history at sea—including an area typically neglected, the participation of women at sea before the twentieth century. While some people may already be familiar with the pirate lovers Anne Bonny and Mary Read, Cordingly has unearthed a wealth of stories that will likely be new to readers. Wives of whalers, lighthouse keepers, even women who dressed in drag to be able to pass as "real" sailors—a surprising number of women found their way onto water. Told in an entertaining, engaging style, these thrilling tales bring a new perspective to maritime history.

> **Subjects:** Sailing • Pirates • Adventure • Travel • History • Maritime History • Seventeenth Century • Eighteenth Century • Nineteenth Century • Global Perspectives

> **Now Try:** For further chronicles of early seafaring women, try *Hen Frigates: Wives of Merchant Captains Under Sail*, by Joan Druett. Packed with diary excerpts, photos, and illustrations, *Hen Frigates* illuminates the lives of nineteenth-century women who joined their men at sea. Oceanic adventures abound, of course—but so do domestic travails, such as the difficulty of raising children on a boat. Also try Druett's book *Petticoat Whalers: Whaling Wives at Sea, 1820–1920*, filled with illuminating examinations of the surprising number of women who joined their husbands in the quest for whales in the nineteenth century.

Erickson, Carolly

The Girl from Botany Bay. Hoboken, NJ: John Wiley & Sons, 2005. 234pp. ISBN 9780471271406.

In England in 1786, the sentence for robbery was hanging, but twenty-year-old Mary Broad was not sent to the gallows. Instead the authorities sentenced her to a lifetime in Australia, where English women were a rare and valuable commodity. The journey was brutal, with food scarce and diseases rampant—and on top of that, Broad was pregnant and in fact delivered a daughter on the overcrowded ship. Nor did things improve much for Broad in the harsh Australian environment, where convicts and guards alike suffered through too many crop failures and too many deaths. With nothing to lose, Broad and several other convicts stole a boat and escaped to Indonesia, where our unlucky heroine was again captured and sentenced to die. Veteran biographer Erickson vividly recreates the grit and the grime of a convict's life in the bleak eighteenth century, but do not despair: a royal pardon for Broad makes for a happy ending after all of the suffering.

> **Subjects:** Broad, Mary • Incarceration • Immigration • Sailing • Adventure • History • Social History • Eighteenth Century • England • Europe • Australia • Biography

> **Now Try:** Learn more about Mary Broad's contemporaries in *The Floating Brothel: The Extraordinary True Story of an Eighteenth-Century Ship and Its Cargo of Female Convicts.* Author Sian Rees, a descendent of English shipbuilders, tells the story of the more than two hundred women prisoners who were shipped off to Australia aboard a ship called the *Lady Julian.* Drawing on myriad primary sources, Rees artfully describes the sexual politics on the vessel, which permitted a lucky few women to earn privileges and perks from their male captors.

Markham, Beryl

West with the Night. Boston: Houghton Mifflin, 1942 (2002). 293pp. ISBN 97808-65471184.

Beryl Markham wrote "so well, and marvelously well, that I am completely ashamed of myself as a writer," said her friend, Ernest Hemingway. Indeed, Markham's gift with the language—her evocative prose, her stunning descriptions, her contemplative musings—would make her autobiography a worthwhile read, even if she'd never done anything spectacular. But fear not: Markham's life was filled with adventures aplenty. Born in England in 1902 but raised by her father in East Africa, Markham spent her childhood hunting with the natives. For her first career, she trained racehorses; for her second, she flew planes. If there is a pinnacle in this uniformly superb book, it is the description of her successful non-stop, solo, east-to-west flight across the Atlantic in 1932, the first ever undertaken by a woman.

> **Subjects:** Aviation • Horse Racing • Hunting • Adventure • Nature • History • Twentieth Century • Kenya • Africa • Atlantic Ocean • Autobiography

> **Now Try:** A natural companion read for *West with the Night* is the classic *Out of Africa.* Isak Dinesen (the pseudonym of Karen Blixen) beautifully describes her life as the Danish owner of a Kenyan plantation in the first part of the twentieth century. Fans of Markham will be delighted with Dinesen's lyrical prose, and they will be intrigued to rediscover the character of the hunter/pilot Denys Finch-Hatton, friend to Markham and lover to Dinesen. Readers who enjoy reading about women explorers in this time period will also want to try *The Lady and the Panda: The True Adventures of the First American Explorer to Bring Back China's Most Exotic Animal.* With a flair for detail and a keen sense of pace, author Vicki Croke tells the story of the little-known Ruth Harkness, an intrepid American who successfully navigated the wilds of China to capture a panda.

Mazel, David, ed.

Mountaineering Women: Stories by Early Climbers. College Station: Texas A&M University Press, 1994. 184pp. ISBN 9780890966167.

"Perhaps we got tired of being taken in hand by men climbers," writes Emily Kelley, in the excerpt that introduces this lovely collection of sixteen essays, all written by early women climbers. The stories they tell are every bit as compelling and daring as those of their more modern counterparts, taking place on mountain peaks and rock summits around the world. But don't just read this for the adventure; read it for an excellent overview of two hundred years' of women's climbing and for the insight into the struggle—sometimes political, sometimes simply personal—for the right of women to participate in a man's sport.

Subjects: Mountain-climbing • History • Nature • Adventure • Travel • Exercise • Feminism • Nineteenth Century • Twentieth Century • Essays • Collection • Anthology • Global Perspectives • Quick Read

Now Try: While *Mountaineering Women* primarily explored the history of women's mountain climbing through primary sources, Rebecca A. Brown's book *Women on High: Pioneers of Mountaineering* continues the exploration with secondary sources and interpretations. Learn about the peculiar challenges of nineteenth-century women's climbing, both societal (such as unsympathetic men) and practical (such as trying to climb a rock while wearing a corset).

Pilkington, Doris

Rabbit-Proof Fence. **(Previously published as** *Follow the Rabbit-Proof Fence.***)** New York: Hyperion, 2002. 136pp. ISBN 9780786887842.

In 1931, a young aboriginal Australian girl named Molly was kidnapped from her home and forced to live in a compound far from her family. Unfortunately, this kidnapping cannot be blamed on rogue criminals but rather on the Australian government itself, which at the time had a policy of separating aboriginal and mixed-race children from their homes for the purpose of indoctrinating them into white culture. This is the story of the teenaged Molly's escape from the Moore River Native Settlement, undertaken with her sister Daisy and her cousin Gracie. Using the lengthy Rabbit-Proof Fence as their landmark, the three girls successfully navigated the thousand-mile journey back home. Molly's story is told by her own daughter, Doris Pilkington, who uses a carefully crafted, minimalist style to describe the harrowing adventures of the three young girls.

Subjects: Incarceration • Adventure • Race • History • Twentieth Century • Australia • Quick Read

Now Try: Lillian Alling would have sympathized with Molly's homesickness. Like the Australian girls, she missed her home so much that she undertook an incredible journey, on foot, to get back to her native lands. In 1927, she walked from New York City to British Columbia, hoping to walk all the way back to Russia. Alling's compelling story so fascinated the writer Cassandra Pybus that she retraced the Russian woman's steps, albeit from the comfort of a car. Blending her own observations with her research into Alling's journey, Pybus creates a most unusual travelogue in *The Woman Who Walked to Russia: A Writer's Search for a Lost Legend*.

Van Tilburg, JoAnne

Among Stone Giants: The Life of Katherine Routledge and Her Remarkable Expedition to Easter Island. New York: Scribner, 2003. 351pp. ISBN 9780743244800.

In the Victorian era, few women studied in college or pursued professional careers, but Katherine Routledge—intelligent, curious, and adventurous —was not the sort to let social norms interfere with her dreams. Her path eased by her family's fortune, Routledge majored in archaeology at Oxford and then went on to organize a groundbreaking expedition to Easter Island in 1914. Biographer Van Tilburg, herself an expert on Easter Island statues, presents a thoroughly researched examination of Routledge's fascinating life and remarkable scientific contributions. Especially interesting is the author's interpretation of Routledge's schizophrenia, a condition that eventually led to the archeologist's death in an insane asylum.

Subjects: Routledge, Katherine • Archaeology • Science • Easter Island • England • Labor • Adventure • Schizophrenia • History • History of Science • Nineteenth Century • Twentieth Century • Biography

Now Try: Katherine Routledge was not the only woman contributing to the field during the birth of modern archeology in the late nineteenth and early twentieth centuries. Meet twelve other remarkable women scientists in *Breaking Ground: Pioneering Women Archaeologists*, edited by Getzel M. Cohen and Martha Joukowsky. In this painstakingly researched collective biography, twelve scholars study twelve women archaeologists, examining not only their triumph over sexist attitudes but also their scientific contributions, most of which were ignored at the time. The writing style is scholarly, but the jargon is worth the effort for anyone interested in knowing the real story of early archaeology.

Whitaker, Robert

The Mapmaker's Wife: A True Tale of Love, Murder, and Survival in the Amazon. New York: Basic Books, 2004. 352pp. ISBN 9780738208084.

Science journalist Robert Whitaker skillfully blends a variety of nonfiction genres—science writing, travel writing, true romance, true crime—into this fast-paced narrative, but the book is, above all, an adventure story of the highest order. During the Enlightenment in Europe, a group of French scientists decided to test their theories about the contours of the planet by mapping equatorial South America. While on their cartographical mission, one of the Frenchmen, Jean Godin, fell in love with an Ecuadorian girl, Isabel Grameson. The two were married, but turbulent political realities forced the couple apart. Twenty years later, the bride undertook a perilous journey through the rainforest in hopes of a reunion with her long-lost husband. So dangerous was the 3,000-mile trip that all of her companions died, but Isabel persevered until she found Jean.

Subjects: Cartography • Relationships • Adventure • Nature • Travel • Science • History of Science • Eighteenth Century • Ecuador • South America

Now Try: For more about Isabel Grameson Godin, try *The Lost Lady of the Amazon: The Story of Isabela Godin and Her Epic Journey*, by Anthony Smith. Whereas Whitaker juggled several different plotlines in *The Mapmaker's Wife*, Smith focuses primarily on Isabel and her travails as she journeys toward her husband. Then learn about early exploration on two other continents. In Pat Shipman's book *To the Heart of the Nile: Lady Florence Baker and the Exploration of Central Africa*, we meet two African explorers, the Hungarian-born Florence and her English husband Sir Samuel Baker. Shirking the conventions of the nineteenth century, the couple traversed dangerous, uncharted territories while fending off illnesses and hostile natives. And in *North of Unknown: Mina Hubbard's Extraordinary Expedition into the Labrador Wilderness*, author Randall Silvis tells the remarkable story of the early-twentieth-century Canadian explorer Mina Hubbard. Hubbard had no intention of leaving home, but when her husband tragically died on an expedition, Hubbard resolved to continue his work, thereby becoming the first white woman to explore the interior of Labrador.

Espionage and War

Stories of female spies, military battles, and other action related to war populate this section.

Whether they wore a uniform or not, women have always served in wars abroad and at home. In the "Espionage and War" section, you'll meet spies, combatants, reporters, and nurses who have risked their lives to serve their countries. Readers interested in women and war will also want to see the "Women Warriors" section of Chapter 1, the "American Civil War" and "Women and War in the Twentieth Century" sections of Chapter 4, the "Women in the Military" section of Chapter 7, and the "War, Violence, and Peace" section of Chapter 8.

Cornum, Rhonda, and Peter Copeland

She Went to War: The Rhonda Cornum Story. Novato, CA: Presidio, 1992. 203pp. ISBN 9780891414636.

Rhonda Cornum isn't your stereotypical Ivy League doctoral graduate: armed with a Ph.D. in biochemistry, she decided to skip the research-lab scene in favor of becoming a battle surgeon in the Army—and to keep things interesting, this wife and mother decided to learn to fly helicopters, too. When her helicopter was shot down during the Gulf War, a badly injured Cornum—one of only three survivors—was captured by the enemy, finally treated for her wounds, and ultimately released. This is the gripping story of her experience, a fast-paced narrative about a remarkable Army major who survived a harrowing wartime ordeal.

> **Subjects:** Warriors • Doctors • Aviation • Adventure • Mothers • Marriage • Relationships • War • Violence • Labor • History • Military History • Women's History • Twentieth Century • Iraq • Middle East • Asia • Memoir • Quick Read

> **Now Try:** Jump ahead in time from the Gulf War of the 1990s to the Iraq War of the 2000s with *I Am a Soldier, Too: The Jessica Lynch Story*. Journalist Rick Bragg tells the story of another American woman who, like Cornum, is wounded and taken prisoner while serving in the Middle East. This is a riveting survival story, replete with scenes of page-turning suspense and, ultimately, a happy ending.

Fawcett, Denby, et al.

War Torn: The Personal Experiences of Women Reporters in the Vietnam War. New York: Random House, 2002. 287pp. ISBN 9780375757822.

In this remarkable collection of essays, nine women who served as war correspondents in the Vietnam War recall their experiences in the jungles and cities of Southeast Asia. Their memoirs present historically valuable insight into America's involvement in Vietnam between 1966 and 1975, while fleshing out the powerful personal trials of each journalist as she struggled to report the war in brutal, sometimes life-threatening conditions. With lucid, compelling storytelling, the journalists recall their dramatic experiences: being captured by the enemy, seeing their friends die, being wounded by enemy fire—and even, amid the tragedies of war, finding love.

Subjects: War Correspondence • Journalism • Adventure • Labor • War • Vietnam War • Violence • History • American History • Twentieth Century • Vietnam • Asia • Essays • Anthology • Collection • Memoir

Now Try: Relatively few books have been written about the Vietnam War, compared with other American conflicts such as the Civil War and World War II; as such, there is no other book quite like *War Torn*. But for readers seeking the gritty descriptions of wartime Vietnam from a woman's perspective, an excellent choice is *Home before Morning: The Story of an Army Nurse in Vietnam*. With courage and painful honesty, author Lynda Van Devanter recalls the gruesome effects of war, while unflinchingly portraying her own psychological battles as she struggled to save lives.

McIntosh, Elizabeth P.

Sisterhood of Spies: The Women of the OSS. Annapolis, MD: Naval Institute Press, 1998. 282pp. ISBN 9781557505989.

In 1943, the precursor to the Central Intelligence Agency, the Office of Strategic Services, hired a young reporter named Elizabeth P. McIntosh as part of its wartime effort against Japan. Fifty years later, McIntosh wrote this captivating memoir of the women spies she worked with. Backed by excellent research and recounted in gripping prose, *Sisterhood of Spies* presents portraits of the undercover women and their daring escapades. Nazi interrogators are thwarted, enemy lines are breached, bad guys are duped through the judicious removal of clothing. Readers will have heard of a few of the spies, such as Marlene Dietrich, but for the most part, these are completely new stories of women risking their lives in World War II.

Subjects: Espionage • Adventure • Labor • History • American History • World War II • Violence • Twentieth Century • Global Perspectives • Memoir

Now Try: America was not the only Allied nation to employ women in unusual roles. Learn about the women of England's Special Operation Executive in the fast-paced, nail-biting mini-biographies in *The Women Who Lived for Danger: The Agents of the Special Operations Executive*. Author Marcus Binney draws extensively on primary sources to paint a picture of the dangerous exploits of ten women spies. And in France, women participated in the French Resistance in remarkable ways, as seen in Margaret Collins Weitz's *Sisters in the Resistance*. Though Weitz does not focus on spies, she presents a fascinating oral history of some extraordinary women and their unorthodox war efforts.

Moran, Lindsay

Blowing My Cover: My Life As a CIA Spy. New York: G.P. Putnam's Sons, 2005. 295pp. ISBN 9780399152399.

"My father," writes Lindsay Moran, "was certain the CIA would never take me. 'You're not their type,' he said. 'They look for people who've been the president of the Young Republicans Club.'" But it has been Moran's lifelong dream to be a spy, so she sent her résumé to the CIA. Turns out her father was wrong: Moran was hired, and she eagerly embarked on her career, itching to uncover plots and to catch bad guys. Except, as it turned out, spying wasn't nearly as fun as she had expected: her work environment was a mix of mind-numbing bureaucratic work and sexist colleagues, and it put a major crimp in her social life; it's very hard to date someone when you can't tell him what you do for a living. Forget James Bond: this is a memoir of what espionage is *really* like, of the inherent loneliness and thrilling but infrequent adventures, related in Moran's enjoyable, fast-paced style.

Subjects: Espionage • Adventure • Labor • Solitude • Sexual Discrimination • America • Young Adult • Memoir

Now Try: Lindsey Moran ultimately chose to leave the CIA when she became disillusioned; for Valerie Plame Wilson, the decision to leave was far more complicated. In *Fair Game: My Life as a Spy, My Betrayal by the White House*, we learn about Wilson's service as a spy (or at least, those parts that the CIA agreed to let her publish)—and, of course, we learn about the whirlwind of events that led to the discovery of her identity: when her husband published an article critical of the Bush administration, Wilson was outed as a spy as political retaliation. This memoir offers a glimpse into the life of a former spy and an insider view of a Washington, D.C., political scandal.

Norman, Elizabeth M.

We Band of Angels: The Untold Story of American Nurses Trapped on Bataan by the Japanese. New York: Random House, 1999. 327pp. ISBN 9780375502453.

Polo and cocktails, palm groves and badminton: this was the allure of the Philippines in 1941, to say nothing of the eligible young men stationed at Fort Stotsenberg; no wonder that Army and Navy nurses vied for this plush assignment. But when America plunged into World War II, the easy living transformed into a living nightmare for the seventy-seven nurses who were captured by the Japanese. Starvation, bombs, and primitive working conditions threatened their very lives, and yet the nurses continued to care for their patients. Drawing on interviews with twenty of those nurses, historian Norman uncovers the courage and bravery of the captives who continued to care for their patients in the jungles of wartime Bataan.

Subjects: Nurses • Adventure • Health Care • War • Violence • History • Military History • American History • World War II • Philippines • Asia • Twentieth Century

Now Try: Supplement Norman's book with another study of nurse prisoners of war in the Philippines, *All This Hell: U.S. Nurses Imprisoned by the Japanese*. Authors Evelyn Monahan and Rosemary Neidel-Greenlee take a similar approach to uncovering the story of the captives by drawing on interviews, letters, and contemporary news pieces. Then consider the Pacific Theater from the perspective of a man in *My Hitch in Hell: The Bataan Death March*. Like the nurses of *We Band of Angels*, author Lester I. Tenney was captured when the Japanese took the Philippines in 1941. With gripping, vivid imagery, this Army soldier details the horrors of the fall of the Philippines and the brutal years he spent laboring as a prisoner of war.

Ruff, Cheryl Lynn, and K. Sue Roper

Ruff's War: A Navy Nurse on the Frontline in Iraq. Annapolis, MD: Naval Institute Press, 2005. 209pp. ISBN 9781591147398.

"People were shooting at us, trying to kill us," recalls Nurse Ruff in her prologue. "Our young Americans were being shot and killed, and I knew that I was in a situation where I was just as much a target of the enemy as were the combat marines." For six months, these dangerous working conditions became the incessant backdrop for Ruff, a Navy nurse anesthetist on the frontlines of Iraq. With a direct, candid style, she recalls the gritty details of her job, from the scorching hot temperatures to the horrific wounds of the soldiers, civilians, and prisoners of war in her care.

Subjects: Nurses • Adventure • Health Care • War • Violence • History • Military History • War on Terror • Iraq • Middle East • Asia • Twenty-first Century • Memoir

Now Try: Now compare Ruff's experience with that of Richard Jadick, who left his civilian career as a doctor to serve in Iraq. In his memoir *On Call in Hell: A Doctor's Iraq War Story*, Jadick describes the war from the thick of the battle; his discussion of the blood and squalor of combat will appeal to Ruff's fans. Then try *Rule Number Two: Lessons I Learned in a Combat Hospital* by Heidi Squier Kraft. This time, the memoirist is not a medical doctor but a psychologist; hers is a thoughtful account of the psychic trauma of war endured not only by soldiers but the doctors who try to heal them.

Shipman, Pat

Femme Fatale: Love, Lies, and the Unknown Life of Mata Hari. New York: W. Morrow, 2007. 450pp. ISBN 9780060817282.

The most famous spy of World War I probably was not a spy at all—or at least, she wasn't a very good one. Mata Hari did indeed accept a job to spy for Germany, but author Shipman convincingly argues that she only did so because she needed the money, not because she had any intention of gathering intelligence evidence. This naïve decision was a result of Mata Hari's self-absorbed personality, lavish lifestyle, and difficult past, artfully examined and chronicled by Shipman. Mata Hari's subsequent decision to spy for France backfired because she was no good at collecting evidence, despite the variety of powerful men in her intimate circle. Shipman's story is both a fascinating biography and a thought-provoking consideration of Mata Hari's famous spying activities, or lack thereof.

Subjects: Hari, Mata • Espionage • Relationships • Exotic Dancing • History • War • World War I • France • Germany • Europe • Twentieth Century • Biography

Now Try: While Mata Hari's role as a spy is iffy at best, many other women most certainly participated in espionage activities in World War I. In *Female Intelligence: Women and Espionage in the First World War*, historian Tammy M. Proctor uses a variety of primary sources to document the role of female espionage in Britain during the Great War, making for a captivating examination of the surprising number of women who contributed to intelligence work. And for readers who can't get enough of Mata Hari, perhaps try Yannick Murphy's excellent novel *Signed, Mata Hari*; of the many fictionalized versions of Mata Hari's life, this is among the best, with lush descriptions of her life and relationships, but tantalizingly few clues as to whether she really spied or not.

Sorel, Nancy Caldwell

The Women Who Wrote the War. New York: Arcade, 1999 (New York: Perennial, 2000). 458pp. ISBN 9781559704939.

Women were not allowed in combat in World War II, and fewer than one hundred served as war correspondents. But from that small number came a great wealth of journalistic achievements, as painstakingly documented by author Sorel. These intrepid women correspondents risked their lives to report news around the globe, covering events everywhere from Asia to Africa to the heart of Nazi Germany. The accessible, anecdotal snapshots of these women, drawn from interviews with the author and primary sources, illustrate both the perils they endured and the larger picture of World War II history.

Subjects: War Correspondence • Journalism • Writing • Labor • History • War • World War II • Violence • Twentieth Century • American History • Global Perspectives

Now Try: For more stories of women wartime journalists, don't miss *Where the Action Was: Women War Correspondents in World War II* by Penny Colman. Though marketed toward a young adult audience, *Where the Action Was* makes for captivating reading for adults as well as teens. The myriad stunning photographs taken by the camerawomen make this a nice supplement to Sorel's book.

Travel

Definition of Travel

Women's journeys away from home provide the focus to titles in this section.

Travel books speak to the joys of pleasure-seeking, the thrills of exploration, the spiritual and emotional growth that comes from trying a new activity or visiting a new place—and women had nothing to do with any of it for the great part of the history of literature. Traveling is mighty hard when you're pregnant or nursing, as any woman with a small child can tell you today; go back to a time when there were no breast pumps and no folding carriages, and travel became well-nigh impossible.

But women did travel in centuries gone by, though not for the same reasons that men did. While Marco Polo was expanding his business opportunities in China in the thirteenth century, while the Arab Ibn Fadlan was journeying to Russia for political reasons in the year 921, most women stayed home: business and politics were fit for men, not women. When they did travel, it was usually either to follow their men, as when their families emigrated to another country, or, less commonly, to satisfy their own needs, as when they went on religious pilgrimages.

For the most part, then, women were not recording their travel writings until the twentieth century, though some wonderful historical exceptions exist; see, for instance, *Unsuitable for Ladies: An Anthology of Women Travellers*, edited by Jane Robinson, and *Women of Discovery: A Celebration of Intrepid Women Who Explored the World* by Milbry Polk and Mary Tiegreen. But just because women were not recording their travel stories en masse does not mean they were not busy exploring, as we see when Englishwoman Isabella L. Bird describes her jaunt into nineteenth-century Colorado in *A Lady's Life in the Rocky Mountains*. And in more recent years, women have been pursuing travel for reasons of business and politics and pleasure, thank you very much. Elizabeth Gilbert traveled to restore her spirit, as we see in her fantastically popular *Eat, Pray, Love*, while Rita Golden Gelman started traveling and decided not to stop, as we see in *Tales of a Female Nomad*.

Appeal of Travel

The best women's travel books are those that inspire their readers to dream. When we as readers start substituting ourselves for the women in the stories, the authors have done their job. Who, when reading Lois Pryce's *Lois on the Loose*, does not secretly wish to buy a motorcycle and take to the roads? Who wouldn't want to travel abroad after reading Marybeth Bond's *A Woman's Europe*?

Setting, of course, plays a crucial role in travel books. Travel writers usually relate a wealth of setting details—not only those that relate to physical environment but also those details that describe atmosphere, mood, and characters. And the way in which those details are relayed takes on critical importance; readers often care as much about an author's writing style and tone as they do about the settings and activities described in a book. Thus the funny anecdotes in Jennifer Leo's anthology *Sand in My Bra* has a very different feel from Annie Dillard's contemplative musings in *Teaching a Stone to Talk*. And, in women's travel writing, the question "What does it mean to be a woman?" gets careful treatment. We travel to reconnect with ourselves and to explore our identities from the perspective afforded by an unfamiliar setting. The authors' revelations about their inner selves speak to unique experiences of women travelers.

The books in this section indulge in women's wanderlust. Some speak to the joys of shared travel, as we see in Wendy Knight's lovely anthology *Making Connections: Mother-Daughter Travel Adventures*. Others, like the anthology *Go Your Own Way: Women Travel the World Solo*, rejoice in the independent woman traveler. Read these to explore distant locales and to reflect on the spiritual discoveries that travel inspires.

Alpine, Lisa, ed.

Stories of World Travel. Guilford, CT: Globe Pequot Press. 2002. 207pp. ISBN 9780762723775.

> In the foreword of *Stories of World Travel*, the Wild Writing Women, a group of adventurous ladies who meet once a month in a San Francisco bar, confess to a "compulsion" to share their travel experiences; the result is an eclectic, enjoyable collection of travelogues that takes readers across the world. The contributors present a variety of stories: some are primarily introspective, with thought-provoking reflections on race and culture; some focus on adventures such as spelunking and motorbiking; some make the pulse race, as when the essayist is nearly killed in an automobile accident. In all cases, the stories of travel are fascinating and educational, told with captivating details and personal insights.

> **Subjects:** Travel • Adventure • Global Perspectives • Essays • Anthology • Collection • Quick Read

> **Now Try:** Consummate travel writer Marybeth Bond, the editor of several anthologies of women's writing, presents another fine collection in *A Woman's Passion for Travel: True Stories of World Wanderlust*. Foreign cultures come alive in the contributors' essays; the exciting adventures and personal revelations of the women travelers will appeal to those who enjoyed *Stories of World Travel*. And for a taste of what it's *really* like in foreign lands, read the reflections of twenty-two expatriates in *Expat: Women's True Tales of Life Abroad*, edited by Christina Henry De Tessan. Humorous mishaps and comedies of error crop up, of course, but the strength of this collection is depth of insight of the various contributors. Difficult questions of nationality, identity, and global culture will leave readers thinking, whether they are armchair travelers or would-be expatriates themselves.

Bond, Marybeth, ed.

A Woman's Europe: True Stories. San Francisco: Travelers' Tales, 2004. 296pp. ISBN 9781932361032.

In *A Woman's Europe,* meet thirty-seven women as they journey through the Old World. Their essays illuminate destinations throughout Europe, ranging from hotspots such as Paris and Rome to places off the beaten path such as Hungary and Bosnia. The anthology presents a broad range of perspectives: some of the stories are adventurous, while others are more contemplative; some of the experiences are universal (parachuting is fun on any continent, after all), while others are distinctly European (riding with a gondolier on a canal could only happen in Venice). But no matter the story or setting, all of the contributors use sensuous, evocative imagery to conjure the places and people they meet.

Subjects: Travel • Europe • Essays • Anthology • Collection

Now Try: Readers who want to revel in a particular country in Europe will be delighted with three books edited by Camile Cusumano: *France, A Love Story: Women Write about the French Experience; Italy, A Love Story: Women Write about the Italian Experience;* and *Greece, A Love Story: Women Write about the Greek Experience.* Each is an anthology of women's travel writing about the country; with vivid descriptions and lush details, the essayists honor the people, culture, food, and history of the countries they visit. Then try *Without Reservations: The Travels of an Independent Woman.* Alice Steinbach was apprehensive at first, fretting over "every bad outcome—from loss of livelihood to loss of life" that could possibly await her; she had just taken a sabbatical from her newspaper job and opened herself to the scary prospect of traveling on her own for months. But her decision to plunge into solo travel turned out to be an extraordinary, life-changing experience. With her flair for words, the Pulitzer Prize–winning columnist chronicles her experiences in the jewels of Europe, from Milan to Oxford to Paris.

Bond, Marybeth, ed.

A Woman's World: True Stories of World Travel. San Francisco: Travelers' Tales, 2003. 430pp. ISBN 9781885211958.

Just as she did in *A Woman's Europe* (see the previous annotation), editor Marybeth Bond carefully included a wide range of perspectives in this anthology of fifty-five essays by women travelers. Some of the women are born adventurers, seeking thrills at both poles and trekking solo through the Australian Outback; others are introspective thinkers, musing over differences in international cuisine or the sweet joys of unexpected romance. But all of the essays, regardless of the writers' destinations or perspectives, are pleasurable to read, filled with the women's insights into foreign cultures and peoples.

Subjects: Travel • Adventure • Global Perspectives • Essays • Anthology • Collection

Now Try: Continue with Bond's sequel, *A Woman's World Again: True Stories of World Travel,* for even more stories of women traveling around the globe. Then try her collection *A Woman's Asia: True Stories.* This time the focus is on the East, with stories about bathing with elephants in Nepal, seeing a wedding in Turkey, and finding the perfect yurt in China. Or try a different continent entirely: visit North America in *Mexico, A Love Story: Women Write about the Mexican Experience;* edited by Camille Cusumano, this anthology explores the history and people of Mexico through the richly crafted essays of women travelers. And be sure to tour Africa in *Stalking the Wild Dik-Dik: One Woman's Solo Misadventures across Africa*, in which solo traveler Marie Javins blends humor and sensitivity as she discovers new people, new places, and new wildlife.

Caperton, Rosemary, et al., eds.

The Unsavvy Traveler: Women's Comic Tales of Catastrophe. Seattle, WA: Seal Press, 2001 (2006). 283pp. ISBN 9781580050586.

Despite the title, not all of the funny stories in this collection of twenty-eight essays spring from bona fide catastrophe. In some case, the humor is gentle and reflective, as when an American of Indian descent realizes that everybody in China seems to love her eyebrows. But in other stories, the humor is side-splittingly funny in the wake of disaster averted, as when a traveler manages not to suffer death by irritated turkey. In countries across the globe, the contributors describe their encounters with foreign cultures and people, giving armchair travelers plenty to make them smile, laugh, and throw hysterical fits.

> **Subjects:** Travel • Humor • Global Perspectives • Essays • Anthology • Collection

> **Now Try:** If reading about other people's mishaps makes you laugh out loud, don't miss *The Risks of Sunbathing Topless: And Other Funny Stories from the Road*, edited by Kate Chynoweth. Encounter comedies of cultural error and ordinary situations gone humorously awry in this collection of writings by twenty-two women travelers. Snicker at misinterpreted translations and chortle at absurd tourist *faux pas* as the writers traverse the globe; the quick wit and cultural insights of the women will appeal to those who enjoyed the range of comedy presented in *The Unsavvy Traveler*.

Conlon, Faith, Ingrid Emerick, and Christina Henry De Tessan, eds.

Go Your Own Way: Women Travel the World Solo. Emeryville, CA: Seal Press, 2007. 301pp. ISBN 9781580051996.

Meet twenty-three women who relish the challenges of solitary adventuring in *Go Your Own Way*. From Senegal to Denmark, Uzbekistan to Egypt, these writers explore the world with no one but themselves to depend on. This is not to say that companions don't crop up along the way; fleeting encounters, even lasting friendships, pepper the women's journeys. But the strength of this collection stems from the contributors' thirst for independence. Their reflections and moments of self-discovery will stir readers' emotions, while their adventures in distant locales will resonate with adventure seekers.

> **Subjects:** Travel • Adventure • Solitude • Global Perspectives • Essays • Anthology • Collection

> **Now Try:** Editors Conlon, Emerick, and De Tessan have compiled another excellent collection in *A Woman Alone: Travel Tales from around the Globe*. Readers thirsting for more stories of solo women travelers will be rewarded with this anthology which, like *Go Your Own Way*, presents the experiences of women from a variety of backgrounds and perspectives; their globe trekking reflects emotional contemplation as well as spirited thrill seeking. Also try Alice Steinbach's adventurous memoir *Kite Strings of the Southern Cross: A Woman's Travel Odyssey*, in which a solo traveler immerses herself in cultures across the globe, from Fiji to New Zealand to Morocco.

Dillard, Annie

Teaching a Stone to Talk: Expeditions and Encounters. New York: Harper & Row, 1982 (New York: HarperPerennial, 1992). 177pp. ISBN 97800-60150303.

1

A literary heir of Henry David Thoreau, Dillard is a giant among contemporary nature writers. With lyrical, evocative language, she transforms ordinary observations into extraordinary works of literature. Her prose very nearly reads like poetry, making *Teaching a Stone to Talk*, in effect, an extended poetical essay on her love of nature. In a variety of far-flung, exotic locales—including the Arctic Circle, the Galapagos Islands, the Amazon jungles of Ecuador—she contemplates the spirituality of adventures in wilderness. Especially compelling is Dillard's relentless examination of her own complicated Christianity against the backdrop of nature.

2

Subjects: Spirituality • Nature • Adventure • Travel • Christianity • Global Perspectives • Essays • Collection • Quick Read

3

Now Try: Dillard's other books of nature writing are a natural progression; try turning to her most famous work, *Pilgrim at Tinker Creek,* set in the Blue Ridge Mountains. Another likely choice is Henry David Thoreau's *Walden*, an extended reflection on living in nature from the grandfather of American nature writing. See also the works of Anne LaBastille, whose enduring popularity is due in no small part to her ability to speak to both extremes of nature readers. Some read nature books to experience vicariously the thrill of the outdoors; others read nature books to tap into the thought-provoking reflection that the wilderness inspires. LaBastille gracefully captures both the exhilarating adventures and the introspective contemplations of nature in her writing. She has written a wide variety of nature books, but a good place to start is with the first in her <u>Woodswoman</u> series, *Woodswoman: Young Ecologist Meets Challenge Living Alone Adirondack Wilderness*, about her struggles to live by herself in the wilds of New York.

4

5

Gelman, Rita Golden

Tales of a Female Nomad: Living at Large in the World. New York: Crown Publishers, 2001. 311pp. ISBN 9780609606421.

6

It's the year 1985. Gelman is leading a charmed life: she writes children's books for a living, and her husband's job brings her into contact with celebrities and gala events. But her marriage of twenty-plus years is feeling some strain, and she yearns for something different. This memoir is the story of Gelman's remarkable transition from urban sophisticate to career adventurer. Shedding the shackles of the modern American lifestyle, Gelman becomes a bona fide nomad: with no plan, no schedule, no one to answer to, she moves freely to Mexico, Israel, Indonesia, anywhere that strikes her fancy, staying as long as she wants. Meet fascinating people and cultures as Gelman's wanderlust propels her across the world.

7

Subjects: Travel • Adventure • Midlife • Seniors • Immigration • Global Perspectives • Memoir

Now Try: First, her twenty-three-year-old child dies; then her thirty-year marriage dissolves. There's nothing for it, decides Nan Watkins, but to travel. And travel she does: at age sixty, armed with a 'round-the-world plane ticket and a strong case of wanderlust, Watkins traverses the globe. *East Toward Dawn: A Woman's Solo Journey around the World* takes readers to Munich and Zurich, to

8

the Himalayas and the Kathmandu Valley, to Jodhpur and Singapore—no destination is too far off the beaten path as Watkins rediscovers herself and begins the slow process of emotional recovery. Though she did not commit to a lifetime of wandering as Gelman did in *Tales of a Female Nomad*, Watkins's emotional openness and spirit of adventure will strike a chord with readers who admire independent, courageous older women.

Gilbert, Elizabeth

Eat, Pray, Love: One Woman's Search for Everything across Italy, India and Indonesia. New York: Viking, 2006 (London: Bloomsbury, 2007). 334pp. ISBN 978067-0034710.

Gilbert was a woman with a mission: following a dissatisfying lifestyle and an unpleasant divorce, she wanted to recapture her *joie de vivre*—and as the legions of fans of *Eat, Pray, Love* can attest, she did it with style. Purposefully choosing travel destinations that would revitalize her body and soul, Gilbert went hunting for fulfillment. In Italy, she feasted on succulent pizzas and wines; in India, she meditated on mental wellness; in Indonesia, she balanced her appetites for bodily and mental health, while entering into a passionate romance. With an engaging style and captivating story, Gilbert's memoir mixes the best of travel writing and spiritual contemplation.

Subjects: Travel • Adventure • Spirituality • Italy • India • Indonesia • Europe • Asia • Relationships • Memoir

Now Try: Like Gilbert, author Laura Fraser turned to travel to help heal her wounds after a nasty divorce. In her memoir *An Italian Affair*, Fraser describes the people and cultures she encounters as she travels to Milan, London, Morocco, and other enticing locales. But the heart of the story is Fraser's ongoing affair with M., a Frenchman she meets in Ischia, an island in the Bay of Naples. The romance nurtures Fraser's wounded soul in this spiritually intense story of healing, love, travel, and adventure.

Knight, Wendy, ed.

Making Connections: Mother-Daughter Travel Adventures. New York: Seal Press, 2003. 332pp. ISBN 9781580050876.

There's no other book quite like *Making Connections*. It is a fine compilation of travel essays, replete with illuminating descriptions of scenery and cultures across the globe. But it is also a tender exploration of the relationship between mothers and daughters. As any experienced traveler can attest, traveling with company brings the parties into close contact—sometimes in wonderful ways, sometimes with people at each other's throats. The frustrations, joys, irritations, and intimacies of mothers and daughters as they travel together are presented in this unusual collection of travelogues, making it a worthwhile anthology not only for armchair travelers but for anyone who enjoys reading about the ups and downs of mothers and daughters.

Subjects: Relationships • Mothers • Daughters • Parents • Children • Travel • Adventure • Global Perspectives • Essays • Anthology • Collection

Now Try: Editor Wendy Knight knows a good thing when she sees it. Like *Making Connections*, her anthology *Far from Home: Father-Daughter Travel Adventures* collects relationship-themed travelogues, but this time, the traveling companions are fathers and daughters. The essays take the reader to countries around the world while exploring the nuances of father-daughter relationships; the vivid descriptions of locations and of familial rapport make for exciting, emotionally satisfying reading.

Leo, Jennifer, ed.

Sand in My Bra and Other Misadventures: Funny Women Write from the Road. San Francisco: Travelers' Tales, 2003 (2004). 194pp. ISBN 978188-5211927.

Wardrobe malfunctions take on a new dimension when your not-very-snug panties capitulate to gravity in a crowded street in Abu Dhabi. The prospect of being trapped on a flight across the Atlantic without a book to read assumes cosmic importance. These misadventures and other escapades comprise the twenty-eight lighthearted essays of *Sand in My Bra*, an anthology of women's travel writing at its funniest. Alternately absurd, silly, and downright hilarious, the stories of travel adventures gone awry will leave readers laughing aloud.

Subjects: Travel • Humor • Global Perspectives • Essays • Anthology • Collection • Quick Read

Now Try: Readers who giggled their way around the world with *Sand in My Bra* can find even more funny stories by women travelers in three subsequent books edited by Jennifer Leo: *More Sand in My Bra: Funny Women Write from the Road, Again*; *The Thong Also Rises: Further Misadventures from Funny Women on the Road*; and *Whose Panties Are These? More Misadventures from Funny Women on the Road*. If that's not enough, turn to Leo's compilation *What Color Is Your Jockstrap?: Funny Men and Women Write from the Road*, with humorous essays by writers of both sexes who find themselves on hilarious, humiliating, and ridiculous adventures across the globe. And don't miss *Dave Barry's Only Travel Guide You'll Ever Need*, a wickedly funny guide to the perils of travel.

McCauley, Lucy, ed.

The Best Women's Travel Writing 2009: True Stories from around the World. Palo Alto, CA: Travelers' Tales, 2009. 327pp. ISBN 9781932361636 .

Since 2005, *The Best Women's Travel Writing* has offered an annual cornucopia of women's travel writing. No matter the year of publication, the authors are guaranteed to entertain readers with their skilled writing about destinations across the globe; past contributors, for instance, include literary superstars Maya Angelou, Jane Smiley, and Barbara Kingsolver. In this 2009 volume, read travel essays that range from adventurous to humorous to anxious as the writers visit places such as Easter Island, Botswana, Sicily, and Jordan. Be sure to catch up on *The Best Women's Travel Writing* from previous years, and keep watch for future editions.

Subjects: Travel • Global Perspectives • Essays • Anthology • Collection

Now Try: Rough Guides, a leading publisher of destination travel guides, produced a lovely volume of women's travel writing in *Women Travel: A Rough Guide Special*, edited by Natania Jansz. Travel the globe with these intrepid essayists as they journey to a variety of destinations, from popular tourist spots to unlikely, even unintended locales. A particular strength of this collection is the focus on the difficulty of travel; these are not pampered tourists but intrepid adventure seekers, women willing to venture into unfamiliar territory—and willing to write about it in vivid detail when they come home.

Pryce, Lois

Lois on the Loose: One Woman, One Motorcycle, 20,000 Miles across the Americas. New York: Thomas Dunne Books/St. Martin's Press, 2007. 294pp. ISBN 9780312352219.

It is not unusual for adults, faced with midlife ennui, to purchase a motorcycle. But that wasn't enough for Lois Pryce. She quit her job, bought the motorcycle, and biked from Anchorage, Alaska, to Ushuaia, Argentina—nearly 20,000 miles in all. In this enjoyable, accessible story, Pryce narrates the highs and lows of traversing two continents. Her encounters in Mexico and South America are especially entertaining, considering that she doesn't speak Spanish. Pryce's droll British humor; her descriptions of climate, scenery, and people; and her zest for adventure make this a fast-paced, breezy read for the armchair traveler.

Subjects: Motorcycling • Adventure • Travel • Canada • America • Mexico • South America • Memoir

Now Try: Author Karen Larsen did not ride quite as far as Pryce did, but her 15,000-mile trip across America and Canada is still mightily impressive. In *Breaking the Limit: One Woman's Motorcycle Journey through North America,* lifelong motorcycle lover Larsen describes the trip she took during the lull between finishing graduate school and starting a career. Vivid descriptions of people and places, along with critical thinking about gender and motorcycling, make this an entertaining and thought-provoking read.

Travel History

This section features tales about women throughout history and where and how they traveled.

In times past, travel was dangerous for men, and even more dangerous for women, as the title of Jane Robinson's anthology *Unsuitable for Ladies* suggests. Nonetheless, the women discussed in the "Travel History" section defied the norms and set out for parts distant.

Bird, Isabella L.

A Lady's Life in the Rocky Mountains. Norman: University of Oklahoma Press, 1960 (2005). 276pp. ISBN 9780806113289.

When her doctor suggested that she travel for her health, Englishwoman Isabella Bird took the advice to heart. Unabashed at traveling solo in the nineteenth century, she ventured to such destinations as Asia, Hawaii, and Australia. In *A Lady's Life in the Rocky Mountains,* we get a peek at one chapter of her globetrotting, the six months she spent exploring Colorado on horseback. Through a series of letters, we discover Bird's intrepid personality and zest for adventure as she scales mountains, evades grizzly bears, and befriends the locals. With her vivid descriptions and disarming candor, she brings to life the terrain and beauty of the American West in 1873.

Subjects: Travel • Adventure • Nature • History • American History • Nineteenth Century • American Old West • America • Memoir • Letters • Collection

Now Try: For another view of Colorado in the late nineteenth century, try the memoir *Tomboy Bride*. This time the narrator is a married woman, but readers who liked Isabella Bird's independent spirit will find a similar streak of self-reliance in Harriet Fish Backus, who persevered through the hardships of raising a daughter in a rugged mining town. And for a collected biography of pioneering Colorado women, try *The Magnificent Mountain Women: Adventures in the Colorado Rockies*, by Janet Robertson. Based on primary documents and illustrated with maps and photographs, the book documents the exploits of mountain climbers, skiers, sportswomen, and others who sought their thrills in the untamed wilds of Colorado.

David-Neel, Alexandra

My Journey to Lhasa: The Classic Story of the Only Western Woman Who Succeeded in Entering the Forbidden City. London: William Heinemann, 1927 (2005). 310pp. ISBN 9780060596552.

Alexandra David-Neel was not your typical Victorian-era woman. That she traveled extensively was unusual in itself; that she left her husband at home while she went exploring in such places as India, Korea, and Japan is extraordinary. In this travel memoir, you'll follow fifty-five-year-old David-Neel on her most intrepid adventure of all, into the Tibetan city of Lhasa. Lhasa is called "The Forbidden City" for a reason; at the time of David-Neel's journey in 1924 it was strictly off limits to Westerners, most especially *women* Westerners. But David-Neel had done her homework: with her insatiable thirst for learning and her prodigious aptitude for studying religions, this Frenchwoman prepared for her expedition by mastering Tibetan dialects and immersing herself in the study of Buddhism. Then, with the aid of a local and a convincing disguise, David-Neel undertook a perilous four-month journey, ultimately becoming the first Western woman to enter Lhasa. Read this remarkable woman's captivating memoir for a rousing good story and for a glimpse at the cultural and religious life of Tibet in the 1920s as seen through the eyes of a foreigner.

Subjects: Travel • Adventure • Midlife • Buddhism • Religion • History • Women's History • Social History • Twentieth Century • Tibet • Asia • Global Perspectives • Memoir

Now Try: *My Journey to Lhasa* focused primarily on David-Neel's exploits in Tibet; now get the full life story of this intrepid adventurer in *The Secret Lives of Alexandra David-Neel: A Biography of the Explorer of Tibet and Its Forbidden Practices* by Barbara M. Foster and Michael Foster. Drawing on her extensive writings, this fascinating biography fleshes out the personality and character of David-Neel, shedding light on her childhood and marriage and, of course, on her world travels, and on the lessons—religious, mystical, and spiritual—that she learned while abroad.

Polk, Milbry, and Mary Tiegreen

Women of Discovery: A Celebration of Intrepid Women Who Explored the World. New York: C. Potter, 2001. 256pp. ISBN 9780609604809.

"Exploration" takes on a broad, refreshing meaning in the hands of author Polk and illustrator Tiegreen. Physical exploration of the sort undertaken by Freya Stark in the Middle East is included, of course, but so are other types of exploration. Venture into male-dominated professions as Amelia

Earhart takes to the skies; uncover secrets of ancient human history with archaeologist Mary Douglas Nicol Leakey; dare to improve the quality of education for American girls with Almira Hart Phelps. Names familiar and obscure come to life in this collective biography of eighty-four women who, throughout time and across the world, explored new territory, physical and otherwise.

> **Subjects:** Travel • Labor • History • Social History • Women's History • Global Perspectives • Biography • Collection

> **Now Try:** Readers hankering for more stories of intrepid women explorers will be richly rewarded with *Maiden Voyages: Writings of Women Travelers*, edited by Mary Morris. Hear the voices of women from the eighteenth, nineteenth, and twentieth centuries as they grapple with practical obstacles, such as foreign dress and raging rhinoceroses, and more abstract difficulties, such as rampant sexism. The determination of these fifty-one writers to embrace new territory will appeal to readers who found themselves energized by the explorers in *Women of Discovery*.

Robinson, Jane, ed.

Unsuitable for Ladies: An Anthology of Women Travellers. Oxford: Oxford University Press, 1994 (2001). 471pp. ISBN 9780192116819.

Historically speaking, travel has been a male-dominated pursuit: men were the ones to go exploring and adventuring in the course of their business and pleasure activities. Nonetheless, a few intrepid women willingly embraced travel even when their social milieus discouraged it. Editor Robinson has collected the writings of nearly two hundred women travelers, spanning sixteen centuries and six continents. The observations and reflections of these pioneering travelers create a fascinating study in social history; the recurring themes of disapproval for their ventures, as well as the women's determination to overcome sexual barriers, will have readers rooting for their cause.

> **Subjects:** Travel • History • Social History • Women's History • Gender • Sexual Discrimination • Labor • Global Perspectives • Essays • Anthology • Collection

> **Now Try:** Continue adventuring into the past with the writings of women travelers in *No Place for a Lady: Tales of Adventurous Women Travelers*, edited by Barbara Hodgson. The anthology collects travel writings from around the globe from the seventeenth, eighteenth, and nineteenth centuries. Read the book not only for the empowering examples of women overcoming sexual discrimination but for the beautiful illustrations and maps throughout.

Simeti, Mary Taylor

Travels with a Medieval Queen. New York: Farrar, Straus, and Giroux, 2001. 318pp. ISBN 9780374278786.

In the year 1194, the political machinations of Emperor Henry VI abruptly altered the plans of his wife, Constance of Hauteville. Records of her life are scarce, but we may safely assume that she would have preferred to stay in her home in Germany; after all, she was forty years old and pregnant. But Constance made the dangerous trip to Sicily (and gave birth along the way!). Approximately eight hundred years later, American expatriate writer Simeti decided to retrace Constance's route to see if she could understand what the journey had been like. By blending historical fact with fictional speculations about the queen's life, Simeti conjures the hardships of medieval travel and fleshes out the story of a little-known queen.

Subjects: Constance of Hauteville • Travel • Royalty • History • Medieval History • Twelfth Century • Roman Empire • Germany • Italy • Europe • Biography

Now Try: Author Tony Perrottet might not have the same political influence as the leader of the Holy Roman Empire, but like Henry VI, he did convince a pregnant woman to go on a journey. The reason? He wanted his girlfriend's company while he researched his quirky historical travelogue. In *Route 66 A.D.: On the Trail of Ancient Roman Tourists*, Perrottet describes travel as it was like in antiquity. The period he describes predates Constance's journey, and the book is lighter in tone, but readers who enjoy reading about travels from the distant past will be delighted with *Route 66 A.D.*

Where to Go and How to Get There

Practical guides for women who travel populate this list.

We all know that people don't read how-to books for pleasure. Or do they? While it is true that these books do not have a continuous, cover-to-cover narrative with traditional plots, they are more than just dull checklists. There are indeed stories in these books, typically in the form of anecdotes and short profiles. They are, in other words, books that can be read for pleasure. The titles here have been chosen for inclusion here based on their ability to mix practical guidance with engaging personal stories and enjoyable prose.

Bond, Marybeth

50 Best Girlfriends Getaways in North America. Washington, DC: National Geographic, 2007. 263pp. ISBN 9781426200519.

No matter what your whim, expert travel writer Bond knows the place to send you and your girlfriends. Recovering from a breakup? Try visiting Hershey, Pennsylvania, to indulge in chocolate. Just want to have a good time? A trip to Quebec is in order. Chock full of practical advice for planning and enjoying a vacation with the girls, this travel guide highlights trips with a theme, whether you're seeking wild adventures or whether you just want to nurture your friendships. Written in a fun, engaging style, and peppered with anecdotes from satisfied women travelers, *50 Best Girlfriends Getaways in North America* suggests places to go and gives the skinny on female-friendly activities including dining, shopping, pampering, and sporting.

Subjects: Travel • Friendships • Relationships • America • Canada • Mexico • How-to

Now Try: *50 Best Girlfriends Getaways in North America* explores destinations for female travelers. Supplement this with Pam Grout's *Girlfriend Getaways: You Go Girl! And I'll Go, Too*, which focuses not on destination but on attitude. Wherever you travel—even if you go no further than your best friend's house—you'll find advice and inspiration in this empowering, positive celebration of time spent traveling and bonding with women. And for female travel with a Christian perspective, try *Girlfriends' Getaway: A Complete Guide to the Weekend Adventure That Turns Friends into Sisters and Sisters into Friends*, by mother-daughter team Kathleen Laing and Elizabeth Butterfield. With a focus on prayer and spirituality, this guide covers ideas for short, rejuvenating trips and retreats with women friends.

Cantrell, Debra Ann

Changing Course: A Woman's Guide to Choosing the Cruising Life. Camden, ME: International Marine/McGraw-Hill, 2001 (2003). 186pp. ISBN 9780071360876.

> When her husband suggested that it would be fun for them to live on a boat, Cantrell didn't take him seriously: "I was afraid of the water. Terrified, actually." Besides, life on a boat would force Cantrell to seriously alter her career, lifestyle, and identity. Yet this doubter now spends about six months of every year living on their boat. *Changing Course* chronicles this remarkable transition, not only from Cantrell's perspective, but from the viewpoints of more than a hundred other women who were faced with the tough choice of moving to a life on water. The psychological and practical difficulties and rewards of moving to a boat are chronicled in a compassionate, accessible text, along with plenty of good advice for women who have decided to take the plunge.

> **Subjects:** Sailing • Nature • Adventure • Travel • Global Perspectives • Memoir • How-to • Quick Read

> **Now Try:** Another excellent preparation for life on a boat is *The Cruising Woman's Advisor* by Diana Jessie, who understands that, while cruising offers the allure of travel and adventure, it also carries serious concerns. Intended to assuage those concerns and to generate enthusiasm for what many women initially see as a daunting change, the book addresses such topics as safety, hygiene, provisioning, and sailing with children and pets.

Griest, Stephanie Elizondo

100 Places Every Woman Should Go. Palo Alto, CA: Travelers' Tales, 2007. 331pp. ISBN 9781932361476.

> The strength of this travel guide is not its vivid examination of destinations or its evocative description of tourist activities, but rather its thematic approach to women's travel. Nine sections such as "Places of Struggle and Renewal" and "Places of Inspiration and Enlightenment" speak to the breadth of women's experiences around the globe. Interested in women's history? Learn about Joan of Arc in Rouen, France, or visit Catherine the Great's stomping grounds in St. Petersburg, Russia. Need pampering? Visit the home of the Brazilian bikini wax in Rio de Janeiro, or indulge the taste buds in Champagne, France. With an accessible, intelligent style, Griest illuminates one hundred destinations and offers convincing reasons for women to pack their bags and go.

> **Subjects:** Travel • Women's History • Global Perspectives

> **Now Try:** For more recommendations of essential travel destinations for women, check out Teresa Rodriguez Williamson's *Fly Solo: The 50 Best Places on Earth for a Girl to Travel Alone.* Aimed at independent travelers but appropriate for any adventure-seeking woman, this how-to guide recommends fifty places to visit and rates them on various issues such as safety, climate, and tourist activities. Especially helpful is the book's emphasis on social interactions on foreign soil.

Lee, Elaine, ed.

Go Girl!: The Black Woman's Guide to Travel and Adventure. Portland, OR: Eighth Mountain Press, 1997. 364pp. ISBN 9780933377431.

Though marketed toward black women, the travel essays in *Go Girl!* will appeal to any armchair traveler. Vivid writing from luminaries such as Maya Angelou and Alice Walker transport the reader to a variety of destinations, from Paris to Beijing, Ghana to Egypt, Jamaica to Peru. View the world from the perspective of fifty-two black women as they reflect on different cultures and pursue adventures in foreign territory. Then turn to the final chapter, "Creating and Sustaining a Trip Around the World," for practical advice for black women travelers.

Subjects: Travel • African Americans • Race • Global Perspectives • Essays • Anthology • Collection • How-to

Now Try: While *Go Girl!* featured only one chapter dedicated to the practicalities of world travel, *The African American Travel Guide to Hot, Exotic and Fun-Filled Places* offers extensive information for planning the trip. Author Jon Haggins details preparations and precautions for aspiring travelers, while illuminating popular destinations such as West Africa, South America, and other locales with flourishing black cultures. Pair it with *Gutsy Women: More Travel Tips and Wisdom for the Road*, written by veteran travel writer Marybeth Bond; loaded with topics ranging from hygiene to traveling with children to romance abroad, this is an essential, comprehensive how-to book for women travelers of any race.

Zepatos, Thalia

A Journey of One's Own: Uncommon Advice for the Independent Woman Traveler. Portland, OR: Eighth Mountain Press, 1992 (2003). 342pp. ISBN 9780933377202.

You want to crawl through ancient Egyptian tombs. Your husband/best gal pal/new fling wants to take in opera in Vienna. Do you surrender your plans? Compromise? Go your own way? Actually—though the title suggests otherwise—*A Journey of One's Own* gives good reasons for all of those approaches. Blending questionnaires, excellent how-to chapters, and insightful thought-pieces from experienced women travelers, author Zepatos covers all aspects of women's travel, in chapters such as "Traveling Alone or with Others?," "Creating Your Own Journey," and "Safe Passage." The accessible, sensible writing will guide women through the ins and outs of fun, safe travel, whether they travel solo or with others.

Subjects: Travel • Solitude • Global Perspectives • How-to

Now Try: Still not convinced you can pull off a solo trip? Let Beth Whitman nudge you along in *Wanderlust and Lipstick: The Essential Guide for Women Traveling Solo*. Chapters such as "Getting beyond the Excuses" and "Mapping Out the Details," written in a conversational, easy-to-understand style, will motivate the hesitant would-be traveler. Follow this with *Safety and Security for Women Who Travel*, in which Sheila Swan and Peter Laufer delve into the nitty-gritty details of safe travel, including such topics as finding secure lodgings, avoiding pickpockets, and keeping a cool head when things go wrong.

Consider Starting With ...

Plunge into Adventure and Travel with some of the most riveting, evocative titles in the genre:

Blum, Arlene. *Annapurna: A Woman's Place*.

David-Neel, Alexandra. *My Journey to Lhasa: The Classic Story of the Only Western Woman Who Succeeded in Entering the Forbidden City*.

Dillard, Annie. *Teaching a Stone to Talk: Expeditions and Encounters*.

Gilbert, Elizabeth. *Eat, Pray, Love: One Woman's Search for Everything across Italy, India and Indonesia*.

Markham, Beryl. *West with the Night*.

Moran, Lindsay. *Blowing My Cover: My Life As a CIA Spy*.

Fiction Read-Alikes

- **Bujold, Lois McMaster.** Interplanetary adventure and tumultuous politics make for a gripping, page-turning read in *Shards of Honor*, part of the Vorkosigan series. Meet Cordelia Naismith, a military career woman and captain of a spaceship who is surprised to find herself falling in love with an enemy when she is marooned on an alien planet.

- **Carey, Jacqueline.** Phèdre nó Delaunay is the captivating heroine of Kushiel's Legacy, a series that deftly blends alternate history with fantasy. Phèdre's job as a spy lands her in any number of adventures, from political intrigues to cloak-and-dagger assassinations to sexual exploits. Read the series in order, starting with *Kushiel's Dart*.

- **Deaver, Jeffery.** As the title of the series suggests, the protagonist of the Lincoln Rhyme series is a man—but every bit as compelling as the quadriplegic criminologist is his girlfriend, Amelia Sachs, a policewoman who uses her considerable intelligence to hunt for criminals. Serial killers, bomb threats, and dangerous environments regularly threaten Sachs; meet her in the first of the series, *The Bone Collector*. Then meet another of Deaver's strong female leads in *The Sleeping Doll*, the first of the Kathryn Dance series, starring an interrogation specialist.

- **Franklin, Ariana.** The setting is twelfth-century Cambridge, and with four Christian children found murdered, the Jews stand accused. In *Mistress of the Art of Death*, a woman medical examiner applies a nascent form of forensic anthropology to catch the murderer; this is a thrilling mystery, with fascinating period details, multifaceted characters, and some thought-provoking observations on gender. Continue with the sequel, *The Serpent's Tale*, in which our heroine, now a new mother, negotiates court politics to find a royal assassin.

- **Gilman, Dorothy.** As a CIA spy, Mrs. Pollifax regularly travels to such locales as Albania, Switzerland, and China for her dangerous assignments. She also happens to be a widowed grandmother. Discover the lighthearted thrills and adventures of the Mrs. Pollifax mysteries with the first in the series, *The Unexpected Mrs. Pollifax*.

- **Moore, Alan.** Despite what you'd expect from the title, the ringleader of the graphic novel *The League of Extraordinary Gentlemen* is Mina Murray, last seen fighting off Count Dracula. Follow Mina and her companions, all drawn from nineteenth-century pop culture, on a series of wild adventures in this cerebral, energetic foray into Victorian England. Subsequent League books follow the same cast of characters in various historical eras.

- **Pratchett, Terry.** Seen from one angle, the Discworld books are a series of fantasy novels; from another, they are a brilliant series of social satires that just happen to be populated by dwarves, vampires, and the like. Dive into Discworld with *Monstrous Regiment*, starring a woman who cross-dresses so that she can join the military; with keen humor and biting insight, the novel considers the role of women in combat.

- **Weber, David.** As an officer in the space navy, Honor Harrington is a math whiz and a navigational genius who regularly participates in spine-tingling intergalactic battles; meet her in *On Basilisk Station*, the first of the Honor Harrington series.

Chapter 6

Feminism and Activism

Never doubt that a small group of thoughtful, committed individuals can change the world; indeed, it's the only thing that ever has.

—*Margaret Mead*

Definition

> According to Wikipedia, feminism is "the belief in the right of women to have political, social, and economic equality with men." Activism is the act of promoting a social cause.

Feminism is difficult to define because there is no universal dogma for feminists. Wikipedia defines feminism as "the belief in the right of women to have political, social, and economic equality with men." Another way to describe feminism is as a "pro-woman" philosphy. But what does it mean to be pro-woman? In fact, feminists differ in their opinions, especially about issues such as birth control, abortion, pornography, and prostitution.

Activism—the act of promoting a social cause—may be somewhat easier to understand, although opinions differ as to the boundaries. Can you call yourself an activist if you write one letter to the editor or march in one protest, or must you fully commit yourself to the cause over a long period of time?

As slippery as these categories are, a few general observations can be made about them. Books written by feminists about feminism are fair game; so, too, are books that discuss activism, especially with regard to social issues that concern women. These are books that speak to feminists and feminism, in times both past and present, and these are books that tell us *why* we should care and *how* we can do it. These are books that question cultural assumptions and the status quo, break down artificial boundaries, and expand what it means to be a woman. Read them, reflect on them, study them. Some will make you happy; some will make you angry; and some just might stir you to march in the streets. Get your comfortable shoes ready, just in case.

Appeal

You'll find a wide array of titles in this chapter—from practical handbooks, mind-bending monologues, and outright rants to reflective treatises, somber tributes, and scholarly investigations. And just as there are many types of books here, we read them for a variety of reasons.

We read Feminism and Activism books for *inspiration*, to meet women from our collective past and present who have fought, and continue to fight, for women's equality, be it in the home, in the workplace, in the government, in the world.

We read Feminism and Activism books for *affirmation*, to rejoice in the qualities that make us unique: our bodies, our rituals, our thoughts, our actions.

We read Feminism and Activism books for *education*, to study the advances made by our foremothers, to learn about the social struggles still faced by women across the world, in our country, in our backyards.

We read Feminism and Activism books for *motivation*, for the powerful and awesome reminder that advances in women's rights have been made, and continue to be made, by women just like us—that it is our duty and privilege to join in their struggles.

For all these reasons and more, we turn to Feminism and Activism. Plot and character can play crucial roles: When we can relive the struggles from the point of view of the characters, when we can participate in the fight for suffrage, for equal pay, for the presidency, the story becomes our own. Tone and writing style are often important appeal factors, too: sometimes we want reflective, thought-provoking, scholarly studies; other times we want edgy, fast-paced, angry books to whip us out of our comfort zones.

Organization

The first section of this chapter, "Feminism," features two subsections. The "History of Feminism" subsection explores the history of feminism and the women's movement, while the "Feminist Theory, Concepts, and Beliefs" subsection presents a range of feminist ideas from the past and present. Note that each title includes at least one of three subject headings: "First-wave Feminism" discusses the first wave of feminism, which occurred in the nineteenth and early twentieth centuries; "Second-wave Feminism" focuses on the second wave of feminism, which occurred in the 1960s and '70s; and "Third-wave Feminism" discusses feminism as it has been practiced from the 1990s through the present. The first section of this chapter covers all three waves of feminism.

The second section, "Activism," features books about social causes that are not necessarily feminist but that nonetheless hold broad interest among women. Some of them are how-to guides, while others are more investigative in approach.

Feminism

*Like Broadway, the novel, and God, feminism has been declared
dead many times.*

—Katha Pollitt

For those of you who haven't studied feminism in depth, a short history lesson is in order: among scholars of feminism and women's studies, the history of feminism is divided into three main waves. The first wave of feminism started with the Seneca Falls convention of 1848 and ended in 1920 with the passage of the twentieth amendment to the United States Constitution, which guaranteed women the right to vote. This first wave is almost synonymous with women's suffrage—a fact that continues to both please and embarrass feminists to this day. The first-wavers fought long and hard for women's right to vote, for which we can be eternally thankful. Unfortunately, they almost completely ignored other social issues of the time, notably race and class; the first wave started, of course, in the slavery era. It was chiefly a movement of white, educated, financially stable women; the needs of women of color and of limited financial means were largely ignored.

During the second wave of feminism, which took place mainly during the 1960s and '70s, women in the margins—women of color, queer women, poor women—began to find their voices, though their needs continued to be shunted to the side; like the preceding first wave, the second-wave agenda was concerned not so much with race or class, but with mainstream (read: "upper middle class white") issues such as birth control and equal wages.

The final wave of feminism had its humble beginnings in the 1980s, though it was in the 1990s that it really took off. In June 1998, a cover of *Time* magazine asked "Is Feminism Dead?" No, no, a thousand times no. Feminism today is alive and well, and concerned with more issues than ever before: race, class, sex, sexual orientation, globalization, the environment, transsexuality, fertility, politics, violence against women, women with disabilities—the list goes on.

With this history lesson in mind, look to the two sections that follow—"History of Feminism," and "Feminist Theory, Concepts, and Beliefs"—to explore feminist thought, and look for the "First-wave Feminism," "Second-wave Feminism," and "Third-wave Feminism" subject headings to determine each book's focus.

History of Feminism

The "History of Feminism" takes us through the evolution of feminism, from the battles for women's suffrage through the various feminist issues of modern times.

You'll find titles on each phase of women's history in this section. The books excel at recreating the social milieus of ages past, and they provoke readers to think about social conditions in their own lives. If you're hungry for more titles on this topic, check for "feminism" in the subject index—there are books about feminism and prominent feminists in other chapters as well.

Baxandall, Rosalyn Fraad, and Linda Gordon, eds.

Dear Sisters: Dispatches from the Women's Liberation Movement. New York: Basic Books, 2000. 322pp. ISBN 9780465070459.

The glory years of the second wave of feminism, 1968–1977, come alive in this exemplary collection of primary historical documents, culled from a dizzying array of sources by historians Baxandall and Gordon. There are essays, as one would expect, but also such various media as song lyrics, leaflets, even cartoons. Contributors include such well-known names as Betty Dodson, Susan Brownmiller, and Adrienne Rich, along with individuals and organizations that have largely been forgotten. Arranged in chapters that cover the gamut of second-wave feminism, from "Feminist Theory" to "Reproductive Rights" to "Objectification, Harassment, Rights," these documents present a vivid, visceral history of the women's liberation movement.

> **Subjects:** Second-wave Feminism • Feminism • Activism • Media • History • Women's History • Social History • Twentieth Century • Collection • Anthology

> **Now Try:** Continue delving into the history of women's liberation, this time with memoirs from the feminists who were there. In *The Feminist Memoir Project: Voices from Women's Liberation*, editors Rachel Blau DuPlessis and Ann Barr Snitow bring together the recollections of women who were actively involved with feminism in the 1960s and '70s. This is a fascinating collection featuring names both familiar and new.

Clift, Eleanor

Founding Sisters and the Nineteenth Amendment. Hoboken, NJ: John Wiley & Sons, 2003. 213pp. ISBN 9780471426127.

Judging from the widespread voter apathy at the polls in all but the high-profile presidential election years, women often take their voting rights for granted. But in this lively, gripping history, *Newsweek* editor Clift shows that women's suffrage was an intense, hotly debated issue for seventy-two long years. Starting with the Seneca Falls Convention of 1848 and going through the down-to-the-wire fight for the nineteenth amendment in 1920, Clift unveils the tumultuous story of the national movement toward women's suffrage. It was no simple matter of men versus women: some enlightened gentlemen did favor the issue, and a surprising number of women opposed it (though obviously there was no way for them to vote against it). In this page-turning social history, meet the stellar cast of historical characters who fought for and against women's suffrage and discover the political intrigues that culminated in the passage of the amendment that guaranteed women the right to vote.

> **Subjects:** First-wave Feminism • Suffrage • Feminism • Activism • Politics • Law • History • Women's History • Social History • American History • Nineteenth Century • Twentieth Century • America

> **Now Try:** Dig deeper into the history of the fight for suffrage in *Votes for Women: The Struggle for Suffrage Revisited*, edited by Jean H. Baker. In essays such as "Pioneers at the

Polls: Woman Suffrage in the West" and "Female Opposition: The Anti-Suf-frage Campaign," twelve scholars consider the various themes, politics, and histories of the suffrage movement. The book is more academic in tone than *Founding Sisters and the Nineteenth Amendment*, but it is well worth the read for those who want to further explore the complicated facets behind the struggle for the right to vote.

Freedman, Estelle B.

No Turning Back: The History of Feminism and the Future of Women. New York: Ballantine Books, 2002. 446pp. ISBN 9780345450548.

If you've ever taken a Women's Studies class, you'll know that there is no such thing as feminism, not really: the more accurate word is *feminisms*, plural. The complicated, divergent, dizzying array of feminism in all its various forms can be overwhelming, but fortunately, historian Freedman has written a succinct synthesis of the many conflicting histories of the feminisms that we know today. Scholarly and thoroughly researched but easily accessible for the lay reader, this vibrant social history considers feminism and all its attendant themes, including race, class, labor, and family. But this is more than just a history: with piercing insight and thoughtful reflections, Freedman shows how feminisms are still relevant today and will continue to affect us in the future.

> **Subjects:** First-wave Feminism • Second-wave Feminism • Third-wave Feminism • History • Women's History • Gender • Sexual Discrimination • Class • Labor • Race • Work/Life Balance • Politics • Sexuality • Violence

> **Now Try:** Supplement *No Turning Back* with, June Hannam's *Feminism*. Written in an accessible, straightforward style, this overview considers the myriad forms of feminism as they have developed over two centuries and across the globe. Historical and contemporary movements—localized, national, and international—are discussed To focus on the history of feminism in America, try Rory Cooke Dicker's *A History of U.S. Feminisms*, which offers a succinct overview of the first, second, and third waves of feminism.

Rosen, Ruth

The World Split Open: How the Modern Women's Movement Changed America. New York: Viking, 2000. 446pp. ISBN 9780670814626.

Readers looking for a primer on the second wave of feminism will find no better introduction than this fabulous social history. Drawing on a variety of primary sources both scholarly and popular, historian Rosen presents a thorough overview of the American climate of the 1960s and '70s, illuminating the sweeping social changes made by feminists in the personal lives and on the political level. Rosen, who was herself an activist during the second wave, is well suited to present this engaging history; she deftly weaves her own memoir with the stories of other feminists, famous and otherwise. Discover the key figures of post–World War II feminism and the highlights of the movement, both good and bad, in this compelling historical survey.

> **Subjects:** Second-wave Feminism • Feminism • Activism • Politics • Sexual Discrimination • History • Women's History • Social History • American History • Twentieth Century • America • Memoir

Now Try: For another excellent chronology of the second wave of feminism, turn to *Moving the Mountain: The Women's Movement in America since 1960*. Like Rosen, journalist Flora Davis researched her topic by interviewing second-wave activists and studying primary documents. The result is a scholarly but thoroughly readable study of both the triumphs and defeats of the movement, bolstered by an analysis of feminism in the 1980s and '90s.

Schneir, Miriam, ed.

Feminism: The Essential Historical Writings. New York: Random House, 1972. 360pp. ISBN 9780394471914.

In this excellent anthology of feminist writings, editor Schneir has collected a variety of pieces—including essays, letters, journal entries, even some fiction—that represent the very best feminist writing from the time of the American Revolution through the first part of the twentieth century. All the big names are here, from Sojourner Truth to Charlotte Perkins Gilman to Lucretia Mott. Feminist men are included, too, with pieces from Frederick Douglass, John Stuart Mill, and Henrik Ibsen. The contributors are each introduced with a brief biographical sketch that gives historical and social context to their writing, making this an excellent overview of feminism as a movement and the classic writings that have defined it.

> **Subjects:** First-wave Feminism • History • Women's History • Eighteenth Century • Nineteenth Century • Twentieth Century • Letters • Essays • Memoir • Biography • Collection • Anthology

> **Now Try:** Though its focus is not on feminist writings per se, readers will find many pieces on feminism and gender in *The Feminist Companion to Literature in English: Women Writers from the Middle Ages to the Present*, by Virginia Blain, Patricia Clements, and Isobel Grundy. This time, the focus is not on the writings of women authors but rather on their biographies; 135 of the most influential women are considered in depth, with detailed literary and biographical analyses, and more than two thousand other writers are discussed in brief.

Schneir, Miriam, ed.

Feminism in Our Time: The Essential Writings, World War II to the Present. New York: Vintage Books, 1994. 503pp. ISBN 9780679745082.

Whereas *Feminism: The Essential Historical Writings* (see the previous annotation) collects writing from the eighteenth, nineteenth, and early twentieth century, Schneir's follow-up anthology considers the cornucopia of feminist writings of roughly the second half of the twentieth century. As in the first anthology, Schneir gives historical and biographical context to the writers, who include such luminaries as Sylvia Plath, Audre Lorde, and Anne Sexton. The collected pieces—including essays, political thought-pieces, court decisions, poems, and fiction—may be read individually, or they may be read collectively for an overview of a the varieties of feminist thought in the latter half of the twentieth century.

> **Subjects:** Second-wave Feminism • Third-wave Feminism • History • Women's History • Twentieth Century • Essays • Memoir • Biography • Collection • Anthology

> **Now Try:** Schneir's collection does a fine job of illuminating the history of feminist thought; now contemplate the feminism of the future with *What Are We Fighting for?: Sex, Race, Class, and the Future of Feminism* by Joanna Russ. With keen insight and appreciation for her topic, Russ considers the state of contemporary feminism and speculates on where it may go and how it may get there. Hers is an energetic brand of feminism, meant to enthuse women who have become complacent about feminist issues.

Siegel, Deborah

Sisterhood, Interrupted: From Radical Women to Grrls Gone Wild. New York: Palgrave Macmillan, 2007. 224pp. ISBN 9781403982049.

It is impossible to comprehend modern feminism without a thorough understanding of second-wave feminism—and in this magnificent social history, scholar Siegel provides just that. In her readable, engaging style, author Siegel first provides a succinct overview of the major themes of the feminist movement in the 1960s and '70s, followed by a discussion of the contemporary feminist movement. But this is far more than a history text; by emphasizing the generational tensions between second-wave feminist foremothers and their third-wave feminist daughters, Siegel paints a vivid picture of both the past and the present, illuminating where we are, where we've been, and where we're going.

> **Subjects:** Second-wave Feminism • Third-wave Feminism • Feminism • Activism • History • Women's History • Social History • Twentieth Century • Twenty-first Century • Quick Read

> **Now Try:** For another engrossing examination of feminism since the 1960s, turn to *Tidal Wave: How Women Changed America at Century's End.* Women's history professor Sara M. Evans offers a detailed, thoroughly researched study of the changing nature of feminism over four decades; written in a scholarly but engaging style, this is a fascinating overview of the organizations, individuals, and strategies that shaped, and continue to shape, American feminism.

Feminist Theory, Concepts, and Beliefs

> Here are titles that probe into the intellectual underpinnings of feminism.

With eighteen titles, "Feminist Theory, Concepts, and Beliefs" is a large section. It's no surprise, because feminism covers a broad range of ideas. This section represents a survey of these various perspectives, from conservative feminists such as Katie Roiphe (see her book *The Morning After*) to radical feminists such as Andrea Dworkin (see *Letters from a War Zone*), from feminists with a niche perspective (try Ana Castillo's *Massacre of the Dreamers*) to feminists with a broad appeal (look to bell hooks's *Feminism Is for Everybody*).

Baumgardner, Jennifer

Look Both Ways: Bisexual Politics. New York: Farrar, Straus and Giroux, 2007. 244pp. ISBN 9780374190040.

Bisexuality: it's the black sheep of sexual orientation. Bisexuals fit in neither with their straight friends nor with the gay crowd. In an attempt to understand where and how bisexuals can find their niche in society, feminist activist Baumgardner presents this eye-opening, provocative examination of bisexual politics and the elusive, ill-defined bisexual lifestyle. Arguing that bisexual women can find answers to their identity within the larger scope of feminism, Baumgardner considers such famous bisexual women as Rebecca Walker, Ani DiFranco, and Anne Heche, as well as her own experiences as a bisexual single mother, in her quest to understand what it means to be a bisexual woman.

> **Subjects:** Bisexuality • Queer Sexuality • Sexuality • Third-wave Feminism • Sociology • Politics • Twenty- first Century • Memoir

> **Now Try:** Learn more about the experience of bisexuals in *Bi America: Myths, Truths, and Struggles of an Invisible Community*, which focuses on both men and women bisexuals. Drawing on anecdotes and his own thought-provoking insights, author William E. Burleson explores the murky territory of the bisexual community in America, uncovering the unique struggles that bisexuals face as they work to forge their identities in a world that doesn't know how to understand them.

Beauvoir, Simone de

The Second Sex. New York: Knopf, 1953 (1997). 746pp. ISBN 9780099744214.

Originally written in French in 1949, the publication of Beauvoir's groundbreaking book caused considerable consternation among traditionalists—and caused relief among those women who were craving an honest discussion of womanhood. In this classic feminist text, Beauvoir considers the definition of sex, gender, and womanhood by examining women's roles throughout history, concluding that "One is not born a woman, one becomes one." This, the most famous line of the book, may not have ruffled too many feathers—but Beauvoir certainly upset a lot of readers with her suggestion that women seek worthwhile employment and disentangle themselves from marriage and motherhood. Though the prose is scholarly and somewhat haltingly translated from the French, this is essential reading for anyone curious about the origins of feminism as we know it today.

> **Subjects:** First-wave Feminism • Gender • Sexual Discrimination • Marriage • Labor • Sociology • History • Women's History • Twentieth Century

> **Now Try:** *The Second Sex* is generally recognized as the first major feminist work of the twentieth century, but for a true understanding of the historical context of feminism, read Mary Wollstonecraft's *A Vindication of the Rights of Woman*. First published in 1792, this essay is dated in style but fresh in thought. Over 150 years before Beauvoir wrote *The Second Sex*, Wollstonecraft criticized the patriarchal demand that women sacrifice intellect and happiness in order to please men.

Castillo, Ana

Massacre of the Dreamers: Essays on Xicanisma. Albuquerque: University of New Mexico Press, 1994. 238pp. ISBN 9780826315540.

What does it mean to be a Chicana, a woman of Mexican descent? "I am commonly perceived as a foreigner everywhere I go, including in the United States and Mexico," writes novelist and poet Castillo. "This international perception is based on my color and features. I am neither black nor white. I am not light skinned and cannot be mistaken for 'white': because my hair is so straight I cannot be mistaken for 'black.'" In this thought-provoking collection of essays, Castillo explores her racial and feminist identity, recasting Chicana feminism into a bolder form of feminism, Xicanisma. This is an erudite, sophisticated collection of thoughts on such complicated themes as spirituality, machismo, and activism, but Castillo's vivid writing and compelling insight make the book accessible for readers interested in the intersection of Chicana identity and feminism.

Subjects: Xicanisma • Latinas • Race • Feminism • Third-wave Feminism • Twentieth Century • Essays • Collection

Now Try: Hear now from other Xicanisma/Chicana feminist voices in *Chicana Feminisms: A Critical Reader*, edited by Gabriela F. Arredondo et al. As with *Massacre of the Dreamers*, this is a scholarly but accessible collection of essays about feminist issues, seen through the lens of Chicana identity. Then turn to *Voicing Chicana Feminisms: Young Women Speak Out on Sexuality and Identity*, edited by Aída Hurtado, for another eye-opening look at race, sex, identity, and feminism.

Daly, Mary

Gyn/Ecology: The Metaethics of Radical Feminism. Boston: Beacon Press, 1978 (1991). 485pp. ISBN 9780807015100.

There is nothing easy about the writings of Mary Daly. Her subject matter invariably provokes deep thought and uneasy conclusions. Her rhetoric elicits strong emotions, both positive and negative. Even her prose style is challenging—but those readers willing to embrace these challenges will be rewarded with a powerful, eloquent discussion of feminist theory. In *Gyn/Ecology*, a classic text of radical feminism, Daly explores topics such as the gendered nature of language and the patriarchy of the Christian church. In no sense is this an easy read, but it is essential for anyone who wants to understand the principles of radical feminism.

Subjects: Third-wave Feminism • Sociology • Religion • Twentieth Century • Gender

Now Try: Before proceeding to the next read, answer the Goldilocks questions: was Daly's feminist porridge too hot, too cold, or just right? If Daly's politics and style overwhelmed you, ease up a bit with *Deborah, Golda, and Me: Being Female and Jewish in America*. Feminist Letty Cottin Pogrebin addresses one of Daly's favorite topics, the influence of patriarchal religion, but she does so in a more accessible, less radical way. If you want a writer similar to Daly in style and politics, try the works of Noam Chomsky. He is perhaps best known as a political activist, but he got his start by developing transformational grammar, an approach to understanding syntax and language usage that profoundly deviates from traditional ways of learning grammar. Readers who agree with Daly's views on the importance of language will be intrigued by Chomsky's perspectives; perhaps start with his book *Syntactic Structures*. And those readers who want someone even more radical and more difficult than Daly should try Judith Butler. Begin with her classic text *Gender Trouble: Feminism and the Subversion of Identity*, about gender, politics, and culture.

Davis, Angela Y.

Women, Race, & Class. New York: Random House, 1981. 271pp. ISBN 9780394510392.

The activists of the first and second waves of feminism fought to make historic changes for women's rights, but too often their focus was narrow: Their gains benefited economically privileged white women, with the needs of poor women and women of color taking the back burner. In this classic feminist text, Davis—an icon both of the Civil Rights and women's rights movements—reexamines the history of feminism with an eye toward race and class. The racism and sexism she exposes is unsettling; even

as well-to-do women were fighting for their own rights, they often deliberately ignored their less privileged sisters. Read this to gain a fuller understanding of the
history of feminism in America.

> **Subjects:** Second-wave Feminism • Feminism • African Americans • Race • Class •
> History • Women's History • Social History • American History • America

> **Now Try:** Continue with Davis's *Women, Culture & Politics*; once again she delves into
> meaty themes of feminism, race, and class, though this time the focus is less on history and
> more on contemporary issues. Then continue with *Sisters in the Struggle: African American
> Women in the Civil Rights-Black Power Movement*, edited by Bettye Collier-Thomas and V. P.
> Franklin; this excellent collection of essays profiles the black women activists and feminists
> who shaped the Civil Rights and Black Power movements.

Dworkin, Andrea

Letters from a War Zone: Writings, 1976–1989. New York: E. P. Dutton, 1989.
337pp. ISBN 9781556521850.

She was angry and strong, passionate and powerful, arrogant and confident: this
is why people loved her, and why people hated her. A women's rights activist
who gained national prominence during the second wave of feminism, Dworkin
was disliked even by some of her feminist sisters, to say nothing of mainstream
and conservative groups. But whatever your feelings, there is no denying that
Dworkin was an extremely influential figure on the feminist scene. Her radical
politics and passionate, eloquent writing helped to define second-wave feminism
not only in terms of her hallmark stance against pornography, but in all areas of
feminist thought, from rape to labor to politics. With speeches and essays on such
topics as sexual violence, free speech, and the exploitation of pornography, *Letters
from a War Zone* serves as an excellent introduction to both Dworkin and to
second-wave feminism at its most radical.

> **Subjects:** Second-wave Feminism • Feminism • Activism • Sexual Discrimination •
> Twentieth Century • America • Essays • Collection

> **Now Try:** Continue learning about Dworkin in her book *Heartbreak: The Political Memoir
> of a Feminist Militant*. With her signature passion and keen social analysis, she further
> discusses her stance about pornography, rape, and sexual subjugation, while illuminat-
> ing the events from her childhood and college years that led her to devote herself to
> feminist activism. Then take a closer look at the topic that galvanized Dworkin, pornog-
> raphy, in a book by Carmine Sarracino and Kevin M. Scott. *The Porning of America: The
> Rise of Porn Culture, What It Means, and Where We Go from Here* takes a critical look at the
> effects of widespread pornography in American culture and media. The authors do not
> share Dworkin's adamantly anti-porn stance, but they do present a thought-provoking
> study that will appeal to Dworkin's fans.

Faludi, Susan

Backlash: The Undeclared War against American Women. New York: Crown, 1991
(2006). 552pp. ISBN 9780517576984.

Pulitzer Prize–winning journalist Faludi doesn't often write books, but when she
does, it's time to sit up straight and pay attention. Her insight into gender and society is nothing short of brilliant, and she writes with a clear, crisp, accessible
prose style. Start here with her first book, *Backlash*, about the public's fear of, and
reaction against, modern feminism. According to feminism's detractors, women
who seek careers and independence are doomed to remain single, to forgo family,
to lose their feminine qualities. With meticulous research into the media and pop-

ular culture, Faludi argues that the backlash against feminism is based on fear and faulty logic. Anyone who worries that feminism is dead will be energized by this spirited defense of feminism and its relevance for women's happiness.

Subjects: Feminism • Third-wave Feminism • Gender • Media • Work/Life Balance • Twenty-first Century • America

Now Try: Looking for more evidence that feminism is necessary and vital in today's world? Turn to *To Be Real: Telling the Truth and Changing the Face of Feminism*, edited by Rebecca Walker. With contributions from such luminaries as bell hooks, Naomi Wolf, and Angela Y. Davis, this exemplary anthology of third-wave voices shows that feminism is evolving to address modern issues such as technology and music.

Findlen, Barbara, ed.

Listen Up!: Voices from the Next Feminist Generation. Seattle, WA: Seal Press, 1995. 264pp. ISBN 9781878067616.

Women have the right to vote and the option to work in any career they choose; where, then, does feminism go next? *Listen Up!* answers the question with a variety of compelling answers. The collection shows that contemporary feminists come from a variety of races, ethnicities, backgrounds, and social classes. Sex and gender, as always, are important, but other concerns —international rights, poverty, health, and religion, among others—take an equally prominent role in these essays. The stories are readable and powerful, written by a new generation of concerned activists.

Subjects: Feminism • Third-wave Feminism • Activism • Gender • Race • Class • Politics • Sexual Discrimination • Body Image • Sexuality • Religion • Abortion • Twentieth Century • Essays • Collection • Anthology • Young Adult

Now Try: For another excellent anthology of contemporary feminist writing, turn to *We Don't Need Another Wave: Dispatches from the Next Generation of Feminists*, edited by Melody Berger. Edgy, hip, politically aware, and powerful, these third-wave writers tackle a variety of subjects, from the media and the government to violence and reproductive choices.

Friedan, Betty

The Feminine Mystique. New York: W. W. Norton, 1963 (2001). 430pp. ISBN 9780393322576.

Simone de Beauvoir's book *The Second Sex* (annotated earlier in the section) is one of the two most important feminist books of the twentieth century; the other is Betty Friedan's 1963 text, *The Feminine Mystique*. Almost single-handedly, it launched the women's rights movement in America, and yet its origins are remarkably simple: Friedan, a newspaper reporter, observed that many women were dissatisfied with their roles as mothers and wives, that the limited domestic sphere was stifling. This "problem that has no name" may seem obvious to us in the twenty-first century, but it was a revolutionary idea at the time, voiced by a woman who herself went on to become a revolutionary as the founder of the National Organization for Women. This is mandatory reading for anyone who wants to understand the origins of feminism and labor in America.

Subjects: Second-wave Feminism • Gender • Labor • Mothers • Children • Marriage • Sexual Discrimination • Mental Health • Psychology • Sociology • America • Twentieth Century

Now Try: It is difficult to find anyone who writes on par with Betty Friedan, but Gloria Steinem is a serious contender. Steinem, a feminist legend in her own right, has written a number of books about women's issues, any of which would be a suitable companion to *The Feminine Mystique*; perhaps start with *Moving beyond Words*, a collection of six essays in which Steinem considers such issues as gender, class, sexuality, and advertising. Written thirty years after Friedan ignited the women's movement, it offers a striking look at the strides that were made and the obstacles that persist even today.

Hernández, Daisy, and Bushra Rehman, eds.

Colonize This!: Young Women of Color on Today's Feminism. New York: Seal Press, 2002. 403pp. ISBN 9781580050678.

It's difficult to define the third wave of feminism, but one thing's for sure: modern feminists think about race and racism in ways their predecessors never dreamed of. In this thought-provoking anthology, young women writers and activists—most of whose names will be unfamiliar to readers—explore race as it relates to sex, gender, class, religion, and various other facets of identity. With chapters such as Taigi Smith's "What Happens When Your Hood Is the Last Stop on the White Flight Express?" and Susan Muaddi Darraj's "It's Not an Oxymoron: The Search for Arab Feminism," this is a fresh, energetic examination of race and contemporary feminism.

Subjects: Race • Feminism • Third-wave Feminism • America • Twenty-first Century • Essays • Collection • Anthology • Young Adult

Now Try: *Colonize This!* presented viewpoints from American writers; now hear what their sisters around the world are thinking in *Sisterhood Is Global: The International Women's Movement Anthology*, edited by Robin Morgan. Each essay—such as "The Harem Window" by Rose Ghurayyib of Lebanon and "The Silent Victims" by Sima Wali of Afghanistan—is prefaced by a brief overview of the status of women in the writer's particular country, making this an insightful, educational look at feminism and women's issues in seventy countries around the globe.

hooks, bell

Ain't I a Woman: Black Women and Feminism. Boston: South End Press, 1981 (1998). 205pp. ISBN 9780896081284.

A classic of both women's studies and African American studies, *Ain't I a Woman* was the book that catapulted bell hooks into the ranks of America's most influential feminist thinkers. In this penetrating work of social history and feminist discourse, hooks examines the dual influences of racism and sexism on American women, starting with slave times and continuing through the present day. Her powerful, angry, insightful analysis of stereotypes and discrimination within the context of black culture and patriarchy is both thought-provoking and deeply troubling. The language is scholarly but accessible, making this a must-read for anyone interested in race and sex in America.

Subjects: African Americans • Race • Gender • Third-wave Feminism • Womanism • Sexual Discrimination • Stereotypes • Class • History • American History • Women's History • Twentieth Century • America

Now Try: hooks has written a wealth of books that will be of interest to fans of *Ain't I a Woman*, any of which make for good follow-ups; perhaps start with *We Real Cool: Black*

Men and Masculinity, in which hooks considers the influence of patriarchy upon black men, and the disturbing cultural norms that affect men in black society. Then, for an excellent companion to *Ain't I a Woman*, turn to another classic of black feminist thought, Audre Lorde's *Sister Outsider: Essays and Speeches*; this remarkable collection brings together some of Lorde's most powerful writings on topics such as race, sex, and sexual orientation.

hooks, bell

Feminism Is for Everybody: Passionate Politics. Cambridge, MA: South End Press, 2000. 123pp. ISBN 9780896086296.

For a concise study of modern feminism, readers will find no better than this marvelous overview, written by none other than feminist icon bell hooks. Compared to her earlier, angrier works, this is a mellow read—but don't worry, there is nothing vanilla about this survey of contemporary feminism: the prose shines with hooks's characteristic passion, but in this case the passion is more inclusive, and less divisive, than in the author's seminal work, *Ain't I a Woman: Black Women and Feminism* (see the previous annotation). Though it has only 205 pages, *Feminism Is for Everybody* packs a punch, covering all the major topics of feminism, including gender, marriage, race, violence, and body image. Excellent for readers new to (or skeptical of) feminism as well as veteran feminists, this is a succinct introduction, presented by one of the most influential feminists of modern times.

> **Subjects:** Feminism • Third-wave Feminism • Twentieth Century • Quick Read
>
> **Now Try:** Those who enjoy hooks's insightful commentary on feminism may wish to continue with *Feminist Theory: From Margin to Center*, though reader beware: this is a less gentle read than *Feminism Is for Everybody*; don't attempt it unless you're willing to face some ugly truths about feminism. Once again, hooks offers a thought-provoking overview of feminism in the past and present, but this time she scrutinizes the feminist movement's uneasy relationship with race, illuminating the ways in which mainstream feminism has marginalized women of color and women of limited economic means.

Pough, Gwendolyn D.

Check It While I Wreck It: Black Womanhood, Hip-Hop Culture, and the Public Sphere. Boston: Northeastern University Press, 2004. 265pp. ISBN 9781555536084.

Who says feminism and hip-hop don't mix? In the scholarly but eminently readable *Check It While I Wreck It*, Women's Studies scholar Pough swiftly dispatches the notion that hip-hop is hostile to women. In chapters such as "My Cipher Keeps Movin' Like a Rollin' Stone: Black Women's Expressive Cultures and Black Feminist Legacies" and "(Re)reconstructing Womanhood : Black Women's Narratives in Hip Hop Culture," Pough applies feminist theory to hip-hop to interpret it as a liberating cultural phenomenon. Drawing on examples ranging from film to spoken-word poetry to successful women rappers, Pough takes a bold new feminist approach to hip-hop, illuminating the empowering nature of a culture that is frequently reviled by other feminists.

> **Subjects:** African Americans • Race • Hip-Hop • Media • Third-wave Feminism • Twenty-first Century

Now Try: Pough isn't the only one who recognizes the feminist appeal of hip-hop. In her *Home Girls Make Some Noise: Hip-Hop Feminism Anthology*, she brings together essays that explore a variety of topics—including sexual orientation, body image, patriarchy, and gender—within the framework of feminism and hip-hop. Then explore popular music as a whole from a feminist perspective in Dorothy Marcic's *Respect: Women and Popular Music*.

Roiphe, Katie

The Morning After: Sex, Fear, and Feminism on Campus. Boston: Little, Brown and Co., 1993. 180pp. ISBN 9780316754316.

Be warned up front: traditional feminists probably won't like this book. Katie Roiphe doesn't have much use for third-wave feminism, and she makes no secret of it—but that is precisely her appeal. Anyone who identifies as a feminist but yearns for a different philosophy will find a breath of fresh air in Roiphe, a "backlash feminist"—that is, someone who embraces feminist theory while rejecting current practice. With clarity and passion, she considers topics such as sexuality and rape to show how contemporary feminism casts women as victims. This is a lucid appeal for returning to the empowered feminism of yesteryear.

> **Subjects:** Third-wave Feminism • Feminism • Sexuality • Rape • Relationships • Sexual Harassment • Twentieth Century • Quick Read

> **Now Try:** If Roiphe's perspective piqued your curiosity, turn to the most famous—and most infamous—of the backlash feminists, Camille Paglia. Controversial and opinionated, she's not afraid to step on anyone's toes, but even her critics must concede that she is intelligent and thoughtful. Try starting with her most famous book, *Sexual Personae: Art and Decadence from Nefertiti to Emily Dickinson*, in which Paglia views art through a lens of backlash feminism.

Sharpley-Whiting, T. Denean

Pimps Up, Ho's Down: Hip Hop's Hold on Young Black Women. New York: New York University Press, 2007. 187pp. ISBN 9780814740149.

T. Denean Sharpley-Whiting is perhaps the perfect person to write this book: she is a feminist scholar with stellar credentials and a brilliant understanding of race, theory, and social criticism; she is also a former fashion model who grew up revering the hip-hop culture. "As a member of the hip-hop generation, I am continually intrigued by the ways in which hip-hop sets the tone for how women—myself included—think and act," she explains. "I have written this book as a way to explore how and why we women do the things we do, what hip-hop has to say about it all, and what we have to say back." With chapters such as "Too Hot to Be Bothered: Black Women and Sexual Abuse" and "'I'm a Hustla, Baby': Groupie Love and the Hip Hop Star," Sharpley-Whiting presents an academic but thoroughly accessible study of the contradictions and intersections of hip-hop culture and feminism; insightful, thoughtful, and at times provocative, this is essential reading for anyone interested in race, women's issues, or popular culture.

> **Subjects:** Hip-Hop • Media • African Americans • Race • Gender • Class • Feminism • Third-wave Feminism • Twenty-first Century • Quick Read

> **Now Try:** Though it's written with a hipper, edgier slant than Sharpley-Whiting's book, fans of *Pimps Up, Ho's Down* won't want to miss Joan Morgan's *When Chickenheads Come Home to Roost: My Life As a Hip-Hop Feminist*. Like Sharpley-Whiting, Morgan embraces the sometimes conflicting cultures of both hip-hop and feminism, and in this

thought-provoking discussion, she considers such topics as race, femininity, feminism, and popular culture.

Stanton, Elizabeth Cady, Susan B. Anthony, and Ellen Carol DuBois

The Elizabeth Cady Stanton-Susan B. Anthony Reader: Correspondence, Writings, Speeches. Boston: Northeastern University Press, 1992. 306pp. ISBN 9781555531492.

Historian Ellen Carol DuBois here selects a fascinating sampling of writings by the two most prominent leaders in the first wave of feminism, Elizabeth Cady Stanton and Susan B. Anthony. With insightful analysis and historical commentary to place the documents in context, DuBois presents a variety of writings by Stanton and Anthony, including diary excerpts, speeches, and letters. Taken collectively, these pieces—including Stanton's history-making "Address Delivered at Seneca Falls"—illuminate a personal, intimate overview of the suffrage movement and the first wave of feminism. These primary documents constitute essential reading for anyone interested in nineteenth-century American history or women's history.

Subjects: Stanton, Elizabeth Cady • Anthony, Susan B. • First-wave Feminism • Feminism • Activism • Suffrage • History • Women's History • Social History • American History • Nineteenth Century • America • Letters • Collection

Now Try: Most folks associate Elizabeth Cady Stanton with the suffrage movement, and understandably so. But she concerned herself with far more than women's voting rights, as we see in *The Woman's Bible: A Classic Feminist Perspective*, Stanton's remarkable feminist analysis of the Christian Bible. Then, for more writing from Susan B. Anthony, turn to *The Trial of Susan B. Anthony*, her account of the legal trial in which she was convicted of illegally casting a vote.

Walker, Alice

In Search of Our Mothers' Gardens: Womanist Prose. San Diego, CA: Harcourt Brace Jovanovich, 1983. 397pp. ISBN 9780151445257.

Alice Walker single-handedly developed a branch of feminism, Womanism, which may be loosely defined as black feminism. Though written in the early 1980s, her first collection of nonfiction still conveys a sense of immediacy and relevancy. Topics range from motherhood to civil rights to body image, from personal memoir to political criticism. Perhaps most compelling is Walker's discussion of her childhood injury that resulted in the loss of an eye and the loss of her confidence, but each piece demonstrates Walker's commitment to feminism and her reverence of black culture. Read this both for the subject matter and to indulge in Walker's stunning, stark prose.

Subjects: Womanism • Feminism • Second-wave Feminism • Gender • Race • African Americans • Essays • Collection • Twentieth Century • Memoir

Now Try: Another formidable figure of Womanist scholarship is Patricia Hill Collins. In *Black Feminist Thought: Knowledge, Consciousness, and the Politics of Empowerment*, she considers the definition of black feminism, placing it in the context of the intersections of the big three—race, gender, and class—as well as less lofty constructions such as conversation and popular culture. Like Walker, she discusses important, thought-provoking themes within an accessible and enjoyable prose style.

Woolf, Virginia

A Room of One's Own. New York: Harcourt, Brace, 1929 (2005). 148pp. ISBN 9780156030410.

Though best known for her fiction, Virginia Woolf produced several remarkable pieces of nonfiction, including one of the early classics of feminist writing, *A Room of One's Own*. Dealing with both class and sex, this lengthy essay criticizes the unfair distribution of money and power under the patriarchal system, arguing that "a woman must have money and a room of her own if she is to write fiction"—or, indeed, to express herself in any creative way. In a particularly memorable passage, Woolf creates a fictional sister for Shakespeare, Judith, who has all of the bard's talents but none of his opportunities, due to her sex and lower economic status. If you already know Woolf from her other, frequently difficult works, you may be pleasantly surprised to discover the accessible style and engaging tone of this landmark feminist essay.

Subjects: First-wave Feminism • Writing • Art • Labor • Class • Sexual Discrimination • Mental Health • Twentieth Century • Quick Read

Now Try: *Well-Behaved Women Seldom Make History* is the catchy title of a book by Laurel Ulrich—but she is not just borrowing the well-known slogan, seen on T-shirts and bumper-stickers everywhere; Ulrich herself coined the phrase in an obscure academic article in 1976. Thirty-odd years later, she returns with a far less obscure book, a series of essays on a variety of feminist issues. The feminist focus will appeal to fans of Woolf, of course, but this is especially appropriate as a companion to *A Room of One's Own* because of the chapter in which Ulrich expands on the story of "Judith Shakespeare."

Activism

> Titles in the "Activism" section focus on women struggling for social change.

The "Activism" section is for people who want to make a difference. Ranging from the quirky (see *The Guerrilla Girls' Bedside Companion to the History of Western Art*) to the deadly serious (see Cheryl Benard and Edit Schlaffer's *Veiled Courage: Inside the Afghan Women's Resistance*), these are books that expose the problems faced by women and encourage us to solve those problems.

Baumgardner, Jennifer, and Amy Richards

Manifesta: Young Women, Feminism, and the Future. New York: Farrar, Straus and Giroux, 2000. 416pp. ISBN 9780374526221.

As former editors of *Ms.* magazine, Baumgardner and Richards understand the state of feminism today. Targeted toward the young adults who have inherited their mothers' second-wave feminism, the book examines modern feminism, allaying any fears that we live in a post-feminist society. With energy and zeal, the authors show how girl culture and third-wave feminism are thriving in harmony, with examples from popular culture ranging from *Bust* magazine to Xena. But this is more than an interesting commentary on the state of feminism; this is also an activist call to arms, a reminder to today's young women that they cannot rest on their laurels; feminism is not dead, but it will be if the next generation becomes complacent.

> **Subjects:** Feminism • Third-wave Feminism • Activism • Media • Twentieth Century • Young Adult
>
> **Now Try:** Rory Cooke Dicker and Alison Piepmeier agree with Baumgardner and Richards: feminism is still alive and kicking, though the onus is on young women to keep the movement going forward. In *Catching a Wave: Reclaiming Feminism for the 21st Century*, Dicker and Piepmeier collect an excellent sampling of essays about third-wave feminism; provocative and edgy, the book illuminates the multitude of perspectives embodied by the third wave and shows why feminist activism is still necessary today.

Benard, Cheryl, and Edit Schlaffer

Veiled Courage: Inside the Afghan Women's Resistance. New York: Broadway Books, 2002. 293pp. ISBN 9780767913010.

As an American white woman, Benard may seem an unlikely person to deliver an insider's view of Afghanistan, but as an adviser to RAWA—the Revolutionary Association of the Women of Afghanistan—and as the wife of an Afghan man, her voice is the perfect vehicle for delivering the story of Afghan women to Western readers. This is the story of RAWA, covering its history, its martyred founder Meena, and its present-day activism. With stories of the women and men whose lives have been affected by RAWA, this is a powerful, page-turning look at the struggles that Afghan women face and the group that is trying to make a difference.

> **Subjects:** Activism • Feminism • Third-wave Feminism • Sexual Discrimination • Politics • History • Afghanistan • Middle East • Asia • Twentieth Century
>
> **Now Try:** Learn more about the remarkable history of RAWA in Anne E. Brodsky's *With All Our Strength: The Revolutionary Association of the Women of Afghanistan*. Based on interviews with RAWA women, this book uncovers the empowering triumphs over patriarchy and discrimination that RAWA has made, showcasing the organization as a model for what can happen when women work together. See also Sally Armstrong's book *Veiled Threat: The Hidden Power of the Women of Afghanistan*, which discusses the human rights abuses faced by women under the Taliban and the women who resisted those abuses.

Borges, Phil

Women Empowered: Inspiring Change in the Emerging World. New York: Rizzoli, 2007. 111pp. ISBN 9780847829279.

In this collection of short photo-essays, breathtaking photography and stirring prose blend to create a remarkable study of women in developing countries. The photos depict women who reside in places where life can be harsh, especially for women, and yet the overall tone of the book is positive: these are women who have triumphed and thrived despite the sexist and cultural barriers of their milieu. Each photo is accompanied by a brief description of the individual and her experience with women's and social issues. The empowering themes and courageous stories will leave readers feeling educated, uplifted, and inspired.

> **Subjects:** Activism • Feminism • Third-wave Feminism • Leadership • Labor • Class • Africa • Asia • South America • Twenty-first Century • Essays • Collection • Quick Read

> **Now Try:** Meet more extraordinary women from the developing world in *Angels in Africa: Portraits of Seven Extraordinary Women*, in which journalist Kimberley Sevcik and photographer Beth O'Donnell assemble a dazzling collection of photo-essays. The inspiring profiles will introduce readers to seven amazing women who have devoted themselves to improving women's issues and social injustices in countries throughout Africa.

Bravo, Ellen

Taking on the Big Boys: Or Why Feminism Is Good for Families, Business, and the Nation. Mariam K. Chamberlain Series on Social and Economic Justice. New York: Feminist Press at the City University of New York, 2007. 294pp. ISBN 978155-8615458.

"The changes feminists want are not favors to women," writes activist Bravo, "but a better way to do business, raise families, build society." She argues that a small minority of people in power—businessmen, politicians, CEOs, and the like—are keen on preserving the status quo for their own gain and at the expense of ordinary working people. In this engagingly written, thoroughly researched social study, Bravo criticizes those people in power—that is, the Big Boys—and shows how feminist goals such as pay equity can reshape the modern workplace into an environment that values women and their work. *Taking on the Big Boys* is both an invigorating thought piece and a practical how-to guide for such issues as combating sexual harassment and forming feminist organizations.

> **Subjects:** Third-wave Feminism • Labor • Activism • Work/Life Balance • Sexual Discrimination • Sociology • Twenty-first Century • America • How-to

> **Now Try:** Though more academic in tone than Bravo's book, *Why So Slow? The Advancement of Women* will appeal to readers for its thought-provoking analysis of gender inequities in the workplace. Drawing on research in such fields as biology, psychology, and social science, author Virginia Valian explores the root causes of sexual discrimination against professional women, exposing how sexism—even when it is subconscious —holds women back from advancement.

Cole, Johnnetta B., and Beverly Guy-Sheftall

Gender Talk: The Struggle for Women's Equality in African American Communities. New York: Ballantine Books, 2003. 298pp. ISBN 9780345454126.

The intersection of racism and sexism with African American communities has a tense, troubled history, with reverberations reaching to the present day. Too often black women's experiences are lost within the discourse on race, with their perspectives ceding to the perspectives of black men. In *Gender Talk*, activists Cole and Guy-Sheftall offer a stirring indictment against this pattern, shifting the discussion on race to emphasize black women and their experiences. Investigating a wide range of topics within black culture, from the black church to hip-hop to black homophobia, the book raises hard questions about racism and sexism, insisting that black women's voices be given their due.

Subjects: African Americans • Gender • Race • Feminism • Third-wave Feminism • Sexual Discrimination • Twenty-first Century • America

Now Try: Listen now to the voices of African American women as they discuss race and sex in *Shifting: The Double Lives of Black Women in America* by Charisse Jones and Kumea Shorter-Gooden. Based on survey responses and interviews, the book unveils the struggles and dissatisfactions faced by black women as they cope with both racism and sexism in their daily lives; as in *Gender Talk*, a great number of topics are considered, including religion, body image, and family.

Durham, Meenakshi Gigi

The Lolita Effect: The Media Sexualization of Young Girls and What We Can Do about It. Woodstock, NY: Overlook Press, 2008. 286pp. ISBN 9781590200636.

For too long, we have allowed the media to sexualize young girls, writes journalism professor Durham. From suggestive children's clothing and sexy dolls to teenage celebrities and the idealized models in magazines, our culture is teaching its daughters to become sexual creatures well before they're of age. With a passionate voice and excellent research, Durham debunks several myths, such as the myth of the perfect body and the myth that younger is sexier. She also suggests practical steps to combat the problem and provides sample questions for parents and children to discuss.

Subjects: Sexuality • Children • Media • Activism • Feminism • Third-wave Feminism • Twenty-first Century • How-to

Now Try: In *The Lolita Effect*, Durham focuses primarily on young girls. Now try a book that considers the media's sexualization of boys and girls alike in *So Sexy So Soon: The New Sexualized Childhood, and What Parents Can Do to Protect Their Kids*. Authors Diane E. Levin and Jean Kilbourne examine the pervasive ways in which boys and girls are subjected to unhealthy images, and they offer realistic suggestions for parents to help their children deal with those images.

Gianturco, Paola

Women Who Light the Dark. New York: PowerHouse, 2007. 239pp. ISBN 9781576873960.

In this beautiful collection of photo-essays, women's rights activist Gianturco shines light on women across the world who are making a positive difference. Travel into some of the grimmest places on the planet, where violence, poverty, and illiteracy poison lives, and discover women who, despite these bleak surroundings, devote themselves to activism. Stunning photographs and powerful essays illuminate the lives of women in fifteen countries as they fight social injustice with positive and creative approaches such as music, art, sport, and poetry. Their stories will provide inspiration and motivation for those readers who worry that nothing they do will make a difference.

Subjects: Activism • Labor • Class • Leadership • Feminism • Third-wave Feminism • Twenty-first Century • Global Perspectives • Essays • Collection

Now Try: Gianturco has written two other collections of photo-essays, each every bit as satisfying as *Women Who Light the Dark*. The book *In Her Hands: Craftswomen Changing the World* looks at women around the globe as they improve their lives with embroidery, weaving, pottery, and other crafts; the women's lives and experiences, as well as their creations, are explored through images and prose. Then turn to the essays and photography in *Celebrating Women*, which profiles women in celebrations around the world, from the vaunted Miss America pageant in the United States to Sankta Lucia day in Sweden.

Guerrilla Girls (Group of Artists)

The Guerrilla Girls' Bedside Companion to the History of Western Art. New York: Penguin Books, 1998. 95pp. ISBN 9780140259971.

"Do women have to be naked to get into the Met. Museum?" In 1989, a group of anonymous feminist activists posed this question, noting that fewer than 5 percent of the artists in the modern art sections of the Metropolitan Museum of Art were women, though 85 percent of the nudes were female. Since then, these women in gorilla masks have dedicated themselves to ending sexism, heterosexism, and racism in art and the world at large. In their *Bedside Companion to the History of Western Art*, replete with artist bios and art reproductions, the Guerrilla Girls reconsider art history from antiquity to the present, putting their own Third Wave spin on art and feminism. Quirky, angry, and powerful, this is revisionist history at its best, an interpretation that proudly restores women artists to the spotlight that should have never been missing.

> **Subjects:** Art • Feminism • Third-wave Feminism • Activism • History • History of Art • Women's History • Twentieth Century • Young Adult • Quick Read

> **Now Try:** The world of art is still dominated by patriarchal norms, but feminism has made proud inroads. *WACK!: Art and the Feminist Revolution*, by Cornelia H. Butler and Lisa Gabrielle Mark, surveys 120 women artists whose work was positively influenced by feminism between 1965 and 1980. Author bios, art reproductions, and critical feminist analysis help readers understand the complicated relationship between art and feminism. *Global Feminisms: New Directions in Contemporary Art*, by Maura Reilly and Linda Nochlin, is a third-wave examination of feminism and contemporary art by women around the globe.

Henry, Astrid

Not My Mother's Sister: Generational Conflict and Third-Wave Feminism. Bloomington: Indiana University Press, 2004. 272pp. ISBN 9780253344540.

How shall we understand third-wave feminism? Is it a reaction to second-wave feminism, or a movement defined on its own terms? It's a little of both, explains Henry, in this thought-provoking look at the tensions between the women's liberation movement of the 1960s and '70s and the current iteration of feminism. Third-wave feminism, with its broader, more inclusive approach to such topics as race and national identity, understandably rejects the more narrow focus of the second wave—but, cautions Henry, the gains of the second movement must not be forgotten. In this insightful analysis of where feminism has been and where it's going, Henry urges contemporary feminists to study the victories of their foremothers so that they can better understand the struggles they face today.

> **Subjects:** Feminism • Third-wave Feminism • Second-wave Feminism • Activism • History • Women's History • Twentieth Century • Twenty-first Century • America

> **Now Try:** One of the best ways to understand the third wave of feminism is to look at the writings that modern feminists produce—and of all the different media they are creating, one of the most fascinating is the zine, whether it is a low-quality paste-up job or a glossy magazine proper. *A Girl's Guide to Taking Over the World: Writings from the Girl Zine Revolution*, edited by Tristan Taormino and Karen Green, collects some of the

best examples of zine writing and photos, arranged into such chapters as "Slumber Party: Friends, Secrets, Sex" and "The Parent Trap: Parents, Siblings, Family."

Maloney, Carolyn

Rumors of Our Progress Have Been Greatly Exaggerated: Why Women's Lives Aren't Getting Any Easier—and How We Can Make Real Progress for Ourselves and Our Daughters. Emmaus, PA: Modern Times, 2008. 254pp. ISBN 9781594863271.

As former co-chair of the Congressional Caucus on Women's Issues, Congresswoman Maloney has a thorough understanding of the issues that affect women at every level of American society. With thorough research, she convincingly demonstrates that gender inequality still persists, in areas from salaries (the gender gap is actually widening!) to health care to reproduction. Anecdotes and stories from a variety of women give the book a personal feel, while "Take-Action Guides" at the end of each chapter offer suggestions to help overcome the inequalities.

Subjects: Activism • Feminism • Third-wave Feminism • Gender • Sexual Discrimination • Twenty-first Century • America • How-to

Now Try: If Maloney's book has you despairing, lighten up with a quirkier activism guide, *It's a Jungle Out There: The Feminist Survival Guide to Politically Inhospitable Environments*. Amanda Marcotte covers similar topics—pay inequality, the work/family balance, reproduction—but with a quirky, tongue-in-cheek sense of humor. Maloney's book will help you save the world; Marcotte's book will help you save your sanity while you're doing it.

Moats, David

Civil Wars: A Battle for Gay Marriage. Orlando, FL: Harcourt, 2004. 288pp. ISBN 9780151010172.

In the late 1990s, the debate over gay marriage raged in Vermont, resulting in the passage of a state law in January 2000 that permitted gay civil unions. For his editorials about that political drama, journalist David Moats won a Pulitzer Prize; now he takes readers behind the scenes of that monumental period of American history. With a magnificent sense of pacing and suspense, Moats brings to life the emotional struggles and triumphs of the lawyers, the legislators, and the same-sex couples whose experiences shaped not only their own lives but also those of queer people throughout the country. This is a riveting, powerful read, an emotionally intense example of investigative journalism at its finest.

Subjects: Queer Sexuality • Activism • Feminism • Third-wave Feminism • Marriage • Politics • History • American History • Social History • Twenty-first Century • America

Now Try: Turn now to another journalist who speaks eloquently about gay marriage, Jonathan Rauch, in his book *Gay Marriage: Why It Is Good for Gays, Good for Straights, and Good for America*. With level-headed arguments and his moving personal perspective (Rauch is himself in a long-term gay relationship), he makes an eloquent case for the dignity and nobility that full marriage would confer upon same-sex couples and the subsequent benefits that America would reap. See also Davina Kotulski's *Why You Should Give a Damn about Gay Marriage*; aimed at gays and lesbians, this book explains the rights and privileges that legally married couples enjoy but that are presently unavailable to same-sex couples.

Miya-Jervis, Lisa, and Andi Zeisler, eds.

BITCHfest: Ten Years of Cultural Criticism from the Pages of Bitch Magazine. New York: Farrar, Straus and Giroux, 2006. 372pp. ISBN 9780374113438.

Founded in 1971, *Ms.* was America's first mainstream feminist magazine, and it has continued to bring attention to feminist issues ever since—but *Ms.* tends to stick to heavy themes, rather than fashion or pop stars. Feminists wanting lighter fare found a lovely alternative in 1996 with the appearance of *Bitch*, the hip, sassy magazine for third-wave feminists who wanted music, books, and celebrities side by side with pressing societal concerns. *BITCHfest* offers a zesty sampling of articles from ten years, covering everything from sexuality and Hollywood to body image and abortion. Pieces such as Lisa Jervis's "Rubyfruit Jungle Gym" and Leigh Shoemaker's "Urinalysis: On Standing Up to Pee" will give readers food for thought.

Subjects: Feminism • Third-wave Feminism • Twenty-first Century • Collection

Now Try: You know about *Bitch*, you know about *Ms.*, but if you don't know about *Bust*, you're in for a treat. Funky, fun, and fabulous, *Bust* is an edgy blend of feminism and fashion, consciousness-raising and pop culture. Go out and buy a current copy for the latest news, and then settle back with *The Bust Guide to the New Girl Order*, edited by Marcelle Karp and Debbie Stoller, to review a sampling of some of the finest articles on culture, feminism, and society from the magazine's illustrious history.

Moraga, Cherríe, and Gloria Anzaldúa, eds.

This Bridge Called My Back: Writings by Radical Women of Color. New York: Kitchen Table, Women of Color Press, 1981 (2002). 261pp. ISBN 9780913175033.

In this stunning anthology of writings from the second wave of feminism, women from all sorts of racial and ethnic backgrounds—including African Americans, Asian Americans, and Native Americans—explore the impact of race in their lives. In letters, stories, and essays, the contributors consider the intersection of race with such themes as sex, orientation, and class, observing how feminism works both for and against racial awareness. Some of the pieces are written for a scholarly audience, but even the more academic entries are accessible to the lay reader. Vivid, visceral, and powerful, the collection presents an eye-opening look at racial issues during the second wave of feminism, with themes that echo through the present day.

Subjects: Race • Second-wave Feminism • Feminism • Activism • Essays • Letters • Collection • Twentieth Century • Anthology

Now Try: Race was obviously a big deal to the women who contributed to *This Bridge Called My Back*, but what was its role in the wider scope of second-wave feminism? In *The Trouble between Us: An Uneasy History of White and Black Women in the Feminist Movement*, we learn the discomfiting answers. With meticulous scholarship and a balanced approach, Wini Breines examines the racial tensions of feminism in the 1960s and '70s, seeking to understand the rifts between black feminists and white feminists that, even today, continue to influence third-wave feminism.

National Council of Women's Organizations

50 Ways to Improve Women's Lives: The Essential Women's Guide for Achieving Equality, Health, and Success. Maui, HI: Inner Ocean, 2005. 182pp. ISBN 9781930722453.

For every thinking woman who recognizes the social ills of the world but isn't quite sure what do to about them, *50 Ways to Improve Women's Lives* holds the answers. From the nonpartisan National Council of Women's Organizations comes a book that honestly addresses the injustices that face people everywhere, be they women, children, ethnic minorities, or any other group that struggles against oppression. In chapters covering a broad scope of issues ranging from pay equity to sex education to human trafficking, women such as Patricia Ireland and Dianne Feinstein discuss social problems—and more important, they offer realistic advice that concerned people can follow to make a difference in their world.

Subjects: Feminism • Third-wave Feminism • Activism • Class • Global Perspectives • Twenty-first Century • How-to • Quick Read

Now Try: If *50 Ways to Improve Women's Lives* inspired you to think about women's issues, turn to *The Fire This Time: Young Activists and the New Feminism*, edited by Vivien Labaton and Dawn Lundy Martin. The contributors don't just write about women's issues; they actually redefine the concept, exploring such new territory as incarceration, theater, and hip-hop. Also try the excellent *Grassroots: A Field Guide for Feminist Activism*, in which Jennifer Baumgardner and Amy Richards show how anyone can become an activist and make a difference.

Rowe-Finkbeiner, Kristin

The F-Word: Feminism in Jeopardy: Women, Politics, and the Future. Emeryville, CA: Seal Press, 2004. 332pp. ISBN 9781580051149.

Think back to the presidential election of 2000, the contentious, mobilizing, historically significant race between Al Gore and George W. Bush. Did you know that 65 percent of women over age forty-four voted? That's compared to only 35 percent of women aged eighteen to twenty-four. Young women who forgo the polls do so at their own peril, warns journalist Rowe-Finkbeiner: "When young women don't vote, their concerns are generally ignored in the public arena. Important issues like education, domestic violence, health-care funding, reproductive rights, college tuition increases, child care, social security, and equitable pay, to name a few, aren't debated with the opinions of young women in mind." *The F-Word* is a rallying cry, an exhortation to women of the younger generation to make their voices heard at the polls. In chapters such as "Are We Postfeminist? Education, Work, and a Nation in Flux" and "Making a Difference: Women in Political Power," Rowe-Finkbeiner makes an impassioned, convincing argument for feminist concerns and the importance of voting.

Subjects: Feminism • Third-wave Feminism • Politics • Twenty-first Century • Sexual Discrimination • America

Now Try: *The F-Word* painted a disturbing portrait of a generation of women who, despite embracing the values of feminism, prefer not to act on it politically. For a further examination of the widespread rejection of feminism proper, turn to *The Female Thing: Dirt, Sex, Envy, Vulnerability* by Laura Kipnis.

Though it does not focus on voting, fans of *The F-Word* will appreciate the insightful, thoughtful discussion of the reluctance of women to embrace modern feminism.

Seely, Megan

Fight Like a Girl: How to Be a Fearless Feminist. New York: New York University Press, 2007. 279pp. ISBN 9780814740019.

What does it mean to fight like a girl? Generally, the phrase suggests that "those who fight like girls, as opposed to fighting like men, don't really know how to fight and that their struggle is not real, not intense, not legitimate—just hair pulling and nail scratching." Feminist activist Megan Seely doesn't buy it: "I know how to fight, and I know plenty of women whose struggles are all too real, all too harrowing, all too dangerous. I'm here to say that not only can we fight like girls; we can win." And in this edgy, empowering book, she tells us exactly how to do it. Based on her own impressive history of activism and drawing on responses from surveys she distributed to young women, Seely presents a succinct overview of the women's movement, focusing especially on contemporary issues such as body image and political advancement. Targeted toward third-wave feminists but accessible for anyone interested in women's issues, the book is an excellent primer on modern feminism and a stirring call to arms, bolstered with practical advice on topics such as writing press releases and getting good media coverage.

Subjects: Feminism • Third-wave Feminism • Activism • Twenty-first Century • How-to • Young Adult

Now Try: Third-wavers inspired by Seely's book will be delighted to find further inspiration in *Third Wave Agenda: Being Feminist, Doing Feminism*, edited by Leslie Heywood and Jennifer Drake. In this collection of thirteen thought-provoking essays, contemporary feminists explore modern feminism and activism, considering such varied topics as class, sexual orientation, and popular culture.

Shah, Sonia, ed.

Dragon Ladies: Asian American Feminists Breathe Fire. Boston: South End Press, 1997. 241pp. ISBN 9780896085763.

Feminism meets activism in bold new ways in this stirring collection of essays, all written by Asian American women with an agenda to make the world a better place. In four sections—"Strategies and Visions," "An Agenda for Change," "Global Perspectives," and "Awakening to Power"—these writers tackle a variety of contemporary issues, from violence to sexual orientation to spirituality to globalism. Featuring contributors who trace their ancestry to countries throughout Asia, the anthology is a high-voltage collection of the fresh, powerful voices of Asian American feminist activism today.

Subjects: Asian Americans • Gender • Race • Sexual Discrimination • Feminism • Third-wave Feminism • Activism • America • Global Perspectives • Twentieth Century • Essays • Collection • Anthology

Now Try: Though with less of an activist agenda, a good companion read is *The Asian Mystique: Dragon Ladies, Geisha Girls, & Our Fantasies of the Exotic Orient*. Author Sheridan Prasso explores many of the same issues covered in *Dragon Ladies*, such as Asian women's sexuality and racial stereotypes, but this time the focus is on understanding Asian women through the distorted, and distorting, lens of Western perspectives. Explore Asian red-light districts and scrutinize the typecasting of Asians on the Hollywood screen in this thought-provoking examination of the image of Asian women in America.

Valenti, Jessica

Full Frontal Feminism: A Young Women's Guide to Why Feminism Matters. Emeryville, CA: Seal Press, 2007. 271pp. ISBN 9781580052016.

"'Feminism' is just too scary and loaded a word for some women," writes Valenti. "Which is really too bad. Because feminism is a pretty amazing thing. When you're a feminist, day-to-day life is better. You have better sex. You understand the struggles you're up against and how best to handle them." With her sassy, snarky, witty style, Valenti discusses the issues that matter to today's young women by way of such chapters as "You're a Hardcore Feminist, I Swear," "Feminists Do It Better (and Other Sex Tips)," and "I Promise I Won't Say 'Herstory.'" Fun but informative, edgy but thought-provoking, the book convincingly shows that feminism is not only relevant but cool.

Subjects: Feminism • Third-wave Feminism • Activism • Humor • Twenty-first Century • Quick Read • Young Adult

Now Try: Continue learning about feminism from more than sixty women in *Sisterhood Is Forever: The Women's Anthology for a New Millennium*, edited by Robin Morgan. Featuring essays by stalwart feminists such as Carol Gilligan, Gloria Steinem, and the Guerrilla Girls, as well as essays by emerging young voices, this collection offers a variety of vibrant perspectives on a wealth of contemporary feminist topics, from globalization and violence to sexual orientation and politics.

Consider Starting With ...

Some of the most popular, accessible titles of Feminism and Activism are the following:

Faludi, Susan. *Backlash: The Undeclared War against American Women.*

Gianturco, Paola. *Women Who Light the Dark.*

Guerrilla Girls. *The Guerrilla Girls' Bedside Companion to the History of Western Art.*

hooks, bell. *Feminism Is for Everybody: Passionate Politics.*

Walker, Alice. *In Search of Our Mothers' Gardens: Womanist Prose.*

Woolf, Virginia. *A Room of One's Own.*

Fiction Read-Alikes

- **Atwood, Margaret.** Each of Atwood's novels pose important questions about social issues, especially those that matter to women. Begin with *The Handmaid's Tale*, which has been called a feminist *1984*. In this near-future dystopia, women can no longer work or have money; instead, they are assigned to be wives, housemaids, or child-bearers, as we learn from the perspective of Offred, a reluctant handmaid—that is, a woman whose role in life is to be raped and consequently breed children.

- **Bechdel, Alison.** All the signature themes of third-wave feminism—race, sex, orientation, nationality, parenthood, the environment—show up with a vengeance in the long-running comic strip *Dykes to Watch Out For*. Meet the lesbian protagonist Mo and her group of racially diverse, left-thinking friends in any of the *DTWOF* collections; the first of the bound collections is *Dykes to Watch Out For.*

- **Flagg, Fannie.** *Fried Green Tomatoes at the Whistle Stop Cafe* is a Southern historical novel with some deeply feminist themes. The elderly Cleo Threadgood reminisces on her life in Depression-era Alabama, recalling two spunky young women who grappled with racism, spousal abuse, and sexism and who became business partners, best friends, and lovers—and as the modern-day Evelyn Couch listens to Mrs. Threadgood's stories, she begins to develop her own feminist awakening. And for more stories told from a feminist slant, try Flagg's other novels, such as *Welcome to the World, Baby Girl!*, about a woman grappling with career, family ties, and identity.

- **Hurston, Zora Neale.** It's hard to believe that Hurston, a star of the Harlem Renaissance, had faded into obscurity before Alice Walker helped restore her to prominence in the 1970s. Discover the story of Janie Crawford, a southern black woman, in Hurston's magnum opus, *Their Eyes Were Watching God*. This is a stunning, thought-provoking look at race, class, violence, love, and marriage in early twentieth-century Florida.

- **Jones, Gayl.** Masterful prose distinguishes the novels of Gayl Jones, which consider hefty themes from the perspectives of utterly believable characters. Start with *Mosquito*, about an African American woman truck driver who finds a young pregnant Mexican woman hitching an illegal ride, or *The Healing*, about a Jane-of-all-trades who spends her time reflecting on the ills of society and practicing her latest profession, faith healing.

- **Le Sueur, Meridel.** We never even learn the name of the protagonist of *The Girl*, but hers is a compelling story, framed by the author's radical Marxist feminism. Set in the 1930s, this is the story of a young woman who grapples with the realities of class, pregnancy, and difficult men; told in a spare, minimalist style, this quick read is a powerful and provocative feminist classic.

- **Pratchett, Terry.** It's hard to know what genre the Discworld series falls into. Fantasy? Satire? Humor? Literary fiction in genre disguise? In all of his novels, Pratchett's focus on the human condition—class, gender, race, religion—will satisfy fans of the Feminist genre, but perhaps start with *Equal Rites*, in which a young woman enters the masculine world of wizardry, much to the patriarchs' dismay.

- **Spinelli, Jerry.** Any woman who has ever felt lonely, outcast, or misunderstood because she stood up for what she believed in will sympathize with the title character of *Stargirl*; this high school girl dares to be true to herself, though doing so bucks the social norms and leaves her friendless. But don't worry: this is ultimately a novel of empowerment and spirit, a tribute to courage and independent thinking. Continue with following our independent-minded heroine in *Love, Stargirl*.

Chapter 7

Women at Work

Definition

> The books in this chapter emphasize women's work in the male-dominated professions.

The old adage is true: a woman's work is never done. Women's work was traditionally relegated to the domestic sphere, but now women participate in every imaginable profession, from those that have a history of embracing females, such as social work, nursing, librarianship, and education, to those that are still chiefly staffed by men, such as politics, the armed forces, and the sciences. (Though, as we all know, women still manage households and raise children; see the "Working Mothers" section of Chapter 8 for books about the pressures of this double burden.)

The books in this chapter emphasize women's work in male-dominated professions. Some of the titles are celebratory, focusing on the lives of women workers and their professional accomplishments; see, for instance, Patricia Fara's *Scientists Anonymous: Great Stories of Women in Science*. (See also the "Women in the Professions" section of Chapter 1, featuring biographies of career women.) Some are more contemplative in nature, giving readers an insider's view of a particular job, as with Eliza Lo Chin's anthology *This Side of Doctoring: Reflections from Women in Medicine*. Others take a critical approach toward investigating the sexist barriers of a profession; try, for example, Kayla Williams's eye-opening memoir *Love My Rifle More Than You: Young and Female in the U.S. Army*.

"Women at Work" books therefore cover a wide range of topics and approaches, reflecting the variety of jobs women hold. Biographical or sociological, historical or contemporary, reflective or practical, the books explore the inroads that women have made into male-dominated careers—though, because of the focus on traditionally male professions, there is no mention here of the most prevalent job among women, motherhood. Look for books on this full-time, lifelong job in Chapter 2.

Appeal

Books about careers give us a glimpse into other people's lifestyles and confirm our own experiences when we read about people who have similar jobs. Women's Nonfiction career books have the added appeal of considering the sociological implications of women laborers. Learning how women have succeeded in areas such as medicine, sports, and business can inspire us to advance in our own careers. Character development can be a big appeal, especially in the biographies and memoirs, as can setting; an author's ability to describe a working environment can take us to settings we would probably never encounter otherwise, as with *Women in Space—Following Valentina*, by David Shayler and Ian A. Moule.

Many of the Women at Work books offer practical advice along with their narratives. Written with the unique career needs of women in mind, these books can inspire us as individuals to advance in our own jobs.

Organization

The first section, "Careers," includes books about women in a wide variety of jobs, from farming to cartooning to winemaking. This section is followed by six subsections: "Women in Science and Technology," "Women Doctors, Lawyers, and Clergy," "Women Athletes," "Women in the Military," "Women in the Business World," and "Women Entrepreneurs." Directly following these career-specific books is the "Professional Guides" section, with books to help women advance in their jobs, regardless of industry.

The "Sexual Harassment" section comes next, with stories of women who have fought sexual harassment as well as books about the broader sociological impact of sexual harassment. This is followed by "Women and Leadership," about women in politics and government, and the chapter concludes with "Women and Finance," featuring practical guides on saving and investing money.

Careers

Women's professions, labor, and occupations are at the core of the stories in this section.

The "Careers" section pays tribute to women's labor in a variety of arenas. Some of the books honor women's work in the (few) professions that have historically embraced women; see, for instance, *Women Who Write*, Stefan Bollman's gorgeous study of women authors, past and present, around the globe. Other books highlight women's work in professions traditionally dominated by men, as we see with the pilots in *Amelia Earhart's Daughters* by Leslie Haynsworth and David M. Toomey. Read these to encounter the individual women who excelled in their careers and to contemplate historical and contemporary barriers that women have faced.

Bollinger, Holly, and Catherine Lee Phillips

Women of the Harvest: Inspiring Stories of Contemporary Farmers. St. Paul, MN: MBI Publishing Company, 2007. 159pp. ISBN 9780760321843.

Though the number of individuals who farm for a living has dropped severely, the percentage of women among those who *do* farm has risen dramatically. Seventeen of those women farmers are profiled in *Women of the Harvest*, a celebration of women's farming in contemporary America. Interviews with the women bring to life the details of farming and farm culture, while gorgeous color photographs illustrate the women and the land they work, taking the reader from mountains to deserts to leafy green landscapes across the country. *Women of the Harvest* serves as a satisfying introduction to an uncommon topic and as a lovely coffee-table book.

Subjects: Farming • Agriculture • Labor • Nature • Business • America • Biography • Collection • Quick Read

Now Try: If *Women of the Harvest* has you pining for a lifestyle that puts you back in touch with the land, don't miss *MaryJane's Ideabook, Cookbook, Lifebook: For the Farmgirl in All of Us*. With down-to-earth wisdom and plentiful photographs, the indomitable MaryJane Butters, author of several books on farming, enlightens readers on a wide variety of topics related to the farming life, including organic farming, starting a farm, food preservation—even games to play with the kids around the farm.

Bollmann, Stefan

Women Who Write. London: Merrell, 2007. 152pp. ISBN 9781858943756.

Stefan Bollmann has created a truly lovely concept with *Women Who Write*, a collective biography of women writers. Each profile pairs a full-page portrait of the author alongside a discussion of her life and the importance of her work. There are plenty of big literary names here, of course (Mary Wollstonecraft, Sylvia Plath, Jane Austen), but also names that are overlooked by the canon (mystery writer Agatha Christie, children's writer Beatrix Potter) and names that you may have never heard of before (poet Ingeborg Bachmann, novelist Zeruya Shalev). This beautifully illustrated book of women writers is not a definitive guide to the best celebrated or most studied authors but rather a celebration of a variety of writers from throughout time and across the globe.

Subjects: Writing • Labor • History • Women's History • Biography • Global Perspectives • Quick Read • Collection

Now Try: The natural companion to *Women Who Write*, of course, is Bollman's *Reading Women*. This visually stunning book features photographs, paintings, and drawings of women reading, paired with Bollman's engaging insights into women, literature, and art. Then try *Women Who Love Books Too Much: Bibliophiles, Bluestockings & Prolific Pens from the Algonquin Hotel to the Ya-Ya Sisterhood*, in which Brenda Knight provides brief, entertaining profiles of women writers throughout the ages; fans of *Women Who Write* will appreciate the entertaining style and the wealth of illustrations.

Haynsworth, Leslie, and David M. Toomey

Amelia Earhart's Daughters: The Wild and Glorious Story of American Women Aviators from World War II to the Dawn of the Space Age. New York: William Morrow, 1998 (New York: Perennial, 2000). 332pp. ISBN 9780688152338.

We all know about Amelia Earhart, but who came after her? To judge by the dearth of women pilots today, one might think that women have never been a significant presence in aviation, but as *Amelia Earhart's Daughters* shows, women played a remarkable role in the history of flight. This book chronicles their extraordinary experiences, from their origins as stunt pilots to their daring escapades in the United States Air Force to their dashed hopes for space flight in the mid-twentieth century. With engaging prose, entertaining anecdotes, and frequently suspenseful circumstances, the authors present stories of the surprising number of American women who had an impact on aviation.

Subjects: Aviation • Labor • Sexual Discrimination • History • Women's History • Social History • American History • Twentieth Century • America

Now Try: For those who enjoyed the celebratory spirit of *Amelia Earhart's Daughters*, an excellent visual companion is *Women and Flight: Portraits of Contemporary Women Pilots*, in which author Carolyn Russo has assembled a stunning array of her photographs of women and their planes. Try also *Yankee Doodle Gals: Women Pilots of World War II*. Amy Nathan's book is written for a young adult audience, but readers of any age will enjoy the stories of the first women to fly American military aircraft.

Heller, Nancy

Women Artists: An Illustrated History. New York: Abbeville Press, 1987 (2003). 255pp. ISBN 9780896597488.

Sure, you've heard of Frida Kahlo and Judy Chicago, but what about Italian Renaissance painter Sofonisba Anguissola or the contemporary Icelandic sculptor Katrin Sigurdardottir? Meet more than one hundred women artists from the Renaissance through the present in this lovely collective biography. Each entry features a brief profile of the artist's life and the importance of her work, along with at least one reproduction of her work. With more than 200 illustrations, including 150 full-color reproductions of paintings and sculptures, this is a visually satisfying, engagingly written survey of women artists; treat it as a reference book or read it from cover to cover for an excellent introduction to those women who are too often ignored in art history books.

Subjects: Art • Artists • Labor • History • Women's History • Art History • Sixteenth Century • Seventeenth Century • Eighteenth Century • Nineteenth Century • Twentieth Century • Twenty-first Century • Global Perspectives • Biography • Collection

Now Try: For another scholarly but accessible survey of women artists, turn to Wendy Slatkin's excellent *Women Artists in History: From Antiquity to the Present*. Profusely illustrated with reproductions of women's creations, the book offers a crisp, detailed introduction not only to women's artwork but also to the artists themselves—their lives, their social milieus, and their struggles to overcome gender barriers.

Matasar, Ann B.

Women of Wine: The Rise of Women in the Global Wine Industry. Berkeley: University of California Press, 2006. 252pp. ISBN 9780520240513.

Perhaps you never realized that winemaking has traditionally been a male-dominated enterprise. *Women of Wine* quickly dispels any confusion over that question, showing that wine production has been the domain of men for millennia. Fortunately that's changing, as author Matasar capably demonstrates through interviews with influential women in today's wine industry. With accessible prose and keen insight, businesswoman Matasar takes the reader through the history of women in wine and considers the various spheres across the globe in which women are influencing wine production today. Issues related to women's needs, such as family, education, and mentorship, are also addressed.

Subjects: Wine • Agriculture • Business • Labor • History • Social History • Women's History • Global Perspectives

Now Try: Though with a less global scope than *Women of Wine*, a great companion piece is Deborah Brenner's *Women of the Vine: Inside the World of Women Who Make, Taste, and Enjoy Wine*. The author, owner of Women of the Vine Cellars, interviews twenty-one women who earn their living in the wine world, including company presidents, sommeliers, and wine writers. Learn about the process of making wine and the gender barriers that women must overcome to succeed in the wine industry.

Robbins, Trina

The Great Women Cartoonists. New York: Watson-Guptill, 2001 (2002). 150pp. ISBN 9780823021703.

Wonder Woman, that luscious babe who fuels adolescent fantasies and gives young girls a female superhero to admire, was actually created by a man; decades passed before a woman took control of her. This seems counterintuitive, but, as Robbins explains, there just weren't many women cartoonists available—not from lack of interest, but because the cartooning world was dominated by men. In this illuminating history of women cartoonists, Robbins—herself an accomplished cartoonist—looks at the intrepid women who managed to publish their art, despite the sexist obstacles. Though written as a scholarly work, the fascinating stories and myriad illustrations make this a captivating read for anyone interested in cartooning, feminism, or women's history.

Subjects: Cartoons • Art • Writing • Labor • History • Social History • Women's History • Twentieth Century • Feminism • Sexual Discrimination • Quick Read

Now Try: To say nothing of her own feminist-inspired cartoons, Robbins is the author of several scholarly works on women and cartooning. A logical follow-up to *The Great Women Cartoonists* is her book *The Great Women Superheroes*, where the emphasis is not on the creators but the creations; with the wealth of illustrations and Robbins's fiery analysis, feminist criticism has never been so fun. To see some of these same superheroes, but with less feminist rhetoric, turn to the stunning art in Louise Simonson's *DC Comics Covergirls*.

Robinson, Jane

Women Out of Bounds: The Secret History of Enterprising Women. New York: Carroll & Graf, 2002 (2003). 222pp. ISBN 9780786710515.

Have you ever heard of Tennessee Claflin, the nineteenth-century clairvoyant and stockbroker? How about Maria de Estrada, the medieval conquistador? Author Jane Robinson has unearthed stories of these and more than one hundred other unusual women, most of whom will be unfamiliar to readers. From pirates to rulers, bricklayers to scientists, *Women Out of Bounds* captures brief profiles of women throughout history who ignored sexual norms to pursue their own gender-defying agendas. Entertaining, informative, and engaging, this collective biography will bring to life new stories for even the most dedicated students of women's history.

Subjects: Labor • History • Social History • Women's History • Global Perspectives • Biography • Collection

Now Try: Though gender rules have weakened in the past century, women still face hurdles when trying to enter professions traditionally dominated by men. In *Conversations with Uncommon Women: Insights from Women Who've Risen above Life's Challenges to Achieve Extraordinary Success*, author Ellie Wymard profiles one hundred women who fought social norms to follow their professional dreams. Readers who enjoyed the sketches in *Women Out of Bounds* will enjoy the inspiring stories of these extraordinary women who have found success in careers ranging from law to politics to the arts.

Women in Science and Technology

Here are stories of women who chose to work in the traditionally male-dominated arenas of science and technology.

Traditionally, the sciences have not been hospitable to women, but the books of the "Women in Science and Technology" section show that women in the past and the present have persevered, despite institutional and societal sexism. Some books featured here consider women's struggles from a broad perspective, as with Margaret Wertheim's *Pythagoras' Trousers: God, Physics, and the Gender Wars*, while others celebrate individuals (see Patricia Fara's *Scientists Anonymous: Great Stories of Women in Science*) and their accomplishments (try *Patently Female* by Ethlie Ann Vare and Greg Ptacek). For more stories of women in science and technology, turn to the "Women in the Professions" section of Chapter 1.

Etzkowitz, Henry, Carol Kemelgor, and Brian Uzzi

Athena Unbound: The Advancement of Women in Science and Technology. Cambridge, UK: Cambridge University Press, 2000. 282pp. ISBN 9780521563802.

Though women have forged tremendous inroads in the workforce over the course of the past several decades, their advances in the sciences have been disappointing. In this wide-reaching study, the authors attempt to understand why men continue to far outnumber women in professional and academic science circles. Based on interviews with hundreds of scientists, *Athena Unbound* unveils the difficult social realities faced by women in science and technology careers. Though scholarly in approach, the accessible writing style and vivid personal anecdotes make this an engaging read, one that invites readers to understand and overcome the barriers to women's advancement in science.

Subjects: Science • Gender • Labor • Sexual Discrimination

Now Try: Learn more about the challenges that women face in science careers in *Who's Afraid of Marie Curie?: The Challenges Facing Women in Science and Technology*. Linley Erin

Hall interviewed more than one hundred women scientists, including doctors, academics, and students, to uncover the biases that they have overcome and the struggles they still continue to face. Then turn to *Unlocking the Clubhouse: Women in Computing*, based on a four-year study of students in computer science, in which authors Jane Margolis and Allan Fisher conclude that the gender gap at the college level and beyond stems from educational biases present in early childhood.

Fara, Patricia

Scientists Anonymous: Great Stories of Women in Science. Thriplow, UK: Wizard, 2005 (2007). 213pp. ISBN 9781840465747.

Sure, you've heard of Marie Curie and Florence Nightingale—but what about Dorothy Crowfoot Hodgkin, winner of the Nobel Prize in Chemistry in 1964, or nineteenth-century mathematician Sophie Germaine? The thorough research of Patricia Fara has unearthed the stories of a wealth of women scientists, many of whom will be unfamiliar to readers. Though intended for a young adult audience, the cogent writing and expansive scope of *Scientists Anonymous* will captivate readers of any age. The inspiring stories of this collective biography, as well as the relentless examples of sexual discrimination, make this welcome reading for anyone interested in the remarkable influence of women in science throughout history.

> **Subjects:** Science • Mathematics • History • History of Science • Labor • Sexual Discrimination • Social History • Women's History • Global Perspectives • Biography • Collection • Young Adult • Quick Read

> **Now Try:** Though not necessarily a cover-to-cover narrative read, a must-have reference for anyone intrigued by *Scientists Anonymous* is Lisa Yount's *A to Z of Women in Science and Math*. Biographies of women scientists from all across the globe, from antiquity to the present, are here collected in one accessible volume. With ample illustrations and a readable style suitable for adults and young adults alike, the book illuminates the life and work of more than 150 scientists and mathematicians and the barriers they faced.

Newitz, Annalee, and Charlie Anders, eds.

She's Such a Geek! Women Write about Science, Technology, and Other Nerdy Stuff. Emeryville, CA: Seal Press, 2006. 231pp. ISBN 9781580051903.

Calling all geek-ladies! If you've ever felt alone because of your competence at building computers, or your enviable skills in the science lab, or your encyclopedic knowledge of the intricate rules of Dungeons & Dragons, this book is for you. This pro-girl, pro-brain anthology highlights the experiences of twenty-four women who don't apologize for their nerdy prowess. In the arenas of science, technology, and male-dominated pastimes, these authors write inspiring, brassy essays that celebrate the geek in all of us. And when sexual discrimination rears its ugly head, they address it head-on, making this both a tribute to brainy women and a reminder that sexist attitudes still threaten the woman who wants to be smart.

> **Subjects:** Geeks • Nerds • Science • Technology • Labor • Gender • Feminism • Sexual Discrimination • Essays • Collection • Anthology

> **Now Try:** Why, exactly, do sexist barriers against smart women still persist, even in the twenty-first century? Find out in *Geek Chic: Smart Women in Popular*

Culture, an anthology edited by Sherrie A. Inness. The essays explore the role of sex and gender in the idea of the smart, geeky woman, drawing on media stereotypes and real-life women in popular culture and society. *Geek Chic* is somewhat more scholarly than *She's Such a Geek!,* but the engaging writing and familiar subject will speak to any woman who has felt stifled because of her brains.

Rayner-Canham, Marelene F., and Geoffrey Rayner-Canham

Women in Chemistry: Their Changing Roles from Alchemical Times to the Mid-Twentieth Century. History of Modern Chemical Sciences. Washington, DC: American Chemical Society, 1998 (Philadelphia, PA: Chemical Heritage Foundation, 2001). 284pp. ISBN 9780841235229.

Marie Curie wasn't the only woman in the history of chemistry, though most people would be hard-pressed to think of another. *Women in Chemistry* seeks to bring attention to the various women who have, throughout history, made their mark in the chemical sciences. With short, informative, engagingly written biographies, the book profiles women chemists ranging from Hypatia, the fifth-century Greek mathematician, to twentieth-century biochemist Icie Macy Hoobler, one of the first scientists to investigate the nutritional needs of pregnant women. The authors give special attention to the discrimination against women in chemistry and the sexual barriers they overcame.

Subjects: Chemistry • Science • Mathematics • Labor • History • Social History • History of Science • Women's History • Sexual Discrimination • Global Perspectives • Biography • Collection

Now Try: For a thorough examination of a slice of chemistry, turn to *A Devotion to Their Science: Pioneer Women of Radioactivity,* also by Rayner-Canham and Rayner-Canham. Focusing on women in the atomic sciences in the early twentieth century, the book presents biographies of twenty-three scientists—including, of course, Marie Curie, but also her lesser-known contemporaries. Their life stories are presented, with special emphasis on their contributions to science at the beginning of the atomic age.

Shayler, David, and Ian A. Moule

Women in Space—Following Valentina. Springer-Praxis Books in Space Exploration. Chichester, UK: Praxis, 2005. 410pp. ISBN 9781852337445.

In 1963, Valentina Tereshkova became the first woman to orbit the Earth. But the story of women in space began long before then—indeed, the authors take us all the way back to 1784, when the first woman flew in a hot-air balloon. In this impressively thorough history, readers learn not only about the dozens of women who have been in space, but about the many, many women who have participated in space programs, including those who worked exclusively on the ground and those who contributed to the development of aviation in general. Both a celebration of women's achievements in space and astronomy and a critical examination of the sexual barriers they overcame, *Women in Space* is a captivating read for anyone interested in women's history, space history, or aviation history.

Subjects: Astronauts • Cosmonauts • Space Exploration • Astronomy • Aviation • Labor • Sexual Discrimination • Travel • Science • History • History of Science • Women's History • Social History • Eighteenth Century • Nineteenth Century • Twentieth Century • Twenty- first Century

Now Try: A little-known chapter of American history quietly passed, unremarked, in the 1960s. The Women in Space Program is a sad example of a what could have been, documented in fascinating detail by Margaret A. Weitekamp in *Right Stuff, Wrong Sex:*

America's First Women in Space Program. Discover the ugly effects of discrimination in action with the story of thirteen women who were thoroughly trained in space flight but who, for political and financial reasons, never made it into space.

Sheffield, Suzanne Le-May

Women and Science: Social Impact and Interaction. Santa Barbara, CA: ABC-CLIO, 2004 (New Brunswick, NJ: Rutgers University Press, 2006). 409pp. ISBN 9781851094608.

"During the Middle Ages and the Renaissance, women had numerous opportunities to study nature," writes Sheffield, "although what we think of as science today did not exist." But with the birth of science as we recognize it today during the Scientific Revolution, and ever since then, women have faced numerous obstacles when trying to participate in the sciences. *Women and Science* critically examines the social barriers of the past three hundred years that have hindered women in science, while celebrating the advances women have made in spite of those barriers. The writing in this well-researched book is scholarly but not arduous, presenting a serious examination of the history of issues such as women in higher education, the recognition of women's scientific achievements, and the feminization of science.

> **Subjects:** Science • History • History of Science • Women's History • Social History • Eighteenth Century • Nineteenth Century • Twentieth Century • Twenty-first Century • Labor • Sexual Discrimination • Feminism

> **Now Try:** Books about women in science written for an adult audience are frustratingly rare—a fact that, in itself, speaks to the continuing under-representation of women in the sciences. Readers willing to explore older books, however, will be rewarded with *Women Scientists in America: Struggles and Strategies to 1940*, written by Margaret W. Rossiter in 1982. With impressive research, Rossiter examines women scientists and the formidable barriers they encountered. See also Rossiter's 1998 sequel *Women Scientists in America: Before Affirmative Action, 1940–1972*, which continues the examination of women scientists and the obstacles that continued to plague them as time progressed.

Vare, Ethlie Ann, and Greg Ptacek

Patently Female: From AZT to TV Dinners: Stories of Women Inventors and Their Breakthrough Ideas. **(Previously known as *Patently Female: Women Inventors and Their Big Ideas.*)** New York: John Wiley & Sons, 2002. 220pp. ISBN 9780471023340.

Everyone knows Eli Whitney invented the cotton gin, right? Actually, Whitney was helped by Catharine Littlefield Greene, who played as big a role in the invention as he did; in fact, an extraordinary number of inventions attributed to men were in fact created by women. *Patently Female* seeks to restore proper credit to those forgotten female inventors, while bringing to light those inventions that have always been properly attributed to their female inventors, such as Kevlar, the fiber worn by law enforcement to deflect bullets, created by Stephanie L. Kwolek. With plentiful photographs and a conversational, engaging style, authors Vare and Ptacek illuminate the achievements of women inventors throughout history.

Subjects: Inventions • Labor • History • Women's History • Biography • Collection

Now Try: *Patently Female* is actually a sequel to Vare and Ptacek's *Mothers of Invention: From the Bra to the Bomb: Forgotten Women and Their Unforgettable Ideas*, well worth reading if you can find the 1988 text. For a more recent examination of women's inventions, try *Feminine Ingenuity: How Women Inventors Changed America*, by Anne MacDonald. With an accessible style and tone, the book examines women patent-holders, their inventions, and the social barriers they overcame to create their inventions.

Wertheim, Margaret

Pythagoras' Trousers: God, Physics, and the Gender Wars. New York: Times Books/Random House, 1995 (New York: W. W. Norton, 1997). 279pp. ISBN 9780-812922004.

Why are there so few women in physics? In this lovely history of science, author Wertheim considers the troubling question of gender inequity with a refreshing, unexpected thesis. The history of physics, argues Wertheim, should be considered in a religious context, with the role of God inseparable from the role of numbers. Seen from this perspective, barriers to women in physics make historical sense, given the barriers to women in Western religion. *Pythagoras' Trousers* is intelligent and scholarly, but not so academic that general readers will be turned off. For fans of feminist, scientific, or religious scholarship, the book brings new meaning to the sexism that continues to plague women physicists to the present day.

Subjects: Physics • Science • History • History of Science • Religion • History of Religion • Women's History • Social History • Sexual Discrimination • Feminism

Now Try: For those readers wanting to know more about women in physics, an excellent choice is *Out of the Shadows: Contributions of Twentieth-Century Women to Physics*, edited by Nina Byers and Gary A. Williams. Though the unusual religious argument of *Pythagoras' Trousers* is absent, the book examines myriad other reasons for the discrimination against women in physics, both in historical and contemporary times. The contributors use scholarly but accessible writing and photographs to illuminate the lives and contributions of women physicists in the twentieth century.

Women Doctors, Lawyers, and Clergy

Women as doctors, lawyers, and clergy provide the focus to these titles.

Time and again, sexism rears its ugly head in the "Women Doctors, Lawyers, and Clergy" section—and each time, women rise to the challenge. In the present and in the past, women have fought to work as doctors, lawyers, and clergy, overcoming sexist opposition that persists even today.

Brooke, Elisabeth

Women Healers: Portraits of Herbalists, Physicians, and Midwives. Rochester, VT: Healing Arts Press, 1996. 168pp. ISBN 9780892815487.

Women have practiced medicine throughout history, usually in defiance of prevailing social norms. *Women Healers* draws on primary sources to examine those women who courageously practiced medicine, including those healers who practiced with the sanction of their societies and, more commonly, those who did not.

Author Brooke reveals portraits of women both famous and forgotten, placing them in social context and examining the prejudices against them. With an enjoyable writing style and a decidedly feminist perspective, the author reconsiders medical history and restores women healers to their rightful place.

Subjects: Doctors • Health Care • Labor • History • History of Medicine • History of Science • Social History • Women's History • Global Perspectives • Quick Read

Now Try: Though published in 1972 and only 48 pages long, *Witches, Midwives, and Nurses: A History of Women Healers* is still very much worth reading. Co-authors Barbara Ehrenreich (most famous for her investigative journalism in *Nickel and Dimed*) and Deirdre English compiled a concise, captivating history of women in medicine that is still relevant today. Another excellent companion piece is Jeanne Achterberg's *Woman as Healer*; like *Women Healers*, it looks at the history of women in medicine and presents a feminist examination of their social and sexual milieu. And for a thorough examination of a slice of women's history in medicine, turn to *The Doctor Wore Petticoats: Women Physicians of the Old West*, by Chris Enss, about ten women medics in the unwelcoming Old West.

Chin, Eliza Lo

This Side of Doctoring: Reflections from Women in Medicine. Thousand Oaks, CA: Sage, 2002 (Oxford, UK: Oxford University Press, 2003). 394pp. ISBN 9780761923541.

In this inspiring anthology of essays and poems, women in medicine use their own voices to describe their experiences as health care providers. More than one hundred women in medicine, both contemporary and historical, reflect on what medicine means to them. *This Side of Doctoring* is illuminating not only for the insider views on practicing medicine, but for the honest, often poignant discussions of the difficulties faced by women doctors as they try to balance their professional dreams with their personal lives. The book is valuable for both scholars of historic and contemporary medicine and for pleasure readers who want to know more about the triumphs and struggles of women in medicine.

Subjects: Doctors • Health Care • Labor • Science • History • History of Medicine • History of Science • Social History • Women's History • Work/Life Balance • Essays • Poems • Collection • Anthology

Now Try: Anyone who appreciates the role of women in medicine will delight in *Women in Medicine: A Celebration of Their Work*. Authors/photographers Ted Grant and Sandy Carter have compiled more than one hundred stunning black-and-white photos of women in health care, from doctors to nurses to medical technicians. The text is deliberately kept to a minimum, allowing the pictures of women practicing medicine to tell their own remarkable stories.

Drachman, Virginia G.

Sisters in Law: Women Lawyers in Modern American History. Cambridge, MA: Harvard University Press, 1998 (2001). 334pp. ISBN 9780674809918.

In the late nineteenth and early twentieth centuries, amid the backdrop of the women's suffrage movement and the first wave of feminism, a handful of courageous women broke into the world of law, first earning the right to enter law school and then campaigning to take the bar exam. In this meticulously researched study of the first women lawyers in America, author Drachman presents an engrossing narrative, part social history and part collective biography. Learn about the stifling social, sexual, and educational barriers that confronted aspiring women attorneys in the Victorian era, and meet the extraordinary women who overcame those barriers to become America's first female lawyers.

> **Subjects:** Law • Lawyers • Labor • History • History of Law • Social History • Women's History • American History • Nineteenth Century • Twentieth Century • Sexual Discrimination • America • Biography • Collection

> **Now Try:** The lawyers profiled in Drachman's book laid the groundwork for the very earliest American women attorneys; now jump ahead a few decades to the Harvard Law School of 1964, where only fifteen students from a class of more than five hundred graduates were women. One of those fifteen women was Judith Hope, who has compiled a mesmerizing account in *Pinstripes & Pearls: The Women of the Harvard Law Class of '64 Who Forged an Old Girl Network and Paved the Way for Future Generations*. Crafted from the memories of Hope, her classmates, and her professors, this is the compelling story of triumph in the face of sexism, of women who attained success in a profession that didn't want them.

Morantz-Sanchez, Regina Markell

Sympathy and Science: Women Physicians in American Medicine. New York: Oxford University Press, 1985 (Chapel Hill; London: University of North Carolina Press, 2000). 464pp. ISBN 9780807848906.

Well before they could formally enter medical school, women in America devised ways to practice as doctors. In this thorough, well-researched text, author Morantz-Sanchez considers the women who practiced medicine, beginning with the midwives and nurses of colonial times and ending with the fully qualified physicians of today. Engagingly written, *Sympathy and Science* examines the historical sexist attitudes that limited women's participation in medicine and the women who overcame them. The triumphs of contemporary women are celebrated, without neglecting the barriers that they continue to struggle against. This is an excellent social study for anyone interested in medicine or women's history.

> **Subjects:** Doctors • Health Care • Labor • Science • History • History of Medicine • History of Science • Social History • Women's History • American History • Sexual Discrimination • America

> **Now Try:** Though her book does not reach as far back into history as *Sympathy and Science*, Ellen Singer More's *Restoring the Balance: Women Physicians and the Profession of Medicine, 1850–1995* makes for an excellent companion read. The writing has a more scholarly tone, but the book's incisive analysis of sexual discrimination and women's issues is essential for anyone trying to understand the social contexts of women's history in medicine. Historical resources and interviews with women physicians flesh out the story of women doctors, while a strong feminist perspective casts the history of sexism into sharp relief. Then try *Doctors: The Illustrated History of Medical Pioneers*, Sherwin B. Nuland's gorgeous survey of medical advances throughout history. The doctors are mostly men, but the historical context and captivating narrative make it a fascinating read.

Nadell, Pamela Susan

Women Who Would Be Rabbis: A History of Women's Ordination, 1889–1985. Boston: Beacon Press, 1998. 300pp. ISBN 9780807036501.

In 1972, Sally Priesand was ordained as America's first woman rabbi—but the story of Jewish women's struggle to be ordained began well before that. In this intelligent, engaging history, author Nadell traces the subject back to 1889, when a Jewish journalist dared to print a provocative question, asking whether women could be rabbis. It seemed laughable at the time, yet as Nadell's scholarship shows, women were listening; even before the first official ordination, women were discussing the question and agitating for change. *Women Who Would Be Rabbis* explores the social and religious history of the major branches of American Judaism, as well as the modern debates over women's roles in Judaism, still unresolved today.

> **Subjects:** Rabbis • Clergy • Judaism • Religion • Labor • History • History of Religion • Nineteenth Century • Twentieth Century • Social History • Women's History • American History • America • Sexual Discrimination

> **Now Try:** Jump across the Atlantic to learn about women rabbis in Britain. Rabbi editor Sybil Sheridan has collected an anthology of essays written by and about Jewish women rabbis in *Hear Our Voice: Women in the British Rabbinate*. Though the contributors are European, their struggles to understand what it means to be a Jewish clergywoman will resonate with readers who enjoyed *Women Who Would Be Rabbis*.

Nossel, Suzanne, and Elizabeth Westfall

Presumed Equal: What America's Top Women Lawyers Really Think about Their Firms. Franklin Lakes, NJ: Career Press, 1998. 392pp. ISBN 9781564143204.

> Even today, with the many remarkable professional advances made by women in law, sex-based barriers abound. In addition to the good-old-boy mentality that still persists at many law firms, there are gendered issues that women lawyers must struggle against, such as the need to balance career and family and the difficulty of getting around the "mommy wall." In *Presumed Equal*, the authors draw on survey responses from almost four thousand women lawyers to get the real story behind sexism in the workplace; what is particularly interesting is that, rather than speaking in generalities, the book identifies details on 105 specific law firms. Though intended for law students, the honest discussion of real-life issues makes this an informative, eye-opening read for anyone curious about the gender climate in modern law practice.

> **Subjects:** Law • Lawyers • Labor • Gender • Sexual Discrimination • America

> **Now Try:** *Presumed Equal* draws on surveys to shed light on gender issues in law firms; *Ending the Gauntlet: Removing Barriers to Women's Success in the Law*, by Lauren Stiller Rikleen, draws on interviews to explore those same issues. The book is valuable not only for its unrelenting examination of sex and sexism in the workplace, but for its practical recommendations for change.

Schneider, Carl J., and Dorothy Schneider

In Their Own Right: The History of American Clergywomen. New York: Crossroad, 1997. 310pp. ISBN 9780824516536.

> Most clergy today in the Christian and Judaic traditions are men, though it is not terribly uncommon for women to serve as clergy; in times past, however, it was most unusual for women to preach, as seen in the excellent book *In Their Own Right: The History of American Clergywomen*. A few

intrepid women, however, managed to overcome the societal and religious barriers of their times to become legitimate members of the clergy. Learn about these courageous women and their modern-day heirs in this painstakingly researched social history, which examines the clergywomen of America's past and present while placing their struggles and triumphs in historical context. A great number of Christian and Judaic denominations and branches are considered, making this a thorough overview of the history of American clergywomen.

Subjects: Clergy • Religion • Christianity • Judaism • Labor • Sexual Discrimination • History • History of Religion • Seventeenth Century • Eighteenth Century • Nineteenth Century • Twentieth Century • Social History • Women's History • American History • America

Now Try: For a more detailed examination of a slice of American clergywomen's history, turn to Susie C. Stanley's *Holy Boldness: Women Preachers' Autobiographies and the Sanctified Self.* Though written with a more scholarly tone than *In Their Own Right*, this text will appeal to readers who want to hear the voices of the women themselves. Drawing from thirty-four autobiographies, author Stanley presents perspectives from Wesleyan/Holiness preachers in the nineteenth and twentieth centuries, while offering her own feminist interpretation of history. Readers who enjoy this feminist approach to the history of clergywomen should also try Beverly Zink-Sawyer's *From Preachers to Suffragists: Woman's Rights and Religious Conviction in the Lives of Three Nineteenth-Century American Clergywomen*, about three preachers whose religious convictions compelled them toward early feminism.

Slotkin, Jacquelyn Hersh, and Samantha Slotkin Goodman, eds.

It's Harder in Heels: Essays by Women Lawyers Achieving Work-Life Balance. Lake Mary, FL: Vandeplas, 2007. 150pp. ISBN 9781600420269.

Every career-minded woman must learn to juggle her work and her personal life, but few must try harder than lawyers. Law is a demanding profession; any lawyer wishing to maintain personal happiness must have courage, creativity, and drive, as seen in this refreshing collection of essays written by and about women lawyers. Topics range from the ugly realities of workplace sexism to the inspiring victories of women who have succeeded in finding balance between work and home. The lively, fresh voices of the contributors will motivate fellow attorneys and illuminate the world of law for curious outsiders.

Subjects: Law • Lawyers • Labor • Work/Life Balance • Sexual Discrimination • Essays • Collection • Anthology • Quick Read

Now Try: Hear more from women lawyers in *Women at Law: Lessons Learned along the Pathways to Success*, in which author Phyllis Horn Epstein interviews more than one hundred women attorneys. Listen to their own voices, couched in Epstein's practical analysis, as they consider the social issues and work/life balance struggles of women in law. For even more interviews with women attorneys, see Mona Harrington's *Women Lawyers: Rewriting the Rules*; though this 1993 text is somewhat dated, many of the same social barriers discussed in the book are still, unfortunately, present today. And for a lighter, brighter read, turn to *Sisters-in-Law: An Uncensored Guide for Women Practicing Law in the Real World* by Lisa G. Sherman, Deborah Turchiano, and Jill Schecter. This is chick lit for the professional lawyer; serious issues are addressed, but the focus is on fun, with topics ranging from personal style to office decorating to interpersonal office relationships.

Women Athletes

Here are stories of women who have participated in sports and other athletic activities.

Male athletes still outpace their women peers in terms of salaries, contracts, and publicity, but the landscape has improved tremendously since the passage of Title IX in 1972. Read this section to discover books about contemporary women athletes in a variety of sports—including basketball, racing, and the martial arts—and for an excellent history of women in sports, try Lissa Smith's *Nike Is a Goddess*. Readers wishing to improve their own games will want to turn to the "Sports and Fitness" section of Chapter 3.

Baker, Christine A.

Why She Plays: The World of Women's Basketball. Lincoln: University of Nebraska Press, 2008. 198pp. ISBN 9780803216334.

Basketball is a sport traditionally dominated by men, so why do some women feel drawn to it? Christine A. Baker is the perfect person to answer that question, as she is a sportswriter, a basketball coach, and a lifelong basketball player. In *Why She Plays*, Baker integrates her own experiences with words of wisdom gleaned from her interviews with women coaches and women players. Covering all levels of basketball playing, from youth and high school teams through college and the WNBA, Baker considers women's experiences in chapters such as "The Fun Factor," "The Slippery Slope of Gender Politics," and "The Superstars and the 'Special' Treatment." With her captivating writing style, Baker gracefully describes and explains the enthusiasm that women players and coaches feel for basketball.

Subjects: Basketball • Sports • Athletes • Exercise • Labor • Memoir • Quick Read

Now Try: *Why She Plays* shows us that some women are drawn to basketball, no matter the obstacles. This lesson is eloquently reinforced with the story of a women's team that nearly won the NCAA Division III championship. That alone makes for a remarkable story, but now consider this: the players were deaf. In *Winning Sounds Like This: A Season with the Women's Basketball Team at Gallaudet, the World's Only University for the Deaf*, sportswriter Wayne R. Coffey details the story of the team's accomplishments in the face of all odds.

McEvoy, John, and Julia McEvoy

Women in Racing: In Their Own Words. Lexington, KY: Eclipse Press, 2001. 288pp. ISBN 9781581500677.

Horse racing is not just about the jockeys. Groomers, trainers, photographers, commentators, clerks—these are just a sampling of occupations among the eighteen women interviewed in *Women in Racing*. Discover the world of horse racing through the variety of perspectives presented in this illuminating compilation of insiders' views. The honesty and fervor of the interviewees' own words captures the best and the worst of racing, from the thrill of victory to the demoralizing reality of sexism. Plentiful black-and-white photos underscore the inspiring, affirming, even shocking stories.

Subjects: Horse Racing • Sports • Athletes • Exercise • Labor • History • Sports History • Social History • Women's History • Twentieth Century • Biography

Now Try: Turn now to the superstars of horse racing, the jockeys themselves. Ten women jockeys present their perspectives in *Great Women in the Sport of Kings: America's Top Women Jockeys Tell Their Stories*, edited by Scooter Toby Davidson and Valerie Anthony. This collection of oral histories sheds light on what it means to participate fully in a male-dominated sport, touching on the competitive aspects as well as the personal and social ramifications of being a woman jockey.

Sey, Jennifer

Chalked Up: Inside Elite Gymnastics' Merciless Coaching, Overzealous Parents, Eating Disorders, and Elusive Olympic Dreams. New York: William Morrow, 2008. 292pp. ISBN 9780061351464.

On one level, we may read *Chalked Up* strictly as a memoir. This is the painful story of Jennifer Sey, a gymnast who won the U.S. national championship at the age of seventeen. Hers is a tale of personal sacrifice, of broken bones, eating disorders, and depression. But the book is also a larger indictment of the sport of gymnastics as a whole. The memoir leaves readers wondering whether the strain, psychological stress, and fierce competitive nature of the sport is healthy for the young women who participate in it. This is a thought-provoking book, written with grace and candor.

Subjects: Gymnastics • Sports • Athletes • Health • Mental Health • Memoir • Young Adult

Now Try: Figure skating is the kissing cousin of gymnastics. Both sports showcase the athletic talents of beautiful, graceful women—and both sports can be physically and mentally brutal for the athletes. Turn now to *A Skating Life*, the memoir of Olympic gold medalist figure skater Dorothy Hamill. Like Sey, Hamill was suffering behind the mask of the successful superstar; read this to see how the rigors of figure skating contributed to Hamill's depression, divorces, and financial problems.

Smith, Lissa

Nike Is a Goddess: The History of Women in Sports. New York: Atlantic Monthly Press, 1998 (2001). 331pp. ISBN 9780871137265.

Thirteen sports, covering a broad spectrum ranging from figure skating to ice hockey to golf, are examined in great detail in the collective biography *Nike Is a Goddess: The History of Women in Sports*. In entertaining, informative essays, various sportswriters examine the women who made their mark in their chosen sport and chronicle the achievements that brought them fame, while placing their triumphs in historical context. Numerous photos, fascinating stories, telling statistics, and frequent anecdotes make this an excellent overview of the female superstars of the nineteenth and twentieth centuries.

Subjects: Sports • Athletes • Exercise • History • Sports History • Social History • Women's History • Nineteenth Century • Twentieth Century • Global Perspectives • Biography • Essays • Collection • Young Adult

Now Try: A delightful companion book is Ernestine G. Miller's *Making Her Mark: Firsts and Milestones in Women's Sports*. Though written as a reference book, the presentation of the text is eminently readable, making it suitable for cover-to-cover reading. Over fifty sports are arranged in alphabetical order, beginning with archery and ending with wrestling, and covering such diverse topics as dogsled racing and judo in between. Highlights of women's achievements in each sport are presented chronologically, alongside black-and-white photos of historic and present-day athletes.

Wiley, Carol A., ed.

Women in the Martial Arts. Io, no. 46. Berkeley, CA: North Atlantic Books, 1992. 145pp. ISBN 9781556431364.

Though published in 1992, *Women in the Martial Arts* is still the best anthology of women's writing about martial arts. With compassion and grace, twenty-three women write about the influence of martial arts in their lives. The physical rigors of such arts as Aikido and T'ai Chi Ch'uan are discussed in detail, but each contributor moves beyond the physical mechanics to discuss the spiritual and emotional impact of martial arts; the stories of healing, personal growth, and enlightenment are moving and provocative. A recurring feminist, pro-woman theme makes this a powerful collection for students of martial arts as well as for anyone seeking inspiration from strong women.

Subjects: Martial Arts • Exercise • Sports • Athletes • Feminism • Essays • Collection • Anthology • Quick Read

Now Try: The emotionally transformative potential of the martial arts shines through in *Sharp Spear, Crystal Mirror: Martial Arts in Women's Lives,* in which author Stephanie T. Hoppe interviews more than twenty women martial artists. As in *Women in the Martial Arts,* the emphasis is on Aikido and T'ai Chi Ch'uan, though other arts are represented. Each interview illustrates the power and discipline of martial arts, while gently exploring the spiritual awakenings of the women who practice them.

Women in the Military

The focus of this section is on women who chose careers in the military and the challenges they have faced.

Should American women be allowed to serve in combat? Of course they should, writes Erin Solaro, in *Women in the Line of Fire.* Oh no they should *not,* writes Brian Mitchell, in *Women in the Military.* And what about lesbian women? Yes, definitely, contends Zsa Zsa Gershick, in *Secret Service.* Whatever your perspective, these books will get you thinking about women's career choices in the armed forces. And for more books about the role of women in war, see the "Women Warriors" section of Chapter 1, the "Espionage and War" section of Chapter 5, the "War, Violence, and Peace" section of Chapter 8, and the "American Civil War" and "Women and War in the Twentieth Century" sections of Chapter 4.

1

2

3

4

5

6

7

8

Gershick, Zsa Zsa

Secret Service: Untold Stories of Lesbians in the Military. Los Angeles, CA: Alyson Books, 2005. 305pp. ISBN 9781555837488.

Gershick, a former reservist with the Army, is perfectly clear in her opinion about the United States military's "Don't Ask, Don't Tell" policy about sexual orientation: she thinks it's absurd. In *Secret Service*, she argues that lesbians can indeed serve their country in uniform and that forcing them to hide their identities hurts the individuals as well as the military itself. The book collects Gerschick's interviews with a wide variety of lesbians from all branches of the military, some of whom are presently serving. By discussing their accomplishments and revealing the struggles they endure to hide their orientations, the interviewees gracefully shatter the myth that lesbians are unfit to serve openly.

Subjects: Lesbian Sexuality • Queer Sexuality • Warriors • Sexual Discrimination • Labor • America

Now Try: Colonel Margarethe Cammermeyer, who wrote the introduction for Gershick's book, understands the cost of revealing a lesbian identity. Despite the accolades she garnered during her long military career—including a Bronze Star for her service in Vietnam and the Nurse of the Year award from the Veterans Administration— she was discharged in 1989 when she admitted that she was a lesbian. In her memoir *Serving in Silence*, Cammermeyer recalls her childhood, her ill-fated marriage, her distinguished career, and the courtroom battles she faced when she fought to be reinstated.

Mirabile, Michele Hunter

Your Mother Wears Combat Boots: Humorous, Harrowing, and Heartwarming Stories of Military Women. Bloomington, IN: AuthorHouse, 2007. 261pp. ISBN 9781434320452.

In *Your Mother Wears Combat Boots*, nearly sixty American servicewomen from every branch of the United States Armed Forces reflect on what it means to be a woman warrior. Compiled by former Air Force brat and Army sergeant Mirabile, these short essays offer glimpses into a variety of issues faced by servicewomen, from lighthearted musings on hair length to profound memories of family, love, and death. A wide range of emotions—courage and ambition, introspection and sorrow—are presented in these straightforward, grittily honest vignettes. This is an excellent sampling of perspectives for anyone curious about modern American women in the armed forces.

Subjects: Warriors • War • Violence • Labor • America • Twentieth Century • Essays • Collection • Anthology

Now Try: To place the contemporary essays of *Your Mother Wears Combat Boots* into historical and visual context, try *Side-by-Side: A Photographic History of American Women in War*. In this readable, beautifully crafted tribute, author/photographer Vickie Lewis documents the impressive history of women soldiers, drawing on primary documents, interviews, and photographs to bring life to the story of American servicewomen.

Mitchell, Brian

Women in the Military: Flirting with Disaster. Washington, DC: Regnery Pub, 1998. 390pp. ISBN 9780895263766.

"With the exception of the medical professions, there is no real need for women in the military," writes Mitchell, a former infantry officer. Furthermore, he contends, the presence of women in uniform threatens national security, leaving the American military "no more disciplined, no more efficient, no more fearsome, no more military than the United States Postal Service." Drawing on his research into gender and military service, Mitchell argues that the acceptance of women in the service is the result of a feminist agenda that values equal gender opportunities more than national defense. Given the book's controversial subject and Mitchell's scathing style, readers will either love or hate *Women in the Military*, but in either case it offers plenty of food for thought.

> **Subjects:** Warriors • Gender • Sexual Discrimination • Labor • America

> **Now Try:** Journalist Stephanie Gutmann does not share Mitchell's belief that women should be barred from service; she thinks that any male or female fit for the job should be accepted. Nonetheless, she has strong reservations about the culture changes in the military that have been kindled by the presence of women. In *The Kinder, Gentler Military: Can America's Gender-Neutral Fighting Force Still Win Wars?*, she argues that, in trying to accommodate women, the military has become too soft. Backed by her interviews with men and women in uniform, Gutmann presents a case for reforming the military's culture to improve its defense capabilities without discriminating against women who want to serve.

Solaro, Erin

Women in the Line of Fire: What You Should Know about Women in the Military. Emeryville, CA: Seal Press, 2006. 411pp. ISBN 9781580051743.

The time has come for women to be fully integrated into America's armed forces, argues author Solaro in her impassioned, magnificently researched study. Based on her time spent in Iraq and Afghanistan studying women's roles in combat, the author has concluded not only that women are fully capable of military service but that America actually needs them. Readers from any number of backgrounds—military or pacifist, liberal or conservative, feminist or traditional—will find a wealth of information in *Women in the Line of Fire*, presented in clear, persuasive prose.

> **Subjects:** Warriors • War • War on Terror • Violence • Gender • Sexual Discrimination • History • Military History • American History • Social History • Twentieth Century • Twenty-first Century • Feminism • Labor • America • Iraq • Afghanistan • Middle East • Asia

> **Now Try:** For more evidence supporting the use of women in combat, see *Band of Sisters: American Women at War in Iraq*, in which author Kirsten A. Holmstedt presents the stories of twelve women serving in Iraq. Tense, gritty, and gripping, the heroism and courageousness of these servicewomen will speak volumes to readers, whatever their position in the debate over women's role in the military. And in *Women at War: Iraq, Afghanistan, and Other Conflicts*, the women's voices speak for themselves; authors James E. Wise and Scott Baron have compiled a powerful volume of oral histories that gives servicewomen the chance to prove their valor in their own words.

Williams, Kayla, and Michael E. Staub

Love My Rifle More Than You: Young and Female in the U.S. Army. New York: W. W. Norton, 2005. 290pp. ISBN 9780393060980.

It was tough, explains Iraq veteran Kayla Williams, for "us females to get our work done without having guys insinuate that 'blow jobs' was part of our Advanced Individual Training. It totally sucked, pun intended." If you prefer to avoid racy language, then steer clear of Williams's book: the dirty, difficult side of war comes through loud and clear on every page—but of course, that is her intent; it is this edgy, raw tone that makes her narrative effective. Visceral and provocative, this is the story of a soldier who had served as an Arabic interpreter in the U.S. Army since 2000; when America went to Iraq, it was inevitable that she would be deployed. Discover the gritty terror of combat and the complicated sexual politics of the modern military in this fast-paced, eye-opening war memoir.

> **Subjects:** Warriors • War • Violence • Labor • Gender • Sexual Discrimination • War on Terror • America • Iraq • Middle East • Asia • Twenty-first Century • Memoir

> **Now Try:** Katherine M. Skiba writes from a somewhat different perspective. As one of only sixty female reporters covering the war in Iraq, she was the only female civilian among more than two thousand soldiers. Read about her experiences as a female outsider in *Sister in the Band of Brothers: Embedded with the 101st Airborne in Iraq*; candid, thoughtful, even funny at times, her memoir shows one journalist's intimate perspective on the war.

Women in the Business World

> Here are titles about and for women who make their professions in the traditionally male-dominated business world.

The male-dominated world of business is not always friendly toward women; for evidence, see *Tough Choices: A Memoir*, by the former CEO of Hewlett-Packard, Carly Fiona. Nonetheless, women must continue to advance in the workplace, as Avivah Wittenberg-Cox and Alison Maitland contend in *Why Women Mean Business*. The "Women in the Business World" section illuminates the experiences of businesswomen through personal stories and thought-provoking cultural analyses and recommends ways for women to improve their careers, as we see in Deborah Tannen's *Talking from 9 to 5*. See also the "Women in the Professions" section of Chapter 1.

Fiorina, Carly

Tough Choices: A Memoir. New York: Portfolio, 2006. 319pp. ISBN 9781591841333.

> As the CEO of Hewlett-Packard for six years, Carly Fiorina was the darling of the business media, a model of women's success in a male-dominated world. And then, in 2005, she was fired. But rather than slink into the shadows, Fiorina chose to write her life story. Of particular interest is her inside scoop on the inner workings of Hewlett-Packard. Did Fiorina really deserve to be sacked? The source is biased, of course, but Fiorina's gleeful airing of Hewlett-Packard's dirty laundry is reason enough to read the book. On top of that, we get to see how Fiorina's childhood and family influenced her, and how this law-school dropout climbed the ranks to become one of the most powerful women in corporate America.

> **Subjects:** Leadership • Business • Labor • America • Autobiography

> **Now Try:** Readers wanting to know more about the Hewlett-Packard/Compaq merger that presaged Fiorina's dismissal may wish to try *Backfire: Carly Fiorina's High-Stakes Battle for the Soul of Hewlett-Packard*. Be forewarned: Peter Burrows is critical of Fiorina,

though he does give her credit where credit is due. This harsher view of the former CEO does give perspective to Fiorina's own account, however, and while Burrow's criticisms may be off-putting to some readers, his insightful analysis of the inner workings of Hewlett-Packard makes for exemplary business writing.

O'Brien, Virginia

Success on Our Own Terms: Tales of Extraordinary, Ordinary Business Women. New York: John Wiley, 1998. 269pp. ISBN 9780471178712.

From one perspective, women are not making impressive inroads in the corporate world; just look at the overwhelming number of men at the top of companies throughout the country. But if you adjust your thinking a little bit, contends author O'Brien, women are actually making remarkable advances. In this inspiring study of top women executives, O'Brien encourages readers not to focus on the lack of women at the top of corporate hierarchies but rather to consider those women who *are* at the top; they are, O'Brien shows, successful and happy. Based on interviews with forty-five women movers-and-shakers, this collection of mini-biographies shows that, while women are not yet storming the gates of the top echelons of the business world, they are contributing to a general culture change that welcomes and encourages women and their perspectives in the workplace.

Subjects: Business • Labor • Gender • America • Biography

Now Try: Now consider success from a somewhat different perspective in *Nine Lives: Stories of Women Business Owners Landing on Their Feet* by Mary Cantando and Laurie Zuckerman. The women profiled in this collective biography are not top executives of major corporations, as we saw in *Success on Our Own Terms,* but they are every bit as successful in their own milieu of small business ownership. Find motivation and inspiration in the stories of nine women who, like their counterparts in bigger corporations, are defining success in their own vision by creating women-friendly business practices.

Pinker, Susan

The Sexual Paradox: Men, Women and the Real Gender Gap. New York: Scribner, 2008. 340pp. ISBN 9780743284707.

"Most women in the West are now in the workplace," writes psychologist Pinker. "But gifted, talented women with the most choices and freedoms don't seem to be choosing the same paths, in the same numbers, as the men around them. Even with barriers stripped away, they don't behave like male clones." A significant reason for the difference between the sexes is biological, argues Pinker. Hormones lead men to gravitate toward competitive, highly focused (and better paying) jobs, and hormones lead women toward less rigid jobs with more social interaction, despite the poorer pay. With clear writing, myriad examples, and thorough research, Pinker convincingly argues that women's needs and desires in the workplace are different from men's and that companies should readjust to accommodate their women employees.

Subjects: Business • Labor • Gender • Biology

Now Try: Though her book does not focus on gender, author Barbara Kellerman presents an intriguing perspective on workplace behaviors that will resonate with those who enjoyed *The Sexual Paradox*. In *Followership: How Followers Are Creating Change and Changing Leaders*, Kellerman examines the followers of the workplace, those who do not have special authority, even though they may well be as qualified as the leaders. With examples from a wide range of professions, she argues that companies must serve the needs of their followers as well as their leaders.

Tannen, Deborah

Talking from 9 to 5: Women and Men at Work. New York: W. Morrow, 1994 (New York: Harper, 2001). 368pp. ISBN 9780688112431.

Conversation expert Tannen is a living, breathing Rosetta Stone of gender. She interprets the indecipherable, puzzling language of men (and women) and translates it for bewildered women (and men) in their own tongue. Liberally illustrated with workplace conversations from real people, Tannen examines the gendered qualities of communication and demonstrates the unintended consequences that arise when the sexes unknowingly misinterpret each other. Told in an academic but easily accessible style, *Talking from 9 to 5* is fascinating for any reader interested in gender and absolutely essential for anyone who works with someone of the other sex.

Subjects: Business • Communication • Gender • Sociology • Labor

Now Try: Readers intrigued by Tannen's analysis of gender and communication should look at the book that made her famous, *You Just Don't Understand: Women and Men in Conversation*. As in *Talking from 9 to 5*, she uses real conversations to illustrate gender differences in communication, but this time she explores interactions in everyday life, not just in the workplace; her analysis of communication within romantic contexts is especially thought-provoking. And for further insight into the quirks of gender communication between romantic partners, don't miss John Gray's *Men Are from Mars, Women Are from Venus: The Classic Guide to Understanding the Opposite Sex*.

Wittenberg-Cox, Avivah, and Alison Maitland

Why Women Mean Business: Understanding the Emergence of Our Next Economic Revolution. Chichester, UK: John Wiley, 2008. 349pp. ISBN 9780470725085.

"Gender is a business issue, not a 'women's issue,'" write the authors. "The under-use of women's talent has an impact on the bottom line." With lucid prose, they develop this argument by looking at examples of business practices from around the world. Wittenberg-Cox, the CEO of 20-First, a company that helps businesses improve their gender policies, and Maitland, a journalist with the *Financial Times*, convincingly demonstrate why companies should revise their workplaces to better suit women; these changes benefit not only the employees but the companies themselves. The authors also offer detailed ideas for creating a more woman-friendly workplace.

Subjects: Business • Labor • Gender • How-to

Now Try: Like Wittenberg-Cox and Maitland, authors Michael Gurian and Barbara Annis argue that it is in the best interests of businesses to pay more attention to the needs of women employees. This time, though, the focus is not sociological as much as biological, as we see in *Leadership and the Sexes: Using Gender Science to Create Success in Business*. The authors discuss the latest findings in research about the difference between men's and women's brains and offer practical suggestions to incorporate workplace strategies that reflect those differences.

Women Entrepreneurs

In these books, you'll find stories about women as business owners, as well as guides for starting a business.

1

A variety of books constitute the "Women Entrepreneurs" section. Some are character studies of successful businesswomen, as we see in *Kitchen Table Entrepreneurs: How Eleven Women Escaped Poverty and Became Their Own Bosses* by Martha Shirk and Anna S. Wadia. Others take a broader approach to women's entrepreneurship, as with Margaret Heffernan's *How She Does It: How Women Entrepreneurs Are Changing the Rules of Business Success.* Yet others offer practical advice; try, for instance, *About My Sister's Business: The Black Woman's Road Map to Successful Entrepreneurship* by Fran Harris.

2

3

Friedman, Caitlin, and Kimberly Yorio

The Girl's Guide to Starting Your Own Business: Candid Advice, Frank Talk, and True Stories for the Successful Entrepreneur. New York: HarperResource, 2003. 257pp. ISBN 9780060521578.

4

> Those who enjoy reading business guides know that it's difficult to escape co-authors Friedman and Yorio—but given the consistently superior quality of their books, it's hard to imagine why anyone would want to avoid them. In *The Girl's Guide to Starting Your Own Business*, the authors bring their considerable expertise and chatty, accessible writing style to a topic that can be intimidating, stressful, even terrifying: entrepreneurship. From the very first step of deciding whether business ownership is the right choice to the complex steps involved in writing a business plan, the book guides women through the complicated process of starting and succeeding in small business. Quizzes, ideas, and interviews with veteran businesswomen make this a lively, informative read for any woman contemplating the difficult but rewarding path of entrepreneurship.

5

> **Subjects:** Entrepreneurs • Business • Labor • Gender • How-to

> **Now Try:** *Ladies Who Launch: Embracing Entrepreneurship & Creativity as a Lifestyle*, like *The Girl's Guide to Starting Your Own Business*, approaches business ownership with a dynamic, infectious enthusiasm. Co-authors Victoria Colligan, Beth Schoenfeldt, and Amy Swift are intimately familiar with what women need to start their own businesses, thanks to their involvement in the Ladies Who Launch program, dedicated to supporting women business owners. In their book, they spell out four steps for starting a business—Imagine It, Speak It, Do It, and Celebrate It—while providing self-analysis quizzes, valuable advice, and anecdotes from successful women entrepreneurs.

6

7

Harris, Fran

About My Sister's Business: The Black Woman's Road Map to Successful Entrepreneurship. New York: Fireside, 1996. 252pp. ISBN 9780684818399.

8

> Though written in the mid-1990s, *About My Sister's Business* is still one of the best books written for black women entrepreneurs. Author Harris

employs a conversational, intimate tone to become a personal cheerleader for the reader, though she doesn't mince words about the difficult side of succeeding in business: "I commend you," she writes "and, in the same breath, warn you." Both a morale booster and an honest guide to entrepreneurship, *About My Sister's Business* takes readers through the ins and outs of starting, developing, and maintaining a successful business. Self-appraisal quizzes, success stories, and quotes from other black women entrepreneurs make this a motivational, informative how-to guide for any black woman trying to navigate the difficult waters of business ownership.

Subjects: Entrepreneurs • Business • Labor • Gender • African Americans • Race • How-to

Now Try: Supplement the advice in *About My Sister's Business* with the empowering messages in *Sister CEO: The Black Woman's Guide to Starting Her Own Business*. With a readable, encouraging style, author Cheryl D. Broussard guides readers through the maze of business ownership, including specific step-by-step instructions as well as general advice and inspiration. For a more recent book, try *The Complete Startup Guide for the Black Entrepreneur* by Bill Boudreaux; though not targeted toward women in particular, the in-depth, no-nonsense advice will be invaluable for any reader.

Heffernan, Margaret

How She Does It: How Women Entrepreneurs Are Changing the Rules of Business Success. New York: Viking, 2007. 274pp. ISBN 9780670038237.

Four hundred and twenty women start businesses each day, and women-run companies are creating jobs at twice the average rate. The numbers are staggering, and the message is clear: women are influencing business ownership in tremendous, positive ways. What is it about women business owners that makes them so successful? To find out, CEO Margaret Heffernan interviewed hundreds of women entrepreneurs. What she discovered is enlightening: women really do approach entrepreneurship differently. For instance, they are more likely to ask for help, more inclined to encourage their employees' family duties, more willing to improvise. With real stories and Heffernan's intelligent analysis, *How She Does It* illuminates the changing culture of women entrepreneurs.

Subjects: Entrepreneurs • Business • Labor • Gender

Now Try: Revel in further exploration of women's entrepreneurial styles in *How to Run Your Business Like a Girl: Successful Strategies from Entrepreneurial Women Who Made It Happen*. Author Elizabeth Cogswell Baskin examines qualities such as intuition and relationship-building that are the hallmarks of successful businesswomen. She offers step-by-step guidance and practical advice for incorporating those qualities into a business model, making this an essential read for entrepreneurs who want to run their businesses in a female-friendly style.

Lavine, Kim

Mommy Millionaire: How I Turned My Kitchen Table Idea into a Million Dollars and How You Can, Too! New York: St. Martin's Press, 2007. 339pp. ISBN 978031-2354572.

When her husband lost his job, stay-at-home mom Kim Levine had to make some tough decisions. She loved being a full-time mother, but her family needed income. This is the story of how she created a multimillion dollar business based on a simple pillow she designed in her own home. But *Mommy Millionaire* is far more than a memoir of Levine's struggles and triumphs; her personal entrepreneurial experience translates into a top-notch guide to launching a business. With detailed advice on such topics as self-promotion, product distribution, and cash-flow analysis, the book offers inspiration and step-by-step instructions for any woman who wants to start a business without sacrificing her family.

Subjects: Entrepreneurs • Business • Labor • Mothers • America • How-to • Memoir

Now Try: Kim Levine is just one of the growing number of mothers who have found extraordinary success by starting their own businesses. Read about others in Tamara Monosoff's *Secrets of Millionaire Moms: Learn How They Turned Great Ideas into Booming Businesses—And How You Can Too!* Engaging profiles of seventeen mommy millionaires—including Julie Clark, founder of The Baby Einstein Company, and Maria de Lourdes Sobrino, founder of LuLu's Dessert—are nestled in chapters such as "The Extreme Sport: Juggling Family and Business" and "Money Matters: Raising Capital"; the solid advice and inspiring stories will help aspiring entrepreneurs balance family and work as they create and nurture their businesses.

Rouda, Kaira Sturdivant

Real You Incorporated: 8 Essentials for Women Entrepreneurs. Hoboken, NJ: John Wiley & Sons, 2008. 243pp. ISBN 047017658X.

There's something infectious about Kaira Sturdivant Rouda's energy. No matter how nervous, hesitant, or timid the reader is feeling, Rouda's enthusiasm will deliver a boost of confidence to any would-be businesswoman. *Real You Incorporated* helps women to identify their own unique talents (an act that, in itself, will improve anyone's morale) and to apply those creative gifts to a business model. With practical advice on such business essentials as marketing and branding, the book will help entrepreneurs channel their ideas into realistic business strategies; profiles of successful businesswomen and thought-provoking anecdotes, interspersed throughout the text, provide additional inspiration.

Subjects: Entrepreneurs • Business • Labor • Gender • How-to

Now Try: Women entrepreneurs seeking further inspiration will do well to turn to *The Woman's Advantage: 20 Women Entrepreneurs Show You What It Takes to Grow Your Business*. Author Mary Cantando interviewed twenty women owners of successful companies to get the inside scoop on starting and growing a small business. Their stories will inspire and motivate women who own, or would like to own, their own enterprises, while Cantando's detailed description of what it takes to increase business will be an invaluable guide to business owners.

Shirk, Martha, and Anna S. Wadia

Kitchen Table Entrepreneurs: How Eleven Women Escaped Poverty and Became Their Own Bosses. Boulder, CO: Westview Press, 2002. 306pp. ISBN 9780813339108.

In different circumstances, this could have been a depressing book: the eleven women profiled here were all, at one time, living on low wages, many of them with young children to provide for. But in fact this is an uplifting collective biography, because every single woman in these pages escaped poverty by starting her own small business, thanks to a boost from various nonprofit organizations underwritten by the Ms. Foundation. You'll meet Ollie, who started Ollie's Mountaineer Knits in West Virginia, and mother-and-daughter team Sharon and Michelle Garza, who serve up hot dogs in Denver in their business Heavenly Dawgs. These and seven other inspiring stories are a tribute to the entrepreneurial skills and courage of women who turned their own creativity and dedication into profit.

Subjects: Entrepreneurs • Business • Labor • Class • America • Biography • Collection

Now Try: Meet even more self-starting women in *Women's Ventures, Women's Visions: 29 Inspiring Stories from Women Who Started Their Own Businesses* by Shoshana Alexander. The women profiled in this collective biography hail from a variety of backgrounds, but they have one thing in common: they all started successful businesses, including cafes, bookstores, and studios. Though not every woman faced the same dire straights as the formerly impoverished business owners in *Kitchen Table Entrepreneurs*, their accomplishments are nonetheless remarkable and will provide inspiration for readers who want to discover further stories of success.

Solovic, Susan Wilson

The Girls' Guide to Building a Million-Dollar Business. New York: AMACOM Books, 2008. 210pp. ISBN 9780814474198.

It can be hard to find information about millionaire businesswomen, writes Solovic: "The incredible stories of these amazing women are one of the world's best kept secrets." Packed with quotes and reflections from financially successful women entrepreneurs, *The Girls' Guide to Building a Million-Dollar Business* neatly fills in the gaps for readers looking for businesswomen's success stories. But the real strength of the book is in its carefully explained, step-by-step advice for women seeking to expand their own businesses. Sections such as "Create the Right Business Plan" and "Venture Capital" detail the entire process of developing a million-dollar enterprise, from articulating a vision during the initial stages to assigning oneself a fair salary once the cash starts flowing in.

Subjects: Entrepreneurs • Business • Labor • Gender • How-to • Quick Read

Now Try: Get inside the heads of twelve phenomenally successful businesswomen in Gregory K. Ericksen's *Women Entrepreneurs Only: 12 Women Entrepreneurs Tell the Stories of Their Success*. Readers will be inspired by profiles of women such as Sheryl Leach, the visionary behind Barney the Dinosaur, while the lessons learned by the entrepreneurs as they negotiated the perils of doing business in a man's world will give invaluable insight to any woman heading her own enterprise.

Whiteley, Sharon, et al.

The Old Girls' Network: Insider Advice for Women Building Businesses in a Man's World. New York: Basic Books, 2003. 246pp. ISBN 9780585482101.

Of all the books written to help people start their own businesses, this one—written with women's unique needs and perspectives in mind—is simply one of the best. The expert advice and wisdom from the authors is enough to make this book stand out; their step-by-step guidance through the nitty-gritty details of starting, cultivating, and maintaining a business is sensible, precise, and comprehensive. An appendix, replete with sample documents and templates, gives readers the tools to act on the authors' advice. And the many profiles of real women entrepreneurs will provide inspiration for readers to follow their own business dreams.

Subjects: Entrepreneurs • Business • Labor • Gender • How-to

Now Try: Owning a business is hard. Owning a business while overcoming sexist obstacles is harder. Supplement the lessons of *The Old Girls' Network* with the frank, honest advice of *Hurdles: Women Building High-Growth Businesses* by Candida G. Brush et al. Based on extensive research and the authors' enviable business acumen, *Hurdles* tells women which barriers to expect and offers strategies to overcome those barriers. Mixing solid business advice and woman-friendly ideas, the book offers expansive, detailed advice to help women succeed in a man's business world.

Wilmerding, Ginny

Smart Women and Small Business: How to Make the Leap from Corporate Careers to the Right Small Enterprise. Hoboken, NJ: John Wiley & Sons, 2006. 281pp. ISBN 9780471778684.

In *Smart Women and Small Business*, author Wilmerding demystifies the frightening prospect of venturing into entrepreneurship. With a warm, candid approach, she explores the various avenues available to women considering the plunge, such as starting a business, entering into partnerships, and purchasing franchises. Though the book offers plenty of practical advice for budding business owners, its real strength is in its careful analysis of the various facets of entrepreneurship; sections such as "Being Realistic about Risk" and "Are Family Businesses More Family-Friendly?" provide food for thought, helping ensure that women consider all their options as they find the business venture that's right for them.

Subjects: Entrepreneurs • Business • Labor • Gender • How-to

Now Try: Entrepreneur Linda Hollander knows what it's like to run a small business; she found out firsthand when she started her packaging enterprise, The Bag Ladies. In her book *Bags to Riches: 7 Success Secrets for Women in Business*, she shares the lessons she learned as a woman entrepreneur, while explaining the process of creating and sustaining a business in straightforward, understandable language. With its detailed, nuts-and-bolts approach to starting a business, the book is a natural complement to the thought-provoking overview of entrepreneurship in *Smart Women and Small Business*.

Professional Guides

These are the "how-to" guides for the aspiring professional woman, with everything you need to know to succeed.

Reading a career guide is one thing. Reading a career guide written for women is something else entirely. The books in the "Professional Guides" section speak to the unique needs of women in the workplace, as well as the obstacles they face in business, an area long dominated by men.

Evans, Gail

She Wins, You Win: The Most Important Rule Every Businesswoman Needs to Know. New York: Gotham Books, 2003. 190pp. ISBN 9781592400256.

Many career advice books focus on the cut-throat, competitive edge that individuals need to foster to succeed. *She Wins, You Win* takes a refreshing new approach, arguing that women need to actively support one another in the corporate world. With numerous real-life situations and anecdotes, Evans—the first female executive vice president of CNN—convincingly demonstrates the need for women to help each other out. Her clear prose and inspired tips, such as "uncover and share information" and "weave a female web," will open doors for women who otherwise would have had to struggle alone in male-dominated work environments.

> **Subjects:** Business • Gender • Relationships • Labor • How-to • Quick Read
>
> **Now Try:** Complement the advice for career advancement found in *She Wins, You Win* with *Her Place at the Table: A Woman's Guide to Negotiating Five Key Challenges to Leadership Success.* Co-authors Deborah M. Kolb, Judith Williams, and Carol Frohlinger have written a book both for women who have already become leaders in their organizations and for those who are poised to enter leadership positions. Based on interviews with businesswomen in demanding leadership roles, the book scrutinizes the difficulties that women encounter in the workplace and offers solid advice for succeeding.

Frankel, Lois P.

Nice Girls Don't Get the Corner Office: 101 Unconscious Mistakes Women Make That Sabotage Their Careers. New York: Warner Business Books, 2004. 268pp. ISBN 9780446531320.

It's always best to collect a census of opinions before making a decision, right? Wrong, says author Frankel. In a male-dominated business culture, seeking input from coworkers usually indicates indecisiveness, not diplomacy. In fact, many behaviors that women employ in the workplace send unintentional, undesirable signals to their male coworkers. Sections such as "Waiting to Be Noticed" and "Using Preambles" illuminate patterns prevalent among women and illustrate how they can backfire with male colleagues. Filled with practical advice and suggestions, *Nice Girls Don't Get the Corner Office* will teach readers about their own subconscious behaviors and show them how to improve their chances for success in the workplace.

> **Subjects:** Business • Gender • Labor • Communication • Leadership • How-to
>
> **Now Try:** *Nice Girls Don't Get the Corner Office* offers general advice for women in the workplace, no matter their ambitions; now try two books that focus on moving women up the career ladder. Uncover the secrets of success in a male-dominated business in Christopher V. Flett's *What Men Don't Tell Women about Business: Opening Up the Heavily Guarded Alpha Male Playbook*; with solid advice about topics such as communication, difficult coworkers, and confidence-building, this book is designed to help women advance their careers in the workplace. And for tips on the nitty-gritty details of negotiation, turn to *Women Don't Ask: Negotiation and the Gender Divide.* Co-authors Linda Babcock and Sara Laschever mix scholarly research and personal anecdotes to help women learn when, how, and why to negotiate for career advancement.

Friedman, Caitlin, and Kimberly Yorio

The Girl's Guide to Kicking Your Career into Gear: Valuable Lessons, True Stories, and Tips for Using What You've Got (A Brain!) to Make Your Worklife Work for You. New York: Broadway Books, 2008. 228pp. ISBN 9780767927666.

Dynamic duo Friedman and Yorio deliver a powerful, take-no-prisoners message: it's up to you to find happiness in your job; and sister, you can do it. The authors interviewed more than one hundred successful businesswomen to cull words of wisdom that will speak to anyone who wants to increase her job satisfaction. Stuck in a dead-end job? Too shy to let your talents shine? Frustrated with difficult coworkers? No matter what problems you grapple with in the workplace, *The Girl's Guide to Kicking Your Career into Gear* will help you learn to cope with them or abandon them altogether if you decide to switch jobs.

Subjects: Business • Labor • Gender • How-to

Now Try: For an excellent companion to *The Girl's Guide to Kicking Your Career into Gear*, turn to *Why Good Girls Don't Get Ahead—But Gutsy Girls Do: Nine Secrets Every Working Woman Must Know*. Author Kate White identifies the common mistakes of the "good girls"—such as rule followers and people pleasers—and helps them transform their behaviors to get the respect and success they deserve. For another perspective on the trials and triumphs of women in the workplace, turn to *From Cinderella to CEO: How to Master the 10 Lessons of Fairy Tales to Transform Your Work Life*. Co-authors Cary Jehl Broussard and Anita Bell examine workplace culture and offer tips to help women succeed by using fairy tales as an extended metaphor for work.

Heim, Pat, and Susan K. Golant

Hardball for Women: Winning at the Game of Business. Los Angeles: Lowell House, 1992 (New York: Plume, 2005). 290pp. ISBN 9780929923819.

Think of business as a game, suggest authors Heim and Golant; as in any game, the players need to be competitive to succeed. Too often, women shy away from competing, preferring to defer to their male colleagues for the sake of harmony. Unfortunately, this humble approach means that many women—even those with superior productivity and capability—are passed over for promotions. With practical advice, anecdotes, and real-life lessons, *Hardball for Women* demystifies the male business culture and suggests ways for women to work within it. Chapters on topics such as body language, verbal communication, and leadership will empower women to shine in their jobs without sacrificing their values.

Subjects: Business • Gender • Labor • Communication • Leadership • How-to

Now Try: If the sports metaphor of *Hardball for Women* struck a chord, dive into *Play Like a Man, Win Like a Woman: What Men Know about Success That Women Need to Learn* by Gail Evans. Chapters such as "Four Ground Rules" and "How to Keep Score" illustrate the competitive nature of business in a man's world and explain the rules, however unfair they may be; see the section titled "They Can Cry. You Can't," for instance. Supplement this no-nonsense advice with *A Woman's Guide to Successful Negotiating: How to Convince, Collaborate, and Create Your Way to Agreement* by Lee E. Miller and Jessica Miller; this readable, practical book teaches women how to be successful in business and in life without forsaking their feminine qualities.

Johnson, Kelly Love

skirt! Rules for the Workplace: An Irreverent Guide to Advancing Your Career. Guilford, CT: skirt! books, 2008. 204pp. ISBN 9781599212234.

Women have come far in the workplace, writes Johnson, but not far enough; they're still expected to perform on par with men while "fetching coffee, stocking the office fridge, wiping the counters, and wearing pantyhose so no one has to be offended by a bare knee, along with earning less money." Edgy, sassy, and unabashedly feminist, *skirt! Rules for the Workplace* is the no-holds-barred guide to shining and succeeding in the workplace without kowtowing to men's gender expectations. Chapters such as "Playing Nice: Alpha and Beta Archetypes at Work" and "Now That You're the Boss" will help women negotiate office politics on their own terms, and the appendix, "Checkpoints for a Higher Paycheck," will help them get the pay they deserve.

Subjects: Business • Labor • Gender • Feminism • How-to • Quick Read

Now Try: Though not as brassy as *skirt! Rules for the Workplace*, the sensible feminism of *The Naked Truth: A Working Woman's Manifesto on Business and What Really Matters* makes it a good companion read. Author Margaret Heffernan has interviewed more than sixty successful businesswomen to explore what it means to be a woman in the corporate world; her practical advice and anecdotes will help women succeed in their jobs without sacrificing their feminine values.

Mindell, Phyllis

How to Say It for Women. **(Previously known as** *A Woman's Guide to the Language of Success: Communicating with Confidence and Power.*) Upper Saddle River, NJ: Prentice Hall, 2001. 298pp. ISBN 9780735202221.

On the very first page, Mindell jumps right to the point for her women readers: "In the workplace, we unwittingly use communication styles that sabotage our messages and our ability to succeed." For instance, two common phrases—"I think" and "I feel"—undermine effectiveness; these mainstays of women's communication are intended to soften their messages, but they come across sounding weak, not diplomatic. With no-nonsense advice and examples galore, *How to Say It for Women* demonstrates the pitfalls of women's communication and shows how to fix them. Sections such as "Words That Make You Invisible" and "Powerful Ways to Say No" offer readers solid suggestions to improve their effectiveness in workplace communication—even if they never before realized that their communication skills could be improved.

Subjects: Business • Communication • Gender • Sociology • Labor • How-to

Now Try: Though not focused specifically on workplace interactions, *Why Men Don't Listen and Women Can't Read Maps: How We're Different and What to Do about It* is an excellent companion read. Using real-life examples and anecdotes, co-authors Barbara Pease and Allan Pease delve into the mysteries of communication differences between men and women. Lighter in tone than *How to Say It for Women*, this is a thought-provoking look at communication—and miscommunication—that will help readers understand how their language choices resonate with members of the other sex, both at work and at play.

Rico, Yrma, and Nancy S. Garascia

La Vida Rica: The Latina's Guide to Success. New York: McGraw-Hill, 2004. 230pp. ISBN 9780071422185.

"Even if your parents were poor," writes Yrma Rico, "you can live in a big house, have nice clothes, drive a fancy car, send your kids to great schools." She should know: as one of seven children of migrant farmers, she went on to earn her GED and then to become a television executive and—most recently—the president and CEO of a company. Blending stories from her own inspiring experience along with stories of other successful Latinas, Rico dispenses practical advice to help women advance in their careers and to improve their finances. Rico gives special attention to the unique cultural and personal challenges that women from a Latino background will face, though all women readers, no matter what their cultural background, will find spirited advice and empowering ideas in this guide to achieving success in careers and in life.

Subjects: Business • Latinas • Labor • Leadership • Finances • How-to

Now Try: Though with less of a focus on careers and more of a focus on success in general, fans of *La Vida Rica* won't want to miss *Empowering Latinas: Breaking Boundaries, Freeing Lives.* Forthright and candid, author Yasmin Davidds-Garrido examines issues that affect Latinas in chapters such as "The Long Legacy of Machismo" and "Empowering Our Daughters to Embrace the World, Not to Fear it." Refreshingly honest, the book discusses the cultural barriers that Latina women face and shows them how to overcome obstacles to success.

Stanny, Barbara

Secrets of Six-Figure Women: Surprising Strategies to Up Your Earnings and Change Your Life. New York: HarperCollins, 2002. 274pp. ISBN 9780060185480.

The reasons why women don't negotiate for higher salaries are varied, writes Stanny: "No time, no energy, no chance, no clue." With an accessible style and straightforward advice, *Secrets of Six-Figure Women* shows women how to stop making excuses and start making more money. Based on interviews with more than 150 high-earning women, the book explores seven strategies for achieving financial success, including "Get in the Game," "Seek Support," and "Obey the Rules of Money." Stanny does not focus on the minutia of what to say during a performance appraisal; instead, she takes a holistic approach, inspiring women to improve their attitudes and financial health in order to see positive results in the workplace.

Subjects: Business • Finances • Gender • Labor • How-to

Now Try: *Secrets of Six-Figure Women* seeks to motivate women toward the right frame of mind for earning more money; supplement this perspective with insider information on the nitty-gritty details of salary negotiation by reading *The Shadow Negotiation: How Women Can Master the Hidden Agendas That Determine Bargaining Success.* Drawing on hundreds of interviews with successful businesswomen, co-authors Deborah M. Kolb and Judith Williams demystify the negotiation experience and suggest key strategies to help women play up their own strengths when they come to the bargaining table.

Wellington, Sheila W., and Betty Spence

Be Your Own Mentor: Strategies from Top Women on the Secrets of Success. New York: Random House, 2001. 302pp. ISBN 9780375500602.

"Mentors are more important to career success than hard work, more important than talent, more important than intelligence," writes author Wellington. "Why? Because you need to learn how to operate in the work world—whether in a corporation, a professional firm, a nonprofit, a university, or the public sector—and mentors can teach you how." As a past president of Catalyst, a nonprofit organization that works to advance women in business, Wellington knows what she's talking about—and in this excellent guide, she offers advice to help women succeed in the workplace; the book is something of a mentor in itself, in fact. Bolstered by words of wisdom from the likes of Carly Fiorina and Andrea Jung, the book delivers practical how-to steps on everything from finding a mentor to learning to network to improving communication skills.

Subjects: Leadership • Business • Labor • Relationships • How-to

Now Try: Those inspired by *Be Your Own Mentor* will certainly want to read Stacy Blake-Beard's essay "The Inextricable Link between Mentoring and Leadership," found in *Enlightened Power: How Women Are Transforming the Practice of Leadership*—but the other essays in the book will appeal, too. Edited by Linda Coughlin, Ellen Wingard, and Keith Hollihan, this excellent collection features a variety of thoughtful, practical pieces related to women's advancement in the workplace.

Sexual Harassment

Sexual harassment refers to the uninvited and unwelcome sexual behavior of one person toward another, generally in the workplace.

The "Sexual Harassment" section features a variety of books. Some are character-driven stories that depict an individual's emotional and legal battles; try, for instance, Clara Bingham's memoir *Class Action*. Others focus on sexual harassment at a societal level, as we see in Daphne Patai's conservative approach to the issue in *Heterophobia*. In all cases, these are books that encourage the reader to think and reflect on sexual harassment (What is it? What is it *not*?) and its affect on women and men.

Baker, Carrie N.

The Women's Movement against Sexual Harassment. New York: Cambridge University Press, 2008. 276pp. ISBN 9780521879354.

Prior to Anita Hill's suit against Clarence Thomas in 1991, the phrase "sexual harassment" was not in the mainstream lexicon. But as women's studies scholar and sociologist Baker shows, American women were fighting against sexual harassment in the 1970s and 1980s. These activists were part of a small, grassroots movement, and yet they managed to win legal gains and foster changes in the workplace. Drawing on meticulous research and writing with a scholarly but accessible style, Baker presents the history of an activist movement that led to permanent improvements for working women.

Subjects: Sexual Harassment • Law • Activism • Feminism • Labor • History • Women's History • American History • History of Labor • Social History • Twentieth Century • Sociology • America

Now Try: Whereas Baker's book is a history of the women's movement against sexual harassment, *Sexual Harassment in the Workplace* is a practical guide to understanding the subject. Lawyer Mary L. Boland demystifies the legalese and helps readers identify what does and does not constitute harassment. She also coaches readers on how to fight against, and recover from, sexual harassment.

Bingham, Clara, and Laura Leedy Gansler

Class Action: The Story of Lois Jenson and the Landmark Case That Changed Sexual Harassment Law. New York: Doubleday, 2002. 390pp. ISBN 9780385496124.

Women who have been sexually harassed oftentimes decline to report the harasser, fearing that they won't be believed or that it won't do any good. The case of *Jenson v. Eveleth*, described here by journalist Bingham and lawyer Gansler, demonstrates this conundrum all too well. In 1975, four women became the first female employees at an iron mine in Minnesota. The sexual harassment began immediately, ranging from insults to salacious propositions to groping. The good news is that the women eventually won their sexual harassment lawsuit against the company; the bad news is that the trial dragged for years through the court system. This is a sobering reminder of the bravery and determination of women who make the difficult choice to take a stand against sexual harassment.

Subjects: Sexual Harassment • Labor • Law • Twentieth Century • America

Now Try: Though we tend to think of women as the victims of sexual harassment, Edwin B. Martin reminds us that it works both ways. He was shocked to find himself the target of sexual harassment from his male colleagues when he took a new job at a railroad in Alabama. In *Stopping the Train*, he recalls the terrible effect of the harassment on his psychological health and discusses the ordeal of his ultimately triumphant legal battle.

Hill, Anita

Speaking Truth to Power. New York: Doubleday, 1997. 374pp. ISBN 978-0385476256.

In 1991, an obscure legal phrase, "sexual harassment," became an irrevocable part of the American consciousness. That was the year that African American lawyer Anita Hill publicly aired her grievances against her African American former colleague, a nominee for the United States Supreme Court named Clarence Thomas. Many derided Hill, claiming that her accusation of sexual impropriety in the workplace was a ploy to bring attention to herself, and the Senate confirmed Thomas in spite of Hill's testimony. But while Hill lost that battle, she single-handedly raised public awareness of sexual harassment. Readers will appreciate Hill's insight into race and sex as she tells her side of the story in this candid memoir.

Subjects: Sexual Harassment • Law • Race • African Americans • America • Memoir

Now Try: For further reflections on race and class as they relate to Anita Hill, try the excellent collection *African American Women Speak Out on Anita Hill-Clarence Thomas*, edited by Geneva Smitherman. These essays are primarily written by scholars, but their perspectives are engaging and thought-provoking, and thoroughly supportive of Hill. Those wishing for the other side of the story, however, can turn directly to Thomas himself with *My Grandfather's Son: A Memoir*. Though staunch Hill supporters will bristle, the book makes for a fascinating glimpse into Thomas's perspective on his life, his career, and his take on the sexual harassment scandal that nearly cost him the nomination.

Patai, Daphne

Heterophobia: Sexual Harassment and the Future of Feminism. Lanham, MD: Rowman & Littlefield, 1998. 276pp. ISBN 9780847689873.

"The experience of sexual interest and sexual play (which can indeed be obnoxious at times) is an ordinary part of human life," writes Women's Studies scholar Patai. "Except for egregious offenses … the petty annoyance of occasional misplaced sexual attentions or sexist putdowns has to be tolerated." Trying to legislate against sexual harassment or to restrict it through workplace codes does very little good, she argues, and often does great harm to the purported harasser. Patai proudly identifies as a feminist but wants nothing to do with male-bashing or radicalism; some readers will find her brand of feminism too conservative, but others will welcome her perspective as she considers the dangers of confusing minor offenses with legitimate sexual harassment in the workplace.

Subjects: Sexual Harassment • Feminism • Labor

Now Try: Though we tend to think of men as having more power, better jobs, and better salaries than women do, Patai showed us how fragile their positions really are; a single accusation of sexual harassment can ruin it all. Warren Farrell expands on this idea in *The Myth of Male Power: Why Men Are the Disposable Sex*, though sexual harassment is but one of the areas he explores. With abundant examples—from suicide rates to violent crime, from birth control to job hazards—he shows that men, too, face their own share of hardships and subordination.

Women and Leadership

Titles in this section focus on women in roles of leading others, whether by example or exercising power and authority.

Books that speak to women's struggles to attain leadership positions in the traditionally male-dominated arenas of politics and business constitute the "Leadership" section, though we must recognize the inherent irony of the situation: these are books about women achieving "leadership" as it is understood in a patriarchal society. Even today, in what some consider a post-feminist society (utter hogwash, in my opinion), we still interpret leadership according to traditional definitions. Thus a woman senator is a leader; a female secretary who works for $20,000 per year, who single-handedly runs the office, orchestrates meetings, plans policy, balances the budget, solves disputes, and brews the coffee in the morning with nary a complaint—she's no leader. She's just the secretary. That said, these are the books that discuss women's advances in government, politics, and business. Some are how-to guides, while others have a more sociological approach. Readers will also want to refer to the "Women and Politics" section of Chapter 8.

Frankel, Lois P.

See Jane Lead: 99 Ways for Women to Take Charge at Work. New York: Warner Business Books, 2007. 279pp. ISBN 9780446579681.

"Women lead all the time," writes best-selling business author Frankel, "they just don't call it leadership. They think of it as working toward a common goal, achieving results through people, or simply doing what needs to be done." This woman-friendly approach is becoming more and more prevalent in the workplace, with the good-old-boys' tradition slowly making room for the feminization of leadership. *See Jane Lead* encourages women to tap into this societal change by playing up their own strengths. Quizzes, tips, self-assessment surveys, and anecdotes provide the knowledge women need to lead on their own terms, without jeopardizing their status in the workplace.

Subjects: Business • Gender • Leadership • Labor • How-to

Now Try: Readers eager to see women leaders in action should turn to *Women and the Leadership Q: The Breakthrough System for Achieving Power and Influence* by Shoya Zichy and Bonnie Kellen. Profiles of more than thirty powerful women offer inspiration, while the book's insightful analysis of leadership will help readers identify and cultivate their own leadership styles. Then turn to *Inside Every Woman: Using the 10 Strengths You Didn't Know You Had to Get the Career and Life You Want Now,* in which Vickie L. Milazzo encourages women to become leaders by using strengths such as intuitive vision, integrity, and endurance.

Friedman, Caitlin, and Kimberly Yorio

The Girl's Guide to Being a Boss (without Being a Bitch): Valuable Lessons, Smart Suggestions, and True Stories for Succeeding as the Chick-in-Charge. New York: Morgan Road, 2006. 224pp. ISBN 9780767922845.

Are you a good witch or a bad bitch? Numerous quizzes throughout the book will help answer that question—but here's a hint: if you've been emulating your male colleagues, you're probably not a good witch. It's unfair, but as the authors explain, women who adopt traditionally masculine leadership styles tend to come across as bitchy. *The Girl's Guide to Being a Boss* will help you draw on your feminine strengths to become a more likeable—but still effective—leader at work. With its chatty style, plentiful anecdotes from women managers, and frank, practical advice, this book is a must-read for women in leadership roles in the workplace.

Subjects: Business • Leadership • Labor • Gender • How-to

Now Try: Co-authors Connie Brown Glaser and Barbara Steinberg Smalley agree with the premise of *The Girl's Guide to Being a Boss*: to succeed as leaders, women need to draw on their own strengths; simply mimicking their male co-workers will only backfire. In *Swim with the Dolphins: How Women Can Succeed in Corporate America on Their Own Terms,* they explore the value of feminine leadership, offering useful checklists to help women assess their own management styles. Interviews with leading women managers and accessible prose make this a valuable guide for women leaders.

Morgan, Angie, and Courtney Lynch

Leading from the Front: No Excuse Leadership Tactics for Women. New York: McGraw-Hill, 2006. 199pp. ISBN 9780071465014.

Not a born leader? Don't worry, effective leadership can be learned—and Angie Morgan and Courtney Lynch are the perfect people to teach you how. As former Marine Corps officers, they know all about leading others, even in situations in which men have traditionally assumed the leadership mantle. In chapters such as "Think before You Act—Especially before You Overreact" and "Say You're Sorry Only When You're at Fault," they offer concrete leadership advice tailored to women's needs. Straightforward, accessible, and practical, this is an excellent guide for both women in leadership positions and those who want to be.

> **Subjects:** Leadership • Labor • How-to • Quick Read

> **Now Try:** Looking for more leadership advice? There's no better role model than First Lady Eleanor Roosevelt. In *Leadership the Eleanor Roosevelt Way: Timeless Strategies from the First Lady of Courage*, Robin Gerber offers a unique blend of biography and leadership advice. By examining Roosevelt's leadership style and approach to life, Gerber shows how contemporary women can apply Roosevelt's example to their own leadership styles. Fans of *Leading from the Front* will appreciate the concrete lessons and illustrative examples.

Myers, Dee Dee

Why Women Should Rule the World. New York: Harper, 2008. 280pp. ISBN 97800-61140402.

While on the job as the first female White House press secretary, Dee Dee Myers had the chance to develop a unique perspective on politics, leadership, and gender. In this captivating book, she clarifies that perspective in no uncertain terms: women ought to be leaders in politics, in business, in the media, and in every arena where men have traditionally dominated. Based on her own experiences and on her research into gender, Myers examines women's leadership in three distinct parts: "Why Women Don't Rule the World," "Why Women Should Rule the World," and "How Women Can Rule the World." Read this for an insider's view on the benefits of women's leadership and for practical suggestions on how to transform leadership at the societal level.

> **Subjects:** Leadership • Gender • Sociology • Sexual Discrimination • How-to

> **Now Try:** Debra Condren agrees with Myers that women need to advance into more leadership roles, though her book focuses less on society at large and more on the individual. In *Ambition Is Not a Dirty Word: A Woman's Guide to Earning Her Worth and Achieving Her Dreams*, she offers practical advice for women who want to step up to more lucrative and powerful roles. Fans of Myers will also enjoy the irreverent observations of Maureen Dowd in *Are Men Necessary?: When Sexes Collide*. Dowd, a columnist with the *New York Times*, examines gender inequity in all areas of life, from personal relationships to public leadership; her deliberately unflattering portrayal of men will appeal to those who embrace Myers's contention that women should rule the world.

Rhode, Deborah L., ed.

The Difference "Difference" Makes: Women and Leadership. Stanford, CA: Stanford Law and Politics, 2003. 232pp. ISBN 9780804746342.

In her introductory chapter, editor Deborah L. Rhode makes an intriguing point: "Gender inequalities in leadership opportunities are pervasive; perceptions of inequality are not. A widespread assumption is that barriers have been coming down, women have been moving up, and equal treatment is an accomplished fact. Two-thirds of surveyed men and three-quarters of male business leaders do not believe that women encounter significant discrimination for top positions in business, the professions, or government." Au contraire, say the contributors to this excellent collection of writings on women in law, business, and politics: barriers to women's leadership do indeed exist. In thought-provoking essays such as Mary B. Cranston's "Some Thoughts on Dealing with Cultural Bias against Women" and Jacob H. Herring's wonderfully titled "Can They Do It? Can Law Firms, Corporate Counsel Departments, and Governmental Agencies Create a Level Playing Field for Women Attorneys?," some of the best scholars, leaders, and feminists of the day consider the obstacles faced by women, as well as the strategies that individuals, companies, and governments can use to eliminate those obstacles.

Subjects: Leadership • Law • Politics • Business • Sexual Discrimination • Essays

Now Try: For more superb commentary on women in leadership, turn to *Women on Power: Leadership Redefined.* Edited by Sue Joan Mendelson Freeman, Susan Carolyn Bourque, and Christine Shelton, this collection of essays considers topics such as motherhood, gender, and activism to explore the nature of women's leadership and the barriers to women in law, business, and other male-dominated fields.

Wilson, Marie

Closing the Leadership Gap: Why Women Can and Must Help Run the World. New York: Penguin Books, 2007. 220pp. ISBN 9780143114031.

Sixty-three percent of workers earning minimum wage are women; only six of the Fortune 500 CEOs are women; only sixteen of the one hundred seats in the Senate are filled by women. These aren't pretty numbers, but is it really a problem worth fixing? Oh yes, says Ms. Foundation President Marie Wilson: "The core of what women bring to leadership—a tendency toward greater inclusiveness, empathy, communication up and down hierarchies, focus on broader issues—makes stronger government and richer business." The leadership gap must be closed, not only as a matter of principle, not only for abstract reasons of equality, but because the values and practices women bring to leadership are indispensable. With eloquence and clarity, Wilson explores the qualities of women's leadership, discussing how individuals, business, and governments can and should make changes to integrate women into leadership roles.

Subjects: Leadership • Labor • Gender • Activism • Feminism • Quick Read

Now Try: Marie Wilson convinced us that the leadership gap needs to close; now continue exploring the theme, and learn how to make it happen, in *Women and Leadership: The State of Play and Strategies for Change*, edited by

Barbara Kellerman and Deborah L. Rhode. Featuring thought-provoking essays from a variety of scholars, the book addresses such topics as the need for flexible working hours, the value of women's leadership, and the pervasive stereotypes that still inhibit women's advancement in the workplace.

Women and Finance

The books of the "Women and Finance" section are practical guides to managing personal finance.

If "women and finance" sounds boring, don't worry: these books offer sound advice in an entertaining, engaging way. Read these to discover the unique challenges faced by women as they save and invest and to seek guidance on managing your money.

Bridgforth, Glinda, and Gail Perry-Mason

Girl, Make Your Money Grow!: A Sister's Guide to Protecting Your Future and Enriching Your Life. New York: Broadway Books, 2003. 244pp. ISBN 9780767914017.

Not exactly sure what a mutual fund is? What does "annualized" mean, anyway? In their chatty, comfortable style, financial gurus Bridgforth and Perry-Mason team up to demystify the world of investing. They explain why investing is a good idea, offering practical strategies to help readers negotiate the intricacies of personal finance. Exercises to help readers practice their financial skills appear throughout the book, while anecdotes about successful African American women investors offer encouragement. The step-by-step advice to investing, told in a positive, empowering tone, will help anyone who has wanted to invest but didn't know where to start.

Subjects: Finances • Investment • African Americans • Race • How-to

Now Try: Bridgforth is the author of two others books designed to help African American women with their finances. *Girl, Get Your Money Straight: A Sister's Guide to Healing Your Bank Account and Funding Your Dreams in 7 Simple Steps* uses a holistic approach to take the stress out of finances; readers can work through the exercises, both financial and mental, to improve their overall financial health. Then turn to *Girl, Get Your Credit Straight!: A Sister's Guide to Ditching Your Debt, Mending Your Credit, and Building a Strong Financial Future*, which helps readers understand, repair, and maintain credit.

Castleberry, Carolyn

Women, Take Charge of Your Money: A Biblical Path to Financial Security. Sisters, OR: Multnomah, 2006. 218pp. ISBN 9781590526620.

Need a role model to show you how to manage your finances? Look at Proverbs 31, says author Castleberry, to see one of the original money-smart women. Written especially for women who have little or no experience in managing personal finances, *Women, Take Charge of Your Money* offers a gentle introduction to the basics of money management. Drawing both on biblical inspiration and the author's own experiences, the book uses accessible, sympathetic language to explain the relevance of biblical passages to today's financial climate. The Christian themes and sound advice will give readers food for thought and practical steps to take.

> **Subjects:** Finances • Christianity • Religion • Gender • How-to

> **Now Try:** Move up to the next level with Castleberry's follow-up title *Women, Get Answers about Your Money*. Though still firmly grounded in biblical text and Christian faith, this book begins to explore more complicated, intricate financial issues such as refinancing loans, buying homes, and investing in real estate. Then, for those who have set their sights as high as possible, turn to C. Thomas Anderson's *Becoming a Millionaire God's Way: Getting Money to You, Not from You*. Though not targeted to women, the book's sensible financial advice, rooted in Christian principles, will appeal to Castleberry's fans.

Frankel, Lois P.

Nice Girls Don't Get Rich: 75 Avoidable Mistakes Women Make with Money. New York: Warner Business Books, 2005. 265pp. ISBN 9780446-577090.

> With her inimitable, unabashedly honest style, author Frankel calls women to task for the mistakes they make with money. She does not blame women for their mistakes—societal values and gender indoctrination are the real culprits—but she does make them aware of their own damaging behaviors. The seventy-five mistakes each have their own sections, such as "Not Playing to Win," "Being a Financial Ostrich," and "Guilt Shopping Trips." Fortunately, Frankel tells women how to correct each of those mistakes; with her blend of sage advice, anecdotes, and quotes, this is a wake-up call to women, even those who never realized they were—literally—shortchanging themselves.

> **Subjects:** Finances • Gender • How-to

> **Now Try:** Like Frankel, authors Candice Bahr and Ginita Wall understand what women need to know to manage their finances. In *It's More than Money, It's Your Life!: The New Money Club for Women*, they help women honestly appraise their own financial habits and fears. Then, in chapters such as "Insuring Your Future" and "When the Vows Break: Getting through Divorce," the authors guide women through the facets of sound financial planning.

Orman, Suze

Women & Money: Owning the Power to Control Your Destiny. New York: Spiegel & Grau, 2007. 255pp. ISBN 9780385519311.

> Financial maven Suze Orman had resisted writing a book about women, reasoning that they were just as capable as men at understanding personal finance. But then she realized that many women were making financial mistakes despite their capabilities; thus *Women & Money* is about empowerment as much as it is about finance. The fundamentals of financial wellness are included, along with a five-month plan to help women get their money under control. But the true strength of the book lies in its inspiring, motivational message for women. With utter sensitivity and never a word of blame, Orman examines the societal pressures that prevent women from embracing their financial potential and helps her readers find the courage to overcome their personal obstacles.

Subjects: Finances • Gender • How-to

Now Try: Like Suze Orman, David Bach understands that women approach personal finance differently than men do. Their emotional, social, and personal needs often dictate—or even interfere with—their financial needs. In *Smart Women Finish Rich: 9 Steps to Achieving Financial Security and Funding Your Dreams*, Bach offers practical advice for getting money under control, both now and in the future; his upbeat, can-do message is tailored to women and their needs, no matter what their present incomes may be.

Thakor, Manisha, and Sharon Kedar

On My Own Two Feet: A Modern Girl's Guide to Personal Finance. Avon, MA: Adams Media, 2007. 191pp. ISBN 9781598691245.

The very first sentence of *On My Own Two Feet* sets the tone for the entire book: "The first step toward financial success is to develop the habit of saving." With accessible, straight-to-the-point language, authors Thakor and Kedar waste no time as they present the basics of personal finance. From understanding credit to investing wisely, from buying a home to saving for retirement, this financial primer explains concepts in concise, clear terms for readers. But this is not a dull economics textbook; filled with realistic examples, practical advice, and occasional snippets of humor, the book is an enjoyable, whirlwind tour of the fundamentals of personal finance.

Subjects: Finances • How-to • Quick Read

Now Try: Readers who enjoyed the positive, straightforward tone of *On My Own Two Feet* should try *Get in the Game!: The Girls' Guide to Money and Investing*. With honest, accessible language, Vanessa Summers illuminates the basics of financial health and stability. Filled with practical advice and sound information, the book presents a message of motivation and inspiration designed to give women the confidence, knowledge, and control they need to manage their personal finances.

Consider Starting With ...

Enter the world of women's work with these thought-provoking titles:

Brooke, Elisabeth. *Women Healers: Portraits of Herbalists, Physicians, and Midwives.*

Haynsworth, Leslie, and David M. Toomey. *Amelia Earhart's Daughters: The Wild and Glorious Story of American Women Aviators from World War II to the Dawn of the Space Age.*

Heffernan, Margaret. *How She Does It: How Women Entrepreneurs Are Changing the Rules of Business Success.*

Newitz, Annalee, and Charlie Anders, eds. *She's Such a Geek! Women Write about Science, Technology, and Other Nerdy Stuff.*

Robbins, Trina. *The Great Women Cartoonists.*

Sey, Jennifer. *Chalked Up: Inside Elite Gymnastics' Merciless Coaching, Overzealous Parents, Eating Disorders, and Elusive Olympic Dreams.*

Tannen, Deborah. *Talking from 9 to 5: Women and Men at Work.*

Fiction Read-Alikes

- **Archer, Jeffrey.** In *The Prodigal Daughter*, we meet the captivating Florentyna Kane, a mother, a businesswoman—and if she has her way, the first female president of the United States; read this page-turner for its deft blend of political intrigue and gender observations. Continue with *Shall We Tell the President?*, in which an assassination plot threatens our female president.

- **Coben, Harlan.** Professional women athletes frequent the pages of Coben's Myron Bolitar mystery series—which is unsurprising, as the protagonist is a sports rep who solves crimes. Try starting with *One False Move*, in which a female basketball star helps the wisecracking sleuth investigate a disappearance. Many of Coben's stand-alone thrillers will also appeal; professional women judges, lawyers, and police appear regularly. Start with *Hold Tight*, featuring a lawyer who must grapple with her duties to her job and her duties to her family when her teenaged son suddenly disappears.

- **L'Engle, Madeleine.** L'Engle is best remembered for her classic young adult novel *A Wrinkle in Time*, starring Meg Murray, the awkward teenager whose parents are both professional scientists—and in subsequent books Meg herself becomes a scientist; see, for instance, *The Arm of the Starfish*. Many of L'Engle's books feature strong, career-minded women; try *A Live Coal in the Sea*, about an astronomer, or *The Small Rain*, about a classical pianist.

- **Reichs, Kathy.** Meet Tempe Brennan, the star of Reich's long-running mystery series. Author Reichs is a forensic anthropologist, allowing her to vividly, and accurately portray the details of Brennan's career as a forensic anthropologist. First in the series is *Déjà Dead*, in which Brennan investigates a serial killer.

- **Willis, Connie.** Professional women scientists frequently star in Willis's science fiction novels. Try *Passage*, about a woman who studies Near Death Experiences, or *The Doomsday Book*, a harrowing novel about a grad student who travels in time to Europe in the Black Plague. Or, for readers who prefer to avoid the genre conventions of science fiction, try *Bellwether*, a light romance starring a social scientist with an interest in chaos theory.

Chapter 8

Women and Society

Definition

> At the core of this chapter is the fact that in the modern world, every dominant form of government, every nation, every mainstream culture—every iteration of society—is rooted in patriarchy, and women are subjugated by patriarchy. These books address those realities.

Consider this: In the modern world, every dominant form of government, every nation, every mainstream culture—every iteration of society—is rooted in patriarchy, a system of beliefs and actions that values men and masculinity over women and femininity. And now consider that, by definition, women are subjugated by patriarchy.

Welcome to Women and Society.

These are the books that take a hard look at the role of women in society. Not all of them are explicitly feminist, of course, and by no means do all of the writers want to topple patriarchy; Caitlin Kelly's *Blown Away: American Women and Guns*, for instance, primarily focuses on the culture and motivations of women gun owners; the influence of men and firearms is a distant secondary concern. But whether they deal explicitly with men or men's dominance, whether they adopt a feminist perspective or a neutral approach, all of the books in "Women and Society" fall into one or two categories: "This is the way things are/this is the way things were" and/or "This is what we're doing about it/this is what we did about it."

Books in this chapter are books with a mission. Some of them want to nudge the reader into action to make the world a better place; others simply want to open the readers' eyes to the way things really are. "The way things really are," of course, is subject to interpretation; these are the books that are in danger of being thrown across the room by irate readers; on the flip side, these are the books that can speak profoundly to women's experiences. The book that one woman slams down in disgust will be the lifelong favorite of another.

Appeal

Readers enjoy books about Women and Society for their educational value. Readers turn to Women and Society books when they want to expand their minds, to learn about women who have a different skin color or country of origin or ideological background. Sometimes the education is inspiring: Judith Stiehm's *Champions for Peace* teaches us about women Nobel Peace Prize winners who have fought social injustice around the world. Other times the education is sobering: Efua Dorkenoo's writing forces us to acknowledge the reality faced by more than one hundred million women and girls in *Female Genital Mutilation: Politics and Prevention*.

Tone also plays a crucial role in Women and Society books, more so than books in any other interest area. Does the reader want gentle inspiration? Does she want righteous indignation? Does she want a book that is angry, triumphant, contemplative? Sassy and snarky or serious and thoughtful? Readers looking for a sober wake-up call on economic hardship will want to try Jennifer Johnson's *Getting by on the Minimum*, whereas readers wanting a more lighthearted overview of women's bodies in society will prefer the witty humor of Susan J. Douglas in *Where the Girls Are: Growing Up Female with the Mass Media*. For more titles that touch on women and social issues, see the "Activism" section in Chapter 6.

Organization

The Women and Society chapter starts with a general section, "General Social Issues," featuring books that cover a variety of social topics of concern to women. It is followed by six subsections. "Abortion and Choice" includes books about birth control and abortion. "Sexual Exploitation" includes books about sexual violence against women and girls, while "Sexual Liberation" includes sex-positive books about topics such as prostitution and exotic dancing. "War, Violence, and Peace" discusses violence (done *to* women and done *by* women) and women's opposition to violence. "Women and Politics" discusses the role of women leaders in government, both in the United States and abroad. Finally, "Working Mothers" examines the conflicts between career and motherhood.

General Social Issues

> The "General Social Issues" section is composed of an assortment of books that don't fall into the other categories in this chapter.

Some titles in this section cover a wide variety of topics, such as Katha Pollitt's *Virginity or Death!*, while others have a specific focus, such as Julia Serano's *Whipping Girl: A Transsexual Woman on Sexism and the Scapegoating of Femininity*. Some are grim in tone, as we see with *The Terror Dream*, by Susan Faludi, while others are just plain sassy, as we see with *Bitches, Bimbos, and Ballbreakers*, by the wickedly irreverent Guerrilla

Girls. Read these books to learn more about women's issues around the world, be it on distant continents or your own backyard.

Douglas, Susan J.

Where the Girls Are: Growing Up Female with the Mass Media. New York: Times Books, 1994. 340pp. ISBN 9780812922066.

Though written in 1994, have no doubt about it: *Where the Girls Are* is as funny, fresh, and relevant today as it was in the mid-1990s. With a wicked sense of humor and spot-on analysis, media scholar Douglas studies the portrayal of women in popular culture in the second half of the twentieth century. In chapters such as "Why the Shirelles Mattered" and "The Rise of the Bionic Bimbo," Douglas considers television, radio, and film, wryly noting the mixed messages delivered by the media concerning women's sexuality, intelligence, politics, and appearance. Especially interesting is her examination of the influence of feminism on the media, and vice versa. Read this for a bizarre stroll down memory lane and a dose of quirky feminism.

> **Subjects:** Media • Body Image • Gender • Feminism • History • Social History • Women's History • America • Twentieth Century • Humor
>
> **Now Try:** Pop-culture addicts won't want to miss *Third Wave Feminism and Television: Jane Puts It in a Box*, edited by Merri Lisa Johnson. This anthology considers society through the framework of television, using such shows as *Buffy the Vampire Slayer* and *Six Feet Under* to discuss a variety of feminist issues, including sexual orientation, monogamy, and rape. Then turn to Maria Elena Buszek's *Pin-up Grrrls: Feminism, Sexuality, Popular Culture*, a delightful social history that relates pin-up girls to feminist thought by studying art, photography, and the media.

Ehrenreich, Barbara, and Arlie Russell Hochschild, eds.

Global Woman: Nannies, Maids, and Sex Workers in the New Economy. New York: Metropolitan Books, 2003. 328pp. ISBN 9780805069952.

In this thought-provoking anthology, sixteen scholars and activists turn their attention to women in the new age of globalization. In particular, they consider the costs and benefits of the nurturing role of global women workers. Though a variety of occupations and locations are discussed —there are Vietnamese maids in China, for instance, and Chicana nannies in America—the theme is clear throughout the book: the countries in which the women work are profiting from the service work of nannies, maids, and sex workers, but the countries they leave behind are suffering, especially when the women workers must leave their children in their native lands. Academic in approach but accessible for the lay reader, *Global Woman* is an eye-opening examination of the economic, social, and personal costs of women's labor in a globalized economy.

> **Subjects:** Labor • Immigration • Class • Sexual Discrimination • Global Perspectives • Essays • Collection • Anthology
>
> **Now Try:** Hear the voices of global women workers come alive in *Sweatshop Warriors: Immigrant Women Workers Take On the Global Factory*. Author Miriam Ching Yoon Louie gathers the stories of Chinese, Korean, and Latina women as they labor in difficult jobs—and as they fight for better wages and working

conditions. See also Pei-Chia Lan's *Global Cinderellas: Migrant Domestics and Newly Rich Employers in Taiwan*, a disturbing but insightful glimpse into the lives of Filipina and Indonesian women employed as domestic workers in Taiwan.

Faludi, Susan

The Terror Dream: Fear and Fantasy in Post-9/11 America. New York: Metropolitan Books, 2007. 351pp. ISBN 9780805086928.

In the wake of the terrorist attacks of September 11, 2001, gender equality in the media took a giant step backward. The media reverted to an old mythos, in which men (police*men*, fire*men*, military *men*) were portrayed as heroes, cowboys, and saviors, while the women were cast as victims, frail and powerless, desperately in need of rescuing. Army Private First Class Jessica Lynch, for instance, after being captured by Iraqi forces, was seen not as a hero but as a female who was rescued by men; and four 9/11 widows who dared to question the government were criticized for their political activism. In her brilliantly argued, impressively researched book, Susan Faludi offers stunning insights into the media landscape in the years following 9/11.

Subjects: Media • Gender • America

Now Try: Though written before 9/11, *Women, Media and Politics* makes for a thoughtful companion read by tackling a thorny question: how does the media reflect and influence the role of women in politics? Editor Pippa Norris brings together essays by twenty-one scholars and journalists that consider how newspapers, radio, and television treat gender issues in the American political landscape. Written for a scholarly audience but accessible for general readers, this is an insightful, thought-provoking examination of the media's influence and bias with regard to gender politics.

Guerrilla Girls (Group of Artists)

Bitches, Bimbos, and Ballbreakers: The Guerrilla Girls' Illustrated Guide to Female Stereotypes. New York: Penguin Books, 2003. 95pp. ISBN 9780142001011.

If you're not already familiar with the Guerrilla Girls, you're in for a treat. Wearing gorilla masks to ensure their anonymity, these feminist activists gleefully tackle sexism wherever they find it. In *Bitches, Bimbos, and Ballbreakers*, they address the stereotypical presentations of women in culture past and present, all within 95 pages—undoubtedly a tall order, but by the end of the book, you'll know all about the tomboy, the femme fatale/vamp, the bimbo/dumb blonde, and the other serious offenders. Campy, artsy, pithy, and brash, the book is a visually satisfying survey of the history of female stereotypes, packed with a healthy dose of feminist anger.

Subjects: Media • Gender • Feminism • Third-wave Feminism • Sociology • History • Women's History • Activism • Stereotypes • Quick Read • Young Adult

Now Try: It's not as kitschy, and the author does not, to my knowledge, wear a gorilla mask, but fans of *Bitches, Bimbos, and Ballbreakers* will nonetheless enjoy *The Girl on the Magazine Cover: The Origins of Visual Stereotypes in American Mass Media*. By examining images of women on magazine covers from the early twentieth century, journalism scholar Carolyn L. Kitch reveals the origins and history of some of the persistent female stereotypes in American culture. The scholarship is engaging, and the reproductions of seventy-five pieces of cover art will sate readers' visual appetites.

Johnson, Jennifer

Getting by on the Minimum: The Lives of Working-class Women. New York: Routledge, 2002. 266pp. ISBN 9780415928007.

"Do secretaries enjoy their jobs as much as attorneys and business-women?" asks sociologist Johnson. "Do day-care providers feel satisfied with their work? Do waitresses?" In interviewing sixty-three working-class women, Johnson attempts to find out. Their life stories, educational backgrounds, and job experiences shine in their own words, illuminating the world of working-class women in vivid, often disturbing detail. And, for comparison, Johnson includes interviews with eighteen middle-class women; the eye-opening contrasts between these two groups, combined with Johnson's excellent research, makes this an exceptional glimpse into the realities of working-class women.

> **Subjects:** Class • Labor • Finances • Mothers • Work/Life Balance • Sociology • America

> **Now Try:** Gain more insight into the lives of working-class women in *Without a Net: The Female Experience of Growing Up Working Class*. Editor Michelle Tea, herself a denizen of the working classes, brings together a startling collection of writings from working-class women in this powerful anthology. Discover their gritty, honest, vivid voices as they discuss the realities of poverty, class, and the struggle to make ends meet.

Levy, Ariel

Female Chauvinist Pigs: Women and the Rise of Raunch Culture. New York: Free Press, 2005. 224pp. ISBN 9780743249898.

Somewhere, somehow, the feminist ideals of the second wave of feminism in the 1970s went wrong, contends *New Yorker* writer Levy. The aspirations toward empowerment and liberation still exist, but now women and girls are seeking their fulfillment in the world of raunch culture. Paris Hilton and Britney Spears are celebrity idols, and women are dressing in uber-sexual outfits. What is so very disturbing is that this trend is powered by women as much as men; in an attempt to be open-minded, to be like "one of the guys," women themselves are encouraging one another to be sexualized and smutty, at the expense of their own identities and desires. With engaging writing and startling insights, *Female Chauvinist Pigs* exposes the perils of women's raunch culture and calls for a return to the true feminist vision of empowerment.

> **Subjects:** Feminism • Sexuality • Sexual Exploitation • History • Women's History • Sociology • Twentieth Century • Twenty-first Century

> **Now Try:** For further evidence of how society has perverted the concept of women's sexual empowerment, turn to *The Body Project: An Intimate History of American Girls*. With primary sources such as magazine ads and diaries, author Joan Jacobs Brumberg traces the social history of the changing self-image of American girls in the nineteenth and twentieth centuries, ending with a discussion of the unsettling current trend toward the hyper-sexualization of today's young women.

Pollitt, Katha

Virginity or Death!: And Other Social and Political Issues of Our Time. New York: Random House Trade Paperbacks, 2006. 265pp. ISBN 9780812976380.

Pollitt, journalist with the left-leaning *The Nation*, here collects nearly ninety of her insightful columns about contemporary social issues. With keen analysis and a biting sense of humor, she tackles subjects ranging from faith-based initiatives to Abu Ghraib to reproductive rights. Though not every column explicitly deals with women's issues, the collection as a whole will appeal to women readers who enjoy the larger scope of social and political writings. Each column shines with Pollitt's feminist political perspective, making it an informative and entertaining lens into one progressive woman's worldview.

> **Subjects:** Feminism • Politics • Twenty-first Century • Essays • Collection
>
> **Now Try:** Pollitt writes with feminist passion about contemporary social issues; now discover the history behind those issues in S. T. Joshi's *In Her Place: A Documentary History of Prejudice against Women.* Based on primary documents, the book looks at women's issues from the perspectives of antifeminist, pro-patriarchal writers. Disturbing but illuminating, the collection assembles a somber history of the hatred and misogyny directed at women by prominent American and European thinkers in the nineteenth and twentieth centuries.

Romero, Mary

Maid in the U.S.A. New York: Routledge, 1992 (2002). 208pp. ISBN 9780415906111.

Themes of class, race, sex, and labor dominate *Maid in the U.S.A.*, a discomfiting but extremely insightful look into the lives of women domestic workers in America. In a scholarly but readable style, author Romero explores the working conditions of working women, most of whom are women of color, migrant laborers, or both. In these pages, anyone with doubts as to the true difficulty of domestic labor will begin to discover how very taxing and demeaning the work is, how low the wages are, and how insufferable the employers can be. Hard questions (but no easy answers) about women and domestic labor will leave readers thinking.

> **Subjects:** Labor • Immigration • Class • Sexual Discrimination • Race • America • Global Perspectives • Essays • Collection
>
> **Now Try:** Follow *Maid in the U.S.A.* with the exploration of women domestic workers in Grace Chang's *Disposable Domestics: Immigrant Women Workers in the Global Economy*, which shows, in no uncertain terms, the value of global women's labor. In addition to exposing the working conditions of domestic laborers and the benefits they bring to the economy, Chang's book offers a rousing, convincing endorsement for immigrant rights and privileges. And for an empowering look at an unusual slice of class and labor history, turn to *Storming Caesar's Palace: How Black Mothers Fought Their Own War on Poverty.* Written by Annelise Orleck, this is the amazing story of how a few angry hotel workers and welfare mothers used protests and demonstrations to win back the health benefits that Nevada had terminated. And that's just the first part of the book; continue reading to learn how some of the protestors pooled their resources and experiences to fight poverty in Las Vegas.

Seager, Joni

The Penguin Atlas of Women in the World. New York: Penguin Books, 2003. 128pp. ISBN 9780142002414.

Women's issues throughout the world are dramatically brought to life in this eye-opening atlas. This broad survey looks at a variety of universal women's issues—including such topics as literacy, leadership, HIV/AIDS, and sexual orientation—in countries across the globe. A color-coded map illustrates each topic, while textual summaries, charts, graphs, and sidebars flesh out the nuances of the various issues. Though many readers will wish to consult the atlas as a reference book, the succinct writing and compelling graphics make *The Penguin Atlas* enjoyable to read as a quick overview of women's issues around the world.

> **Subjects:** Global Perspectives • Feminism • Sexual Discrimination • Twenty-first Century • Atlas • Quick Read

> **Now Try:** Supplement the facts in *The Penguin Atlas* with the powerful contributions collected in *Imagining Ourselves: Global Voices from a New Generation of Women*. Edited by Paula Goldman and Hafsat Abiola, this anthology showcases the fiction, nonfiction, poetry, and visual art of 105 women from 57 countries. With arresting visual images and magnificent presentation, the book is both inspiring and educational as it presents women's issues from across the globe in the voices of the women themselves.

Serano, Julia

Whipping Girl: A Transsexual Woman on Sexism and the Scapegoating of Femininity. Emeryville, CA: Seal Press, 2007. 390pp. ISBN 9781580051545.

Transsexuality: it's a topic steeped in misunderstanding—not only in mainstream culture, but even within the gender-conscious queer community. In *Whipping Girl*, biologist Serano, herself a transsexual woman, demystifies transsexuality in a series of articulate, thought-provoking chapters such as "Boygasms and Girlgasms: A Frank Discussion about Hormones and Gender Differences" and "Skirt Chasers: Why the Media Depicts the Trans Revolution in Lipstick and Heels." In presenting her own experiences in conjunction with her research in such areas as biology, psychology, and sociology, Serano considers transsexuality as it relates to feminism, femininity, and society at large. This eye-opening investigation is scholarly in tone but accessible for readers who want to understand transsexuality as it exists today.

> **Subjects:** Transsexuality • Transgender • Gender • Queer Sexuality • Sexuality • Relationships • Biology • Psychology • Sociology • Feminism • Third-wave Feminism • Memoir

> **Now Try:** Now discover other transsexual voices in two anthologies of tranny writing: *Nobody Passes: Rejecting the Rules of Gender and Conformity* by Matt "Mattilda" Bernstein Sycamore, and *Genderqueer: Voices from beyond the Sexual Binary*, edited by Joan Nestle, Clare Howell, and Riki Anne Wilchins. Both books collect writings by and about transsexuals, and though the essays within the two books tend to be less academic in tone than Serano's *Whipping Girl*, they will appeal to readers for their candor and the breadth of experience they represent.

Abortion and Choice

Here is a sampling of titles that address the issues of birth control, abortion, and a woman's right to choose.

No subject is more politically and emotionally charged than Abortion and Choice. In an effort to use the most neutral language possible, the annotations that follow refer to the "pro-choice" and "anti-abortion" sides (i.e., I avoid the more contentious "pro-abortion," "pro-life," and "anti-choice"). I have tried to present a balanced sampling of texts representing both sides. For books on the history of abortion and contraception, see the section "Women's Bodies and Sexuality throughout History" in Chapter 4.

Bachiochi, Erika, ed.

The Cost of Choice: Women Evaluate the Impact of Abortion. San Francisco: Encounter Books, 2004. 180pp. ISBN 9781594030512.

Whereas most voices in the debate over abortion fall into two major factions, with the anti-abortion camp speaking for the rights of the fetus and the pro-choice camp speaking for the rights of the woman, this insightful collection of essays presents an unusual perspective, arguing against abortion because of women's best interests. *The Cost of Choice* presents twelve essays by prominent women professionals and academics who examine the negative implications of abortion—not as they relate to the fetus but as they relate to the women who undergo the operation. Read about the steep legal, medical, societal, and psychological costs of abortion from a new type of feminist perspective, one that values the needs and rights of women while recognizing that abortion can undermine those needs and rights.

Subjects: Abortion • Anti-Abortion • Feminism • Birth Control • Health • Sexual Health • Politics • Essays • Collection • Anthology • Quick Read

Now Try: For a stirring argument against abortion by a woman who truly understands the full ramifications of it, turn to *Won by Love: Norma McCorvey, Jane Roe of Roe V. Wade, Speaks Out for the Unborn as She Shares Her New Conviction for Life.* Author Norma McCorvey, more commonly known as Jane Roe of *Roe v. Wade*, relates her experience as a long-time abortion rights activist and her eventual ideological transformation into an anti-abortionist Christian. Fans of *The Cost of Choice* may also appreciate the thoughtful, insightful arguments against abortion found in Randy C. Alcorn's book *Pro Life Answers to Pro Choice Arguments;* though it is more conservative, and less feminist, than *The Cost of Choice*, it presents well-reasoned answers for readers who want to understand the logical—and not just ideological—stance against abortion.

Maguire, Daniel C., ed.

Sacred Rights: The Case for Contraception and Abortion in World Religions. Oxford, UK: Oxford University Press, 2003. 295pp. ISBN 9780195160000.

It is a commonly held belief that religions, in general, teach against contraception and abortion. In this thought-provoking collection of essays, twelve contributors show this to be a simplistic view, that religious teachings about birth control are complicated and, surprisingly, frequently pro-choice. Each essay is written by a scholar who practices the religion about which he or she writes; the world's five major religions (Christianity, Judaism, Islam, Hinduism, and Buddhism) are discussed, as well as other religious perspectives such as Native American traditions, Confucianism, and Taoism. With accessible prose and illuminating insights, these essays unveil the startlingly complex ways in which the world's religions treat birth control.

> **Subjects:** Religion • Birth Control • Abortion • Pro-Choice • Health • Sexual Health • Global Perspectives • Essays

> **Now Try:** Though not written specifically about birth control, fans of *Sacred Rights* may also enjoy *Sacred Energies: When the World's Religions Sit Down to Talk about the Future of Human Life and the Plight of This Planet*, also by Daniel Maguire. As in *Sacred Rights*, the scope of the book explores the teachings and beliefs of a variety of world religions, though in this case the topics range from race to class to the global environment.

Mathewes-Green, Frederica

Real Choices: Listening to Women, Looking for Alternatives to Abortion. Ben Lomond, CA: Conciliar Press, 1997. 211pp. ISBN 9781888212075.

> "When circumstances make a woman feel so desperate that killing her own child seems the only way to survive, the problem is not inside her body, but outside it," writes Mathewes-Green in this remarkable book. With common sense, compassion, and sensitivity, she breathes fresh air into the abortion debate, showing the steps that we as a society can take to reduce the abortion rate while still valuing the needs of women. Based on surveys and interviews with people who have faced unwanted pregnancies, *Real Choices* humanizes the women who have endured abortions, placing them—and not their fetuses—at the center of the anti-abortion debate. Succinctly and intelligently written, the book offers level-headed strategies to help women prevent unwanted pregnancies and to find workable alternatives to abortion when unwanted conception does occur.

> **Subjects:** Abortion • Anti-Abortion • Health • Sexual Health • Activism • Feminism • Birth Control

> **Now Try:** Mathewes-Green espouses an unusual anti-abortion/pro-feminist perspective, one that argues against abortion without demonizing women who suffer unwanted pregnancies; now, for more feminist writings in this school of thought, turn to *Prolife Feminism: Yesterday and Today*, edited by Mary Krane Derr, Rachel MacNair, and Linda Naranjo-Huebl. Collecting historical and contemporary writings by feminists such as Susan B. Anthony and Mary Wollstonecraft, the anthology documents the long history of feminist opposition to abortion—and the negative consequences of abortion on women.

Messer, Ellen, and Kathryn E. May

Back Rooms: Voices from the Illegal Abortion Era. New York: St. Martin's Press, 1988 (1994). 234pp. ISBN 9780312017323.

> Before the landmark Supreme Court decision in *Roe v. Wade* in 1973, abortions were illegal, extremely difficult to come by, and all too often lethal. Worried that America might go back to criminalizing abortion, authors Messer and May conducted interviews with women who sought abortions when they were illegal. The women's moving stories, presented here

in their own words, are collected into chilling sections such as "Back Alleys, Dark Streets" and "Leaving the Country." Also included are the stories of women who were unable to obtain the abortions they wanted. Candid, emotional, and heart-wrenching, these stories work together to warn against denying reproductive choice to women.

Subjects: Abortion • Pro-Choice • Health • Sexual Health • Birth Control • History • Women's History • Social History • History of Medicine • Twentieth Century

Now Try: A natural companion to *Back Rooms* is Leslie J. Reagan's book *When Abortion Was a Crime: Women, Medicine, and Law in the United States, 1867–1973*. Learn the stories of pregnant women, their lovers, doctors, and midwives who tried, often unsuccessfully and at risk of legal prosecution, to perform abortions. The methods they used, including poisons, needles, and scissors, make for a heart-breaking examination of the desperate measures that American women undertook to terminate their pregnancies before abortions were legalized.

Page, Cristina

How The Pro-choice Movement Saved America. New York: Basic Books, 2006. 236pp. ISBN 9780465054893.

"If you don't want people to have abortions, then why not help them prevent unwanted pregnancies?" asks NARAL Pro-Choice America activist Page. "Why would those so adamantly against abortion seek to hamper practical, simple, and safe attempts to actually prevent abortions?" The unfortunate answer, she explains, is that the anti-abortion movement is not just against abortion, but rather against sex for any purpose other than reproduction. Thus, they fight against contraception, even though condoms help prevent the spread of HIV; thus, they do not sanction same-sex couplings; thus, they argue against the HPV vaccine because it might encourage young women to be promiscuous. Engagingly written, fast-paced, and thought-provoking, the book exposes the hypocrisy inherent to much of the anti-abortion movement and argues for a society where sex may be enjoyed with protection against diseases and unintended pregnancies.

Subjects: Birth Control • Abortion • Pro-Choice • Feminism • Activism • Sociology • Health • Sexual Health • America

Now Try: Turn now to another famous feminist activist, Gloria Feldt, the president of Planned Parenthood. In *The War on Choice: The Right-Wing Attack on Women's Rights and How to Fight Back*, she echoes Page's worries over the influence of the anti-abortion movement, arguing that they are corroding women's access to affordable reproductive choices, not just abortion. With a compelling sense of urgency, she calls readers to action and presents steps they can take to preserve women's rights to reproductive options.

Sexual Exploitation

The stories of women whose bodies are sexually used and abused for profit populate this section.

Even in the twenty-first century, women and girls around the globe—even in the United States—are being exploited. From flagrant abuses such as human trafficking to more subtle poisons such as pornography, sex is being used to abuse, devalue, and dehumanize women. Books in the "Sexual Exploitation" section expose these practices and provoke readers to thought—and maybe even to action.

Bales, Kevin

Disposable People: New Slavery in the Global Economy. Berkeley: University of California Press, 1999 (2004). 298pp. ISBN 9780520217973.

"Slavery is not a horror safely confined to the past," writes activist scholar Bales. "It continues to exist throughout the world, even in developed countries like France and the United States.... This is the new slavery, which focuses on big profits and cheap lives. It is not about owning people in the traditional sense of the old slavery, but about controlling them completely." Horrifying, shocking, and unbearably vivid, *Disposable People* investigates this new type of slavery, exposing the inhumane treatment of more then 27 million people with real-life stories from Thailand, Mauritania, Brazil, Pakistan, and India. Many of these slaves are women and children; some of them labor as manufacturers, others as service providers, still others as prostitutes. With stark, unforgettable imagery, the book lays bare the realities of slavery as it exists today, while offering realistic actions that people can take to reduce—and possibly even end—slavery in the modern world.

> **Subjects:** Slavery • Violence • Sexual Exploitation • Children • Labor • Class • Activism • Global Perspectives • Twenty-first Century

> **Now Try:** For more heart-wrenching stories of modern slavery, turn to *Enslaved: True Stories of Modern Day Slavery*, edited by Jesse Sage and Liora Kasten. With seven stories of former slaves and one story of a slave owner-cum-abolitionist, the collection reveals the horrifying conditions that people are forced to endure for the sake of other people's profit; also included are practical, simple guidelines to help people consume products that do not exploit slaves. Then turn to the harrowing memoir *Slave* by Mende Nazer, in which the author recounts her abduction into slavery after a happy childhood in the Sudan, followed by her escape after seven years of physical, sexual, and emotional slavery.

Dorkenoo, Efua

Female Genital Mutilation: Politics and Prevention. London: Hurst & Co., 2006. 272pp. ISBN 9780231143462.

Each year, more than two million girls and women undergo female genital mutilation (FGM); the World Health Organization (WHO) estimates that between 100 million and 140 million have endured an FGM procedure. Activist Dorkenoo, the first WHO expert on female genital mutilation, presents an informative, eye-opening, and disturbing look at the practice as it exists today. In clear, crisp prose, she explains the history of FGM, the religious and cultural forces that support its continued existence, and the psychological, physical, and sexual effects on girls and women who have undergone genital cutting. Stark and straightforward, this is an excellent overview of FGM, appropriate both as an introductory text and as a resource for further information for those readers who already have some familiarity with the practice.

Subjects: Female Genital Mutilation • Violence • Health • Sexual Health • Activism • Global Perspectives • Twenty-first Century

Now Try: Alice Walker, known for her novels, essays, and poems about a variety of social issues, teams up now with filmmaker Pratibha Parmar to expose the violent practice of FGM in *Warrior Marks*, the companion book to Parmar's documentary of the same name. Interviews with FGM victims and their families, activists, and even people who perform the procedure make this an eye-opening exposé. Readers may also wish to turn to the photojournalism in *The Day Kadi Lost Part of Her Life*, by Isabel Ramos and Kim Manresa, but be forewarned: the pictures of the genital mutilation of four-year-old Kadi are graphic and vivid; they tell the story of FGM in horrific visual detail, and readers will not wish to open the book casually.

Stepp, Laura Sessions

Unhooked: How Young Women Pursue Sex, Delay Love and Lose at Both. New York: Riverhead Books, 2007. 288pp. ISBN 9781594489389.

Hooking up: it's the common parlance for casual sex in the modern era, typified by solitary or repeated encounters between two people who don't know each other very well—who may not even know each other's names—but who nonetheless have physical relations together. Having followed the sexual lives of nine young women for a year in preparation for writing *Unhooked*, *Washington Post* reporter Stepp is gravely concerned that hooking up is becoming the norm among high school and college students. The utter lack of commitment or emotional rapport inherent to the hook-up leaves young women unprepared to enter into lasting, stable relationships as they mature, Stepp argues; we as a culture should be encouraging women at this age to date, not to settle for meaningless sexual encounters.

Subjects: Sexuality • Dating • Relationships • Sociology

Now Try: Though written with a somewhat different scope, Wendy Shalit's *Girls Gone Mild: Young Women Reclaim Self-Respect and Find It's Not Bad to Be Good* makes for a nice companion read. Whereas Stepp focuses on replacing the hook-up culture with a dating culture, Shalit takes a broader perspective, arguing that young women and girls are being sexualized in every context; relationships such as the hook-up fall under her fire, but so, too, do celebrity models for sexuality and over-sexualized dolls and toys marketed toward young girls. Her insightful criticism of the sexualization of society at large gives context to the hook-up phenomenon described by Stepp.

Whisnant, Rebecca, and Christine Stark, eds.

Not for Sale: Feminists Resisting Prostitution and Pornography. North Melbourne, Australia: Spinifex Press, 2004. 445pp. ISBN 9781876756499.

A current trend in feminist thought is to embrace and celebrate the sex industries for the empowerment and liberation that they can give to sex workers. The more traditional feminist viewpoint, that sex work harms and exploits women, is still alive and well, however, as seen in this thought-provoking collection of feminist essays. More than thirty contributors from around the globe, including activists, writers, and women with experience in sex work, share their insights into the perils of prostitution and pornography, showing that adult entertainment does not empower women but subjugates them. With heavy themes of race, nationality, gender, and class permeating the anthology, the book is not a light read, but rather a somber, serious collection of feminist arguments that convincingly demonstrate the harmfulness of women's sex work.

Subjects: Prostitution • Pornography • Sexual Exploitation • Feminism • Third-wave Feminism • Activism • Global Perspectives • Essays • Collection • Anthology

Now Try: Continue learning about the harmful consequences of prostitution and pornography in two additional books. In Mary Lucille Sullivan's *Making Sex Work: A Failed Experiment with Legalised Prostitution*, discover the threats to women's health and safety that persisted in Australia even after the State of Victoria legalized prostitution. Then turn to *Pornified: How Pornography Is Transforming Our Lives, Our Relationships, and Our Families*, in which author Pamela Paul sensibly deconstructs the modern feminist notion that porn is empowering to women; her research and her interviews with porn viewers, to the contrary, show that porn continues to negatively affect adults' relationships and children's sexual innocence.

Sexual Liberation

The "Sexual Liberation" section features books about women who are empowered by their sexuality.

The authors of the books in this section take a sex-positive approach to adult entertainment, showing that exotic dancing, pornography, and prostitution can be liberating for women.

Barton, Bernadette

Stripped: Inside the Lives of Exotic Dancers. New York: New York University Press, 2006. 195pp. ISBN 0814799337.

"What kind of woman dances naked for money?" asks sociologist Barton in the very first sentence of *Stripped*; the rest of the book is an attempt to answer that question. Based on Barton's interviews with hundreds of exotic dancers and her five years spent haunting strip clubs in three American cities, the book paints a complex picture of the lifestyle of exotic dancers: Initially the job can be fun and lucrative, but as time passes, troubles such as drug problems and difficult personal relationships often crop up. The feminist perspective that stripping is a degrading, exploitive job is given due consideration, but so too is the alternative feminist perspective that stripping is an empowering job that celebrates women's sexualities. Barton refrains from advocating either view, but instead lets her readers make up their own minds in this fascinating, fast-paced investigation.

Subjects: Exotic Dancing • Labor • Sexuality • Sexual Exploitation • Feminism • America • Quick Read

Now Try: For another feminist investigation into stripping, turn to R. Danielle Egan's *Dancing for Dollars and Paying for Love: The Relationships between Exotic Dancers and Their Regulars*. Like Barton, Egan uses interviews and her own field observations to understand the people who frequent strip clubs, both the dancers and their regular customers. Then turn to *Flesh for Fantasy: Producing and Consuming Exotic Dance*, edited by Egan, Katherine Frank, and Merri Lisa Johnson—all three of whom are scholars who have worked as exotic dancers. Their anthology collects essays by and about strippers, giving readers a feel for what it's really like inside a strip club.

Milne, Carly, ed.

Naked Ambition: Women Who Are Changing Pornography. New York: Carroll & Graf, 2005. 352pp. ISBN 9780585314723.

Author Carly Milne has written extensively about the pornography industry, making her the perfect editor for this unusual anthology of essays, which showcases the inroads that women have been making in the adult entertainment industry. Women are doing far more than taking off their clothes in front of the camera, as seen in sections such as "Porn Purveyors," "Erotic Envisioners," and "Wanton Webmistresses." Get the insider scoop on women behind the scenes from such writers as Regina Lynn, who writes about the marriage of sex and technology, and Theresa Flynt, who writes about her experience in restructuring *Hustler*. Fun and informative, these essays illuminate the ways in which women are influencing pornography and adult entertainment.

> **Subjects:** Pornography • Labor • Business • Essays • Collection • Anthology

> **Now Try:** *Naked Ambition* shows that women are changing the production and distribution of pornography; now try two books that show how women are changing the consumption of pornography. In *The Smart Girl's Guide to Porn*, sex educator Violet Blue offers a how-to guide to help women enjoy porn, with chapters such as "Find the Right Porn for You" and "Porn Resources for Smart Girls." Then try *At Home with Pornography: Women, Sexuality, and Everyday Life* by Jane Juffer. Scholarly in approach and tone, the book makes for heavier reading than *Naked Ambition*, but readers looking for excellent research into the changing role of pornography within normal women's day-to-day lives will find it a thought-provoking, eye-opening read.

Nagle, Jill, ed.

Whores and Other Feminists. New York: Routledge, 1997. 291pp. ISBN 97804159-18213.

When it comes to adult entertainment, feminism offers two main schools of thought: there are those who think that stripping, prostitution, and the like exploit women, and then there are those who insist that sex work can be empowering and liberating. Coming down firmly in this second camp are the contributors to *Whores and Other Feminists*, who are themselves sex workers. Hear from pornographers, prostitutes, exotic dancers, and other women in the adult entertainment industry as they explore the feminist underpinnings of sex work. With a decidedly scholarly bent, this is no light read, but rather a serious academic exploration of feminism by feminists who will open readers' eyes to the personal politics of adult entertainment.

> **Subjects:** Labor • Feminism • Third-wave Feminism • Exotic Dancing • Pornography • Prostitution • Sexuality • Essays • Collection • Anthology

> **Now Try:** Like *Whores and Other Feminists*, the book *Live Sex Acts: Women Performing Erotic Labor* is a scholarly, feminist treatment of women's sex work. Based on her interviews with sex workers, author Wendy Chapkis illuminates the experiences and perspectives of women who work in the adult entertainment industry, showing both the gritty side of sex work and the potential for feminist empowerment for women sex workers.

Ringdal, Nils Johan

Love for Sale: A World History of Prostitution. New York: Grove Press, 2004. 435pp. ISBN 9780802117458.

Prostitution: it's the oldest profession, and perhaps the most fascinating. In this thoroughly researched social history, author Ringdal examines the practice and influence of prostitution across time and across the globe, fleshing out the changing social, moral, and political attitudes toward prostitution in various cultures and times. Drawing on primary documents, myths, and literature, Ringdal surveys prostitution through the centuries, from the ancient world through the Victorian era through contemporary times. Engrossing and accessible, the book breathes life into the stories of famous prostitutes from history, uncovering the consequences, both good and bad, for women who have exchanged sex for money in the past and in the present.

Subjects: Prostitution • History • Labor • History of Labor • Social History • Women's History • Global Perspectives

Now Try: Supplement the history of *Love for Sale* with the more contemporary focus of *Sex Work: Writings by Women in the Sex Industry*, edited by Frédérique Delacoste and Priscilla Alexander. With its blend of academic essays about sex work with the stories of women sex workers, the insightful discussion of legal and feminist issues surrounding prostitution and other sex jobs should appeal to Ringdal's fans.

War, Violence, and Peace

Issues of war and peace take center stage in these books, which often seek to promote a more humane approach but sometimes justify women's use of violence as a means of self-defense.

In the "War, Violence, and Peace" section, we find that women have a long tradition of writing about war and violence; see, for instance, Daniela Gioseffi's anthology *Women on War*. Perhaps more surprising is that women themselves participate in violence, as we learn in Tara McKevley's anthology *One of the Guys: Women as Aggressors and Torturers*. On the flip side, we see that women can and should oppose violence, as Jean Shinoda Bolen urges us to do in *Urgent Message from Mother: Gather the Women, Save the World*.

Bolen, Jean Shinoda

Urgent Message from Mother: Gather the Women, Save the World. York Beach, ME: Conari Press, 2005. 187pp. ISBN 9781573242653.

"It is time to 'gather the women'—for only when women are *strong together* can women be fiercely protective of what we love," writes Bolen, a psychiatrist and internationally known activist. "Only then, will children be safe and peace a real possibility." With her thoughtful, emotionally moving style, Bolen demonstrates the power and potential of women to end violence and promote peace. She discusses the nurturing qualities that underpin women's psychologies, and she offers practical ways for women to come together for a cause. Passionate and compassionate, insightful and profound, the book is both a contemplative thought-piece and a powerful call to action.

> **Subjects:** Peace • Violence • Gender • Psychology • Spirituality • Activism • Feminism • How-to • Quick Read

> **Now Try:** If Bolen's vision of a world transformed by women's activism struck a chord with you, turn to *If Women Ruled the World: How to Create the World We Want to Live In: Stories, Ideas, and Inspiration for Change*, edited by Sheila Ellison. Like *Urgent Message from Mother*, this is a call for action; this time, however, the call comes from a variety of different voices. Essays, reflections, stories, and meditations from women around the world, from all walks of life—politicians, writers, mothers, teenagers—speak to the power of women to change things for the better.

Gioseffi, Daniela, ed.

Women on War: An International Anthology of Women's Writings from Antiquity to the Present. New York: Feminist Press at the City University of New York, 2003. 375pp. ISBN 9781558614086.

Since ancient times, women have felt compelled to write about, and against, war. Though the combatants have (usually) been men, the tragedy, despair, and violence of war has always affected women, as seen in this exemplary anthology of women's voices. Editor Gioseffi has gathered writings from a wide variety of women—including authors, activists, soldiers, and protestors—in a collection that covers war from 2300 B.C.E. to modern times. Some of the contributors, such as Adrienne Rich and Isabelle Allende, will be familiar to readers, while other voices will be lesser-known figures from history—but in all cases, the writing is excellent, speaking from women's perspectives about the costs of war.

> **Subjects:** War • Violence • History • Social History • Women's History • Feminism • Global Perspectives • Essays • Collection • Anthology

> **Now Try:** For a quicker but no less profound read, turn to the photo-essays in *The Other Side of War: Women's Stories of Survival & Hope*. As the president of a charity group dedicated to improving the lives of women survivors of war, author Zainab Salbi was the perfect person to write this moving collection of short profiles of women war survivors. Powerful stories and stunning photographs of women around the globe reveal the despair and triumph of those who have survived war. Those who enjoyed *Women on War* may also like reading the essays in *Nothing Sacred: Women Respond to Religious Fundamentalism and Terror*; edited by Betsy Reed, this anthology presents feminist viewpoints of the social and political ramifications of religious fundamentalism on war, violence, and terror.

Kelly, Caitlin

Blown Away: American Women and Guns. New York: Pocket Books, 2004. 324pp. ISBN 9780743464185.

We tend to associate firearms with masculine pursuits, but as journalist Kelly reveals in her thought-provoking study, 17 million American women own guns. Their motivations for gun ownership, however, tend not toward leisure but toward self-defense and crime prevention. In this investigation into women and guns in American society, Kelly draws on American history, pop culture, and interviews with women gun owners to determine why women choose to own guns and to illuminate the consequences, both positive and negative, of women's gun ownership. The book is neither pro-gun nor anti-gun; instead, it is a balanced examination of a topic that rarely receives such thoughtful treatment.

Subjects: Guns • Violence • America

Now Try: Unravel the complicated but fascinating history of American women and guns in Laura Browder's book *Her Best Shot: Women and Guns in America*. This scholarly but accessible social history examines the different eras and social settings in which women have owned guns, from the Civil War and the old American West through modern times. Rediscover women gunslingers such as Annie Oakley and Ma Barker as Browder analyzes women's gun ownership in the contexts of feminism and sexual discrimination

McKelvey, Tara, ed.

One of the Guys: Women as Aggressors and Torturers. Emeryville, CA: Seal Press, 2007. 266pp. ISBN 9781580051965.

Common wisdom holds women to be gentler than men, more diplomatic in dealing with conflict, and more compassionate toward enemies. While this may be true in general, the anthology *One of the Guys* destroys any doubt about the capacity for women to engage in aggression and torture. With disturbing insights and sobering conclusions, the essays swiftly dispatch assumptions about the inherent nonviolence of women by examining the question of women and torture in settings such as Guantánamo and Abu Ghraib. Stellar contributions from writers such as Eve Ensler, Barbara Ehrenreich, and Angela Y. Davis make this a thought-provoking, scholarly read.

Subjects: Violence • War • Psychology • Gender • Global Perspectives • Essays • Collection • Anthology

Now Try: For visceral evidence of the link between women and torture, turn to the story that shocked America and the world in *One Woman's Army: The Commanding General of Abu Ghraib Tells Her Story*. As the person in charge at Abu Ghraib, the site of torture by American servicepeople against prisoners, author Janis L. Karpinski accepts responsibility for her role in this shameful chapter of American history—but as this compelling memoir shows, violence is too complicated to reduce to simple concepts of sex or gender.

Stiehm, Judith

Champions for Peace: Women Winners of the Nobel Peace Prize. Lanham, MD: Rowman & Littlefield, 2006. 233pp. ISBN 9780742540255.

Though it was first awarded in 1901, only twelve recipients of the annual Nobel Peace Prize have been women. In this collective biography, author Stiehm profiles those twelve women, all of whom hail from markedly different backgrounds. They come from across the globe, from different classes, from different educational backgrounds—yet all of them are united in their tireless efforts to make the world a better place. Despite their high-profile prizes, most of these women are, sadly, unknown to most readers; fortunately, Stiehm's deft prose brings their stories to life, while assuring the reader that individuals can, and do, make a difference.

Subjects: Nobel Peace Prize • Peace • Activism • Labor • Global Perspectives • Biography • Collection

> **Now Try:** A good companion to *Champions for Peace* is *Women Nobel Peace Prize Winners*. Though more scholarly in tone, readers wishing to know more about the twelve winners will appreciate the detailed approach of author Anita Prize Davis as she continues Stiehm's examination of the lives of the winners, paying special attention to the accomplishments of each woman that led to the Nobel Prize.

Women and Politics

Women in political roles are described by titles in this section.

As congresswomen, as governors, as presidents (though not in the United States), women are serving as politicians. Some of the books in the "Women and Politics" section focus on the personal stories of these women, while others take a more sociological approach, examining the affect of women as political leaders along with the role of public policy in women's lives. Readers who enjoy this section will also want to see the "Women and Leadership" section of Chapter 7.

Clift, Eleanor, and Tom Brazaitis

Madam President: Shattering the Last Glass Ceiling. New York: Scribner, 2000 (2003). 349pp. ISBN 9780684856193.

Wife-and-husband team Clift and Brazaitis know their stuff: as journalists with insider knowledge of the workings of Washington, D.C., they are privy to the thoughts and behaviors that shape America's politics. Granted, they wrote *Madam President* prior to Hillary Rodham Clinton's bid for the presidency in 2008, but even so, this is a fascinating, relevant look at the intersection of politics and gender. With examples of women senators, governors, and other key leadership positions, the book considers why women have succeeded—or, as is still so often the case, why they have not. Filled with anecdotes, trivia, and thought-provoking insights, this is a fun, engaging study of where women are now and where they will someday be.

> **Subjects:** Politics • Gender • Leadership • History • Women's History • Social History • American History • Twentieth Century • Twenty-first Century • America

> **Now Try:** For a more in-depth look at could-have-been women presidents, turn to Nichola D. Gutgold's *Paving the Way for Madam President*. Like *Madam President*, this book was written prior to Hillary Rodham Clinton's 2008 campaign, but it is still valuable for the insight it gives into other women who have run for president. In this collective biography, you'll discover the lives and the politics of Carol Moseley Braun, Shirley Chisholm, Elizabeth Dole, Patricia Schroeder, and Margaret Chase Smith.

Conway, M. Margaret, David W. Ahern, and Gertrude A. Steuernagel

Women & Public Policy: A Revolution in Progress. Washington, DC: CQ Press, 1995 (2004). 213pp. ISBN 9780871879233.

The oft-cited slogan of the second wave of feminism got it right: the personal is political. The issues that affect women's everyday lives—such as education, health care, housing, and child care—are matters of national politics and law. Published by CQ Press, a publisher celebrated for accessible, informative analyses of social and political topics, *Women & Public Policy* offers a thorough, readable survey of

American policies that directly affect women. Especially valuable are the sections on the history of public policy, which vividly illustrate the strides that have been made. Read this to discover where we've been, where we are, and where we're going.

Subjects: Politics • Law • Gender • History • Women's History • Twentieth Century • Twenty-first Century • America

Now Try: *Women & Public Policy* considers the policies that affect women's lives; now turn to two books that discuss the role women have had in shaping those policies. The essays of *Women Transforming Politics: An Alternative Reader*, edited by Cathy J. Cohen, Kathleen B. Jones, and Joan C. Tronto, analyzes the strides women have made, emphasizing the role of women outside the privileged white mainstream. *The Impact of Women in Public Office*, edited by Susan J. Carroll, collects essays that consider elected and appointed women officials, with special emphasis on their work with policies that relate to women's issues.

Enloe, Cynthia H.

Bananas, Beaches & Bases: Making Feminist Sense of International Politics. Berkeley: University of California Press, 1990 (2000). 244pp. ISBN 9780520069848.

"If we don't take women's experiences—in all their diversity—seriously, if we act as though manipulations of ideas about femininity and masculinity are not political, but merely 'cultural,' we risk, I think, underestimating how much of our lives are indeed political. We thereby risk being globally naïve," warns scholar Enloe. To compensate for the neglect of women's issues in the current discourse on global politics, she has written this compelling, thought-provoking study of gender on the international stage. In chapters such as "On the Beach: Sexism and Tourism" and "'Just Like One of the Family': Domestic Servants in World Politics," Enloe considers gender in a variety of international topics, including disease, diplomacy, labor, and the sex trade. The book's insight analysis and eye-opening photos make this a fascinating, informative read.

Subjects: Feminism • Gender • Politics • Global Perspectives • Twentieth Century

Now Try: A good complement to *Bananas, Beaches & Bases* is *Participation and Protest: Women and Politics in a Global World* by Sarah Henderson and Alana S. Jeydel. This thoughtful overview of international politics considers not only the gendered nature of global issues but also the role of women activists in such areas as human rights, women's rights, and economic development.

Han, Lori Cox, and Caroline Heldman, eds.

Rethinking Madam President: Are We Ready for a Woman in the White House? Boulder, CO: Lynne Rienner Publishers, 2007. 229pp. ISBN 9781-588265197.

In 2008, Hillary Rodham Clinton came closer than any other woman to reaching the presidency, just barely losing the Democratic nomination to Barack Obama. *Rethinking Madam President*, published the year prior, is therefore somewhat dated, but its insightful essays are nonetheless relevant to understanding the modern climate of gender and politics. The collection takes a hard look at the American public's willingness—or lack thereof—to support women presidential candidates in essays such as "Money and the Art and Science of Candidate Viability" by Victoria Farrar-Myers and "Shaping Women's Chances: Stereotypes and the Media," by Gina Serignese Woodall and Kim L. Fridkin. With fine political writing and thought-provoking observations, this is an excellent overview of gender and national politics in twenty-first century America.

> **Subjects:** Politics • Gender • Leadership • Sociology • America • Twenty-first Century • Essays • Collection • Anthology

> **Now Try:** To further understand the role, or lack of role, of women in public office, turn to *It Takes a Candidate: Why Women Don't Run for Office* by Jennifer L. Lawless and Richard Logan Fox. Based on the authors' survey of nearly four thousand "potential candidates," the book provides hard data for understanding why women are less likely to run for office; women, for instance, are less likely to be recruited to run, and they tend to feel less qualified than men. This is a fascinating, if somewhat disheartening, study of women, gender, and politics.

Kunin, Madeleine

Pearls, Politics, & Power: How Women Can Win and Lead. White River Junction, VT: Chelsea Green, 2008. 233pp. ISBN 9781603580106.

> "Women are not supposed to want power, somewhat like sex. It's OK if they just receive it," writes Kunin. "Women tend to look at power differently than men. Rather than having *power over* others, they are more comfortable to *share power with* others." Kunin knows what she's talking about; she has served as the governor of Vermont and as ambassador to Switzerland. To illustrate the nature of women's leadership, she draws on her own experiences and offers profiles of influential women such as Bella Abzug and Abigail Adams. Engaging and thought-provoking, the book demonstrates the benefits of women's political leadership and offers practical steps to help women get elected.

> **Subjects:** Politics • Leadership • Labor • Sociology • Gender • America • Memoir • Biography • Collection • How-to

> Now Try: Kunin's book was published in 2008, the year that saw two women reach unprecedented heights in the quest for national office. While neither woman won the office, their stories illuminate the realities of women's political influence described by Kunin. Read about Hillary Rodham Clinton's bid for the presidency in *Her Way: The Hopes and Ambitions of Hillary Rodham Clinton* by Jeff Gerth and Don Van Natta. With a relatively neutral approach to a controversial woman, the authors discuss Clinton's history in politics, concluding with her presidential campaign. Then learn about the woman who almost became vice president in *Sarah: How a Hockey Mom Turned the Political Establishment Upside Down.* Though the focus is more on Sarah Palin's entire life than on her political achievements per se, author Kaylene Johnson deftly explores Palin's meteoric rise on the national scene.

Liswood, Laura A.

Women World Leaders: Fifteen Great Politicians Tell Their Stories. London: Pandora, 1995 (2007). 179pp. ISBN 9780044409045.

> While the United States of America has yet to elect a female president, women have served at the top in other countries around the globe. Meet fifteen of them in this fascinating collective biography, based on author Liswood's personal interviews with women presidents and prime ministers. Liswood, the Secretary General of the Council of Women World Leaders, brings out the stories of women who

may or may not be familiar to American audiences; there is Benazir Bhutto, of course, who was twice elected as Prime Minister of Pakistan and whose political assassination wrenched her into international fame; but there is also Cory Aquino, former president of the Philippines, whose name may be new to readers. This inspiring collection of profiles presents a thought-provoking glimpse into gender, politics, and leadership around the world.

Subjects: Leadership • Gender • Global Perspectives • Biography • Collection • Quick Read

Now Try: Looking for more information on women leaders around the globe? Try Rosemarie Skaine's *Women Political Leaders in Africa*, which looks at women serving at the national level in countries across Africa, including the president of Liberia and the prime minister of Mozambique. Or perhaps try *Women and Power in the Middle East* by Suad Joseph and Susan Slyomovics; though the focus is less on individual leaders and more on the general power of women across the political spectrum, fans of *Women World Leaders* will enjoy the discussion of gender and politics in the Middle East.

Palmer, Barbara, and Dennis Michael Simon

Breaking the Political Glass Ceiling: Women and Congressional Elections. Women in American Politics. New York: Routledge, 2006 (2008). 235pp. ISBN 9780415950879.

Women comprise more than half of the American population, but as of this writing, they hold only fifteen of the one hundred seats in the Senate. Any number of intellectuals, pundits, and armchair theorists have speculated on the causes of women's continued underrepresentation, but scholars Palmer and Simon go a step further by looking at hard facts. Drawing on data from congressional races since 1956, they examine the factors that help women get into office (women fare better in wealthy urban communities, for instance) and the issues that women consider when they decide whether to campaign for Congress. In scholarly but accessible chapters such as "Why So Few, and Why So Slow?" and "Where Women Run: Women and the Competitive Environment," the authors paint a fascinating picture of gender in the modern American political climate.

Subjects: Politics • Leadership • Gender • Sexual Discrimination • America • Twenty-first Century

Now Try: Readers eager to learn more about women in Congress would do well to turn to *Women and Congress: Running, Winning, and Ruling*, edited by Karen O'Connor. This collection of thought-provoking essays considers the successes and struggles of women seeking congressional seats by exploring such topics as the glass ceiling, the portrayal of women in the media, and political incumbency.

Sanbonmatsu, Kira

Where Women Run: Gender and Party in the American States. Ann Arbor: University of Michigan Press, 2006. 250pp. ISBN 9780472099344.

Women are sorely underrepresented in local, state, and federal political offices—but not because voters don't want them. "The scarcity of women candidates, rather than a failure of women to win their races, is the primary reason for the dearth of women in public office; election results reveal that women candidates typically win their races at rates similar to those of men," explains political scientist Sanbonmatsu. To understand this paucity of women candidates, Sanbonmatsu considers the influence of political parties: do they encourage or discourage women to run? Do they facilitate their campaigns? Do the traditional rules of political parties invite women's participation? To answer these questions, Sanbonmatsu surveyed legislators and performed in-depth case studies of party leaders; her findings, presented in a scholarly but accessible style, paint a fascinating picture of the gender politics of candidacy in American political parties.

Subjects: Politics • Leadership • Gender • America • Twenty-first Century

Now Try: Continue exploring the obstacles faced by women candidates in *Voting for Women: How the Public Evaluates Women Candidates*. Author Kathleen A. Dolan uses hard facts to analyze the voter demographics that influence women's successes (or lack thereof) at the polls in this fascinating study of the public's attitudes toward women candidates. Readers may also enjoy *Anticipating Madam President*, edited by Robert P. Watson and Ann Gordon; though somewhat dated in light of Hillary Rodham Clinton's campaign in 2008, this collection of essays is nonetheless an intriguing investigation of the struggles faced by women who run for office.

Working Mothers

The dual role of motherhood and career that many contemporary women take provides the focus for titles in this section.

The primary job of women throughout history has been to raise children. Even today, with unprecedented career choices available to women and with child-raising rendered optional, motherhood still commands our attention. These books discuss the societal implications of motherhood in an age when career and family often conflict. For books about relationships between mothers and their children, see the "Motherhood," "Fertility and Adoption," and "Pregnancy, Childbirth, and Nursing" sections of Chapter 2.

Bennetts, Leslie

The Feminine Mistake: Are We Giving Up Too Much? New York: Voice/Hyperion, 2007. 350pp. ISBN 9781401303068.

Motherhood, as any woman with children can tell you, is a full-time job—but in the past few decades, women have entered the workforce in droves, opting either to forsake having children or to carry the dual burden of motherhood and career. In response to the stress of this burden, many women have recently been making the conscious decision to stay at home with their kids, depending on husbands to support them financially—but as Bennetts warns in this excellent study, that can be a dangerous choice. Based on interviews with financial experts, lawyers, and other professionals and on interviews with hundreds of women who ceded their financial autonomy, Bennetts convincingly demonstrates that women who give up their income risk losing their retirement nest eggs and their access to health care, especially as they age. *The Feminine Mistake* is a thought-provoking entry in the debate over the mommy wars, a book that asks not whether women *should* give up their careers, but whether they can even afford to.

Subjects: Labor • Finances • Class • Mothers • Work/Life Balance • Sociology • America • Twenty-first Century

Now Try: Bennetts amply demonstrates the risk of giving up financial security for the sake of raising children; those women who consequently want to contemplate a return to the workforce can follow up with *Back on the Career Track: A Guide for Stay-at-Home Moms Who Want to Return to Work*. Written by Carol Fishman Cohen and Vivian Steir Rabin, two mothers who discovered first-hand the difficulties inherent to resuming work after having children, this book presents seven practical steps for relaunching a career. Readers may also enjoy *Dispatches from a Not-So-Perfect Life: Or How I Learned to Love the House, the Man, the Child*. In this wry, witty memoir, feminist Faulkner Fox reflects on many of the same issues in Bennets's book—motherhood, finances, economics—as they relate to her own marriage, career, and motherhood.

Blades, Joan, and Kristin Rowe-Finkbeiner

The Motherhood Manifesto: What America's Moms Want and What to Do about It. New York: Nation Books, 2006. 248pp. ISBN 9781560258841.

"Motherhood in America is at a critical juncture," write activists Blades and Rowe-Finkbeiner. "More women than ever are in the workforce, and more children than ever are raised in homes without a stay-at-home parent." In this stirring call for change, the authors insist that now is the time to make careers and motherhood compatible, to empower families to find the resources they need to arrange for quality, affordable child care. Drawing on eye-opening anecdotes of overworked mothers and success stories of progressive employers, *The Motherhood Manifesto* presents a scathing critique of a society that properly accommodates neither stay-at-home nor working mothers. The book proposes a list of actions that families, lawmakers, and employers can take to make sure that mothers can balance their jobs, their families, and their child-care needs.

Subjects: Labor • Mothers • Children • Activism • Feminism • Work/Life Balance • Sociology • America • Twenty-first Century

Now Try: For further evidence of the financial risk of motherhood in modern America, turn to *The Price of Motherhood: Why the Most Important Job in the World Is Still the Least Valued*. Author Ann Crittenden draws on economics and social science to paint a grim picture of the cost of motherhood, showing that stay-at-home-moms—and even working mothers—are at risk for loss of income, even poverty, because their jobs as mothers do not come with Social Security, health benefits, workers' compensation, or any of the other benefits of paid positions. See also *Mothers on the Fast Track: How a New Generation Can Balance Family and Careers*, in which mother/daughter authors Mary Ann Mason and Eve Mason Ekman offer career advice targeted to mothers of all ages and to women who are thinking about having children.

Hays, Sharon

Flat Broke with Children: Women in the Age of Welfare Reform. Oxford, UK: Oxford University Press, 2003. 290pp. ISBN 9780195132885.

In the mid-1990s, welfare reform was introduced as a cure for a broken system, a means to nudge women out of poverty and into self-sufficiency. In this thoroughly researched social critique, author Hays examines the effects of welfare reform on the mothers, who constitute more than 90 percent of adult welfare recipients. Based on her interactions with welfare mothers and her observations of welfare offices, Hays presents a grim picture of reality, showing that welfare reform pushed single mothers into low-paying, dead-end jobs. The stories of women struggling to support their families in the wake of welfare reform dispel myths about welfare mothers getting rich off the state.

> **Subjects:** Welfare • Labor • Class • Mothers • Work/Life Balance • Sociology • America • Twentieth Century
>
> **Now Try:** For a further look at the difficulties of transitioning from welfare to low-paying jobs, turn to *Making Ends Meet: How Single Mothers Survive Welfare and Low-Wage Work* by Kathryn Edin and Laura Lein. Based on interviews with welfare mothers and the working poor, the book paints a disturbing picture of the economic impossibility of surviving on low wages without government assistance. Then turn to *Promises I Can Keep: Why Poor Women Put Motherhood before Marriage*, in which Kathryn Edin and Maria Kefalas interview low-income women to discover why they choose to raise children they cannot afford; the insights are both surprising and thought-provoking, essential for anyone concerned about welfare and the working poor.

Peskowitz, Miriam

The Truth behind the Mommy Wars: Who Decides What Makes a Good Mother? Emeryville, CA: Seal Press, 2005. 243pp. ISBN 9781580051293.

The media would have us believe that mothers fall into two camps: those who selfishly commit themselves to their careers and those who languish at home with their children, with nary a thought for personal identity. This is a myopic view, argues Peskowitz, one that misrepresents both sides and which completely neglects the parents who work part-time. The true problem is that parents are often pushed into an all-or-nothing side approach to parenthood: "mothers and fathers want to spend time with their kids, perhaps stay home during their youngest years and work reduced hours later on, and the workplace generally doesn't allow this." Re-entry into the workplace after an extended absence is difficult, and balancing family duties with careers is, at best, complicated. In this engaging investigation into contemporary parenthood, Peskowitz debunks the prevailing myths about working parents and stay-at-home moms, while exposing the common workplace barriers that force women to choose between work and family.

> **Subjects:** Mothers • Labor • Work/Life Balance • Sociology • America • Twenty-first Century
>
> **Now Try:** Peskowitz's view of motherhood as a social issue is, essentially, a feminist perspective. Readers looking for a contrasting view may wish to turn to the witty Caitlin Flanagan of *New Yorker* fame. In her book *To Hell with All That: Loving and Loathing Our Inner Housewife*, Flanagan takes a proud stand in favor of stay-at-home mothering and housework. Her values and her privileged lifestyle will be a turnoff to some, but her nuanced discussion of the conflicts of motherhood, work, and identity make for a thought-provoking counterpoint to *The Truth behind the Mommy Wars*.

Steiner, Leslie Morgan

Mommy Wars: Stay-at-Home and Career Moms Face Off on Their Choices, Their Lives, Their Families. New York: Random House, 2006. 336pp. ISBN 978140-0064151.

In this stimulating collection of essays, twenty-six mothers relate twenty-six different approaches to balancing work and family. With excellent writing from such luminaries as Jane Smiley and Susan Cheever, these essays show readers a glimpse into the struggles faced by successful career women as they try to juggle work and children. Some of the contributors put in long hours at their jobs every week; some deliberately stay at home to be with their children; others find a middle ground between reduced workday hours and staying at home. Every woman's experience is different, but in all cases, the essays present captivating, provocative stories of the various perspectives in the mommy wars.

Subjects: Labor • Class • Mothers • Children • Work/Life Balance • America • Sociology • Twenty-first Century • Essays • Collection • Anthology

Now Try: Those readers who prefer the stay-at-home approach to mothering will wish to turn to *Opting Out?: Why Women Really Quit Careers and Head Home*, in which Pamela Stone interviewed fifty-four career women who chose to leave their jobs in favor of full-time mothering. Those readers who prefer the career approach to mothering will enjoy *This Is How We Do It: The Working Mothers' Manifesto*, in which Carol Evans offers practical advice on making careers compatible with raising children.

Consider Starting With ...

The following list represents a small sampling of the many celebrated, engaging Women and Society books:

Bennetts, Leslie. *The Feminine Mistake: Are We Giving Up Too Much?*

Bolen, Jean Shinoda. *Urgent Message from Mother: Gather the Women, Save the World.*

Douglas, Susan J. *Where the Girls Are: Growing Up Female with the Mass Media.*

Kunin, Madeleine. *Pearls, Politics, & Power: How Women Can Win and Lead.*

Levy, Ariel. *Female Chauvinist Pigs: Women and the Rise of Raunch Culture.*

Ringdal, Nils Johan. *Love for Sale: A World History of Prostitution.*

Fiction Read-Alikes

- **Eugenides, Jeffrey.** This is the story of Callie, a girl born in Detroit in the 1960s. This is also the story of Cal, the man who was "born" when Calliope turned out not to be a female, after all. *Middlesex* is a fascinating look at gender norms, intersexuality, and identity, told from the perspective of a believable, likeable protagonist. Eugenides is known for his thoughtful, and thought-provoking, exploration of social issues; try also *The Virgin Suicides*, which considers heavy themes of death, adolescence, and depression in young women.

- **Hernandez, Jaime.** Meet Maggie, a bisexual with bad taste in men, and her true love Hopey, a lesbian punk rocker, in the <u>Locas</u> stories of the <u>Love and Rockets</u> comic. These two Chicana women grapple with sexual identity, of course, but also with themes of race, nationality, and culture; though their lives have been chronicled in many books, the best place to discover them is in the mammoth collection *Locas: The Maggie and Hopey Stories*.

- **Irving, John.** Despite having grown up as an orphan who never got adopted, Homer Wells refused to perform abortions, though his mentor and father figure Dr. Wilbur Larch nonetheless taught him the mechanics of performing the procedure. *The Cider House Rules* will leave readers thinking not only about the morality of abortion (Irving gives no clear answers, one way or the other) but about race, marital fidelity, class, and parenthood. Irving's other novels will also entrance readers for their exploration of social themes. Try *The World According to Garp*, which considers such varied topics as transsexuality, sexual happiness and fidelity, and rape and violence.

- **Mootoo, Shani.** On a fictional Caribbean island, two sisters, Mala and Asha, suffer horrible sexual and physical abuse from their tyrannical father. Though *Cereus Blooms at Night* is ultimately an empowering novel of recovery and growth, much of the story is grim; read it not only for the disturbing plot, told in Mootoo's lyrical prose, but for the reflections on race, culture, and sexuality.

- **Perry, Thomas.** Jane Whitefield disappears people: when the FBI Witness Protection Program isn't enough, she helps them start a new life where no one can find them. These are page-turning thrillers, fun in their own right, but they can be read on a deeper level: as a half-white/half-Native American woman, Jane grapples with issues of gender, race, spirituality, religion, and identity, even while she is whisking victims to safety. Start with the first in the Jane Whitefield series, *Vanishing Act*.

- **Sittenfeld, Curtis.** In all of her novels, Sittenfeld creates believable, vividly detailed women protagonists. Try *Prep* for the story of a young woman's painful introduction to a world of rigid class and social structures, or turn to *American Wife* for a fictional speculation on First Lady Laura Bush's personal and public politics.

- **Walker, Alice.** In an attempt to understand and support her African heritage, Tashi submits to female genital mutilation in *Possessing the Secret of Joy*—and for the rest of her life, both in Africa and America, she must grapple with the terrible consequences, including the loss of sexual pleasure, the birth deformities that her son suffers from being birthed through a narrow vagina, and madness. Walker always treats her readers to thought-provoking novels about women and their place in society; perhaps continue with *Now Is the Time to Open Your Heart*, featuring themes of spirituality, race, politics, and religion.

- **Willingham, Bill.** Characters familiar from childhood stories, including the Big Bad Wolf and Goldilocks, have repatriated themselves in contemporary New York in the graphic novel series Fables. Lots of folks read the series for a rollicking good time—the books are nothing if not fun—but lurking just beneath the twisted fairy-tale motif are deep social themes. War, violence, and peace—with a healthy dose of Middle East politics—predominate, along with questions of gender, work/life balance, and family. Start with the first in the series, *Fables: Legends in Exile*.

Appendix

Further Resources

I. Women's Bookstores

Women's bookstores are a great resource for Women's Nonfiction. If you're lucky enough to have one nearby, visit it frequently. Many women's bookstores have online presences as well; find them by using a search engine, or start with the directory of the Feminist Bookstore Network: http://www.litwomen.org/WIP/stores.html.

II. Print Resources

Try these four books for more great reading ideas:

Bauermeister, Erica, Jesse Larsen, and Holly Smith

500 Great Books by Women: A Reader's Guide. New York: Penguin Books, 1994. 425pp. ISBN 9780140175905.

> Arranged thematically into such categories as "Art," "Growing Old," and "Power," this is a wonderful collection of five hundred fiction and nonfiction books by women writers.

Felder, Deborah G.

A Bookshelf of Our Own: Works That Changed Women's Lives. New York: Citadel Press, 2005. 302pp. ISBN 9780806526140.

> Discover and rediscover fifty fiction and nonfiction favorites, from Thomas Hardy's *Tess of the D'Urbervilles* to Adrienne Rich's *Of Woman Born*, in this collection of short essays about books that have influenced women's lives. Each entry includes literary and historical analysis, as well as information about the author.

Hammond, Margo, and Ellen Heltzel

Between the Covers: The Book Babes' Guide to a Woman's Reading Pleasures.
Philadelphia: Da Capo Press, 2008. 282pp. ISBN 9780738212296.

> Featuring both fiction and nonfiction, *Between the Covers* is a lovely guide to books that women want to read. Thematic chapters such as "Family & Friends" and "Home, Work, & Taking Care" include a variety of lists, from "10 That Tap Your Inner Artist" to "10 about Adultery, Betrayal, & Moving On." Each title is described with a short, engaging annotation.

Krikos, Linda A., Cindy Ingold, and Catherine Loeb

Women's Studies: A Recommended Bibliography. Westport, CT: Libraries Unlimited, 2004. 828pp. ISBN 9781563085666.

> Though the books covered in this impressively thorough bibliography are intended to support women's studies curricula, many of them are appropriate for general readers. The books, most of which are nonfiction titles, are arranged into categories such as" "Feminist Theories and Women's Movements" and" "Business, Economics, and Labor."

III. Presses

Women's Nonfiction titles can be published by any press, but these in particular have a history of publishing quality Women's Nonfiction titles: Alyson Books and the Cleis Press both publish fiction and nonfiction titles of interest to the LGBT community, while the Feminist Press, Seal Press, and skirt! books all publish Women's Nonfiction titles.

Title/Author Index

Entries in bold refer to primary annotations.

The 5-Minute Face: The Quick and Easy Makeup Guide for Every Woman, 193

The 19th Wife, 180–81

100 Christian Women Who Changed the Twentieth Century, 121

100 Most Important Women of the 20th Century, 9

The 100 Most Influential Women of All Time: A Ranking Past and Present, 202

100 Places Every Woman Should Go, 276

1001 Things Everyone Should Know about Women's History, 201–202

50 Best Girlfriends Getaways in North America, 275

50 Boyfriends Worse than Yours, 84

50 Ways to Improve Women's Lives: The Essential Women's Guide for Achieving Equality, Health, and Success, 303

500 Self-Portraits, 74

A to Z of Women in Science and Math, 313

Abiola, Hafsat, 355

About My Sister's Business: The Black Woman's Road Map to Successful Entrepreneurship, 329–30

About What Was Lost: 20 Writers on Miscarriage, Healing, and Hope, 179

Abu-Jaber, Diana, 56

The Accidental Explorer, 256

Achterberg, Jeanne, 317

Across Boundaries: The Journey of a South African Woman Leader, 35

Across the Savage Sea: The First Woman to Row across the North Atlantic, 253

Adair, Suzanne, 224

Adam, Eve, and the Serpent, 124

Adams, Jeremy duQuesnay, 10–11

Addicted, 137

Adelman, Penina V., 125–26

Adielé, Faith, 61

Adler, Felicia Rose, 84

Adler, Margot, 135

Adventures in Natural Childbirth: Tales from Women on the Joys, Fears, Pleasures, and Pains of Giving Birth Naturally, 111

Aebi, Tania, 254

The African American Travel Guide to Hot, Exotic and Fun-Filled Places, 277

African American Women Speak Out on Anita Hill-Clarence Thomas, 340

African Women: A Modern History, 237

African Women in Revolution, 237–38

After Silence: Rape and My Journey Back, 184

Afzal-Khan, Fawzia, 128

Against Our Will: Men, Women, and Rape, 26

The Age of Innocence, 247

Agrippina: Sex, Power, and Politics in the Early Empire, 212–13

Ahern, David W., 366–67

Ahmed, Leila, 127–28

Ain't I a Beauty Queen?: Black Women, Beauty, and the Politics of Race, 148

Ain't I a Woman: Black Women and Feminism, 292

Aizley, Harlyn, 41

Alcorn, Randy C., 356

Alcorn, Susan, 250–51

Alexander, Gemma, 7–8

Alexander, Priscilla, 363

Alexander, Shoshana, 332

Ali, Ayaan Hirsi, 183

Ali, Kecia, 204

All the Daring of the Soldier: Women of the Civil War Armies, 234

All This Hell: U.S. Nurses Imprisoned by the Japanese, 263

Allen, Marie, 179

Allen, Paula Gunn, 44, 47, 113

Allison, Stacy, 251

Alone across the Arctic: One Woman's Epic Journey by Dog Team, 252
Alper, Nicole, 211
Alpert, Rebecca T., 57
Alpine, Lisa, 266
Alspaugh, Nancy, 175, 177
Altared: Bridezillas, Bewilderment, Big Love, Breakups, and What Women Really Think about Contemporary Weddings, 85
Alvrez, Alicia, 72
Amazing Women of the Civil War, 235
am-BITCH-ous, 69
Ambition Is Not a Dirty Word: A Woman's Guide to Earning Her Worth and Achieving Her Dreams, 342
Amelia Earhart's Daughters: The Wild and Glorious Story of American Women Aviators from World War II to the Dawn of the Space Age, 310
American Chica: Two Worlds, One Childhood, 44–45
American Heroines: The Spirited Women Who Shaped Our Country, 8
American Jezebel: The Uncommon Life of Anne Hutchinson, the Woman Who Defied the Puritans, 58
American Wife, 374
American Women in World War I: They Also Served, 243
America's Joan of Arc: The Life of Anna Elizabeth Dickinson, 15
America's Women: Four Hundred Years of Dolls, Drudges, Helpmates, and Heroines, 209
America's Working Women: A Documentary History 1600 to the Present, 210
Ames, John, 43
Among Stone Giants: The Life of Katherine Routledge and Her Remarkable Expedition to Easter Island, 259–60
Amt, Emilie, 220
Anchee Min, 21
Ancient African Queens (In Praise of Black Women), 204–205
Anders, Charlie, 313
Anderson, Carol M., 95
Anderson, C. Thomas, 345
Anderson, Laurie Halse, 195
Anderson, Susan, 172

Angel of Vengeance: The "Girl Assassin," the Governor of St. Petersburg, and Russia's Revolutionary World, 228
Angelides, Steven, 91
Angelou, Maya, 24–25
Angels, 196
Angels in Africa: Portraits of Seven Extraordinary Women, 298
Angier, Natalie, 72
Annapurna: A Woman's Place, 252
Anne Frank, Beyond the Diary: A Photographic Remembrance, 48
Annis, Barbara, 328
Anthony, Valerie, 322
Anticipating Madam President, 370
Antoine-Dariaux, Geneviève, 185
Antony and Cleopatra, 246
Antoun, Rob, 144–45
Anway, Carol Anderson, 56
Anzaldúa, Gloria, 302
Apostolides, Marianne, 158
Appearance Is Everything: The Hidden Truth Regarding Your Appearance Discrimination, 149
Appelbaum, Arlene, 181
Apter, T. E., 76
Arana, Marie, 44–45
Archer, Jeffrey, 347
Are Men Necessary?: When Sexes Collide, 342
The Arm of the Starfish, 347
Armstrong, Penny, 110
Armstrong, Sally, 297
An Army of Angels: A Novel of Joan of Arc, 11
Arnesen, Liv, 251–52
Arnstein, Walter L., 22
Arons, Katie, 82
Aronson, Robin, 142
Arredondo, Gabriela F., 288
The Art of Being Satisfied, Fulfilled and Independent, 96
The Art of Meeting Women. A Guide for Gay Women: How to Meet the Women You Want to Meet, 91
The Asian Mystique: Dragon Ladies, Geisha Girls, & Our Fantasies of the Exotic Orient, 304
Ashworth, Trisha, 103
Asian American Women: The Frontiers Reader, 54
Asian Women United of California, 54

Asian/Pacific Islander American Women: A Historical Anthology, 54

Askowitz, Andrea, 107

At Grandmother's Table: Women Write about Food, Life and the Enduring Bond between Grandmothers and Granddaughters, 78

At Home with Pornography: Women, Sexuality, and Everyday Life, 362

Athena Unbound: The Advancement of Women in Science and Technology, 312

Atwood, Margaret, 305

Aucoin, Kevyn, 192

Aung San Suu Kyi, 30–31

Autobiography of a Blue-Eyed Devil: My Life and Times in a Racist, Imperialist Society, 76

Autobiography of a Geisha, 33

The Autobiography of Eleanor Roosevelt, 6

Avalon series, 246

The Awakening, 62

Axelrod, Toby, 57

Baar, Karen, 177

Babcock, Linda, 334

Babes in the Woods: The Woman's Guide to Eating Well, Sleeping Well, and Having Fun in the Backcountry, 146

Baby Love: Choosing Motherhood after a Lifetime of Ambivalence, 102

Bach, David, 346

Bachiochi, Erika, 356

Backfire: Carly Fiorina's High-Stakes Battle for the Soul of Hewlett-Packard, 326–27

Backlash: The Undeclared War against American Women, 290–91

Back on the Career Track: A Guide for Stay-at-Home Moms Who Want to Return to Work, 371

Backpacking, 146

Back Rooms: Voices from the Illegal Abortion Era, 357–58

Backus, Harriet Fish, 273

Baer, Ann, 220

Bags to Riches: 7 Success Secrets for Women in Business, 333

Bahr, Candice, 345

Bainbridge, David, 70

Baker, Carrie N., 338–39

Baker, Christine A., 321

Baker, Dan, 71

Baker, Jean H., 4, 284–85

Bales, Kevin, 359

The Ballad of Frankie Silver, 62–63

Ballad series, 62–63

Bananas, Beaches & Bases: Making Feminist Sense of International Politics, 367

Bancroft, Ann, 251–52

Band of Sisters: American Women at War in Iraq, 325

Bandel, Betty, 37

bandele, asha, 83

Banks, Ingrid, 148

The BAP Handbook: The Official Guide to the Black American Princess, 174

Barash, Susan Shapiro, 77–78

Barber, E. J. W., 200

Barefoot Heart: Stories of a Migrant Child, 49–50

Barker-Benfield, G. J., 8

Barlas, Asma, 129

Baron, Beth, 219

Baron, Scott, 325

Barrett, Anthony, 212–13

Barrett, Nina, 99

Barry, Dave, 271

Barry, Kathleen, 3–4

Barstow, Anne Llewellyn, 221–22

Barton, Bernadette, 361

Baskin, Elizabeth Cogswell, 330

Battle Cries and Lullabies: Women in War from Prehistory to the Present, 202

Baumgardner, Jennifer, 287–88, 296, 303

Baxandall, Rosalyn Fraad, 210, 284

Be Your Own Mentor: Strategies from Top Women on the Secrets of Success, 338

Beanland, Ame Mahler, 78

Beasley, Ruth, 166

Beauman, Francesca, 72

Beautiful Shadow: A Life of Patricia Highsmith, 42

Beauty, 196

The Beauty Bible: The Ultimate Guide to Smart Beauty, 193

Beauty by the Book, 191

Beauty Junkies, 149–50

Beautylicious!: The Black Girl's Guide to the Fabulous Life, 174

The Beauty Myth: How Images of Beauty Are Used against Women, 153

Beauty: The New Basics, 186
Beauvoir, Simone de, 288
*Because I Remember Terror, Father, I
    Remember You*, 180
Bechdel, Alison, 40–41, 306
*Becoming a Millionaire God's Way: Getting
    Money to You, Not from You*, 345
*Becoming a Woman: A Biography of Christine
    Jorgensen*, 43
***Becoming Judy Chicago: A Biography of
    the Artist,*** 8
*Beginnings: Lesbians Talk about the First
    Time They Met Their Long-Term
    Partner*, 90
Begoun, Paula, 193
Behan, Mona, 216
Behind Every Choice Is a Story, 30
Behrmann, Barbara L., 109
Bek, Anna Nikolaevna, 32
Belenky, Mary Field, 67–68
*Believing in Myself: Self Esteem Daily
    Meditations for Healing and Building
    Self-esteem*, 114
*"Believing Women" in Islam: Unreading
    Patriarchul Interprelations of the
    Qur'an*, 129
Bell, Anita, 335
Bell, Julian, 74
Bellis, Alice Ogden, 217
Bellwether, 347
Beloved, 196
Belsky, Gail, 169
Benard, Cheryl, 297
A Bend in the Road, 136–37
Bennett, Amanda, 156
Bennetts, Leslie, 370
Ben-Ozer, Snunit, 105
Benson, Lorri Antosz, 158
Benson, Taryn Leigh, 158
***Bento Box in the Heartland: My Japanese
    Girlhood in Whitebread America,***
    48
Berg, Rona, 186
Berger, Iris, 204
Berger, Melody, 291
Berkeley, Ellen Perry, 78
Berkin, Carol, 224–26
Berman, Jennifer, 164
Berman, Laura, 164
Bernell, Bonnie, 149
Bernstein, Carl, 4
Berry, Carmen Renee, 80

Bess, Savitri L., 132
Best Friends, 81
Best of Covered Wagon Women, 231
The Best Tips from Women Abroad, 145
***The Best Women's Travel Writing 2009:
    True Stories from around the
    World,*** 271
Bettelyoun, Susan Bordeaux, 46
Better than Beauty: A Guide to Charm, 185
***Better than I Ever Expected: Straight Talk
    about Sex after Sixty,*** 87
Between a Rock and a Hard Place, 255
*Between Mothers and Sons: Women Writers
    Talk about Having Sons and Raising
    Men*, 98
***Between the Fields and the City: Women,
    Work, and Family in Russia,
    1861–1914,*** 227–28
***Beyond Stitch and Bitch: Reflections on
    Knitting and Life,*** 119
*Beyond the Flower: The Autobiography of a
    Feminist Artist*, 9
***Beyond the Limits: A Woman's Triumph
    on Everest,*** 251
*Bi America: Myths, Truths, and Struggles of
    an Invisible Community*, 288
*Bi Any Other Name: Bisexual People Speak
    Out*, 91
***Bi Lives: Bisexual Women Tell Their
    Stories,*** 91
Bich Minh Nguyen, 48
Bickman, Connie, 73
Biddle, Geoffrey, 146
Bidwell, John, 110
*Big Big Love: A Sourcebook on Sex for People
    of Size and Those Who Love Them*, 83
The Big Book of Women Saints, 60
Big Breasts and Wide Hips, 31
The Big Coloring Book of Vaginas, 151
*The Big Rumpus: A Mother's Tale from the
    Trenches*, 100
*Bike Lust: Harleys, Women, and American
    Society*, 239
Biko, 35
Billinghurst, Jane, 207
Bingham, Clara, 339
Bingying, Xie, 39
Binney, Marcus, 262
Bird, Isabella L., 272
*The Bisexual's Guide to the Universe: Quips,
    Tips, and Lists for Those Who Go Both
    Ways*, 92

Bishop, Jan Galen, 147

Biskupic, Joan, 11

Bitches, Bimbos, and Ballbreakers: The Guerrilla Girls' Illustrated Guide to Female Stereotypes, 352

BITCHfest: Ten Years of Cultural Criticism from the Pages of Bitch Magazine, 302

Black Feminist Thought: Knowledge, Consciousness, and the Politics of Empowerment, 295–96

Black Like Me, 152

Black Ships, 213

The Blacksmith's Daughter, 224

Black Titan: A.G. Gaston and the Making of a Black American Millionaire, 46

Black, White and Jewish: Autobiography of a Shifting Self, 102

Black Women in White America: A Documentary History, 211

Black Women's Lives: Stories of Pain and Power, 54

Blackledge, Catherine, 73

Blades, Joan, 371

Blain, Virginia, 286

Blair, Pamela D., 175

Blank, Hanne, 83

Blanks, Derek, 82

Blanton, DeAnne, 234

Blech, Susan, 143

Blessed by Thunder: Memoir of a Cuban Girlhood, 47

Blixen, Karen, 258

Bloch, Avital H., 236

Block, Jennifer, 107–108

Blood & Irony: Southern White Women's Narratives of the Civil War, 1861–1937, 236

Blowing My Cover: My Life As a CIA Spy, 262

Blown Away: American Women and Guns, 364–65

The Bluest Eye, 196

Blue, Violet, 362

Blum, Arlene, 252

Blum, Deborah, 71

Blum, Louise A., 41

Blum, Virginia L., 150

Blume, E. Sue, 178

Bly, Robert, 68–69

Bobbi Brown Beauty Evolution: A Guide to a Lifetime of Beauty, 186

Bock, Caroline, 143

Bock, Gisela, 201

Body Drama, 151

Bodylove: Learning to Like Our Looks—and Ourselves, 160

The Body Myth: Adult Women and the Pressure to Be Perfect, 160

The Body Project: An Intimate History of American Girls, 353

Body Outlaws: Rewriting the Rules of Beauty and Body Image, 148

Body Wars: Making Peace with Women's Bodies: An Activist's Guide, 160

Bogle, Kathleen, 167

Bohjalian, Chris, 135

Boland, Mary L., 339

Bolden, Tonya, 211

Bold in Her Breeches: Women Pirates across the Ages, 16

Bolen, Jean Shinoda, 68, 113–14, 175, 363–64

Bollet, Alfred J., 235

Bollinger, Holly, 309

Bollmann, Stefan, 309

Bombeck, Erma, 98

Bonavoglia, Angela, 30

Bond, Marybeth, 266–67, 275, 277

Bone Black: Memories of Girlhood, 50

The Bone Collector, 278

Bonk: The Curious Coupling of Science and Sex, 190

B.O.O.B.S.: A Bunch of Outrageous Breast-Cancer Survivors Tell Their Stories of Courage, Hope, & Healing, 154

Boobs: A Guide to Your Girls, 190

The Book about Blanche and Marie, 12

The Book of African American Women: 150 Crusaders, Creators, and Uplifters, 211

The Book of Eleanor: A Novel of Eleanor of Aquitaine, 23

The Book of Latina Women: 150 Vidas of Passion, Strength, and Success, 75

The Book of Margery Kempe: A New Translation, 56–57

Book of Shadows: A Modern Woman's Journey into the Wisdom of Witchcraft and the Magic of the Goddess, 55

The Book of Splendour, 246–47

Border-Line Personalities: A New Generation of Latinas Dish on Sex, Sass, and Cultural Shifting, 51

Bordo, Susan, 147–48
Borges, Phil, 297–98
Born for Liberty: A History of Women in America, 211
Born in the Big Rains: A Memoir of Somalia and Survival, 181
Born in the USA: How a Broken Maternity System Must Be Fixed to Put Women and Children First, 107–108
Borysenko, Joan, 114, 118
Borzello, Frances, 74
Boston Women's Health Book Collective, 141, 169–70
Boucher, Sandy, 129–30
Bouchéz, Colette, 164, 171
Boudica Quadrilogy, 16
Boudica: Dreaming the Eagle, 16
Boudica: Iron Age Warrior Queen, 16
Boudica: The British Revolt Against Rome AD 60, 16
Boudica: The Life of Britain's Legendary Warrior Queen, 16
Boudreaux, Bill, 330
Bountiful Women: Large Women's Secrets for Living the Life They Desire, 149
Bourland, Julia, 173
Bourque, Susan Carolyn, 343
Bové, Jennifer, 252
Boyd, Helen, 25
Boyd, Loree, 45
Boylan, Jennifer Finney, 43
Bra: A Thousand Years of Style, Support and Seduction, 189
Brabner, Joyce, 157
Bradford, Ernle Dusgate Selby, 19
Bradley, Marion Zimmer, 246
Bragg, Rick, 261
Brain Gender, 70
Brain Sex: The Real Difference between Men and Women, 68
Brashares, Ann, 80
Brave Bird, Mary, 45–46
Bravo, Ellen, 298
Brazaitis, Tom, 366
Brazilian Waxes, Lazy Ovaries & Outrageous Orgasms: Embarrassing Questions and Sassy Answers on Women's Sexual Health, 168
Breaking Ground: Pioneering Women Archaeologists, 260
Breaking the Limit: One Woman's Motorcycle Journey through North America, 272

Breaking the Political Glass Ceiling: Women and Congressional Elections, 369
The Breastfeeding Cafe: Mothers Share the Joys, Challenges, and Secrets of Nursing, 109
Breastfeeding Made Simple: Seven Natural Laws for Nursing Mothers, 110
Breasts: The Women's Perspective on an American Obsession, 192
Breeder: Real-Life Stories from the New Generation of Mothers, 100
Breines, Wini, 302
Brenner, Deborah, 311
The Brethren: Inside the Supreme Court, 12
Bridgforth, Glinda, 344
Bright Evening Star: Mystery of the Incarnation, 124
Bringing Home the Light: A Jewish Woman's Handbook of Rituals, 125
Brinley, Maryann Bucknum, 14
Briscoe, Connie, 176
Briscoe, Jill, 121
Brissman, Barry, 39
Brissman, Lily Chia, 39
Brizendine, Louann, 68
Brkic, Courtney Angela, 242
Brock, Ann Graham, 217
Brodsky, Anne E., 297
Broner, E. M., 125
Brontë, Charlotte, 135
Brooke, Elisabeth, 316–17
Brosius, Shirley, 121–22
Brothels, Bordellos & Bad Girls: Prostitution in Colorado, 1860–1930, 232
Broude, Norma, 9
Broussard, Cary Jehl, 335
Broussard, Cheryl D., 330
Browder, Laura, 365
Brown, Bobbi, 185–86
Brown, Harriet, 89
Brown, Mary Crist, 115
Brown, Nancy Marie, 220
Brown, Rebecca A., 259
Brown, Rita Mae, 62
Browne, Jill Conner, 84, 93–94
Brownmiller, Susan, 26
Brownsey, Mo, 91–92
Bruhns, Karen Olsen, 213
Brumberg, Joan Jacobs, 353
Brush, Candida G., 333
Buchanan, Andrea J., 98–99, 103

Buckingham, Jane, 173

Budapest, Zsuzsanna Emese, 133

Buddhist Women on the Edge: Contemporary Perspectives from the Western Frontier, 131

Buff, Sheila, 160

Bugbee, Sylvia J., 37

Bujold, Lois McMaster, 278

Bullitt-Jonas, Margaret, 158

Bullough, Vern L., 203

Bumiller, Elisabeth, 4–5, 164

Bundles, A'Lelia Perry, 46

Burgos-Debray, Elisabeth, 34

Burke, Theresa Karminski, 183

Burleson, William E., 288

Burma: The State of Myanmar, 31

Burroughs, Augusten, 162, 184

Burrows, Peter, 326–27

Bussel, Rachel Kramer, 168

The Bust Guide to the New Girl Order, 302

Buszek, Maria Elena, 351

Butler, Cornelia H., 300

Butler, Judith, 288

Butler, Octavia, 246

Butterfield, Elizabeth, 275

Butters, MaryJane, 309

Byers, Nina, 316

Byrd, Ayana D., 148

By the Grace of the Sea: A Woman's Solo Odyssey around the World, 254

Cahill, Susan Neunzig, 115–16

Cammermeyer, Margarethe, 324

Cancer Made Me a Shallower Person: A Memoir in Comics, 157

The Cancer Poetry Project: Poems by Cancer Patients and Those Who Love Them, 154

Cancer Schmancer, 154

Cancer Vixen: A True Story, 157

Canfield, Jack, 79–81

Can She Bake a Cherry Pie?: American Women and the Kitchen in the Twentieth Century, 240

Cantando, Mary, 327, 331

Cantarella, Eva, 214

Cantrell, Debra Ann, 276

Capel, Anne K., 214

Caperton, Rosemary, 268

Card, Orson Scott, 123

Carey, Jacqueline, 278

Carl, Ann, 37–38

Carlin, Patricia, 83

Carlin, Peter, 251

Carlson, Amy Greimann, 118

Carmindy, 193

Carol, Joy, 81

Caron, Ann F., 98

Carr, Kris, 153–54

Carr, Toni, 240

Carroll, Susan J., 367

Carter, Jennifer, 253

Carter, Sandy, 317

Cartledgehayes, Mary, 60

Casey, Karen, 114

Caster, Wendy, 168

Castillo, Ana, 288

Castillo-Speed, Lillian, 51

Castleberry, Carolyn, 344–45

Catalyst, 195

Catching a Wave: Reclaiming Feminism for the 21st Century, 297

Catfight: Rivalries among Women—From Diets to Dating, from the Boardroom to the Delivery Room, 78

Catherine De' Medici, 18

Catherine de Medici: Renaissance Queen of France, 18

Catherine, Empress of Russia, 20

Catherine the Great, 20

Catherine the Great. *See* Catherine, Empress of Russia,

Catherine the Great: Love, Sex, and Power, 20

Celebrating Women, 300

The Center Cannot Hold: My Journey through Madness, 155

Cereus Blooms at Night, 374

Chabrillan, Céleste Vénard de, comtesse, 228

The Chalice and the Blade: Our History, Our Future, 115

Chalked Up: Inside Elite Gymnastics' Merciless Coaching, Overzealous Parents, Eating Disorders, and Elusive Olympic Dreams, 322

Chalker, Rebecca, 165

Challenging the Pacific: The First Woman to Row the Kon-Tiki Route, 253

Chambers, Anne, 16

Champions for Peace: Women Winners of the Nobel Peace Prize, 365

Chang, Grace, 354

Changing Course: A Woman's Guide to Choosing the Cruising Life, 276

Chapin, Andrea, 89

Chapkis, Wendy, 362

Chase, Carole F., 124

Chavoya, C. Ondine, 70

Check It While I Wreck It: Black Womanhood, Hip-Hop Culture, and the Public Sphere, 293

Cherokee Women: Gender and Culture Change, 1700–1835, 226

Chesler, Ellen, 5

Chicago, Judy, 8

Chicana Feminisms: A Critical Reader, 288

Chicken Soup for the Grandma's Soul: Stories to Honor and Celebrate the Ageless Love of Grandmothers, 79

Chicken Soup for the Mother & Daughter Soul: Stories to Warm the Heart and Honor the Relationship, 80

Chicken Soup for the Sister's Soul, 81

Chicken Soup for the Sister's Soul 2, 81

Chicken Soup series, 81

Child of the Jungle: The True Story of a Girl Caught between Two Worlds, 51

Childbirth without Fear: The Principles and Practice of Natural Childbirth, 109

Chin, Eliza Lo, 317

China Men, 52

The Chocolate Cake Sutra: Ingredients for a Sweet Life, 130–31

Choices: Finding God's Way in Dating, Sex, Singleness, and Marriage, 87

The Choices We Made: Twenty-Five Women and Men Speak Out About Abortion, 30

Chomsky, Noam, 288

Chopin, Kate, 62

Chow, Claire S., 53

Christ, Carol P., 133

Chynoweth, Kate, 268

The Cider House Rules, 374

Circle of Stones: Woman's Journey to Herself, 28

Citizen Bacchae: Women's Ritual Practice in Ancient Greece, 216

The Civil Rights Movement: A Photographic History, 1954–68, 53

Civil Wars: A Battle for Gay Marriage, 301

Clairmont, Patsy, 121

Clark, Melissa, 142

Class Action: The Story of Lois Jenson and the Landmark Case That Changed Sexual Harassment Law, 339

Clements, Alan, 30–31

Clements, Marcelle, 96

Clements, Patricia, 286

Cleopatra (Ernle Dusgate Selby Bradford), 19

Cleopatra **(Michael Grant),** 18–19

Clift, Eleanor, 284, 366

Climbing High: A Woman's Account of Surviving the Everest Tragedy, 252

Clin, Marie-Véronique, 10–11

Clinton, Catherine, 8, 229

Clinton, Hillary Rodham, 4

Clipped Wings: The Rise and Fall of the Women Airforce Service Pilots (WASPS) of World War II, 244

The Clitoral Truth: The Secret World at Your Fingertips, 165

Closing the Leadership Gap: Why Women Can and Must Help Run the World, 343

Clunis, D. Merilee, 103

Clyman, Toby W., 32

Coast Road, 195

Cobble, Dorothy Sue, 210

Coben, Harlan, 347

Cocaine: An Unauthorized Biography, 162–63

Cochran, Jackie, 14

Coffey, Wayne R., 321

Cohen, Carol Fishman, 371

Cohen, Cathy J., 367

Cohen, Getzel M., 260

Cohen, Leah Hager, 70

Cohen, Marisa, 108

Cohen-Sandler, Roni, 79

Cold Mountain, 235

Cole, Jean Hascall, 244

Cole, Johnnetta B., 298

Cole, Joni B., 26

Colgate, Doris, 145

The Collection of the Kyoto Costume Institute: A History from the 18th to the 20th Century, 188

Colley, Linda, 15

Collier-Thomas, Bettye, 290

Colligan, Victoria, 329

Collingridge, Vanessa, 16

Collins, Gail, 209

Collins, Patricia Hill, 295–96

Colman, Penny, 264–65

Colonize This!: Young Women of Color on Today's Feminism, 292

The Color Purple, 25, 63–64

The Colors of Courage: Gettysburg's Hidden History: Immigrants, Women, and African-Americans in the Civil War's Defining Battle, 235

The Comfort Women: Japan's Brutal Regime of Enforced Prostitution in the Second World War, 209

Comfort Women: Sexual Slavery in the Japanese Military during World War II, 208–209

Coming into Our Fullness: On Women Turning Forty, 175

The Complete Gods and Goddesses of Ancient Egypt, 218

The Complete Startup Guide for the Black Entrepreneur, 330

Condoleezza Rice: An American Life, 4–5

Condren, Debra, 69, 342

Confessions of a Carb Queen: The Lies You Tell Others & the Lies You Tell Yourself: A Memoir, 143

Confessions of a Failed Southern Lady, 41–42

Confessions of a True Romantic: The Secrets of a Sizzling Relationship from America's Romance Coach, 92

Confessions of the Other Mother: Nonbiological Lesbian Moms Tell All, 41

Conlon, Faith, 268

Connecting: The Enduring Power of Female Friendship, 81

Connelly, Joan Breton, 216

Connor, Carolyn L., 219

The Conscious Bride: Women Unveil Their True Feelings about Getting Hitched, 85

Contraception and Abortion from the Ancient World to the Renaissance, 207

Conversations with Uncommon Women: Insights from Women Who've Risen above Life's Challenges to Achieve Extraordinary Success, 312

Conway, Jill K., 27

Conway, M. Margaret, 366–67

Cook, Blanche Wiesen, 5–6

Cook, Lauren M., 38, 234

Cook, Sharon A., 237

Coontz, Stephanie, 89

Coopersmith, Geralyn, 143

Copeland, David, 84

Copeland, Peter, 261

Coquery-Vidrovitch, Catherine, 237

Cordingly, David, 257

Corinne, Tee, 151

Cornell, Kari A., 119

Cornell, Rkia Elaroui, 129

Cornum, Rhonda, 261

Corral, Jill, 84

The Corset: A Cultural History, 190–91

The Cost of Choice: Women Evaluate the Impact of Abortion, 356

Coughlin, Linda, 338

The Courage to Be Yourself: A Woman's Guide to Emotional Strength and Self-Esteem, 114

Courtesans: Money, Sex, and Fame in the Nineteenth Century, 228

Coverdale, Linda, 182–83

Cowen, Lauren, 79–80

Cowgirls of the Rodeo: Pioneer Professional Athletes, 232

Craig, Maxine Leeds, 148

Crane, Kathleen, 254

Crazy Sexy Cancer Tips, 153–54

Creighton, Margaret S., 235

Crittenden, Ann, 371

Croke, Vicki, 258

Crones Don't Whine: Concentrated Wisdom for Juicy Women, 175

Cross, Robin, 200

Crossing: A Memoir, 42–43

Crossing to Avalon: A Woman's Midlife Quest for the Sacred Feminine, 113

Crowns: Portraits of Black Women in Church Hats, 186

The Crucible, 225

The Cruising Woman's Advisor, 276

Cunningham, Michael, 176, 186

Cunt: A Declaration of Independence, 76

Cunt Coloring Book: Drawings, 151

Cuny, Marie-Thérèse, 182–83

Curie, Eve, 12

Curott, Phyllis W., 55

Curran, Colleen, 85

The Curse: Confronting the Last Unmentionable Taboo: Menstruation, 170–71

Cusumano, Camile, 267–68

Dahle, Cheryl, 251–52

Daly, Mary, 288

Dammann, Gordon, 235

The Damned and the Beautiful: American Youth in the 1920's, 241

The Dance of the Dissident Daughter: A Woman's Journey from Christian Tradition to the Sacred Feminine, 28

Dancing for Dollars and Paying for Love: The Relationships between Exotic Dancers and Their Regulars, 361

Danowski, Debbie, 158

Da Silva, Rachel, 251

Daughter of Persia: A Woman's Journey from Her Father's Harem through the Islamic Revolution, 34

Daughters and Mothers, 80

Daughters and Mothers: Making It Work, 79

Daughters of Another Path: Experiences of American Women Choosing Islam, 56

Daughters of Caliban: Caribbean Women in the Twentieth Century, 239

Daughters of Men: Portraits of African-American Women and Their Fathers, 82

Daughters of the Goddess: The Women Saints of India, 58

Dave Barry's Only Travel Guide You'll Ever Need, 271

Davidds-Garrido, Yasmin, 337

David-Neel, Alexandra, 273

Davidson, Scooter Toby, 322

Davis, Angela Y., 289–90

Davis, Anita Prize, 366

Davis, Deborah L., 181

Davis, Elizabeth, 108

Davis, Flora, 286

Davis, Natalie Zemon, 201

Davis-Kimball, Jeannine, 216

Day, H. Alan, 12

A Day in the Life of the American Woman: How We See Ourselves, 75

The Day Kadi Lost Part of Her Life, 360

Daymond, M. J., 205

Days of a Russian Noblewoman: The Memories of Anna Labzina, 1758–1821, 32

DC Comics Covergirls, 311

Deadly Persuasion: Why Women and Girls Must Fight the Addictive Power of Advertising, 153

Deakin, Michael A. B., 6

Dear G-Spot: Straight Talk about Sex and Love, 168

Dear Sisters: Dispatches from the Women's Liberation Movement, 284

Deaver, Jeffery, 278

Deborah, Golda, and Me: Being Female and Jewish in America, 288

Decades of Beauty, 188

Deerskin, 196

De Ferrari, Gabriella, 45

Defiant Muse: Hebrew Feminist Poems from Antiquity to the Present, 126–27

De Grandis, Francesca, 173

De Hart, Jane Sherron, 210

Déjà Dead, 347

Delacoste, Frédérique, 363

Delaney, Lisa, 142

Delinsky, Barbara, 154, 195

Deliver This!: Make the Childbirth Choice That's Right for You—No Matter What Everyone Else Thinks, 108

Deliver Us from Evie, 90

A Delusion of Satan: The Full Story of the Salem Witch Trials, 225

DePaulo, Bella M., 94

De Pauw, Linda Grant, 202

De Puy, Candace, 178

Derr, Mary Krane, 357

The Descent of Woman, 73

Desert Flower: The Extraordinary Journey of a Desert Nomad, 182

De Tessan, Christina Henry, 266, 268

Devices and Desires: A History of Contraceptives in America, 208

Devi: Goddesses of India, 132

The Devil Wears Prada, 196

A Devotion to Their Science: Pioneer Women of Radioactivity, 314

Diamant, Anita, 62

Diary of an Anorexic Girl, 159

The Diary of a Young Girl: The Definitive Edition, 47–48

Diaw, Aminata, 205

Dicker, Rory Cooke, 285, 297

Dickey, Eric Jerome, 135–36

Dick-Read, Grantly, 109

The Difference "Difference" Makes: Women and Leadership, 343

Dillard, Annie, 269

Dillon, Matthew, 216

Dillow, Linda, 85, 165

Dimidjian, Sona, 95

Dinesen, Isak, 258

The Dinner Party: From Creation to Preservation, 9

Dirie, Waris, 182

Disarming the Nation: Women's Writing and the American Civil War, 235–36

Disco Divas: Women and Popular Culture in the 1970s, 239

Discovering Eve: Ancient Israelite Women in Context, 214

Discworld series, 279, 306

Dispatches from a Not-So-Perfect Life: Or How I Learned to Love the House, the Man, the Child, 371

Disposable Domestics: Immigrant Women Workers in the Global Economy, 354

Disposable People: New Slavery in the Global Economy, 359

Distorted: How a Mother and Daughter Unraveled the Truth, the Lies, and the Realities of an Eating Disorder, 158

Divining Women, 136

Dixon, Ann, 252

Docter, Richard F., 43

The Doctor Wore Petticoats: Women Physicians of the Old West, 317

Doctors: The Illustrated History of Medical Pioneers, 318

Dodson, Betty, 95, 165

Doherty, P. C., 24

Dolan, Brian, 223

Dolan, Kathleen A., 370

Don't Go Shopping for Hair Care Products without Me: Over 4,000 Brand Name Products Reviewed, Plus the Latest Hair Care Information, 193

Don't Go to the Cosmetics Counter without Me: A Unique Guide to Over 35,000 Products, Plus the Latest Skin-Care Research, 193

Don't Play in the Sun: One Woman's Journey through the Color Complex, 48–49

The Doomsday Book, 347

Dorkenoo, Efua, 359

Do They Hear You When You Cry?, 181–82

Do You Think I'm Beautiful?: The Question Every Woman Asks, 191

Douglas, Ann, 111

Douglas, Susan J., 102–103

Douglas, Susan J., 351

Dovitch, Dana, 178

Dowd, Maureen, 342

Down the Common, 220

Drachman, Virginia G., 12–13, 317–18

Dragon Ladies: Asian American Feminists Breathe Fire, 304

Dragon Lady: The Life and Legend of the Last Empress of China, 21

Drake, Jennifer, 304

Drawing Down the Moon: Witches, Druids, Goddess-Worshippers, and Other Pagans in America, 135

Draznin, Yaffa, 229

Dreaming Me: From Baptist to Buddhist, One Woman's Spiritual Journey, 61

Drescher, Fran, 154

Dresser, Marianne, 131

Drinking: A Love Story, 162

A Drinking Life, 162

Druett, Joan, 257

Dry, 162

DuBois, Ellen Carol, 211, 295

Duerk, Judith, 28

Dumenil, Lynn, 211

Duncan, Karen A., 178

Dundas, Barbara, 243

Dunnewold, Ann, 102

DuPlessis, Rachel Blau, 284

Durham, Meenakshi Gigi, 299

Dworkin, Andrea, 290

Dykes to Watch Out For, 306

Dzielska, Maria, 6

Each Day a New Beginning: Daily Meditations for Women, 114

Early Embraces: True-Life Stories of Women Describing Their First Lesbian Experience, 90

Early Embraces II, 90

Early Embraces III, 90

Early Sufi Women: Dhikr An-Niswa Al-Muta 'Abbidat as Sufiyyat, 128

The Earth, My Butt, and Other Big Round Things, 74, 196

Earthly Bodies & Heavenly Hair: Natural and Healthy Personal Care for Every Body, 195

The Eastern Region (Women Writing Africa), 205

East Toward Dawn: A Woman's Solo Journey around the World, 269–70

Eat, Pray, Love: One Woman's Search for Everything across Italy, India and Indonesia, 270

Ebadi, Shirin, 35
Ebershoff, David, 180–81
Eden, Dawn, 165–66
Edin, Kathryn, 372
The Edge of Winter, 136
Edmonds, S. Emma E., 38
Edut, Ophira, 148
Egan, R. Danielle, 361
Ehrenreich, Barbara, 152–53, 317, 351
Ehrlich, Elizabeth, 55–56
Ehrman, Bart D., 124
Eicher, Joanne Bubolz, 73
Eichhorst, Sabine, 181
Eisenberg, Arlene, 111
Eisler, Riane Tennenhaus, 115
Eisner, Lisa, 232
Ekman, Eve Mason, 371
Elder, Lindsey, 90
Eleanor of Aquitaine: A Life, 22
Eleanor of Aquitaine and the Four Kings, 23
Eleanor Roosevelt, 5–6
Eleanor Roosevelt Mysteries, 6
Elia, Tómas de, 7
Elizabeth & Leicester: Power, Passion, and Politics, 23
The Elizabeth Cady Stanton-Susan B. Anthony Reader: Correspondence, Writings, Speeches, 295
Elizabeth I, 23
Ellen Foster, 136
Ellis, Anne, 230–31
Ellison, Sheila, 364
Elman, Leslie Gilbert, 72
Elwell, Ellen Sue Levi, 57
Embracing Menopause Naturally: Stories, Portraits, and Recipes, 172
Embroideries, 36
Emerging Feminism from Revolution to World War (A History of Women in the West), 201
Emerick, Ingrid, 268
Empowering Latinas: Breaking Boundaries, Freeing Lives, 337
Empress Orchid, 21
Empty Arms: Coping after Miscarriage, Stillbirth and Infant Death, 181
Empty Cradle, Broken Heart: Surviving the Death of Your Baby, 181
Encountering Kali: In the Margins, at the Center, in the West, 132
Ending the Gauntlet: Removing Barriers to Women's Success in the Law, 319

Engaged Surrender: African American Women and Islam, 56
Engel, Barbara Alpern, 227–28
Engelberg, Miriam, 157
English, Deirdre, 317
The English Patient, 245
Enlightened Power: How Women Are Transforming the Practice of Leadership, 338
Enloe, Cynthia H., 367
Enquist, Per Olov, 12
Enslaved: True Stories of Modern Day Slavery, 359
Ensler, Eve, 74
Enss, Chris, 231–32, 317
Enterprising Women: 250 Years of American Business, 12–13
Ephron, Nora, 176
Epp, Eldon Jay, 59
Epstein, Phyllis Horn, 320
Equal Rites, 306
Erdman, Cheri K., 148–49
Erdoes, Richard, 45
Erdrich, Heid E., 46–47
Ericksen, Gregory K., 332
Erickson, Carolly, 17, 257–58
Erickson, John, 244
Erlbaum, Janice, 163
Escape, 180
Eskenazi, Tamara Cohn, 126
Esquivel, Laura, 227
Estés, Clarissa Pinkola, 68
Etcoff, Nancy L., 149
Etzkowitz, Henry, 312
Eugenides, Jeffrey, 373
Evans, Carol, 373
Evans, Gail, 334–35
Evans, Sara M., 211, 287
Even God Is Single: (So Stop Giving Me a Hard Time), 97
Even June Cleaver Would Forget the Juice Box: Cut Yourself Some Slack (and Still Raise Great Kids) in the Age of Extreme Parenting, 102
Every Day Is a Good Day: Reflections of Contemporary Indigenous Women, 20
Everyday Magic: Spells & Rituals for Modern Living, 134
Everyday Moon Magic: Spells & Rituals for Abundant Living, 134
Everyday Sun Magic: Spells & Rituals for Radiant Living, 134

Everything but the Kitchen Sink: What Every Modern Woman Needs to Know, 72

Eve's Herbs: A History of Contraception and Abortion in the West, 208

Evita (Eva Perón), 7

Evita: An Intimate Portrait of Eva Perón, 7

Evita: In My Own Words, 7

Evita: The Real Life of Eva Perón, 7

An Exact Replica of a Figment of My Imagination: A Memoir, 181

Expat: Women's True Tales of Life Abroad, 266

Experiencing Abortion: A Weaving of Women's Words, 178

Extraordinary Women of the Medieval and Renaissance World: A Biographical Dictionary, 222

Extreme Beauty: The Body Transformed, 187–88

Fables: Legends in Exile, 374

The Fabric of Friendship: Celebrating the Joys, Mending the Tears in Women's Relationships, 81

The Face behind the Veil: The Extraordinary Lives of Muslim Women in America, 56

Face Forward, 192

Faderman, Lillian, 238

Fair Game: A Complete Book of Soccer for Women, 145

Fair Game: My Life as a Spy, My Betrayal by the White House, 263

Fair, Lorrie, 145

Falconi, Dina, 195

Faldet, Rachel, 179

Fall of Atlantis, 246

Faludi, Susan, 290–91, 352

Fantham, Elaine, 215

Fant, Maureen B., 215

Far from Home: Father-Daughter Travel Adventures, 270

Fara, Patricia, 313

Farge, Arlette, 201

Farman-Farmaian, Sattareh, 34

Farmworker's Daughter: Growing Up Mexican in America, 51

Farquhar, Michael, 206

Farr, Kendall, 190

Farrar, Janet, 134

Farrar, Stewart, 134

Farrell, Warren, 340

Farrell-Beck, Jane, 189

The Far Traveler: Voyages of a Viking Woman, 220

Fashions of the Roaring '20s, 241

Fass, Paula S., 241

The Fat Girl's Guide to Life, 151–52

Fat! So?: Because You Don't Have to Apologize for Your Size!, 152

Fawcett, Denby, 261

Fearless Women: Midlife Portraits, 177

Felber, Edith, 24

Felder, Deborah G., 202

Feldhahn, Shaunti Christine, 86

Feldman, Christina, 130

Feldon, Barbara, 95

Feldt, Gloria, 30, 358

Fellman, Anita Clair, 237

Fels, Anna, 69

The Female Brain, 68

Female Chauvinist Pigs: Women and the Rise of Raunch Culture, 353

Female Genital Mutilation: Politics and Prevention, 359

Female Intelligence: Women and Espionage in the First World War, 264

The Female Thing: Dirt, Sex, Envy, Vulnerability, 303–304

Feminine Ingenuity: How Women Inventors Changed America, 316

The Feminine Mistake: Are We Giving Up Too Much?, 370

The Feminine Mystique, 291

Feminism, 285

Feminism in Our Time: The Essential Writings, World War II to the Present, 286

Feminism Is for Everybody: Passionate Politics, 293

Feminism: The Essential Historical Writings, 286

The Feminist Companion to Literature in English: Women Writers from the Middle Ages to the Present, 286

The Feminist Memoir Project: Voices from Women's Liberation, 284

Feminist Theory: From Margin to Center, 293

Femme Fatale: Love, Lies, and the Unknown Life of Mata Hari, 264

Fernandez Barrios, Flor, 47

Ferrar, Ann, 238

Fessler, Ann, 105

Fetterman, Peter, 75

Fies, Brian, 157

Fifty Years of Fashion: New Look to Now, 189

Figes, Kate, 99

Fight Like a Girl: How to Be a Fearless Feminist, 304

Filipovic, Zlata, 242

Find a Husband after 35 Using What I Learned at Harvard Business School: A Simple 15-Step Action Program, 86

Findlen, Barbara, 291

Finney, Kathryn, 187

Fiorina, Carly, 326

The Fire This Time: Young Activists and the New Feminism, 303

Firman, Dorothy, 79

Firman, Julie, 79

First Buddhist Women: Poems and Stories of Awakening, 60

First Generations: Women in Colonial America, 225

Fisher, Allan, 313

Fisher, Ann Kempner, 154

Fit and Female: The Perfect Fitness and Nutrition Game Plan for Your Unique Body Type, 143

Fitness through Aerobics, 147

Fitton, Karen, 179

Fitton, Karen, 179

Fitzgerald, F. Scott, 241–42

Five Books of Miriam: A Woman's Commentary on the Torah, 126

Flagg, Fannie, 306

Flake, Emily, 161

Flanagan, Caitlin, 372

Flannery, Sarah, 6

Flapper: A Madcap Story of Sex, Style, Celebrity, and the Women Who Made America Modern, 241

Flat Broke with Children: Women in the Age of Welfare Reform, 371–72

Flesh for Fantasy: Producing and Consuming Exotic Dance, 361

Flesh Wounds: The Culture of Cosmetic Surgery, 150

Flett, Christopher V., 334

The Floating Brothel: The Extraordinary True Story of an Eighteenth-Century Ship and Its Cargo of Female Convicts, 258

Flowers, Pam, 252

Fly Solo: The 50 Best Places on Earth for a Girl to Travel Alone, 276

Flying for Her Country: The American and Soviet Women Military Pilots of World War II, 244

Flying Solo: Single Women in Midlife, 95

Flyy Girl, 63

Follow the Rabbit-Proof Fence, 259

Follow the Stars Home, 136

Followership: How Followers Are Creating Change and Changing Leaders, 328

Fontanel, Béatrice, 191

Fontenoy, Maud, 253

The Forgotten Queens of Islam, 219

For Freedom's Sake: The Life of Fannie Lou Hamer, 53

For Keeps: Women Tell the Truth about Their Bodies, Growing Older, and Acceptance, 176

For My Next Act . . .: Women Scripting Life after Fifty, 177

For Women Only: A Revolutionary Guide to Overcoming Sexual Dysfunction and Reclaiming Your Sex Life, 164

For Women Only: What You Need to Know about the Inner Lives of Men, 86

Forbidden Grief: The Unspoken Pain of Abortion, 183

Ford, Judy, 96

Ford-Grabowsky, Mary, 115, 120

Forever Cool: How to Achieve Ageless, Youthful and Modern Personal Style, 188

Forsythe, Cassandra E., 142

Foster, Barbara M., 273

Foster, Frances Smith, 230

Foster, Michael, 273

Founding Mothers & Fathers: Gendered Power and the Forming of American Society, 225

Founding Mothers: The Women Who Raised Our Nation, 226

Founding Sisters and the Nineteenth Amendment, 284

The Fourth Estate: A History of Women in the Middle Ages, 220

Fox, Faulkner, 371

Fox, Richard Logan, 368

Fraisse, Genevieve, 201

Framing Our Past: Canadian Women's History in the Twentieth Century, 237

France, A Love Story: Women Write about the French Experience, 267

France, Kim, 187
Francina, Suza, 170
Francisco, Patricia Weaver, 184
Frank, Anne, 47–48
Frank, Katherine, 361
Frank, Otto, 47–48
Frankel, Ellen, 126
Frankel, Lois P., 334, 341, 345
Franklin, Ariana, 278
Franklin, V. P., 290
Fraser, Antonia, 17, 200, 222–23
Fraser, Laura, 270
Fraser, Nicholas, 7
Fraulein Rabbiner Jonas: The Story of the First Woman Rabbi, 57
Frazier, Charles, 235
Free to Believe: Liberating Images of God for Women, 115
Freedman, Estelle B., 285
Freedman, Rita Jackaway, 160
Freedom from Fear: And Other Writings, 31
Freeman, Sue Joan Mendelson, 343
French Women Don't Get Fat, 143–44
French Women for All Seasons: A Year of Secrets, Recipes & Pleasure, 144
Fresh Milk: The Secret Life of Breasts, 109
Fried Green Tomatoes at the Whistle Stop Cafe, 306
Frieda, Leonie, 18
Friedan, Betty, 291
Friedman, Caitlin, 329, 335, 341
Friedman, David M., 192
The Friend Who Got Away: Twenty Women's True Life Tales of Friendships That Blew Up, Burned Out or Faded Away, 80
Frohlinger, Carol, 334
From Ancient Goddess to Christian Saints (A History of Women in the West), 201
From Bananas to Buttocks: The Latina Body in Popular Film and Culture, 151
From Cinderella to CEO: How to Master the 10 Lessons of Fairy Tales to Transform Your Work Life, 335
From Deborah to Esther: Sexual Politics in the Hebrew Bible, 123
From Out of the Shadows: Mexican Women in Twentieth-Century America, 241
From Pocahontas to Power Suits: Everything You Need to Know about Women's History in America, 203

From Preachers to Suffragists: Woman's Rights and Religious Conviction in the Lives of Three Nineteenth-Century American Clergywomen, 320
From the Heart: A Woman's Guide to Living Well with Heart Disease, 155
Frymer-Kensky, Tikva Simone, 216–17
Fukai, Akiko, 188
Fulda, Jennette, 143
Full Frontal Feminism: A Young Women's Guide to Why Feminism Matters, 305
Fumia, Molly, 179
Fun Home: A Family Tragicomic, 40
Furiya, Linda., 48
The F-Word: Feminism in Jeopardy: Women, Politics, and the Future, 303

Gaining: The Truth about Life after Eating Disorders, 160
Gallick, Sarah, 60
Gallion, Mari, 112
Gallman, J. Matthew, 15
Game Face: What Does a Female Athlete Look Like?, 146
Gammelgaard, Lene, 252
Ganahl, Jane, 94–95
Gansler, Laura Leedy, 339
Gansler, Laura Leedy, 38
Garascia, Nancy S., 337
Gardner, Sarah E., 236
Garrard, Mary D., 9
Garrett, Sheryl, 88
Garrison, Webb B., 235
Garza, Hedda, 241
Gaskin, Ina May, 109
Gates, Janice, 116
Gather Together in My Name, 25
Gau, Colleen, 189
Gavin, Lettie, 243
Gay Marriage: Why It Is Good for Gays, Good for Straights, and Good for America, 301
Geek Chic: Smart Women in Popular Culture, 313–14
Gehrke-White, Donna, 56
Geisha of Gion: The Memoir of Mineko Iwasaki, 33
Gelman, Rita Golden, 269

Gender Talk: The Struggle for Women's Equality in African American Communities, 298

Gender Trouble: Feminism and the Subversion of Identity, 288

Genderqueer: Voices from Beyond the Sexual Binary, 355

Genevieve, 135

The Gentleman's Daughter: Women's Lives in Georgian England, 223

George, Margaret, 18–19, 217

Gerber, Robin, 342

Gershick, Zsa Zsa, 324

Gerth, Jeff, 368

Get in the Game!: The Girls' Guide to Money and Investing, 346

Get Me Out of Here: My Recovery from Borderline Personality Disorder, 156

Get On with It!: How to be Sassy, Successful & Single, 97

Getting by on the Minimum: The Lives of Working-class Women, 353

Gianturco, Paola, 299–300

Gibbons, Kaye, 136

Gidgets and Women Warriors: Perceptions of Women in the 1950s and 1960s, 236–37

Giesemann, Suzanne, 145

A Gift of Prayer: The Spirituality of Jewish Women, 127

Gifts of the Wild: A Woman's Book of Adventure, 255

Gift-Wrapped by God: Secret Answers to the Question, "Why Wait?", 85

Gilbert, Elizabeth, 270

Giles, Fiona, 109

Gillespie, Peggy, 103

Gilliam, Connally, 96

Gilligan, Carol, 69

Gillow, John, 200

Gilman, Dorothy, 278

Gilman, Susan Jane, 173

Gimbutas, Marija, 116

Gioseffi, Daniela, 364

The Girl, 306

The Girl from Botany Bay, 257–58

Girl, Get Your Credit Straight!: A Sister's Guide to Ditching Your Debt, Mending Your Credit, and Building a Strong Financial Future, 344

Girl, Get Your Money Straight: A Sister's Guide to Healing Your Bank Account and Funding Your Dreams in 7 Simple Steps, 344

Girl, Interrupted, 156

The Girl on the Magazine Cover: The Origins of Visual Stereotypes in American Mass Media, 352

Girl, Make Your Money Grow!: A Sister's Guide to Protecting Your Future and Enriching Your Life, 344

Girlbomb: A Halfway Homeless Memoir, 163

Girlfriend Getaways: You Go Girl! And I'll Go, Too, 275

Girlfriends Are the Best Friends of All: A Tribute to Laughter, Secrets, Girl Talk, Chocolate, Shopping—and Everything Else Women Share, 79

The Girlfriends' Bible, 78

Girlfriends: Invisible Bonds, Enduring Ties, 80

Girlfriends' Getaway: A Complete Guide to the Weekend Adventure That Turns Friends into Sisters and Sisters into Friends, 275

Girls and Women in Classical Greek Religion, 216

Girls Gone Mild: Young Women Reclaim Self-Respect and Find It's Not Bad to Be Good, 360

The Girl's Guide to Absolutely Everything, 173

The Girl's Guide to Being a Boss (without Being a Bitch): Valuable Lessons, Smart Suggestions, and True Stories for Succeeding as the Chick-in-Charge, 341

The Girls' Guide to Building a Million-Dollar Business, 332

The Girl's Guide to Kicking Your Career into Gear: Valuable Lessons, True Stories, and Tips for Using What You've Got (A Brain!) to Make Your Worklife Work for You, 335

The Girl's Guide to Starting Your Own Business: Candid Advice, Frank Talk, and True Stories for the Successful Entrepreneur, 329

A Girl's Guide to Taking Over the World: Writings from the Girl Zine Revolution, 300–301

The Girls Who Went Away: The Hidden History of Women Who Surrendered Children for Adoption in the Decades before Roe v. Wade, 105

Glaser, Connie Brown, 341
The Glass Castle: A Memoir, 184
Glimpses of Grace: Daily Thoughts and Reflections, 124
Global Cinderellas: Migrant Domestics and Newly Rich Employers in Taiwan, 352
Global Feminisms: New Directions in Contemporary Art, 300
Global Woman: Nannies, Maids, and Sex Workers in the New Economy, 351
Gloria Steinem: A Biography, 29
The Gnostic Gospels, 124
Go Girl: Finding Adventure Wherever Your Travels Lead, 118
The Go-Girl Guide: Surviving Your 20s with Savvy, Soul, and Style, 173
Go Girl!: The Black Woman's Guide to Travel and Adventure., 277
Go Your Own Way: Women Travel the World Solo, 268
God Has No Religion: Blending Traditions for Prayer, 122
Goddess Bless!: Divine Affirmations, Prayers, and Blessings, 134
Goddess Companion: Daily Meditations on the Goddess, 133–34
Goddesses in Everywoman: A New Psychology of Women, 68
Goddesses, Whores, Wives, and Slaves: Women in Classical Antiquity, 215
Godek, Gregory J. P., 92
Goer, Henci, 108
Goff, Barbara E., 216
Going Alone: Women's Adventures in the Wild, 256
Going Gray: What I Learned about Beauty, Sex, Work, Motherhood, Authenticity, and Everything Else That Really Matters, 176
Gola, Mark, 145
Golant, Susan K., 335
Goldberg, Nieca, 155–56
Golden, Arthur, 62
Golden, Marita, 48–49
Goldman, Leslie, 150
Goldman, Paula, 355
Goldsmith, Barbara, 12
Gondor, Emery I., 185
Gone with the Wind, 246
The Good Body, 74
Good Harbor, 62
Good in Bed, 83

Good Time Girls of the Alaska-Yukon Gold Rush, 232
Goodman, Nancy, 158
Goodman, Samantha Slotkin, 320
The Good Women of China: Hidden Voices, 39
Gordon, Ann, 370
Gordon, Beate, 32
Gordon, Linda, 208, 210, 284
Gore, Ariel, 99–100
The Gospel of Mary of Magdala: Jesus and the First Woman Apostle, 217
Gotsch, Gwen, 110
Gottesman, Jane, 146
Gottlieb, Lori, 126, 159
Gottman, John, 86
Goulart, Frances Sheridan, 122
Gourley, Catherine, 236–38
Grace: A Memoir, 60
Grace (Eventually): Thoughts on Faith, 123
The Graceful Guru: Hindu Female Gurus in India and the United States, 58
Graham, Jo, 213
Graham, Michelle, 191
Graña, Mari, 14
Grandes Horizontales: The Lives and Legends of Four Nineteenth-Century Courtesans, 228
Grandmothers, 79
Grandmothers of the Light: A Medicine Woman's Sourcebook, 113
Grant, Michael, 18–19
Grant, Ted, 317
Granuaile: Ireland's Pirate Queen C. 1530–1603, 16
Grassroots: A Field Guide for Feminist Activism, 303
Gray, John, 328
The Great Cosmic Mother: Rediscovering the Religion of the Earth, 116
The Great Gatsby, 241–42
The Great Goddesses of Egypt, 218
The Great Women Cartoonists, 311
Great Women in the Sport of Kings: America's Top Women Jockeys Tell Their Stories, 322
Great Women Masters of Art, 74
The Great Women Superheroes, 311
Greece, A Love Story: Women Write about the Greek Experience, 267
Green, Anne Bosanko, 37
The Green Belt Movement: Sharing the Approach and the Experience, 28

Green, G. Dorsey, 103
Green, Karen, 300–301
Greenberg, Cathy, 71
Greene, Melissa Fay, 104–105
Greenfield, Lauren, 159
Greenlaw, Linda, 253–54
Greenwald, Rachel, 86
Gregory, Peter N., 130
Griest, Stephanie Elizondo, 276
Griffin, John Howard, 152
Gringa Latina: A Woman of Two Worlds, 45
Gristwood, Sarah, 23
Gross, Jessica Berger, 179
Grout, Pam, 275
*The Grown-Up Girl's Guide to Style: A
    Maintenance Bible for Fashion, Beauty,
    and More,* 185–86
Gruhzit-Hoyt, Olga, 245
Grundy, Isobel, 286
Guerin-Williams, Mirranda, 54
*The Guerrilla Girls' Bedside Companion
    to the History of Western Art,* 300
Guerrilla Girls (Group of Artists), 300,
    352
*A Guide to Elegance: For Every Woman
    Who Wants to Be Well and
    Properly Dressed on All Occasions,*
    185
Guilbault, Rose Castillo, 51
Guiliano, Mireille, 143–44
Gurian, Michael, 328
Gutgold, Nichola D., 366
Gutmann, Stephanie, 325
*Gutsy Women: More Travel Tips and Wisdom
    for the Road,* 277
Guy, J. A., 17–18
Guy-Sheftall, Beverly, 298
Guzman, Sandra, 75
*Gyn/Ecology: The Metaethics of Radical
    Feminism,* 288

Hachemi, Chékéba, 33
Haddad, Yvonne Yazbeck, 128
Haggins, Jon, 277
Haiken, Elizabeth, 150
*Hair Matters: Beauty, Power, and Black
    Women's Consciousness,* 148
*Hair Story: Untangling the Roots of Black
    Hair in America,* 148
Hakakian, Roya, 36
Half-Assed: A Weight-loss Memoir, 143
Hall, Adrienne, 146, 256

Hall, Linley Erin, 312–13
Hall, Meredith, 105
Hall, Richard, 233–34
Halliday, Ayun, 100
Halpin, Mary Ann, 177
Hambly, Gavin, 219
Hamel, Debra, 213–14
Hamill, Dorothy, 322
Hamill, Pete, 162
Hamilton, Cathy, 78
Hammer, Jill, 125
The Handmaid's Tale, 305
Han, Lori Cox, 367–68
Handbags: The Power of the Purse, 187
*Handbags: What Every Woman Should
    Know,* 187
Hanin, Jennifer S., 106
Hannam, June, 285
*The Happy Hook-Up: A Single Girl's Guide
    to Casual Sex,* 167
*Hardball for Women: Winning at the
    Game of Business,* 335
Hardin, Nikki, 172
Harding, Elizabeth U., 133
Harper, Lisa, 121
Harrington, Mona, 320
Harris, Fran, 329–30
Harris, Juliette, 186
Harrison, Kathryn, 180
Harris-Watkins, Patricia, 122
Hart, Elva Treviño, 49–50
Haskett, Robert Stephen, 213
Hastings, Morgan, 151
Hathaway, Sandee Eisenberg, 111
*Having a Baby—When the Old-fashioned
    Way Isn't Working: Hope and Help
    for Everyone Facing Infertility,* 105
Hawass, Zahi A., 214
Hawley, John Stratton, 132
Haynsworth, Leslie, 310
Hays, Charlotte, 94
Hays, Sharon, 371–72
The Healing, 306
*The Healing Choice: Your Guide to
    Emotional Recovery after an
    Abortion,* 178
*Healing from the Trauma of Childhood
    Sexual Abuse: The Journey for
    Women,* 178
*Healthy Transitions: A Woman's Guide to
    Perimenopause, Menopause & Beyond,*
    170

Hear Me Roar: Women, Motorcycles, and the Rapture of the Road, 238

Hear Our Voice: Women in the British Rabbinate, 319

Heart and Hands: A Midwife's Guide to Pregnancy & Birth, 108

Heartbreak: The Political Memoir of a Feminist Militant, 290

Hearts West: True Stories of Mail Order Brides on the Frontier, 232

Heffernan, Margaret, 330, 336

Heim, Pat, 335

Heldman, Caroline, 367–68

Hell Hath No Fury: True Stories of Women at War from Antiquity to Iraq, 200

Heller, Nancy, 310

Helminski, Camille Adams, 128

Helpmates, Harlots, and Heroes: Women's Stories in the Hebrew Bible, 217

Hen Frigates: Wives of Merchant Captains Under Sail, 257

Henderson, Carol, 182

Henderson, Sarah, 367

Henry, Astrid, 300

Henry, Pat, 254

Her Best Shot: Women and Guns in America, 365

Her Choice to Heal, 183

Her Dream of Dreams: The Rise and Triumph of Madam C. J. Walker, 46

Her Last Death: A Memoir, 163

Her Place at the Table: A Woman's Guide to Negotiating Five Key Challenges to Leadership Success, 334

Her Share of the Blessings: Women's Religions among Pagans, Jews, and Christians in the Greco-Roman World, 217–18

Her Voice, Her Faith: Women Speak on World Religions, 120

Her Way: The Hopes and Ambitions of Hillary Rodham Clinton, 368

Herman, Eleanor, 206

Hernández, Daisy, 292

Hernandez, Jaime, 373–74

Heroines of the Slavery Era (In Praise of Black Women), 204–205

Herrera Mulligan, Michelle, 51

Herrin, Judith, 219

Herring, Cedric, 49

Herzog, David B., 159

Heterophobia: Sexual Harassment and the Future of Feminism, 340

Heywood, Leslie, 304

Hibbert, Christopher, 22

Hichens, Mark, 22

Hickman, Katie, 228

Hicks, George L., 209

The Hidden Diary of Marie Antoinette: A Novel, 17

Highsmith, Patricia, 42

Highsmith: A Romance of the 1950's, a Memoir, 42

Hijas Americanas: Beauty, Body Image, and Growing Up Latina, 150

Hill, Anita, 339

Hill, Frances, 225

Hill, Sarah H., 226

Himalayan Hermitess: The Life of a Tibetan Buddhist Nun, 59

Hindu Goddesses: Visions of the Divine Feminine in the Hindu Religious Tradition, 132

Hines, Elizabeth Gardner, 46

Hines, Melissa, 70

Hingley, Richard, 16

The Hip Mama Survival Guide, 99–100

Hiratsuka Raicho, 32

A History of Bisexuality, 91

A History of the Breast, 191–92

A History of the Wife, 89

A History of U.S. Feminisms, 285

A History of Women in the Canadian Military, 243

A History of Women in the West, 201

The Hite Report on Male Sexuality, 166

The Hite Report: A Nationwide Study on Female Sexuality, 166

Hite, Shere, 166

Hoadley, Bobbi, 146

Hochschild, Arlie Russell, 351

Hodgson, Barbara, 274

Hodgson, Marion Stegeman, 38

Hoffer, Peter Charles, 208

Hold Tight, 347

Holden, Kate, 161

Holland, Barbara, 7

Hollander, Linda, 333

Hollern, Susie, 239

Hollihan, Keith, 338

Holloway, Kris, 110

Holmes, Kenneth L., 231

Holmes, Sarah, 91

Holmstedt, Kirsten A., 325

*Holy Boldness: Women Preachers'
    Autobiographies and the Sanctified
    Self,* 320

The Holy Book of Women's Mysteries,
    133

Holy Hunger: A Memoir of Desire, 158

*Home before Morning: The Story of an Army
    Nurse in Vietnam,* 262

*Home Girls Make Some Noise: Hip-Hop
    Feminism Anthology,* 294

*Home Was the Land of Morning Calm: A
    Saga of a Korean-American Family.,* 52

*The Honeymoon's Over: True Stories of Love,
    Marriage, and Divorce,* 89

Honor Harrington series, 279

*Hooking Up: Sex, Dating, and Relationships
    on Campus,* 167

**The Hookup Handbook: A Single Girl's
    Guide to Living It Up,** 167

hooks, bell, 50–51, 292–93

**Hope in a Jar: The Making of America's
    Beauty Culture,** 194

Hope, Judith, 318

Hoppe, Stephanie T., 323

Hornbacher, Marya, 155, 159

Horowitz, Leslie, 226

Horton, Hayward Derrick, 49

Hosier, Helen Kooiman, 121

Houppert, Karen, 170–71

*Households and Holiness: The Religious
    Culture of Israelite Women,* 215

The House of Mirth, 247

Howard, Jane, 36

Howard, Keith, 209

Howell, Clare, 355

*How My Breasts Saved the World:
    Misadventures of a Nursing Mother,*
    109–10

**How Not to Look Old: Fast and Effortless
    Ways to Look 10 Years Younger, 10
    Pounds Lighter, 10 Times Better,**
    188

**How She Does It: How Women
    Entrepreneurs Are Changing the
    Rules of Business Success,** 330

**How The Pro-choice Movement Saved
    America,** 358

**How to Be a Budget Fashionista: The
    Ultimate Guide to Looking
    Fabulous for Less,** 187

**How to Be a Happy Lesbian: A Coming
    Out Guide,** 92

**How to Date Men: Dating Secrets from
    America's Top Matchmaker,** 88

*How to Get Married after 35: A User's Guide
    to Getting to the Altar,* 86

*How to Run Your Business Like a Girl:
    Successful Strategies from
    Entrepreneurial Women Who Made It
    Happen,* 330

How to Say It for Women, 336

How to Succeed with Men, 84

**How to Tell If Your Boyfriend Is the
    Antichrist: (And If He Is, Should
    You Break Up with Him?),** 83

Huber, Cheri, 131

Huggins, Kathleen, 110

Hull, N. E. H., 208

Hune, Shirley, 54

**The Hungry Ocean: A Swordboat
    Captain's Journey,** 253

Hunt, Swanee, 242

Hunter, Margaret L., 49

*Hurdles: Women Building High-Growth
    Businesses,* 333

Hurston, Zora Neale, 306

Hurtado, Aída, 288

Husain, Sarah, 128

Hutcherson, Hilda, 164, 166–67

Hutchins, Loraine, 91

Hutchison, Kay Bailey, 8, 210

Hwang, David Henry, 62

Hypatia of Alexandria, 6

**Hypatia of Alexandria: Mathematician
    and Martyr,** 6

I Am a Soldier, Too: The Jessica Lynch Story,
    261

**Ice Bound: A Doctor's Incredible Battle
    for Survival at the South Pole,** 255

Idelson, Shirley, 57

**I Feel Bad about My Neck: And Other
    Thoughts on Being a Woman,** 176

*If Women Ruled the World: How to Create the
    World We Want to Live In: Stories,
    Ideas, and Inspiration for Change,* 364

I Know Why the Caged Bird Sings, 24–25

*The Illustrated Virago Book of Women
    Travellers,* 8

Ilse, Sherokee, 181

*Images of Civil War Medicine: A
    Photographic History,* 235

Imagining Ourselves: Global Voices from a New Generation of Women, 355

I'm Not in the Mood: What Every Woman Should Know about Improving Her Libido, 164

I'm Not Mad, I Just Hate You!: A New Understanding of Mother-Daughter Conflict, 79

The Impact of Women in Public Office, 367

Impossible to Hold: Women and Culture in the 1960's, 236

The Improvised Woman: Single Women Reinventing Single Life, 96

In a Different Voice: Psychological Theory and Women's Development, 69

Ina May's Guide to Childbirth, 109

In Beauty May She Walk: Hiking the Appalachian Trail at 60, 251

Incidents in the Life of a Slave Girl: Written by Herself, 51

In Code: A Mathematical Journey, 6

Inconceivable: A Woman's Triumph over Despair and Statistics, 106–107

Incorporating Women: A History of Women and Business in the United States, 13

The Indelible Alison Bechdel: Confessions, Comix, and Miscellaneous Dykes to Watch Out For, 40–41

Indian Women of Early Mexico, 213

Indichova, Julia, 106–107

I Never Called It Rape: The Ms. Report on Recognizing, Fighting, and Surviving Date and Acquaintance Rape, 26

Infidel, 183

In Her Hands: Craftswomen Changing the World, 299–300

In Her Place: A Documentary History of Prejudice against Women, 354

In My Skin: A Memoir, 161

Inner Hunger: A Young Woman's Struggle through Anorexia and Bulimia, 158

Inner Peace for Busy Women: Balancing Work, Family, and Your Inner Life, 114

Inness, Sherrie A., 239, 313–14

In Our Time: Memoir of a Revolution, 26

In Praise of Black Women, 204–205

In Search of Our Mothers' Gardens: Womanist Prose, 295

In the Beginning, Woman Was the Sun: The Autobiography of a Japanese Feminist, 32

In Their Own Right: The History of American Clergywomen, 319–20

In the Name of Honor: A Memoir, 182–83

Inside Every Woman: Using the 10 Strengths You Didn't Know You Had to Get the Career and Life You Want Now, 341

Inside Iran: Women's Lives, 36

Intended for Pleasure, 165

Intimate Issues: Conversations Woman to Woman: 21 Questions Women Ask about Sex, 165

Inventing Beauty: A History of the Innovations That Have Made Us Beautiful, 194

Inventing the Rest of Our Lives: Women in Second Adulthood, 176–77

Invincible Spirits: A Thousand Years of Women's Spiritual Writings, 61

The Invisible Bond: How to Break Free from Your Sexual Past, 87

Iran Awakening: A Memoir of Revolution and Hope, 35

I, Rigoberta Menchú: An Indian Woman in Guatemala, 34

Iron John: A Book about Men, 68–69

Irving, John, 374

Isabel the Queen: Life and Times, 19

Isabella and the Strange Death of Edward II, 24

Isabella of Castile: The First Renaissance Queen, 19

Is It a Date or Just Coffee?: The Gay Girl's Guide to Dating, Sex, and Romance, 91–92

Is It Hot in Here? Or Is It Me?: The Complete Guide to Menopause, 170

An Italian Affair, 270

It Gets Easier! And Other Lies We Tell New Mothers, 103

It's a Boy: Women Writers on Raising Sons, 98

It's a Chick Thing: Celebrating the Wild Side of Women's Friendships, 78

It's a Girl: Women Writers on Raising Daughters, 98–99

It's a Jungle Out There: The Feminist Survival Guide to Politically Inhospitable Environments, 301

It's Harder in Heels: Essays by Women Lawyers Achieving Work-Life Balance, 320

It's More than Money, It's Your Life!: The New Money Club for Women, 345

It's Your Boat Too: A Woman's Guide to Greater Enjoyment on the Water, 145

Italy, A Love Story: Women Write about the Italian Experience, 267

It Takes a Candidate: Why Women Don't Run for Office, 368

It Was Food vs. Me—and I Won, 158

Iversen, Leslie L., 162

Iwasaki Mineko, 33

I Was Amelia Earhart, 14

I Was a Really Good Mom before I Had Kids: Reinventing Modern Motherhood, 103

I Wish Someone Had Told Me: A Realistic Guide to Early Motherhood, 99

Iyengar, Geeta S., 144

Jackie Cochran: An Autobiography, 14

Jackie Cochran: Pilot in the Fastest Lane, 14

Jacobs, Harriet A., 51

Jadick, Richard, 264

Jamison, Kay R., 155

Jane Eyre, 135

Jane Whitefield series, 374

Jansz, Natania, 271

Japanese Women Don't Get Old or Fat: Secrets of My Mother's Tokyo Kitchen, 144

Jarrell, Donna, 152

Javins, Marie, 268

Jeffries, Steve, 149

Jenkins, Carol, 46

Jensen, Jane Richardson, 122

Jensen, Karol L., 93

Jesch, Judith, 220

Jessel, David, 68

Jessie, Diana, 276

Jessop, Carolyn, 180

Jewels: 50 Phenomenal Black Women Over 50, 176

Jewels of the Tsars: The Romanovs and Imperial Russia, 20–21

Jeydel, Alana S., 367

Joan of Arc: By Herself and Her Witnesses, 11

Joan of Arc: Her Story, 10–11

Joan: The Mysterious Life of the Heretic Who Became a Saint, 11

Joans, Barbara, 239

Jochens, Jenny, 220

Joffrey, Rebecca, 26

Johnsen, Linda, 58, 131–32

Johnson, Anna, 187

Johnson, Jennifer, 353

Johnson, Kalyn, 174

Johnson, Kaylene, 368

Johnson, Kelly Love, 336

Johnson, Merri Lisa, 351, 361

Johnson, Pamela, 186

Jones, Charisse, 299

Jones, Constance, 201–202

Jones, Daniel, 84

Jones, David E., 202

Jones, Gayl, 306

Jones, Kathleen B., 367

Jones, Robert, 193

Joseph, Suad, 369

Joshi, S. T., 354

Joukowsky, Martha, 260

Joulwan, Melissa, 240

Journey from the Land of No: A Girlhood Caught in Revolutionary Iran, 36

Journey into Motherhood: Inspirational Stories of Natural Birth, 111

A Journey North: One Woman's Story of Hiking the Appalachian Trail, 256

A Journey of One's Own: Uncommon Advice for the Independent Woman Traveler, 277

The Joy Luck Club, 52, 63

Juana Inés de la Cruz, Sister, 122

Juffer, Jane, 362

Julian of Norwich, 57

Jung Chang, 31

Junger, Sebastian, 253

Junia: The First Woman Apostle, 59

Kaahumanu, Lani, 91

Kabul Beauty School: An American Woman Goes Behind the Veil, 27

Kaeser, Gigi, 103

Kali: The Black Goddess of Dakshineswar, 133

Kali: The Feminine Force, 133

Kanable, Kathy, 105

Kanafani, Deborah, 27

Kane, Emily, 172

Kang, K. Connie, 52

Kantrowitz, Barbara, 170

Karp, Marcelle, 302

Karpinski, Janis L., 365

Kasher, Steven, 53
Kassindja, Fauziya, 181–82
Kastan, Kathy, 155
Kasten, Liora, 359
Kathryn Dance series, 278
Katigbak-Sillick, Marie Clare, 185
Kauder-Nalebuff, Rachel, 91
Kaufman, Pamela, 23
Kaufman, Shirley, 126–27
Kay, Devra, 127
Kaysen, Susanna, 156
Kedar, Sharon, 346
Keddie, Nikki R., 219
Keeping Faith, 136
Keeping You a Secret, 63
Kefalas, Maria, 372
Keil, Sally Van Wagenen, 244
Keith, Verna, 49
Kellen, Bonnie, 341
Kellerman, Barbara, 328, 343–44
Kelly, Amy R., 23
Kelly, Caitlin, 364–65
Kelly, Joe, 160
Kelsey, Marion, 243
Kemelgor, Carol, 312
Kempe, Margery, 56–57
Kendall-Tackett, Kathleen A., 110
Kent, Debra, 166
Kentz, Marilyn, 175, 177
Kerber, Linda K., 210
Kessler-Harris, Alice, 210
Keyes, Marian, 195–96
Khalsa, Hari Kaur, 116
Khandelwal, Meena, 58
The Kid: What Happened after My Boyfriend and I Decided to Go Get Pregnant: An Adoption Story, 107
Kidd, Sue Monk, 28, 136
Kilbourne, Jean, 153, 299
Kim, Edmund S., 170
The Kinder, Gentler Military: Can America's Gender-Neutral Fighting Force Still Win Wars?, 325
Kindred, 246
Kindred, Ursula Inga, 54
King, Florence, 41–42
King, Karen L., 217
King, Margaret L., 222
King, Stephen, 196
Kingston, Maxine Hong, 52
Kinsella, Bridget, 83
Kinsey, Alfred, 166

The Kinsey Institute New Report on Sex: What You Must Know to Be Sexually Literate, 166
Kinsley, David R., 132
Kipnis, Laura, 303–304
Kirsch, Melissa, 173
The Kiss, 180
Kiss My Tiara: How to Rule the World as a Smartmouth Goddess, 173
Kitch, Carolyn L., 352
Kitchen Table Entrepreneurs: How Eleven Women Escaped Poverty and Became Their Own Bosses, 331–32
Kite Strings of the Southern Cross: A Woman's Travel Odyssey, 268
Klapheck, Elisa, 57
Klapisch-Zuber, Christiane, 201
Klein, Lillian R., 123
Kluger-Bell, Kim, 181
Knapp, Caroline, 162
Knecht, R. J., 18
Knight, Brenda, 309
Knight, Sirona, 55, 134
Knight, Wendy, 270
KnitLit: Sweaters and Their Stories and Other Writing about Knitting, 119
Knitting Yarns and Spinning Tales: A Knitter's Stash of Wit and Wisdom, 119
Knockdown Knits: 30 Projects from the Roller Derby Track, 240
Knock Yourself Up: No Man? No Problem!: A Tell-all Guide to Becoming a Single Mom, 112
Knowledge, Difference, and Power: Essays Inspired by Women's Ways of Knowing, 68
Koda, Harold, 187–88
Kolb, Deborah M., 334, 337
Kolodiejchuk, Brian, 60
Korn, Fadumo, 181
Korrol, Virginia Sánchez, 204
Kotulski, Davina, 301–302
Kozlowski, Karen, 194
Kraemer, Ross Shepard, 217–18
Kraft, Heidi Squier, 264
Kreamer, Anne, 176
Kripal, Jeffrey John, 132
Kristal, Nicole, 92
Kristeva, Julia, 219
Kristin Lavransdatter trilogy, 247
Krupp, Charla, 188

Kuczynski, Alex, 149–50
Kuebelbeck, Amy, 182
Kuegler, Sabine, 51
Kunin, Madeleine, 368
Kushi, Gabriele, 172
Kushiel's Dart, 278
Kushiel's Legacy, 278
Kushner, Eve, 178
Kwolek-Folland, Angel, 13

LaBastille, Anne, 253, 269
Labaton, Vivien, 303
Labzina, Anna Evdokimovna, 32
Ladies of the Grand Tour: British Women in
    Pursuit of Enlightenment and
    Adventure in Eighteenth-Century
    Europe, 223
The Ladies' Room Reader Quiz Book: 1,000
    Questions and Answers about Women
    and the Things They Love, 72
The Ladies' Room Reader Revisited: A
    Curious Compendium of Fascinating
    Female Facts, 72
The Ladies' Room Reader: The Ultimate
    Women's Trivia Book, 72
Ladies Who Launch: Embracing
    Entrepreneurship & Creativity as a
    Lifestyle, 329
The Lady and the Panda: The True
    Adventures of the First American
    Explorer to Bring Back China's Most
    Exotic Animal, 258
A Lady's Life in the Rocky Mountains,
    272
Laing, Kathleen, 275
Lakota Woman, 45
Lamb, Amanda, 103
Lamott, Anne, 101, 123
Lan, Pei-Chia, 352
Lane, Helen R., 7
The Language of Baklava, 56
The Language of the Goddess: Unearthing
    the Hidden Symbols of Western
    Civilization, 116
LaPlante, Eve, 58
Lapsley, Jacqueline E., 123
Larkin, Geri, 130–31
Larkin, Joan, 90
Larrington, Carolyne, 220
Larsen, Earnest, 114
Larsen, Karen, 272
Laschever, Sara, 334

Lash, Jennifer, 113
The Last Days of Dogtown, 62
The Last Empress, 21
The Last Girls, 136
Latifa, 33
Latina: Women's Voices from the Borderlands,
    51
The Latina's Bible: The Nueva Latina's
    Guide to Love, Spirituality,
    Family, and La Vida, 75
Latinas: Hispanic Women in the United
    States, 241
Latteier, Carolyn, 192
Laubner, Ellie, 241
Laufer, Peter, 277
Lavender, Bee, 100
Lavine, Kim, 330–31
Lavinthal, Andrea, 167
Lawler, Jennifer, 70
Lawless, Jennifer L., 368
Lazaro, Pedro, 158
Lazy B: Growing Up on a Cattle Ranch in the
    American Southwest, 12
Leadership and the Sexes: Using Gender
    Science to Create Success in Business,
    328
Leadership the Eleanor Roosevelt Way:
    Timeless Strategies from the First Lady
    of Courage, 342
Leading from the Front: No Excuse
    Leadership Tactics for Women, 342
Leading Ladies: American Trailblazers, 210
Leading Out: Women Climbers Reaching for
    the Top, 251
The League of Extraordinary Gentlemen, 279
Leaving Church: A Memoir of Faith, 60
Leaving Deep Water: Asian American Women
    at the Crossroads of Two Cultures, 53
LeCompte, Mary Lou, 232
LeDai, Marlee, 118
Lee, Chana Kai, 53
Lee, Elaine, ed., 277
Lee, Mary Paik, 52
Lefkowitz, Mary R., 215
Legato, Marianne J., 70–71
Legends 2: Women Who Have Changed the
    World through the Eyes of Great
    Women Writers, 10
Legends: Women Who Have Changed the
    World through the Eyes of Great
    Women Writers, 10
Leibovitz, Annie, 75

Lein, Laura, 372
Leng, Felicity, 61
L'Engle, Madeleine, 124, 347
Leo, Jennifer, 118
Leo, Jennifer, 271
León, Vicki, 202–203
Leonard, Elizabeth D., 234
Lerner, Gerda, 211
Lesbian Epiphanies: Women Coming Out in Later Life, 93
The Lesbian Parenting Book: A Guide to Creating Families and Raising Children, 103
Lesbian Rabbis: The First Generation, 57
The Lesbian Sex Book: A Guide for Women Who Love Women, 168
Lesko, Barbara S., 218
Le Sueur, Meridel, 306
Letters from a War Zone: Writings, 1976–1989, 290
Letters of a Woman Homesteader, 233
Levack, Brian P., 222
Lever, Evelyne, 17
Levin, Carole, 222
Levin, Diane E., 299
Levin, Gail, 8
Levine, Suzanne, 176–77
Levy, Ariel, 353
Lewis, Brenda Ralph, 245
Lewis, Karen Gail, 95
Lewis, Vickie, 324
Liberty: The Lives and Times of Six Women in Revolutionary France, 222–23
Liberty's Daughters: The Revolutionary Experience of American Women, 1750–1800, 224
Life after Birth: What Even Your Friends Won't Tell You about Motherhood, 99
Life and Death in Shanghai, 31
Life in the Treetops: Adventures of a Woman in Field Biology, 254
The Life of a Russian Woman Doctor: A Siberian Memoir, 1869–1954, 32
The Life of an Ordinary Woman, 230
The Life of Elizabeth I, 23
Life's Spices from Seasoned Sistahs: A Collection of Life Stories from Mature Women of Color, 176
Lighting the Way: Nine Women Who Changed Modern America, 8

Lihamba, Amandina, 205
<u>Lincoln Rhyme</u> series, 278
Linett, Andrea, 187
Ling, Lisa, 73
Lipstick, 193–94
Liss, Peggy K., 19
Listen Up!: Voices from the Next Feminist Generation, 291
Liswood, Laura A., 368–69
Litoff, Judy Barrett, 29
Liu, Aimee, 160
A Live Coal in the Sea, 124, 347
Live Large! Affirmations for Living the Life You Want in the Body You Already Have, 149
Live Sex Acts: Women Performing Erotic Labor, 362
Livia: First Lady of Imperial Rome, 213
Living Alone & Loving It: A Guide to Relishing the Solo Life, 95
Living Beauty, 185
The Living Goddess: Reclaiming the Tradition of the Mother of the Universe, 131–32
Living History, 4
Livoti, Carol, 167
Locas: The Maggie and Hopey Stories, 373–74
Locker Room Diaries: The Naked Truth about Women, Body Image, and Re-imagining the "Perfect" Body, 150
Lois on the Loose: One Woman, One Motorcycle, 20,000 Miles across the Americas, 272
The Lobster Chronicles: Life on a Very Small Island, 253–54
Longing to Tell: Black Women Talk about Sexuality and Intimacy, 168
Look Both Ways: Bisexual Politics, 287–88
The Lolita Effect: The Media Sexualization of Young Girls and What We Can Do about It, 299
López Springfield, Consuelo, 239
Lorde, Audre, 293
Losing Malcolm: A Mother's Journey through Grief, 182
The Lost Apostle: Searching for the Truth about Junia, 59
The Lost Lady of the Amazon: The Story of Isabela Godin and Her Epic Journey, 260
Louden, Jennifer, 117–19

Louie, Miriam Ching Yoon, 351–52

Louis, Ron, 84

Love and Hate in Jamestown: John Smith, Pocahontas, and the Start of a New Nation, 44

Love and Louis XIV: The Women in the Life of the Sun King, 223

Love and Rockets series, 373–74

Love Comes Softly, 63

Love for Sale: A World History of Prostitution, 363

Love Makes a Family: Portraits of Lesbian, Gay, Bisexual, and Transgender Parents and Their Families, 103

Love My Rifle More Than You: Young and Female in the U.S. Army, 325–26

The Love Spell: An Erotic Memoir of Spiritual Awakening, 55

Love, Stargirl, 306

Lowman, Margaret, 254

Lowry, Beverly, 46

Lucas, Geralyn, 156

Luchetti, Cathy, 233

Lucky, 183–84

The Lucky Shopping Manual: Building and Improving Your Wardrobe Piece by Piece, 187

Lucy Sullivan Is Getting Married, 196

Luna, 63

Luu, Cindy, 167

Lying Awake, 63

Lynch, Courtney, 342

M. Butterfly, 62

M.E. Kerr, 90

Maathai, Wangari, 28

Mabe, Catherine, 240

MacDonald, Anne, 316

MacKell, Jan, 232

Mackler, Carolyn, 74, 196

MacNair, Rachel, 357

Madam President: Shattering the Last Glass Ceiling, 366

Madame Curie: A Biography, 12

Madariaga, Isabel de, 20

Maddox, Brenda, 13

Madness: A Bipolar Life, 155

The Magnificent Mountain Women: Adventures in the Colorado Rockies, 273

Maguire, Daniel C., 356–57

Mai, Mukhtar, 182–83

Maid in the U.S.A., 354

Maiden Voyage, 254

Maiden Voyages: Writings of Women Travelers, 274

Maine, Margo, 160

Maines, Rachel, 73

Maitland, Alison, 328

The Majesty of the Law: Reflections of a Supreme Court Justice, 12

The Majority Finds Its Past: Placing Women in History, 211

Makeup Makeovers: Expert Secrets for Stunning Transformations, 193

Making a Change for Good: A Guide to Compassionate Self-Discipline, 131

Making Connections: Mother-Daughter Travel Adventures, 270

Making Ends Meet: How Single Mothers Survive Welfare and Low-Wage Work, 372

Making Faces, 192

Making Her Mark: Firsts and Milestones in Women's Sports, 322–23

Making More Waves: New Writing by Asian American Women, 54

Making Sex Work: A Failed Experiment with Legalised Prostitution, 361

Making Waves: An Anthology of Writings by and about Asian American Women, 54

Malinche, 227

Maloba, Wunyabari O., 237–38

Maloney, Carolyn, 301

Maltz, Wendy, 178–79

The Mammoth Book of Heroic & Outrageous Women, 7–8

Managing Menopause Naturally: Before, During, and Forever, 172

Manheim, Camryn, 152

Manifesta: Young Women, Feminism, and the Future, 296–97

Mankiller: A Chief and Her People, 20

Mankiller, Wilma Pearl, 20

Manning, Brennan, 123

Manresa, Kim, 360

Mansfield, L. G., 190

Mao: The Unknown Story, 31

Mapes, Diane, 96

The Mapmaker's Wife: A True Tale of Love, Murder, and Survival in the Amazon, 260

Marcantel, Pamela, 11

Marcello, Patricia Cronin, 29

Marchetto, Marisa Acocella, 157

Marcic, Dorothy, 294

Marcotte, Amanda, 301

Margolis, Cindy, 105

Margolis, Jane, 313

Margolis, Jonathan, 73

Marie Antoinette: The Journey, 17

Marie Antoinette: The Last Queen of France, 17

Marie Curie: A Life, 12

Marker, Gary, 32

Markey, Kevin, 9

Markham, Beryl, 258

Mark, Lisa Gabrielle, 300

Markoe, Glenn, 214

Marks, Lara, 206

Marks, Shelly, 179

Márquez, María Teresa, 70

Marriage, a History: From Obedience to Intimacy, or How Love Conquered Marriage, 89

Married Women Who Love Women, 93

Marshall, Jennifer A., 96

Martin, Courtney E., 150

Martin, Dawn Lundy, 303

Martin, Edwin B., 339

Martin, Katherine, 10, 76

Martínez, Tomás Eloy, 6

Mary, Called Magdalene, 217

MaryJane's Ideabook, Cookbook, Lifebook: For the Farmgirl in All of Us, 309

Mary Magdalene, the First Apostle: The Struggle for Authority, 217

Mary Queen of Scotland and the Isles: A Novel, 18

Mary, Queen of Scots, 17

Mary, Queen of Scots, and the Murder of Lord Darnley, 18

The Mask of Motherhood: How Becoming a Mother Changes Everything and Why We Pretend It Doesn't, 100

Mason, Mary Ann, 371

Mass, Leslie, 251

Massacre of the Dreamers: Essays on Xicanisma, 288

Massé, Sydna, 183

Massey, Mary Elizabeth, 234–45

Massotty, Susan, 47–48

Master Dating: How to Meet & Attract Quality Men!, 84

Masuda Sayo, 33

Matasar, Ann B., 310–11

Mathewes-Green, Frederica, 357

Mathieson, Sherrie, 188

Mattioni, Gloria, 9–10

Maurine, Camille, 117

Maushart, Susan, 100

May, Kathryn E., 357–58

May, Rachel, 32

Mazel, David, 258

McCall Smith, Alexander, 196

McCauley, Lucy, 118, 255, 271

McCloskey, Deirdre N., 42

McCorvey, Norma, 356

McCracken, Elizabeth, 181

McCrumb, Sharyn, 62–63

McCullough, Colleen, 246

McDermott, Rachel Fell, 132

McEvoy, John, 321–22

McEvoy, Julia, 321–22

McFeely, Mary Drake, 240

McGovern, George S., 162

McIntosh, Elizabeth P., 262

McKelvey, Tara, 365

McKinley, Robin, 196

McLean, Lorna R., 237

McPhillips, Caitilin, 172

Meaker, Marijane, 42–43

Meditation Secrets for Women: Discovering Your Passion, Pleasure, and Inner Peace, 117

Meditations for Women Who Do Too Much, 118

Meeting Faith: The Forest Journals of a Black Buddhist Nun, 61

Mellor, Christie, 102

Memoirs of a Courtesan in Nineteenth-Century Paris, 228

Memoirs of a Geisha, 62

Memoirs of a Soldier, Nurse, and Spy: A Woman's Adventures in the Union Army, 38

The Memoirs of Catherine the Great, 20

The Memoirs of Cleopatra: A Novel, 19

Men Are from Mars, Women Are from Venus: The Classic Guide to Understanding the Opposite Sex, 328

Men Are Like Fish: What Every Woman Needs to Know about Catching a Man, 88

Menchú, Rigoberta, 34

Mendelsohn, Jane, 14

Mendible, Myra, 151

Mendoza, Sylvia, 75

Menelli, Sheri, 111
Menocal, Maria Rosa, 19
Menzie, Morgan, 159
A Mercy, 51
The Mermaid Chair, 136
Mernissi, Fatima, 219
Merryman, Molly, 244
Messer, Ellen, 357–58
Metcalfe, Gayden, 94
Mexico, A Love Story: Women Write about the Mexican Experience, 267–68
Meyers, Carol L., 214
Michaels, Meredith W., 102–103
Middlesex, 373
A Midwife's Story, 110
Midwives, 135
Migrations of the Heart: An Autobiography, 49
Milazzo, Vickie L., 341
A Mile in Her Boots: Women Who Work in the Wild, 252
Miles, Rosalind, 200, 203
Miller, Arthur, 225
Miller, Ernestine G., 322–23
Miller, Jean Baker, 69
Miller, Jessica, 335
Miller, John, 10
Miller, Karin B., 154
Miller, Lee E., 335
Miller, Marshall, 88
Miller, Michael, 83
Miller, Neil, 238
Millman, Marcia, 76
Mills, Kay, 53, 203
Milne, Carly, 362
Min, Anchee, 21
Mindell, Phyllis, 336
A Mind of Its Own: A Cultural History of the Penis, 192
Mineko, Iwasaki, 33
Minkin, Mary Jane, 164
Mirabile, Michele Hunter, 324
Miriam's Kitchen: A Memoir, 55–56
Miriam's Well: Rituals for Jewish Women around the Year, 126
Mirror, Mirror: Self-Portraits by Women Artists, 74
Miscarriage, Women Sharing from the Heart, 179
Misconceptions: Truth, Lies, and the Unexpected on the Journey to Motherhood, 101

Misquoting Jesus: The Story behind Who Changed the Bible and Why, 124
Mistress of the Art of Death, 278
Mistress of the House, Mistress of Heaven: Women in Ancient Egypt, 214
The Mists of Avalon, 246
Mitchell, Brian, 324–25
Mitchell, Margaret, 246
Mitchell, S. E., 205
Miya-Jervis, Lisa, 84, 302
Mo, Yan, 31
Mo'Nique, 152
Moats, David, 301
Modern African Women (In Praise of Black Women), 204–205
The Modern Girl's Guide to Life, 173
The Modern Goddess' Guide to Life: How to Be Absolutely Divine on a Daily Basis, 173
Modern Love: 50 True and Extraordinary Tales of Desire, Deceit, and Devotion, 84
Modern Women of the Diaspora (In Praise of Black Women), 204–205
Mohrbacher, Nancy, 110
Moir, Anne, 68
Molinary, Rosie, 150
Momfidence!: An Oreo Never Killed Anybody and Other Secrets of Happier Parenting, 101
Mommy Millionaire: How I Turned My Kitchen Table Idea into a Million Dollars and How You Can, Too!, 330–31
The Mommy Myth: The Idealization of Motherhood and How It Has Undermined All Women, 102–103
Mommy Wars: Stay-at-Home and Career Moms Face Off on Their Choices, Their Lives, Their Families, 372–73
Mom's Cancer, 157
Momsen, Janet Henshall, 239
Monaghan, Patricia, 133–34
Monahan, Evelyn, 263
Money without Matrimony: The Unmarried Couple's Guide to Financial Security, 88
Monique and the Mango Rains: Two Years with a Midwife in Mali, 110
Monosoff, Tamara, 331
Monstrous Regiment, 279
Montoya, Delilah, 70

Mookerjee, Ajit, 133
Moore, Alan, 279
Moore, Kathleen M., 128
Moore, Lucy, 222–23
Moore, Suzanne, 79
Mootoo, Shani, 374
The Moral Property of Women: A History of Birth Control Politics in America, 208
Mor, Barbara, 116
Moraga, Cherríe, 302
Moran, Lindsay, 262
Moran, Michelle, 214
Morantz-Sanchez, Regina Markell, 318
More Sand in My Bra: Funny Women Write from the Road, Again, 271
More, Ellen Singer, 318
More, Now, Again: A Memoir of Addiction, 162
Moreno, Robyn, 51
Morgan, Angie, 342
Morgan, Elaine, 73
Morgan, Joan, 294–95
Morgan, Lael, 232
Morgan, Robin, 292, 305
Moriyama, Naomi, 144
The Morning After: Sex, Fear, and Feminism on Campus, 294
Morris, Desmond, 73
Morris, Mary, 8, 274
Morrison, Dorothy, 134
Morrison, Susan, 4
Morrison, Toni, 51, 196
Moses, Kate, 100
Mosquito, 306
Mother, Daughter, Sister, Bride: Rituals of Womanhood, 73
Motherhood Is Not for Wimps: No Answers, Just Stories, 98
The Motherhood Manifesto: What America's Moms Want and What to Do about It, 371
Motherhood: The Second Oldest Profession, 98
The Mother of All Pregnancy Books, 111
Mothers & Daughters, 80
Mothers and Daughters in the Twentieth Century: A Literary Anthology, 99
Mothers and Daughters: Women of the Intelligentsia in Nineteenth Century Russia, 228
Mother Shock: Loving Every (Other) Minute of It, 103

Mothers of Invention: From the Bra to the Bomb: Forgotten Women and Their Unforgettable Ideas, 316
Mothers on the Fast Track: How a New Generation Can Balance Family and Careers, 371
Mothers Who Think: Tales of Real-life Parenthood, 100
Mother Teresa: A Complete Authorized Biography, 60
Mother Teresa: Come Be My Light: The Private Writings of the "Saint of Calcutta, 60
The Mother Trip: Hip Mama's Guide to Staying Sane in the Chaos of Motherhood, 100
Moule, Ian A., 314
Mountaineering Stories of Adventurous Women, 251
Mountaineering Women: Stories by Early Climbers, 258
Moving beyond Words, 292
Moving the Mountain: The Women's Movement in America since 1960, 286
Mr. Wrong: Real-Life Stories about the Men We Used to Love, 89
Mrozik, Susanne, 130
Mrs. Pollifax mysteries, 278
Ms. and the Material Girls: Perceptions of Women from the 1970s through the 1990s, 238
Mulvey, Kate, 188
Munker, Dona, 34
Murcott, Susan, 60
Murder and the First Lady, 6
Murder in Byzantium, 219
Murder of a Medici Princess, 18
Murkoff, Heidi Eisenberg, 111
Murphy, Caroline P., 18
Murphy, Yannick, 264
Muscio, Inga, 76
Muslim Women in America: The Challenge of Islamic Identity Today, 128
Myers, Dee Dee, 342
My Forbidden Face: Growing Up under the Taliban: A Young Woman's Story, 33
My Grandfather's Son: A Memoir, 340
My Hitch in Hell: The Bataan Death March, 263

My Husband Betty: Love, Sex, and Life with a Crossdresser, 25

My Husband Wears My Clothes: Crossdressing from the Perspective of a Wife, 25

My Journey to Lhasa: The Classic Story of the Only Western Woman Who Succeeded in Entering the Forbidden City, 273

Myles, Bruce, 244

My Little Red Book, 91

My Miserable, Lonely, Lesbian Pregnancy, 107

Myron Bolitar series, 347

My Sister, My Self: Understanding the Sibling Relationship That Shapes Our Lives, Our Loves, and Ourselves, 76

My Soul Is a Woman: The Feminine in Islam, 128

The Mysterious Private Thompson: The Double Life of Sarah Emma Edmonds, Civil War Soldier, 38

The Myth of Male Power: Why Men Are the Disposable Sex, 340

Nadell, Pamela Susan, 318–19

Nafisi, Azar, 34

Nagle, Jill, 362

Nakamoto, Steve, 88

Naked Ambition: Women Who Are Changing Pornography, 362

Naked on the Page: The Misadventures of My Unmarried Midlife, 94

The Naked Truth: A Working Woman's Manifesto on Business and What Really Matters, 336

The Naked Woman: A Study of the Female Body, 73

Nam, Vickie, 53

Naranjo-Huebl, Linda, 357

Nashat, Guity, 204

Nathan, Amy, 310

National Council of Women's Organizations, 303

Navarro, Marysa, 7, 204

Nazer, Mende, 359

Necessary Dreams: Ambition in Women's Changing Lives, 69

Nefertiti, 214

Neidel-Greenlee, Rosemary, 263

Neiman, Debra A., 88

Nemat, Marina, 35

Nestle, Joan, 355

Neuburger, Karen, 78

Neuls-Bates, Carol, 204

The New Feminine Brain: Developing Your Intuitive Genius, 71

Newitz, Annalee, 313

Newman, Catherine, 101

Newman, Felice, 168

Newman, Janis Cooke, 106

The New Single Woman, 94

The Next Fifty Years: A Guide for Women at Mid-Life and Beyond, 175

Nguyen, Bich Minh, 48

Nice Girls Don't Get Rich: 75 Avoidable Mistakes Women Make with Money, 345

Nice Girls Don't Get the Corner Office: 101 Unconscious Mistakes Women Make That Sabotage Their Careers, 334

Nickel and Dimed: On (Not) Getting by in America, 152–53

Nielsen, Jerri, 255

Nien Cheng, 31

Nies, Judith, 4

Night Witches: The Untold Story of Soviet Women in Combat, 244

Nike Is a Goddess: The History of Women in Sports, 322

Nine Lives: Stories of Women Business Owners Landing on Their Feet, 327

Nine Women: Portraits from the American Radical Tradition, 4

The No. 1 Ladies' Detective Agency, 196

Nobile, Amy, 103

Nobody Passes: Rejecting the Rules of Gender and Conformity, 355

Nochlin, Linda, 300

No Horizon Is So Far: Two Women and Their Extraordinary Journey across Antarctica, 251–52

Nomura, Gail M., 54

No Place for a Lady: Tales of Adventurous Women Travelers, 274

Norman, Elizabeth M., 263

Norris, Pippa, 352

The Northern Region (Women Writing Africa), 205

North of Unknown: Mina Hubbard's Extraordinary Expedition into the Labrador Wilderness, 260

Northrup, Christiane, 141–42, 171

The Norton Book of Women's Lives, 26
The Nursing Mother's Companion, 110
Norton, Mary Beth, 224–25
Nossel, Suzanne, 319
No Time to Die: Living with Ovarian Cancer, 155
Not for Sale: Feminists Resisting Prostitution and Pornography, 360
Nothing Sacred: Women Respond to Religious Fundamentalism and Terror;, 364
Nothing to Do but Stay, 231
Not My Mother's Sister: Generational Conflict and Third-Wave Feminism, 300
No Turning Back: The History of Feminism and the Future of Women, 285
Not Your Mother's Midlife: A Ten-Step Guide to Fearless Aging, 175
Nothing to Lose: A Guide to Sane Living in a Larger Body, 148–49
Now and Not Yet: Making Sense of Single Life in the Twenty-First Century, 96
No Way Renée: The Second Half of My Notorious Life, 43
Now Is the Time to Open Your Heart, 374
Nuland, Sherwin B., 318

O: The Intimate History of the Orgasm, 73
O'Brien, Virginia, 327
Obsessive Genius: The Inner World of Marie Curie, 12
O'Connor, Karen, 369
O'Connor, Larry, 8
O'Connor, Sandra Day, 12
Odd Girls and Twilight Lovers: A History of Lesbian Life in Twentieth-Century America, 238
An Officer and a Lady: The World War II Letters of Lt. Col. Betty Bandel, Women's Army Corps, 37
Offill, Jenny, 80
Ogden, Gina, 167
Ohitika Woman, 46
O'Keeffe, Linda, 189
Oke, Janette, 63
The Old Girls' Network: Insider Advice for Women Building Businesses in a Man's World, 332
Olwell, Carol, 233
On Agate Hill, 136
On Basilisk Station, 279

On Call in Hell: A Doctor's Iraq War Story, 264
Ondaatje, Michael, 245
One False Move, 347
One of the Guys: Women as Aggressors and Torturers, 365
One Woman's Army: The Commanding General of Abu Ghraib Tells Her Story, 365
One Woman's War: Letters Home from the Women's Army Corps, 1944–1946, 37
The One Year Book of Devotions for Women, 121
On Her Own Ground: The Life and Times of Madam C.J. Walker, 46
The Only Woman in the Room: A Memoir, 32
On My Own Two Feet: A Modern Girl's Guide to Personal Finance, 346
On Pilgrimage: A Time to Seek, 113
On the Pill: A Social History of Oral Contraceptives, 1950–1970, 207
On the Trail of the Women Warriors: The Amazons in Myth and History, 215
On Women Turning 30: Making Choices, Finding Meaning, 175
On Women Turning 50: Celebrating Mid-Life Discoveries, 175
On Women Turning 60: Embracing the Age of Fulfillment, 175
On Women Turning 70: Honoring the Voices of Wisdom, 175
On Your Own: The Complete Guide to Adopting as a Single Parent, 103
Opening the Lotus: A Woman's Guide to Buddhism, 129–30
Operating Instructions: A Journal of My Son's First Year, 101
Opting Out?: Why Women Really Quit Careers and Head Home, 373
The Ordeal of Elizabeth Marsh: A Woman in World History, 15
Orenstein, Peggy, 106
Orleck, Annelise, 354
Orman, Suze, 345
The Ornament of the World: How Muslims, Jews and Christians Created a Culture of Tolerance in Medieval Spain, 19
Orndorff, Kata, 91
O'Rourke, Kate, 237
Ostler, Sue, 97
The Other Civil War: American Women in the Nineteenth Century, 229

The Other Side of War: Women's Stories of Survival & Hope, 364

The Other Woman, 136

The Other Woman: Twenty-one Wives, Lovers, and Others Talk Openly about Sex, Deception, Love, and Betrayal, 89

Ouchi, Rande Brown, 33

Our Bodies, Ourselves: A New Edition for a New Era, 141

Our Bodies, Ourselves: Menopause, 169–70

Our Cancer Year, 157

Our Lady of Weight Loss: Miraculous and Motivational Musings from the Patron Saint of Permanent Fat Removal, 142

Our Mothers' War: American Women at Home and at the Front During World War II, 245

Our Stories of Miscarriage: Healing with Words, 179

Outing Yourself: How to Come Out as Lesbian or Gay to Your Family, Friends, and Coworkers, 92–93

Out of Africa, 258

Out of the Past: Gay and Lesbian History from 1869 to the Present, 238

Out of the Shadows: Contributions of Twentieth-Century Women to Physics, 316

Out to Work: A History of Wage-Earning Women in the United States, 210

Outrageous Acts and Everyday Rebellions, 29

Over the Hill and between the Sheets: Sex, Love, and Lust in Middle Age, 169

Page, Cristina, 358

Pagels, Elaine H., 124

Paglia, Camille, 294

Pallingston, Jessica, 193–94

Palmer, Barbara, 369

Palmer, Laura, 180

Pandora's Daughters: The Role and Status of Women in Greek and Roman Antiquity, 214

Paris Fashion: A Cultural History, 224

Parmar, Pratibha, 360

Participation and Protest: Women and Politics in a Global World, 367

Passage, 347

Passionate Minds: Women Rewriting the World, 9

Passport to Beauty: Secrets and Tips from around the World for Becoming a Global Goddess, 194

Patai, Daphne, 340

Patently Female: From AZT to TV Dinners: Stories of Women Inventors and Their Breakthrough Ideas, 315

The Path of the Mother, 132

Paul, Pamela, 361

Paul, Sheryl, 85

Paving the Way for Madam President, 366

Paz, Octavio, 122

Pearls, Politics, & Power: How Women Can Win and Lead, 368

Pease, Allan, 336

Pease, Barbara, 336

Peavy, Linda S., 233

Peay, Pythia, 118

Pechilis, Karen, 58

Pedersen, Stephanie, 187, 189

Pederson, Rena, 59

Peiss, Kathy Lee, 194

Pekar, Harvey, 157

Pendle, Karin, 203–204

The Penguin Atlas of Women in the World, 355

Pennington, Reina, 244

Perdue, Theda, 45, 226

Perfect Girls, Starving Daughters: The Frightening New Normalcy of Hating Your Body, 150

Perfect Madness: Motherhood in the Age of Anxiety, 102

Perfection Salad: Women and Cooking at the Turn of the Century, 240

The Perfect Sister: What Draws Us Together, What Drives Us Apart, 76

The Perfect Storm: A True Story of Men against the Sea, 253

Peri, Camille, 100

Pernoud, Régine, 10–11

Perón, Eva, 6

Perrot, Michelle, 201

Perrottet, Tony, 275

Perry, Thomas, 374

Perry-Mason, Gail, 344

Persepolis, 36

Persepolis 2: The Story of a Return, 36

Personal Recollections of Joan of Arc, 247

Peskowitz, Miriam, 372
Peters, Julie Ann, 63
*Petticoat Whalers: Whaling Wives at Sea,
    1820–1920,* 257
Phillips, Catherine Lee, 309
Phillips, Joan, 183
Picoult, Jodi, 136
*A Piece of My Heart: Living through the Grief
    of Miscarriage, Stillbirth, or Infant
    Death,* 179
*A Piece of My Heart: The Stories of 26
    American Women Who Served in
    Vietnam,* 245
Piepmeier, Alison, 297
Pierpont, Claudia Roth, 9
Pilgrim at Tinker Creek, 269
Pilkington, Doris, 259
The Pilot's Wife, 136
*Pimps Up, Ho's Down: Hip Hop's Hold
    on Young Black Women,* 294
Pinker, Susan, 327
*Pinstripes & Pearls: The Women of the
    Harvard Law Class of '64 Who Forged
    an Old Girl Network and Paved the
    Way for Future Generations,* 318
Pintus, Lorraine, 85, 165
*Pin-up Grrrls: Feminism, Sexuality, Popular
    Culture,* 351
*Pioneer Doctor: The Story of a Woman's
    Work,* 14
*Pioneer Women: The Lives of Women on
    the Frontier,* 233
*The Pirate Queen: In Search of Grace
    O'Malley and Other Legendary
    Women of the Sea,* 16
*Pistol Packin' Madams: True Stories of
    Notorious Women of the Old West,*
    231
The Pivot of Civilization, 5
*'Plain Anne Ellis'; More about the Life of an
    Ordinary Woman,* 231
Plan B: Further Thoughts on Faith, 123
*Plant Seed, Pull Weed: Nurturing the
    Garden of Your Life,* 130
Plante, Ellen M., 229
*Play Like a Man, Win Like a Woman: What
    Men Know about Success That Women
    Need to Learn,* 335
*Pleasure: A Woman's Guide to Getting
    the Sex You Want, Need, and
    Deserve,* 166–67
Plunkett, John, 22

PMS [Problems Men Started], 172
*Pocahontas: Medicine Woman, Spy,
    Entrepreneur, Diplomat,* 44
*Pocahontas, Powhatan, Opechancanough:
    Three Indian Lives Changed by
    Jamestown,* 44
*The Pocket Stylist: Behind-the-Scenes
    Expertise from a Fashion Pro on
    Creating Your Own Unique Look,* 190
Poemas de Amor, 122
*Poems, Protest, and a Dream: Selected
    Writings,* 122
Pogrebin, Letty Cottin, 288
Pokorny, Sydney, 92
*The Politics of Women's Bodies: Sexuality,
    Appearance, and Behavior,* 148
Polk, Milbry, 273–74
Pollitt, Katha, 354
Pomeroy, Sarah B., 215
Pop: A Celebration of Black Fatherhood, 82
Porn for Women, 172
*Pornified: How Pornography Is Transforming
    Our Lives, Our Relationships, and Our
    Families,* 361
*The Porning of America: The Rise of Porn
    Culture, What It Means, and Where
    We Go from Here,* 290
*Portrait of a Priestess: Women and
    Ritual in Ancient Greece,* 216
*Portraits of American Women: From
    Settlement to the Present,* 8
Posner, Trisha, 171–72
Possessing the Secret of Joy, 374
Potter, Daniel A., 106
Pough, Gwendolyn D., 293
*The Power of Feminist Art: The American
    Movement of the 1970s, History and
    Impact,* 9
*Praise Her Works: Conversations with
    Biblical Women,* 125
Prasso, Sheridan, 304
Pratchett, Terry, 279, 306
*Pregnancy and Power: A Short History of
    Reproductive Politics in America,*
    208
*Pregnancy: The Ultimate Week-by-Week
    Pregnancy Guide,* 111
Prep, 374
Pressler, Mirjam, 47–48
*Presumed Equal: What America's Top
    Women Lawyers Really Think
    about Their Firms,* 319

Pretty Is What Changes: Impossible Choices, the Breast Cancer Gene, and How I Defied My Destiny, 156–57
Price, David A., 44
Price, Joan, 87
The Price of Motherhood: Why the Most Important Job in the World Is Still the Least Valued, 371
The Price of Salt, 42
Prime: Adventures and Advice on Sex, Love, and the Sensual Years, 87
Prince Michael of Greece, 20–21
Prioleau, Elizabeth Stevens, 207
Prisoner of Tehran: A Memoir, 35
The Prisoner's Wife: A Memoir, 83
Proctor, Tammy M., 264
The Prodigal Daughter, 347
Pro Life Answers to Pro Choice Arguments, 356
Prolife Feminism: Yesterday and Today, 357
Promises I Can Keep: Why Poor Women Put Motherhood before Marriage, 372
Prozac Nation: Young and Depressed in America, 163
Pryce, Lois, 272
Pryor, Liz, 80
Ptacek, Greg, 315
The Pumpkin Patch: A Single Woman's International Adoption Journey, 106
Punch! Why Women Participate in Violent Sports, 70
Pushed: The Painful Truth about Childbirth and Modern Maternity Care, 107–108
Pybus, Cassandra, 259
Pythagoras' Trousers: God, Physics, and the Gender Wars, 316

Queen Isabella: Treachery, Adultery, and Murder in Medieval England, 23–24
Queen of Fashion: What Marie Antoinette Wore to the Revolution, 223
Queen of Scots: The True Life of Mary Stuart, 17–18
Queen of Shadows: A Novel of Isabella, Wife of King Edward II, 24
Queen Victoria (Lytton Strachey), 21
Queen Victoria (Walter L. Arnstein), 22
Queen Victoria: A Personal History, 22
Queen Victoria: First Media Monarch, 22
Queens: Portraits of Black Women and Their Fabulous Hair, 186

Queiroz, Juan Pablo, 7
Queller, Jessica, 156–57
Quiet as a Nun, 200
Quiet Odyssey: A Pioneer Korean Woman in America, 52
The Quiet Room: A Journey Out of the Torment of Madness, 156
Quinn, Susan, 12
Qur'an and Woman: Rereading the Sacred Text from a Woman's Perspective, 129

Rabbit-Proof Fence, 259
Rabin, Vivian Steir, 371
Race, Gender, and the Politics of Skin Tone, 49
Rachel's Holiday, 195
Racz, Justin, 84
The Ragamuffin Gospel: Good News for the Bedraggled, Beat-Up, and Burnt Out, 123
Ragas, Meg Cohen, 194
Raicho, Hiratsuka, 32
Raine, Nancy Venable, 184
Raines, Jenyne M., 174
Rakhra, B. K., 26
Ralston, Aron, 255
Ramos, Isabel, 360
Ramphele, Mamphela, 35
Ramusack, Barbara N., 204
Rassweiler, Anne Dickason, 32
Rauch, Jonathan, 301
Rayner-Canham, Geoffrey, 314
Rayner-Canham, Marelene F., 314
Reading Lolita in Tehran: A Memoir in Books, 34
Reading the Women of the Bible, 216–17
Reading Women, 309
Read My Lips: A Cultural History of Lipstick, 194
Reagan, Leslie J., 358
Real Choices: Listening to Women, Looking for Alternatives to Abortion, 357
Real Sex: The Naked Truth about Chastity, 86–86
Real You Incorporated: 8 Essentials for Women Entrepreneurs, 331
Reardon, David C., 183
Rebirth of the Goddess: Finding Meaning in Feminist Spirituality, 133

Reckless: The Outrageous Lives of Nine Kick-Ass Women, 9–10
Redd, Nancy Amanda, 151
Redgrove, Peter, 171
The Red Tent, 62
Redworth, Glyn, 59
Reed, Betsy, 364
Reed, Kit, 150
Rees, Sian, 258
Reflections in a Jaundiced Eye, 42
Regaining Your Self: Breaking Free from the Eating Disorder Identity: A Bold New Approach, 160
Rehman, Bushra, 292
Reichman, Judith, 164
Reichs, Kathy, 347
Reid, Constance, 28–29
Reiland, Rachel, 156
Reilly, Maura, 300
Reinisch, June Machover, 166
Renaissance and Enlightenment Paradoxes (A History of Women in the West), 201
Respect: Women and Popular Music, 294
Restoring the Balance: Women Physicians and the Profession of Medicine, 1850–1995, 318
Restoring Women to History series, 204
Rethinking Canada: The Promise of Women's History, 237
Rethinking Madam President: Are We Ready for a Woman in the White House?, 367–68
Revelations of a Single Woman: Loving the Life I Didn't Expect, 96
Revelations of Divine Love, 57
Reverby, Susan, 210
Revolution from Within: A Book of Self-Esteem, 174
Revolutionary Mothers: Women in the Struggle for America's Independence, 224
Rhode, Deborah L., 343–44
Rhys, Jean, 63
Rice, Luanne, 136
Rich, Doris L., 14
Richards, Amy, 296–97, 303
Richards, Melissa, 188
Richards, Renée, 43
Rico, Yrma, 337
Riddle, John M., 207
Rideal, Liz, 74

Right Stuff, Wrong Sex: America's First Women in Space Program, 314–15
Rigoberta Menchú and the Story of All Poor Guatemalans, 34
Rikleen, Lauren Stiller, 319
Riley, Laura, 111
Rinehart, Paula, 87
Rinehart, Stacy, 87
Ringdal, Nils Johan, 363
Riordan, Teresa, 194
The Risks of Sunbathing Topless: And Other Funny Stories from the Road, 268
Rivenbark, Celia, 42
Roach, Mary, 190
Roar Softly and Carry a Great Lipstick: 28 Women Writers on Life, Sex, and Survival, 174
Robbins, Trina, 311
Roberts, Cokie, 226
Robertson, Janet, 273
Robinson, Alex, 161
Robinson, Jane, 274, 311–12
Roche, Lorin, 117
Rodeo Girl, 232
Rodriguez, Deborah, 27
Roe v. Wade: The Abortion Rights Controversy in American History, 208
Rogers, Susan Fox, 256
Roghaar, Linda, 119
Rohrer, Lynette, 211
Roiphe, Katie, 294
Roller Derby: The History and All-Girl Revival of the Greatest Sport on Wheels, 240
Rollergirl: Totally True Tales from the Track, 240
Romero, Mary, 354
A Room of One's Own, 296
Roosevelt, Eleanor, 6
Roosevelt, Elliott, 6
Roper, K. Sue, 263
Rosalind Franklin and DNA, 13
Rosalind Franklin: The Dark Lady of DNA, 13
Rose Madder, 196
Rose, Phyllis, 26
Rose, Tricia, 168
Rosen, Ruth, 285
Rosenau, Douglas, 166
Rosenberg, Helena Hacker, 86
Ross, Carol, 82
Rossiter, Margaret W., 315

Roston, Miles, 105

Rouda, Kaira Sturdivant, 331

Rounding, Virginia, 20, 228

Rountree, Cathleen, 175

Rountree, Helen C., 44

Rouse, Carolyn Moxley, 56

Route 66 A.D.: On the Trail of Ancient Roman Tourists, 275

Rowe-Finkbeiner, Kristin, 303, 371

Rozler, Jessica, 167

Rubin, Courtney, 143

Rubyfruit Jungle, 62

Rudd, Peggy J., 25

Ruff, Cheryl Lynn, 263

Ruff's War: A Navy Nurse on the Frontline in Iraq, 263

Ruíz, Vicki, 241

Rule Number Two: Lessons I Learned in a Combat Hospital, 264

Rumors of Our Progress Have Been Greatly Exaggerated: Why Women's Lives Aren't Getting Any Easier—and How We Can Make Real Progress for Ourselves and Our Daughters, 301

Running with Scissors: A Memoir, 184

Russ, Joanna, 287

Russell, Maria, 145

The Russian Word for Snow: A True Story of Adoption, 106

Russia through Women's Eyes: Autobiographies from Tsarist Russia, 32

Russo, Carolyn, 310

Ruttenberg, Danya, 126

Saboura, Sam, 190

Sacker, Ira M., 160

Sacks, Rhona, 91

Sacred Energies: When the World's Religions Sit Down to Talk about the Future of Human Life and the Plight of This Planet, 357

The Sacred Hoop: Recovering the Feminine in American Indian Traditions, 113

Sacred Rights: The Case for Contraception and Abortion in World Religions, 356–57

Sacred Voices: Essential Women's Wisdom through the Ages, 115

Safety and Security for Women Who Travel, 277

Sage, Jesse, 359

Sailing, 145

Saks, Elyn R., 155

Salbi, Zainab, 364

The Salem Witch Trials Reader, 225

Saline, Carol, 75, 80–81

Salmansohn, Karen, 97

Salzman, Mark, 63

Sam Saboura's Real Style: Style Secrets for Real Women with Real Bodies, 190

Sanbonmatsu, Kira, 369–70

Sand in My Bra and Other Misadventures: Funny Women Write from the Road, 271

Sandoz, Joli, 146

Sandra Day O'Connor: How the First Woman on the Supreme Court Became Its Most Influential Justice, 11

Sanger, Margaret, 5

Santa Evita, 7

Santiago, Esmeralda, 47

Sarah, 123

Sarah: How a Hockey Mom Turned the Political Establishment Upside Down, 368

Sark, 174

Sarracino, Carmine, 290

Satrapi, Marjane, 36

Savage, Dan, 107

Sayo, Masuda, 33

Sayre, Anne, 13

Schaef, Anne Wilson, 118

Schaeffer, Kurtis R., 59

Schappell, Elissa, 80

Schecter, Jill, 320

Schell, Patience A., 205

Schenone, Laura, 211

Schiff, Karenna Gore, 8

Schiller, Lori, 156

Schimmel, Annemarie, 128

Schlaffer, Edit, 297

Schmitt Pantel, Pauline, 201

Schneider, Carl J., 319–20

Schneider, Dorothy, 319–20

Schneir, Miriam, 286

Schoenfeld, Brad, 147

Schoenfeldt, Beth, 329

Schroeder, Susan, 213

Schultz, Jane E., 235
Schulz, Mona Lisa, 71
Schwab, Christine, 185–86
Schwartz, Margaret L., 106
Schwartz, Pepper, 87
Schwarz-Bart, André, 204–105
Schwarz-Bart, Simone, 204–105
Schwarzer, Elizabeth Soutter, 98
Schwegel, Janet, 111
Sciachitano, Marian, 54
Science Has No Sex: The Life of Marie Zakrzewska, M.D., 14
Scientists Anonymous: Great Stories of Women in Science., 313
Scoot Over, Skinny: The Fat Nonfiction Anthology, 152
Scott, Kevin M., 290
Scott, Manda, 16
Scruggs, Afi, 119
Sculpting Her Body Perfect, 147
Sea Legs: Tales of a Woman Oceanographer, 254
Seafaring Women: Adventures of Pirate Queens, Female Stowaways, and Sailors' Wives, 257
Seager, Joni, 355
Seagrave, Peggy, 21
Seagrave, Sterling, 21
Seagraves, Anne, 231
Sebold, Alice, 183–84
The Second Sex, 288
The Secret Language of Girlfriends: Talking Loudly, Laughing Wildly, and Making the Most of Our Most Important Friendships, 78
The Secret Life of Bees, 136
The Secret Lives of Alexandra David-Neel: A Biography of the Explorer of Tibet and Its Forbidden Practices, 273
Secret Service: Untold Stories of Lesbians in the Military, 324
Secret Survivors: Uncovering Incest and Its Aftereffects in Women, 178
Secrets of a Former Fat Girl: How to Lose Two, Four (or More!) Dress Sizes, and Find Yourself along the Way, 142
Secrets of Millionaire Moms: Learn How They Turned Great Ideas into Booming Businesses—And How You Can Too!, 331

Secrets of Six-Figure Women: Surprising Strategies to Up Your Earnings and Change Your Life, 337
Seductress: Women Who Ravished the World and Their Lost Art of Love, 207
See Jane Lead: 99 Ways for Women to Take Charge at Work, 341
Seeing Ourselves: Women's Self-Portraits, 74
Seely, Megan, 304
Seibel, Machelle M., 116
Self-Made Man: One Woman's Journey into Manhood and Back Again, 152
Seligson, Susan, 190
Sentance, Bryan, 200
Serano, Julia, 355
The Serpent's Tale, 278
Serving in Silence, 324
Sevcik, Kimberley, 298
Sex and the Seasoned Woman: Pursuing the Passionate Life, 169
Sex and the Soul of a Woman: The Reality of Love & Romance in an Age of Casual Sex, 87
Sex for One: The Joy of Selfloving, 95, 165
The Sex of Class: Women Transforming American Labor, 210
Sex on the Brain: The Biological Differences between Men and Women, 71
Sex with Kings: 500 Years of Adultery, Power, Rivalry, and Revenge, 206
Sex with the Queen: 900 Years of Vile Kings, Virile Lovers, and Passionate Politics, 206
Sex Work: Writings by Women in the Sex Industry, 363
Sexual Behavior in the Human Female, 166
Sexual Behavior in the Human Male, 166
Sexual Chemistry: A History of the Contraceptive Pill, 206
Sexual Harassment in the Workplace, 339
The Sexual Healing Journey: A Guide for Survivors of Sexual Abuse, 178–79
The Sexual Paradox: Men, Women and the Real Gender Gap, 327
Sexual Personae: Art and Decadence from Nefertiti to Emily Dickinson, 294
Sexy at Any Size: The Real Woman's Guide to Dating and Romance, 82
Sey, Jennifer, 322

Seyder Tkhines: The Forgotten Book of Common Prayer for Jewish Women, 127

Shacking Up: The Smart Girl's Guide to Living in Sin without Getting Burned, 88

The Shadow Negotiation: How Women Can Master the Hidden Agendas That Determine Bargaining Success, 337

Shah, Sonia, 304

Shahar, Shulamith, 220

Shalit, Wendy, 360

Shall We Tell the President?, 347

Shame on It All, 137

Shanker, Wendy, 151–52

Shannon, Jacqueline, 82

Shapiro, Laura, 240

Shapiro, Lisa Wood, 109–10

Shards of Honor, 278

Sharma, Arvind, 120

Sharp Spear, Crystal Mirror: Martial Arts in Women's Lives, 323

Sharpley-Whiting, T. Denean, 294

Shattering the Stereotypes: Muslim Women Speak Out, 128

Shayler, David, 314

The She-Apostle: The Extraordinary Life and Death of Luisa de Carvajal, 59

Sheean, Vincent, 12

Sheehy, Gail, 169

Sheehy, Sandy, 81

Sheffield, Suzanne Le-May, 315

Sheggeby, Dawn, 75

Shelton, Brenda K., 203

Shelton, Christine, 343

Sheridan, Sybil, 319

Sherman, Alexa Joy, 167

Sherman, Lisa G., 320

Sherwood, Frances, 246–47

She's Not the Man I Married: My Life with a Transgender Husband, 25

She's Not There: A Life in Two Genders, 43

She's Such a Geek! Women Write about Science, Technology, and Other Nerdy Stuff, 313

She Went to the Field: Women Soldiers of the Civil War, 234

She Went to War: The Rhonda Cornum Story, 261

She Who Dwells Within: A Feminist Vision of a Renewed Judaism, 126

She Who Prays: A Woman's Interfaith Prayer Book, 122

She Wins, You Win: The Most Important Rule Every Businesswoman Needs to Know, 334

Shifting: The Double Lives of Black Women in America, 299

The Shining, 196

Shipman, Pat, 260, 264

Shirk, Martha, 331–32

Shoes: A Celebration of Pumps, Sandals, Slippers & More, 189

Shoes: What Every Woman Should Know, 189

Shorter-Gooden, Kumea, 299

Showings, 57

Shreve, Anita, 136

Shreve, Susan Richards, 49

Shulman, Neil, 170

Shuttle, Penelope, 171

Side-by-Side: A Photographic History of American Women in War, 324

Siegel, Deborah, 287

Sievers, Sharon L., 204

Sifters: Native American Women's Lives, 45

Signed, Mata Hari, 264

Signorile, Michelangelo, 92–93

The Silenced Cry: One Woman's Diary of a Journey to Afghanistan, 33

Silences of the Middle Ages (A History of Women in the West), 201

Silent Images: Women in Pharaonic Egypt, 214

Siljak, Ana, 228

Silko, Leslie, 113

Silver, Michelle, 79

Silverman, Sue William, 180

Silvis, Randall, 260

Simeti, Mary Taylor, 274

Simon, Dennis Michael, 369

Simonson, Louise, 311

Simpson, Sherry, 256

Since You Went Away: World War II Letters from American Women on the Home Front, 29

Singled Out: How Singles Are Stereotyped, Stigmatized, and Ignored, and Still Live Happily Ever After, 94

The Single Girl's Manifesta: Living in a Stupendously Superior Single State of Mind, 97

Single State of the Union: Single Women Speak Out on Life, Love, and the Pursuit of Happiness, 96

The Single Truth: Challenging the Misconceptions of Singleness with God's Consuming Truth, 96

Single Woman of a Certain Age: 29 Women Writers on the Unmarried Midlife—Romantic Escapades, Heavy Petting, Empty Nests, Shifting Shapes, and Serene Independence, 95

The Single Woman's Guide to a Happy Pregnancy, 112

Sippy Cups Are Not for Chardonnay, and Other Things I Had to Learn as a New Mom, 103

Sister CEO: The Black Woman's Guide to Starting Her Own Business, 330

Sister Gumbo: Spicy Vignettes from Black Women on Life, Sex and Relationships, 54

Sisterhood, Interrupted: From Radical Women to Grrls Gone Wild, 287

Sisterhood Is Forever: The Women's Anthology for a New Millennium, 305

Sisterhood Is Global: The International Women's Movement Anthology, 292

Sisterhood of Faith: 365 Life-Changing Stories about Women Who Made a Difference, 121–22

Sisterhood of Spies: The Women of the OSS, 262

Sisterhood of the Traveling Pants, 80

Sister in the Band of Brothers: Embedded with the 101st Airborne in Iraq, 326

Sister Juana, 122

The Sister Knot: Why We Fight, Why We're Jealous, and Why We'll Love Each Other No Matter What, 76

Sister Nations: Native American Women Writers on Community, 46–47

Sister Outsider: Essays and Speeches, 293

Sisters, 81

Sisters at Sinai: New Tales of Biblical Women, 125

Sisters in Law: Women Lawyers in Modern American History, 317–18

Sisters in the Resistance, 262

Sisters in the Struggle: African American Women in the Civil Rights-Black Power Movement, 290

Sisters: The Lives of America's Suffragists, 4

Sisters-in-Law: An Uncensored Guide for Women Practicing Law in the Real World, 320

Sittenfeld, Curtis, 374

Six Women's Slave Narratives, 51

Sjoholm, Barbara, 16

Sjoo, Monica, 116

Skaine, Rosemarie, 369

A Skating Life, 322

Skee, Mickey, 92

Skiba, Katherine M., 326

Skin Deep: Black Women & White Women Write about Race, 49

Skin Deep: How Race and Complexion Matter in the "Color-Blind" Era, 49

Skinner, John, 56–57

The Skinny: How to Fit into Your Little Black Dress Forever: The Eat-What-You-Want Way to Lose Weight and Keep It Off, 142

Skinny Women Are Evil: Notes of a Big Girl in a Small-minded World, 152

skirt! Rules for the Workplace: An Irreverent Guide to Advancing Your Career, 336

Slacks and Calluses: Our Summer in a Bomber Factory, 28–29

Slatkin, Wendy, 310

Slave, 359

Slavin, Sarah, 203

The Sleeping Doll, 278

Sloan, Louise, 112

Slotkin, Jacquelyn Hersh, 320

Slyomovics, Susan, 369

Smalley, Barbara Steinberg, 341

The Small Rain, 347

The Smart Girl's Guide to Porn, 362

Smart Women and Small Business: How to Make the Leap from Corporate Careers to the Right Small Enterprise, 333

Smart Women Finish Rich: 9 Steps to Achieving Financial Security and Funding Your Dreams, 346

Smashed: Story of a Drunken Girlhood, 163

Smith, Anthony, 260

Smith, Bonnie G., 204

Smith, David C., 29

Smith, Jane I., 128

Smith, Lee, 136

Smith, Lissa, 322
Smith, Lori, 96
Smith, Ursula, 233
Smitherman, Geneva, 340
*Smotherhood: Wickedly Funny Confessions
     from the Early Years,* 103
Snitow, Ann Barr, 284
Socolow, Susan Migden, 227
Soiled Doves: Prostitution in the Early West,
     231
Solaro, Erin, 325
Solinger, Rickie, 208
Solitaire: A Narrative, 160
Solomon, Rivka, 76
Solo: On Her Own Adventure, 256
Solot, Dorian, 88
Solovic, Susan Wilson, 332
*Somebody Is Going to Die if Lilly Beth
     Doesn't Catch That Bouquet: The
     Official Southern Ladies' Guide to
     Hosting the Perfect Wedding,* 94
Somerset, Anne, 23
Sonnenberg, Susanna, 163
Sontag, Susan, 75
Sorel, Nancy Caldwell, 264
Sor Juana, 122
Sor Juana, or, The Traps of Faith, 122
Sor Juana's Love Poems, 122
*So Sexy So Soon: The New Sexualized
     Childhood, and What Parents Can Do
     to Protect Their Kids,* 299
**Soul Sisters: The Five Divine Qualities of
     a Woman's Soul,** 118
Soul Virgins: Redefining Single Sexuality,
     166
Southern Discomfort, 62
*The Southern Region (Women Writing
     Africa),* 205
**Sovereign Ladies: The Six Reigning
     Queens of England,** 22
*So You Want to Be a Lesbian?: A Guide for
     Amateurs and Professionals,* 92
Sparks, Nicholas, 136–37
Sparrowe, Linda, 144
Speak, 195
Speaking Truth to Power, 339
*Speed, Ecstasy, Ritalin: The Science of
     Amphetamines,* 162
Spence, Betty, 338
Spencer, Paula, 101

*Spider Woman's Granddaughters: Traditional
     Tales and Contemporary Writing by
     Native American Women,* 47
Spilner, Maggie, 170
Spindel, Janis, 88
Spinelli, Jerry, 306
Spink, Kathryn, 60
**The Spiral Dance: A Rebirth of the
     Ancient Religion of the Great
     Goddess,** 134
**Spirit Moves: The Story of Six
     Generations of Native Women,** 45
Spiritual Midwifery, 109
Spook: Science Tackles the Afterlife, 190
Spoto, Donald, 11
Squires, Elisabeth, 190
**Stacked: A 32DDD Reports from the
     Front,** 190
Stafford, Nancy, 191
*Stalking the Wild Dik-Dik: One Woman's
     Solo Misadventures across Africa,* 268
Stanley, Jo, 16
Stanley, Susie C., 320
Stanny, Barbara, 337
Stanton, Elizabeth Cady, 295
Stargirl, 306
Starhawk, 134
Stark, Christine, 360
Stark, Vikki, 76
Staub, Michael E., 325–26
Stealing Buddha's Dinner: A Memoir, 48
Steele, Valerie, 190–91
Steele, Valerie, 189, 223
Steinbach, Alice, 267–68
Steinberg, David I., 31
Steinem, Gloria, 29, 174, 292
Steiner, Leslie Morgan, 372–73
Stendhal, Renate, 92
Stephens, Autumn, 229
Stephens, Autumn, 10, 174
Stepp, Laura Sessions, 360
Sterling, Dorothy, 230
Steuernagel, Gertrude A., 366–67
Stevens, Patricia, 98
Stevens, Tracey, 92
Stewart, Barbara, 146
Stewart, Elinore Pruitt, 233
Stewart, Jerusha, 97
Stewart, Susan, 95
Stick Figure: A Diary of My Former Self, 159
Stiehm, Judith, 365

Stiff: The Curious Lives of Human Cadavers, 190

Stitch 'N Bitch: The Knitter's Handbook, 119

Stoff, Laurie S., 243

Stolen Innocence: My Story of Growing Up in a Polygamous Sect, Becoming a Teenage Bride, and Breaking Free of Warren Jeffs, 180

Stoll, David, 34

Stoller, Debbie, 119, 302

The Stone Fields: An Epitaph for the Living, 242

Stone, Merlin, 115

Stone, Pamela, 373

Stopping the Train, 339

Stories of World Travel, 266

Storming Caesar's Palace: How Black Mothers Fought Their Own War on Poverty, 354

The Story of V: A Natural History of Female Sexuality, 73

Stothert, Karen E., 213

Stoumbos, Helen, 146

Strachey, Lytton, 21

Streatfeild, Dominic, 162–63

Strebe, Amy Goodpaster, 244

Stripped: Inside the Lives of Exotic Dancers, 361

Strober, Michael, 159

Strock, Carren, 93

Strong-Boag, Veronica Jane, 237

Strong Mothers, Strong Sons: Raising the Next Generation of Men, 98

Stuart, Nancy Rubin, 19

The Subordinated Sex: A History of Attitudes toward Women, 203

The Sweet Potato Queens' Book of Love, 84

The Sweet Potato Queens' Field Guide to Men: Every Man I Love Is Either Married, Gay, or Dead, 93–94

Success on Our Own Terms: Tales of Extraordinary, Ordinary Business Women, 327

Succulent Wild Woman: Dancing with Your Wonder-Full Self!, 174

Sucheng Chan, 52

Sukrungruang, Ira, 152

Sulami, Muhammad ibn al-Husayn, 129

Sullivan, Mary Lucille, 361

Summers, Vanessa, 346

Suoh, Tamami, 188

Support and Seduction: The History of Corsets and Bras, 191

Survival of the Prettiest: The Science of Beauty, 149

Susan B. Anthony, 295

Susan B. Anthony: A Biography of a Singular Feminist, 3–4

Sussman, Lisa, 168

Sutherland-Addy, Esi, 205

Swan, Sheila, 277

Sweatshop Warriors: Immigrant Women Workers Take On the Global Factory, 351–52

Sweet Potato Queens, 84

Swift, Amy, 329

Swim with the Dolphins: How Women Can Succeed in Corporate America on Their Own Terms, 341

Sycamore, Matt "Mattilda" Bernstein, 355

Sympathy and Science: Women Physicians in American Medicine, 318

Syntactic Structures, 288

Taking Away the Distance: A Young Orphan's Journey and the AIDS Epidemic in Africa, 105

Taking Charge of Your Fertility: The Definitive Guide to Natural Birth Control, Pregnancy Achievement, and Reproductive Health, 106

Taking on the Big Boys: Or Why Feminism Is Good for Families, Business, and the Nation, 298

Tales of a Female Nomad: Living at Large in the World, 269

Talking from 9 to 5: Women and Men at Work, 328

Tan, Amy, 52, 63

Tanenbaum, Leora, 78

Tannen, Deborah, 79, 328

Taormino, Tristan, 300–301

Taylor, Barbara Brown, 60

Taylor, Janice, 142

Tea, Michelle, 353

Teaching a Stone to Talk: Expeditions and Encounters, 269

The Technology of Orgasm: "Hysteria," the Vibrator, and Women's Sexual Satisfaction, 73

Telling: A Memoir of Rape and Recovery, 184

Temperance Brennan series, 347

Temptress: From the Original Bad Girls to Women on Top, 207

Tenderheaded: A Comb-Bending Collection of Hair Stories, 186

Tenneson, Joyce, 177

Tenney, Lester I., 263

The Terror Dream: Fear and Fantasy in Post–9/11 America, 352

Terry, Emily Miles, 78

Terry: My Daughter's Life-and-Death Struggle with Alcoholism, 162

Testimonies: Lesbian and Bisexual Coming-out Stories, 91

Thakor, Manisha, 346

Thanks for the Mammogram!: Fighting Cancer with Faith, Hope, and a Healthy Dose of Laughter, 154

Tharps, Lori L., 148

That Takes Ovaries!: Bold Females and Their Brazen Acts, 76

Thébaud, Franc͵oise, 201

Their Eyes Were Watching God, 306

There Is No Me without You: One Woman's Odyssey to Rescue Her Country's Children, 104–105

These Things Ain't Gonna Smoke Themselves: A Letter to a Very Bad Habit, 161

They Fought for the Motherland: Russia's Women Soldiers in World War I and the Revolution, 243

They Fought Like Demons: Women Soldiers in the Civil War, 234

They Went Whistling: Women Wayfarers, Warriors, Runaways, and Renegades, 7

Thiébaux, Marcelle, 220

Thin, 159

The Thinking Woman's Guide to a Better Birth, 108

Thinner Than Thou, 150

The Third Man of the Double Helix: The Autobiography of Maurice Wilkins, 13

Third Wave Agenda: Being Feminist, Doing Feminism, 304

Third Wave Feminism and Television: Jane Puts It in a Box, 351

Thirty Ways of Looking at Hillary: Reflections by Women Writers, 4

This Bridge Called My Back: Writings by Radical Women of Color, 302

This Common Secret: My Journey as an Abortion Doctor, 30

This Day in the Life: Diaries from Women Across America, 26

This Day: Diaries from American Women, 26

This Is How We Do It: The Working Mothers' Manifesto, 373

This Is Not Your Mother's Menopause: One Woman's Natural Journey through Change, 171–72

This Little Light of Mine: The Life of Fannie Lou Hamer, 53

This Side of Doctoring: Reflections from Women in Medicine, 317

This Was Not Our War: Bosnian Women Reclaiming the Peace, 242

Thoele, Sue Patton, 114, 117

Thomas, Angela, 191

Thomas, Clarence, 340

Thompson, Alice, 185

The Thong Also Rises: Further Misadventures from Funny Women on the Road, 271

Thoreau, Henry David, 269

The Thorn Birds, 246

Those Wonderful Women in Their Flying Machines: The Unknown Heroines of World War Two, 244

A Thousand Years over a Hot Stove: A History of American Women Told Through Food, Recipes, and Remembrances, 211

The Three-Martini Playdate: A Practical Guide to Happy Parenting, 102

The Thrill of the Chaste: Finding Fulfillment While Keeping Your Clothes On, 165–66

Through the Flower: My Struggle as a Woman Artist, 9

Through Women's Eyes: An American History with Documents, 211

Tidal Wave: How Women Changed America at Century's End, 287

Tiegreen, Mary, 273–74

Tilberis, Liz, 155

A Time Remembered: American Women in the Vietnam War, 245

The Times and Trials of Anne Hutchinson: Puritans Divided, 58

Tisdale, Sallie, 131

Titanic Adventure: One Woman's True Life Voyage Down to the Legendary Ocean Liner, 253

To Be Real: Telling the Truth and Changing the Face of Feminism, 291

Tocantins, Nicole, 167

Tohe, Laura, 46–47

To Hell with All That: Loving and Loathing Our Inner Housewife, 372

Tomboy Bride, 273

Tomorrow Begins Today: African American Women as We Age, 176

Tone, Andrea, 208

Too Cool to Be Forgotten, 161

Toomey, David M., 310

Topp, Elizabeth, 167

The Torah: A Women's Commentary, 126

Torgus, Judy, 110

Tortajada, Anna, 33

To the Heart of the Nile: Lady Florence Baker and the Exploration of Central Africa, 260

To the Scaffold: The Life of Marie Antoinette, 17

Tough Choices: A Memoir, 326

Toward a Cultural Identity in the Twentieth Century (A History of Women in the West), 201

Toward a New Psychology of Women, 69

Tracey, Liz, 92

Traeder, Tamara, 80

Trans-Sister Radio, 135

Traveling Mercies: Some Thoughts on Faith, 123

Travels with a Medieval Queen, 274

A Treasury of Royal Scandals: The Shocking True Stories of History's Wickedest, Weirdest, Most Wanton Kings, Queens, Tsars, Popes, and Emperors, 206

The Trial of Susan B. Anthony, 295

Tribe of Women: A Photojournalist Chronicles the Lives of Her Sisters around the Globe, 73

Trimberger, Ellen Kay, 94

Tripping the Prom Queen: The Truth about Women and Rivalry, 77–78

Tronto, Joan C., 367

The Trouble between Us: An Uneasy History of White and Black Women in the Feminist Movement, 302

Troyat, Henri, 20

True Secrets of Lesbian Desire: Keeping Sex Alive in Long-Term Relationships, 92

True Stories of the Korean Comfort Women, 209

The Truth behind the Mommy Wars: Who Decides What Makes a Good Mother?, 372

Trying Neaira: The True Story of a Courtesan's Scandalous Life in Ancient Greece, 213–14

Tsui, Bonnie, 234

Tuchman, Arleen, 14

Tucker, Judith E., 204

Tucker, Laura, 70–71

Tuñón, Julia, 205

Turchiano, Deborah, 320

Turning the Wheel: American Women Creating the New Buddhism, 130

Turpin, Joanne, 61

Tust, Jenn, 91

Twain, Mark, 247

Two in the Wild, 256

Tyree, Omar, 63

Ulrich, Laurel, 296

Umansky, Lauri, 236

Unbearable Weight: Feminism, Western Culture, and the Body, 147–48

Unbowed: A Memoir, 28

An Uncommon Soldier: The Civil War Letters of Sarah Rosetta Wakeman, Alias Private Lyons Wakeman, 153rd Regiment, New York State Volunteers, 38

Undset, Sigrid, 247

The Unexpected Mrs. Pollifax, 278

Unhooked: How Young Women Pursue Sex, Delay Love and Lose at Both, 360

Unlocking the Clubhouse: Women in Computing, 313

Unmarried to Each Other: The Essential Guide to Living Together as an Unmarried Couple, 88

An Unquiet Mind: A Memoir of Moods and Madness, 155

The Unsavvy Traveler: Women's Comic Tales of Catastrophe, 268

Unspeakable Losses: Understanding the Experience of Pregnancy Loss, Miscarriage, and Abortion, 181

Unsuitable for Ladies: An Anthology of Women Travellers, 274

Unveiled: A Woman's Journey through Politics, Love, and Obedience, 27

Unwin, Christina, 16

Uplift: Secrets from the Sisterhood of Breast Cancer Survivors, 154

Uplift: The Bra in America, 189

Uppity Women of Ancient Times, 202

Uppity Women of Medieval Times, 202

Uppity Women of the New World, 202

Uppity Women of the Renaissance, 202

Uppity Women series, 202

Urgent Message from Mother: Gather the Women, Save the World, 363–64

Uzzi, Brian, 312

The V Zone: A Woman's Guide to Intimate Health Care, 164

Vadhera, Shalini, 194

The Vagina Monologues, 74

Vaginas: An Owner's Manual, 167

Valenti, Jessica, 305

Valentine, Helen, 185

Valian, Virginia, 298

van der Rol, Ruud, 48

Van Devanter, Lynda, 262

Vanishing Act, 374

Van Natta, Don, 368

Van Tilburg, JoAnne, 259–60

Vare, Ethlie Ann, 315

Varon, Lee, 103

Vassel, Rachel, 82

Vegan Virgin Valentine, 196

Veiled Courage: Inside the Afghan Women's Resistance, 297

Veiled Threat: The Hidden Power of the Women of Afghanistan, 297

Velazquez, Loreta Janeta, 39

Venus Envy: A History of Cosmetic Surgery, 150

Venus Envy: A Sensational Season inside the Women's Tennis Tour, 145

Verhoeven, Rian, 48

Vickery, Amanda, 223

Victorian London's Middle-Class Housewife: What She Did All Day, 229

Victory Harvest: Diary of a Canadian in the Women's Land Army, 1940–1944, 243

La Vida Rica: The Latina's Guide to Success, 337

Vigue, Jordi, 74

Vilette, 135

Vincent, Norah, 152

Vindication, 247

A Vindication of the Rights of Woman, 288

Virginity or Death!: And Other Social and Political Issues of Our Time, 354

The Virgin Suicides, 373

Visiting Life: Women Doing Time on the Outside, 83

Võ, Linda Trinh, 54

The Voice of Hope, 30–31

Voices of Resistance: Muslim Women on War, Faith and Sexuality, 128

Voices of the Matriarchs: Listening to the Prayers of Early Modern Jewish Women, 127

Voicing Chicana Feminisms: Young Women Speak Out on Sexuality and Identity, 288

Vollers, Maryanne, 255

Von Prondzynski, Heather, 99

Vorkosigan series, 278

Votes for Women: The Struggle for Suffrage Revisited, 284–85

Voting for Women: How the Public Evaluates Women Candidates, 370

Vowles, Judith, 32

WACK!: Art and the Feminist Revolution, 300

Wadia, Anna S., 331–32

Wadud, Amina, 129

Wadyka, Sally, 186

Wagner, Marsden, 107–108

Waiting for Birdy: A Year of Frantic Tedium, Neurotic Angst, and the Wild Magic of Growing a Family, 101

Waiting for Daisy: A Tale of Two Continents, Three Religions, Five Infertility Doctors, an Oscar, an Atomic Bomb, a Romantic Night, and One Woman's Quest to Become a Mother, 106

Waiting with Gabriel: A Story of Cherishing a Baby's Brief Life, 182

Wakeman, Sarah Rosetta, 38

Wake Up, I'm Fat!, 152

Walden, 269

Walden, Patricia, 144

Walk Your Way through Menopause: 14 Programs to Get in Shape, Boost Your Mood, and Recharge Your Sex Life No Matter What Your Current Fitness Level, 170

Walker, Alice, 25, 63–64, 295, 360, 374

Walker, Barbara G., 120

Walker, Keith, 245

Walker, Laura Jensen, 154

Walker, Rebecca, 102

Walking Home: A Woman's Pilgrimage on the Appalachian Trail, 256

Wall, Elissa, 180

Wall, Ginita, 345

Waller, Maureen, 22

Wallis, Michael, 20

Walls, Jeannette, 184

Wanderlust and Lipstick: The Essential Guide for Women Traveling Solo, 277

Wann, Marilyn, 152–53

Wanting to Be Her: Body Image Secrets Victoria Won't Tell You, 191

The War on Choice: The Right-Wing Attack on Women's Rights and How to Fight Back, 358

The Warrior Queens, 200

War Torn: The Personal Experiences of Women Reporters in the Vietnam War, 261

Ward, Vicki L., 176

Warner, Judith, 102

Warrior Marks, 360

Warrior Women: An Archaeologist's Search for History's Hidden Heroines, 216

Warshaw, Robin, 26

A WASP Among Eagles: A Woman Military Test Pilot in World War II, 37–38

Wasted: A Memoir of Anorexia and Bulimia, 159

Watkins, Elizabeth Siegel, 207

Watkins, Nan, 269–70

Watson, Robert P., 370

The Weaker Vessel, 222

We Are Your Sisters: Black Women in the Nineteenth Century, 230

We Band of Angels: The Untold Story of American Nurses Trapped on Bataan by the Japanese, 263

We Don't Need Another Wave: Dispatches from the Next Generation of Feminists, 291

We Real Cool: Black Men and Masculinity, 292–93

We're in the Mountains, Not over the Hills: Tales and Tips from Seasoned Women Backpackers, 250–51

We're Just Like You, Only Prettier: Confessions of a Tarnished Southern Belle, 42

Weaving New Worlds: Southeastern Cherokee Women and Their Basketry, 226

Weber, Caroline, 223

Weber, David, 279

Webster, Graham, 16

The Weight of Water, 136

The Weight-Loss Diaries, 143

Weiner, Jennifer, 83

Weir, Alison, 18, 22–24

Weisberger, Lauren, 196

Weiss, Andrea L., 126

Weissler, Chava, 127

Weitekamp, Margaret A., 314–15

Weitz, Margaret Collins, 262

Weitz, Rose, 148

Welcome to the World, Baby Girl!, 306

Well-Behaved Women Seldom Make History, 296

Wellington, Sheila W., 338

Wertheim, L. Jon, 145

Wertheim, Margaret, 316

Weschler, Toni, 106

West Africa and the Sahel (Women Writing Africa), 205

West with the Night, 258

Westfall, Elizabeth, 319

Wexler, Jayne, 79–80

Wharton, Edith, 247

What Are We Fighting for?: Sex, Race, Class, and the Future of Feminism, 286

What Color Is Your Jockstrap?: Funny Men and Women Write from the Road, 271

What Did I Do Wrong?: When Women Don't Tell Each Other the Friendship Is Over, 80

What Happy Women Know: How New Findings in Positive Psychology Can Change Women's Lives for the Better, 71

What Men Don't Tell Women about Business: Opening Up the Heavily Guarded Alpha Male Playbook, 334

What the Bible Is All about for Women: A Devotional Reading for Every Book of the Bible, 121

What to Do When You Can't Get Pregnant: The Complete Guide to All the Technologies for Couples Facing Fertility Problems, 106

What to Expect When You're Expecting, 111

What Your Mother Never Told You about S.E.X., 164

Whatever It Takes: Women on Women's Sport, 146

Wheat, Ed, 165

Wheat, Gaye, 165

Wheeler, Bonnie, 10–11

When Abortion Was a Crime: Women, Medicine, and Law in the United States, 1867–1973, 358

When Chickenheads Come Home to Roost: My Life As a Hip-Hop Feminist, 294–95

When God Was a Woman, 115

When I Was Puerto Rican, 47

Where the Action Was: Women War Correspondents in World War II, 264–65

Where the Girls Are: Growing Up Female with the Mass Media, 351

Where Women Run: Gender and Party in the American States, 369–70

Whipping Girl: A Transsexual Woman on Sexism and the Scapegoating of Femininity, 355

Whisnant, Rebecca, 360

Whispering the Word: Hearing Women's Stories in the Old Testament, 123

Whitaker, Robert, 260

White, E. Frances, 204

White, Kate, 335

Whiteley, Sharon, 332

Whitman, Beth, 277

Whitman, Stacy, 88

Whitman, Wynne, 88

Who Cooked the Last Supper?: The Women's History of the World, 203

The Whole Lesbian Sex Book: A Passionate Guide for All of Us, 168

A Whole Other Ball Game: Women's Literature on Women's Sport, 146

Who's Afraid of Marie Curie?: The Challenges Facing Women in Science and Technology, 312–13

Whores and Other Feminists, 362

Whose Panties Are These? More Misadventures from Funny Women on the Road, 271

Why Can't I Stop Eating?: Recognizing, Understanding, and Overcoming Food Addiction, 158

Why Good Girls Don't Get Ahead—But Gutsy Girls Do: Nine Secrets Every Working Woman Must Know, 335

Why I Wore Lipstick to My Mastectomy, 156

Why Marriages Succeed or Fail: And How You Can Make Yours Last, 86

Why Men Don't Listen and Women Can't Read Maps: How We're Different and What to Do about It, 336

Why Men Never Remember and Women Never Forget, 70–71

Why She Plays: The World of Women's Basketball, 321

Why So Slow? The Advancement of Women, 298

Why Women Mean Business: Understanding the Emergence of Our Next Economic Revolution, 328

Why Women Should Rule the World, 342

Why You Should Give a Damn about Gay Marriage, 301–302

Wicklund, Susan, 30

Wide Sargasso Sea, 63

Wilchins, Riki Anne, 355

Wild Swans: Three Daughters of China, 31

Wild Women in the Kitchen: 101 Rambunctious Recipes & 99 Tasty Tales, 211

Wild Women: Crusaders, Curmudgeons, and Completely Corsetless Ladies in the Otherwise Virtuous Victorian Era, 229

Wild Words from Wild Women: An Unbridled Collection of Candid Observations & Extremely Opinionated Bon Mots, 10

Wilde, Lyn Webster, 215

Wilder-Taylor, Stefanie, 103

Wiley, Carol A., 323

Wilkins, Maurice, 13

Wilkinson, Richard H., 218

Williams, Gary A., 316

Williams, Judith, 334, 337
Williams, Kayla, 325–26
Williamson, Teresa Rodriguez, 276
Willingham, Bill, 374
Willis, Connie, 347
Willis, Janice Dean, 61
Wilmerding, Ginny, 333
Wilson, Andrew, 42
Wilson, Barbara, 87
Wilson, Marie, 343
Wilson, Michael Todd, 166
Wilson, Valerie Plame, 263
Winans, Joby, 146
Wingard, Ellen, 338
Wingert, Pat, 170
Wings, Women, and War: Soviet Airwomen in World War II Combat, 244
Winner, Lauren F., 86–86
Winning My Wings: A Woman Airforce Service Pilot in World War II, 38
Winning Sounds Like This: A Season with the Women's Basketball Team at Gallaudet, the World's Only University for the Deaf, 321
Winship, Michael P., 58
Winters, Kelly, 256
The Wisdom of Menopause: Creating Physical and Emotional Health and Healing During the Change, 171
Wise, James E., 325
Wise Women: A Celebration of Their Insights, Courage, and Beauty, 177
Wise Women: Over Two Thousand Years of Spiritual Writing by Women, 115–16
The Wise Wound: Eve's Curse and Everywoman, 171
Witchcraze: A New History of the European Witch Hunts, 221–22
A Witches' Bible: The Complete Witches' Handbook, 134
Witches, Midwives, and Nurses: A History of Women Healers, 317
The Witch-Hunt in Early Modern Europe, 222
A Witch Like Me: The Spiritual Journeys of Today's Pagan Practitioners, 55
With All Our Strength: The Revolutionary Association of the Women of Afghanistan, 297

With My Own Eyes: A Lakota Woman Tells Her People's History, 46
With or Without a Man: Single Women Taking Control of Their Lives, 95
Without a Map: A Memoir, 105
Without a Net: The Female Experience of Growing Up Working Class, 353
Without Apology: Girls, Women, and the Desire to Fight, 70
Without Reservations: The Travels of an Independent Woman, 267
Wittenberg-Cox, Avivah, 328
Wives of the Kings of England: From Hanover to Windsor, 22
Wofford-Girand, Sally, 89
Wohlmuth, Sharon J., 75, 80–81
Wolf, Molly, 119
Wolf, Naomi, 101, 153
Wolk, Claudine, 103
Wollstonecraft, Mary, 288
Woman: A Celebration, 75
A Woman Alone: Travel Tales from around the Globe, 268
Woman: An Intimate Geography, 72
Woman as Healer, 317
Woman Awake: Women Practicing Buddhism, 130
The Woman in Battle: A Narrative of the Exploits, Adventures, and Travels of Madame Loreta Janeta Velazquez, 39
A Woman in Charge: The Life of Hillary Rodham Clinton, 4
A Woman Like That: Lesbian and Bisexual Writers Tell Their Coming Out Stories, 90
Woman of Valor: Margaret Sanger and the Birth Control Movement in America, 5
The Womanly Art of Breastfeeding, 110
WomanPrayers: Prayers by Women throughout History and around the World, 120
A Woman Soldier's Own Story: The Autobiography of Xie Bingying, 39
The Woman Warrior: Memoirs of a Girlhood among Ghosts, 52
The Woman Who Walked to Russia: A Writer's Search for a Lost Legend, 259
The Woman's Advantage: 20 Women Entrepreneurs Show You What It Takes to Grow Your Business, 331
A Woman's Asia: True Stories, 267

The Woman's Bible: A Classic Feminist Perspective, 295

The Woman's Book of Confidence: Meditations for Strength and Inspiration, 117

The Woman's Book of Courage: Meditations for Empowerment & Peace of Mind, 117

A Woman's Book of Meditation: Discovering the Power of a Peaceful Mind, 117

The Woman's Book of Soul: Meditations for Courage, Confidence, and Spirit, 117

A Woman's Book of Yoga: Embracing Our Natural Life Cycles, 116

The Woman's Book of Yoga and Health: A Lifelong Guide to Wellness, 144

The Woman's Comfort Book: A Self-Nurturing Guide for Restoring Balance in Your Life, 117–18

The Woman's Dictionary of Symbols and Sacred Objects, 120

The Woman's Encyclopedia of Myths and Secrets, 120

A Woman's Europe: True Stories, 267

A Woman's Guide to Sexual Health, 164

A Woman's Guide to Successful Negotiating: How to Convince, Collaborate, and Create Your Way to Agreement, 335

A Woman's Guide to the Language of Success: Communicating with Confidence and Power, 336

A Woman's Journey to God: Finding the Feminine Path, 118

A Woman's Passion for Travel: True Stories of World Wanderlust, 266

A Woman's Path: Women's Best Spiritual Travel Writing, 118

The Woman's Retreat Book: A Guide to Restoring, Rediscovering, and Reawakening Your True Self—in a Moment, an Hour, a Day, or a Weekend., 118

A Woman's Spirit: More Meditations from the Author of Each Day a New Beginning, 114

A Woman's World Again: True Stories of World Travel, 267

A Woman's World: True Stories of World Travel, 267

Women, 75

Women & Change in the Caribbean: A Pan-Caribbean Perspective, 239

Women and Congress: Running, Winning, and Ruling, 369

Women and Flight: Portraits of Contemporary Women Pilots, 310

Women and Gender in Islam: Historical Roots of a Modern Debate, 127–28

Women and Leadership: The State of Play and Strategies for Change, 343–44

Women and Motorcycling: The Early Years, 239

Women & Money: Owning the Power to Control Your Destiny, 345

Women & Music: A History, 203–204

Women and Power in the Middle East, 369

Women & Public Policy: A Revolution in Progress, 366–67

Women and Science: Social Impact and Interaction, 315

Women and the Leadership Q: The Breakthrough System for Achieving Power and Influence, 341

Women and Wilderness, 253

Women and Writing in Medieval Europe: A Sourcebook, 220

Women Are Not Small Men: Life-Saving Strategies for Preventing and Healing Heart Disease in Women, 155–56

Women Artists in History: From Antiquity to the Present, 310

Women Artists: An Illustrated History, 310

Women at Home in Victorian America: A Social History, 229

Women at Law: Lessons Learned along the Pathways to Success, 320

Women at the Front: Hospital Workers in Civil War America, 235

Women at War: Iraq, Afghanistan, and Other Conflicts, 325

Women at War: The Women of World War II—at Home, at Work, on the Front Line, 245

Women Boxers: The New Warriors, 70

Women, Culture & Politics, 290

Women Don't Ask: Negotiation and the Gender Divide, 334

Women Empowered: Inspiring Change in the Emerging World, 297–98

Women Entrepreneurs Only: 12 Women Entrepreneurs Tell the Stories of Their Success, 332

Women, Get Answers about Your Money, 345

Women Healers: Portraits of Herbalists, Physicians, and Midwives, 316–17

Women in Ancient America, 213

Women in Asia: Restoring Women to History, 204

Women in Chemistry: Their Changing Roles from Alchemical Times to the Mid-Twentieth Century, 314

Women in Church History: 21 Stories for 21 Centuries, 61

Women in European History, 201

Women in Latin America and the Caribbean: Restoring Women to History, 204

Women in Medicine: A Celebration of Their Work, 317

Women in Mexico: A Past Unveiled, 205

Women in Middle Eastern History: Shifting Boundaries in Sex and Gender, 219

Women in Music: An Anthology of Source Readings from the Middle Ages to the Present, 204

Women in Ochre Robes: Gendering Hindu Renunciation, 58

Women in Old Norse Society, 220

Women in Purple: Rulers of Medieval Byzantium, 219

Women in Racing: In Their Own Words, 321–22

Women in Space—Following Valentina, 314

Women in Sub-Saharan Africa: Restoring Women to History, 204

Women in the Civil War, 234–45

Women in the Classical World: Image and Text, 215

Women in the Line of Fire: What You Should Know about Women in the Military, 325

Women in the Martial Arts, 323

Women in the Medieval Islamic World: Power, Patronage, and Piety, 219

Women in the Middle East and North Africa: Restoring Women to History, 204

Women in the Military: Flirting with Disaster, 324–25

Women in the Viking Age, 220

Women in the Wild: True Stories of Adventure and Connection, 255

Women Lawyers: Rewriting the Rules, 320

Women Nobel Peace Prize Winners, 366

Women of Byzantium, 219

The Women of Colonial Latin America, 227

Women of Courage: Inspiring Stories from the Women Who Lived Them, 76

Women of Discovery: A Celebration of Intrepid Women Who Explored the World, 273–74

The Women of Faith Daily Devotional, 121

Women of Genesis series, 123

Women of Reform Judaism (U.S.), 127

Women of Spirit: Stories of Courage from the Women Who Lived Them, 10

Women of Sufism: A Hidden Treasure: Writings and Stories of Mystic Poets, Scholars & Saints, 128

Women of the Harvest: Inspiring Stories of Contemporary Farmers, 309

The Women of the House: How a Colonial She-Merchant Built a Mansion, a Fortune, and a Dynasty, 15

Women of the Renaissance, 222

Women of the Vine: Inside the World of Women Who Make, Taste, and Enjoy Wine, 311

Women of the Way: Discovering 2,500 Years of Buddhist Wisdom, 131

Women of the West, 233

Women of Wine: The Rise of Women in the Global Wine Industry, 310–11

Women on High: Pioneers of Mountaineering, 259

Women on Power: Leadership Redefined, 343

Women on the Civil War Battlefront, 233–34

Women on War: An International Anthology of Women's Writings from Antiquity to the Present, 364

Women Out of Bounds: The Secret History of Enterprising Women, 311–12

Women Pilots of World War II, 244

Women Political Leaders in Africa, 369

Women Practicing Buddhism: American Experiences, 130

Women Sailors and Sailors' Women: An Untold Maritime History, 257

Women Scientists in America: Before Affirmative Action, 1940–1972, 315

Women Scientists in America: Struggles and Strategies to 1940, 315

Women, Take Charge of Your Money: A Biblical Path to Financial Security, 344–45

Women Transforming Politics: An Alternative Reader, 367

Women Travel: A Rough Guide Special, 271

Women Warriors: A History, 202

Women Who Light the Dark, 299

The Women Who Lived for Danger: The Agents of the Special Operations Executive, 262

Women Who Love Books Too Much: Bibliophiles, Bluestockings & Prolific Pens from the Algonquin Hotel to the Ya-Ya Sisterhood, 309

Women Who Love Sex: Ordinary Women Describe Their Paths to Pleasure, Intimacy, and Ecstasy, 167

The Women Who Wrote the War, 264

Women Who Run with the Wolves: Myths and Stories of the Wild Woman Archetype, 68

Women Who Would Be Rabbis: A History of Women's Ordination, 1889–1985, 318–19

Women Who Write, 309

Women World Leaders: Fifteen Great Politicians Tell Their Stories, 368–69

Women Writing Africa, 205

Women, Media and Politics, 352

Women, Race, & Class, 289–90

Women's America: Refocusing the Past, 210

Women's Bodies, Women's Wisdom: Creating Physical and Emotional Health and Healing, 141–42

Women's Health Perfect Body Diet: The Ultimate Weight Loss and Workout Plan to Drop Stubborn Pounds and Get Fit for Life, 142

Women's History in Global Perspective, 204

Women's Life in Greece and Rome: A Source Book in Translation, 215

Women's Lives in Medieval Europe: A Sourcebook, 220

The Women's Movement against Sexual Harassment, 338–39

Women's Religions in the Greco-Roman World: A Sourcebook, 218

The Women's Revolution in Mexico, 1910–1953, 205

Women's Soccer: The Passionate Game, 146

Women's Tennis Tactics, 144–45

Women's Ventures, Women's Visions: 29 Inspiring Stories from Women Who Started Their Own Businesses, 332

Women's Voices, Women's Lives: Documents in Early American History, 226

Women's Ways of Knowing: The Development of Self, Voice, and Mind, 67–68

Women's Work: The First 20,000 Years: Women, Cloth, and Society in Early Times, 200

Won by Love: Norma McCorvey, Jane Roe of Roe V. Wade, Speaks Out for the Unborn as She Shares Her New Conviction for Life, 356

Wood, Stephanie Gail, 213

Woodruff, Cheryl D., 176

Woods, Donald, 35

Woodswoman: Young Ecologist Meets Challenge Living Alone Adirondack Wilderness, 269

Woodward, Bob, 12

Woolf, Virginia, 296

Working IX to V: Orgy Planners, Funeral Clowns, and Other Prized Professions of the Ancient World, 203

The World According to Garp, 374

The World Split Open: How the Modern Women's Movement Changed America, 285

World Textiles: A Visual Guide to Traditional Techniques, 200

Wounds of Passion: A Writing Life, 51

The Wreath, 247

Wright, Carol V., 164

A Wrinkle in Time, 347

The Writings of Medieval Women: An Anthology, 220

Written by Herself: An Anthology, 27

Written by Herself: Literary Production by African American Women, 1746–1892, 230

Written by Herself, Volume II: Women's Memoirs from Britain, Africa, Asia, and the United States, 27

Wulff, Donna Marie, 132

Wunder, Katherine, 92
Wurtzel, Elizabeth, 162–63
Wymard, Ellie, 312

*The X in Sex: How the X Chromosome
    Controls Our Lives,* 70
Xie Bingying, 39
Xinran, 39

Yalof, Ina L., 71
Yalom, Marilyn, 89, 191–92
*Yankee Doodle Gals: Women Pilots of World
    War II,* 310
Yan Mo, 31
Yellin, Emily, 245
*YELL-Oh Girls! Emerging Voices Explore
    Culture, Identity, and Growing Up
    Asian American,* 53
*Yellow Woman and a Beauty of the Spirit:
    Essays on Native American Life Today,*
    113
*Yentl's Revenge: The Next Wave of Jewish
    Feminism,* 126
Yoga: A Gem for Women, 144
*Yoga and the Wisdom of Menopause: A
    Guide to Physical, Emotional, and
    Spiritual Health at Midlife and
    Beyond,* 170
Yogini: The Power of Women in Yoga, 116
Yorio, Kimberly, 329, 335, 341
Yoshimi, Yoshiaki, 208–209
*You Just Don't Understand: Women and Men
    in Conversation,* 328

*You're Not from Around Here, Are You?: A
    Lesbian in Small-Town America,* 41
*You're Wearing That?: Understanding
    Mothers and Daughters in
    Conversation,* 79
Young, Carrie, 231
Young, Elizabeth, 235–36
Young, Katherine K., 120
*Young Wives' Tales: New Adventures in
    Love and Partnership,* 84
Yount, Lisa, 313
*Your Mother Wears Combat Boots:
    Humorous, Harrowing, and
    Heartwarming Stories of Military
    Women,* 324
*Your Perfectly Pampered Menopause: Health,
    Beauty, and Lifestyle Advice for the
    Best Years of Your Life,* 171

Zackheim, Victoria, 89, 176
Zailckas, Koren, 163
Zane, 137, 168
Zeisler, Andi, 302
Zeitz, Joshua, 241
Zepatos, Thalia, 277
Zichy, Shoya, 341
Zimmerman, Jean, 15, 99
Zink-Sawyer, Beverly, 320
Zlata's Diary: A Child's Life in Sarajevo,
    242
Zook, Kristal Brent, 54
Zuckerman, Laurie, 327

Subject Index

Bold numbers refer to designated chapter sections.

Abortion, 5, 178, 181, 183, 207–208; anti-abortion, **356–57**; pro-choice, 30, **356–58**

Abu-Jaber, Diana, 55

Activism, 74, 76, 141, 160, 236, **284–85, 287, 290–91, 295–305**, 338–39, 343, 352, 357–60, 363–67, 371; autobiographies, 20, 32, 34–35, 39; biographies, 3–6, 8, 29, 46, 53, 60, 104–105, 110, 222–23, **298**; memoirs, 28–31, 34, 110, 181–83, **284–85, 290**, 356

Addiction, 155, **161–63**; alcoholism, **162–63**; drugs, **161–63**; smoking, **161**

Adielé, Faith, 61

Adoption, **104–107**

Adventure, 7–10, 76, 145–46, 239–40, **249–56,** 266–70, 272–77; espionage, 38, **262–64**; war, 37–39; historical, 15, **257–265**

Aebi, Tania, 254

Afghanistan, 27, 33, 297, 325

Africa, 204–205, 237–38, 260, 268, 297–98, 369; Egypt, 18–19, 214–15, 218; Ethiopia, 104–105; Kenya, 28, 258; Mali, 110; Nigeria, 49; Somalia, 181–83; South Africa, 35; Sudan, 359; Togo, 182

African Americans, 82, 148, 168, 174, 211, 230, 235, 277, 289–90, 292–95, 298–99, 329–30, 344; autobiographies, 24–25, **51**; biographies, **46, 53–54**, 176, 186, 204–205, 211, 290; memoirs, **48–51**, 61, 83, 102, 295, 339–40

Aging, **174–77**; midlife, 86, 93, 94–95, 113, 169–72, **175–77**, 185–86, 188, 254, 269, 273; seniors, 87, 129–30, 169–70, **175–77**, 185–86, 188, 250–51, 254, 269

Agriculture, 49–50, **309–11;** farming, 309

Agrippina, 212–13

AIDS, 104–105

Alcoholism, 162–63

Ali, Ayaan Hirsi, 183

Allen, Clara Marie, 28–29

Allison, Stacy, 251

Amazons, 215–16

America, 75, 113, 128, 130, 150, 166, 275, 301, 288–92, 298–304, 309, 316, 319, 322, 324–26, 338–40, 352–54, 358, 361, 364–65, 367–73; autobiographies, 41–42, 45–46, biographies, 4–5, 46–47, 56, 58, 366; memoirs, 26, 29, 41, 44–45, 48, 50, 61, 262–63, 272, 324, 365, 368. See also American history

American history, 8, 12–13, 194, **202–205, 208–12**, 289–90, 318, 324; and the Civil War, 38–39, **233–36**; and the Gulf War, 261; and the Vietnam War, 245, 261–62; and the War on Terror, 261, 263–64, 325–26, 365; and World War I, 243; and World War II, 14, 28–29, 37–38, **208–209, 244–45**, 262–64, 310; colonial and revolutionary, 15, 44, 58, **224–27**; in the Old West, 14, **230–33**, 272–73, 317; in the nineteenth century, 3, 14, 46, 51, **229–30**, 284–85, 295, 317–20, 353; in the twentieth century, 4–6, 13–14, 20, 24–26, 41–42, 52–53, 148, **232, 236–45**, 284–85, 292, 310, 314–15, 317–20, 324–25, 338–39, 351–52, 366–67, 371–72

Ancient history, 16, 116, **200–203, 207, 212–18**; Classical, 6, 18–19, **201–203, 207, 212–18**, 275; religious life in, 59, **123–24, 215–18**

Angelou, Maya, 24–25

Annapurna, 252

Anne (Queen of England), 22

Anorexia, 155, **158–60**, 162. See also Eating disorders

Antarctica, 251–52, 255

Anthologies: Chapter 1, Life Stories, 31, 46–47, 53–54; Chapter 2, Personal Growth, 73, 75–76, 78, 84–85, 89–90, 95–96, 98–100, 111, 114–15, 117–122, 124, 126–128, 130–34; Chapter 3, Health, Wellness, and Beauty, 146, 174, 179; Chapter 4, Women's History, 204, 210, 219, 221, 226, 231, 236, 238; Chapter 5, Adventure and Travel, 251–52, 255–56, 258, 261, 266–68, 271, 274, 277; Chapter 6, Feminism and Activism, 284, 286, 289–92, 290, 293–96, 300–302, 304–305; Chapter 7, Women at Work, 313–14, 317–319–20, 322–25, 338, 340, 343–44; Chapter 8, Women and Society, 351–53, 355–57, 360–63, 365–70, 372–73

Anthony, Susan B., 3–4, 295
Apartheid, 35
Apostles, 59, 217
Apostolides, Marianne, 158
Appalachian Trail, 251, 256
Appearance (physical). *See* Beauty
Arana, Marie, 44–45
Archaeology, 113, 116, 200, 213–16, 259–60
Arctic, The, 251
Argentina, 7
Armstrong, Penny, 110
Arnesen, Liv, 251–52
Art and artists, 8–9, 20, 73–75, 116, 187–88, 254, 296, 299–300, 310–11, 352; art history, 8–9, 74, 113, 116, 187–88, **213–14, 219, 225**, 294, 300, 310, 352; cartoons, 311
Asia, 204, 267, 297–98; China, 20, 31, 39, 251, 258; India, 58, 60–61, 131–32, 270; Indonesia, 270; Japan, 32–33, 208–209; Korea, 209; Myanmar, 30–31; Nepal, 61, 251–52; Philippines, 263; Taiwan, 352; Tibet, 59, 61, 251, 273; Vietnam, 245, 261–62. *See also* Middle East
Asian Americans, 304; autobiographies, **52**; memoirs, **48, 52–54**
Askowitz, Andrea, 107
Astronauts, **314**
Astronomy, 6 **314–15**
Athletes, 70, 144–46, 232, 240, **321–23**. *See also* Sports
Atlantic Ocean, 253, 258
Atlases, 355

Aung San Suu Kyi, 30–31
Australia, 161, 257–59, 361
Autobiographies, 20, 326; collective, **27**; global voices, **32–35**, 39, 243, 258, 359; motherhood, 35, 45, 56–57; queer identity, 39, **41–42**; racial identity, 20, 24–25, 29, 34, **45–46, 51–52**; religious identity, 51, **56–67, 320**; warriors, **39**, 243
Aviation, 14, 37–38, 244, 258, 261, **310, 314–15**

Babcock, Mollie, 14
Backpacking, 146, 250–51, 256
Backus, Harriet Fish, 273
Baker, Christine A., 321
Baker, Florence, 260
Baker, Samuel, 260
Bancroft, Ann, 251–52
bandele, asha, 83
Bandel, Betty, 37
Basketball, 321
Baumgardner, Jennifer, 287–88
Beauty, 27, 176, **184–92**; body image, 48–49, 74, 82–83, 142–43, **147–53**, 154, 156–161, 186, **189–92**, 194, 351; bras, **189, 191**; clothing, **185, 187–91**, 200; corsets, **190–91**; cosmetics, 46, 185–86, 188, **192–95**; cosmetic surgery, 148–49; fashion, 157, **184–92**, 192–94, 223–24, 241; hair, **186, 193**; hats, **186**; purses, **187**; shoes, **189**
Bechdel, Alison, 40–41
Bek, Anna Nikolaevna, 32
Benson, Lorri Antosz, 158
Benson, Taryn Leigh, 158
Bich Minh Nguyen, 48
Bickman, Connie, 73
Biko, Steve, 35
Bingying, Xie, 39
Biographies, **3–11**, 212–14, 257–60, 264; collective, **4, 7–10, 12, 16, 22, 46–47, 54, 56, 58, 60–61**, 116, 121, 128, 153–54, 176, 194, 200, 202, 204–207, 210–12, 219, 222–23, 228–29, 231–32, 235, 241, 260, 262, 273–74, 286, 309–18, 321–22, 327, 331–32, 365–66, 368–69; global voices, 6–7, 9–12, 16–21, 60, 105, 110, 115, 121, 128, 131, 220, 222, 273–74, **309–14, 322–23**; motherhood, 18–20, 22–23,

31, 55–56, 104–105; queer identity, **40, 42–43**; racial identity, **44–47, 53–54,** 75, 176, 186, 204–205, 211, 290; religious identity, 6, 10–11, 13, 17–19, 23, **56–61**; royalty and rulers, 4, **15–24,** 274; warriors, 10–11, **38,** 200, 202, 261; women in the professions, **11–15,** 259–60, **309–18, 321–22, 327, 331–32, 342**

Biology, 13, 28, 68, 70–73, 149, 164, 167, 171–72, 254, 327–28, 355

Bird, Isabella L., 272

Birth, 41, 99–103, **107–12,** 182

Birth control, 5, 206–208, 356–58. *See also* Abortion

Bisexuality, **90–93,** 287–88; autobiographies, 39, **41–42;** memoirs, **93,** 287–88

Blum, Louise A., 41

Body image, 48–49, 74, 82–83, 142–43, **147–53,** 154, 156–161, 186, **189–92,** 194, 351. *See also* Beauty

Bolen, Jean Shinoda, 113

Bombeck, Erma, 98

Borderline personality disorder, 156

Bosnia and Herzegovina, 242

Botany, 254

Boucher, Sandy, 129–30

Boudica, 16

Boxing, 70

Boyd, Helen, 25

Boyd, Loree, 45

Boylan, Jennifer Finney, 43

Brabner, Joyce, 157

Bras, 189, 191

Brave Bird, Mary, 45–46

Breast-feeding, **107–12**

Breasts, 190–92

Brkic, Courtney Angela, 242

Broad, Mary, 257–58

Brownmiller, Susan, 26

Buchanan, Andrea J., 103

Buddhism, **129–31;** autobiographies, **59;** memoirs, 30–31, **61, 129–30,** 273; nuns, 59–61

Bulimia, **158–59.** *See also* Eating disorders

Bullitt-Jonas, Margaret, 158

Burma, 30–31

Burroughs, Augusten, 162, 184

Business, 170–71, **309–11, 326–28, 341, 343,** 362; and entrepreneurs, 12–13, 15, 46, 194, 231–32, **329–33;** and

professional guides, **333–38;** history of, 12–13, 46, 194

Byzantium, 219–20

Cammermeyer, Margarethe, 325

Canada, 45, 237, 243, 259–60, 272, 275

Cancer, **153–57;** breast, 11–12 **154, 156–57,** 255; ovarian, 13, **155;** uterine, **154**

Cantrell, Debra Ann, 276

Careers, 69, 298, **308–12;** athletes, 146, 232, **321–23;** aviators, 14, 37–38, 244, 258, 261, **310, 314–15;** clergy, 57, 60–61, **318–20;** entrepreneurs, 12–13, 15, 46, 194, 231–32, **329–33;** in adult entertainment, 33, 213–14, 228, 231–32, 264, **360–63;** in agriculture, 49–50, **309–11;** in health care, 5, 14, 30, 32, 35, 38, 104–105, 108, 110, 235, 255, 261–64, **316–18;** in politics, 4–7, 53, **343, 366–70;** in science and technology, 6, 12–13, 28–29, 253–54, 259–60, **312–16;** in the arts, 8–9, 20, 73–75, 116, 187–88, 203–104, 254, 296, 299–300, 310–11, 352, **309–11;** in the business world, **309–11, 326–28, 341, 343;** in the military, 16–17, **37–39,** 200, 202, **223–24, 243–45,** 261–65, **310, 323–26;** in the wild, 252–53; lawyers, 4, 11–12, 35, **317–20, 343;** professional guides, **333–38;** spies, 38, **262–64;** war correspondents, 261, 264–65, 326; working mothers, 353–54, **370–73.** *See also* Labor; *and* Prostitution; *and* Rulers; *and* Royalty; *and* Sexual harassment

Caribbean, 204–205, 227, 239; Cuba, 47; Puerto Rico, 47

Carl, Ann, 37–38

Cartledgehayes, Mary, 60

Cartography, 260

Cartoons, 311

Carvajal, Luisa de, 59

Catherine the Great, 20

Chabrillan, Céleste Vénard de, comtesse, 228

Chang, Jung, 31

Chastity, 85–87, 360

Chemistry, 12–13, 206–207, **314**

Cheng, Nien, 31

Chicago, Judy, 8–9

Chicanisma, 241, 288–89; Xicanisma, 288

Chick lit, 157
Children, 42, 51, 55–56, **98–107**, 180, 299, 359, 371–73. *See also* Daughters; *and* Sons
China, 20, 31, 39, 251, 258
Chokyi, Orgyan, 59
Christianity, 6, 85–87, 96, **120–24**, 165–66, 183, 191, 216–22, 275, 295, 344–45; apostles, 59, 217; autobiographies, 51, **56–67, 320**; biographies, 10–11, 17–19, 23, **58–61**; clergy, **60, 319–20**; memoirs, 28, 35, **60**, 96, **123**, 158, 182; nuns, **60**; saints, **60**
Civil War, American, 38–39, **233–36**
Class (economic), 100, 148, 152–53, 208, 210, 227–28, 241, 285, 289–300, 303, 331–32, 351–54, 359, 370–73; memoirs, 47, 50, 52, 184
Classical history, 6, 18–19, **201–203, 207, 212–18**, 275
Cleopatra, 18–19
Clergy: Christian, **60, 319–20**; Jewish, **57, 318–20**
Clinton, Hillary Rodham, 4, 368
Clitorises, 164. *See also* Cunts
Clothing. *See under* Fashion
Cochran, Jackie, 14
Cohabitation, 88
Collection: anthologies and miscellanea, 31, 46–47, 53–54, 73, 75–76, 78, 84–85, 89–90, 95–96, 98–100, 111, 114–15, 117–122, 124, 126–128, 130–34, 146, 174, 179, 204, 210, 219, 221, 226, 231, 236, 238, 251–52, 255–56, 258, 261, 266–68, 271, 274, 277, 284, 286, 289–92, 290, 293–96, 300–302, 304–305, 313–14, 317–319–20, 322–25, 338, 340, 343–44, 351–53, 355–57, 360–63, 365–70, 372–73; of autobiographical writing, **27**; of biographical writing, **4, 7–10, 12, 16, 22, 46–47, 54, 56, 58, 60–61**, 116, 121, 128, 153–54, 176, 194, 200, 202, 204–207, 210–12, 219, 222–23, 228–29, 231–32, 235, 241, 260, 262, 273–74, 286, 309–18, 321–22, 327, 331–32, 365–66, 368–69; global voices, 6–7, 9–12, 16–21, 60, 105, 110, 115, 121, 128, 131, 220, 222, 273–74, **309–14, 322–23**; of diary writing, 26, 231; of essays, 20, 29, 41, 46–47, 49–50, 53–54, 57–58, 68,

74, 76, 78, 80–82, 84–85, 89–91, 95–96, 98–100, 103, 109, 111, 113, 116, 118–120, 123, 125–26, 130–32, 146–48, 154, 174–76, 179, 186, 201, 210–11, 213–14, 219, 236–39, 251–52, 255–56, 258, 261, 266–71, 274, 277, 284–85, 288–92, 295–300, 304–305, 313–14, 319–20, 322–24, 338, 340, 343–44, 351–53, 355–57, 360–63, 365–70, 372–73; of letters, 29, 38, 60, 231, 233, 272, 351–52, 354–57, 360–63, 365–70, 372–73; of memoirs, 45, 50, 53–54, 261, 284–85, 290
Comfort women, 208–209
Coming of age, 24–25, 33, 36, 40–42, 44–45, 47–48, 50–53, 184, 242, 254
Communication, 86, 92, 328, 334–36
Computer science, 313
Constance of Hauteville, 274
Cornum, Rhonda, 261
Corsets, 190–91
Cosmonauts, **314**
Cosmetic surgery, 148–49
Cosmetics, 46, 185–86, 188, **192–95**
Courtesans, 228
Cowgirls, 232
Crossdressing, 25, 39, 152. *See also* Transgender
Cuba, 47
Cunts, 76. *See also* Vaginas
Curie, Marie, 12
Curott, Phyllis W., 55

Dark Ages, 16, 113, **201–202, 207, 218–21**
Dating, 41–42, **82–88, 90–92**, 93–95, 97, 157, 165, 167, 360
Daughters, 24–25, 31, 41–42, 51, **79–80, 82, 98–99,** 158, 180, 184, 270. *See also* Children
David-Neel, Alexandra, 273
De Ferrari, Gabriella, 45
de Medici, Isabella, 18
Dembele, Monique, 110
Devotionals, 121
Diaries, 26, 32, 47–48, 242–43, 254; collections of diary writing, 26, 231
Dickinson, Anna Elizabeth, 15
Dieting, **142–44**, 171–72
Dillard, Annie, 269
Dirie, Waris, 182
Discrimination. *See* Sexual discrimination

Disease, **153–57**; alcoholism, **162–63**; addiction, 155, **161–63**; AIDS, 104–105; borderline personality disorder, **156**; eating disorders, 150, 155, **157–60**; heart disease, **155–56**; manic depression, **155**; schizophrenia, **155**, 259–60; schizoaffective disorder, **156**. *See also* Cancer

DNA, 13

Doctors, 14, 30, 32, 35, 110, 255, 261, 264, **316–18**

Drescher, Fran, 154

Drugs, 161–63

Dworkin, Andrea, 290

Earhart, Amelia, 14

Easter Island, 259–60

Eating disorders, 150, **157–60**; anorexia, 155, **158–60**, 162; bulimia, **158–59**; overeating disorder, **158**

Ebadi, Shirin, 35

Ecuador, 260

Edmonds, Sarah Emma, 38

Education, 34–35, 67–68

Egypt, 18–19, 214–15, 218

Ehrlich, Elizabeth, 55–56

Eighteenth century history, 8, 12–13, 18, 20, 32, **201–202, 208–210, 222–24, 226–27, 230**, 257–58, 260, 274, 286, 288, 314–15, 319–20

Eighth century history, **219**

Eleanor of Aquitaine, 22

Elizabeth I (Queen of England), 22–23

Elizabeth II (Queen of England), 22

Ellis, Anne, 230–31

Emotional wellness and mental health, 94–97, 99–102, 114, 116–19, 142–44, 151–52, 155, 170–71, **172–77**, 254, 291, 296, 322; recovery from trauma, **177–84**, 269–70

Encyclopedias, 120

England, 15–17, 21–24, 58–59, 113, 223, 228, 244, 257–60, 262, 264

Engelberg, Miriam, 157

Entrepreneurs, 12–13, 15, 46, 194, 231–32, **329–33**

Erlbaum, Janice,

Espionage, 38, **262–64**

Essays: Chapter 1, Life Stories, 20, 29, 41, 46–47, 49–50, 53–54, 57–58; Chapter 2, Personal Growth, 68, 74, 76, 78,

80–82, 84–85, 89–91, 95–96, 98–100, 103, 109, 111, 113, 116, 118–120, 123, 125–26, 130–32; Chapter 3, Health, Wellness, and Beauty, 146–48, 154, 174–76, 179, 186; Chapter 4, Women's History, 201, 210–11, 213–14, 219, 236–39; Chapter 5, Adventure and Travel, 251–52, 255–56, 258, 261, 266–71, 274, 277; Chapter 6, Feminism and Activism, 284–85, 288–92, 295–300, 304–305; Chapter 7, Women at Work, 313–14, 319–20, 322–24, 338, 340, 343–44; Chapter 8, Women and Society, 351–53, 355–57, 360–63, 365–70, 372–73

Ethiopia, 104–105

Euphrosyne (Byzantine empress), 219

Europe, 113, 116, 201, 206–208, 220–23, 267; Bosnia and Herzegovina, 242; England, 15–17, 21–24, 58–59, 113, 223, 228, 244, 257–60, 262, 264; France, 10–12, 17–18, 22–24, 113–14, 222–24, 228, 262, 264, 267; Germany, 14, 57, 264, 274; Greece, 6, 18–19, 213, 215–18, 267; Iceland, 220; Ireland, 16; Italy, 18, 267, 270, 274; Netherlands, 47–48; Norway, 220; Poland, 12; Russia, 20–21, 32, 106, 227–28, 243–44; Scotland, 17, 113; Spain, 19, 59, 113–14; Ukraine, 106, 215; Yugoslavia, 60

Everest, 251–52

Evita, 7

Exercise, 116, **142–47**, 150, 170, 172; backpacking, 146, 250–51, 256; martial arts, 323; mountain climbing, 250–52, 255–56, 258. *See also* Sports

Exotic dancing, 264, **361–62**

Farman-Farmaian, Sattareh, 34

Farming, 309

Fashion 157, **184–92**, 192–94, 223–24, 241; bras, **189, 191**; clothing, **185, 187–91**, 200; corsets, **190–91**; cosmetics, 46, 185–86, 188, **192–95**; hair, **186, 193**; hats, **186**; purses, **187**; shoes, **189**

Fathers, **82**, 180, 270

Feldon, Barbara, 95

Female Genital Mutilation, 181–83, **359–60**

Feminism, 8–9, 28, 32, 39, 67–70, 84, 92,
102, 107–108, 113, 115–16, 120,
122–34, 141, 147–48, 150–53, 170–71,
173, 201, 205, 207, 217, 238–41, 258,
283–305, 311, 313–16, 323, 325, 336,
338–40, 343; Chicanisma, 241,
288–89; first wave, 3–6, **284–86, 288,
295–96,** 320, 351–58, 361–64, 367,
371; history, **283–87**; second wave,
26, 29, 236, 238, **284–86, 289–92, 300,
302;** theory, concepts, and beliefs,
287–96; third wave, 49, 54, 74, 76,
99–100, 102–103, **285–305,** 352, 355,
360, 362; Womanism, 217, 292–93,
295–96

Fernandez Barrios, Flor, 47
Fertility, 41, **104–107**
Fies, Brian, 157
Fifteenth-century history, 10–11, 19,
56–57, **202, 222, 227**
Figure skating, 322
Fiorina, Carly, 326–27
Finances, 88, 187, 337, **344–46**, 353, 370–71
First-century history, 16, 59, **212–13**
First-century B.C.E. history, 18–19
First ladies, 4–6, 342
Fishing, 253–54
Fitness, physical, **144–47**
Flake, Emily, 161
Flannery, Sarah, 6
Flappers, 241
Flowers, Pam, 252
Fontenoy, Maud, 253
Food, 48, 55–56, 78, 143–44, 212, 240;
dieting, **142–44,** 171–72; recipes, 48,
55–56, 78, 93–94, 130–31, 143–44,
212
Fourteenth-century history, 23–24, 56–57,
202, 222
Fourth-century history, 6
Fourth-century B.C.E. history, 213–14
Fox, Faulkner, 371
France, 10–12, 17–18, 22–24, 113–14,
222–24, 228, 262, 264, 267
Francisco, Patricia Weaver, 184
Frank, Anne, 47–48
Franklin, Rosalind, 13
Fraser, Laura, 270
Friendships, 21–23, **78–80**, 275
Fundamentalist Church of Jesus Christ of
Latter Day Saints, 180–81
Furiya, Linda, 48

Gammelgaard, Lene, 252
Ganahl, Jane, 95
Gardening, 130
Gaston, A. G., 46
Geeks, 313–14
Geishas, 33
Gelman, Rita Golden, 269
Gender: Chapter 1, Life Stories, 12–13, 22,
25, 27, 35–36, 38–39, 45, 49–59,
52–54, 56, 58, 59; Chapter 2,
Personal Growth, 67–71, 86, 98–99,
113, 115–16, 118, 120, 127–30;
Chapter 3, Health, Wellness, and
Beauty, 147–48, 151–52, 163, 166,
168, 172; Chapter 4, Women's
History, 205, 211, 213, 219, 221–22,
225–28, 233–34, 240–41; Chapter 5,
Adventure and Travel, 272, 274;
Chapter 6, Feminism and Activism,
285–86, 289–95, 298–99, 301, 304;
Chapter 7, Women at Work, 310–14,
316, 319, 324–37, 341–45; Chapter 8,
Women and Society, 351–52, 355,
364–70
Germany, 14, 57, 264, 274
Gilbert, Elizabeth, 270
Gilliam, Connally, 96
Global perspectives, 7–10, 75, 122, 187–88,
191–92, 194, 200–207, 212, 221, 252,
254–58, 262, 264–71, 274, 276–77,
292, 299–300, 303–304, 310–11,
316–17, 351–52, 354, 356–57, 359–60,
363–69; autobiographies, **32–35**, 39,
243, 258, 359; biographies, 6–7,
9–12, 16–21, 60, 105, 110, 115, 121,
128, 131, 220, 222, 273–74, **309–14,
322–23;** memoirs, 28, **31–36**, 44–45,
53–54, 73, 181–83, 228, 242, 253–54,
269, 273, 276. *See also under names of
specific countries*
Goddesses, **55, 113, 116, 131–34, 218**. *See
also* Paganism
Godin, Isabel Grameson, 260
Golden, Marita, 48–49
Gordon, Beate, 32
Gore, Ariel, 100
Gottlieb, Lori, 159
Grammar, 289
Granddaughters, 24–25, 31, 51, **78**
Grandmothers, 20, 31, 41–42, 55–56, **78–79**
Granuaile, 16
Graphic novel, 36, 40, 157, 161

Greece, 6, 18–19, 213, 215–18, 267

Green, Anne Bosanko, 37

Green Belt Movement, 28

Greene, Melissa Fay, 104–105

Greenlaw, Linda, 253–54

Guatemala, 34

Gudrid, 220

Guilbault, Rose Castillo, 50

Gulf War, 261

Gymnastics, 322

Guns, 364–65

Hair, **186, 193**

Hakakian, Roya, 36

Hall, Adrienne, 256

Hall, Meredith, 105

Halliday, Ayun, 100

Hamer, Fannie Lou, 53

Hamill, Dorothy, 322

Hamill, Pete, 162

Hardenbroeck, Margaret, 15

Hari, Mata, 264

Harrison, Kathryn, 180

Hart, Elva Treviño, 49–50

Hats, 186

Health, **141–44**; dieting, **142–44,** 171–72;
    exercise, 116, **142–47,** 150, 170, 172,
    250–52, 255–56, 258, 323; fertility,
    pregnancy, and birth, **99, 102,
    104–11;** history of medicine, 73,
    206–208, 235, 316–18, 357–58;
    menopause and menstruation, 91,
    169–72; sexual health, 5, 30, 36,
    82–83, 86–87, 95, **163–72,** 207–208,
    356–60; weight, 82–83, 142–43,
    147–49, 151–52. *See also* Cancer; *and*
    Disease; *and* Health care; *and*
    Emotional wellness and mental
    health

Health care, **107–112,** 141, 155–57, 164,
    169–72, 317; doctors, 14, 30, 32, 35,
    110, 255, 261, 264, **316–18;** nurses,
    38, 235, 262–63

Heart disease, 155–56

Henderson, Carol, 182

Henry, Pat, 254

Highsmith, Patricia, 42–43

Hill, Anita, 339–40

Hinduism, **131–33;** biographies, **58**

Hip-Hop, 293–95

Hiratsuka Raicho, 32

History: adventures in, 15, **257–265;**
    Ancient and Classical, 6, 16, 18–19,
    59, 116, **123–24, 200–203, 207,
    212–18,** 275; and travel, 15–16,
    56–57, **220, 223, 272–75;** Dark Ages,
    16, 113, **201–202, 207, 218–21;** of art,
    8–9, 74, 113, 116, 187–88, **213–14,
    219, 225,** 294, 300, 310, 352; of
    business, 12–13, 46, 194; of
    feminism, **283–87;** of labor, 28–29,
    200, 203, 210, 212, 227–28, 273–74,
    311–12, 338–39, 363; of law, 58, 208,
    214, 284–85, 295, 317–18, 358; of
    medicine, 73, **206–208, 235,** 316–18,
    357–58; of music, **203–204;** of
    religion, 10–11, 18–19, 56–61, 89,
    113, 115–16, **120–24, 127–35, 216–18,**
    219–22, 316, 318–20; of science, 6,
    12–13, 73, 206–208, 259, 313–316; of
    sports, 70, **232;** of the military and
    war, 10–11, 14, 16, 28–29, 31, 37–39,
    47–48, 57, 128, **200, 202, 208–209,**
    222–23, **233–36, 242–45,** 261–65, **310,
    324–26, 364–65;** maritime history,
    257; Medieval (Middle Ages),
    10–11, 19, 22–24, 56–57, **201–202,
    207, 218–21,** 274; Prehistory, 113,
    116, **200, 213;** social history, 3–5,
    7–8, 16–26, 28–29, 33, 35, 39, 50–53,
    72–74, 89, 148, 171, 187–94, **199–245,**
    257–58, 273–74, 284–85, 287, 289–90,
    292, 295, 301, 309–323, 325, 338–39,
    351–54, 356, 363–67; women's
    bodies and sexuality throughout,
    73, 124, **206–209, 228, 238,** 258;
    women's history, 7, 9–10, 14, 45, 89,
    115–16, 127–29, 187–88, **199–245,**
    273–74, 276, 284–92, 295, 300,
    309–323, 325, 338–39, 351–54, 356,
    363–67. *See also specific centuries and
    countries*

Hodgson, Marion Stegeman, 38

Holden, Kate, 161

hooks, bell, 50–51

Hornbacher, Marya, 159

Horse racing, 258, **321–22**

How-to: Chapter 1, Life Stories, 55;
    Chapter 2, Personal Growth, 70–71,
    75, 77, 79–88, 91–93, 95–97, 99–101,
    103–106, 108–12, 114, 117–19, 125,
    129–31, 133–34; Chapter 3, Health,
    Wellness, and Beauty, 160, 164–68,

170–71, 173–75, 178, 183, 185–88, 190, 192–95; Chapter 4, Women's History, 239; Chapter 5, Adventure and Travel, 250–51, 275–77; Chapter 6, Feminism and Activism, 298–99, 301, 303–304; Chapter 7, Women at Work, 328–39, 341–46; Chapter 8, Women and Society, 358, 362–64, 368, 373

Humor: Chapter 1, Life Stories, 28–29, 41–42; Chapter 2, Personal Growth, 83–84, 91–94, 97–98, 101–103, 106–107, 112, 123; Chapter 3, Health, Wellness, and Beauty, 142, 151–54, 161, 167, 172–73, 176, 190; Chapter 4, Women's History, 202–203; Chapter 5, Adventure and Travel, 268, 271; Chapter 6, Feminism and Activism, 301, 305; Chapter 8, Women and Society, 351

Hunting, 258
Hutchinson, Anne, 58
Hypatia, 6

Iceland, 220
Immigration, 257–58, 269, 351–52, 354
Incarceration, 83, 257–59
Incest, 178–80
India, 58, 60–61, 131–32, 270
Indichova, Julia, 106
Indonesia, 270
Infidelity, 89
Inventions, 315–16
Iran, 34–36
Iraq, 261, 263–64, 325–26, 365
Ireland, 16
Irene (Byzantine empress), 219
Isabella of Castile, 19
Isabella of France, 23–24
Islam, **127–29**, 219; biographies, **56**; memoirs, 33–36; Sufism, 128–29
Israel, 214–15
Italy, 18, 267, 270, 274
Iwasaki Mineko, 33

Jacobs, Harriet A., 51
Jadick, Richard, 264
Jamestown, Virginia, 44
Jamison, Kay R., 155
Japan, 32–33, 208–209
Javins, Marie, 268
Jessop, Carolyn, 180

Joan of Arc, 10–11
Jonas, Regina, 57
Jorgensen, Christine, 43
Juana Inés de la Cruz, Sister, 122
Judaism, 123, **125–27**, 216–18; biography, 13, **57**; memoir, 36, **47–48, 55–56**, 102, 289; rabbis, **57, 318–20**
Judges, 11–12
Julian of Norwich, 57
Junia, 59
Jung Chang, 31

Kali, 132–33
Kanafani, Deborah, 27
Kang, K. Connie, 52
Karpinski, Janis L., 365
Kassindja, Fauziya, 181–82
Kaysen, Susanna, 156
Kelsey, Marion, 243
Kempe, Margery, 56–57
Kenya, 28, 258
Kidd, Sue Monk, 28
King, Florence, 41–42
Kingston, Maxine Hong, 52
Kinsella, Bridget, 83
Knitting, 119, 240
Korea, 209
Korn, Fadumo, 181
Knapp, Caroline, 162
Kraft, Heidi Squier, 264
Kuegler, Sabine, 51
Kuebelbeck, Amy, 182
Kunin, Madeleine, 368

LaBastille, Anne, 269
Labor (work), 51, 240, 288, 291, 297–99, **342–43**, 351–54, 359, 365–66; history of, 28–29, **200, 203, 210, 212, 227–28**, 273–74, **311–12**, 338–39, 363; work–life balance, 69, 113, 290–91, 298, 317, 320, 353, 370–73; sexual harassment, 294, **338–40**. *See also* Careers; *and* Working mothers
Labor (childbirth). *See* Birth
Labzina, Anna Evdokimovna, 32
Lamb, Amanda, 103
Lamott, Anne, 101, 123
Larsen, Karen, 272
Lash, Jennifer, 113–14
Latifa (Afghan teenager), 33
Latin America, 204, 227, 297–98; Argentina, 7; Caribbean, 204–205,

227, 239; Cuba, 47; Ecuador, 260;
Guatemala, 34; Mexico, 122, 205,
213, 267–68, 272, 275; Peru, 44–45;
Puerto Rico, 47; South America,
204–205, 213, 272
Latinas, 75, 150, 205, 227, 239, 241, 288–89,
337; autobiographies, 29, 34;
biographies, 75; memoirs, **44–45, 47,
49–50**
Lavine, Kim, 330–31
Law, 182–83, 338–39, 343, 366–67; and
lawyers, 4, 11–12, 35, **317–20, 343**;
history of, 58, 208, 214, 284–85, 295,
317–18, 358
Lawyers, 4, 11–12, 35, **317–20, 343**
Leadership, 297–99, **328, 334–35, 337–38,
341–44**, 366–70; life stories of
leaders, **16–24, 28, 35**, 200, **326**, 366,
368–69. *See also* Rulers; *and* Royalty
Lee, Mary Paik, 52
Leicester, Earl of, 23
L'Engle, Madeleine, 124
Lesbian sexuality, 57, **90–93**, 104, 107, 168,
238, 324; autobiographies, **41–42**,
76; biographies, **42–43**; memoirs,
40–42, 129–30, 324
Letters, 29, 37–38
Lifestyle, 75, 88, 95–97, 173–74, 119
Lipstick, 193–94
Literature, 34
Liu, Aimee, 160
Livia, 213
Lowman, Margaret, 254
Louis XIV, 223
Lucas, Geralyn, 156
Lynch, Jessica, 261

Maathai, Wangari, 28
Magdalene, Mary, 217
Mai, Mukhtar, 182–83
Mao (Chairman), 31
Mali, 110
Manic depression, 155
Marchetto, Marisa Acocella, 157
Margolis, Cindy, 105
Marie Antoinette, Queen of France, 17,
223
Maritime history, 257
Markham, Beryl, 258
Marriage, 19–25, 31–32, 42–45, 56–57,
83–86, 89, 93, 157, 165, 180, 213–14,
232, 251, 260–61, 288, 291, 301–302

Marsh, Elizabeth, 15
Martial arts, 323
Martin, Edwin B., 339
Mary I (Queen of England), 22
Mary II (Queen of England), 22
Mary, Queen of Scots, 17
Mass, Leslie, 251
Masuda Sayo, 33
Mathematics, 6, 313–14
McCloskey, Deirdre N., 42
McCorvey, Norma, 356
McCracken, Elizabeth , 181
McGovern, Terry, 162
McIntosh, Elizabeth P., 262
Meaker, Marijane, 42–43
Media, 22, 48–49, 148, 151, 153, 238, 284,
290–91, 293–97, 299–301
Medieval history (Middle Ages), 10–11,
19, 22–24, 56–57, **201–202, 207,
218–21**, 274
Meditation, **114, 116–19, 121, 124, 127,
129–30, 132–34**, 144, 149, 174
Memoirs, 8, **24–30**, 87, 107, 151–63,
171–72, 174, 180–84, 230–31 ,
251–56, 261–64, 267–70, 272–73, 276;
collective, 45, 50, 53–54, 261, 284–85,
290; global voices, 28, **31–36**, 44–45,
53–54, 73, 181–83, 228, 242, 253–54,
269, 273, 276; motherhood, 41, **98,
100–107, 109–10, 112**, 150, 180, 261,
330–31, 371; queer identity, 25,
40–43, 76, **93**, 107, **129–30**, 184,
287–88, 324, 355; racial identity,
44–45, 47–54, 49–50; religious
identity, 28, 30–31, 33–36, **47–48,
55–56, 60–61**, 96, 102, **123, 129–30**,
158, 182, 273, 289; warriors, **37–39**,
261, 263, **324–26**; women in the
professions, 28–30, 254–55, 261–62,
264, **321–22, 326, 330–31, 339**, 365
Menchú, Rigoberta, 34
Menopause, **169–72**
Menstruation, 91, **170–71**
Mental Health. *See* Emotional wellness
and mental health
Mexico, 122, 205, 213, 267–68, 272, 275
Middle Ages. *See* Medieval history
Middle East, 59, 123, 204, 216–17, 219, 369;
Afghanistan, 27, 33, 297, 325; Iran,
34–36; Iraq, 261, 263–64, 325–26,
365; Israel, 214–15; Pakistan, 33,
182–83; Palestine, 27

Midlife. *See under* Aging

Mineko, Iwasaki 33

Miscarriage, 179, 181

Moran, Lindsay, 262

Motherhood and mothers, **79–80, 97–112**, 270, 291; autobiographies, 35, 45, 56–57; biographies, 18–20, 22–23, 31, 55–56, 104–105; fertility and adoption, 41, **104–107**; memoirs, 41, **98, 100–107, 109–10, 112**, 150, 180, 261, 330–31, 371; pregnancy, birth, and breast-feeding, 99–103, **107–12**, 182; working mothers, 353–54, **370–73**

Mother Teresa, 60

Motorcycling, 239, 272

Mountain climbing, 250–52, 255–56, 258

Muscio, Inga, 76

Music, 294; history, **203–204**

Muslim perspectives. *See* Islam

Myanmar, 30–31

Nafisi, Azar, 34

Native Americans, 20, 113, 213, 226; autobiographies, 20, 34, **45–46**; biographies, **44–47**

Nature, 146, 250–56, 258–60, 269, 272–73, 276, 309

Nazer, Mende, 359

Neaira, 213–14

Nemat, Marina, 35

Nepal, 61, 251–52

Nerds, 313

Netherlands, 47–48

New Guinea, 51

Newman, Catherine, 101

Newman, Janis, 106

Nguyen, Bich Minh, 48

Nielsen, Jerri, 255

Nien Cheng, 31

Nigeria, 49

Nineteenth-century history, 3–6, 8, 12–14, 20–22, 32, 45–46, 51, 188, **201–202, 208–211, 226–30, 237**, 257–60, 259, 274, 284–86, 295, 314–15, 317–22, 353–54; and the American Civil War, 38–39, **233–36**; and the American Old West, 14, **230–33**, 272–73, 317

Ninth-century history, **219**

Nobel Peace Prize, 28, 30–31, 34, 60, 365–66

Nobel Prize in Chemistry, 12

Nobel Prize in Physics, 12

Norway, 220

Nuns: Buddhist, 59–61; Christian, 60

Nurses, 38, 235, 262–63

Nursing. *See* Breast-feeding

Oceanography, 254

O'Connor, Sandra Day, 11–12

Old West, history of the American, 14, **230–33**, 272–73, 317

O'Malley, Grace, 16

Opechancanough, 44

Orenstein, Peggy, 106

Orgasms, 73

Overeating disorder, 158. *See also* Eating disorders

Paganism, 113, 116, **133–35**, 216–18, 220; biographies, 6; memoirs, 28, **55**; Wicca, **55, 133–35**. *See also* Goddesses

Palin, Sarah, 368

Pakistan, 33, 182–83

Palestine, 27

Pacific Ocean, 253

Peace, **363–66;** Nobel Prize in, 28, 30–31, 34, 60, 365–66

Pekar, Harvey, 157

Penises, 192

Perón, Eva, 7

Peru, 44–45

Philippines, 263

Physics, 12, 316

Pirates, 16, 257

Pocahontas, 44

Poland, 12

Politics, 206, 208, 284–85, 287–90, 295–97, 301–303, 343, 352, 354, 356, **366–70**; autobiographies, 20, 35; biographies, 3–8, 11–12, 16–24, 31, 44–45, 53, 58, 212–13, 219, 366, 368–69; memoirs, 8, 12, 20, 27–28, 30–31, 35–36, 37, 263, 368

Polygmy, 180

Pornography, 290, **360–62**

Posner, Trisha, 171–72

Powhatan, 44

Prayer, 114–15, 117–22, 127, 134

Pregnancy, 41, 99–103, **107–12**, 182

Prehistory, 113, 116, **200, 213**

Priestesses, 216
Professional guides, **333–38**
Prostitution and prostitutes, 161, 231–32, **360–63**; courtesans, 228
Pryce, Lois, 272
Psychology, 42, **67–71**, 149, 160, 164, 174–75, 178, 181, 225, 264, 291, 342, 355, 363–65
Puerto Rico, 47
Purses, 187

Queer sexuality, 301–302; autobiographies, 39, **41–42**; biographies, **40, 42–43**; memoirs, 25, **40–43, 93,** 107, **129–30,** 184, **287–88, 324,** 355. *See also* Bisexuality; Lesbian sexuality; Transgender sexuality; Transsexuality
Quick read: Chapter 1, Life Stories, 6–7, 9–10, 12–13, 28–29, 32–33, 36–38, 48–52, 57; Chapter 2, Personal Growth, 69–70, 72–76, 78–84, 86–87, 90–92, 96, 98, 103, 114, 117, 119, 122–24, 127–32; Chapter 3, Health, Wellness, and Beauty, 98, 145–46, 148–49, 152–54, 156–57, 159, 161, 167, 171–77, 179, 180–183, 185–93 , 116, 153–54, 176; Chapter 4, Women's History, 202, 205, 207, 213–14, 224, 231, 233, 239–40, 242; Chapter 5, Adventure and Travel, 253, 258, 261, 266, 269, 271, 276; Chapter 6, Feminism and Activism, 287, 293–94, 300, 303, 305; Chapter 7, Women at Work, 309, 311, 313, 316–17, 320–21, 323, 332, 334, 336, 342–43, 346; Chapter 8, Women and Society, 352, 355–56, 361, 363–64, 368–69

Rabbis, 57, 318–20
Race, 35, 49, 76, 102, 128, 152, 194, 208, 259, 285, 289–93, 302, 354; *See also under specific races*
Raicho, Hiratsuka, 32
Raine, Nancy Venable, 184
Ralston, Aron, 255
Ramphele, Mamphela, 35
Rape, 26, 208–209, 294; autobiographies, 24, 45; memoirs, 182–84
Recipes, 48, 55–56, 78, 93–94, 130–31, 143–44, 212

Reid, Constance, 28–29
Reiland, Rachel, 156
Relationships, 4, 20, 23–24, 33–34, 36, 47–48, **76–97,** 168–69, 206, 212–13, 223, 228, 256, 264, 270, 294, 328, 334, 337; children, 42, 51, 55–56, **98–107,** 180, 299, 359, 371–73; dating, 41–42, **82–88, 90–92,** 93–95, 97, 157, 165, 167, 360; daughters, 24–25, 31, 41–42, 51, **79–80, 82, 98–99,** 158, 180, 184, 270; fathers, **82,** 180, 270; friendships, 21–23, **78–80,** 275; granddaughters, 24–25, 31, 51, **78**; grandmothers, 20, 31, 41–42, 55–56, **78–79**; marriage, 19–25, 31–32, 42–45, 56–57, **83–86, 89, 93,** 157, 165, 180, 213–14, 232, 251, 260–61, 288, 291, 301–302; sisters, **77, 81,** 184; sons, **98, 101.** *See also* Motherhood
Religion, 34, 45, 61, 115, 118, **120–135,** 289, 356–57, 364; devotionals, **121**; history of, 10–11, 18–19, 56–61, 89, 113, 115–16, **120–24, 127–35, 216–18,** 219–22, 316, 318–20; in antiquity, 59, **123–24, 215–18**; prayer, **114–15, 117–22, 127, 134**; spells, **55, 134.** *See also under specific religions; and* Spirituality
Rice, Condoleezza, 4–5
Richards, Renée, 43
Rivalry, 77–78
Rodeo, 232
Rodriguez, Deborah, 27
Roller derby, 240
Roman Empire, 18–19, 212–13, 215, 217–18, 274–75
Roosevelt, Eleanor, 5–6, 342
Rosen, Ruth, 285
Routledge, Katherine, 259–60
Rowing, 253
Royalty, 206, 219; biographies, **15–24**
Ruff, Cheryl Lynn, 263
Rulers, 206 219; biographies, 4, **15–24,** 219
Russia, 20–21, 32, 106, 227–28, 243–44

Sailing, 145, 254, 257–58, 276
Saints, 60
Sanger, Margaret, 5
Santiago, Esmeralda, 47
Satrapi, Marjane, 36
Savage, Dan, 107
Sayo, Masuda, 33

Schiller, Lori, 156
Schizoaffective disorder, **156**
Schizophrenia,**155**, 259–60
Schwartz, Margaret L., 106
Schwartz, Pepper, 87
Science, 212–13, 313; and technology, careers in, 6, 12–13, 28–29, 253–54, 259–60, **312–16**; archaeology, 113, 116, 200, 213–16, 259–60; astronomy, 6, **314–15**; biology, 13, 28, 68, 70–73, 149, 164, 167, 171–72, 254, 327–28, 355; botany, 254; cartography, 260; chemistry, 12–13, 206–207, **314**; computer science, **313**; history of, 6, 12–13, 73, 206–208, 259, 313–316; oceanography, 254; physics, 12, **316**. *See also* Psychology; *and* Sociology
Scotland, 17, 113
Sebold, Alice, 183–84
Second-century history, **217**
Senators, 4
Seniors. *See under* Aging
Serano, Julia, 355
Seventeenth-century history, 15, 58–59, 122, **201–202, 207, 209–210, 221–22, 225, 227**, 257, 274, 319–20
Sexual discrimination: Chapter 1, Life Stories, 12–14, 24–29, 33–34, 36–39, 52, 54, 58–59; Chapter 2, Personal Growth, 124, 127–28; Chapter 4, Women's History, 211, 221–22, 233–34, 243–44; Chapter 5, Adventure and Travel, 262, 274; Chapter 6, Feminism and Activism, 285, 288, 290–92, 296–98, 301, 303–304; Chapter 7, Women at Work, 310–320, 325–26, 342–43; Chapter 8, Women and Society, 351–52, 354–55, 365
Sexual exploitation, 33, 51, 178–83, 208–209, 213–14, 299, 353, **358–62**
Sexual harassment, 294, **338–40**
Sexual health, 5, 30, 36, 82–83, 86–87, 95, **163–72**, 207–208, 356–60; birth control, 5, 206–208, 356–58
Sexuality, 24–25, 33, 47–48, 82, 85, 87, 89, 128, **164–69**, 289, 294, 299, 353, **360–63**; and women's bodies throughout history, 73, 124, **206–209, 228, 238**, 258. *See also* Queer sexuality

Sexual liberation, **361–63**
Sey, Jennifer, 322
Shapiro, Lisa Wood, 109–10
Shoes, 189
Silverman, Sue William, 180
Simpson, Sherry, 256
Single woman, The (lifestyle), **93–97**, 104, 112
Sister Juana, 122
Sisters, **77, 81**, 184
Sixteenth-century history, 16–18, 23, 44, 59, **201–202, 207, 221–22, 226–27**
Skating, 322
Skiba, Katherine M., 326
Slavery, 51, 359
Sloan, Louise, 112
Smith, John, 44
Smoking, 161
Soccer, 145–46
Social history, 3–5, 7–8, 16–26, 28–29, 33, 35, 39, 50–53, 72–74, 89, 148, 171, 187–94, **199–245**, 257–58, 273–74, 284–85, 287, 289–90, 292, 295, 301, 309–323, 325, 338–39, 351–54, 356, 363–67
Sociology, 48–49, 69–70, 72, 149, 152–53, 168, 171, 190–91, 194, 287–89, 291, 298, 328, 336, 338–39, 342, 352–55, 358, 360, 367–73
Solitude, 105, 254, 256, 262, 268, 276–77; and the single lifestyle, **93–97**, 104, 112
Somalia, 181–83
Sonnenberg, Susanna, 163
Sons, **98, 101**. *See also* Children
Sor Juana, 122
South Africa, 35
South America, 204–205, 213, 272; Argentina, 7; Ecuador, 260; Peru, 44–45
Space exploration, 314–15
Spain, 19, 59, 113–14
Spells, 55, 134
Spirituality, 34, 61, 109, **112–120**, 122, 124, 127–31, 133–34, 170, 175, 269–70, 363–64; autobiographies, 45; biographies, 10–11, 45; meditation, **114, 116–19, 121, 124, 127, 129–30, 132–34**, 144, 149, 174; memoirs, 28, 30–31, 45, 47–48, **113–14**, 254; prayer, 114–15, 117–22, 127, 134. *See also* Religion

Sports, 70, **144–47**; backpacking, 146, 250–51, 256; basketball, **321**; boxing, 70; figure skating, **322**; gymnastics, **322**; history of, 70, **232**; horse racing, 258, **321–22**; hunting, 258; martial arts, 323; mountain climbing, 250–52, 255–56, 258; rodeo, 232; roller derby, 240; rowing, 253; sailing, 145, 254, 257–58, 276; soccer, 145–46; tennis, 144–45. *See also* Athletes

Stanton, Elizabeth Cady, 295

Steinbach, Alice, 267–68

Steinem, Gloria, 29, 174

Stereotypes, 150, 128, 172, 292, 304, 313–14, 352

Stewart, Elinore Pruitt, 233

Strock, Carren, 93

Sudan, 359

Suffrage, 3–4, 284–85, 295

Sufism, 128–29

Supreme Court, 11–12

Taiwan, 352

Taylor, Barbara Brown, 60

Technology, 313; and science, careers in, 6, 12–13, 28–29, 253–54, 259–60, **312–16**. *See also* Science

Teferra, Haregewoin, 104–105

Tenney, Lester I., 263

Tennis, 144–45

Thomas, Clarence, 340

Theodora (Byzantine empress), 219

Third-century history, 6

Tibet, 59, 61, 251, 273

Tilberis, Liz, 155

Togo, 182

Transgender sexuality, 25, **42**, 152

Transsexuality, 355; memoirs, **42**, 355

Travel, 33, 73, 110, 113–14, 118, 250–52, 254–260, **265–72**; destinations and means of, 145–46, **275–77**; historical, 15–16, 56–57, **220, 223, 272–75**

Trauma, recovery from, **177–84**, 269–70

Trivia, 72

Tsu Hsi, 20

Twelfth-century history, 22, 274

Twentieth-century history, 7, 9–10, 12, 32–33, 45, 47, 52, 188–89, **201–202, 205–211, 227–28, 236–45**, 258–60, 273, 284–97, 300, 302, 304, 310–11, 314–22, 354, 358, 367; American, 4–6, 13–14, 20, 24–26, 41–42, 52–53, 148, **232, 236–45**, 284–85, 292, 310, 314–15, 317–20, 324–25, 338–39, 351–52, 366–67, 371–72; and women and war, 14, 31, 39, **242–45, 324–25**; Gulf War, 261; Vietnam War, 245, 261–62; World War I, 243, 264; World War II, 14, 28–29, 37–38, 47–48, 57, **208–209, 243–45**, 262–65, 310

Twenty-first century, 4, 50, 96, 240, 287–88, 290–95, 297–305, 314–15, 352–55, 359–60, 366–73; War on Terror, 261, 263–64, 325–26, 365

Ukraine, 106, 215

Vaginas, 73–74, 151, 167–68. *See also* Cunts

Velazquez, Loreta Janeta, 39

Van Devanter, Lynda, 262

Vibrators, 73

Victoria (Queen of England), 21–22

Vietnam, 245, 261–62

Vietnam War, 245, 261–62

Violence, 19, 23–4, 31, 33–35, 45, 70, 222, 225, **363–65**, 359–60; rape, 24, 26, 45, 182–84, 208–209, 294. *See also* Trauma, recovery from; *and* War

Wakeman, Sarah Rosetta, 38

Walker, Alice, 102, 295

Walker, Laura Jensen, 154

Walker, Madam C. J., 46

Walker, Rebecca, 102

Wall, Elissa, 180

Walls, Jeannette, 184

War, 128, 222–23, **324, 364–65**; American Civil, 38–39, **233–36**; and adventure, 37–39; and military history, 10–11, 16, **200, 202,**; and espionage, 38, **262–64**; and women in the twentieth century, 14, 31, 39, **242–45, 324–25**; Gulf War, 261; Vietnam War, 245, 261–62; war correspondence, 261, 264–65, 326; War on Terror, 261, 263–64, 325–26, 365; World War I, 243, 264; World War II, 14, 28–29, 37–38, 47–48, 57, **208–209, 243–45**, 262–65, 310. *See also* Warriors

War correspondence, 261, 264–65, 326

War on Terror, 261, 263–64, 325–26, 365

Warriors, 202, 215–16, **223–24, 243–45, 323–36**; autobiographies, 39, **243**; biographies, 10–11, **38**, 200, 202, 261; memoirs, **37–39**, 261, 263, **324–26**

Watkins, Nan, 269–70

Weight, 82–83, 142–43, 147–49, 151–52; dieting, **142–44,** 171–72

Welfare, 354, 371–72

Wellness, emotional. *See* Emotional wellness

Wicca, **55, 133–35**

Wicklund, Susan, 30

Wilder-Taylor, Stefanie, 103

Wilkins, Maurice, 13

Williams, Kayla, 325–26

Willis, Janice Dean, 61

Wilson, Valerie Plame, 263

Wine, 310–11

Winters, Kelly, 256

Witches, 221–22, 225

Wittman, Blanche, 12

Womanism, 217, 292–93, 295–96

Women's history. *See under* History

Work. *See* Labor

Working mothers, 353–54, **370–73**

Work–life balance, 69, 113, 290–91, 298, 317, 320, 353, 370–73

World War I, 243, 264

World War II, 14, 28–29, 37–38, 47–48, 57, **208–209, 243–45**, 262–65, 310

Writing, 9, 42, 230, 235, 296, **309, 311**; war correspondence, 261, 264–65, 326

Wurtzel, Elizabeth, 162

Xicanisma, 288

Xie Bingying, 39

Yoga, 116–17, 144, 170

Young adult: Chapter 1, Life Stories, 8–10, 24–25, 33, 36, 44–50, 53; Chapter 2, Personal Growth, 76, 90; Chapter 3, Health, Wellness, and Beauty, 143, 150–51, 156, 158–59, 163, 180, 184; Chapter 4, Women's History, 201–203, 229, 231, 242; Chapter 5, Adventure and Travel, 251–53, 262, 264–65; Chapter 6, Feminism and Activism, 291–92, 296–97, 300, 304–305; Chapter 7, Women at Work, 310, 313, 322–23; Chapter 8, Women and Society, 352

Yugoslavia, 60

Zailckas, Koren, 163

Zakrzewska, Marie, 14

About the Author

JESSICA ZELLERS is the Electronic Resources Librarian at the Williamsburg Regional Library in Virginia. She helped create the library's daily book-review Web site, Blogging for a Good Book (http://bfgb.wordpress.com), and she regularly contributes Author Read-Alike pieces to the NoveList Plus database. She also enjoys writing about books, libraries, and assorted miscellany at her personal blog, http://www.thelesbrarian.com, though she refuses to write anything for anyone unless she's had her fix of graphic novels, paperback vampire romances, and Russian classics.